British regional employment statistics
1841–1971

British regional employment statistics 1841 - 1971

C.H. LEE

Senior Lecturer in Economic History, University of Aberdeen

CAMBRIDGE UNIVERSITY PRESS

CAMBRIDGE

LONDON · NEW YORK · MELBOURNE

Published by the Syndics of the Cambridge University Press
The Pitt Building, Trumpington Street, Cambridge CB2 1RP
Bentley House, 200 Euston Road, London NW1 2DB
32 East 57th Street, New York, NY 10022, USA
296 Beaconsfield Parade, Middle Park, Melbourne 3206, Australia

© Cambridge University Press 1979

First published 1979

Printed in Great Britain at the
University Press, Cambridge

Library of Congress cataloguing in publication data

Lee, Clive Howard.
British regional employment statistics, 1841–
1971.

1. Labour supply – Great Britain – Statistics.
2. Labour supply – Great Britain – History.
I. Title.
HD5765.A6L43   331.1'1'0941   78-25698
ISBN 0 521 22666 X

Contents

Preface

My thanks are due to a number of public bodies and individuals for assistance in producing this study over the course of several years. The Social Science Research Council provided a grant to employ a research assistant to help in the arduous task of preparing the statistical data contained in the tables in Parts II and III. The Houblon-Norman Fund and the Twenty-Seven Foundation both gave generous financial assistance towards the cost of publishing the final volume. My especial personal thanks are due to Mrs. Meg Irving who, as the research assistant on the project for three years, processed the great bulk of the statistical data. Lynne Cockburn and Pat Smith typed the draft and made light of that burdensome task. My wife helped prepare the final manuscript for publication. Without the assistance of all these individuals and institutions, this work could never have been completed.

August 1978   C.H. Lee

PART I

1　The census as a source of employment data

One of the greatest problems facing the historian of the nineteenth and twentieth centuries, and facing the social scientist who often necessarily and wisely
reverts to the use of historical data to test theoretical constructs, lies in the
acquisition of statistical data which are both analytically useful and internally
consistent over time. The present volume presents one set of statistical data,
employment by industrial order, in such a form. The data presented here are
derived exclusively from the successive decennial censuses which represent
the best source, and indeed the only comprehensive source for such data
throughout the period covered. Furthermore, the census data allow disaggregation at county and regional level thus making possible spatial as well as
temporal analysis. Since there are no comprehensive data on income or prod-
uct comparable to those relating to employment, the latter measure is likely
to provide the best single indicator of structural change in the British economy
and its component regions in the nineteenth and early twentieth centuries. In
this lies the justification for this volume.

The first British census was published in 1801 and decenially thereafter
until the present day with the single exception of 1941 which, of course, fell
unfortunately during wartime. Prior to 1841, however, the census data relating
to employment are of very limited use to the historian, so the tables presented
in this study commence at that date. The 1801 census classified people under
three general occupational headings only, those who were 'chiefly' in agriculture, those who were 'chiefly' in trade, manufactures and handicrafts, and
thirdly the residual of those employed. Since the collection and presentation
of the data were entrusted to the parish overseers, there was no uniformity of
treatment in the enumeration of women, children or domestic servants. The
following three censuses, taken in 1811, 1821 and 1831, attempted to over-
come such inconsistency of classification by collecting returns not for individuals but for entire families according to their 'principal activity'. The lack of
detail, uncertain classification criteria, and the method of data collection,
render these early censuses both of doubtful value and certainly not consistent
with the later enumerations.

In the 1841 census the method of collecting the information was changed
so that, as at the present day, each householder had to fill up a separate
schedule giving the requisite information about himself and his family. 'Hitherto the returns had been merely numerical summaries prepared by the Overseer
for the whole of his parish or district from information elicited by personal
enquiry of the several householders. From 1841 onwards the householder

himself recorded the particulars for each individual person, and the enumerator has been responsible only for seeing that obvious errors were corrected in the schedules, and that the necessary particulars were not omitted'.* Further in 1841 the previous practice of classifying employment groups by family was discontinued and individual categorisation returned. In 1841, for the first time, employment information was collected and published in detail greater than two or three general groups.

*Census of England and Wales 1911, General Report p. 5.

The published data for 1841 were made available in the form of an alphabetical list of 877 occupations. In 1851 this extremely inconvenient format was abandoned and the data was presented grouped into 17 orders, comprising 91 sub-orders and a total of some 400 separately identifiable groups or 'headings'. This format, with some adjustment in the number and definition of orders has been used ever since. Fortunately, indeed essentially, the level of disaggregation with the 400 or so headings has been maintained, and it is the rearrangement of these groups which has formed the essence of this study.

While the 1841 census marked a new departure and a vast improvement from previous practice, uncertainties about both the data and their collection must remain. The General Register Office itself had continuing doubts about the competence of both householder and enumerator as sources of information, especially concerning employment. As late as 1891 it was noted that 'The main difficulty arises from the extremely inaccurate and inadequate manner in which uneducated, and often, indeed, even educated persons, describe their calling . . . A census taken on the ordinary method, where the schedule is filled up by the householder himself or some member of his family, who, too commonly, neither cares for accuracy nor is capable of it, does not supply data which are suitable for minute classification, or admit a profitable examination in detail. The most that it is reasonable to expect from data so collected is that they shall give the means of drawing such a picture of the occupational distribution of the people as shall be fairly true in its main lines, though little value can be attached to the detailed features.'† Against this may be set the optimistic view of the 1861 census. 'Several of the enumerators who had acted in the same capacity ten years before remarked that a more intelligent appreciation of the objects and uses of the enquiry, combined with the utmost willingness to furnish the returns, was evinced by the poorer population; a result which may be fairly ascribed to the co-operation of the educated and influential classes of society, particularly of the clergy of all denominations and of public writers in the press.'* It is similarly possible to find mixed views on the competence of the enumerators. The 1861 census was again optimistic. 'The enumerators were required to be intelligent and active, able to read and write well, not younger than 18 years of age or older than 60; they were to be respectable persons likely to conduct themselves with strict propriety and courtesy in the discharge of their duties, and well acquainted with the district in which they were to act. No difficulty was experienced in procuring the services of a highly respectable body of enumerators, including clergymen and many other professional men who undertook the work from public motives.'† Conversely, it was stated two decades later that 'Out of an army of thirty five thousand enumerators, there could not be but a certain proportion of unintelligent or careless men, and the

†Census of England and Wales 1891, General Report p. 35.

*Census of England and Wales 1861, General Report p. 3.

†Ibid. p. 1.

requisite precision of statement as to occupations was far from being univer-
sally observed.'* It may well be that greater criticism found in later censuses
reflects both a greater desire for precision and a greater competence within
the General Register Office. Such errors cannot be quantified by the historian,
who can only make allowance for such inadequacies by careful use of the
resultant data.

The main problem involved in the derivation of employment data from the
census lies in the choice of classification categories. Armstrong, on the basis
of Booth's pioneer study completed in the 1880s, has argued the merits of a
highly detailed classification.† This involves the difficulty of overstraining the
credibility of precise disaggregated figures. Such an approach was rejected in
this study because the level of detail which would be involved would preclude
the provision of a series of data which would be sufficiently compact to be
easily manipulated. The choice here was to favour spatial disaggregation
rather than category disaggregation. The 'model' chosen as the basis for
classification was the standard industrial classification, as revised in 1968, by
which the General Register Office divides employment into twenty-seven
industrial orders. Besides being a most appropriate measure of employment,
the standard industrial classification does make it possible to obtain a great
deal of comparability between present-day and Victorian data. Having chosen
this model, the next step was to ascertain the degree to which the data in the
censuses could be reclassified to conform to the requirements of the twenty-
seven industrial orders. Inspection of the twentieth-century data confirmed
that a high degree of comparability between successive censuses could be
obtained in terms of this categorisation, and they were used as the basis for
Series B, 1901–1971. A major discontinuity was found between the data for
Series B and the nineteenth-century data with regard to the distributive trades.
In part, this reflects the fact that whereas the manufacture and distribution of
many commodities are today quite separate and distinct activities, in the
nineteenth century this was not so. In the food trades especially, the processor
was often also the retail distributor. It was a common practice in nineteenth-
century censuses not to distinguish, either by accident or intent, between the
two types of activity. For this reason, a single continuous series from 1841 to
1971 is not feasible within the classification system adopted. Accordingly the
earlier data were formed into Series A, 1841–1911, in which distributors in a
given industry were included under the same order as the manufacturers.
Hence the industrial order for distributive trades in Series A contains only
those generally described as shopkeepers, costermongers or street sellers. With
this prime exception the criteria of the standard industrial classification industrial orders apply fairly well to the nineteenth-century data, and thus the composition of orders by a completely different set of definitions is avoided. In section 4 below the data for Great Britain in 1911 is shown categorised by the
criteria of both Series A and Series B, with 89 per cent of those employed
remaining in the same industrial order by either definition. The data for 1901
and 1911 were included in both series to provide as long a time sequence as
possible for each classification.

The administrative changes in the taking of the census in 1841 also provided
the basis for spatial disaggregation of employment data. These changes followed

*Census of England and
Wales 1881*, General Report
p. 27. See also: M. Drake,
The Census 1801–1891, in
E.A. Wrigley (ed.) *Nine-
teenth Century Society:
Essays in the use of Quan-
titative Methods for the
Study of Social Data.*
(Cambridge University
Press 1972)

†W.A. Armstrong, The Use
of Information about
Occupations, in Wrigley
Nineteenth Century Society,
and C. Booth, Occupations
of the People of the United
Kingdom 1801–1881,
*Journal of the Royal
Statistical Society*, June,
1886.

upon the reorganisation of the Poor Law through the legislation of 1834 which created Poor Law Unions as the basis for giving local relief. Two years later the Registration Act established the civil registration of births and deaths, and adopted the same Poor Law Unions as areas for registration districts. The 1841 census then took the registration district as the basic unit for its enumeration and placed the local registrar in the role of supervisor over the enumerators in his district. The adoption of the registration county as the basic unit of spatial measurement in 1841, and its continued use thereafter until the reorganisation of local government in 1894, provides an appropriately disaggregated unit of analysis and one which has the advantage of consistency over time.

As a result of the 1894 legislation, the registration county was replaced by the newly constituted administrative county which fulfilled the same requirements as its predecessor until the further local government changes in the mid 1970s. The regional definitions used in this study are necessarily aggregates of these county units and are, given that constraint, as far as possible based on the current standard regions as defined by the Office of Population Censuses and Surveys. In the case of Scotland and Wales, for economy of space and because many of the counties in both countries have always had relatively small populations, the data have been presented at sub-regional rather than county level, although these sub-regions are aggregates of counties. The eight Scottish sub-regions are based fairly closely on the new 1975 Scottish local government regions. In the case of Wales, the two sub-regions used here approximate closely to amalgamations, four in each case, of the new Welsh local government regions. A large measure of spatial consistency is thus possible over a long period broken only by the local government changes of the 1890s. Even then there was considerable consistency between the old registration county and the administrative county which replaced it as shown in the comparison of the two in tables 5.2 and 5.3 below.

2   Employment data – Series A classification

2.1. General problems

This section falls into three parts, a general discussion of the major problems involved in the Series A classification, notes on specific industrial orders, and a list of occupations included within each industrial order. The first problem concerns the conflicting requirements and different composition of an industrial classification, under which employment is related to an industrial group such as shipbuilding, steel manufacture or banking, and an occupational classification under which employment is viewed in terms of type of activity such as clerk, manual labourer, self employed, etc. The first industrial classification in the census does not appear until 1921, while the first truly occupational classification is to be found in approximate form in 1911. In fact the nineteenth-century censuses adopted classification procedures which combined industrial and occupational categorisation, although the latter title is to be found at the head of each table until 1921. Thus we find coal miners and cotton weavers, industrially classified, and labourers and clerks, occupationally classified. Only in 1911 does there appear the beginnings of an appreciation of the divergent criteria and meaning of industrial and occupation groupings. Earlier censuses had tended to dismiss such problems. The general report for 1851 stated baldly, 'It would be out of place here to insert a disquisition on the principles of classification; to attempt to show the impracticable nature or the imperfection of other classifications; and to vindicate in all its details the arrangement that has been adopted. But this arrangement possesses one advantage that should not be overlooked: it is not a mere arrangement on paper such as that of people into producers, distributors and consumers; but an arrangement in which it has been found practicable to find a place for every one of the twenty-one millions of people in Great Britain, and in which we can pass them rapidly and distinctly in review.'* The imperfection of information supplied probably contributed to the combination of industrial and occupational categorisation and to the fact that successive census takers wavered between the two courses. Generally the censuses of 1851, 1861 and 1871 inclined to an industrial classification, while those from 1881 to 1911 tended in the opposite direction. At the latter date it was observed that 'it is quite certain that for a very large proportion of workers following certain occupations common to many industries no statement was made in the schedule as to the industry with which they were connected, and the limited information derived from the single question as to occupation must be held to have given unsatisfactory returns both as to personal occupation and to industry.'† At the 1911 census an additional question was added asking the nature of the employer's business, and this was doubtless responsible for the marked fall in those returned as general labourers in that year. Both series in this study have adopted an industrial classification as the basis of analysis, because this seemed technically more feasible and practically useful than an occupational classification. This imposes the constraint that some occupations cannot be divided between the appropriate industrial orders, such as ironmongers, while others cannot be allocated at all. In the former case, groups such as ironmongers were assigned to the order where they would be found in greatest numbers. In the latter case, labourers and clerks had to be assigned to the unfortunately large 'not classified' residual category. Each of these problems is discussed below under specific industrial orders.

The first problem to be resolved in compiling employment categories is to decide who should or should not be counted as employed. This apparently obvious question was both a source of constant debate amongst census takers and a subject which received varying treatment from them. In general the constraint of including those who were economically active was not observed, so that a large number of persons who were not in current or even recent employment found their way into the statistics. Up to and including 1871 those who were retired from work were classified under the occupation they had previously followed, thus giving an obvious but undetectable boost to the activity rate. This is suggested by table 2.1 below which gives the activity

Census of Great Britain 1851, Report p. lxxxii.

†*Census of England and Wales 1911*, Report on Tables on Occupations and Industries, vol. X, p. viii.

Table 2.1. *Activity rates for population aged 65 and above (per cent)*

	Male	Female
1851	88.3	30.0
1861	92.3	33.3
1871	70.9	32.7
1881	72.6	18.3
1891	64.8	16.0
1901	60.6	13.2
1911	56.0	11.5

rate, that is the proportion of the population returned as being economically active, for the over 65 age group. There is not sufficient disaggregation by age in 1841 to derive a figure for that date. It is impossible to quantify either the proportion of these people who were actually active or how that proportion shifted over time. It would be inaccurate to exclude all over 65 from the employment categories, nor would it be possible at county level since such disaggregation by age and employment is not provided in either 1881 or 1891. From 1881 it was decided to exclude the retired; further an investigation carried out at the same time 'found by careful examination of the enumeration books for an entire county, including a large town, that, had we included the "retired" as was done in 1871, the persons returned by us under any heading would on average have been about 2 per cent more than they actually are. On the whole, seeing that the difference was so small, we thought it best altogether to omit those who had retired from business.'* Even so a small number of people, retired from certain professions were still classified as active in the later decades of the century. Clergy of the established church, members of the medical profession, and officers in the armed services were thus treated.

Census of England and Wales 1881, General Report p. 28.

At the lower end of the age scale, the problem is rather easier. After 1871 all children under the age of 10 were unoccupied. In the earlier censuses the numbers of children under this age and economically active was small, and declining from 2.0 per cent males and 1.4 per cent females in 1851 to 0.8 per cent and 0.7 per cent respectively in 1871.

Prior to 1881 it was also usual practice to include by occupation lunatics in asylums, hospital patients and criminals in jail, all of whom were, at least temporarily, inactive. From that date such persons were omitted and there was even an attempt to exclude those 'out of employ'. But it should be generally assumed that little or no allowance has been made for unemployment nor, and perhaps equally important in this period, the underemployment characteristic of casual labour. A further inclusion in the censuses prior to 1881 which probably inflates the number of those employed was a small number of entries under vague headings like landowner, householder, capitalist and shipowner.

A further area of uncertainty affecting the activity rate, and of course the size of certain categories lay in the criteria for the inclusion of women as economically active. The general report to the 1851 census expressed views which suggested that this problem should never have arisen. 'The duties of a wife, a mother, and a mistress of a family can only be efficiently performed by unremitting attention; accordingly it is found that in districts where the women are much employed from home, children and parents perish in great numbers.'[†] In spite of this dire warning, women continued to seek and find employment. Some, however, were returned as employed when they were probably not so engaged. 'On examining the occupational tables it will be seen that sometimes women are returned as following the occupations that are practically confined to the stronger sex . . . This arises in part from the not uncommon incident that a woman carries on the business of her defunct husband or father, employing men for work she cannot herself perform. But this can scarcely be the whole explanation; for, were it so, all the women returned under these masculine occupations would be returned as "employers", whereas many of them appear as "employed" . . . The explanation is to be found in the fact that women not infrequently returned themselves by their husband's vocation; and, indeed, an instruction put by order of the Local Government Board upon the Householder's Schedule, that wives assisting their husbands in their trade should be returned as employed by them, has given some sanction to this practice, for assisting a husband in his occupation is capable of a very wide interpretation, and may be understood to cover keeping his petty accounts, taking orders, or receiving payments for him.'[*] Since the most common sources of female employment are found in agriculture, domestic service, retail, and board and lodging, activities in which women might be expected to find employment which might be full time, part time or casually occasional, it is not possible to assess the quantitative significance of such employment. To complicate the problem of female employment even further, in 1891, perhaps the most eccentric of censuses, women engaged in domestic duties about the home were for the first and last time classified not as unoccupied but under the heading of domestic service.

All the above problems have concerned the inflation of the labour force beyond its true limits. The 1881 census made a point which at least suggests the possibility of error in the opposite direction. 'Of the 182,282 males in the working period of life (20–65) without specific occupations, a large number, doubtless, were busily engaged in vocations which were none the less serious or less important because not recognised in our classification. They were managing their estates and property; directing charitable institutions, prosecuting literary or scientific researches; or engaged in other of the multifarious channels by which unpaid energy finds vent. If these were deducted from the 182,282 unoccupied males, a further deduction were also made for those who were incapacitated for work by physical defects, the remainder, constituting the really idle portion of the community, would probably prove to be but very small.'[†] Lack of additional comment suggests that the writer seemed less anxious to show or did not believe that the number of females returned under this heading as 'really idle' was overstated.

The problem of activity rates in the nineteenth-century data is thus a very real one, and clearly shows that the overall figures as well as those for indi-

[†] *Census of Great Britain 1851*, Report p. lxxxviii.

[*] *Census of England and Wales 1891*, General Report pp. 57–8.

[†] *Census of England and Wales 1881*, General Report pp. 49–50

vidual industrial orders must be treated with great caution. All that can be safely stated is that the problem almost certainly diminishes with the passage of time and in relation to fuller and better data collection. There is a clear break in practice between 1871 and 1881 and this is reflected in the data with a fall of about five per cent in the male activity rate and eight per cent in the female equivalent. It is not improbable that these imperfect statistics mask divergent trends within the true pattern of activity rates. Improving data collection and categorisation reduces the activity rate over time, while the real activity rate may have been rising over time as more casual labour and female labour was drawn into full-time employment. This must be kept in mind when interpreting long-run trends over the entire period.

Having considered the problems involved in the identification of the labour force, it remains to consider some of the principal problems concerned with the allocation of people into the industrial orders. Foremost among such problems is the difficulty of classification. The task which faced the census makers in classifying a host of diverse and often obscure job titles was formid-able. The general report to the 1881 census plaintively lists a selection of these including blabber, bull-dog burner, crutter, glan rider, muck roller, ponty sticker, shore woman, sparable cutter, tingle maker and whim driver. In order to cope with this problem, a book of instruction was compiled in 1861 for the use of enumerators, using the occupational terminology used in the trade directories of London and other major cities. Unfortunately, this volume was not published. In 1881 'a more extended compilation was made from infor-mation compiled by means of circulars sent out to leading manufacturers and supplemented by a preliminary examination of the census returns from the chief industrial centres. By this means books of instruction were prepared, and have subsequently been revised from time to time, with the object of obtaining uniformity of treatment of the returns at each census. These instructions have also served to promote continuity of treatment at successive censuses.'* This was written in 1911, at which time the census first contained the detailed analysis of occupational categories together with a comparison with the classifications used in the three previous censuses. This showed how a large number of jobs, estimated in 1881 at 11,000–12,000, were reduced to about 400 headings and thence into the much smaller number of orders. While revisions were made in nearly every census in the latter half of the nine-teenth century, the pairs of 1861/1871, 1881/1891 and 1901/1911 are each very similar in composition.

Even within the bounds of the 400 headings from which the twenty-seven industrial orders used here have been derived, there were considerable prob-lems of definition, since quite different occupations are sometimes described by the same term. 'By drummer may either be meant a Musician or a Black-smith's hammerman; by Muffin Maker, either a man who makes the eatable that bears that name, or the man who makes what is known as a muffin in China manufacture. An Engineer may be either a maker or driver of engines. A Collar Maker may be a Seamstress or a Harness Maker.'† In cases where the entry was so general as to preclude meaningful assignment to an industrial order, as in occupational groups termed labourers, merchants, commercial clerks or commercial travellers resort has been had to the 'Not classified'

Census of England and Wales 1911, General Report p. 96 and vol. X Appendix: Classified and Alphabetical Lists of Occupations and Rules Adopted for Classifi-cation. See also vol. X, tables 25 and 26.

†*Census of England and Wales 1881*, General Report p. 27.

category. Where a group should be divided between several industrial orders, such as those returned as 'blacksmith' the group has been assigned to that order which appeared to claim the greater part of its members. Similarly in 1871 and earlier censuses, each group of occupational headings is often followed by a group termed 'others'. Such cases have been resolved by adding the 'others' to the largest heading in the sub-group, again in the hope of minimising error. Finally, no amount of care or rule of practice can completely account for the influence of human vanity. As was sceptically observed in 1881, 'Who can say how many of the 7,962 persons who were returned as Artists, Painters were really such, and how many were house decorators, who had magnified their office? We shall, therefore, pass over a good many of the headings without comment.'*

*Ibid. p. 30.

Two further definitional problems emerge from the nature of the Victorian economy. One, which relates primarily to the decades before 1881, concerns the fact that some people had more than one occupation. This was observed as early as the 1841 census. 'In many small towns, the spectacle-maker would merge with the optician, who would perhaps also be the watch-maker, the barometer-seller, and the bell-hanger of his neighbourhood. The coffin-maker would be doing the last offices to his former customers in the cabinet-making line; while the hatter would figure in the list as draper, grocer, bookseller or shopkeeper, according as he might prefer one name to the other.'† In 1861 it was decided to take the first of several occupations offered by a respondent on the assumption that a man would enter his prime activity first. In 1881 the rule became more specific: 'Firstly, that a mechanical handicraft or constructive occupation should invariably be preferred to a mere shopkeeping occupation; secondly, that, if one of the diverse occupations seemed of more importance than the others, it should be selected; and, thirdly, that in default of such apparent difference the occupation first mentioned should be taken, on the ground that a person would be likely to mention his main business first.'*

†*Census of Great Britain 1841*, Occupation Abstract with Preface p. 8.

Census of England and Wales 1881, General Report p. 28.

The second source of definitional inaccuracy related to the contemporary economy, and one which is relevant throughout the period covered in Series A, was the failure of the census to distinguish fully and consistently between manufacturers and distributors. In many trades such a distinction would have been misleading. 'We would say that, though in economical treatises a broad line is drawn between production and distribution, in actual life the two are by no means so distinct, the maker and the retail seller being very frequently one and the same person; and further that, when the two are distinct persons, they very generally have one and the same occupational title. The man, for instance, who makes bread, and the man who only sells bread, are alike called 'baker' and the man who sells shoes calls himself a shoemaker, as much as the man who actually does the cutting and sewing.'† Such a distinction, between dealer and producer, is of course increasingly more valid in the later decades of the century than in 1841–51. For this reason and to obtain continuity over a long period, the general practice in Series A has been to include dealers under the same industrial order as manufacturers in a given industrial order. Thus, for example, the clothing and footwear industrial order includes clothiers and haberdashers as well as manufacturers. Before 1901 it is not

†*Census of England and Wales 1891*, General Report p. 36.

possible to make a sufficiently universal distinction between producers and distributors to justify the attempt. By that date, the distinction is becoming clearer in most trades, and the census classification merely confirms the economic trend. By 1911 the clerks taking the census were given instructions to classify all persons in such a way as to show clearly whether they were makers or dealers. In Series B, this problem, like many of the difficulties described above with regard to Series A, was of little importance.

2.2. Specific problems: industrial orders

1. Agriculture, forestry and fishing

It was noted in 1911 that: 'The totals as they stand cannot fairly be compared with those for the earlier censuses, and in order to carry the comparison back to 1851 they must be modified by the inclusion of domestic gardeners, and by the exclusion of farmers' sons and other male relatives under 15 years, and of female relatives of all ages who were returned as assisting in the work of the farm, since the procedure adopted included more of these persons at some censuses than at others.'*

The problem of domestic gardeners relates, in fact, only to the census of 1891 when they were not disaggregated from other gardeners. In view of this, only the 1891 data break the continuity of the sequence, although there was some confusion in earlier censuses about the classification of gardeners. 'In 1881, when a man simply returned himself as a Gardener, he was taken, in the absence of any certainty, to be a Domestic Gardener, on the grounds that this was likely to be the more numerous class. But our predecessors in 1871 took the contrary view, and considered the gardener undefined to be a market gardener.'†

Female relatives, as noted above, have been classified under 'Not occupied' throughout Series A, but are included in the Series B tables for which period the returns are clearly more accurate. Farmers' male relatives under the age of fifteen years cannot be excluded from the regional tables since disaggregation by age is often not provided at county level in the data. Hence such persons contribute a small inflationary addition to the figures under this order in Series A.

The principal source of inaccuracy in this order for which allowance cannot be made is probably the result of better definition of labouring occupations with the passage of time. Thus some may be accurately returned as 'agricultural labourers' in later censuses who had earlier been returned simply as 'labourers'. This is, of course, a general problem with regard to nineteenth-century data. There is also some loss of accuracy in earlier censuses owing to the lumping together of persons under occupational rather than industrial headings. Thus some horsekeepers, trainers etc. classed under industrial order 22 (Transport and communication) doubtless include some who might more accurately be classed under this order.

2. Mining and quarrying

The main problem in this order is the heading 'coalheavers, coal porters'. As was noted in the 1911 census report 'Coalheavers, Coal Porters to the number of 8,928 were returned as in the employ of coal merchants, and a

*Census of England and Wales 1911, General Report p. 113.

†*Census of England and Wales 1881*, General Report p. 38.

further 2,130 as working in connexion with harbour, dock, wharf service; altogether 13,190 out of the 32,533 coal heavers were returned according to the industry or service in which they were employed.'* There is also some degree of overlap with other industrial orders especially, apart from distribution, the inclusion of manufacturers of cement and asbestos which in Series B came under the industrial order 16. In the later years covered by Series A it was also assigned to industrial order 16 but was included in this order in some of the earlier years of this Series.

*Census of England and Wales 1911, vol. X, Occupations and Industries Report, p. xlv.

3. Food, drink and tobacco

There are no apparent problems in this order in later years. Earlier censuses include 'butcher's wife' as a heading. Such women were probably active in some kind of assistant capacity, but it has been thought more reliable to omit them from this order and include those so returned under 'Not occupied'. Those women returned as 'butcher' etc. have been included in this order.

4/5. Coal and petroleum products/Chemical and allied industries

These industrial orders have been amalgamated in all censuses prior to 1961 when distinction was first made between different branches of the chemical industry. There are no major problems with regard to this order. In 1851 dealers in surgical instruments are lumped together with druggists and thus included here instead of in industrial order 12.

6. Metal manufacture

There is a very large overlap between this industrial order and industrial order 12. To attain a large measure of accuracy, the two industrial orders should be taken together. Since in many cases the manufacturers of a metal are not distinguished from the workers and manipulators of that metal, in Series A both groups have been included under this industrial order. As was stated in 1911, 'The Separation of the producers from the workers in the metals was attempted for the first time in 1901. In the Report on that census it was stated that "the persistent efforts made, both before the census was taken and subsequently by local enquiry, to ensure the completeness and accuracy of returns have been only partially successful." The same may be said at this census, and further experience leads to the conclusion that complete separation cannot be attained, not only owing to the incompleteness of description in the census schedules and to the general looseness of occupational nomenclature, but also to the organisation of industry. In many cases the production of metals and the manufacture of commodities from the metals are carried on in the same works and a distinction between the two classes of workers is, therefore, impracticable.'† There is also the problem that lack of clarity of employment terminology together with quirks of everyday usage makes meaningful allocation of some jobs between different metal working trades both impossible and pointless. Thus 'the term "Brassfounders" and "Brass Foundry" [was] being apparently largely used by workers in factories where no brass founding was carried on, but stamped goods only were made'.* Especially problematic from the viewpoint of industrial classification are all-

†Ibid. p. lxii.

*Ibid. pp. lxvi–lxvii.

embracing occupational titles, such as that of blacksmith. 'The occupation "Blacksmith" is one which is found in connexion with many different industries, and out of a total of 125,305 males shown under this heading as many as 61,101 are assigned in the industry tables to the business carried on by their employers. Thus 17,099 were employed in iron foundries, in boiler making, or in engineering or machine making works, 10,091 in connexion with coal mines, 2,947 in railway coach, wagon making, or in tram car making, 740 in motor car making, 2,244 in the construction of coaches, carriages, and other vehicles, 5,514 in shipbuilding works, 3,640 on railways, and 2,600 in iron and steel manufacture.'† Similarly there are a number of categories which include employment groups which should be split between industrial orders 6 and 12. Here the needs of continuity over time often determine allocation.

†Ibid. p. lxv.

Generally, industrial order 6 contains the manufacture and working of metals, while industrial order 12 covers the manufacture of specified metal goods such as tools, cutlery, nuts and bolts, as well as working in silver and gold.

7. Mechanical engineering

There are a number of uncertainties in this order, owing to definitional lack of clarity. 'Patternmakers', 'fitters' and 'erectors' are all headings which may include some who should be classed elsewhere within the engineering and metal trades. Further there are two groups which should be in this order but which are, in fact, excluded. 'Constructional engineering' and 'iron bridge building' are included in the general group 'other iron goods makers' and cannot, therefore, be removed from industrial order 12. For complete continuity and accuracy, therefore, industrial order 7 should be amalgamated with industrial orders 6 and 12.

8. Instrument engineering

This industrial order maintains a high level of internal consistency over time.

9. Electrical engineering

Wide definitions of 'electrician' probably include some who should be classed elsewhere. Otherwise there are no problems, nor indeed any entries under this order prior to 1881.

10. Shipbuilding and marine engineering

The only apparent inconsistency here lies in the fact that in 1891 and in earlier censuses, ship's chandlers are included under this order, and thereafter excluded.

11. Vehicles

This industrial order maintains a high level of internal consistency over time.

12. Metal goods not elsewhere specified

See notes to industrial orders 4, 6 and 7.

13. Textiles

There is some overlap with dress trades, industrial order 15. The census of 1911 noted that drapers, linen drapers and mercers were to a large extent makers and sellers of dress as well as of materials for its fabrication. In censuses prior to 1881 dyers, printers and bleachers are included under general chemical industries. It has been assumed that most people so occupied would in fact follow their trade within the context of the textile industries, and accordingly these people have been classified under this order.

14. Leather, leather goods and fur

This industrial order maintains a high level of internal consistency over time.

15. Clothing and footwear

See notes to industrial order 13. Some small errors with regard to this order include the classification of wig makers along with hairdressing under industrial order 26, and the classification of waterproof clothing under industrial order 19 since it cannot be disaggregated from rubber, elastic and other waterproof goods manufacture.

16. Bricks, pottery, glass, cement, etc.

This industrial order maintains a high level of internal consistency over time.

17. Timber, furniture, etc.

The only problem apparent regarding this order is the fact that undertakers are not distinguished from funeral furniture makers prior to 1921, and thus in Series A they are included under this rather than under industrial order 26

18. Paper, printing and publishing

Bill posting and advertising are included in this order to maintain comparability. Prior to the disaggregation of these groups, they were included under the heading 'other workers in paper'.

19. Other manufacturing industries

This industrial order maintains a high level of internal consistency over time.

20. Construction

See notes to industrial order 7 regarding constructional engineering. The composition of this order was influenced by improved definition of labouring occupations with the passage of time. Those hitherto classed as general labourers are latterly defined more accurately as builders' labourers. On the other hand, carpenters more accurately defined may latterly go to industrial order 17, and stone masons to industrial order 2.

21. *Gas, electricity and water*
This industrial order maintains a high level of internal consistency over time.

22. *Transport and communication*
There are some problems of vague definition regarding this order. In particular it is difficult to assign 'horsekeepers, grooms, stablemen' whole-heartedly to transport, since it includes those clearly occupied elsewhere, such as headman (racing stables), jockey, whipper-in (to hunt), as well as gentleman riders. It appears, however, that horse-drawn transport constituted the majority of those included under this heading, and thus they were assigned to this order. By the same criteria, 'coalheaver, coal porter' was included under industrial order 2, some of which group should properly be in this order. See also notes to order 26.

23. *Distributive trades*
This very general order maintains a high level of internal consistency.

24. *Insurance, banking, finance and business services*
See notes to 'Not classified' order.

25. *Professional and scientific services*
The major problem with this occupational group is that it includes subordinates who by modern definition would not qualify as professional people. In earlier censuses farriers returned themselves as veterinary surgeons, and in 1901 their ranks were depleted by the call of the South African War. As the introduction to the 1891 census noted, 'We regard, however, these returns with much suspicion, and think it probable that no few unqualified persons return themselves as medical practitioner. Such, certainly, is the case with dentists, for we found that many lads and girls were so returned, though they were merely employed in the manufacture of false teeth and dental apparatus.'*

*Census of England and Wales 1891, General Report p. 39.

This industrial order includes a number of people who might be classed under two different occupations, particularly members of the clergy who were employed as teachers. In interpreting this, the 1891 census followed the principle that a manufacturing trade should always be taken in preference to a selling trade so that the occupations of clergyman and schoolmaster in combination were always referred to as schoolmaster.

Another problem of double occupation was noted in 1861, 'The parish clerk is occupied in his church duties chiefly on Sundays; hence he has other secular occupations of more or less importance. This is a striking example of double occupation; and of the officiating parish clerks of the kingdom only 2,140 are so returned, the others appearing under other heads. So it is of sextons, or gravediggers, as they often call themselves.'†

†Census of England and Wales 1861, General Report p. 32.

There is the usual problem of better definition of occupation with the passage of time. In 1911 the decline in the number of 'architects' was accounted for by the transfer of draughtsmen and assistants from that profession to the less exalted heading of 'art, music and theatre service' in order

26. Similarly better information showed a number of 'surveyors' to be mere 'auctioneers' in 1911. Perhaps the most significant example of this, however, concerned the teaching profession. The 1911 census noted that 'It should be observed, however, that the figures are affected for comparison by the great change in the system of training teachers. Formerly a large proportion of the pupil teachers and probationers were part-time or whole-time teachers, and were accordingly classified to the heading "teacher"; now, however, intending teachers are mainly whole-time "students", and have been classified accordingly.'*

Census of England and Wales 1911, vol. X, Occupations and Industries Report, p. xxi.

This industrial order also includes a divided group 'hospital, institution and Benevolent Society – service' which includes mental nurses, matrons etc. who should be in industrial order 25, but also welfare and charitable institutions which should be in industrial order 26 by twentieth-century classification.

26. *Miscellaneous services*

For divided categories affecting this order, see notes to industrial orders 17 and 25. The data for 1891 are diminished by the failure to disaggregate domestic service from others in gardening (industrial order 1) and coachmen (industrial order 22).

27. *Public administration and defence*

There is possibly some inflation of the numbers in armed forces. The 1911 census notes that those given as being active in the armed forces at that census exceeded the numbers returned as being on the regimental strength in that year, as indicated by the annual report on the army.

N.C. *Not classified*

The inclusion of merchants, commercial clerks, commercial travellers in this order was necessary because of the impossibility of allocating them to industrial groups. As was noted in 1881, 'What constitutes a Merchant? Probably it would be said that the term applies to any wholesale dealer on a large scale. But there are many large wholesale dealers who do not call themselves merchants, and many retail dealers who give themselves this designation . . . The rule adopted by us was, that whenever the nature of the goods in which the merchant dealt was stated, the individual should be classed by the character of his merchandise; but when that kind of goods was not stated, the simple return being "Merchant" without further specification, or when the name of the country only was given with which the merchant traded, e.g. East India Merchant, he should be placed under the heading "Merchant".'†

†*Census of England and Wales 1881*, General Report pp. 33–4.

There was some discontinuity of treatment of these general titles, as was also observed in the 1881 census report. 'The Commercial Clerks numbered 181,457, and were also twice as many as were so classed in 1871, but the term was used in different ways on the two occasions. In 1871 the clerks in factories were placed to the account of the special manufacture in the office of which they were engaged. For instance, a clerk in a cotton warehouse was placed to Cotton Manufacture; but in 1881 all clerks, employed in any branch of commerce or industry were assigned, not to that special branch, but to the general heading "Commercial Clerk". The heading was thus made to include all clerks excepting Civil Service, Army, Navy, Law, Bank, Insurance, and Railway Clerks.'*

2.3. Series A industrial orders by component occupations

1. Agriculture, forestry and fishing

farmers, graziers
farmers', graziers' — sons etc. assisting in work of farm (not females)
farm bailiffs, foremen
shepherds
agricultural labourers
woodmen
nurserymen, seedsmen, florists

market gardeners
other gardeners (not domestic)
agricultural machinery — proprietors, attendants
others in agriculture
fishermen
cattle, sheep, pig — dealers
drovers, lairmen
dog, bird, animal — dealers

knackers, catsmeat dealers
farm servants (indoor)
vermin destroyers
thatchers
hay and straw dealers
horse proprietors, dealers
horse breeders
land drainage service (not in towns)

2. Mining and quarrying

coal and shale mine — workers at face
coal and shale mine — others below ground
coal and shale mine — workers above ground
coal and shale mine — owners, agents, managers
coal and shale mine — others
iron miners, quarriers
copper miners

lead miners
tin miners
miners in other minerals
metalliferous mine — owners, managers, etc.
metalliferous mine — others
stone, slate, etc. mine, quarry — owners, agents
stone — miners, quarriers
stone — cutters, dressers
slate — miners, quarriers

slate workers
limeburners
clay, sand, gravel, chalk — pit, etc. workers
other workers in products of quarries
coal, coke — merchants, dealers
dealers in stone, slate, etc.
coalheavers, coal porters, labourers
fossil, coprolite — diggers, dealers

3. Food, drink and tobacco

creamery workers
milksellers, dairymen
provision curers
cheesemongers, buttermen, provision dealers
slaughterers
butchers, meat salesmen
fish curers
fishmongers, poulterers, game dealers
millers, cereal food manufacture
corn, flour, seed — merchants dealers
bread, biscuit, cake — makers

bakers, confectioners (dealers)
sugar refiners
jam, preserve, sweet — makers
chocolate, cocoa — makers
grocers; tea, coffee, chocolate — dealers
greengrocers, fruiterers
ginger beer, mineral water — manufacture
mustard, vinegar, spice, pickle, etc. — makers
other dealers in food
tobacco manufacture
tobacconists

maltsters
brewers
distillers, spirit manufacture
beer bottlers
cellarmen
wine and spirit — merchants, agents
flour dealers, agents
fruit, flower — vendors
potato merchants

4. Coal and petroleum products

5. Chemicals and allied industries

coke burners
patent fuel manufacture
dye, paint, ink, blacking –
 manufacture
gunpowder, guncotton,
 explosive –
 manufacture
cartridge, fireworks,
 explosive –
 manufacture
lucifer match manufacture
salt makers

manufacturing chemists
alkali manufacture
chemists, druggists
oil – millers, refiners; oil
 cake makers
candle, grease –
 manufacture
soap – boilers, makers
manure manufacture
glue, size, varnish, etc. –
 manufacture
oil and colourmen

other dealers
drysalters
coke, charcoal, peat –
 cutters, burners
percussion cap makers
cartridge, annite makers
others dealing in drugs and
 surgical instruments
others dealing in grease,
 bones, etc.

6. Metal manufacture

pig iron manufacture (blast
 furnace)
puddling furnaces; iron and
 steel rolling mills
tube manufacture
steel – manufacture,
 smelting, founding
tinplate manufacture
copper manufacture
lead manufacture
zinc manufacture
brass, bronze –
 manufacture
manufacture of other
 metals

ironfounders
brassfounders
blacksmiths, strikers
brass finishers
coppersmiths
type – cutters, founders
stove, grate, range, fire iron
 – makers
bedstead makers (iron or
 brass)
tinplate goods makers
copper workers
leaden goods makers
zinc workers
brass, bronze – workers

iron workers (undefined)
metal – refiner, worker,
 turner, burnisher,
 lacquerer
tin manufacture
tinplate workers, tinmen
tinkers
others
white metal manufacturers
other workers, dealers in
 mixed metals

7. Mechanical engineering

patternmakers
millwrights
erectors, fitters, turners
erectors' fitters' turners' –
 labourers
metal machinists
labourers in engineering
 works
boiler makers

others in engineering –
 textile machinery –
 other
roller engravers, block
 cutters
gunsmiths, gun
 manufacturers
sword, bayonet – makers,
 cutlers

weighing and measuring
 apparatus makers
spinning and weaving
 machine makers
agricultural machine and
 implement makers
ordnance manufacture
pattern designers

8. Instrument engineering

watchmakers and clock-
 makers
scientific instrument
 makers, opticians
photographic apparatus
 makers

surgical and dental instrument and apparatus
 makers

9. Electrical engineering

electrical cable
 manufacture
electric lamp manufacture
other electrical apparatus
 makers, electrical fitters

electricians (undefined)
electricity supply

(No entries under this order
 prior to 1881.)

10. Shipbuilding and marine engineering

ship – platers, rivetters, etc.
ship – other workers in
  iron
shipwrights
ship – other workers in
  wood
ship painters

shipyard labourers
others in ship and boat
  building
ship – riggers, fitters; mast,
  yard, oar, block –
  makers
sail makers

ship's chandlers

11. Vehicles

railway – coach, wagon
  makers
tram car makers
cycle makers
motor car chassis makers;
  mechanics

motor car body makers
coach, carriage – makers
wheelwrights
others in construction of
  vehicles

12. Metal goods not elsewhere specified

galvanised sheet
  manufacturers
tool makers
file makers
saw makers
cutlers, scissor makers
needle, pin – makers
steel pen makers
die, seal, coin, medal –
  makers
nail manufacture
bolt, nut, screw, rivet,
  staple – makers
anchor, chain –
  manufacture
wire – drawers, workers,
  weavers, makers

lamp, lantern, candlestick
  – makers
white metal – plated ware
  manufacturers,
  pewterers
other iron goods makers
other metal workers
ironmongers; hardware –
  dealers, merchants
other dealers in metals,
  machines, etc.
goldsmiths, silversmiths,
  jewellers
lapidaries and other
  workers
dealers in precious metals,
  jewels, watches

japanners
domestic machinery and
  implement makers,
  dealers
gold, silver beaters
clasp, buckle, hinge –
  makers
blade – makers, forgers
knife makers
razor makers
grinders (branch
  undefined)

13. Textiles

cotton – card and blowing
  room processes
cotton – spinning
  processes
cotton – winding, warping,
  etc. processes
cotton – weaving processes
cotton – workers in other
  processes
cotton – workers
  undefined
fustian cutters
wool – sorting processes
wool – carding and comb-
  ing processes
wool and worsted – spin-
  ning processes
wool and worsted –
  weaving processes
wool and worsted –
  workers in other
  processes
wool and worsted –
  workers undefined
silk - spinning processes
silk - weaving processes

silk – workers in other
  processes
silk – workers undefined
flax, linen – manufacture
hemp manufacture
jute manufacture
cocoa fibre manufacture
rope, twine, cord –
  manufacture
mat makers
canvas, sailcloth, sacking,
  net – manufacture
thread manufacture
hosiery manufacture
lace manufacture
carpet, rug, felt –
  manufacture
smallware manufacture
fancy goods (textile)
  manufacture
weavers of sundry fabrics
other workers in sundry
  fabrics
factory hands (textile)
  undefined
textile bleachers

textile printers
textile dyers
textile – calenderers and
  finishers
drapers, linen drapers,
  mercers
other dealers in textile
  fabrics
woolstapler
flannel, blanket –
  manufacture
crape, gauze –
  manufacture
tape manufacture
Manchester warehousemen
trimming makers,
  embroiderers
fullers
stuff manufacture
ribbon manufacture
packers and pressers
  (cotton)

14. Leather, leather goods and fur

furriers, skinners
tanners
curriers
leather goods, port-
    manteau, bag, strap,
    etc. – makers
saddlers; harness, whip –
    makers

brush, broom – makers;
    hair, bristle – workers
quill, feather – dressers
dealers in skins, leather,
    hair and feathers
parchment, vellum –
    makers, dealers
fellmongers

15. Clothing and footwear

straw plait manufacture
straw hat, bonnet – manu-
    facture
felt hat manufacture
makers of cloth hats and
    caps
makers of other hats and
    caps
milliners
hat, bonnet, straw, plait,
    etc. – dealers
tailors

clothiers, outfitters, dealers
dressmakers
stay, corset – makers
shirt makers, seamstresses
glove makers
hosiers, haberdashers
boot, shoe – makers
slipper makers
patten, clog – makers
boot, shoe, patten, clog –
    dealers
artificial flower makers

umbrella, parasol, stick –
    makers
other workers in dress
other dealers in dress
accoutrement makers
old clothes dealers and
    others
shawl manufacture

16. Bricks, pottery, glass, cement, etc.

brick, plain tile, terra cotta
    – makers
plaster, cement – manu-
    facture
earthenware, china,
    porcelain – manu-
    facture

sheet, plate glass –
    manufacture
glass bottle manufacture
other workers in glass
    manufacture
brick, cement – dealers

earthenware, china, glass –
    dealers

17. Timber, furniture, etc.

cabinet makers
french polishers
upholsterers
house and shop fittings
    makers
undertakers, funeral
    furniture makers
wood carvers; carvers and
    gilders
willow, cane, rush –
    workers; basket makers

sawyers, wood cutting
    machinists
lath, wooden fence, hurdle
    – makers
wood turners
wooden box, packing case
    – makers
coopers, hoop makers,
    benders
cork, bark – cutters,
    workers

other workers in wood
furniture, etc. – dealers
timber, wood, cork, bark –
    merchants, dealers
blind makers
chair makers
picture frame makers
bedstead, mattress makers

18. Paper, printing and publishing

paper manufacture
paper stainers
stationery manufacture
envelope makers
paper bag makers
cardboard box makers
other workers in paper,
    etc.
stationers, law stationers
other dealers in paper
printers
– hand compositors

– machine compositors
– printing machine
    minders
– stereotypers, electro-
    typers
– others in printing
lithographers; copper and
    steel plate printers
bookbinders
book, print – publishers,
    sellers
newspaper publishers

newspaper agents, news
    room keepers
circular, envelope –
    addressers
advertising, bill posting –
    agents
bill posters
card, pattern card –
    makers
ticket, label – writers

19. *Other manufacturing industries*

piano, organ – makers
other musical instrument
  makers
fishing tackle, toy game
  apparatus – maker
dealers in instruments,
  toys, etc.
india rubber, gutta percha
  – workers

waterproof goods makers
elastic web manufacture
button makers
celluloid – makers,
  workers
tobacco, pipe, snuff box,
  etc. – makers
bone, horn, ivory, tortoiseshell – workers

floor cloth, oil cloth –
  manufacture
pencil makers (wood)
comb makers

20. *Construction*

platelayers, gangers,
  packers
railway labourers
lock, key – makers
gas fittings makers
builders
builders' labourers
carpenters, joiners
carpenters' joiners' –
  labourers
bricklayers
bricklayers' – labourers
masons
masons' – labourers

slaters, tilers
plasterers
plasterers' – labourers
paperhangers, white-
  washers
painters, decorators
glaziers
architectural, monumental
  – carvers, sculptors
monumental masons
plumbers
gasfitters
locksmiths, bellhangers

railway, canal, harbour,
  etc. – contractors
navvies; railway, etc. –
  contractors, labourers
well, mine – sinkers,
  borers
road – contractors, sur-
  veyors, inspectors
paviours, road labourers
marble masons

21. *Gas, electricity and water*

gas works service
waterworks service
drainage and sanitary
  service
scavenging and disposal of
  refuse
dust collectors

22. *Transport and communication*

railway – officials, clerks
railway ticket – examiners,
  collectors, checkers
railway engine – drivers,
  stokers, cleaners
railway guards
signalmen
pointsmen, level crossing
  men
railway porters
other railway servants
livery stable keepers; coach,
  cab – owners
coachmen (not domestic),
  cabmen
horsekeepers, grooms,
  stablemen (not
  domestic)
motor car drivers (not
  domestic), motor cab
  drivers

carmen, carriers, carters,
  wagoners (not farm)
motor van, etc. – drivers
van, etc. – guards, boys
others connected with
  carrying or cartage
omnibus service
 – horse drivers
 – motor drivers
 – conductors
 – others
tramway service
 – drivers
 – conductors
 – others
others on roads
merchant service; seamen
 – navigation
 – engineering
 – cooks, stewards, etc.
pilots, boatmen on seas

bargemen, lightermen,
  watermen
navigation service (on
  shore)
dock labourers, wharf
  labourers
harbour, dock, wharf,
  lighthouse – officials
warehousemen
messengers, porters, watchmen
telegraph, telephone
  service (not govern-
  ment)
toll collectors, turnpike
  gate keepers
wheel chair – proprietors,
  attendants, etc.
meter, weighers
horsekeepers, horsemen,
  teamsters, carters

23. Distributive trades

dealers in works of art
rag – gatherers, dealers
multiple shop, multiple
store – proprietors,
workers

general or unclassified
shopkeepers, general
dealers
pawnbrokers

costermongers, hawkers,
street sellers
news – boys, vendors
(street or undefined)
marine store dealers

24. Insurance, banking, finance and business services

auctioneers, appraisers,
valuers, house agents
bankers; bank – officials,
clerks
bill – discounters, brokers;
finance agents

life, house, ship, etc. –
insurance – officials,
clerks
insurance agents

25. Professional and scientific services

clergymen (established
church)
Roman Catholic priests
ministers, priests of other
religious bodies
itinerant preachers, scripture readers, mission
workers
monks, nuns, Sisters of
Charity
church, chapel, cemetery
– officers
barristers
solicitors
law clerks
physicians, surgeons,
registered practitioners
dentists (including
assistants)

veterinary surgeons
midwives
sick nurses, invalid
attendants
subordinate medical
services
schoolmasters, teachers,
professors, lecturers
others connected with
education
authors, editors, journalists,
reporters
persons engaged in
scientific pursuits
others connected with
literature, etc.
civil, mining – engineers
land, house, ship –
surveyors

professional engineers',
surveyors' – assistants
painters, sculptors, artists
architects
engravers
hospital, institution and
benevolent society –
service
accountants
institution service
officers of law court
parish clerk
other church officers

26. Miscellaneous services

photographers
musicians, music masters,
singers
actors
art, music, theatre –
service, etc.
performers, showmen;
exhibition, games –
service
domestic indoor servants
in hotels, lodging
houses, eating houses
other domestic servants
domestic – coachmen,
grooms
domestic – motor car
drivers, motor car
attendants
domestic gardeners

gamekeepers
college, club – service
park, lodge, gate, etc. –
keepers
caretakers, office keepers
cooks (not domestic)
day girls, day servants (so
returned)
charwomen
laundry workers; washers,
ironers, manglers, etc.
bath and wash house
service
others engaged in service
officers of commercial
guilds, societies, etc.
motor garage – proprietors,
attendants
wig makers, hairdressers

coffee house, eating house
– keepers
lodging house, boarding
house – keepers
inn, hotel – keepers;
publicans, beer sellers,
cider dealers
barmen
waiters
others in inn, hotel, eating
house etc. service
chimney sweeps
receiving shop, receiving
office – keepers, assist-
ants (laundry, dyers
and cleaners)

27. *Public administration and defence*

post office – telegraphists, telephone operators
other post office officers and clerks
postmen
post office messengers, etc.
other civil service officers and clerks
other civil service messengers, etc.
police
Poor Law service
municipal, parish and other local county officers

army officers (effective)
army officers (retired)
soldiers and N.C.O.s
officers of the navy (effective)
officers of the navy (retired)
men of the navy
officers of the marines (effective)
officers of the marines (retired)
men of the marines
prison officer, etc.

East Indian and colonial service
magistrate (so returned)
municipal, parish, union officer
militia, volunteers
coastguard, royal naval reserve
Inland Revenue
Customs
dockyard artificers

Not classified

merchants (commodity undefined)
brokers, agents, factors
salesmen, buyers (not otherwise described)
commercial travellers
commercial or business clerks
sandwich men, bill distributors
other workers in sundry industries

other dealers in sundry industries
contractors, manufacturers, managers, superintendants, foremen (undefined)
general labourers
engine – drivers, stokers, firemen (not railway, marine or agricultural)
artisans, mechanics, apprentices (undefined)

factory – hands, labourers (undefined)
machinists, machine workers (undefined)
figure, image – makers, dealers
animal, bird – preserver; naturalist
stock broker

Not occupied

retired from business (not army or navy)
pensioners
old age pensioners
private means
students
scholars
others
Peers, M.P.s, Privy Councillors
army pensioners
navy pensioners
theological students
law students
medical students, assistants

art students
agricultural students
persons returned by property, rank, and not by special occupation
children under 5 years of age
land proprietors
house proprietors
vagrants, gipsies
gentlemen – independent, annuitant, dependent on relatives
almspersons (no stated occupation)

paupers, lunatics (no stated occupation)
prisoners
housewives, etc.
capitalists, shareholders
farmer's daughters
Chelsea Pensioner
Greenwich Pensioner
others supported by the community
persons of no stated occupation or condition

Not all occupations given in the above list appear in every census; often they appear in a much condensed form. The exception is the extremely detailed census for 1841. All occupations given in that year have not been reproduced here. Most are easily identifiable, but where this is not so, reference should be made to the appendix to volume X of the Census of England and Wales 1911, where an extremely full classification may be found.

3   Employment data – Series B classification

As might be expected, the problems encountered here are less daunting than those relating to the data in Series A. The industrial/occupational dichotomy has been resolved in favour of the former classification, the data no longer include inflationary bias of retired persons and others permanently out of the labour force, and the definitional problems relating to industrial orders are much simpler. The only 'bad' census during the twentieth century from the point of view of this analysis is that taken in 1921. The data on industry dis-aggregated at county level are published in the form of a condensed list which groups some information in such a way as to preclude the building up of orders from the requisite Minimum List Headings in all cases. Even so, the net result of this was to reallocate 'wrongly' only 3.28 per cent of those employed.

The definitional basis for this series is the standard industrial classification as revised in 1968, and which provides the basis for the 1971 census classifi-cation. However, rather than stick rigidly to achieving comparability with this model, which in some cases is easier for 1931 than for 1951, comparability between successive censuses has also been taken into account. Quite often it has been found possible to achieve comparability over 1921–1961 with a break between 1961 and 1971. This procedure has been followed, in the interest of long-term consistency. Generally speaking there has been a high level of continuity over the entire series with a general improvement of continuity as the data approach the present. The only notable departure from this is found in industrial order 24 where 1951 and 1961 break the continuity of the sequence.

There is a problem involved in the estimation of the degree of continuity obtained. Primarily this reflects the fact that changes in classification made by the office of the Registrar General often involve the splitting of groups contained within a Minimum List Heading. From the published data it is, of course, possible only to deal with whole Minimum List Headings. With regard to the degree of comparability between 1951 and 1961, this may be quanti-fied since the data for 1951 are given by 1951 and 1961 criteria in the latter census. The 1951 census gives a list of changes adopted since 1931 but not in a form which enables quantification of the degree of comparability. The errors detected in this series seem sufficiently small for the data to be used with some considerable confidence, with the possible exception of the data for 1921.

Notes on industrial orders in Series B
1. 1911 class includes 'drovers' who were relegated to the 'Not classified' category in 1921 and 1931, and later restored to this industrial order.

2. Mining employment in coal mines was omitted from the 1921 industry tables. However the census notes that 'In this case the industrial classification coincides so closely with the occupational classification that the local distribution shown in the occupational tables appeared to meet all practical purposes.'† In 1921 and 1931 this industrial order also included 'coal, iron, and steel companies – branch of industry not known' who were fortunately small in number.

† *Census of England and Wales 1921*, Industry Tables, p. 339, footnotes.

3. There is a small discrepancy between 1971 and earlier censuses in the classification of 'vegetable and animal oils and fats' which was included here in 1971, whereas hitherto it came under industrial order 5.

4/5. These two industrial orders have only been separated in 1961 and 1971. In 1951 'patent fuel' workers were entered under industrial order 16 instead of industrial order 4/5. In 1921, due to the presentation of a condensed list this order contained 'ganister manufacture' and 'other manufacture' in stone, cement, etc. which should be in industrial order 16.

6. There is some lack of clarity in earlier censuses as to the precise distribution of employees within metal industries. 1911 contained 'ironfounders' and 'iron workers (undefined)' which groups have been included under this industrial order, but which may contain some who should not have been so classed.

In 1921 this industrial order included 'patternmakers' who were otherwise in industrial order 7, and lost 'typefounders' to industrial order 12.

7. There is a lack of comparability between 1971 in which 'engineer's small tools and gauges' are classed under industrial order 12, instead of here as had previously been the practice. In 1921 'patternmakers' were lost to industrial order 6. But 'steam locomotives, road & rail, and railway plant' were included here. This Minimum List Heading should have been under industrial order 11. Here again occurs the problem of lack of clarity in 1911 data which were partly occupationally based. 'Millwrights' and 'erectors, fitters, turners' were included here, some of whom should doubtless be elsewhere, particularly in the other metal and engineering trades.

8. Prior to 1961 the repairing of watches was included under this order. Later and correctly it was included in industrial order 23. 'Watchmaking' in 1921 was omitted from this industrial order and included in industrial order 12. The manufacture of photographic plate, etc. was included in industrial order 19 from 1921 to 1951. In 1961 it was included in this industrial order, as it probably was in 1911. In 1971 it was transferred again this time to industrial order 5.

9. Prior to 1961 this industrial order did not contain the manufacture of gramophones and records, which were included in industrial order 19. Prior to 1951 this industrial order included 'wiring and contracting' which group contained some who later would probably be elsewhere, particularly in industrial order 20.

10. There are no apparent problems relating to this industrial order.

11. In 1971 'perambulators, hand carts, etc.' were removed from this industrial order to industrial order 7. See notes on industrial order 7 above regarding 1921 census.

12. See notes to industrial order 7 regarding 1971, and notes to industrial orders 6 and 8 regarding 1921. Censuses for 1921 and 1931 included the

manufacture of lamps under this order. There was probably some overlap with industrial order 9 in this regard.

13. There are no apparent problems relating to this industrial order.

14. There are no apparent problems relating to this industrial order.

15. Prior to 1971 rubber footwear was classed in industrial order 19. In 1921 artificial flowers were classed in industrial order 19. In 1911 waterproof clothing was grouped under the general heading 'waterproof goods' in industrial order 19.

16. See notes to industrial order 4/5.

17. In 1921 'dealers in timber' were allocated to this order; this group should have been in industrial order 23. In 1911 undertakers were classed in this industrial order instead of industrial order 26 as on subsequent occasions.

18. There are no apparent problems relating to this industrial order.

19. 'Photographic paper, plate, film, etc.' was included here from 1921 to 1951, but was allocated to industrial order 8 in 1911 and 1961, and to industrial order 5 in 1971. See also notes to industrial orders 9 and 15 above.

20. There are no apparent problems relating to this industrial order.

21. There are no apparent problems relating to this industrial order.

22. In 1921 employees of 'Post Office' were erroneously classed in industrial order 27. In 1911 coalporters were classed in industrial order 23.

23. In 1931 this industrial order included some money lenders who might properly belong to industrial order 24. In 1921 both pawnbrokers and dealers in timber were excluded from this industrial order to 24 and 17 respectively. In 1911 some coalheavers from industrial order 22 and some newsroom keepers from 26 slightly inflate this industrial order.

24. This is probably the most 'messy' order in Series B. In 1961 business services were included in industrial order 26 instead of here. In 1951 business services were included in industrial order 25. On other occasions they were included in this industrial order. The data for 1921 included pawnbrokers here instead of in industrial order 23.

25. See notes to industrial order 24 regarding 1951. The data for 1921 are badly distorted by the loss of 'education' to industrial order 27. The same census includes 'political and industrial associations' in this industrial order instead of in industrial order 26. There was a small inflation in the 1911 data due to the inclusion of a split category here. Some classed under 'hospital, institution and Benevolent Society service' should have been in industrial order 26.

26. See notes on industrial order 24 regarding 1961. Prior to 1961 this order was diminished by the classification of motor maintenance, footwear repairing and similar services under other industrial orders. In 1921 'service of foreign governments' was excluded from this industrial order to 'not classified'. See also notes to industrial order 25 regarding 1921.

27. The data for 1921 were very badly affected by the inclusion of 'Post Office' and 'education' which should have been in industrial orders 22 and 25 respectively.

N.C. In 1921 this industrial order included 'service of foreign governments' which should have been in industrial order 26.

Composition of industrial orders by Minimum List Heading. 1921

1. 000–019
2. 039–049 (plus 030 for county tables)
3. 360–390
4/5. 050–052, 056–059, 070–109
6. 110–133, 134, 137–140, 149, 243
7. 150, 153–159, 151–152, 222, 227, 230, 237, 241–242
8. 489–490
9. 160–169
10. 190–201
11. 170–189
12. 135–136, 141, 210–221, 223–226, 228–229, 231–236, 238–240, 244–259
13. 260–324
14. 330–338
15. 340–359
16. 053–055, 060–069, 460–461
17. 400–419, 641
18. 420–433, 439–447, 459
19. 434–435, 480–487, 491–492, 493–509
20. 462–479
21. 510–529
22. 530–599
23. 600–670 (not 641)
24. 680–685, 686–699
25. 730–749
26. 448, 750–789
27. 700–729
N.C. 790, 809, 899, X

Composition of industrial orders by Minimum List Heading. 1931

1. 000–019
2. 030–049
3. 360–390
4/5. 050–051, 070–109
6. 110–133, 137–140, 245–247
7. 134, 150, 153–169, 222, 227, 232, 240, 243–244
8. 253, 497–498
9. 170–179
10. 200–209
11. 151–152, 180–199
12. 135–136, 141, 210–221, 223–226, 228–231, 233–239, 241–242, 249–250, 254–259
13. 260–324
14. 330–339
15. 340–359, 502
16. 053–069, 460–461
17. 400–419
18. 420–433, 439–447, 459
19. 434–435, 470–471, 480–496, 499–501, 508–509
20. 462–469
21. 510–529
22. 530–591, 710
23. 600–670, 686
24. 680–685, 687–699
25. 711, 722, 730–741, 749
26. 448, 742–744, 750–790
27. 700, 719–720, 728–729
N.C. 809, X

Composition of industrial orders by Minimum List Heading. 1951

1. 1–3
2. 10–19
3. 150–169
4/5. 30–39

6. 40–49
7. 52–69
8. 100–101
9. 70–79
10. 50–51
11. 80, 82–89
12. 90–99, 102
13. 110–129
14. 130–132
15. 140–148
16. 20–29
17. 170–179
18. 180–189
19. 103, 190–194, 199
20. 200–202
21. 210–212
22. 220–239
23. 240–246
24. 250
25. 270–279
26. 81, 149, 195, 280–299
27. 260–265
Not stated and ill defined

Composition of industrial orders by Minimum List Heading. 1961

1. 001–003
2. 101–109
3. 211–240
4. 261–263
5. 271–277
6. 311–322
7. 331–349
8. 351–352
9. 361–369
10. 370
11. 381–389
12. 391–399
13. 411–429
14. 431–433
15. 441–450
16. 461–469
17. 471–479
18. 481–489
19. 491–499
20. 500
21. 601–603
22. 701–709
23. 810–832
24. 860
25. 871–879
26. 881–899
27. 901–906
Industry inadequately described; place of work outside UK

Composition of industrial orders by Minimum List Heading. 1971

1. 001–003
2. 101–109
3. 211–240
4. 261–263
5. 271–279
6. 311–323
7. 331–349
8. 351–354
9. 361–369
10. 370
11. 380–385
12. 390–399
13. 411–429
14. 431–433
15. 441–450
16. 461–469
17. 471–479
18. 481–489
19. 491–499
20. 500
21. 601–603
22. 701–709
23. 810–832
24. 860–866
25. 871–879
26. 881–899
27. 901–906

Industry inadequately described; place of work outside UK

4 Comparison of Series A and Series B (1911)

1. Agriculture, forestry and fishing

farmers, graziers	(67,530 females)
farmers', graziers' – sons, daughters or other relatives assisting in the work of the farm	
farm bailiffs, foremen	
shepherds	
agricultural labourers, farm servants – distinguished as in charge of cattle	
agricultural labourers, farm servants – distinguished as in charge of horses	
agricultural labourers, farm servants – not otherwise distinguished	
woodmen	
nurserymen, seedsmen, florists	
market gardeners (including labourers)	
other gardeners (not domestic)	
agricultural machine – proprietors, attendants	
others engaged or connected with agriculture	
fishermen	
drovers, lairmen	1,490,857
cattle, sheep – dealers, salesmen	
dog, bird, animal – keepers, dealers	
knackers; catsmeat dealers	9,674
	1,500,531

A.	1,500,531		B.	1,500,531
less	67,530 (to not occupied)		less	9,674 (to 23)
	1,433,001			1,490,857

2. Mining and quarrying

coal and shale mine – workers at face	
coal and shale mine – other workers below ground	
coal and shale mine – workers above ground	
coal and shale mine – owners, agents, managers	
coal and shale mine – other mine service	
iron miners, quarriers	
copper miners	
tin miners	
lead miners	
miners in other minerals	
metalliferous mine – owners, general managers, captains	
metalliferous mine – other mine service	
stone, slate, etc. mine, quarry – owners, agents, managers	
stone – miners, quarriers	
slate – miners, quarriers	
clay, sand, gravel, chalk – pit, etc. workers	1,143,893
stone – cutters, dressers	
slate workers	
limeburners	
other workers in products of quarries	20,330
coal, coke – merchants, dealers	
dealers in stone, slate, etc.	
coalheavers, coal porters	70,107
	1,234,330

A.	1,234,330		B.	1,234,330
			less	20,330 (to 16)
				1,214,000
			less	70,107 (to 23)
	1,234,330			1,143,893

3. Food, drink and tobacco

creamery workers
provision curers
slaughterers
fish curers
millers, cereal food manufacture
bread, biscuit, cake etc. − makers
jam, preserve, sweet − makers
sugar refiners
chocolate, cocoa − makers
ginger beer, mineral water − manufacture
mustard, vinegar, spice, pickle, etc −
    makers
tobacco manufacture
maltsters
brewers
distillers, spirit manufacture
beer bottlers
cellarmen   333,855

milksellers, dairymen
cheesemongers, buttermen, provision dealers
butchers, meat salesmen
fishmongers, poulterers, game dealers
corn, flour, seed − merchants, dealers
bakers, confectioners (dealers)
grocers; tea, coffee, chocolate − dealers
greengrocers, fruiterers
other dealers in food
tobacconists
wine and spirit − merchants, agents   798,643

     1,132,498

A.	1,132,498	B.	1,132,498
		less	798,643 (to 23)
	1,132,498		333,855

4. Coal and petroleum products
5. Chemicals and allied industries

coke burners
patent fuel manufacture
oil − millers, refiners; oil cake makers
dye, paint, ink, blacking − manufacture
gunpowder, guncotton, explosive substance −
    manufacture
cartridge, fireworks, explosive article −
    manufacture
lucifer match manufacture
salt makers
manufacturing chemist
alkali manufacture
candle, grease − manufacture
soap − boilers, makers
manure manufacture
glue, size, varnish, etc. − makers   122,628

chemists, druggists
oil and colourmen
other dealers   51,557

     174,185

A.	174,185	B.	174,185
		less	51,557 (to 23)
	174,185		122,628

6. Metal manufacture

pig iron manufacture (blast furnaces)
puddling furnaces; iron and steel rolling
    mills
tube manufacture
steel − manufacturing, smelting, founding
ironfounders
stove, grate, range, fire iron − makers
iron workers (undefined)
brassfounder
type cutters, founders
tinplate manufacture
copper manufacture
lead manufacture
zinc manufacture
brass, bronze − manufacture
manufacture of these or unspecified metals   355,346

galvanised sheet manufacture   4,844

blacksmith, striker
brass finisher
coppersmith
bedstead makers (iron or brass)
tinplate goods makers
copper workers
leaden goods makers
zinc workers
brass, bronze − workers   234,748

     594,938

A.	594,938	B.	594,938
less	4,844 (to 12)	less	234,748 (to 12)
	590,094		360,190

7. Mechanical engineering

weighing and measuring apparatus makers
gunsmith, gun manufacturers
sword, bayonet – makers, cutlers
millwrights
erectors, fitters, turners
erectors', fitters', turners' – labourers
boiler makers
metal machinists
patternmakers
labourers (undefined) in engineering
    works
others in engineering or machine making
    – textiles
    – other
roller engravers, block cutters (for textile,
    printing)

Total for Series A and B	516,326

8. Instrument engineering

watchmakers and clockmakers
scientific instrument makers, opticians
photographic apparatus makers
surgical and dental instrument and
    apparatus makers

Total for Series A and B	38,578

9. Electrical engineering

electrical cable manufacture
electric lamp manufacture
other electrical apparatus makers,
    electrical fitters
electricians (undefined)   101,245

electricity supply   15,649
                             116,894

A.	116,894	B.	116,894
		less	15,649 (to 21)
	116,894		101,245

10. Shipbuilding and marine engineering

ship – platers, riveters etc.
ship – other workers in iron
shipwrights
ship – other workers in wood
ship painters
shipyard labourers (undefined)
others in ship and boat building

Total for Series A and B	155,885

11. Vehicles

railway – coach, wagon makers
tram car makers
cycle makers
motor car chassis makers;
    motor car mechanics
motor car body makers
coach, carriage – makers
wheelwrights
others in construction of vehicles

Total for Series A and B	192,738

12. Metal goods not elsewhere specified

goldsmiths, silversmiths, jewellers
lapidaries and other workers
tool makers
file makers
saw makers
cutlers, scissors makers
needle, pin – makers
steel pen makers
nail manufacture
bolt, nut, rivet, screw, staple – makers
anchor, chain – manufacture
wire – drawers, makers, workers, weavers
lamp, lantern, candlestick – makers
white metal – plated ware manufacturers,
    pewterers
other iron goods makers
other metal workers
die, seal, coin, medal – makers
japanners   245,278

lock, key – makers
gas fittings makers   14,489

ironmongers; hardware – dealers, merchants
other dealers in metals, machines, etc.
dealers in precious metals, jewellery, watches   71,618

                                       331,385

A.	331,385		B.	331,385	
add	4,844 (from 6)		add	234,748 (from 6)	
	336,229			566,133	
less	14,489 (to 20)		less	71,618 (to 23)	
	321,740			494,515	

13. Textiles

cotton — card and blowing room processes
cotton — spinning processes
cotton — winding, warping, etc. processes
cotton — weaving processes
cotton — workers in other processes
cotton — workers undefined
fustian cutters
wool — sorting processes
wool — carding and combing processes
wool and worsted — spinning processes
wool and worsted — weaving processes
wool and worsted — workers in other processes
wool and worsted — workers undefined
silk — spinning processes
silk — weaving processes
silk — workers in other processes
silk — workers undefined
flax, linen — manufacture
hemp manufacture
jute manufacture
cocoa fibre manufacture
rope, twine, cord — manufacture
mat makers
canvas, sailcloth, sacking, net, etc. —
    manufacture
hosiery manufacture
lace manufacture
carpet, rug, felt — manufacture
thread manufacture
smallware manufacture
fancy goods (textile) etc. manufacture
weavers of sundry fabrics and undefined
other workers in sundry fabrics and undefined
factory hands (textile) undefined
textile bleachers
textile printers
textile dyers
textile — calenderers and finishers   1,294,274

drapers, linen drapers, mercers
other dealers in textile fabrics   214,461

elastic web manufacture   3,777

        1,512,512

A.	1,512,512		B.	1,512,512	
less	3,777 (to 19)		less	214,461 (to 23)	
	1,508,735			1,298,051	

14. Leather, leather goods and fur

furriers, skinners
tanners
curriers
leather goods, portmanteau, bag, strap, etc. —
    makers
saddlers; harness, whip — makers   89,749

brush, broom — makers; hair, bristle — workers
quill, feather — dressers   22,538

dealers in skins, leather, hair and feathers   8,973

        121,260

A.	121,260		B.	121,260	
			less	22,538 (to 19)	
			less	8,973 (to 23)	
	121,260			89,749	

15. Clothing and footwear

straw plait manufacture
straw hat, straw bonnet — manufacture
felt hat manufacture
makers of cloth caps and hats
makers of other caps and hats
milliners
dressmakers
stay, corset — makers
shirt makers, seamstresses
tailors
glove makers
boot, shoe — makers
slipper makers
patten, clog — makers
artificial flower makers
umbrella, parasol, stick — makers
other workers in dress   1,143,559

hat, bonnet, shawl, plait, etc. — dealers
clothiers, outfitters — dealers
hosiers, haberdashers
boot, shoe, patten, clog — dealers
other dealers in dress   107,406

        1,250,965

A.	1,250,965	B.	1,250,965
		less	107,406 (to 23)
	1,250,965		1,143,559

16. Bricks, pottery, glass, cement etc.

brick, plain tile, terra cotta — makers
plaster, cement — manufacture
earthenware, china, porcelain — manufacture
sheet, plate glass — manufacture
glass bottle manufacture
other workers in glass manufacture — 174,290

brick, cement — dealers
earthenware, china, glass — dealers — 12,566

186,856

A.	186,856	B.	186,856
		less	12,566 (to 23)
			174,290
		add	20,330 (from 2)
	186,856		194,620

17. Timber, furniture etc.

cabinet makers
upholsterers
french polishers
house and shop fittings makers
undertakers, funeral furniture makers
wood carvers; carvers and gilders
willow, cane, rush -- workers; basket
    makers
sawyers, wood cutting machinists
lath, wooden fence, hurdle — makers
wood turners
wooden box, packing case — makers
coopers; hoop makers, benders
cork, bark — cutters, workers
other workers in wood — 276,191

furniture, etc. — dealers
timber, wood, cork, bark — merchants,
    dealers — 41,256

317,447

A.	317,447	B.	317,447
		less	41,256 (to 23)
	317,447		276,191

18. Paper, printing and publishing

paper manufacture
paper stainers
envelope makers
paper bag makers
cardboard box makers
other workers in paper
stationery manufacture
printers — hand compositors
    — machine compositors
    — printing machine minders
    — stereotypers, electrotypers
    — others in printing
lithographers; copper and steel plate
    printers
bookbinders
newspaper publishers
book, print — publishers, sellers — 335,657

newspaper agents, newsroom keepers
stationers, law stationers
other dealers in paper — 53,924

advertising, bill posting — agents
circular, envelope-addressers, etc.
bill posters — 7,726

397,307

A.	397,307	B.	397,307
		less	53,924 (to 23)
			343,383
		less	7,726 (to 24)
	397,307		335,657

19. Other manufacturing industries

piano, organ — makers
other musical instrument makers
fishing tackle, toy, game apparatus — makers
celluloid — makers, workers
india rubber, gutta percha — workers
waterproof goods makers
button makers
tobacco pipe, snuff box, etc. — makers
bone, horn, tortoiseshell, ivory — workers
floor cloth, oil cloth — manufacture — 83,121

elastic web manufacture — 3,777

brush, broom — makers; hair, bristle — workers
quill, feather — dressers — 22,538

dealers in instruments, toys, etc. — 7,948

117,384

A.	117,384		B.	117,384	
less	22,538 (to 14)		less	3,777 (to 13)	
				113,607	
			less	7,948 (to 23)	
	94,846			105,659	

drainage and sanitary service
scavenging and disposal of refuse   27,183

113,440

A.	113,440		B.	113,440	
less	15,649 (to 9)		less	27,183 (to 27)	
	97,791			86,257	

20. Construction

builders
builders' labourers
carpenters, joiners
carpenters', joiners' – labourers
bricklayers
bricklayers' labourers
architectural, monumental – carvers,
    sculptors
monumental masons
masons
masons' labourers
slaters, tilers
plasterers
plasterers' labourers
paperhangers, whitewashers
painters, decorators
glaziers
plumbers
gasfitters
locksmiths, bellhangers
railway, canal, harbour – contractors
navvies; railway, etc. – contractors'
    labourers
platelayers, gangers, packers
railway labourers
well, mine – sinkers, borers
road – contractors, surveyors, inspectors
paviours, road labourers   1,138,881

gas fittings makers
lock, key – makers   14,489

1,153,370

A.	1,153,370		B.	1,153,370	
			less	14,489 (to 12)	
	1,153,370			1,138,881	

21. Gas, electricity and water

gas works service
waterworks service   70,608

electricity supply   15,649

22. Transport and communication

railway engine – drivers, stokers, cleaners
railway guards
pointsmen, level crossing men
signalmen
railway ticket – examiners, collectors,
    checkers
railway porters
other railway servants
railway – officials, clerks
livery stable keepers; coach, cab – proprietors
coachmen (not domestic), cabmen
horsekeepers, grooms, stablemen (not
    domestic)
omnibus service – horse drivers
                – motor drivers
                – conductors
                – others
motor car drivers (not domestic), motor cab
    drivers
motor van, etc. drivers
carmen, carriers, carters, wagoners (not farm)
van, etc. – guards, boys
others connected with carrying or cartage
tramway service – drivers
                – conductors
                – others
others on roads
merchant service; seamen
    – navigating department
    – engineering department
    – cooks, stewards and others
pilots, boatmen on seas
bargemen, lightermen, watermen
navigation service
dock labourers, wharf labourers
harbour, dock, wharf, lighthouse –
    officials, servants
warehousemen
messengers, porters, watchmen (not
    railway or government)
telegraph telephone operators (not
    government)   1,476,483

post office – telegraphists, telephone operators
post office clerks, etc.   142,070

1,618,553

A. 1,618,553   B. 1,618,553
  less   142,070 (to 27)

     1,476,483   1,618,553

23. Distributive trades

cattle, sheep – dealers
dog, bird, animal – keepers, dealers
knackers, catsmeat dealers
coal, coke – merchants, dealers
dealers in stone, slate, etc.
coalheavers, coal porters
milksellers, dairymen
cheesemongers, buttermen, provision dealers
butchers, meat salesmen
fishmongers, poulterers, game dealers
corn, flour, seed – merchants, dealers
bakers, confectioners (dealers)
grocers; tea, coffee, chocolate – dealers
greengrocers, fruiterers
other dealers in food
tobacconists
wine and spirit merchants, agents
chemists, druggists
oil and colourmen
other dealers
ironmongers; hardware – dealers,
     merchants
other dealers in metals, machines, etc.
dealers in precious metals, jewellery and
     watches
drapers, linen drapers, mercers
other dealers in textile fabrics
dealers in skins, leather, hair and feathers
hat, bonnet, shawl, plait, etc. – dealers
clothiers, outfitters – dealers
hosiers, haberdashers
boot, shoe, patten, clog – dealers
other dealers in dress
brick, cement – dealers
earthenware, china, glass – dealers
furniture, etc. – dealers
timber, wood, cork, bark – merchants,
     dealers
stationers, law stationers
other dealers in paper
newspaper agents, newsroom keepers
dealers in instruments, toys, etc.   1,448,133

dealers in works of art
rag – gatherers, dealers
multiple shop, multiple store –
     proprietors, workers
general or unclassified shopkeepers,
     general dealers
pawnbrokers
costermongers, hawkers, street sellers
news – boys, vendors (street or undefined)   225,316

other dealers in sundry industries   1,812

                                            227,128

A. 227,128   B.   227,128
  less   1,812 (to   add 1,448,133 (from
       ——— N.C.)   ——— 1–19)
     225,316   1,675,261

24. Insurance, banking, finance and business services

bankers; bank – officials, clerks
bill-discounters, brokers; finance agents
life, house, ship, etc. – insurance –
     officials, clerks, etc.
insurance agents
auctioneers, appraisers, valuers, house agents   178,052

circular, envelope – addressers
advertising, bill posting agents
bill posters   7,726

sandwichmen, bill distributors   1,303

                                             187,081

A. 187,081   B.   187,081
  less   7,726 (to 18)   add 55,375 (from
                                       N.C.)
     179,355
  less   1,303 (to
       ——— N.C.)
     178,052   242,456

25. Professional and scientific services

clergymen (Established Church)
Roman Catholic priests
ministers, priests of other religious bodies
itinerant preachers, scripture readers,
     mission workers
monks, nuns, Sisters of Charity
church, chapel, cemetery – officers, etc.
barristers
solicitors
law clerks
physicians, surgeons, registered practitioners
dentists (including assistants)
midwives
sick nurses, invalid attendants
subordinate medical service
schoolmasters, teachers, professors,
     lecturers
others connected with education
veterinary surgeons
authors, editors, journalists, reporters

persons engaged in scientific pursuits
others connected with literature, etc.
painters, sculptors, artists
engravers
architects
civil, mining – engineers
land, house, ship – surveyors
professional engineers', professional
   surveyors' – assistants
accountants
hospital, institution and Benevolent
   Society – service

    Total for Series A and B   730,740

26. Miscellaneous services

photographers
musicians, music masters, singers
actors
art, music, theatre – service, etc.
performers, showmen; exhibition, games –
   service
officers of commercial gilds, societies
coffee house, eating house – keepers
lodging house, boarding house – keepers
inn, hotel – keepers, publicans, beersellers,
   cider dealers
barmen
waiters (not domestic)
others in inn, hotel, eating house, etc. –
   service
domestic indoor service in hotels, lodging
   houses, etc.
other domestic indoor service
day girls, day servants (so returned)
domestic – coachmen, grooms
domestic – motor car drivers, attendants
domestic gardeners
gamekeepers
motor garage – proprietor, workers
college, club – service
park, lodge, gate – keepers
caretakers, office keepers
cooks (not domestic)
charwomen
laundry workers; washers, ironers,
   manglers, etc.
bath and wash house service
others engaged in service
chimney sweeps
receiving shop, receiving office – keepers,
   assistants (laundry; dyers and cleaners)
wig makers, hair dressers

    Total for Series A and B   2,888,363

27. Public administration and defence

post office – telegraphists, telephone operators
other post office officers and clerks
postmen
post office messengers, etc.   142,070

other civil service officers and clerks
other civil service messengers
police
Poor Law service
municipal, parish and other local or county
   officers
army officers (effective)
soldiers and N.C.O.s
officers of the navy (effective)
officers of the marines (effective)
men of the navy
men of the marines   410,754

         552,824

A.	552,824	B.	552,824
		less	142,070 (to 22)
			410,754
		add	27,183 (from 21)
	552,824		437,937

Not classified

general labourers
engine – drivers, stokers, firemen (not
   railway marine or agriculture)
artisans, mechanics, apprentices
factory – hands, labourers (undefined)
machinists, machine workers (undefined)
contractors, managers, manufacturers,
   foremen (undefined)
other workers in sundry industries
commercial travellers
commercial or business clerks
salesmen, buyers (not otherwise described) 1,138,722

merchants (commodity undefined)
brokers, agents, factors
sandwichmen, bill distributors   56,678

other dealers in sundry industries   1,812

        1,197,212

A.	1,197,212	B.	1,197,212
		less	1,812 (to 23)
			1,195,400
		less	56,678 (to 24)
	1,197,212		1,138,722

Table 4.1. *Comparison between industrial orders by Series A and Series B definitions*

| Industrial order | Changed involved in transformation from Series A to Series B | | Common* core (per cent) |
	Gain	Loss	
1. Agriculture, forestry and fishing	+ 67,530 (N.O.)	− 9,674 (23)	94.8
2. Mining and quarrying		− 20,330 (16) − 70,107 (23)	92.7
3. Food, drink and tobacco		−798,643 (23)	29.5
4/ Coal and petroleum products 5. Chemicals and allied industries		− 51,557 (23)	70.4
6. Metal manufacture	+ 4,844 (12)	−234,748 (12)	59.7
7. Mechanical engineering			100.0
8. Instrument engineering			100.0
9. Electrical engineering		− 15,649 (21)	86.6
10. Shipbuilding and marine engineering			100.0
11. Vehicles			100.0
12. Metal goods not elsewhere specified	+ 234,748 (6) + 14,489 (20)	− 4,844 (6) − 71,618 (23)	43.0
13. Textiles	+ 3,777 (19)	−214,461 (23)	85.5
14. Leather, leather goods and fur		− 22,538 (19) − 8,973 (23)	74.0
15. Clothing and footwear		−107,406 (23)	91.4
16. Bricks, pottery, glass, cement etc.	+ 20,330 (2)	− 12,566 (23)	84.1
17. Timber, furniture etc.		− 41,256 (23)	87.0
18. Paper printing and publishing		− 53,924 (23) − 7,726 (24)	84.5
19. Other manufacturing industries	+ 22,538 (14)	− 3,777 (13) − 7,948 (23)	70.8
20. Construction		− 14,489 (12)	98.7
21. Gas, electricity and water	+ 15,649 (9)	− 27,183 (27)	62.2
22. Transport and communication	+ 142,070 (27)		91.2
23. Distributive trades	+ 1,812 (N.C.) + 1,448,133 (1−19)		13.5
24. Insurance, banking, finance and business services	+ 7,726 (18) + 1,303 (N.C.) + 55,375 (N.C.)		73.4
25. Professional and scientific services			100.0
26. Miscellaneous services			100.0
27. Public administration and defence	+ 27,183 (21)	−142,070 (22)	95.3
Not classified		− 1,812 (23) − 1,303 (24) − 55,375 (24)	95.1

*The 'common core' is that proportion of people classified in a given industrial order who appear in that category under both Series A and Series B definitions expressed as a percentage of the total number of people who appear in the category under either definition. Thus, in the case of Agriculture, forestry and fishing, 1,500,531 people are classed in this industrial order under Series A definition, Series B definition, or both. Of them, 67,530 are in B but not A, while 9,674 are in A but not B. Thus 77,204 people are members of the total set but not common to A and B. The remainder, 1,423,327, appear in industrial order 1 by both A and B definitions and are thus the 'common core', and account for 94.8 per cent of the total set.

5   County and regional classification

The only possible basis for a comprehensive analysis of the component regions of Great Britain using the census data is to take the county as the basic unit. Wherever pertinent, data have been presented for counties. In the case of Scotland and Wales pressure of space together with the smallness of population of some of the component counties of those countries has made such detail impracticable. Data for Scotland and Wales have therefore been presented at sub-regional level, as indicated in table 5.1. The basic model taken for the regions of England and the sub-regions of Scotland and Wales is the composition of the New Standard Regions as defined in April 1974 in England and Wales, and the new local government areas of Scotland as defined in April 1975. These definitions have been modified by the need in the present study to have all regions and sub-regions comprised of undivided counties. The 'common core' or degree of 'overlap' between the officially defined areas and those used in this study has been quantified and the results presented in table 5.4. below. As can be seen from that table the comparability is very good both for the English regions and for the Scottish and Welsh sub-regions. Such a comparison between English counties and the new areas which became new counties and metropolitan counties in April 1974 does not show a close comparability with the old administrative county in many cases, principally because of the creation of the new metropolitan counties.†

As a result of the local government reorganisation of the 1830s, the districts of the superintendent registrars of births and deaths were created to be co-extensive with the poor law unions. The 1841 census used this duality as the basis for the registration counties, which were simply aggregates of poor law unions. This registration county was the area for which employment and population data were presented in the census from 1841 until 1901. By then the effect of further local government reorganisation in England and Wales under the Local Government Acts of 1888 and 1894 was reflected in the adoption of the administrative county. The administrative county was adopted as the spatial basis for employment analysis in England and Wales in 1901, and thenceforward until the further changes in local government in 1974, which made quite radical changes at county level with the introduction of several new metropolitan counties.

There are thus two breaks in comparability over time, the first being in the switch from registration counties in 1891 to administrative counties in 1901, and the second in 1974 which falls outside the present study but which makes for considerable discrepancies at county level between the areas used in the present study and the new counties of England and Wales. Fortunately the 1901 census provided population data for each county by both the new

†See Office of Population Censuses and Surveys, *Reorganisation of Local Government Areas: Correlation of New and Old Areas*, (H.M.S.O. 1975), table 2.

administrative county criteria and by the old registration county definition.
Thus it is possible to compare the two forms of definition in terms of the 1901
population. The results of this are presented below in table 5.2. In most cases,
at county level, the degree of overlap is encouragingly high, although there
are exceptions, especially Worcestershire, Huntingdonshire, Rutland and
Derbyshire. At regional level, however, the degree of overlap is extremely
high in all cases. The changes in county boundaries which were reflected in
the 1901 census, were effected in Scotland in 1891 as a result of the Local
Government (Scotland) Act of 1889. Thus in 1891 the registration county
was replaced by the civil county as the basis for employment data. A comparison of regional population in Scotland by civil and registration county in
1891 shows a very high level of overlap, as shown in table 5.4.

Table 5.1. *Composition of regions and sub-regions by county*

(a) Regions of Great Britain:

South East	London, Middlesex, Kent, Surrey, Sussex, Hamp-shire, Berkshire, Oxford, Buckingham, Bedford, Hertford, Essex.
East Anglia	Cambridge, Huntingdon, Norfolk, Suffolk.
South West	Cornwall, Devon, Somerset, Gloucester, Wiltshire, Dorset.
West Midlands	Hereford, Shropshire, Stafford, Warwick, Worcester.
East Midlands	Derby, Nottingham, Leicester, Lincoln, Northampton, Rutland.
North West	Cheshire, Lancashire.
Yorkshire and Humberside	West Riding, East Riding.
North	North Riding, Westmorland, Cumberland, Northumberland, Durham.
Wales	Wales.
Scotland	Scotland.

(b) Welsh sub-regions:

Glamorgan and Monmouth	Glamorgan, Monmouth.
North and West Wales	All Wales except Glamorgan and Monmouth.

(c) Scottish sub-regions:

Strathclyde	Argyll, Ayr, Bute, Dunbarton, Lanark, Renfrew.
Dumfries and Galloway	Dumfries, Kirkcudbright, Wigtown.
Borders	Berwick, Peebles, Roxburgh, Selkirk.
Lothian	East Lothian (Haddington), Midlothian (Edinburgh), West Lothian (Linlithgow).
Central and Fife	Clackmannan, Fife, Stirling.
Tayside	Angus (Forfar), Kinross, Perth.
Grampian	Aberdeen, Banff, Kincardine, Moray (Elgin).
Highland	Caithness, Inverness, Nairn, Orkney and Shetland, Ross and Cromarty, Sutherland.

Table 5.2. *Comparison between populations of registration counties and administrative counties in 1901*

| Registration county | Changes involved in transformation from registration county to administrative county | | Common core (per cent)* |
	Gain	Loss	
London	No change		100.00
Middlesex	+23,456 (Surrey)	− 6,549 (Essex) −34,899 (Herts)	92.2
Kent	+22,465 (Surrey) + 3,530 (Sussex)		97.3
Surrey	+11,895 (Berks)	−30,974 (Hants) −22,465 (Kent) −23,456 (Middlesex)	87.8
Sussex		− 3,530 (Kent)	99.4
Hampshire	+30,974 (Surrey)		96.1
Berkshire		− 1,179 (Gloucs) −10,792 (Oxford) −11,895 (Surrey) − 7,094 (Wilts)	89.1
Oxford	+10,792 (Berks) + 429 (Northants)	− 6,527 (Bucks) − 2,414 (Northants) − 2,518 (Warwick)	88.5
Bucks	+ 7,639 (Bedford) + 792 (Herts) + 9,027 (Northants) + 6,527 (Oxford)		87.8
Bedford	+ 3,336 (Hunts) + 1,038 (Northants)	− 7,639 (Bucks)	93.3
Hertford	+34,899 (Middlesex)	− 792 (Bucks) − 8,556 (Cambs) − 6,888 (Essex)	81.4
Essex	+ 528 (Cambs) + 6,888 (Herts) + 6,549 (Middlesex) + 7,388 (Suffolk)		98.0
Cambridge	+ 8,556 (Herts) + 2,638 (Hunts) + 1,799 (Northants)	− 528 (Essex) − 746 (Hunts) −14,602 (Norfolk) −13,038 (Suffolk)	80.4
Huntingdon	+ 746 (Cambs) + 426 (Lincoln) +12,177 (Northants)	− 3,336 (Bedford) − 2,638 (Cambs)	67.8
Norfolk	+14,602 (Cambs)	− 5,803 (Suffolk)	95.8
Suffolk	+13,038 (Cambs) + 5,803 (Norfolk)	− 7,388 (Essex)	93.1
Cornwall	+ 6,203 (Devon)	− 2,460 (Devon)	97.3
Devon	+ 2,460 (Cornwall) + 3,337 (Somerset)	− 6,203 (Cornwall) − 2,095 (Dorset)	97.9
Somerset		− 3,337 (Devon) −27,906 (Gloucs)	93.3

*See sidenote to table 4.1 for explanation of the 'common core'.

Gloucester	+ 1,179 (Berks)	− 356 (Wilts)	
	+ 1,293 (Hereford)	− 3,894 (Worcester)	
	+23,814 (Monmouth)		
	+27,906 (Somerset)		90.4
	+ 6,926 (Warwick)		
	+ 2,944 (Worcester)		
Wiltshire	+ 7,094 (Berks)		
	+ 356 (Gloucs)		97.3
Dorset	+ 2,095 (Devon)		99.0
Hereford	+ 1,550 (Monmouth)	− 1,293 (Gloucs)	
	+ 2,415 (Shrops)	− 583 (Monmouth)	
	+ 934 (Worcester)	− 1,406 (Worcester)	88.3
	+ 2,094 (N & W Wales)	− 2,944 (N & W Wales)	
	+ 809 (N & W Wales)		
Shropshire	+ 140 (Staffs)	− 4,488 (Cheshire)	
	+ 1,233 (Worcester)	− 2,415 (Hereford)	
	+ 3,539 (N & W Wales)	− 7,296 (Staffs)	
	+ 1,846 (N & W Wales)	− 2,150 (Worcester)	87.6
		− 3,956 (N & W Wales)	
		− 5,057 (N & W Wales)	
		− 701 (N & W Wales)	
Stafford	+ 4,054 (Derby)	−35,838 (Derby)	
	+ 7,296 (Shrops)	− 140 (Shrops)	
	+96,157 (Worcester)	−12,596 (Warwick)	83.1
		−73,924 (Worcester)	
Warwick	+ 1,581 (Leics)	− 6,926 (Gloucs)	
	+ 2,518 (Oxford)	− 1,373 (Leics)	
	+12,596 (Staffs)	− 2,284 (Northants)	84.9
	+75,426 (Worcester)	−48,235 (Worcester)	
Worcester	+ 1,406 (Hereford)	− 934 (Hereford)	
	+ 2,150 (Shrops)	− 2,944 (Gloucs)	
	+73,924 (Staffs)	− 1,233 (Shrops)	51.4
	+48,235 (Warwick)	−96,157 (Staffs)	
	+ 3,894 (Gloucs)	−75,426 (Warwick)	
Derby	+ 6,988 (Leics)	− 6,223 (Leics)	
	+83,878 (Notts)	− 2,827 (Cheshire)	
	+35,838 (Staffs)	− 8,286 (Notts)	74.3
	+14,176 (West Riding)	− 4,054 (Staffs)	
Nottingham	+ 8,286 (Derby)	−83,878 (Derby)	
	+ 4,032 (Leics)	− 464 (Leics)	
	+ 3,618 (Lincoln)	− 8,141 (Lincoln)	81.1
	+ 960 (West Riding)	− 6,659 (West Riding)	
Leicester	+ 6,223 (Derby)	− 6,988 (Derby)	
	+ 2,995 (Lincoln)	− 4,202 (Northants)	
	+ 464 (Notts)	− 4,032 (Notts)	93.4
	+ 2,306 (Rutland)	− 1,581 (Warwick)	
	+ 1,373 (Warwick)		
Lincoln	+ 2,747 (Northants)	− 426 (Hunts)	
	+ 8,141 (Notts)	− 2,995 (Leics)	
	+ 9,449 (West Riding)	− 1,462 (Northants)	93.8
		− 3,618 (Notts)	
		− 2,835 (Rutland)	
Northants	+ 4,202 (Leics)	− 1,038 (Bedford)	
	+ 1,462 (Lincoln)	− 9,027 (Bucks)	
	+ 2,414 (Oxford)	− 1,799 (Cambs)	
	+ 1,563 (Rutland)	−12,177 (Hunts)	89.1
	+ 2,284 (Warwick)	− 2,747 (Lincoln)	
		− 429 (Oxford)	

Rutland	+ 2,835 (Lincoln)	− 2,306 (Leics) − 1,563 (Northants)	71.6
Cheshire	+ 2,827 (Derby) +63,380 (Lancs) + 4,488 (Shrops)	−18,142 (Lancs) −18,275 (N & W Wales)	87.6
Lancashire	+18,142 (Cheshire)	−63,380 (Cheshire) − 5,237 (West Riding)	98.0
West Riding	+ 5,237 (Lancs) + 6,659 (Notts) + 1,960 (East Riding)	−14,176 (Derby) − 9,449 (Lincoln) − 960 (Notts) − 3,100 (East Riding) − 2,149 (North Riding)	98.4
East Riding	+14,769 (North Riding) + 3,100 (West Riding)	− 6,924 (North Riding) − 1,960 (West Riding)	94.3
North Riding	+ 7,116 (Durham) + 6,924 (East Riding) + 2,149 (West Riding)	−14,769 (East Riding)	92.1
Westmorland	No change		100.0
Cumberland	No change		100.0
Northumberland	No change		100.0
Durham		− 7,116 (North Riding)	99.4
Glamorgan and Monmouth	+ 4,781 (N & W Wales) + 583 (Hereford) + 5,993 (N & W Wales)	−11,100 (N & W Wales) −23,814 (Gloucs) − 1,550 (Hereford)	96.0
North and West Wales	+18,275 (Cheshire) + 2,944 (Hereford) + 3,956 (Shrops) + 5,057 (Shrops) + 701 (Shrops) +11,100 (Glamorgan & Monmouth)	− 2,094 (Hereford) − 809 (Hereford) − 5,993 (Glamorgan & Monmouth) − 3,539 (Shrops) − 1,846 (Shrops) − 4,781 (Glamorgan & Monmouth)	93.0

Source: *Census of England and Wales 1901*, County Tables, vols. I−V

Table 5.3. *Comparison between population of regions by registration county and administrative county in 1901*

Registration county region	Changes involved in transformation from registration county to administrative county		Common core (per cent)*
	Gain	Loss	
South East	+11,252 (East Anglia) +10,494 (East Midlands)	− 8,273 (South West) − 2,414 (East Midlands) − 2,518 (West Midlands) − 8,556 (East Anglia)	99.6
East Anglia	+ 8,556 (South East) +14,402 (East Midlands)	−11,252 (South East)	96.9
South West	+ 8,273 (South East) +11,163 (West Midlands) +23,814 (Wales)	− 3,894 (West Midlands)	98.2
West Midlands	+ 2,518 (South East) + 5,635 (East Midlands) + 9,838 (Wales) + 3,894 (South West)	−11,163 (South West) −39,495 (East Midlands) − 4,488 (North West) −13,241 (Wales)	97.0
East Midlands	+ 2,414 (South East) +39,495 (West Midlands) +24,585 (Yorkshire & Humberside)	−10,494 (South East) −14,402 (East Anglia) − 5,635 (West Midlands) − 2,827 (North West) − 6,659 (Yorkshire & Humberside)	95.7
North West	+ 4,488 (West Midlands) + 2,827 (East Midlands)	−18,275 (Wales) − 5,237 (Yorkshire & Humberside)	99.4
Yorkshire & Humberside	+ 6,659 (East Midlands) + 5,237 (North West) +14,769 (North)	−24,585 (East Midlands) − 9,073 (North)	98.1
North	+ 9,073 (Yorkshire & Humberside)	−14,769 (Yorkshire & Humberside)	99.0
Wales	+13,241 (West Midlands) +18,275 (North West)	−23,814 (South West) − 9,838 (West Midlands)	96.8
Scotland	No change		100.0

*See sidenote to table 4.1 for explanation of the 'common core'.

Source: *Census of England and Wales 1901*, County Tables, vols. I–V

Table 5.4. *Comparison between populations of Scottish sub-regions by registration county and by civil county in 1891*

Sub-region by registration county	Changes involved in transformation from registration county to civil county		Common core (per cent)*
	Gain	Loss	
Strathclyde	+ 3,519 (Central) + 4,510 (Highland) + 139 (Borders)	− 24 (Dumfries) − 203 (Highland)	99.5
Dumfries and Galloway	+ 24 (Strathclyde)		100.0†
Borders		− 40 (Lothian) − 95 (Lothian) − 139 (Strathclyde)	99.8
Lothian	+ 40 (Borders) + 95 (Borders)		100.0†
Central and Fife	+ 165 (Tayside) + 197 (Tayside) + 450 (Tayside)	− 107 (Tayside) − 3,615 (Tayside) − 1,511 (Tayside) − 3,519 (Strathclyde)	97.1
Tayside	+ 107 (Central) + 3,615 (Central) + 1,511 (Central)	− 165 (Central) − 197 (Central) − 450 (Central)	98.6
Grampian	+ 12 (Highland) + 437 (Highland)		99.9
Highland	+ 203 (Strathclyde)	− 12 (Grampian) − 437 (Grampian) − 4,510 (Strathclyde)	98.0

*See sidenote to table 4.1.

†The degree of non-overlap in each of these cases was too small to be significant.

Table 5.5. *Comparison between 'county' regions and 1974–75 new standard regions, measured by 1971 population*

County region	Changes involved in transformation from county region to new standard region	Common core (per cent)*
South East	−188,240 (Hampshire to Dorset)	98.9
East Anglia	No change	100.0
South West	+188,240 (To Dorset from Hampshire)	95.4
West Midlands	No change	100.0
East Midlands	−305,570 (Lincolnshire to Humberside) − 1,670 (Nottinghamshire to South Yorkshire) − 1,480 (To Derbyshire from Cheshire)	92.2
North West	−107,030 (Lancashire to Cumbria) − 1,480 (Cheshire to Derbyshire) + 20,550 (To Greater Manchester from West Riding) + 20,480 (To Lancashire from West Riding)	97.8
Yorkshire and Humberside	− 20,550 (West Riding to Greater Manchester) − 20,480 (West Riding to Lancashire) − 3,680 (West Riding to Cumbria) +266,800 (To North Yorks from North Riding) +305,570 (To Humberside from Lincolnshire) + 1,670 (To South Yorkshire from Nottinghamshire)	87.1
North	−266,800 (North Riding to North Yorks) +107,030 (To Cumbria from Lancashire) + 3,680 (To Cumbria from West Riding)	88.9
Wales	No change	100.0
Scotland	No change	100.0
County sub-regions		
Monmouth and Glamorgan	+ 5,780 (To Mid Glamorgan from Breconshire) + 9,880 (To Gwent from Breconshire)	99.1
North and West Wales	− 5,780 (Breconshire to Mid Glamorgan) − 9,880 (Breconshire to Gwent)	98.5
Strathclyde	− 2,922 (Strathclyde to Highland) + 20,715 (To Strathclyde from Central)	99.1
Dumfries and Galloway	No change	100.0
Borders	+ 1,190 (To Borders from Lothian)	98.8
Lothian	− 13,367 (Lothian to Central − 1,190 (Lothian to Borders)	98.1
Central and Fife	− 20,715 (Central to Strathclyde) + 13,367 (To Central from Lothian) + 14,348 (To Central from Tayside)	92.0
Tayside	− 14,348 (Tayside to Central)	96.5
Grampian	− 2,464 (Grampian to Highland)	99.4
Highland	+ 2,464 (To Highland from Grampian) + 2,922 (To Highland from Strathclyde)	97.8

*See sidenote to table 4.1.

Sources: Office of Population Censuses and Surveys, *Reorganisation of Local Government Areas; Correlation of Old and New Areas.* (H.M.S.O. 1975) table 3, pp. 38–42. Scottish Office, *Scottish Abstract of Statistics* no. 4, 1974. (H.M.S.O.) p. vi. *Census of Scotland 1971*, County Tables.

6 Sources

Census of Great Britain 1841. Part 13. Occupation Abstract.

Census of Great Britain 1851. Vols. I and II. Occupation Tables.

Census of England and Wales 1861. Vol. II. County Divisions: Occupations.

Census of Scotland 1861. Vol. I. Table III. Occupations.

Census of England and Wales 1871. Vol. III. Divisional Tables: Occupations.

Census of Scotland 1871. Table XIV. Occupations.

Census of England and Wales 1881. Vol. III. Divisional Tables. Table 10.

Census of Scotland 1881. Vol. II Part XV. Occupations.

Census of England and Wales 1891. Vol. III. Divisional Tables. Table 7.

Census of Scotland 1891. Vol. II Part II. Occupations.

Census of England and Wales 1901. County Reports. Vols. I–V. Table 32.

Census of Scotland 1901. Vol. III. Occupations.

Census of England and Wales 1911. Vol. X. Occupations and Industries. Table 12.

Census of Scotland 1911. Vol. I. County Tables. Table XXII.

Census of England and Wales 1921. Industry Tables. Table 4.

Census of Scotland 1921. Vol. III. Industry Tables. Table 13.

Census of England and Wales 1931. Industries. Table 2.

Census of Scotland 1931. Vol. III. Industries. Table 16.

Census of England and Wales 1951. Industry Tables. Table 2.

Census of Scotland 1951. Industry Tables. Table 2.

Census of England and Wales 1961. Occupation, Industry and Socio-Economic Group. County Tables. Industry and Status. Table 3.

Census of Scotland 1961. County Tables. Industry and Status. Table 3.

Census of England and Wales 1971. Economic Activity County Leaflet. Industry and Status. Table 3.

Census of Scotland 1971. Economic Activity County Leaflet. Industry and Status. Table 3.

PART II

STATISTICAL TABLES

Series A, county and regional employment 1841–1911

MALE EMPLOYMENT: 1841

South East

	1. London	2. Middlesex	3. Kent	4. Surrey	5. Sussex	6. Hants.	7. Berks.	8. Oxon
1.	17,807		48,057	25,129	35,964	35,406	19,507	19,689
2.	2,696		505	1,096	214	184	78	116
3.	31,353		8,078	10,666	4,337	4,623	2,264	2,203
4.	–		–	–	–	–	–	–
5.	4,584		655	1,529	289	302	118	118
6.	10,769		3,216	3,895	1,761	2,391	1,022	848
7.	2,394		430	641	164	203	93	98
8.	4,498		302	521	144	160	82	81
9.	–		–	–	–	–	–	–
10.	2,231		2,341	978	245	1,445	76	33
11.	5,832		1,139	1,633	859	817	519	451
12.	8,212	Data for this	479	1,409	269	441	150	137
13.	22,682	county included	2,127	3,269	842	1,404	815	1,102
14.	6,190	under 'London'	973	4,176	698	700	350	334
15.	43,342		7,832	12,119	4,501	5,635	2,536	2,837
16.	3,004		764	1,189	423	449	190	174
17.	18,345		2,598	5,341	1,481	2,039	873	991
18.	12,428		1,328	3,605	337	432	243	432
19.	3,876		202	881	64	79	33	38
20.	37,872		9,431	13,948	6,059	7,096	2,900	3,075
21.	643		50	160	29	16	9	6
22.	30,407		7,011	8,905	2,219	3,787	761	617
23.	5,358		670	1,758	389	527	307	251
24.	986		228	315	128	146	48	47
25.	20,155		3,190	5,180	1,719	1,949	836	1,030
26.	52,357		11,214	12,592	6,085	6,904	4,228	3,243
27.	13,391		14,381	3,357	1,632	6,032	1,630	282
N.C.	71,250		16,658	29,414	7,561	10,987	4,002	3,153
Total Employed	432,662		143,859	153,706	78,413	94,154	43,670	41,386
Total Population	738,904		272,532	278,203	147,604	175,023	80,233	80,436

9. Bucks.	10. Beds.	11. Herts.	12. Essex	13. Cambridge	14. Hunts.	15. Norfolk	16. Suffolk	
21,351	14,801	19,763	50,301	22,321	8,248	50,142	43,581	1.
44	23	79	127	55	8	422	172	2.
2,016	1,418	2,275	4,537	2,166	785	5,037	4,027	3.
–	–	–	–	–	–	–	–	4.
88	67	99	278	106	37	293	212	5.
771	507	922	1,891	815	300	2,699	2,138	6.
144	56	92	163	140	53	287	204	7.
74	50	74	145	70	29	233	146	8.
–	–	–	–	–	–	–	–	9.
5	1	15	185	81	20	517	294	10.
384	281	475	1,068	395	169	1,171	1,122	11.
123	71	120	210	103	29	300	212	12.
466	283	667	1,408	360	144	4,623	1,451	13.
260	164	337	728	250	128	978	699	14.
2,253	2,024	2,464	4,507	2,632	960	7,937	5,361	15.
178	145	153	561	237	211	576	491	16.
1,120	404	579	1,315	530	171	1,919	1,364	17.
404	70	352	254	298	61	383	332	18.
20	19	18	46	30	23	108	44	19.
2,286	1,653	2,971	5,534	2,473	915	7,106	5,159	20.
5	4	12	16	9	3	40	18	21.
473	218	801	2,800	691	231	3,339	2,018	22.
305	185	266	688	218	77	1,179	704	23.
35	25	57	102	35	16	135	99	24.
727	478	858	1,737	805	258	1,908	1,519	25.
3,830	1,911	4,321	6,611	3,706	1,353	7,057	4,738	26.
211	154	317	1,172	166	73	1,033	889	27.
3,086	2,059	4,411	8,326	3,076	960	7,888	4,458	N.C
40,659	27,071	42,498	94,710	41,768	15,262	107,310	81,452	
76,482	52,190	77,617	172,348	81,611	29,072	199,101	154,095	

MALE EMPLOYMENT: 1841

South West							West Midlands	
	17.Corn-wall	18. Devon	19.Som-erset	20.Gloucs.	21.Wilts.	22.Dorset	23.Here-ford	24.Shrops
1.	27,021	53,671	43,094	29,424	33,495	18,926	15,790	27,347
2.	24,271	2,191	4,276	3,808	293	558	104	7,204
3.	2,357	5,535	5,114	5,670	2,434	2,170	999	2,460
4.	−	−	−	−	−	−	−	−
5.	185	504	371	580	146	83	85	259
6.	3,181	3,864	2,948	3,438	1,374	1,005	765	3,220
7.	99	252	197	662	149	71	73	167
8.	124	248	199	302	90	71	30	114
9.	−	−	−	−	−	−	−	−
10.	700	1,947	266	453	18	192	8	64
11.	269	968	618	947	311	169	371	1,052
12.	160	511	592	1,120	162	137	225	1,253
13.	1,096	3,749	4,265	5,579	4,497	1,290	309	1,363
14.	504	1,327	1,070	1,140	556	322	263	577
15.	4,903	10,403	8,373	9,001	3,447	3,145	2,126	4,784
16.	39	240	413	583	239	132	91	737
17.	924	2,804	2,361	3,239	1,120	831	711	1,234
18.	204	828	525	789	189	139	85	284
19.	44	76	74	281	23	24	8	46
20.	6,492	12,520	10,812	10,398	4,712	3,871	2,749	4,067
21.	13	35	36	41	12	8	1	13
22.	2,336	4,120	2,059	3,747	955	1,098	274	1,003
23.	273	497	591	793	359	219	144	327
24.	64	166	169	183	63	59	39	65
25.	1,360	3,050	2,865	3,177	1,071	786	585	1,279
26.	7,640	14,921	7,304	9,773	3,633	2,998	4,965	4,333
27.	1,003	5,240	962	1,464	589	794	180	389
N.C.	4,781	10,454	13,602	15,656	8,208	3,645	2,577	6,901
Total Employed	90,043	140,121	113,156	112,248	68,145	42,743	33,557	70,542
Total Population	164,757	252,760	209,383	205,543	128,240	83,554	56,978	119,355

East Midlands

25.Staffs.	26.War-wick	27.Worcs.	28.Derby	29.Notts.	30.Leics.	31.Lincs.	32.North-ants.	
28,425	23,764	20,541	18,399	20,067	16,759	56,615	25,530	1.
19,410	1,608	2,565	7,317	1,337	1,055	211	97	2.
4,722	5,416	2,467	2,538	3,271	2,879	4,321	2,703	3.
-	-	-	-	-	-	-	-	4.
557	490	307	253	229	152	393	116	5.
11,543	7,784	2,946	2,389	1,743	986	2,271	1,022	6.
1,695	2,879	218	357	725	579	293	73	7.
369	1,251	88	139	107	95	180	97	8.
								9.
190	81	76	49	67	20	173	13	10.
1,601	1,098	651	704	636	519	1,404	532	11.
6,044	7,487	5,803	2,120	432	388	376	160	12.
3,193	7,834	3,458	11,965	17,207	14,018	1,435	1,351	13.
1,917	1,734	833	531	601	450	896	638	14.
9,642	7,683	4,819	4,929	5,031	4,302	6,769	7,829	15.
14,443	1,773	903	1,177	500	609	883	221	16.
2,609	2,762	1,114	1,104	988	746	1,249	847	17.
407	923	251	455	298	179	307	156	18.
292	3,512	227	35	106	71	74	25	19.
11,162	7,902	3,916	4,736	3,360	3,101	6,059	3,500	20.
53	55	15	8	15	10	13	14	21.
2,398	2,638	1,437	1,055	1,274	1,054	1,779	702	22.
639	752	403	553	458	376	526	470	23.
142	144	72	64	55	55	104	48	24.
1,977	2,378	1,101	1,185	1,067	962	1,795	880	25.
6,305	6,850	3,669	6,603	4,076	5,748	7,391	3,659	26.
652	1,294	406	325	621	344	504	1,006	27.
19,375	12,558	6,520	9,720	5,082	3,342	5,541	2,774	N.C.
149,762	112,650	64,806	78,710	69,353	58,799	101,562	54,463	
258,864	195,679	114,664	135,620	121,731	105,616	181,758	98,977	

MALE EMPLOYMENT: 1841

	East Midlands	North West	Yorks. & Humberside			North		
	33.Rut-land	34.Cheshire	35.Lancs.	36. West Riding	37. East Riding	38. North Riding	39.West-morland	40.Cum-berland
1.	3,246	25,102	47,993	47,760	23,364	26,331	6,274	13,936
2.	8	2,965	19,439	18,093	205	1,680	323	3,801
3.	258	3,366	15,201	10,488	2,635	2,138	473	1,622
4.	–	–	–	–	–	–	–	–
5.	11	859	2,725	1,350	364	387	64	162
6.	113	2,464	13,350	9,307	1,528	1,696	371	1,382
7.	9	527	5,614	4,148	342	165	47	153
8.	7	144	2,483	434	118	106	22	118
9.	–	–	–	–	–	–	–	–
10.	–	354	2,175	251	606	581	4	448
11.	72	939	2,507	1,770	552	442	49	112
12.	11	563	5,624	18,302	267	182	96	356
13.	53	27,251	138,158	100,229	1,153	2,012	1,491	5,270
14.	58	686	3,180	2,544	636	628	140	482
15.	368	8,858	31,105	18,970	4,495	4,809	1,067	3,307
16.	22	648	3,237	2,267	471	613	32	244
17.	91	1,713	8,924	3,336	1,324	675	479	741
18.	8	536	4,432	1,603	291	158	89	238
19.	–	145	1,107	947	85	38	37	91
20.	384	6,936	34,283	20,263	3,636	4,209	1,253	3,849
21.	1	40	204	121	13	5	–	9
22.	74	3,000	22,856	7,073	2,366	1,252	175	1,176
23.	25	840	5,067	2,102	301	233	48	200
24.	4	98	514	263	68	79	21	55
25.	109	1,716	7,814	4,619	1,022	1,157	344	934
26.	503	8,460	18,900	12,171	2,977	3,577	1,438	4,484
27.	13	1,034	6,097	2,233	1,005	307	90	561
N.C.	343	13,898	75,554	33,744	5,701	2,520	654	2,682
Total Employed	5,791	113,142	478,543	324,388	55,525	55,980	15,081	46,413
Total Population	10,721	193,646	814,847	574,120	96,018	100,482	28,213	86,292

	Wales			Scotland				
41.North- umberland	42.Durham	43.Glam- organ & Monmouth	44.North & West Wales	45.Strathclyde	46.Dumfries & Galloway	47.Borders	48.Lothian	
16,486	13,677	18,148	88,667	46,911	18,069	13,259	15,111	1.
10,173	18,886	23,405	20,573	16,139	553	122	2,564	2.
3,029	3,268	2,140	4,207	8,882	1,179	873	5,127	3.
–	–	–	–	–	–	–	–	4.
417	714	435	469	945	49	35	438	5.
3,801	5,384	10,591	6,026	9,281	991	714	3,408	6.
668	745	337	309	1,699	103	227	409	7.
161	163	155	294	386	74	60	245	8.
–	–	–	–	–	–	– –	–	9.
1,006	3,293	407	1,113	1,782	107	2	413	10.
458	485	203	966	517	104	37	420	11.
529	948	665	749	1,797	222	86	991	12.
1,814	3,118	1,021	5,407	55,611	2,904	3,102	3,037	13.
914	673	491	1,387	1,404	254	274	1,226	14.
5,400	5,535	5,211	12,811	15,805	2,578	1,666	7,172	15.
1,168	1,744	314	512	1,591	84	63	706	16.
1,588	1,680	1,553	2,401	4,997	585	363	2,988	17.
569	530	292	494	1,829	128	117	2,118	18.
88	109	22	38	503	6	5	250	19.
6,053	7,567	6,899	13,115	18,766	2,888	2,494	6,918	20.
5	25	13	17	113	6	10	62	21.
3,853	5,438	1,892	3,582	10,165	912	521	4,304	22.
466	423	548	1,046	1,322	132	136	360	23.
99	101	86	171	219	47	20	168	24.
1,466	1,605	1,362	3,383	4,940	938	656	4,264	25.
2,615	4,044	4,639	11,290	9,681	1,813	1,424	4,701	26.
1,023	895	1,311	1,430	3,553	299	210	2,448	27.
7,430	11,194	15,297	14,313	37,575	1,941	1,537	10,234	N.C.
71,279	92,244	97,437	194,770	256,413	36,966	28,013	80,082	
121,268	160,073	158,475	359,838	437,646	71,283	47,589	133,742	

MALE EMPLOYMENT: 1841

Scotland

	49.Central & Fife	50.Tayside	51.Gram-pian	52.High-land	53. South East	54. East Anglia	55. South West	56. West Midlands
1.	17,282	26,349	43,138	41,464	307,775	124,292	205,631	115,867
2.	4,330	757	422	148	5,162	657	35,397	30,891
3.	2,583	3,071	2,444	1,068	73,770	12,015	23,280	16,064
4.	-	-	-	-	-	-	-	-
5.	199	129	177	45	8,127	648	1,869	1,698
6.	2,256	2,406	2,390	1,032	27,993	5,952	15,810	26,258
7.	384	804	377	77	4,478	684	1,430	5,032
8.	95	146	172	59	6,131	478	1,034	1,852
9.	-	-	-	-	-	-	-	-
10.	294	544	583	364	7,555	912	3,576	419
11.	99	95	310	274	13,458	2,857	3,282	4,773
12.	714	268	215	58	11,621	644	2,682	20,812
13.	15,996	21,590	4,999	1,441	35,065	6,578	20,476	16,157
14.	388	442	398	130	14,910	2,055	4,919	5,324
15.	3,478	5,362	5,491	3,912	90,050	16,890	39,272	29,054
16.	344	144	84	29	7,230	1,515	1,646	17,947
17.	1,022	1,519	1,825	1,554	35,086	3,984	11,279	8,430
18.	509	354	428	95	19,885	1,074	2,674	1,950
19.	31	55	225	16	5,276	205	522	4,085
20.	4,668	7,068	5,781	3,874	92,825	15,653	48,805	29,796
21.	25	33	32	4	950	70	145	137
22.	1,962	2,775	2,380	1,237	57,999	6,279	14,315	7,750
23.	153	213	218	171	10,704	2,178	2,732	2,265
24.	67	110	86	46	2,117	285	704	462
25.	1,263	1,955	1,777	1,323	37,859	4,490	12,309	7,320
26.	2,227	3,609	2,913	3,797	113,296	16,854	46,269	26,122
27.	672	988	995	868	42,559	2,161	10,052	2,921
N.C.	7,366	7,291	5,929	3,139	160,907	16,382	56,346	47,931
Total Employed	68,407	88,077	83,789	66,225	1,192,788	245,792	566,456	431,317
Total Population	116,105	148,548	144,875	142,074	2,151,572	463,879	1,044,237	745,540

57. East Midlands	58. North West	59. Yorks. & Humberside	60. North	61. Wales	62. Scotland	63. Great Britain	
140,616	73,095	73,232	76,704	106,815	221,583	1,445,610	1.
10,025	22,404	18,337	34,863	43,978	25,035	226,749	2.
15,970	18,567	13,843	10,530	6,347	25,227	215,613	3.
-	-	-	-	-	-	-	4.
1,154	3,584	1,807	1,744	904	2,017	23,552	5.
8,524	15,814	11,187	12,634	16,617	22,478	163,267	6.
2,036	6,141	4,524	1,778	646	4,080	30,829	7.
625	2,627	590	570	449	1,237	15,593	8.
-	-	-	-	-	-	-	9.
322	2,529	857	5,332	1,520	4,089	27,111	10.
3,867	3,446	2,471	1,546	1,169	1,856	38,725	11.
3,487	6,187	18,704	2,111	1,414	4,351	72,013	12.
46,029	165,409	101,768	13,705	6,428	108,680	520,295	13.
3,174	3,866	3,408	2,837	1,878	4,516	46,887	14.
29,228	39,963	24,691	20,118	18,022	45,464	352,752	15.
3,412	3,885	2,876	3,801	826	3,045	46,183	16.
5,025	10,637	5,018	5,163	3,954	14,853	103,429	17.
1,403	4,968	2,113	1,584	786	5,578	42,015	18.
311	1,252	1,162	363	60	1,091	14,327	19.
21,140	41,219	24,965	22,931	20,014	52,457	369,805	20.
61	244	138	44	30	285	2,104	21.
5,938	25,856	9,760	11,894	5,474	24,256	169,521	22.
2,408	5,907	2,493	1,370	1,594	2,705	34,356	23.
330	612	349	355	257	763	6,234	24.
5,998	9,530	6,038	5,506	4,745	17,116	110,911	25.
27,980	27,360	16,041	16,158	15,929	30,165	336,174	26.
2,813	7,131	3,367	2,876	2,741	10,033	86,654	27.
26,802	89,452	40,768	24,480	29,610	75,012	567,690	N.C.
368,678	591,685	390,507	280,997	292,207	707,972	5,068,399	
654,423	1,008,493	688,311	496,328	518,313	1,241,862	9,012,958	

FEMALE EMPLOYMENT: 1841

South East

	1. London	2. Middlesex	3. Kent	4. Surrey	5. Sussex	6. Hants.	7. Berks.	8. Oxon
1.	1,034		972	520	665	848	1,774	1,248
2.	100		17	32	2	4	3	5
3.	3,182		728	2,102	373	449	183	177
4.	–		–	–	–	–	–	–
5.	197		10	68	11	9	3	2
6.	148		28	30	24	17	17	–
7.	56		1	9	–	–	1	–
8.	94		4	16	2	6	2	–
9.	–		–	–	–	–	–	–
10.	10		11	5	2	3	1	–
11.	70		8	15	8	7	3	–
12.	381		15	72	14	33	17	9
13.	7,404	Data for this	264	652	75	455	401	687
14.	1,193	county included	11	381	11	16	25	20
15.	35,418	under 'London'	3,717	8,623	2,378	3,173	1,163	1,156
16.	222		22	29	10	11	9	5
17.	1,266		51	354	47	52	17	20
18.	1,801		403	302	50	73	15	24
19.	384		23	102	14	20	7	4
20.	239		25	60	30	37	7	5
21.	25		–	3	–	–	–	–
22.	251		40	117	24	33	15	15
23.	1,995		363	551	72	227	111	88
24.	3		1	5	25	–	–	–
25.	8,599		2,065	3,170	1,065	1,123	507	473
26.	135,962		30,905	40,857	18,993	19,431	8,894	7,853
27.	213		24	50	10	17	20	8
N.C.	2,394		481	649	237	481	243	264
Total Employed	202,641		40,189	58,774	24,142	26,525	13,438	12,063
Total Population	837,732		275,805	304,475	152,149	179,981	80,916	81,207

East Anglia

9. Bucks.	10. Beds.	11. Herts.	12. Essex	13. Cambridge	14. Hunts.	15. Norfolk	16. Suffolk	
656	194	505	1,832	1,064	343	1,430	1,122	1.
1	2	4	3	-	-	11	3	2.
188	123	218	312	176	81	399	327	3.
-	-	-	-	-	-	-	-	4.
1	-	8	19	5	1	10	4	5.
12	9	16	53	8	2	-	23	6.
-	2	1	11	23	1	1	1	7.
-	-	1	6	1	-	3	7	8.
-	-	-	-	-	-	-	-	9.
-	-	1	1	-	1	-	1	10.
3	3	3	12	4	1	6	5	11.
14	5	6	25	8	-	3	11	12.
4,467	2,619	414	1,400	41	66	2,658	851	13.
12	8	12	15	6	1	21	96	14.
2,057	3,053	5,343	2,112	1,150	327	3,878	2,232	15.
3	1	5	20	2	1	11	13	16.
15	10	9	32	35	4	94	48	17.
43	1	54	17	4	23	30	42	18.
2	2	4	10	2	1	6	4	19.
8	12	12	44	15	2	24	35	20.
-	-	-	-	-	-	-	-	21.
8	7	19	41	19	3	16	20	22.
63	33	148	224	96	35	374	227	23.
-	-	-	-	-	-	-	1	24.
359	280	564	1,148	562	184	1,311	1,036	25.
5,996	3,711	7,406	16,094	7,349	2,704	19,701	15,383	26.
9	5	11	17	3	2	37	13	27.
96	66	144	471	211	49	695	249	N.C.
14,013	10,146	14,908	23,919	10,784	3,832	30,719	21,754	
79,501	55,746	79,590	172,631	82,848	29,477	213,563	160,978	

FEMALE EMPLOYMENT: 1841

South West   West Midlands

	17.Corn-wall	18. Devon	19.Som-erset	20.Gloucs.	21.Wilts.	22.Dorset	23.Here-ford	24.Shrops
1.	1,414	2,482	2,140	2,280	3,201	908	989	863
2.	3,289	42	106	36	9	22	4	111
3.	601	791	419	629	214	234	103	238
4.	-	-	-	-	-	-	-	-
5.	27	19	4	21	2	2	1	9
6.	15	17	13	48	19	12	13	50
7.	-	5	1	13	1	2	-	3
8.	3	4	2	4	-	-	2	-
9.	-	-	-	-	-	-	-	-
10.	2	5	2	5	-	-	-	1
11.	-	4	4	7	-	2	1	4
12.	13	34	42	395	11	11	9	315
13.	403	4,631	3,503	4,474	3,344	1,133	70	318
14.	19	30	37	32	14	11	3	37
15.	3,394	7,154	7,244	6,335	1,612	1,666	883	1,419
16.	3	14	28	50	9	7	4.	190
17.	39	99	135	208	26	19	8	32
18.	23	120	46	64	17	8	7	19
19.	3	26	26	186	8	207	-	21
20.	18	47	45	30	45	16	16	18
21.	-	-	-	-	-	-	-	1
22.	28	50	45	77	40	13	15	45
23.	291	469	442	601	148	132	62	147
24.	-	1	-	2	-	1	-	-
25.	656	1,802	1,457	1,628	594	487	238	454
26.	14,470	31,627	26,531	26,987	11,082	7,815	7,007	15,055
27.	26	43	30	55	12	10	3	21
N.C.	794	1,734	1,441	946	645	339	293	788
Total Employed	25,531	51,250	43,743	45,113	21,053	13,057	9,731	20,159
Total Population	176,522	280,700	226,599	225,840	130,493	91,489	56,900	119,693

25.Staffs.	26.Warwick	27.Worcs.	28.Derby	29.Notts.	30.Leics.	31.Lincs.	32.Northants.	
933	661	3,124	1,081	547	465	1,418	426	1.
262	29	36	49	15	14	6	3	2.
441	561	208	220	257	262	421	221	3.
-	-	-	-	-	-	-	-	4.
33	48	15	8	7	11	7	4	5.
162	296	25	13	8	13	22	14	6.
11	70	-	4	3	4	2	1	7.
5	37	2	2	3	2	4	1	8.
-	-	-	-	-	-	-	-	9.
-	2	2	-	-	-	-	-	10.
10	11	2	2	6	5	8	3	11.
1,594	1,547	2,895	103	8	14	16	3	12.
2,530	7,298	689	10,054	7,635	5,438	176	2,881	13.
77	226	35	7	49	9	35	13	14.
2,965	4,457	2,849	2,111	2,625	2,487	2,550	1,637	15.
6,651	115	97	115	9	22	16	4	16.
68	255	39	22	36	20	34	14	17.
134	222	28	77	16	17	12	14	18.
96	1,654	61	3	10	17	21	11	19.
80	49	21	11	10	17	18	14	20.
-	-	-	1	-	-	-	-	21.
84	370	38	26	25	32	21	32	22.
319	417	257	204	170	105	161	93	23.
1	-	-	-	2	-	-	-	24.
874	1,278	695	496	620	555	1,217	513	25.
20,442	21,370	9,346	10,612	11,456	9,700	21,926	8,502	26.
29	14	8	10	5	3	17	9	27.
632	855	608	391	735	374	198	66	N.C.
38,433	41,842	21,080	25,622	24,257	19,586	28,306	14,479	
251,640	206,036	118,672	136,597	128,179	110,251	180,844	100,251	

FEMALE EMPLOYMENT: 1841

East Midlands	North West	Yorks. & Humberside			North		
33.Rut- land	34.Cheshire	35.Lancs.	36. West Riding	37. East Riding	38. North Riding	39.West- morland	40.Cum berlan
1.	88	1,927	2,458	2,060	749	2,410	359	1,882
2.	1	30	1,159	550	3	5	–	20
3.	34	413	2,806	1,541	297	306	157	593
4.	–	–	–	–	–	–	–	–
5.	2	13	67	51	12	2	4	8
6.	2	16	79	179	18	24	2	3
7.	–	9	253	909	2	2	2	–
8.	–	2	19	4	1	1	–	–
9.	–	–	–	–	–	–	–	–
10.	–	2	6	3	4	9	–	1
11.	–	4	18	10	6	2	–	1
12.	–	16	437	779	8	8	1	25
13.	32	25,650	112,163	44,237	366	324	545	2,299
14.	–	39	130	307	15	11	2	7
15.	108	2,737	15,886	7,592	1,887	1,387	434	1,768
16.	–	137	237	218	12	114	14	23
17.	–	43	667	166	43	20	28	16
18.	2	20	375	150	13	17	3	17
19.	–	16	105	177	12	2	10	2
20.	2	19	96	81	23	15	5	13
21.	–	1	–	9	–	–	–	1
22.	1	35	263	291	21	9	9	21
23.	6	410	2,528	1,160	169	92	43	204
24.	–	–	1	3	–	–	–	–
25.	59	768	2,864	1,681	517	358	143	340
26.	1,121	18,645	70,081	37,910	11,966	11,737	3,466	9,089
27.	1	14	31	29	9	9	5	8
N.C.	16	414	5,288	4,531	158	409	102	403
Total Employed	1,475	51,380	218,017	104,628	16,311	17,273	5,334	16,744
Total Population	10,581	202,014	852,207	579,981	98,918	103,640	28,241	91,746

	Wales			Scotland					
41.North-umberland	42.Durham	43.Glam-organ & Monmouth	44.North & West Wales	45.Strathclyde	46.Dumfries & Galloway	47.Borders	48.Lothian	
1,470	1,240	823	5,514	3,032	3,632	2,395	2,092	1.
52	55	601	509	323	33	28	335	2.
539	472	366	931	1,416	285	177	961	3.
-	-	-	-	-	-	-	-	4.
9	21	22	34	117	2	3	47	5.
6	11	351	118	52	3	1	12	6.
-	-	6	2	143	-	-	3	7.
1	1	2	3	1	-	-	3	8.
-	-	-	-	-	-	-	-	9.
5	11	-	1	5	-	-	2	10.
1	-	-	4	1	-	-	1	11.
8	8	8	30	68	4	3	17	12.
257	481	320	2,013	41,366	949	875	1,257	13.
5	14	9	46	86	3	2	107	14.
2,079	1,646	2,028	3,011	14,544	1,338	689	4,767	15.
64	39	51	46	202	11	10	70	16.
21	17	33	20	145	2	4	56	17.
87	37	20	78	275	2	31	150	18.
4	6	14	6	53	-	1	27	19.
-	10	12	43	36	8	9	17	20.
-	-	-	-	1	-	-	2	21.
43	13	26	105	265	31	19	75	22.
350	228	261	462	726	120	60	380	23.
-	-	-	1	-	-	-	-	24.
352	432	310	612	563	187	142	610	25.
13,156	13,126	14,772	46,790	41,490	8,252	5,896	23,977	26.
4	13	7	21	23	14	51	16	27.
273	480	632	1,090	4,311	310	112	985	N.C.
18,786	18,361	20,674	61,490	109,244	15,186	10,508	35,969	
129,010	164,211	147,068	380,577	466,161	81,861	51,363	154,470	

FEMALE EMPLOYMENT: 1841

Scotland

	49.Central & Fife	50.Tayside	51.Grampian	52.Highland	53. South East	54. East Anglia	55. South West	56. Mi
1.	1,078	1,939	3,465	4,995	10,248	3,959	12,425	6,
2.	389	4	-	-	173	14	3,504	
3.	401	705	608	137	8,035	983	2,888	1.
4.	-	-	-	-	-	-	-	
5.	16	3	1	15	328	20	75	
6.	5	6	6	1	354	33	124	
7.	6	3	1	2	81	26	22	
8.	-	-	-	-	131	11	13	
9.	-	-	-	-	-	-	-	
10.	2	1	1	-	34	2	14	
11.	-	-	-	1	132	16	17	
12.	9	21	1	-	591	22	506	6.
13.	8,344	16,723	6,756	1,540	18,838	3,616	17,488	10.
14.	18	4	2	-	1,704	124	143	
15.	1,440	2,107	1,523	1,985	68,193	7,587	27,405	12.
16.	35	21	19	11	337	27	111	7.
17.	7	8	6	1	1,873	181	526	
18.	79	18	95	1	2,783	99	278	
19.	3	4	37	4	572	13	456	1.
20.	15	13	7	10	479	76	201	
21.	-	-	-	-	28	-	-	
22.	45	32	26	6	570	58	253	
23.	104	122	116	34	3,875	732	2,083	1.
24.	-	-	-	-	34	1	4	
25.	251	333	713	263	19,353	3,093	6,624	3.
26.	9,561	16,895	22,919	17,067	296,102	45,137	118,512	73.
27.	17	7	26	13	384	55	176	
N.C.	1,038	1,143	802	542	5,526	1,204	5,899	3.
Total Employed	22,863	40,112	37,130	26,628	440,758	67,089	199,747	131
Total Population	125,247	168,125	165,278	165,817	2,299,733	486,866	1,131,643	752

57. East Midlands	58. North West	59. Yorks. & Humberside	60. North	61. Wales	62. Scotland	63. Great Britain	
4,025	4,385	2,906	7,361	6,337	22,628	80,844	1.
88	1,189	557	132	1,110	1,112	8,321	2.
1,415	3,219	1,921	2,067	1,297	4,690	28,066	3.
-	-	-	-	-	-	-	4.
39	80	66	44	56	204	1,018	5.
72	95	201	46	469	86	2,026	6.
14	262	912	4	8	158	1,571	7.
12	21	5	3	5	4	251	8.
-	-	-	-	-	-	-	9.
-	8	7	26	1	11	108	10.
24	22	17	4	4	3	267	11.
144	453	791	50	38	123	9,078	12.
26,216	137,813	44,675	3,906	2,333	77,810	343,600	13.
113	169	330	39	55	222	3,277	14.
11,518	18,623	9,975	7,314	5,039	28,393	196,620	15.
166	374	231	254	97	379	9,033	16.
126	710	231	102	53	229	4,433	17.
138	395	171	161	98	651	5,184	18.
62	121	190	24	20	129	3,419	19.
72	115	117	43	55	115	1,457	20.
1	1	9	1	-	3	44	21.
137	298	319	95	131	499	2,912	22.
739	2,938	1,389	917	723	1,662	16,260	23.
2	1	3	-	1	-	47	24.
3,460	3,632	2,336	1,625	922	3,062	47,646	25.
63,317	88,726	52,831	50,574	61,562	146,057	996,038	26.
45	45	42	39	28	167	1,056	27.
1,780	5,702	4,743	1,667	1,722	9,243	40,662	N.C.
113,725	269,397	124,975	76,498	82,164	297,640	1,803,238	
666,703	1,054,221	699,047	516,848	527,645	1,378,322	9,513,969	

TOTAL EMPLOYMENT: 1841

South East

	1. London	2. Middlesex	3. Kent	4. Surrey	5. Sussex	6. Hants.	7. Berks.	8. Oxon
1.	18,841		49,029	25,649	36,629	36,254	21,281	20,937
2.	2,796		522	1,128	216	188	81	121
3.	34,535		8,806	12,768	4,710	5,072	2,447	2,380
4.	-		-	-	-	-	-	-
5.	4,781		665	1,597	300	311	121	120
6.	10,917		3,244	3,925	1,785	2,408	1,039	848
7.	2,450		431	650	164	203	94	98
8.	4,592		306	537	146	166	84	81
9.	-		-	-	-	-	-	-
10.	2,241		2,352	983	247	1,448	77	33
11.	5,902		1,147	1,648	867	824	522	451
12.	8,593		494	1,481	283	474	167	146
13.	30,086	Data for this	2,391	3,921	917	1,859	1,216	1,789
14.	7,383	county included	984	4,557	709	716	375	354
15.	78,760	under 'London'	11,549	20,742	6,879	8,808	3,699	3,993
16.	3,226		786	1,218	433	460	199	179
17.	19,611		2,649	5,695	1,528	2,091	890	1,011
18.	14,229		1,731	3,907	387	505	258	456
19.	4,260		225	983	78	99	40	42
20.	38,111		9,456	14,008	6,089	7,133	2,907	3,080
21.	668		50	163	29	16	9	6
22.	30,658		7,051	9,022	2,243	3,820	776	632
23.	7,353		1,033	2,309	461	754	418	339
24.	989		229	320	153	146	48	47
25.	28,754		5,255	8,350	2,784	3,072	1,343	1,503
26.	188,319		42,119	53,449	25,078	26,335	13,122	11,096
27.	13,604		14,405	3,407	1,642	6,049	1,650	290
N.C.	73,644		17,139	30,063	7,798	11,468	4,245	3,417
Total Employed	635,303		184,048	212,480	102,555	120,679	57,108	53,449
Total Population	1,576,636		548,337	582,678	299,753	355,004	161,149	161,643

East Anglia

9. Bucks.	10. Beds.	11. Herts.	12. Essex	13. Cambridge	14. Hunts.	15. Norfolk	16. Suffolk	
22,007	14,995	20,268	52,133	23,385	8,591	51,572	44,703	1.
45	25	83	130	55	8	433	175	2.
2,204	1,541	2,493	4,849	2,342	866	5,436	4,354	3.
–	–	–	–	–	–	–	–	4.
89	67	107	297	111	38	303	216	5.
783	516	938	1,944	823	302	2,699	2,161	6.
144	58	93	174	163	54	288	205	7.
74	50	75	151	71	29	236	153	8.
–	–	–	–	–	–	–	–	9.
5	1	16	186	81	21	517	295	10.
387	284	478	1,080	399	170	1,177	1,127	11.
137	76	126	235	111	29	303	223	12.
4,933	2,902	1,081	2,808	401	210	7,281	2,302	13.
272	172	349	743	256	129	999	795	14.
4,310	5,077	7,807	6,619	3,782	1,287	11,815	7,593	15.
181	146	158	581	239	212	587	504	16.
1,135	414	588	1,347	565	175	2,013	1,412	17.
447	71	406	271	302	84	413	374	18.
22	21	22	56	32	24	114	48	19.
2,294	1,665	2,983	5,578	2,488	917	7,130	5,194	20.
5	4	12	16	9	3	40	18	21.
481	225	820	2,841	710	234	3,355	2,038	22.
368	218	414	912	314	112	1,553	931	23.
35	25	57	102	35	16	135	100	24.
1,086	758	1,422	2,885	1,367	442	3,219	2,555	25.
9,826	5,622	11,727	22,705	11,055	4,057	26,758	20,121	26.
220	159	328	1,189	169	75	1,070	902	27.
3,182	2,125	4,555	8,797	3,287	1,009	8,583	4,707	N.C.
54,672	37,217	57,406	118,629	52,552	19,094	138,029	103,206	
155,983	107,936	157,207	344,979	164,459	58,549	412,664	315,073	

TOTAL EMPLOYMENT: 1841

South West   West Midlands

	17.Corn-wall	18. Devon	19.Som-erset	20.Gloucs.	21.Wilts.	22.Dorset	23.Here-ford	24.Shrops
1.	28,435	56,153	45,234	31,704	36,696	19,834	16,779	28,210
2.	27,560	2,233	4,382	3,844	302	580	108	7,315
3.	2,958	6,326	5,533	6,299	2,648	2,404	1,102	2,698
4.	-	-	-	-	-	-	-	-
5.	212	523	375	601	148	85	86	268
6.	3,196	3,881	2,961	3,486	1,393	1,017	778	3,270
7.	99	257	198	675	150	73	73	170
8.	127	252	201	306	90	71	32	114
9.	-	-	-	-	-	-	-	-
10.	702	1,952	268	458	18	192	8	65
11.	269	972	622	954	311	171	372	1,056
12.	173	545	634	1,515	173	148	234	1,568
13.	1,499	8,380	7,768	10,053	7,841	2,423	379	1,681
14.	523	1,357	1,107	1,172	570	333	266	614
15.	8,297	17,557	15,617	15,336	5,059	4,811	3,009	6,203
16.	42	254	441	633	248	139	95	927
17.	963	2,903	2,496	3,447	1,146	850	719	1,266
18.	227	948	571	853	206	147	92	303
19.	47	102	100	467	31	231	8	67
20.	6,510	12,567	10,857	10,428	4,757	3,887	2,765	4,085
21.	13	35	36	41	12	8	1	14
22.	2,364	4,170	2,104	3,824	995	1,111	289	1,048
23.	564	966	1,033	1,394	507	351	206	474
24.	64	167	169	185	63	60	39	65
25.	2,016	4,852	4,322	4,805	1,665	1,273	823	1,733
26.	22,110	46,548	33,835	36,760	14,715	10,813	11,972	19,388
27.	1,029	5,283	992	1,519	601	804	183	410
N.C.	5,575	12,188	15,043	16,602	8,853	3,984	2,870	7,689
Total Employed	115,574	191,371	156,899	157,361	89,198	55,800	43,288	90,701
Total Population	341,279	533,460	435,982	431,383	258,733	175,043	113,878	239,048

East Midlands

25.Staffs.	26.Warwick	27.Worcs.	28.Derby	29.Notts.	30.Leics.	31.Lincs.	32.Northants.	
29,358	24,425	23,665	19,480	20,614	17,224	58,033	25,956	1.
19,672	1,637	2,601	7,366	1,352	1,069	217	100	2.
5,163	5,977	2,675	2,758	3,528	3,141	4,742	2,924	3.
–	–	–	–	–	–	–	–	4.
590	538	322	261	236	163	400	120	5.
11,705	8,080	2,971	2,402	1,751	999	2,293	1,036	6.
1,706	2,949	218	361	728	583	295	74	7.
374	1,288	90	141	110	97	184	98	8.
–	–	–	–	–	–	–	–	9.
190	83	78	49	67	20	173	13	10.
1,611	1,109	653	706	642	524	1,412	535	11.
7,638	9,034	8,698	2,223	440	402	392	163	12.
5,723	15,132	4,147	22,019	24,842	19,456	1,611	4,232	13.
1,994	1,960	868	538	650	459	931	651	14.
12,607	12,140	7,668	7,040	7,656	6,789	9,319	9,466	15.
21,094	1,888	1,000	1,292	509	631	899	225	16.
2,677	3,017	1,153	1,126	1,024	766	1,283	861	17.
541	1,145	279	532	314	196	319	170	18.
388	5,166	288	38	116	88	95	36	19.
11,242	7,951	3,937	4,747	3,370	3,118	6,077	3,514	20.
53	55	15	9	15	10	13	14	21.
2,482	3,008	1,475	1,081	1,299	1,086	1,800	734	22.
958	1,169	660	757	628	481	687	563	23.
143	144	72	64	57	55	104	48	24.
2,851	3,656	1,796	1,681	1,687	1,517	3,012	1,393	25.
26,747	28,220	13,015	17,215	15,532	15,448	29,317	12,161	26.
681	1,308	414	335	626	347	521	1,015	27.
20,007	13,413	7,128	10,111	5,817	3,716	5,739	2,840	N.C.
188,195	154,492	85,886	104,332	93,610	78,385	129,868	68,942	
510,504	401,715	233,336	272,217	249,910	215,867	362,602	199,228	

TOTAL EMPLOYMENT: 1841

	East Midlands	North West		Yorks. & Humberside		North		
	33.Rutland	34. Cheshire	35.Lancs.	36. West Riding	37. East Riding	38. North Riding	39.Westmorland	40.Cumberland
1.	3,334	27,029	50,451	49,820	24,113	28,741	6,633	15,81?
2.	9	2,995	20,598	18,643	208	1,685	323	3,82?
3.	292	3,779	18,007	12,029	2,932	2,444	630	2,21?
4.	-	-	-	-	-	-	-	-
5.	13	872	2,792	1,401	376	389	68	17?
6.	115	2,480	13,429	9,486	1,546	1,720	373	1,38?
7.	9	536	5,867	5,057	344	167	49	15?
8.	7	146	2,502	438	119	107	22	11?
9.	-	-	-	-	-	-	-	-
10.	-	356	2,181	254	610	590	4	44?
11.	72	943	2,525	1,780	558	444	49	11?
12.	11	579	6,061	19,081	275	190	97	38?
13.	85	52,901	250,321	144,466	1,519	2,336	2,036	7,56?
14.	58	725	3,310	2,851	651	639	142	48?
15.	476	11,595	46,991	26,562	6,382	6,196	1,501	5,07?
16.	22	785	3,474	2,485	483	727	46	26?
17.	91	1,756	9,591	3,502	1,367	695	507	75?
18.	10	556	4,807	1,753	304	175	92	25?
19.	-	161	1,212	1,124	97	40	47	9?
20.	386	6,955	34,379	20,344	3,659	4,224	1,258	3,86?
21.	1	41	204	130	13	5	-	1?
22.	75	3,035	23,119	7,364	2,387	1,261	184	1,19?
23.	31	1,250	7,595	3,262	470	325	91	40?
24.	4	98	515	266	68	79	21	5?
25.	168	2,484	10,678	6,300	1,539	1,515	487	1,27?
26.	1,624	27,105	88,981	50,081	14,943	15,314	4,904	13,57?
27.	14	1,048	6,128	2,262	1,014	316	95	56?
N.C.	359	14,312	80,842	38,275	5,859	2,929	756	3,08?
Total Employed	7,266	164,522	696,560	429,016	71,836	73,253	20,415	63,15?
Total Population	21,302	395,660	1,667,054	1,154,101	194,936	204,122	56,454	178,03?

	Wales			Scotland				
41.North-umberland	42.Durham	43.Glam-organ & Monmouth	44.North & West Wales	45.Strathclyde	46.Dumfries & Galloway	47.Borders	48.Lothian	
17,956	14,917	18,971	94,181	49,943	21,701	15,654	17,203	1.
10,225	18,941	24,006	21,082	16,462	586	150	2,899	2.
3,568	3,740	2,506	5,138	10,298	1,464	1,050	6,088	3.
-	-	-	-	-	-	-	-	4.
426	735	457	503	1,062	51	38	485	5.
3,807	5,395	10,942	6,144	9,333	994	715	3,420	6.
668	745	343	311	1,842	103	227	412	7.
162	164	157	297	387	74	60	248	8.
-	-	-	-	-	-	-	-	9.
1,011	3,304	407	1,114	1,787	107	2	415	10.
459	485	203	970	518	104	37	421	11.
537	956	673	779	1,865	226	89	1,008	12.
2,071	3,599	1,341	7,420	96,977	3,853	3,977	4,294	13.
919	687	500	1,433	1,490	257	276	1,333	14.
7,479	7,181	7,239	15,822	30,349	3,916	2,355	11,939	15.
1,232	1,783	365	558	1,793	95	73	776	16.
1,609	1,697	1,586	2,421	5,142	587	367	3,044	17.
656	567	312	572	2,104	130	148	2,268	18.
92	115	36	44	556	6	6	277	19.
6,053	7,577	6,911	13,158	18,802	2,896	2,503	6,935	20.
5	25	13	17	114	6	10	64	21.
3,896	5,451	1,918	3,687	10,430	943	540	4,379	22.
816	651	809	1,508	2,048	252	196	740	23.
99	101	86	172	219	47	20	168	24.
1,818	2,037	1,672	3,995	5,503	1,125	798	4,874	25.
15,771	17,170	19,411	58,080	51,171	10,065	7,320	28,678	26.
1,027	908	1,318	1,451	3,576	313	261	2,464	27.
7,703	11,674	15,929	15,403	41,886	2,251	1,649	11,219	N.C.
90,065	110,605	118,111	256,260	365,657	52,152	38,521	116,051	
250,278	324,284	305,543	740,415	903,807	153,144	98,952	288,212	

TOTAL EMPLOYMENT: 1841

Scotland

	49.Central & Fife	50.Tayside	51.Grampian	52.Highland	53. South East	54. East Anglia	55. South West	56. West Midland
1.	18,360	28,288	46,603	46,459	318,023	128,251	218,056	122,437
2.	4,719	761	422	148	5,335	671	38,901	31,333
3.	2,984	3,776	3,052	1,205	81,805	12,998	26,168	17,615
4.	-	-	-	-	-	-	-	-
5.	215	132	178	60	8,455	668	1,944	1,804
6.	2,261	2,412	2,396	1,033	28,347	5,985	15,934	26,804
7.	390	807	378	79	4,559	710	1,452	5,116
8.	95	146	172	59	6,262	489	1,047	1,898
9.	-	-	-	-	-	-	-	-
10.	296	545	584	364	7,589	914	3,590	424
11.	99	95	310	275	13,590	2,873	3,299	4,801
12.	723	289	216	58	12,212	666	3,188	27,172
13.	24,340	38,313	11,755	2,981	53,903	10,194	37,964	27,062
14.	406	446	400	130	16,614	2,179	5,062	5,702
15.	4,918	7,469	7,014	5,897	158,243	24,477	66,677	41,627
16.	379	165	103	40	7,567	1,542	1,757	25,004
17.	1,029	1,527	1,831	1,555	36,959	4,165	11,805	8,832
18.	588	372	523	96	22,668	1,173	2,952	2,360
19.	34	59	262	20	5,848	218	978	5,917
20.	4,683	7,081	5,788	3,884	93,304	15,729	49,006	29,980
21.	25	33	32	4	978	70	145	138
22.	2,007	2,807	2,406	1,243	58,569	6,337	14,568	8,302
23.	257	335	334	205	14,579	2,910	4,815	3,467
24.	67	110	86	46	2,151	286	708	463
25.	1,514	2,288	2,490	1,586	57,212	7,583	18,933	10,859
26.	11,788	20,504	25,832	20,864	409,398	61,991	164,781	99,342
27.	689	995	1,021	881	42,943	2,216	10,228	2,996
N.C.	8,404	8,434	6,731	3,681	166,433	17,586	62,245	51,107
Total Employed	91,270	128,189	120,919	92,853	1,633,546	312,881	766,203	562,562
Total Population	241,352	316,673	310,153	307,891	4,451,305	950,745	2,175,880	1,498,481

57. East Midlands	58. North West	59.Yorks. & Humberside	60. North	61. Wales	62. Scotland	63. Great Britain	
144,641	77,480	76,138	84,065	113,152	244,211	1,526,454	1.
10,113	23,593	18,894	34,995	45,088	26,147	235,070	2.
17,385	21,786	15,764	12,597	7,644	29,917	243,679	3.
-	-	-	-	-	-	-	4.
1,193	3,664	1,873	1,788	960	2,221	24,570	5.
8,596	15,909	11,388	12,680	17,086	22,564	165,293	6.
2,050	6,403	5,436	1,782	654	4,238	32,400	7.
637	2,648	595	573	454	1,241	15,844	8.
-	-	-	-	-	-	-	9.
322	2,537	864	5,358	1,521	4,100	27,219	10.
3,891	3,468	2,488	1,550	1,173	1,859	38,992	11.
3,631	6,640	19,495	2,161	1,452	4,474	81,091	12.
72,245	303,222	146,443	17,611	8,761	186,490	863,895	13.
3,287	4,035	3,738	2,876	1,933	4,738	50,164	14.
40,746	58,586	34,666	27,432	23,061	73,857	549,372	15.
3,578	4,259	3,107	4,055	923	3,424	55,216	16.
5,151	11,347	5,249	5,265	4,007	15,082	107,862	17.
1,541	5,363	2,284	1,745	884	6,229	47,199	18.
373	1,373	1,352	387	80	1,220	17,746	19.
21,212	41,334	25,082	22,974	20,069	52,572	371,262	20.
62	245	147	45	30	288	2,148	21.
6,075	26,154	10,079	11,989	5,605	24,755	172,433	22.
3,147	8,845	3,882	2,287	2,317	4,367	50,616	23.
332	613	352	355	258	763	6,281	24.
9,458	13,162	8,374	7,131	5,667	20,178	158,557	25.
91,297	116,086	68,872	66,732	77,491	176,222	1,332,212	26.
2,858	7,176	3,409	2,915	2,769	10,200	87,710	27.
28,582	95,154	45,511	26,147	31,332	84,255	608,352	N.C.
482,403	861,082	515,482	357,495	374,371	1,005,612	6,871,637	
1,321,126	2,062,714	1,387,358	1,013,176	1,045,958	2,620,184	18,526,927	

MALE EMPLOYMENT: 1851

South East

	1. London	2. Middlesex	3. Kent	4. Surrey	5. Sussex	6. Hants.	7. Berks.	8. Oxon
1.	15,510	13,508	59,474	26,492	47,738	45,586	31,202	27,462
2.	6,588	251	862	277	383	391	245	255
3.	63,144	3,529	9,896	4,180	7,002	7,399	3,987	3,316
4.	-	-	-	-	-	-	-	-
5.	10,469	406	722	342	367	454	218	144
6.	21,263	899	2,983	1,330	2,339	3,073	1,452	965
7.	10,173	273	683	133	342	815	188	145
8.	6,425	114	296	107	239	285	112	100
9.	-	-	-	-	-	-	-	-
10.	5,069	31	992	32	346	1,583	82	32
11.	6,953	516	1,239	563	1,109	960	637	440
12.	11,716	186	401	186	380	473	191	316
13.	27,439	617	2,269	1,009	1,259	1,774	916	1,243
14.	11,910	287	987	666	782	886	517	369
15.	64,823	1,982	7,184	2,754	5,301	6,715	3,193	3,180
16.	6,983	1,063	1,470	466	1,003	909	454	396
17.	31,549	922	2,629	1,206	2,364	2,908	1,279	1,046
18.	21,474	230	1,545	492	468	598	406	523
19.	4,414	39	137	33	81	89	23	39
20.	69,202	3,931	10,652	5,985	10,824	9,697	4,660	4,616
21.	2,148	102	131	72	83	79	62	26
22.	91,253	2,885	11,317	3,068	5,897	9,214	2,562	1,859
23.	12,564	487	1,052	455	681	917	431	307
24.	1,133	85	162	74	146	106	53	43
25.	39,385	1,739	3,453	1,980	2,745	2,908	1,577	1,437
26.	52,169	3,355	7,214	4,656	5,872	6,319	3,634	3,030
27.	32,565	1,270	14,604	1,515	2,191	14,644	1,812	383
N.C.	78,880	5,017	10,713	5,220	5,911	9,637	4,221	2,997
Total Employed	705,201	43,724	153,067	63,293	105,853	128,419	64,114	54,669
Total Population	1,106,558	73,331	242,282	100,412	167,189	200,301	99,486	85,550

East Anglia

9. Bucks.	10. Beds.	11. Herts.	12. Essex	13. Cambridge	14. Hunts.	15. Norfolk	16. Suffolk	
23,695	21,812	28,287	57,971	32,767	11,102	65,779	57,335	1.
135	132	161	499	306	42	807	475	2.
2,523	2,194	3,568	6,498	3,356	1,153	7,671	5,884	3.
-	-	-	-	-	-	-	-	4.
80	113	146	389	143	48	467	309	5.
769	718	1,165	2,318	1,088	349	3,373	2,950	6.
111	82	164	540	192	45	497	438	7.
79	66	87	156	94	37	298	201	8.
-	-	-	-	-	-	-	-	9.
12	3	14	258	57	21	357	299	10.
390	344	532	1,219	515	173	1,380	1,239	11.
84	109	140	253	162	52	542	282	12.
500	406	895	2,076	469	156	4,539	1,753	13.
298	202	322	807	341	134	1,214	904	14.
2,313	2,522	2,408	4,619	3,205	1,066	9,885	5,844	15.
396	317	297	717	541	300	1,472	914	16.
2,865	2,790	1,929	1,791	720	228	2,545	1,756	17.
594	90	502	324	395	90	618	452	18.
15	23	16	67	43	21	109	47	19.
2,762	2,490	4,272	6,563	3,643	1,341	9,596	6,800	20.
28	12	35	66	36	4	71	43	21.
1,290	1,163	2,277	5,605	2,377	561	7,593	4,489	22.
357	275	399	870	361	97	1,227	800	23.
37	28	38	94	51	12	111	81	24.
963	675	1,113	2,269	1,417	394	2,945	2,188	25.
2,008	1,485	2,733	4,343	2,504	663	5,093	3,798	26.
345	255	509	2,177	506	119	1,699	1,328	27.
2,845	2,406	4,053	7,339	3,706	909	6,390	4,136	N.C.
45,494	40,712	56,062	109,828	58,995	19,117	136,278	104,745	
70,928	62,539	86,465	172,717	95,704	30,024	210,759	165,701	

MALE EMPLOYMENT: 1851

South West   West Midlands

	17.Corn-wall	18. Devon	19.Som-erset	20.Gloucs.	21.Wilts.	22.Dorset	23.Here-ford	24.Shrops
1.	36,802	71,959	54,525	36,794	40,204	26,229	18,872	35,240
2.	32,342	4,450	7,375	3,403	600	1,235	332	7,309
3.	3,653	8,241	7,746	8,017	3,507	2,632	1,213	3,470
4.	–	–	–	–	–	–	–	–
5.	328	804	500	826	218	139	104	223
6.	4,259	5,054	3,496	3,287	1,674	1,316	830	4,517
7.	551	618	459	963	505	146	45	292
8.	174	396	243	345	117	88	54	109
9.	–	–	–	–	–	–	–	–
10.	797	1,744	276	506	16	218	9	34
11.	326	1,262	767	865	324	251	390	1,173
12.	231	810	851	1,121	222	185	164	453
13.	1,345	4,491	5,247	6,414	4,688	1,628	306	1,404
14.	604	1,604	1,410	1,159	641	381	240	616
15.	5,481	11,979	10,019	8,850	3,714	3,318	1,868	5,036
16.	103	644	926	966	345	287	178	904
17.	1,262	3,611	3,079	3,862	1,345	1,093	842	1,490
18.	302	1,048	712	953	205	200	91	289
19.	26	70	58	320	16	32	1	36
20.	7,622	16,539	12,387	11,754	5,656	4,915	2,823	5,090
21.	28	77	181	117	47	35	18	44
22.	4,965	8,838	5,178	9,380	2,336	2,663	638	1,810
23.	554	762	695	921	389	287	101	373
24.	78	142	141	149	62	43	44	72
25.	1,829	4,625	3,817	4,309	1,603	1,220	789	1,982
26.	2,017	6,074	5,856	5,953	2,799	2,256	1,448	3,580
27.	1,521	9,044	1,527	2,134	778	1,155	243	559
N.C.	2,749	9,195	10,903	12,122	4,867	4,318	1,055	3,983
Total Employed	109,949	174,081	138,374	125,490	76,878	56,270	32,698	80,088
Total Population	172,193	272,063	217,050	198,569	118,959	85,828	49,809	122,297

East Midlands

25.Staffs.	26.War-wick	27.Worcs.	28.Derby	29.Notts.	30.Leics.	31.Lincs.	32.North-ants.	
35,436	30,345	21,967	20,227	26,915	23,216	68,677	31,857	1.
33,078	2,849	3,194	10,641	4,817	2,339	642	256	2.
8,827	8,790	3,636	3,534	4,937	4,045	6,569	3,702	3.
-	-	-	-	-	-	-	-	4.
966	1,125	527	385	389	290	606	184	5.
26,496	16,048	7,317	4,115	2,561	1,457	2,972	1,380	6.
4,441	5,121	1,026	986	758	278	743	473	7.
410	2,637	133	149	164	117	233	103	8.
-	-	-	-	-	-	-	-	9.
189	116	101	34	27	22	182	17	10.
1,805	1,550	699	651	864	654	1,430	558	11.
6,989	9,440	6,912	1,607	627	424	483	198	12.
4,151	10,481	4,535	14,208	22,219	19,029	1,555	1,193	13.
1,681	2,112	939	608	804	525	910	806	14.
12,281	9,933	4,845	5,330	7,552	5,171	6,974	12,130	15.
20,054	2,753	2,701	1,531	1,180	1,186	2,146	513	16.
3,999	4,741	1,482	1,444	2,204	1,521	1,398	1,203	17.
616	1,292	374	643	522	280	384	210	18.
215	2,836	195	45	97	50	81	33	19.
15,942	12,111	5,057	5,696	5,887	4,050	9,837	4,509	20.
187	173	77	56	55	39	76	39	21.
7,100	7,744	3,428	2,985	3,150	2,736	5,540	2,372	22.
1,018	909	386	605	652	560	703	406	23.
116	192	78	49	59	76	102	46	24.
3,508	3,776	1,911	1,428	1,676	1,437	2,671	1,347	25.
5,956	7,517	4,056	2,513	3,294	3,207	4,869	2,575	26.
1,281	1,612	633	484	789	490	830	1,338	27.
14,977	10,562	6,471	5,949	4,366	2,800	6,232	3,678	N.C.
211,719	156,765	82,680	85,903	96,565	75,999	126,845	71,126	
320,903	235,859	127,038	129,501	144,600	115,451	201,416	106,747	

MALE EMPLOYMENT: 1851

	East Midlands	North West	Yorks. & Humberside		North		
	33.Rut- land	34.Cheshire	35.Lancs.	36. West Riding	37. East Riding	38. North Riding	39.West- morland	40.Cun berla
1.	4,099	34,337	67,848	66,170	27,722	31,239	8,441	21,01
2.	51	3,733	36,411	30,871	519	2,307	493	6,17
3.	406	5,849	28,989	17,815	5,495	2,939	760	2,57
4.	–	–	–	–	–	–	–	–
5.	25	1,976	5,573	3,171	1,069	635	88	29
6.	137	3,400	23,861	26,331	2,433	1,792	434	1,87
7.	5	1,822	17,229	7,510	912	156	77	32
8.	9	242	3,374	803	220	115	31	10
9.	–	–	–	–	–	–	–	–
10.	–	481	3,406	358	667	324	11	67
11.	87	1,339	3,850	2,128	791	432	61	16
12.	11	873	6,908	17,081	463	165	100	41
13.	59	27,519	190,476	145,848	2,765	1,690	1,508	6,34
14.	82	762	3,833	3,416	1,028	664	182	55
15.	421	9,353	37,993	25,064	6,216	4,927	1,149	3,97
16.	39	1,591	7,161	4,072	1,101	597	54	58
17.	102	2,345	15,094	6,580	2,042	700	859	1,24
18.	12	608	5,382	2,923	650	240	104	29
19.	–	92	813	983	183	19	19	3
20.	735	9,547	45,916	31,084	5,937	4,802	1,537	5,04
21.	4	125	1,033	472	97	20	10	4
22.	181	8,114	59,992	16,773	8,627	2,286	416	3,20
23.	31	1,197	6,858	3,595	702	278	72	24
24.	2	77	504	232	94	52	19	2
25.	180	2,750	12,064	6,901	2,169	1,400	461	1,29
26.	501	3,844	16,794	9,352	2,979	2,151	625	1,50
27.	48	1,450	9,017	2,548	1,822	517	121	60
N.C.	481	11,267	59,743	20,615	5,138	1,712	726	2,12
Total Employed	7,708	134,693	670,122	452,696	81,841	62,159	18,358	60,68
Total Population	12,286	207,008	1,008,824	666,912	124,572	96,620	29,134	96,24

	Wales			Scotland				
41.North- umberland	42.Durham	43.Glam- organ & Monmouth	44.North & West Wales	45.Strathclyde	46.Dumfries & Galloway	47.Borders	48.Lothian	
22,204	17,426	25,876	108,284	51,864	22,224	14,693	15,939	1.
12,726	34,284	38,065	27,333	34,185	1,258	295	6,044	2.
4,870	5,737	4,304	7,048	16,766	1,784	1,479	8,151	3.
–	–	–	–	–	–	–	–	4.
638	1,657	366	720	2,303	84	54	753	5.
5,883	9,329	20,940	8,371	18,539	1,171	848	4,629	6.
2,120	1,758	1,119	498	5,985	156	221	1,205	7.
265	219	183	359	545	87	55	355	8.
–	–	–	–	–	–	–	–	9.
1,299	4,528	539	1,052	2,047	81	9	261	10.
519	673	383	1,203	1,011	128	57	476	11.
819	1,303	869	867	2,175	212	80	1,155	12.
2,100	3,435	1,710	6,709	60,831	2,844	4,055	3,292	13.
1,019	784	586	1,570	1,568	242	261	1,204	14.
6,249	7,093	6,832	14,317	20,505	2,732	1,807	7,389	15.
2,242	3,390	563	740	2,854	189	104	795	16.
1,917	2,235	2,275	3,109	7,535	673	436	3,317	17.
803	772	413	682	2,699	134	153	3,263	18.
70	167	51	21	354	1	1	198	19.
8,046	10,512	10,369	15,454	23,631	3,818	3,265	9,820	20.
67	104	55	51	475	21	24	211	21.
8,688	13,476	8,414	8,790	21,505	1,912	940	7,520	22.
710	578	645	1,317	2,591	385	172	1,042	23.
54	73	64	155	209	35	15	130	24.
1,999	2,189	2,109	4,679	6,842	1,113	827	5,595	25.
2,459	2,476	3,368	6,013	5,609	1,045	903	3,278	26.
1,927	1,003	1,323	3,243	3,848	423	267	3,095	27.
6,575	7,970	15,898	13,972	22,224	2,944	1,426	6,703	N.C.
96,268	133,171	147,319	236,557	318,700	45,696	32,447	95,820	
149,515	207,088	217,388	377,405	499,533	77,744	52,859	152,188	

MALE EMPLOYMENT: 1851

Scotland

	49.Central & Fife	50.Tayside	51.Grampian	52.Highland	53. South East	54. East Anglia	55. South West	56. W Midl
1.	17,009	27,612	51,106	55,167	398,737	166,983	266,513	141,
2.	8,348	1,343	1,055	618	10,179	1,630	49,405	46,
3.	3,724	4,841	4,304	2,051	117,236	18,064	33,796	25,
4.	–	–	–	–	–	–	–	
5.	366	206	277	99	13,850	967	2,815	2,
6.	3,912	2,960	2,733	1,315	39,274	7,760	19,086	55,
7.	739	1,089	540	141	13,649	1,172	3,242	10,
8.	124	203	233	101	8,066	630	1,363	3,
9.	–	–	–	–	–	–	–	
10.	223	678	659	437	8,454	734	3,557	
11.	267	273	577	394	14,902	3,307	3,795	5,
12.	807	386	231	122	14,435	1,038	3,420	23,
13.	17,508	25,970	4,425	1,511	40,403	6,917	23,813	20,
14.	471	532	438	163	18,033	2,593	5,799	5,
15.	3,950	6,088	6,179	4,606	106,994	20,000	43,361	33,
16.	573	245	262	67	14,471	3,227	3,271	26,
17.	1,350	2,141	2,066	1,632	53,278	5,249	14,252	12,
18.	430	528	700	176	27,246	1,555	3,420	2,
19.	13	30	569	2	4,976	220	522	3,
20.	6,175	8,473	6,592	4,873	135,654	21,380	58,873	41,
21.	71	119	71	20	2,844	154	485	
22.	4,149	5,204	4,241	2,925	138,390	15,020	33,360	20,
23.	410	556	522	414	18,795	2,485	3,608	2,
24.	51	100	64	33	1,999	255	615	
25.	1,590	2,391	2,397	1,645	60,244	6,944	17,403	11,
26.	1,183	2,110	1,821	1,588	96,818	12,058	24,955	22,
27.	683	1,096	1,175	1,020	72,270	3,652	16,159	4,
N.C.	4,267	6,308	4,974	4,292	139,239	15,141	44,154	37,
Total Employed	78,393	101,482	98,211	85,412	1,570,436	319,135	681,042	563,
Total Population	126,751	158,966	161,029	146,409	2,467,758	502,188	1,064,662	855,

57. East Midlands	58. North West	59. Yorks. & Humberside	60. North	61. Wales	62. Scotland	63. Great Britain	
174,991	102,185	93,892	100,323	134,160	255,614	1,835,258	1.
18,746	40,144	31,390	55,982	65,398	53,146	372,782	2.
23,193	34,838	23,310	16,879	11,352	43,100	347,704	3.
–	–	–	–	–	–	–	4.
1,879	7,549	4,240	3,316	1,086	4,142	42,789	5.
12,622	27,261	28,764	19,313	29,311	36,107	274,706	6.
3,243	19,051	8,422	4,436	1,617	10,076	75,833	7.
775	3,616	1,023	739	542	1,703	21,800	8.
–	–	–	–	–	–	–	9.
282	3,887	1,025	6,834	1,591	4,395	31,208	10.
4,244	5,189	2,919	1,853	1,586	3,183	46,595	11.
3,350	7,781	17,544	2,798	1,736	5,168	81,228	12.
58,263	217,995	148,613	15,079	8,419	120,436	660,815	13.
3,735	4,595	4,444	3,201	2,156	4,879	55,023	14.
37,578	47,346	31,280	23,391	21,149	53,256	418,318	15.
6,595	8,752	5,173	6,805	1,303	5,089	81,276	16.
7,872	17,439	8,622	6,957	5,384	19,150	150,757	17.
2,051	5,990	3,573	2,217	1,095	8,083	57,892	18.
306	905	1,166	314	72	1,168	12,932	19.
30,714	55,463	37,021	29,943	25,823	66,647	502,541	20.
269	1,158	569	242	106	1,012	7,338	21.
16,964	68,106	25,400	28,068	17,204	48,396	411,628	22.
2,957	8,055	4,297	1,882	1,962	6,092	52,920	23.
334	581	326	226	219	637	5,694	24.
8,739	14,814	9,070	7,346	6,788	22,400	165,714	25.
16,959	20,638	12,331	9,216	9,381	17,537	242,450	26.
3,979	10,467	4,370	4,170	4,566	11,607	135,568	27.
23,506	71,010	25,753	19,107	29,870	53,138	457,966	N.C.
464,146	804,815	534,537	370,637	383,876	856,161	6,548,735	
710,001	1,215,832	791,484	578,601	594,793	1,375,479	10,156,704	

FEMALE EMPLOYMENT: 1851

South East

	1. London	2. Middlesex	3. Kent	4. Surrey	5. Sussex	6. Hants.	7. Berks.	8. Oxon.
1.	939	1,027	2,684	936	2,148	1,780	4,548	2,458
2.	189	7	36	9	9	21	11	6
3.	6,659	283	875	334	599	819	297	301
4.	–	–	–	–	–	–	–	–
5.	955	52	40	15	13	18	2	7
6.	430	20	42	11	36	33	19	20
7.	72	–	2	–	–	–	1	–
8.	93	2	3	2	2	202	2	1
9.	–	–	–	–	–	–	–	–
10.	4	–	2	–	–	2	–	1
11.	81	6	2	5	6	1	2	1
12.	390	2	7	6	11	10	5	32
13.	16,104	266	454	200	205	662	532	2,045
14.	3,406	4	21	13	41	32	27	19
15.	96,649	2,357	7,734	2,769	6,038	9,169	4,261	4,970
16.	493	14	16	7	13	19	15	13
17.	3,109	148	94	65	157	164	52	46
18.	4,893	56	1,487	132	77	134	95	70
19.	615	4	19	15	26	18	11	7
20.	129	19	30	16	18	29	14	17
21.	2	2	3	1	2	–	–	–
22.	688	32	202	32	76	94	77	58
23.	4,657	150	368	163	227	327	195	138
24.	–	–	–	–	–	–	–	–
25.	20,566	1,267	3,008	1,469	2,569	2,671	1,379	1,050
26.	219,768	13,059	29,475	15,937	25,651	25,992	11,914	8,574
27.	226	23	80	35	57	76	39	28
N.C.	1,145	63	146	85	30	128	246	62
Total Employed	382,262	18,863	46,830	22,257	38,011	42,401	23,744	19,924
Total Population	1,255,678	77,275	242,739	102,109	172,415	201,715	99,738	84,697

9. Bucks.	10. Beds.	11. Herts.	12. Essex	13. Cambridge	14. Hunts.	15. Norfolk	16. Suffolk	
1,347	964	1,493	3,312	3,388	792	6,418	4,483	1.
5	1	6	9	7	1	11	3	2.
475	184	342	563	330	124	785	624	3.
–	–	–	–	–	–	–	–	4.
3	1	8	18	2	1	32	12	5.
15	7	20	44	11	2	31	36	6.
–	–	1	1	–	–	28	1	7.
–	–	2	5	–	–	3	1	8.
–	–	–	–	–	–	–	–	9.
–	–	–	–	–	–	1	1	10.
–	–	–	1	2	–	3	2	11.
3	1	–	10	4	1	9	13	12.
10,924	5,793	831	3,111	190	1,041	4,797	2,089	13.
12	3	12	35	11	2	34	296	14.
2,275	7,023	3,875	5,308	3,150	869	11,479	6,570	15.
11	4	13	22	6	3	32	17	16.
3,154	10,095	8,800	3,103	204	24	175	2,257	17.
262	11	312	34	69	103	201	135	18.
8	3	7	21	3	3	13	10	19.
10	6	9	18	11	4	18	21	20.
–	–	–	1	1	–	–	–	21.
24	33	48	88	81	11	247	111	22.
92	80	150	367	190	39	518	272	23.
–	–	–	–	–	–	–	–	24.
773	634	1,039	2,425	1,275	383	2,871	2,273	25.
5,738	4,240	7,919	16,039	9,423	2,255	20,821	14,658	26.
19	10	33	68	23	7	85	67	27.
39	17	41	98	175	3	240	73	N.C.
25,189	29,110	24,961	34,701	18,556	5,668	48,852	34,025	
72,727	67,266	87,497	171,413	96,190	30,295	222,957	170,435	

FEMALE EMPLOYMENT: 1851

South West   West Midlands

	17.Corn-wall	18. Devon	19.Som-erset	20.Gloucs.	21.Wilts.	22.Dorset	23.Here-ford	24.Shrops
1.	6,229	9,248	7,837	4,920	8,414	3,398	1,638	2,880
2.	3,807	215	81	40	13	4	3	623
3.	1,283	1,839	1,024	1,239	461	328	174	515
4.	–	–	–	–	–	–	–	–
5.	64	43	23	51	32	8	1	8
6.	2,268	193	56	104	20	16	11	206
7.	–	–	1	–	1	–	–	1
8.	–	5	3	1	–	–	–	2
9.	–	–	–	–	–	–	–	–
10.	–	–	–	1	–	–	–	–
11.	–	3	3	1	–	1	1	1
12.	–	12	188	160	4	1	3	8
13.	840	9,725	6,439	7,513	5,080	2,686	74	513
14.	10	42	128	92	55	19	4	133
15.	7,624	19,442	20,498	13,633	3,922	5,754	2,317	3,494
16.	11	96	41	158	12	15	9	394
17.	46	275	241	345	70	66	41	53
18.	39	479	232	222	23	19	10	37
19.	13	65	41	175	4	682	–	45
20.	3	17	10	19	14	8	4	7
21.	–	1	–	–	–	2	–	–
22.	177	328	188	178	130	93	75	171
23.	281	755	767	949	207	226	136	267
24.	–	–	–	–	–	–	–	–
25.	1,597	3,860	3,080	2,877	1,409	1,143	403	1,033
26.	13,399	34,295	29,365	32,326	11,052	8,572	6,370	15,096
27.	52	103	84	53	49	38	18	48
N.C.	395	326	494	540	179	148	197	243
Total Employed	38,138	81,367	70,824	65,597	31,151	23,227	11,489	25,778
Total Population	184,448	300,267	239,209	220,945	122,007	91,267	49,311	122,601

East Midlands

25.Staffs.	26.Warwick	27.Worcs.	28.Derby	29.Notts.	30.Leics.	31.Lincs.	32.Northants.	
2,127	2,137	2,240	2,617	2,653	1,546	2,166	2,279	1.
691	71	109	20	47	14	12	5	2.
1,107	1,151	458	433	557	490	654	344	3.
-	-	-	-	-	-	-	-	4.
59	522	78	9	23	27	18	9	5.
1,982	4,179	433	45	22	12	27	16	6.
18	159	6	-	-	1	1	1	7.
2	52	2	1	1	1	2	-	8.
-	-	-	-	-	-	-	-	9.
-	-	1	1	-	-	1	-	10.
2	14	3	3	1	1	3	1	11.
5,097	2,387	5,110	75	11	19	9	7	12.
4,154	15,387	1,744	17,258	20,960	17,577	335	10,696	13.
323	434	138	6	26	12	31	25	14.
10,477	11,899	9,096	5,307	10,565	7,250	6,460	5,801	15.
9,782	232	409	103	25	91	24	3	16.
127	511	96	55	93	88	37	64	17.
121	684	72	314	202	69	30	62	18.
96	3,129	80	47	20	11	16	8	19.
18	37	13	2	2	5	24	7	20.
-	9	2	1	-	-	-	-	21.
596	1,572	223	118	113	472	210	92	22.
760	837	441	298	249	186	264	149	23.
-	-	-	-	-	-	-	-	24.
2,046	2,187	1,226	995	1,437	1,216	2,381	1,298	25.
26,260	26,956	15,815	9,423	12,396	10,416	24,597	8,598	26.
51	49	44	30	32	31	54	32	27.
267	352	416	22	58	35	89	29	N.C.
66,163	74,947	38,255	37,183	49,493	39,570	37,445	29,526	
309,642	244,261	131,695	131,192	149,780	119,506	198,820	107,097	

FEMALE EMPLOYMENT: 1851

	East Midlands	North West		Yorks. & Humberside		North		
	33.Rut-land	34. Cheshire	35.Lancs.	36. West Riding	37. East Riding	38. North Riding	39.West-morland	40.Cum-berland
1.	112	2,723	4,649	6,655	1,709	3,423	1,382	4,757
2.	1	21	426	182	8	2	9	83
3.	33	937	6,589	2,979	584	448	269	914
4.	–	–	–	–	–	–	–	–
5.	–	28	347	389	18	16	8	10
6.	2	29	204	1,550	33	80	6	27
7.	–	186	46	208	3	1	–	1
8.	–	1	27	38	–	–	1	
9.	–	–	–	–	–	–	–	
10.	–	1	3	1	2	1	–	–
11.	–	6	13	6	3	–	–	1
12.	–	12	378	510	8	4	–	3
13.	117	27,915	184,502	102,162	1,556	381	812	4,239
14.	1	20	164	691	20	6	5	16
15.	355	6,252	38,423	20,991	5,819	3,373	928	3,482
16.	1	40	899	442	37	18	10	112
17.	–	100	1,373	367	101	23	16	54
18.	1	48	833	396	49	90	49	44
19.	–	52	107	162	16	3	2	6
20.	–	20	38	45	12	6	4	2
21.	–	2	1	1	–	–	–	–
22.	13	342	1,294	2,033	384	55	29	72
23.	12	762	6,129	2,269	367	118	43	235
24.	–	–	–	–	–	–	–	–
25.	124	1,567	5,454	4,102	1,403	737	213	553
26.	1,429	22,894	104,364	44,092	16,441	10,884	3,048	8,372
27.	10	48	141	64	23	38	14	26
N.C.	2	146	1,248	313	141	98	31	169
Total Employed	2,213	64,152	357,652	190,648	28,737	19,805	6,879	23,178
Total Population	11,986	216,518	1,058,477	673,139	129,780	98,024	29,253	99,248

	Wales			Scotland				
41.North-umberland	42.Durham	43.Glam-organ & Monmouth	44.North & West Wales	45.Strathclyde	46.Dumfries & Galloway	47.Borders	48.Lothian	
5,994	3,764	4,938	28,097	11,434	4,451	4,738	5,282	1.
15	54	1,203	613	176	3	3	76	2.
1,196	1,032	986	2,304	3,243	615	336	1,520	3.
-	-	-	-	-	-	-	-	4.
89	49	9	28	503	9	1	95	5.
25	26	1,529	581	69	1	4	11	6.
-	-	3	-	11	-	-	2	7.
1	1	2	1	-	-	-	-	8.
-	-	-	-	-	-	-	-	9.
-	2	1	1	-	-	-	-	10.
1	1	1	2	3	-	-	1	11.
6	3	7	9	197	10	9	69	12.
508	1,115	497	3,936	74,284	2,094	1,855	2,353	13.
20	27	14	63	134	2	5	154	14.
5,403	6,000	6,025	9,800	23,713	4,075	1,436	8,455	15.
302	338	117	108	545	17	14	103	16.
91	53	64	111	332	20	12	131	17.
149	213	56	87	862	7	115	1,526	18.
7	16	30	8	82	1	-	27	19.
13	8	7	13	14	4	2	13	20.
6	2	3	1	1	-	-	3	21.
80	104	130	366	665	67	44	172	22.
559	462	413	939	1,760	255	127	1,037	23.
-	-	-	-	-	-	-	-	24.
791	1,126	974	1,378	1,467	323	246	1,475	25.
14,826	15,776	17,316	29,885	41,143	8,789	4,743	25,961	26.
40	49	33	115	87	39	22	45	27.
138	297	607	446	325	353	40	349	N.C.
30,260	30,518	34,965	78,892	161,050	21,135	13,752	48,860	
154,053	204,591	199,837	394,284	532,594	86,889	55,627	173,768	

FEMALE EMPLOYMENT: 1851

Scotland

	49.Central & Fife	50.Tayside	51.Grampian	52.Highland	53. South East	54. East Anglia	55. South West	56. West Midlands
1.	4,223	6,666	10,403	13,446	23,636	15,081	40,046	11,022
2.	190	13	10	14	309	22	4,160	1,497
3.	795	1,083	1,135	379	11,731	1,863	6,174	3,405
4.	-	-	-	-	-	-	-	-
5.	21	12	187	2	1,132	47	221	668
6.	4	6	5	3	697	80	2,657	6,811
7.	2	-	-	-	77	29	2	184
8.	-	-	-	-	314	4	9	58
9.	-	-	-	-	-	-	-	-
10.	1	-	-	-	9	2	1	1
11.	-	-	1	-	105	7	8	21
12.	15	17	10	2	477	27	365	12,605
13.	15,181	29,845	7,420	3,659	41,127	8,117	32,283	21,872
14.	7	9	15	7	3,625	343	346	1,032
15.	3,573	5,031	3,915	2,438	152,428	22,068	70,873	37,283
16.	57	41	23	11	640	58	333	10,826
17.	18	38	46	671	28,987	2,660	1,043	828
18.	242	33	367	5	7,563	508	1,014	924
19.	5	6	1	1	754	29	980	3,350
20.	3	1	-	1	315	54	71	79
21.	-	-	-	4	11	1	3	11
22.	145	105	108	47	1,452	450	1,094	2,637
23.	354	362	306	94	6,914	1,019	3,185	2,441
24.	-	-	-	-	-	-	-	-
25.	472	734	1,267	582	38,850	6,802	13,966	6,895
26.	8,491	12,873	18,493	13,241	384,306	47,157	129,009	90,497
27.	37	41	55	33	694	182	379	210
N.C.	182	200	149	521	2,100	491	2,082	1,475
Total Employed	34,018	57,116	43,916	35,161	708,253	107,101	310,304	216,632
Total Population	135,983	179,882	178,731	169,789	2,635,269	519,877	1,158,143	857,510

57. East Midlands	58. North West	59. Yorks. & Humberside	60. North	61. Wales	62. Scotland	63. Great Britain	
11,373	7,372	8,364	19,320	33,035	60,643	229,892	1.
99	447	190	163	1,816	485	9,188	2.
2,511	7,526	3,563	3,859	3,290	9,106	53,028	3.
-	-	-	-	-		-	4.
86	375	407	172	37	830	3,975	5.
124	233	1,583	164	2,110	103	14,562	6.
3	232	211	2	3	15	758	7.
5	28	38	3	3	-	462	8.
-	-	-	-	-	-	-	9.
2	4	3	3	2	1	28	10.
9	19	9	3	3	5	189	11.
121	390	518	16	16	329	14,864	12.
66,943	212,417	103,718	7,055	4,433	136,691	634,656	13.
101	184	711	74	77	333	6,826	14.
35,738	44,675	26,810	19,186	15,825	52,636	477,522	15.
247	939	479	780	225	811	15,338	16.
337	1,473	468	237	175	1,268	37,476	17.
678	881	445	545	143	3,157	15,858	18.
102	159	178	34	38	123	5,747	19.
40	58	57	33	20	38	765	20.
1	3	1	8	4	8	51	21.
1,018	1,636	2,417	340	496	1,353	12,893	22.
1,158	6,891	2,636	1,417	1,352	4,295	31,308	23.
-	-	-	-	-	-	-	24.
7,451	7,021	5,505	3,420	2,352	6,566	98,828	25.
66,859	127,258	60,533	52,906	47,201	133,734	1,139,460	26.
189	189	87	167	148	359	2,604	27.
235	1,394	454	733	1,053	2,119	12,136	N.C.
195,430	421,804	219,385	110,640	113,857	415,008	2,818,414	
718,381	1,274,995	802,919	585,169	594,121	1,513,263	10,659,647	

TOTAL EMPLOYMENT: 1851

South East

	1. London	2. Middlesex	3. Kent	4. Surrey	5. Sussex	6. Hants.	7. Berks.	8. Oxon
1.	16,449	14,535	62,158	27,428	49,886	47,366	35,750	29,920
2.	6,777	258	898	286	392	412	256	261
3.	69,803	3,812	10,771	4,514	7,601	8,218	4,284	3,617
4.	-	-	-	-	-	-	-	-
5.	11,424	458	762	357	380	472	220	151
6.	21,693	919	3,025	1,341	2,375	3,106	1,471	985
7.	10,245	273	685	133	342	815	189	145
8.	6,518	116	299	109	241	487	114	101
9.	-	-	-	-	-	-	-	-
10.	5,073	31	994	32	346	1,585	82	33
11.	7,034	522	1,241	568	1,115	961	639	441
12.	12,106	188	408	192	391	483	196	348
13.	43,543	883	2,723	1,209	1,464	2,436	1,448	3,288
14.	15,316	291	1,008	679	823	918	544	388
15.	161,472	4,339	14,918	5,523	11,339	15,884	7,454	8,150
16.	7,476	1,077	1,486	473	1,016	928	469	409
17.	34,658	1,070	2,723	1,271	2,521	3,072	1,331	1,092
18.	26,367	286	3,032	624	545	732	501	593
19.	5,029	43	156	48	107	107	34	46
20.	69,331	3,950	10,682	6,001	10,842	9,726	4,674	4,633
21.	2,150	104	134	73	85	79	62	26
22.	91,941	2,917	11,519	3,100	5,973	9,308	2,639	1,917
23.	17,221	637	1,420	618	908	1,244	626	445
24.	1,133	85	162	74	146	106	53	43
25.	59,951	3,006	6,461	3,449	5,314	5,579	2,956	2,487
26.	271,937	16,414	36,689	20,593	31,523	32,311	15,548	11,604
27.	32,791	1,293	14,684	1,550	2,248	14,720	1,851	411
N.C.	80,025	5,080	10,859	5,305	5,941	9,765	4,467	3,059
Total Employed	1,087,463	62,587	199,897	85,550	143,864	170,820	87,858	74,593
Total Population	2,362,236	150,606	485,021	202,521	339,604	402,016	199,224	170,247

East Anglia

9. Bucks.	10. Beds.	11. Herts.	12. Essex	13. Cambridge	14. Hunts.	15. Norfolk	16. Suffolk	
25,042	22,776	29,780	61,283	36,155	11,894	72,197	61,818	1.
140	133	167	508	313	43	818	478	2.
2,998	2,378	3,910	7,061	3,686	1,277	8,456	6,508	3.
–	–	–	–	–	–	–	–	4.
83	114	154	407	145	49	499	321	5.
784	725	1,185	2,362	1,099	351	3,404	2,986	6.
111	82	165	541	192	45	525	439	7.
79	66	89	161	94	37	301	202	8.
–	–	–	–	–	–	–	–	9.
12	3	14	258	57	21	358	300	10.
390	344	532	1,220	517	173	1,383	1,241	11.
87	110	140	263	166	53	551	295	12.
11,424	6,199	1,726	5,187	659	1,197	9,336	3,842	13.
310	205	334	842	352	136	1,248	1,200	14.
4,588	9,545	6,283	9,927	6,355	1,935	21,364	12,414	15.
407	321	310	739	547	303	1,504	931	16.
6,019	12,885	10,729	4,894	924	252	2,720	4,013	17.
856	101	814	358	464	193	819	587	18.
23	26	23	88	46	24	122	57	19.
2,772	2,496	4,281	6,581	3,654	1,345	9,614	6,821	20.
28	12	35	67	37	4	71	43	21.
1,314	1,196	2,325	5,693	2,458	572	7,840	4,600	22.
449	355	549	1,237	551	136	1,745	1,072	23.
37	28	38	94	51	12	111	81	24.
1,736	1,309	2,152	4,694	2,692	777	5,816	4,461	25.
7,746	5,725	10,652	20,382	11,927	2,918	25,914	18,456	26.
364	265	542	2,245	529	126	1,784	1,395	27.
2,884	2,423	4,094	7,437	3,881	912	6,630	4,209	N.C.
70,683	69,822	81,023	144,529	77,551	24,785	185,130	138,770	
143,655	129,805	173,962	344,130	191,894	60,319	433,716	336,136	

TOTAL EMPLOYMENT: 1851

South West   West Midlands

	17.Corn- wall	18. Devon	19.Som- erset	20.Gloucs.	21.Wilts.	22.Dorset	23.Here- ford	24.Shrops
1.	43,031	81,207	62,362	41,714	48,618	29,627	20,510	38,120
2.	36,149	4,665	7,456	3,443	613	1,239	335	7,932
3.	4,936	10,080	8,770	9,256	3,968	2,960	1,387	3,985
4.	-	-	-	-	-	-	-	-
5.	392	847	523	877	250	147	105	231
6.	6,527	5,247	3,552	3,391	1,694	1,332	841	4,723
7.	551	618	460	963	506	146	45	293
8.	174	401	246	346	117	88	54	111
9.	-	-	-	-	-	-	-	-
10.	797	1,744	276	507	16	218	9	34
11.	326	1,265	770	866	324	252	391	1,174
12.	231	822	1,039	1,281	226	186	167	461
13.	2,185	14,216	11,686	13,927	9,768	4,314	380	1,917
14.	614	1,646	1,538	1,251	696	400	244	749
15.	13,105	31,421	30,517	22,483	7,636	9,072	4,185	8,530
16.	114	740	967	1,124	357	302	187	1,298
17.	1,308	3,886	3,320	4,207	1,415	1,159	883	1,543
18.	341	1,527	944	1,175	228	219	101	326
19.	39	135	99	495	20	714	1	81
20.	7,625	16,556	12,397	11,773	5,670	4,923	2,827	5,097
21.	28	78	181	117	47	37	18	44
22.	5,142	9,166	5,366	9,558	2,466	2,756	713	1,981
23.	835	1,517	1,462	1,870	596	513	237	640
24.	78	142	141	149	62	43	44	72
25.	3,426	8,485	6,897	7,186	3,012	2,363	1,192	3,015
26.	15,416	40,369	35,221	38,279	13,851	10,828	7,818	18,676
27.	1,573	9,147	1,611	2,187	827	1,193	261	607
N.C.	3,144	9,521	11,397	12,662	5,046	4,466	1,252	4,226
Total Employed	148,087	255,448	209,198	191,087	108,029	79,497	44,187	105,866
Total Population	356,641	572,330	456,259	419,514	240,966	177,095	99,120	244,898

East Midlands

25. Staffs.	26.Warwick	27.Worcs.	28.Derby	29.Notts.	30.Leics.	31.Lincs.	32.Northants.	
37,563	32,482	24,207	22,844	29,568	24,762	70,843	34,136	1.
33,769	2,920	3,303	10,661	4,864	2,353	654	261	2.
9,934	9,941	4,094	3,967	5,494	4,535	7,223	4,046	3.
-	-	-	-	-	-	-	-	4.
1,025	1,647	605	394	412	317	624	193	5.
28,478	20,227	7,750	4,160	2,583	1,469	2,999	1,396	6.
4,459	5,280	1,032	986	758	279	744	474	7.
412	2,689	135	150	165	118	235	103	8.
-	-	-	-	-	-	-	-	9.
189	116	102	35	27	22	183	17	10.
1,807	1,564	702	654	865	655	1,433	559	11.
12,086	11,827	12,022	1,682	638	443	492	205	12.
8,305	25,868	6,279	31,466	43,179	36,606	1,890	11,889	13.
2,004	2,546	1,077	614	830	537	941	831	14.
22,758	21,832	13,941	10,637	18,117	12,421	13,434	17,931	15.
29,836	2,985	3,110	1,634	1,205	1,277	2,170	516	16.
4,126	5,252	1,578	1,499	2,297	1,609	1,435	1,267	17.
737	1,976	446	957	724	349	414	272	18.
311	5,965	275	92	117	61	97	41	19.
15,960	12,148	5,070	5,698	5,889	4,055	9,861	4,516	20.
187	182	79	57	55	39	76	39	21.
7,696	9,316	3,651	3,103	3,263	3,208	5,750	2,464	22.
1,778	1,746	827	903	901	746	967	555	23.
116	192	78	49	59	76	102	46	24.
5,554	5,963	3,137	2,423	3,113	2,653	5,052	2,645	25.
32,216	34,473	19,871	11,936	15,690	13,623	29,466	11,173	26.
1,332	1,661	677	514	821	521	884	1,370	27.
15,244	10,914	6,887	5,971	4,424	2,835	6,321	3,707	N.C.
277,882	231,712	120,935	123,086	146,058	115,569	164,290	100,652	
630,545	480,120	258,733	260,693	294,380	234,957	400,236	213,844	

TOTAL EMPLOYMENT: 1851

	West Midlands	North West		Yorks. & Humberside		North		
	33.Rutland	34. Cheshire	35.Lancs.	36. West Riding	37. East Riding	38. North Riding	39.Westmorland	40.Cumberland
1.	4,211	37,060	72,497	72,825	29,431	34,662	9,823	25,77
2.	52	3,754	36,837	31,053	527	2,309	502	6,25
3.	439	6,786	35,578	20,794	6,079	3,387	1,029	3,48
4.	-	-	-	-	-	-	-	-
5.	25	2,004	5,920	3,560	1,087	651	96	3(
6.	139	3,429	24,065	27,881	2,466	1,872	440	1,90
7.	5	2,008	17,275	7,718	915	157	77	3?
8.	9	243	3,401	841	220	115	32	1(
9.	-	-	-	-	-	-	-	-
10.	-	482	3,409	359	669	325	11	67
11.	87	1,345	3,863	2,134	794	432	61	16
12.	11	885	7,286	17,591	471	169	100	41
13.	176	55,434	374,978	248,010	4,321	2,071	2,320	10,58
14.	83	782	3,997	4,107	1,048	670	187	56
15.	776	15,605	76,416	46,055	12,035	8,300	2,077	7,45
16.	40	1,631	8,060	4,514	1,138	615	64	63
17.	102	2,445	16,467	6,947	2,143	723	875	1,30
18.	13	656	6,215	3,319	699	330	153	34
19.	-	144	920	1,145	199	22	21	4
20.	735	9,567	45,954	31,129	5,949	4,808	1,541	5,04
21.	4	127	1,034	473	97	20	10	4
22.	194	8,456	61,286	18,806	9,011	2,341	445	3,27
23.	43	1,959	12,987	5,864	1,069	396	115	47
24.	2	77	504	232	94	52	19	2
25.	304	4,317	17,518	11,003	3,572	2,137	674	1,85
26.	1,930	26,738	121,158	53,444	19,420	13,035	3,673	9,87
27.	58	1,498	9,158	2,612	1,845	555	135	62
N.C.	483	11,413	60,991	20,928	5,279	1,810	757	2,29
Total Employed	9,921	198,845	1,027,774	643,344	110,578	81,964	25,237	83,85
Total Population	24,272	423,526	2,067,301	1,340,051	254,352	194,644	58,387	195,49

		Wales		Scotland			
41.North- umberland	42.Durham	43.Glam- organ & Monmouth	44.North & West Wales	45.Strathclyde	46.Dumfries & Galloway	47.Borders	48.Lothian	
28,198	21,190	30,814	136,381	63,298	26,675	19,431	21,221	1.
12,741	34,338	39,268	27,946	34,361	1,261	298	6,120	2.
6,066	6,769	5,290	9,352	20,009	2,399	1,815	9,671	3.
-	-	-	-	-	-	-	-	4.
727	1,706	375	748	2,806	93	55	848	5.
5,908	9,355	22,469	8,952	18,608	1,172	852	4,640	6.
2,120	1,758	1,122	498	5,996	156	221	1,207	7.
266	220	185	360	545	87	55	355	8.
-	-	-	-	-	-	-	-	9.
1,299	4,530	540	1,053	2,047	81	9	261	10.
520	674	384	1,205	1,014	128	57	477	11.
825	1,306	876	876	2,372	222	89	1,224	12.
2,608	4,550	2,207	10,645	135,115	4,938	5,910	5,645	13.
1,039	811	600	1,633	1,702	244	266	1,358	14.
11,652	13,093	12,857	24,117	44,218	6,807	3,243	15,844	15.
2,544	3,728	680	848	3,399	206	118	898	16.
2,008	2,288	2,339	3,220	7,867	693	448	3,448	17.
952	985	469	769	3,561	141	268	4,789	18.
77	183	81	29	436	2	1	225	19.
8,059	10,520	10,376	15,467	23,645	3,822	3,267	9,833	20.
73	106	58	52	476	21	24	214	21.
8,768	13,580	8,544	9,156	22,170	1,979	984	7,692	22.
1,269	1,040	1,058	2,256	4,351	640	299	2,079	23.
54	73	64	155	209	35	15	130	24.
2,790	3,315	3,083	6,057	8,309	1,436	1,073	7,070	25.
17,285	18,252	20,684	35,898	46,752	9,834	5,646	29,239	26.
1,967	1,052	1,356	3,358	3,935	462	289	3,140	27.
6,713	8,267	16,505	14,418	22,549	3,297	1,466	7,052	N.C.
126,528	163,689	182,284	315,449	479,750	66,831	46,199	144,680	
303,568	411,679	417,225	771,689	1,032,127	164,633	108,486	325,956	

TOTAL EMPLOYMENT: 1851

Scotland

	49.Central & Fife	50.Tayside	51.Grampian	52.Highland	53. South East	54. East Anglia	55. South West	56. Mic
1.	21,232	34,278	61,509	68,613	422,373	182,064	306,559	152
2.	8,538	1,356	1,065	632	10,488	1,652	53,565	48
3.	4,519	5,924	5,439	2,430	128,967	19,927	39,970	29
4.	-	-	-	-	-	-	-	
5.	387	218	464	101	14,982	1,014	3,036	3
6.	3,916	2,966	2,738	1,318	39,971	7,840	21,743	62
7.	741	1,089	540	141	13,726	1,201	3,244	11
8.	124	203	233	101	8,380	634	1,372	3
9.	-	-	-	-	-	-	-	
10.	224	678	659	437	8,463	736	3,558	
11.	267	273	578	394	15,007	3,314	3,803	5
12.	822	403	241	124	14,912	1,065	3,785	36
13.	32,689	55,815	11,845	5,170	81,530	15,034	56,096	42
14.	478	541	453	170	21,658	2,936	6,145	6
15.	7,523	11,119	10,094	7,044	259,422	42,068	114,234	71
16.	630	286	285	78	15,111	3,285	3,604	37
17.	1,368	2,179	2,112	2,303	82,265	7,909	15,295	13
18.	672	561	1,067	181	34,809	2,063	4,434	3
19.	18	36	570	3	5,730	249	1,502	6
20.	6,178	8,474	6,592	4,874	135,969	21,434	58,944	41
21.	71	119	71	24	2,855	155	488	
22.	4,294	5,309	4,349	2,972	139,842	15,470	34,454	23
23.	764	918	828	508	25,709	3,504	6,793	5
24.	51	100	64	33	1,999	255	615	
25.	2,062	3,125	3,664	2,227	99,094	13,746	31,369	18
26.	9,674	14,983	20,314	14,829	481,124	59,215	153,964	113
27.	720	1,137	1,230	1,053	72,964	3,834	16,538	4
N.C.	4,449	6,508	5,123	4,813	141,339	15,632	46,236	38
Total Employed	112,411	158,598	142,127	120,573	2,278,689	426,236	991,346	780
Total Population	262,734	338,848	339,760	316,198	5,103,027	1,022,065	2,222,805	1,713

57. East Midlands	58. North West	59.Yorks. & Humberside	60. North	61. Wales	62. Scotland	63.Great Britain	
186,364	109,557	102,256	119,643	167,195	316,257	2,065,150	1.
18,845	40,591	31,580	56,145	67,214	53,631	381,970	2.
25,704	42,364	26,873	20,738	14,642	52,206	400,732	3.
-	-	-	-	-	-	-	4.
1,965	7,924	4,647	3,488	1,123	4,972	46,764	5.
12,746	27,494	30,347	19,477	31,421	36,210	289,268	6.
3,246	19,283	8,633	4,438	1,620	10,091	76,591	7.
780	3,644	1,061	742	545	1,703	22,262	8.
-	-	-	-	-	-	-	9.
284	3,891	1,028	6,837	1,593	4,396	31,236	10.
4,253	5,208	2,928	1,856	1,589	3,188	46,784	11.
3,471	8,171	18,062	2,814	1,752	5,497	96,092	12.
125,206	430,412	252,331	22,134	12,852	257,127	1,295,471	13.
3,836	4,779	5,155	3,275	2,233	5,212	61,849	14.
73,316	92,021	58,090	42,577	36,974	105,892	895,840	15.
6,842	9,691	5,652	7,585	1,528	5,900	96,614	16.
8,209	18,912	9,090	7,194	5,559	20,418	188,233	17.
2,729	6,871	4,018	2,762	1,238	11,240	73,750	18.
408	1,064	1,344	348	110	1,291	18,679	19.
30,754	55,521	37,078	29,976	25,843	66,685	503,306	20.
270	1,161	570	250	110	1,020	7,389	21.
17,982	69,742	27,817	28,408	17,700	49,749	424,521	22.
4,115	14,946	6,933	3,299	3,314	10,387	84,228	23.
334	581	326	226	219	637	5,694	24.
16,190	21,835	14,575	10,766	9,140	28,966	264,542	25.
83,818	147,896	72,864	62,122	56,582	151,271	1,381,910	26.
4,168	10,656	4,457	4,337	4,714	11,966	138,172	27.
23,741	72,404	26,207	19,840	30,923	55,257	470,102	N.C.
659,576	1,226,619	753,922	481,277	497,733	1,271,169	9,367,149	
1,428,382	2,490,827	1,594,403	1,163,770	1,188,914	2,888,742	20,816,351	

MALE EMPLOYMENT: 1861

South East

	1. London	2. Middlesex	3. Kent	4. Surrey	5. Sussex	6. Hants.	7. Berks.	8. Oxon.
1.	14,424	13,706	59,875	27,414	45,152	40,675	31,155	27,547
2.	6,588	324	1,032	414	592	549	275	381
3.	69,309	4,306	11,010	5,480	7,988	8,386	4,533	3,479
4.	-	-	-	-	-	-	-	-
5.	11,446	458	716	401	429	484	211	136
6.	24,518	1,078	3,224	1,527	2,392	3,355	1,508	1,108
7.	16,913	1,436	1,278	252	571	1,136	310	242
8.	7,747	195	342	199	243	315	132	99
9.	-	-	-	-	-	-	-	-
10.	8,284	82	950	63	502	2,377	76	36
11.	8,006	635	1,354	794	1,164	1,040	639	426
12.	12,521	330	498	326	437	503	219	257
13.	26,684	694	2,045	1,254	1,445	1,777	850	1,188
14.	14,979	318	1,057	826	838	856	505	379
15.	66,714	2,308	6,937	3,218	5,326	6,545	2,960	2,884
16.	5,263	1,453	2,999	840	1,031	1,309	485	336
17.	44,082	1,034	3,042	1,553	2,786	3,440	1,442	1,290
18.	30,752	577	2,090	683	668	794	429	621
19.	7,152	111	261	67	114	86	41	31
20.	87,257	5,339	14,544	9,077	11,082	13,094	5,730	4,375
21.	3,866	188	272	182	176	204	65	40
22.	117,859	3,802	12,228	4,308	8,536	12,683	2,735	1,905
23.	12,012	416	936	492	614	949	396	354
24.	3,365	182	415	278	271	330	148	117
25.	38,757	2,447	3,922	2,926	3,325	3,314	1,728	1,429
26.	55,077	4,567	8,869	7,129	7,215	7,988	4,430	3,302
27.	42,426	2,249	27,744	15,610	4,048	24,202	2,183	607
N.C.	91,357	6,069	10,361	6,122	5,516	12,221	3,030	2,686
Total Employed	827,358	54,304	178,001	91,435	112,461	148,612	66,215	55,255
Total Population	1,307,781	89,888	274,567	138,565	176,573	228,039	101,437	84,905

East Anglia

9. Bucks.	10. Beds.	11. Herts.	12. Essex	13.Cambridge	14. Hunts.	15. Norfolk	16. Suffolk	
22,957	22,564	27,789	58,826	31,862	10,957	66,894	56,203	1.
169	184	261	591	423	74	987	660	2.
2,606	2,517	3,941	7,312	3,282	1,168	8,096	6,193	3.
–	–	–	–	–	–	–	–	4.
86	103	176	718	155	73	693	347	5.
907	945	1,128	2,669	1,024	381	3,366	3,024	6.
484	98	204	892	194	57	638	696	7.
68	72	95	223	85	32	289	169	8.
–	–	–	–	–	–	–	–	9.
13	7	29	897	73	12	498	459	10.
387	373	542	1,320	488	156	1,353	1,241	11.
124	159	162	323	151	55	542	356	12.
506	475	888	2,184	446	160	3,469	2,059	13.
308	209	359	833	345	136	1,191	988	14.
2,622	4,481	2,997	4,534	2,755	965	9,343	5,381	15.
422	387	292	1,031	331	195	1,071	951	16.
2,901	594	937	1,838	742	190	2,596	1,651	17.
547	119	847	536	526	109	791	506	18.
27	23	19	80	20	12	95	51	19.
3,171	3,087	4,549	8,609	3,129	1,129	9,801	6,917	20.
30	41	75	144	65	30	208	101	21.
1,477	1,303	2,537	8,452	2,437	660	6,652	4,957	22.
301	286	424	765	258	121	1,169	861	23.
113	61	147	207	88	36	238	159	24.
951	773	1,218	2,491	1,503	401	2,893	2,233	25.
2,311	1,748	3,552	5,653	2,677	664	5,606	4,088	26.
581	433	669	5,138	540	169	1,971	1,607	27.
3,511	2,886	2,957	6,358	3,480	1,122	3,821	3,231	N.C
47,580	43,928	56,794	122,624	57,079	19,064	134,271	105,089	
72,529	66,425	86,757	190,501	88,889	29,131	205,451	164,144	

MALE EMPLOYMENT: 1861

South West   West Midlands

	17. Corn-wall	18. Devon	19.Som-erset	20.Gloucs.	21.Wilts.	22.Dorset	23.Here-ford	24.Shrops.
1.	33,443	63,718	54,704	36,497	38,699	25,326	18,463	35,830
2.	34,353	6,426	7,808	4,295	803	1,310	387	8,213
3.	3,756	9,358	8,102	8,850	4,015	3,686	1,377	3,827
4.	-	-	-	-	-	-	-	-
5.	277	811	550	1,060	202	133	120	259
6.	4,992	4,995	3,706	3,701	1,964	1,406	847	5,233
7.	801	1,197	686	1,419	1,000	173	123	475
8.	177	421	251	339	120	105	56	126
9.	-	-	-	-	-	-	-	-
10.	1,076	2,988	339	719	26	285	5	37
11.	424	1,301	1,026	1,126	352	293	395	1,221
12.	274	848	779	1,188	224	205	162	584
13.	1,234	3,462	4,228	5,360	3,728	1,521	260	1,041
14.	597	1,550	1,515	1,331	615	426	255	639
15.	4,621	10,876	8,910	8,562	3,233	2,970	1,693	4,732
16.	102	678	920	1,129	378	701	230	1,144
17.	1,484	4,017	3,425	4,470	1,435	1,053	903	1,711
18.	330	1,330	967	1,245	275	271	126	354
19.	26	97	144	322	39	35	12	60
20.	7,952	17,550	13,816	12,978	6,403	5,716	4,434	7,138
21.	45	164	128	295	78	47	24	64
22.	7,274	11,037	6,112	10,403	2,817	3,203	920	2,742
23.	326	784	640	832	357	303	154	379
24.	151	313	252	260	132	79	81	169
25.	1,908	4,584	4,006	4,413	1,749	1,268	857	1,831
26.	2,006	6,476	5,584	6,301	3,054	2,427	1,460	3,973
27.	2,262	18,775	2,146	2,558	899	2,176	391	753
N.C.	3,429	9,628	9,439	13,475	3,916	3,564	2,780	5,025
Total Employed	113,320	183,384	140,183	133,128	76,513	58,682	36,515	87,560
Total Population	174,148	281,657	218,781	207,898	115,898	88,707	54,126	130,290

East Midlands

25.Staffs.	26.Warwick	27.Worcs.	28.Derby	29.Notts.	30.Leics.	31.Lincs.	32.Northants.	
34,109	31,207	24,076	20,160	27,390	25,472	71,004	33,076	1.
42,319	3,778	4,098	16,977	8,295	3,691	695	507	2.
11,500	10,399	4,413	4,138	5,987	4,242	7,444	4,021	3.
-	-	-	-	-	-	-	-	4.
1,458	1,272	788	620	446	272	679	211	5.
37,577	18,892	8,641	5,111	3,161	1,516	3,327	1,597	6.
5,674	9,750	1,520	1,712	1,225	377	1,173	1,045	7.
534	3,847	171	155	186	135	244	111	8.
-	-	-	-	-	-	-	-	9.
331	136	119	43	40	13	330	38	10.
2,194	2,336	781	859	928	694	1,641	620	11.
8,705	13,311	8,045	1,925	1,129	862	583	210	12.
4,345	9,994	2,841	13,580	20,780	15,159	1,600	1,106	13.
2,192	2,492	1,084	602	891	595	943	882	14.
12,529	10,214	4,845	4,849	6,527	6,027	6,430	14,257	15.
21,882	2,837	3,046	1,188	1,063	1,138	1,273	525	16.
4,570	5,522	1,757	1,595	1,713	1,264	1,639	1,296	17.
901	2,064	611	827	872	378	548	307	18.
254	2,539	506	68	117	136	76	38	19.
17,569	14,150	6,953	9,370	6,862	4,721	8,376	5,374	20.
363	389	127	122	192	117	136	66	21.
10,946	9,664	4,428	3,621	3,670	3,042	5,625	2,885	22.
925	974	392	486	731	497	759	444	23.
460	326	214	147	195	123	283	100	24.
3,671	3,747	2,243	1,637	1,856	1,581	2,941	1,521	25.
7,003	6,510	3,772	2,936	3,497	3,259	5,120	3,058	26.
1,674	2,229	941	702	759	655	1,220	1,279	27.
19,492	11,986	6,907	5,297	4,851	2,279	5,408	3,157	N.C.
253,177	180,565	93,319	98,727	103,363	78,245	129,497	77,731	
388,530	273,894	143,844	146,816	156,810	118,723	200,472	115,213	

MALE EMPLOYMENT: 1861

	East Midlands	North West		Yorks. & Humberside		North		
	33.Rut-land	34. Cheshire	35.Lancs.	36. West Riding	37. East Riding	38. North Riding	39.West-morland	40.Cum-berland
1.	4,359	35,901	70,642	67,848	28,210	30,630	8,255	20,171
2.	32	4,618	51,854	42,850	652	4,385	528	8,295
3.	400	6,839	35,793	21,845	5,796	3,293	798	2,854
4.	-	-	-	-	-	-	-	-
5.	16	2,760	6,912	3,818	1,435	298	55	286
6.	131	5,448	43,860	32,458	3,140	2,134	426	2,444
7.	11	3,210	20,579	9,761	1,745	241	150	620
8.	8	276	3,934	969	256	132	31	133
9.	-	-	-	-	-	-	-	-
10.	1	1,237	6,366	550	1,187	474	11	805
11.	76	1,378	4,998	2,769	936	414	46	182
12.	20	1,033	9,936	30,622	521	226	491	723
13.	48	25,313	207,595	134,161	2,290	1,332	1,256	4,954
14.	65	934	4,489	4,386	999	668	197	530
15.	366	9,379	38,170	23,616	5,610	4,449	1,098	3,498
16.	32	1,742	8,312	5,800	867	482	42	322
17.	89	2,429	17,488	7,865	2,728	1,256	329	1,116
18.	10	782	8,313	3,604	779	276	123	439
19.	-	106	997	1,115	250	34	28	50
20.	472	11,521	59,433	36,825	7,022	5,987	3,100	6,179
21.	3	230	2,125	1,187	145	68	16	69
22.	197	11,357	78,065	22,273	9,519	2,977	518	3,418
23.	40	685	4,923	2,759	570	278	82	200
24.	15	326	1,919	829	195	148	42	89
25.	199	3,031	13,689	8,222	2,249	1,563	509	1,385
26.	392	4,486	20,017	11,051	3,189	2,516	731	1,647
27.	65	1,790	9,925	4,029	1,838	783	177	760
N.C.	341	12,192	66,027	22,653	5,636	2,023	615	2,676
Total Employed	7,388	149,003	796,361	503,865	87,764	67,067	19,654	63,845
Total Population	11,646	228,146	1,190,480	752,612	134,359	104,855	30,770	100,333

| | Wales | | | Scotland | | | | |
41.North-umberland	42.Durham	43.Glam-organ & Monmouth	44.North & West Wales	45.Strathclyde	46.Dumfries & Galloway	47.Borders	48.Lothian	
21,854	17,331	24,941	104,381	48,576	20,803	13,779	15,477	1.
15,360	42,503	44,164	32,610	40,277	883	252	7,690	2.
5,180	6,987	5,602	7,545	21,199	1,939	1,430	8,554	3.
-	-	-	-	-	-	-	-	4.
921	3,535	1,055	857	2,473	119	82	824	5.
7,405	17,094	28,214	9,400	25,524	1,095	806	4,942	6.
4,107	4,449	2,179	978	9,734	157	236	1,782	7.
245	275	262	372	703	94	63	397	8.
-	-	-	-	-	-	-	-	9.
2,243	6,758	1,126	2,017	6,048	102	23	392	10.
576	687	491	1,296	932	158	61	486	11.
884	1,405	1,374	1,001	2,697	274	122	1,190	12.
1,959	2,593	1,756	5,454	47,952	2,474	4,016	2,538	13.
984	748	612	1,563	1,754	274	311	1,267	14.
6,070	7,143	6,865	13,050	20,695	2,418	1,676	6,588	15.
2,014	4,191	718	814	3,700	114	86	974	16.
2,119	2,908	2,471	3,338	8,326	689	450	3,699	17.
1,021	989	569	866	4,266	197	210	4,487	18.
83	186	54	43	897	12	22	432	19.
9,950	13,821	13,230	18,578	28,529	4,803	5,102	10,727	20.
119	207	164	126	861	35	39	370	21.
12,153	19,980	13,053	11,369	26,664	2,091	1,145	8,840	22.
553	632	692	1,097	1,776	266	157	490	23.
229	271	249	418	1,021	175	155	619	24.
2,036	2,668	2,841	5,098	7,620	1,129	851	5,245	25.
2,688	3,005	3,759	6,594	5,383	1,327	1,157	3,254	26.
1,306	1,381	1,433	4,803	5,344	515	368	4,088	27.
7,977	13,732	19,460	14,618	30,749	2,501	1,443	8,044	N.C.
109,976	175,479	177,334	248,286	353,700	44,644	34,042	103,396	
170,665	275,859	268,845	386,300	559,255	74,871	54,619	164,364	

MALE EMPLOYMENT: 1861

Scotland

	49.Central & Fife	50. Tayside	51.Grampian	52.Highland	53. South East	54. East Anglia	55. South West	56. West Midlands
1.	17,062	28,563	51,022	53,180	392,084	165,916	252,387	143,685
2.	9,799	1,282	1,174	656	11,360	2,144	54,995	58,795
3.	3,866	5,161	4,287	2,130	130,867	18,739	37,767	31,516
4.	-	-	-	-	-	-	-	-
5.	407	270	359	72	15,364	1,268	3,033	3,897
6.	4,378	3,323	2,931	1,343	44,359	7,795	20,764	71,190
7.	1,052	1,509	715	168	23,816	1,585	5,276	17,542
8.	130	207	248	116	9,730	575	1,413	4,734
9.	-	-	-	-	-	-	-	-
10.	316	859	917	489	13,316	1,042	5,433	628
11.	247	320	356	269	16,680	3,238	4,522	6,927
12.	765	500	345	103	15,859	1,104	3,518	30,807
13.	12,158	17,839	3,413	1,143	39,990	6,134	19,533	18,481
14.	408	497	435	149	21,467	2,660	6,034	6,662
15.	3,409	5,159	5,844	3,801	111,526	18,444	39,172	34,013
16.	635	291	242	42	15,848	2,548	3,908	29,139
17.	1,381	2,287	2,260	1,558	64,939	5,179	15,884	14,463
18.	518	782	987	205	38,663	1,932	4,418	4,056
19.	76	104	699	5	8,012	178	663	3,371
20.	5,762	9,619	8,685	5,324	169,914	20,976	64,415	50,244
21.	121	242	104	33	5,283	404	757	967
22.	4,936	5,374	4,545	3,199	177,825	14,706	40,846	28,700
23.	289	391	431	351	17,945	2,409	3,242	2,824
24.	235	379	302	191	5,634	521	1,187	1,250
25.	1,655	2,723	2,494	1,808	63,281	7,030	17,928	12,349
26.	1,419	2,509	2,238	1,876	111,841	13,035	25,848	22,718
27.	1,404	1,604	1,624	1,328	125,890	4,287	28,816	5,988
N.C.	5,165	10,275	5,435	4,183	153,074	11,654	43,451	46,190
Total Employed	77,593	102,069	102,092	83,722	1,804,567	315,503	705,210	651,136
Total Population	125,943	160,599	169,399	140,798	2,817,967	487,615	1,087,089	990,684

57. East Midlands	58. North West	59. Yorks. & Humberside	60. North	61. Wales	62. Scotland	63. Great Britain	
181,461	106,543	96,058	98,241	129,322	248,462	1,814,159	1.
30,197	56,472	43,502	71,071	76,774	62,013	467,323	2.
26,232	42,632	27,641	19,112	13,147	48,566	396,219	3.
-	-	-	-	-	-	-	4.
2,244	9,672	5,253	5,095	1,912	4,606	52,344	5.
14,843	49,308	35,598	29,503	37,614	44,342	355,316	6.
5,543	23,789	11,506	9,567	3,157	15,353	117,134	7.
839	4,210	1,225	816	634	1,958	26,134	8.
-	-	-	-	-	-	-	9.
465	7,603	1,737	10,291	3,143	9,146	52,804	10.
4,818	6,376	3,705	1,845	1,787	2,829	52,727	11.
4,729	10,969	31,143	3,729	2,375	5,996	110,229	12.
52,273	232,908	136,451	12,094	7,210	91,533	616,607	13.
3,978	5,423	5,385	3,127	2,175	5,095	62,006	14.
38,456	47,549	29,226	22,258	19,915	49,590	410,149	15.
5,219	10,054	6,667	7,051	1,532	6,084	88,050	16.
7,596	19,917	10,593	7,728	5,809	20,650	172,758	17.
2,942	9,095	4,383	2,848	1,435	11,652	81,424	18.
435	1,103	1,365	381	97	2,247	17,852	19.
35,175	70,954	43,847	39,037	31,808	78,551	604,921	20.
636	2,355	1,332	479	290	1,805	14,308	21.
19,040	89,422	31,792	39,046	24,422	56,794	522,593	22.
2,957	5,608	3,329	1,745	1,789	4,151	45,999	23.
863	2,245	1,024	779	667	3,077	17,247	24.
9,735	16,720	10,471	8,161	7,939	23,525	177,139	25.
18,262	24,503	14,240	10,587	10,353	19,163	270,550	26.
4,680	11,715	5,867	4,407	6,236	16,275	214,161	27.
21,333	78,219	28,289	27,023	34,078	67,795	511,106	N.C.
494,951	945,364	591,629	436,021	425,620	901,258	7,271,259	
749,680	1,418,626	886,971	682,482	655,145	1,449,848	11,226,107	

FEMALE EMPLOYMENT: 1861

South East

	1. London	2. Middlesex	3. Kent	4. Surrey	5. Sussex	6. Hants.	7. Berks.	8. Oxon.
1.	831	750	1,254	532	753	1,552	2,977	2,434
2.	159	12	21	11	13	12	14	9
3.	7,923	418	1,327	652	855	1,231	490	397
4.	-	-	-	-	-	-	-	-
5.	934	86	16	12	19	11	4	3
6.	446	13	26	18	29	19	10	9
7.	236	34	11	-	2	-	1	-
8.	355	5	6	2	13	180	5	3
9.	-	-	-	-	-	-	-	-
10.	37	1	2	2	1	4	-	-
11.	117	2	5	3	6	2	5	1
12.	807	15	20	13	35	23	2	42
13.	16,131	295	562	343	324	780	329	1,774
14.	3,835	19	29	24	37	36	13	11
15.	122,421	3,418	9,437	4,013	7,606	11,266	4,437	5,033
16.	572	54	108	22	14	33	8	17
17.	5,106	140	148	104	214	226	190	77
18.	7,301	88	1,746	167	119	223	108	58
19.	1,028	39	40	28	29	40	21	14
20.	225	10	30	31	49	37	14	14
21.	3	1	2	-	-	1	-	-
22.	743	33	95	45	101	100	51	56
23.	5,407	210	322	203	235	396	149	172
24.	-	-	-	-	-	-	-	-
25.	24,067	1,563	3,539	2,067	3,416	3,291	1,470	1,017
26.	259,989	18,499	35,739	24,834	35,337	31,526	14,497	11,397
27.	462	111	123	61	102	134	84	54
N.C.	2,658	111	230	79	244	239	137	109
Total Employed	461,793	25,927	54,838	33,266	49,553	51,362	25,016	22,701
Total Population	1,496,208	97,437	270,705	134,699	190,263	228,615	104,198	86,328

East Anglia

9. Bucks.	10. Beds.	11. Herts.	12. Essex	13. Cambridge	14. Hunts.	15. Norfolk	16. Suffolk	
1,008	304	1,021	1,693	3,870	626	5,421	2,010	1.
1	3	5	14	6	-	8	7	2.
255	249	418	735	405	161	1,027	712	3.
-	-	-	-	-	-	-	-	4.
3	4	5	28	8	-	13	10	5.
6	10	20	30	9	4	25	24	6.
-	1	-	7	1	-	-	-	7.
-	-	1	6	2	-	6	6	8.
-	-	-	-	-	-	-	-	9.
-	-	-	1	-	-	1	-	10.
1	-	1	3	1	-	2	5	11.
12	7	4	18	5	2	50	17	12.
9,557	6,827	1,061	3,795	218	742	4,932	2,821	13.
18	5	15	36	11	5	157	636	14.
6,075	21,917	13,415	9,140	3,635	1,040	12,976	9,334	15.
14	6	16	33	8	5	18	22	16.
438	14	40	93	47	17	203	91	17.
271	11	439	52	225	171	236	77	18.
10	16	9	31	8	2	29	14	19.
8	6	8	19	12	5	19	16	20.
1	-	-	-	-	-	-	-	21.
42	27	32	48	48	22	94	61	22.
76	41	145	310	174	39	509	247	23.
-	-	-	-	-	-	-	-	24.
696	558	924	2,100	913	290	2,391	1,832	25.
7,454	6,128	10,269	22,279	10,359	3,208	25,717	19,300	26.
40	31	49	99	46	13	131	85	27.
45	57	43	144	151	29	466	151	N.C.
26,031	36,222	27,940	40,714	20,162	6,381	54,431	37,478	
74,678	74,054	90,695	189,204	92,696	30,006	222,015	171,265	

South West   West Midlands

	17.Corn-wall	18. Devon	19.Som-erset	20.Gloucs.	21.Wilts.	22.Dorset	23.Here-ford	24.Shrops
1.	3,105	2,949	4,053	3,771	5,968	2,270	1,437	2,654
2.	29	29	67	39	5	2	14	594
3.	1,839	2,139	1,430	1,533	568	452	191	622
4.	-	-	-	-	-	-	-	-
5.	18	19	11	28	30	2	-	15
6.	6,739	449	16	29	19	9	7	642
7.	1	1	-	1	-	-	1	-
8.	1	7	4	12	1	2	2	1
9.	-	-	-	-	-	-	-	-
10.	1	4	1	-	-	1	-	-
11.	2	5	2	5	2	-	-	-
12.	26	53	80	104	8	4	16	40
13.	1,166	8,466	5,571	6,643	4,630	2,748	83	468
14.	23	42	272	125	37	2	6	113
15.	9,332	21,423	21,915	16,064	4,353	7,226	2,398	4,113
16.	233	136	78	113	24	26	25	320
17.	71	356	271	453	56	51	50	69
18.	44	643	293	310	76	34	13	52
19.	20	73	55	229	8	65	8	87
20.	7	15	13	11	15	11	3	19
21.	1	2	-	-	-	-	-	1
22.	117	217	165	155	117	59	64	126
23.	213	729	590	727	158	168	114	230
24.	-	-	-	-	-	-	-	-
25.	1,405	3,011	2,863	2,904	1,371	1,074	482	1,155
26.	17,810	44,382	35,591	37,538	13,916	11,029	7,462	18,608
27.	94	156	130	106	82	58	39	72
N.C.	365	462	638	596	260	128	131	208
Total Employed	42,662	85,768	74,109	71,496	31,704	25,421	12,546	30,209
Total Population	190,700	307,728	244,480	235,637	120,129	93,486	52,670	130,119

East Midlands

5.Staffs.	26.War-wick	27.Worcs.	28.Derby	29.Notts.	30.Leics.	31.Lincs.	32.North-ants.	
2,503	1,664	2,399	1,580	1,131	1,129	4,854	861	1.
917	68	40	22	32	17	8	8	2.
1,617	1,640	608	698	830	631	755	456	3.
-	-	-	-	-	-	-	-	4.
22	140	104	26	12	38	10	5	5.
786	2,950	244	21	14	18	22	13	6.
27	365	4	-	1	2	-	-	7.
22	173	8	3	2	2	2	3	8.
-	-	-	-	-	-	-	-	9.
-	-	-	-	-	-	-	-	10.
1	25	2	5	5	-	2	1	11.
7,420	5,789	5,169	91	15	16	15	12	12.
4,415	15,945	1,120	16,717	21,758	15,169	420	8,619	13.
647	755	279	16	31	12	38	12	14.
12,544	14,087	9,911	5,267	10,101	9,197	6,862	8,288	15.
11,055	295	659	165	51	124	17	12	16.
239	1,297	146	78	105	126	60	40	17.
170	994	110	377	368	57	42	44	18.
256	3,445	338	44	27	8	13	8	19.
18	58	10	3	12	10	14	8	20.
1	1	-	-	-	-	-	1	21.
686	1,864	155	89	214	306	47	70	22.
724	789	394	194	334	178	226	173	23.
-	-	-	-	-	-	-	-	24.
2,765	2,621	1,564	1,039	1,290	1,149	1,941	1,098	25.
33,308	32,585	20,378	13,687	16,963	12,935	25,850	11,851	26.
112	92	72	43	46	54	89	59	27.
325	440	364	562	674	258	46	65	N.C.
80,580	88,082	44,078	40,727	54,016	41,436	41,333	31,707	
381,011	287,440	151,109	147,058	166,974	124,925	203,671	115,866	

FEMALE EMPLOYMENT: 1861

	East Midlands	North West		Yorks. & Humberside		North		
	33.Rut-land	34. Cheshire	35.Lancs.	36. West Riding	37. East Riding	38. North Riding	39.West-morland	40.Cum-berland
1.	228	2,819	5,459	4,662	1,465	2,951	696	3,12
2.	1	34	836	122	17	6	7	11
3.	45	1,281	9,335	4,104	738	498	279	1,01
4.	-	-	-	-	-	-	-	
5.	-	30	229	81	11	6	2	
6.	-	37	205	771	28	60	3	3
7.	-	-	6	23	2	-	-	-
8.	-	4	66	53	1	1	-	-
9.	-	-	-	-	-	-	-	
10.	-	-	8	1	2	-	-	
11.	-	1	9	6	-	1	1	-
12.	2	175	1,672	2,746	12	6	3	2
13.	78	30,458	240,188	109,965	1,601	569	713	4,39
14.	-	44	314	610	42	6	14	
15.	350	8,488	47,217	24,436	6,277	3,564	1,084	3,87
16.	3	91	972	607	28	23	18	8
17.	1	129	1,866	697	124	23	18	6
18.	2	79	1,668	765	59	57	39	6
19.	-	47	264	299	28	1	2	1
20.	1	12	91	42	16	11	1	1
21.	-	-	-	1	-	-	-	
22.	4	115	838	1,198	51	37	22	4
23.	11	612	4,895	1,902	339	126	47	22
24.	-	-	-	-	-	-	-	-
25.	132	1,963	7,002	4,452	1,435	781	214	63
26.	1,479	29,139	121,173	60,758	19,673	13,374	4,416	12,56
27.	13	71	200	159	49	57	15	4
N.C.	3	216	1,472	2,452	257	140	64	36
Total Employed	2,353	75,845	445,985	220,912	32,255	22,298	7,658	26,71
Total Population	11,833	242,028	1,274,886	777,395	140,066	106,254	30,176	104,94

		Wales			Scotland			
41.North-umberland	42.Durham	43.Glam-organ & Monmouth	44.North & West Wales	45.Strathclyde	46. Dumfries & Galloway	47.Borders	48.Lothian	
5,228	2,409	2,257	14,911	9,204	4,880	3,845	4,848	1.
26	62	1,050	316	184	10	2	111	2.
1,311	1,339	1,485	2,642	4,844	704	349	1,825	3.
-	-	-	-	-	-	-	-	4.
60	40	8	13	372	7	6	221	5.
39	28	1,827	758	29	5	1	20	6.
-	-	1	-	7	1	-	1	7.
3	1	1	1	13	-	-	5	8.
-	-	-	-	-	-	-	-	9.
-	6	1	-	3	1	-	1	10.
-	2	1	1	-	-	-	1	11.
9	19	34	32	277	15	19	81	12.
338	914	482	3,365	65,333	2,240	1,952	2,013	13.
15	14	20	58	207	2	2	97	14.
6,274	7,907	8,897	12,025	27,969	3,077	1,460	8,092	15.
293	336	414	153	743	24	14	214	16.
108	82	90	48	907	19	6	264	17.
142	210	48	141	1,530	7	158	2,130	18.
14	17	61	13	211	-	1	59	19.
12	11	6	6	30	3	4	24	20.
2	4	1	1	-	-	-	-	21.
104	124	74	227	1,346	65	51	234	22.
595	523	458	769	2,026	175	169	715	23.
-	-	-	-	-	1	-	-	24.
799	1,436	1,386	1,509	1,861	373	248	1,613	25.
18,468	21,129	25,454	50,148	48,464	9,028	5,530	26,524	26.
68	83	64	164	145	50	42	61	27.
200	261	653	343	6,980	326	109	971	N.C.
34,108	36,957	44,773	87,644	172,685	21,013	13,968	50,125	
172,360	266,266	254,386	403,303	603,367	85,623	57,301	186,400	

FEMALE EMPLOYMENT: 1861

Scotland

	49.Central & Fife	50.Tayside	51.Grampian	52.Highland	53. South East	54. East Anglia	55. South West	56. W Mid
1.	4,120	5,283	5,996	10,748	15,109	11,927	22,116	10
2.	206	11	2	-	274	21	171	1
3.	966	1,361	1,353	337	14,950	2,305	7,961	4
4.	-	-	-	-	-	-	-	
5.	11	9	40	6	1,125	31	108	
6.	19	8	4	7	636	62	7,261	4
7.	-	11	6	-	292	1	3	
8.	-	-	-	-	576	14	27	
9.	-	-	-	-	-	-	-	
10.	-	1	-	-	48	1	7	
11.	-	-	1	-	146	8	16	
12.	26	78	9	2	998	74	275	18
13.	14,272	23,466	6,297	3,892	41,778	8,713	29,224	22
14.	8	9	18	-	4,078	809	501	1
15.	3,673	5,436	4,387	2,928	218,178	26,985	80,313	43
16.	120	38	40	4	897	53	610	12
17.	41	62	108	6	6,790	358	1,258	1
18.	245	117	789	6	10,583	709	1,400	1
19.	10	10	153	-	1,305	53	450	4
20.	1	1	2	1	451	52	72	
21.	-	1	-	1	8	-	3	
22.	84	87	65	33	1,373	225	830	2
23.	356	442	379	150	7,666	969	2,585	2
24.	-	-	-	-	-	-	-	
25.	516	791	1,194	553	44,708	5,426	12,628	8
26.	9,783	16,286	22,621	18,955	477,948	58,584	160,266	112
27.	45	86	75	38	1,350	275	626	
N.C.	187	8,141	705	211	4,096	797	2,449	1
Total Employed	34,689	61,735	44,244	37,878	855,363	118,452	331,160	255
Total Population	137,338	188,080	189,037	165,300	3,037,084	515,982	1,192,160	1,002

57. East Midlands	58. North West	59. Yorks. & Humberside	60. North	61. Wales	62. Scotland	63. Great Britain	
9,783	8,278	6,127	14,404	17,168	48,924	164,493	1.
88	870	139	216	1,366	526	5,304	2.
3,415	10,616	4,842	4,438	4,127	11,739	69,071	3.
-	-	-	-	-	-	-	4.
91	259	92	117	21	672	2,797	5.
88	242	799	167	2,585	93	16,562	6.
3	6	25	-	1	26	754	7.
12	70	54	5	2	18	984	8.
-	-	-	-	-	-	-	9.
-	8	3	7	1	6	81	10.
13	10	6	4	2	2	235	11.
151	1,847	2,758	62	66	507	25,172	12.
62,761	270,646	111,566	6,926	3,847	119,465	676,957	13.
109	358	652	57	78	343	8,785	14.
40,065	55,705	30,713	22,705	20,922	57,022	595,661	15.
372	1,063	635	757	567	1,197	18,505	16.
410	1,995	821	297	138	1,413	15,281	17.
890	1,747	824	511	189	4,982	23,174	18.
100	311	327	50	74	444	7,248	19.
48	103	58	46	12	66	1,016	20.
1	-	1	8	2	2	28	21.
730	953	1,249	336	301	1,965	10,857	22.
1,116	5,507	2,241	1,519	1,227	4,412	29,493	23.
-	-	-	-	-	1	1	24.
6,649	8,965	5,887	3,860	2,895	7,149	106,754	25.
82,765	150,312	80,431	69,953	75,602	157,191	1,425,393	26.
304	271	208	266	228	542	4,457	27.
1,608	1,688	2,709	1,025	996	17,630	34,466	N.C.
211,572	521,830	253,167	127,736	132,417	436,337	3,243,529	
770,327	1,516,914	917,461	679,999	657,689	1,612,446	11,902,411	

TOTAL EMPLOYMENT: 1861

South East

	1. London	2. Middlesex	3. Kent	4. Surrey	5. Sussex	6. Hants.	7. Berks.	8. Oxon.
1.	15,255	14,456	61,129	27,946	45,905	42,227	34,132	29,981
2.	6,747	336	1,053	425	605	561	289	390
3.	77,232	4,724	12,337	6,132	8,843	9,617	5,023	3,876
4.	-	-	-	-	-	-	-	-
5.	12,380	544	732	413	448	495	215	139
6.	24,964	1,091	3,250	1,545	2,421	3,374	1,518	1,117
7.	17,149	1,470	1,289	252	573	1,136	311	242
8.	8,102	200	348	201	256	495	137	102
9.	-	-	-	-	-	-	-	-
10.	8,321	83	952	65	503	2,381	76	36
11.	8,123	637	1,359	797	1,170	1,042	644	427
12.	13,328	345	518	339	472	526	221	299
13.	42,815	989	2,607	1,597	1,769	2,557	1,179	2,962
14.	18,814	337	1,086	850	875	892	518	390
15.	189,135	5,726	16,374	7,231	12,932	17,811	7,397	7,917
16.	5,835	1,507	3,107	862	1,045	1,342	493	353
17.	49,188	1,174	3,190	1,657	3,000	3,666	1,632	1,367
18.	38,053	665	3,836	850	787	1,017	537	679
19.	8,180	150	301	95	143	126	62	45
20.	87,482	5,349	14,574	9,108	11,131	13,131	5,744	4,389
21.	3,869	189	274	182	176	205	65	40
22.	118,602	3,835	12,323	4,353	8,637	12,783	2,786	1,961
23.	17,419	626	1,258	695	849	1,345	545	526
24.	3,365	182	415	278	271	330	148	117
25.	62,824	4,010	7,461	4,993	6,741	6,605	3,198	2,446
26.	315,066	23,066	44,608	31,963	42,552	39,514	18,927	14,699
27.	42,888	2,360	27,867	15,671	4,150	24,336	2,267	661
N.C.	94,015	6,180	10,591	6,201	5,760	12,460	3,167	2,795
Total Employed	1,289,151	80,231	232,839	124,701	162,014	199,974	91,231	77,956
Total Population	2,803,989	187,325	545,272	273,264	366,836	456,654	205,635	171,233

9. Bucks.	10. Beds.	11. Herts.	12. Essex	13. Cambridge	14. Hunts.	15. Norfolk	16. Suffolk	
23,965	22,868	28,810	60,519	35,732	11,583	72,315	58,213	1.
170	187	266	605	429	74	995	667	2.
2,861	2,766	4,359	8,047	3,687	1,329	9,123	6,905	3.
–	–	–	–	–	–	–	–	4.
89	107	181	746	163	73	706	357	5.
913	955	1,148	2,699	1,033	385	3,391	3,048	6.
484	99	204	899	195	57	638	696	7.
68	72	96	229	87	32	295	175	8.
–	–	–	–	–	–	–	–	9.
13	7	29	898	73	12	499	459	10.
388	373	543	1,323	489	156	1,355	1,246	11.
136	166	166	341	156	57	592	373	12.
10,063	7,302	1,949	5,979	664	902	8,401	4,880	13.
326	214	374	869	356	141	1,348	1,624	14.
8,697	26,398	16,412	13,674	6,390	2,005	22,319	14,715	15.
436	393	308	1,064	339	200	1,089	973	16.
3,339	608	977	1,931	789	207	2,799	1,742	17.
818	130	1,286	588	751	280	1,027	583	18.
37	39	28	111	28	14	124	65	19.
3,179	3,093	4,557	8,628	3,141	1,134	9,820	6,933	20.
31	41	75	144	65	30	208	101	21.
1,519	1,330	2,569	8,500	2,485	682	6,746	5,018	22.
377	327	569	1,075	432	160	1,678	1,108	23.
113	61	147	207	88	36	238	159	24.
1,647	1,331	2,142	4,591	2,416	691	5,284	4,065	25.
9,765	7,876	13,821	27,932	13,036	3,872	31,323	23,388	26.
621	464	718	5,237	586	182	2,102	1,692	27.
3,556	2,943	3,000	6,502	3,631	1,151	4,287	3,382	N.C
73,611	80,150	84,734	163,338	77,241	25,445	188,702	142,567	
147,207	140,479	177,452	379,705	181,585	59,137	427,466	335,409	

TOTAL EMPLOYMENT: 1861

South West   West Midlands

	17.Corn-wall	18. Devon	19.Som-erset	20.Gloucs.	21.Wilts.	22.Dorset	23.Here-ford	24.Shrops.
1.	36,548	66,667	58,757	40,268	44,667	27,596	19,900	38,484
2.	34,382	6,455	7,875	4,334	808	1,312	401	8,807
3.	5,595	11,497	9,532	10,383	4,583	4,138	1,568	4,449
4.	–	–	–	–	–	–	–	–
5.	295	830	561	1,088	232	135	120	274
6.	11,731	5,444	3,722	3,730	1,983	1,415	854	5,875
7.	802	1,198	686	1,420	1,000	173	124	475
8.	178	428	255	351	121	107	58	127
9.	–	–	–	–	–	–	–	–
10.	1,077	2,992	340	719	26	286	5	37
11.	426	1,306	1,028	1,131	354	293	395	1,221
12.	300	901	859	1,292	232	209	178	624
13.	2,400	11,928	9,799	12,003	8,358	4,269	343	1,509
14.	620	1,592	1,787	1,456	652	428	261	752
15.	13,953	32,299	30,825	24,626	7,586	10,196	4,091	8,845
16.	335	814	998	1,242	402	727	255	1,464
17.	1,555	4,373	3,696	4,923	1,491	1,104	953	1,780
18.	374	1,973	1,260	1,555	351	305	139	406
19.	46	170	199	551	47	100	20	147
20.	7,959	17,565	13,829	12,989	6,418	5,727	4,437	7,157
21.	46	166	128	295	78	47	24	65
22.	7,391	11,254	6,277	10,558	2,934	3,262	984	2,868
23.	539	1,513	1,230	1,559	515	471	268	609
24.	151	313	252	260	132	79	81	169
25.	3,313	7,595	6,869	7,317	3,120	2,342	1,339	2,986
26.	19,816	50,858	41,175	43,839	16,970	13,456	8,922	22,581
27.	2,356	18,931	2,276	2,664	981	2,234	430	825
N.C.	5,794	10,090	10,077	14,071	4,176	3,692	2,911	5,233
Total Employed	155,982	269,152	214,292	204,624	108,217	84,103	49,061	117,769
Total Population	364,848	589,385	463,261	443,535	236,027	182,193	106,796	260,409

East Midlands

25.Staffs.	26.Warwick	27.Worcs.	28.Derby	29.Notts.	30.Leics.	31.Lincs.	32.Northants.	
36,612	32,871	26,475	21,740	28,521	26,601	75,858	33,937	1.
43,236	3,846	4,138	16,999	8,327	3,708	703	515	2.
13,117	12,039	5,021	4,836	6,817	4,873	8,199	4,477	3.
–	–	–	–	–	–	–	–	4.
1,480	1,412	892	646	458	310	689	216	5.
38,363	21,842	8,885	5,132	3,175	1,534	3,349	1,610	6.
5,701	10,115	1,524	1,712	1,226	379	1,173	1,045	7.
556	4,020	179	158	188	137	246	114	8.
–	–	–	–	–	–	–	–	9.
331	136	119	43	40	13	330	38	10.
2,195	2,361	783	864	933	694	1,643	621	11.
16,125	19,100	13,214	2,016	1,144	878	598	222	12.
8,760	25,939	3,961	30,297	42,538	30,328	2,020	9,725	13.
2,839	3,247	1,363	618	922	607	981	894	14.
25,073	24,301	14,756	10,116	16,628	15,224	13,292	22,545	15.
32,937	3,132	3,705	1,353	1,114	1,262	1,290	537	16.
4,809	6,819	1,903	1,673	1,818	1,390	1,699	1,336	17.
1,071	3,058	721	1,204	1,240	435	590	351	18.
510	5,984	844	112	144	144	89	46	19.
17,587	14,208	6,963	9,373	6,874	4,731	8,390	5,382	20.
364	390	127	122	192	117	136	67	21.
11,632	11,528	4,583	3,710	3,884	3,348	5,672	2,955	22.
1,649	1,763	786	680	1,065	675	985	617	23.
460	326	214	147	195	123	283	100	24.
6,436	6,368	3,807	2,676	3,146	2,730	4,882	2,619	25.
40,311	39,095	24,150	16,623	20,460	16,194	30,970	14,909	26.
1,786	2,321	1,013	745	805	709	1,309	1,338	27.
19,817	12,426	7,271	5,859	5,525	2,537	5,454	3,222	N.C.
333,757	268,647	137,397	139,454	157,379	119,681	170,830	109,438	
769,541	561,334	294,953	293,874	323,784	243,648	404,143	231,079	

TOTAL EMPLOYMENT: 1861

	East Midlands	North West		Yorks. & Humberside		North		
	33.Rutland	34.Cheshire	35.Lancs.	36. West Riding	37. East Riding	38. North Riding	39.Westmorland	40.Cumberland
1.	4,587	38,720	76,101	72,510	29,675	33,581	8,951	23,291
2.	33	4,652	52,690	42,972	669	4,391	535	8,410
3.	445	8,120	45,128	25,949	6,534	3,791	1,077	3,865
4.	-	-	-	-	-	-	-	-
5.	16	2,790	7,141	3,899	1,446	304	57	295
6.	131	5,485	44,065	33,229	3,168	2,194	429	2,481
7.	11	3,210	20,585	9,784	1,747	241	150	620
8.	8	280	4,000	1,022	257	133	31	133
9.	-	-	-	-	-	-	-	-
10.	1	1,237	6,374	551	1,189	474	11	806
11.	76	1,379	5,007	2,775	936	415	47	182
12.	22	1,208	11,608	33,368	533	232	494	748
13.	126	55,771	447,783	244,126	3,891	1,901	1,969	9,346
14.	65	978	4,803	4,996	1,041	674	211	538
15.	716	17,867	85,387	48,052	11,887	8,013	2,182	7,374
16.	35	1,833	9,284	6,407	895	505	60	409
17.	90	2,558	19,354	8,562	2,852	1,279	347	1,182
18.	12	861	9,981	4,369	838	333	162	502
19.	-	153	1,261	1,414	278	35	30	66
20.	473	11,533	59,524	36,867	7,038	5,998	3,101	6,190
21.	3	230	2,125	1,188	145	68	16	71
22.	201	11,472	78,903	23,471	9,570	3,014	540	3,467
23.	51	1,297	9,818	4,661	909	404	129	428
24.	15	326	1,919	829	195	148	42	89
25.	331	4,994	20,691	12,674	3,684	2,344	723	2,015
26.	1,871	33,625	141,190	71,809	22,862	15,890	5,147	14,213
27.	78	1,861	10,125	4,188	1,887	840	192	803
N.C.	344	12,408	67,499	25,105	5,893	2,163	679	3,036
Total Employed	9,741	224,848	1,242,346	724,777	120,019	89,365	27,312	90,560
Total Population	23,479	470,174	2,465,366	1,530,007	274,425	211,109	60,946	205,276

	Wales			Scotland				
41.North-umberland	42.Durham	43.Glam-organ & Monmouth	44.North & West Wales	45.Strathclyde	46.Dumfries & Galloway	47.Borders	48.Lothian	
27,082	19,740	27,198	119,292	57,780	25,683	17,624	20,325	1.
15,386	42,565	45,214	32,926	40,461	893	254	7,801	2.
6,491	8,326	7,087	10,187	26,043	2,643	1,779	10,379	3.
-	-	-	-	-	-	-	-	4.
981	3,575	1,063	870	2,845	126	88	1,045	5.
7,444	17,122	30,041	10,158	25,553	1,100	807	4,962	6.
4,107	4,449	2,180	978	9,741	158	236	1,783	7.
248	276	263	373	716	94	63	402	8.
-	-	-	-	-	-	-	-	9.
2,243	6,764	1,127	2,017	6,051	103	23	393	10.
516	689	492	1,297	932	158	61	487	11.
893	1,424	1,408	1,033	2,974	289	141	1,271	12.
2,297	3,507	2,238	8,819	113,285	4,714	5,968	4,551	13.
999	762	632	1,621	1,961	276	313	1,364	14.
12,344	15,050	15,762	25,075	48,664	5,495	3,136	14,680	15.
2,307	4,527	1,132	967	4,443	138	100	1,188	16.
2,227	2,990	2,561	3,386	9,233	708	456	3,963	17.
1,163	1,199	617	1,007	5,796	204	368	6,617	18.
97	203	115	56	1,108	12	23	491	19.
9,962	13,832	13,236	18,584	28,559	4,806	5,106	10,751	20.
121	211	165	127	861	35	39	370	21.
12,257	20,104	13,127	11,596	28,010	2,156	1,196	9,074	22.
1,148	1,155	1,150	1,866	3,802	441	326	1,205	23.
229	271	249	418	1,021	176	155	619	24.
2,835	4,104	4,227	6,607	9,481	1,502	1,099	6,858	25.
21,156	24,134	29,213	56,742	53,847	10,355	6,687	29,778	26.
1,374	1,464	1,497	4,967	5,489	565	410	4,149	27.
8,177	13,993	20,113	14,961	37,729	2,827	1,552	9,015	N.C.
144,084	212,436	222,107	335,930	526,385	65,657	48,010	153,521	
343,025	542,125	523,231	789,603	1,162,622	160,494	111,920	350,764	

TOTAL EMPLOYMENT: 1861

Scotland

	49.Central & Fife	50.Tayside	51.Grampian	52.Highland	53. South East	54. East Anglia	55. South West	56. West Midlands
1.	21,182	33,846	57,018	63,928	407,193	177,843	274,503	154,342
2.	10,005	1,293	1,176	656	11,634	2,165	55,166	60,428
3.	4,832	6,522	5,640	2,467	145,817	21,044	45,728	36,194
4.	–	–	–	–	–	–	–	–
5.	418	279	399	78	16,489	1,299	3,141	4,178
6.	4,397	3,331	2,935	1,350	44,995	7,857	28,025	75,819
7.	1,052	1,520	721	168	24,108	1,586	5,279	17,939
8.	130	207	248	116	10,306	589	1,440	4,940
9.	–	–	–	–	–	–	–	–
10.	316	860	917	489	13,364	1,043	5,440	628
11.	247	320	357	269	16,826	3,246	4,538	6,955
12.	791	578	354	105	16,857	1,178	3,793	49,241
13.	26,430	41,305	9,710	5,035	81,768	14,847	48,757	40,512
14.	416	506	453	149	25,545	3,469	6,535	8,462
15.	7,082	10,595	10,231	6,729	329,704	45,429	119,485	77,066
16.	755	329	282	46	16,745	2,601	4,518	41,493
17.	1,422	2,349	2,368	1,564	71,729	5,537	17,142	16,264
18.	763	899	1,776	211	49,246	2,641	5,818	5,395
19.	86	114	852	5	9,317	231	1,113	7,505
20.	5,763	9,620	8,687	5,325	170,365	21,028	64,487	50,352
21.	121	243	104	34	5,291	404	760	970
22.	5,020	5,461	4,610	3,232	179,198	14,931	41,676	31,595
23.	645	833	810	501	25,611	3,378	5,827	5,075
24.	235	379	302	191	5,634	521	1,187	1,250
25.	2,171	3,514	3,688	2,361	107,989	12,456	30,556	20,936
26.	11,202	18,795	24,859	20,831	589,789	71,619	186,114	135,059
27.	1,449	1,690	1,699	1,366	127,240	4,562	29,442	6,375
N.C.	5,352	18,416	6,140	4,394	157,170	12,451	45,900	47,658
Total Employed	112,282	163,804	146,336	121,600	2,659,930	433,955	1,036,370	906,631
Total Population	263,281	348,679	358,436	306,098	5,855,051	1,003,597	2,279,249	1,993,033

57. East Midlands	58. North West	59.Yorks. & Humberside	60. North	61. Wales	62. Scotland	63. Great Britain	
191,244	114,821	102,185	112,645	146,490	297,386	1,978,652	1.
30,285	57,342	43,641	71,287	78,140	62,539	472,627	2.
29,647	53,248	32,483	23,550	17,274	60,305	465,290	3.
-	-	-	-	-	-	-	4.
2,335	9,931	5,345	5,212	1,933	5,278	55,141	5.
14,931	49,550	36,397	29,670	40,199	44,435	371,878	6.
5,546	23,795	11,531	9,567	3,158	15,379	117,888	7.
851	4,280	1,279	821	636	1,976	27,118	8.
-	-	-	-	-	-	-	9.
465	7,611	1,740	10,298	3,144	9,152	52,885	10.
4,831	6,386	3,711	1,849	1,789	2,831	52,962	11.
4,880	12,816	33,901	3,791	2,441	6,503	135,401	12.
115,034	503,554	248,017	19,020	11,057	210,998	1,293,564	13.
4,087	5,781	6,037	3,184	2,253	5,438	70,791	14.
78,521	103,254	59,939	44,963	40,837	106,612	1,005,810	15.
5,591	11,117	7,302	7,808	2,099	7,281	106,555	16.
8,006	21,912	11,414	8,025	5,947	22,063	188,039	17.
3,832	10,842	5,207	3,359	1,624	16,634	104,598	18.
535	1,414	1,692	431	171	2,691	25,100	19.
35,223	71,057	43,905	39,083	31,820	78,617	605,937	20.
637	2,355	1,333	487	292	1,807	14,336	21.
19,770	90,375	33,041	39,382	24,723	58,759	533,450	22.
4,073	11,115	5,570	3,264	3,016	8,563	75,492	23.
863	2,245	1,024	779	667	3,078	17,248	24.
16,384	25,685	16,358	12,021	10,834	30,674	283,893	25.
101,027	174,815	94,671	80,540	85,955	176,354	1,695,943	26.
4,984	11,986	6,075	4,673	6,464	16,817	218,618	27.
22,941	79,907	30,998	28,048	35,074	85,425	545,572	N.C.
706,523	1,467,194	844,796	563,757	558,037	1,337,595	10,514,788	
1,520,007	2,935,540	1,804,432	1,362,481	1,312,834	3,062,294	23,128,518	

MALE EMPLOYMENT: 1871

South East

	1. London	2. Middlesex	3. Kent	4. Surrey	5. Sussex	6. Hants.	7. Berks.	8. Oxon
1.	14,506	12,888	56,908	24,354	44,428	41,951	27,680	24,764
2.	5,904	372	1,315	567	630	699	314	346
3.	80,634	5,482	12,945	7,611	9,362	9,902	5,403	3,593
4.	-	-	-	-	-	-	-	-
5.	12,316	564	948	561	536	562	212	162
6.	26,439	1,298	4,341	2,029	2,603	3,674	1,790	1,376
7.	17,224	1,880	2,140	439	700	1,498	510	219
8.	7,398	249	430	322	328	322	165	99
9.	-	-	-	-	-	-	-	-
10.	6,135	109	2,169	100	418	2,208	90	47
11.	8,492	737	1,633	930	1,307	1,160	676	427
12.	15,100	515	640	490	562	642	272	225
13.	25,285	1,023	2,309	1,461	1,695	1,740	802	1,068
14.	15,891	377	1,051	835	732	744	487	337
15.	64,354	2,471	6,132	3,679	4,688	5,885	2,638	2,653
16.	5,665	1,053	2,498	767	1,084	1,001	525	314
17.	47,405	1,261	3,345	1,851	2,830	3,230	1,467	1,231
18.	40,225	894	2,597	1,120	1,004	1,084	523	767
19.	8,855	352	316	209	153	114	52	43
20.	106,815	9,116	18,019	13,228	14,158	14,681	7,124	4,918
21.	4,656	333	453	366	292	315	120	98
22.	141,152	5,588	15,619	6,708	9,114	13,260	3,283	2,180
23.	15,636	691	1,695	910	1,165	1,610	565	438
24.	7,961	517	635	766	417	453	196	119
25.	43,452	3,586	4,680	4,354	4,023	3,935	2,025	1,541
26.	63,001	5,477	10,140	8,210	8,775	9,799	5,089	3,701
27.	46,310	3,432	23,820	13,251	3,768	31,457	2,477	664
N.C.	161,362	15,296	24,729	18,027	13,946	18,377	8,462	5,480
Total Employed	992,173	75,561	201,507	113,145	128,718	170,303	72,947	56,810
Total Population	1,523,151	126,141	312,931	176,327	201,250	262,207	111,920	87,560

East Anglia

9. Bucks.	10. Beds.	11. Herts.	12. Essex	13. Cambridge	14. Hunts.	15. Norfolk	16. Suffolk	
21,460	20,374	24,209	55,600	30,530	10,593	56,634	50,776	1.
189	231	276	741	299	81	671	407	2.
2,728	2,819	4,098	8,752	3,478	1,168	8,316	6,509	3.
–	–	–	–	–	–	––	–	4.
195	134	168	862	173	55	693	517	5.
924	1,108	1,186	3,507	1,109	346	3,658	3,200	6.
314	209	276	1,679	227	86	904	1,026	7.
82	78	120	297	91	39	293	196	8.
–	–	–	–	–	–	–	–	9.
12	2	22	695	58	7	547	503	10.
599	374	581	1,432	545	203	1,362	1,276	11.
117	114	150	432	177	57	538	317	12.
476	537	944	2,001	543	156	2,582	2,051	13.
348	242	423	939	386	121	1,331	967	14.
2,345	4,239	2,760	4,177	2,559	788	8,324	4,818	15.
280	237	356	984	413	151	960	823	16.
3,258	593	929	1,915	799	181	2,434	1,632	17.
669	173	769	833	646	120	992	669	18.
21	30	46	389	35	14	133	48	19.
3,904	4,006	5,948	10,720	5,227	1,226	9,670	7,664	20.
72	54	117	465	94	47	242	162	21.
1,520	1,592	3,056	10,444	1,949	346	6,841	5,665	22.
389	512	531	1,320	458	145	1,782	1,095	23.
94	84	144	477	124	37	358	258	24.
1,014	898	1,405	2,949	1,367	419	3,045	2,290	25.
2,574	1,967	3,766	5,891	2,515	770	6,612	5,044	26.
575	513	824	7,308	641	221	2,055	1,658	27.
5,490	5,545	8,850	17,275	7,468	1,396	14,489	10,279	N.C.
49,649	46,665	61,954	142,084	61,911	18,773	135,466	109,850	
75,748	71,544	95,178	221,277	94,301	28,387	207,159	170,163	

MALE EMPLOYMENT: 1871

South West   West Midlands

	17.Corn-wall	18. Devon	19.Som-erset	20.Gloucs.	21.Wilts.	22.Dorset	23.Here-ford	24.Shrops
1.	32,045	55,178	45,659	31,285	32,422	22,685	17,653	30,078
2.	25,874	4,423	7,345	5,174	1,067	1,299	425	7,530
3.	3,923	9,643	8,974	9,795	4,216	4,049	1,551	3,756
4.	-	-	-	-	-	-	-	-
5.	320	817	639	1,178	205	125	121	327
6.	4,395	4,612	3,749	4,142	2,366	1,331	917	5,510
7.	828	1,169	1,031	1,747	1,701	221	161	786
8.	155	469	267	393	121	106	64	140
9.	-	-	-	-	-	-	-	-
10.	1,223	2,233	333	714	22	176	8	39
11.	466	1,417	1,058	1,299	602	320	427	1,073
12.	324	755	750	1,149	216	194	163	482
13.	1,164	3,163	3,773	4,789	3,301	1,409	307	1,049
14.	586	1,556	1,636	1,370	586	406	283	568
15.	3,916	9,376	7,714	8,653	2,777	2,531	1,627	3,869
16.	78	630	1,018	1,337	383	539	187	1,134
17.	1,290	3,508	3,207	4,446	1,306	989	786	1,484
18.	405	1,672	1,496	1,751	352	304	169	446
19.	24	109	158	360	61	18	14	48
20.	8,453	18,717	14,967	15,802	7,021	5,492	3,678	6,520
21.	72	252	251	386	112	66	42	117
22.	6,378	11,216	6,386	10,206	2,110	2,407	841	2,422
23.	495	1,068	946	1,241	539	523	216	466
24.	195	549	377	509	187	168	96	187
25.	2,119	5,115	4,135	4,891	1,806	1,348	972	1,961
26.	2,404	7,907	6,677	6,918	3,259	2,792	2,009	4,073
27.	2,580	18,979	2,518	2,914	1,153	3,263	470	962
N.C.	6,905	18,911	20,938	24,488	10,672	7,595	5,927	10,807
Total Employed	106,617	183,444	146,002	146,937	78,563	60,356	39,114	85,834
Total Population	167,839	287,211	228,027	229,583	120,434	92,574	60,170	132,854

East Midlands

25.Staffs.	26.Warwick	27.Worcs.	28.Derby	29.Notts.	30.Leics.	31.Lincs.	32.Northants.	
29,587	27,110	21,149	17,217	22,883	20,982	66,433	28,649	1.
44,844	4,113	3,751	19,184	12,584	4,752	902	1,169	2.
13,662	11,651	4,970	4,575	6,471	4,692	8,101	4,097	3.
-	-	-	-	-	-	-	-	4.
1,435	1,450	965	724	564	340	911	213	5.
42,540	20,781	10,396	6,841	3,963	1,643	4,612	1,840	6.
6,558	11,334	2,375	2,800	2,503	1,045	1,682	782	7.
616	4,443	228	191	208	153	322	130	8.
-	-	-	-	-	-	-	-	9.
368	138	103	21	38	11	506	34	10.
2,474	2,374	954	997	940	742	1,716	848	11.
8,850	16,769	7,428	1,390	600	593	596	248	12.
4,263	6,790	3,739	11,235	19,521	12,715	1,796	772	13.
3,794	2,653	1,158	872	1,001	638	920	1,109	14.
11,453	9,213	4,423	3,840	5,440	9,366	5,624	16,121	15.
25,055	2,894	3,325	1,155	932	1,117	1,243	452	16.
4,741	5,845	1,873	1,481	1,864	1,292	1,711	1,144	17.
1,123	2,500	912	1,047	1,233	487	613	380	18.
242	2,851	608	516	194	1,410	49	92	19.
22,261	16,338	7,599	9,329	9,246	6,697	9,262	6,176	20.
634	649	208	245	283	173	209	123	21.
11,484	11,198	4,318	4,585	4,250	3,193	6,085	2,839	22.
1,342	1,428	507	701	963	758	1,003	650	23.
526	453	362	170	293	169	322	135	24.
4,023	4,028	2,690	1,892	2,110	1,765	3,060	1,591	25.
8,098	7,058	4,497	3,354	3,968	3,870	5,513	2,965	26.
2,008	2,414	1,177	908	955	809	1,370	1,234	27.
31,238	24,056	13,985	12,102	11,598	8,672	12,426	8,075	N.C.
283,219	200,531	103,700	107,372	114,605	88,084	136,987	81,868	
441,411	307,410	161,985	162,040	173,286	134,134	212,500	123,364	

MALE EMPLOYMENT: 1871

	East Midlands	North West		Yorks. & Humberside		North		
	33.Rutland	34. Cheshire	35.Lancs.	36. West Riding	37. East Riding	38. North Riding	39.Westmorland	40.Cumberland
1.	3,606	31,597	60,438	58,976	26,595	27,802	7,401	17,723
2.	26	5,199	60,833	55,068	809	8,244	563	10,900
3.	395	7,980	41,594	27,498	6,529	3,640	834	2,765
4.	-	-	-	-	-	-	-	-
5.	17	3,374	9,093	4,897	2,249	324	73	294
6.	131	7,220	48,090	41,983	4,417	3,530	458	4,204
7.	8	6,070	29,040	17,764	2,622	421	483	1,109
8.	12	288	3,570	1,196	315	137	39	156
9.	-	-	-	-	-	-	-	-
10.	-	1,413	6,373	486	1,658	336	5	617
11.	85	1,397	6,200	3,641	1,040	400	74	208
12.	21	796	6,560	31,824	596	218	66	467
13.	46	21,878	197,185	137,635	1,862	1,277	1,008	3,572
14.	70	1,083	4,849	5,931	1,131	553	218	525
15.	307	9,830	35,988	24,972	4,824	3,823	1,171	3,295
16.	43	1,306	9,194	7,522	836	415	69	2,196
17.	86	2,505	17,878	9,231	2,974	2,025	391	926
18.	12	1,113	11,711	5,124	1,026	322	228	527
19.	-	126	2,072	1,117	278	24	38	45
20.	555	14,931	76,072	54,730	9,220	6,833	3,650	6,621
21.	4	364	3,261	2,038	233	122	25	90
22.	126	12,994	95,363	30,348	11,341	2,655	668	4,240
23.	46	1,169	7,768	4,442	779	482	89	393
24.	11	551	2,579	1,397	338	172	52	176
25.	203	3,743	17,151	10,283	2,586	1,797	557	1,580
26.	416	6,593	25,261	14,238	3,499	3,146	738	1,860
27.	52	3,310	13,427	6,163	2,132	887	61	860
N.C.	961	23,520	123,668	56,812	8,852	5,285	2,033	5,940
Total Employed	7,239	170,350	915,218	615,316	98,741	74,870	20,992	71,289
Total Population	11,667	261,604	1,372,664	914,662	151,434	117,730	33,052	109,079

		Wales			Scotland			
41.North-umberland	42. Durham	43.Glam-organ & Monmouth	44.North & West Wales	45.Strathclyde	46.Dumfries & Galloway	47.Borders	48.Lothian	
19,007	15,021	21,289	88,769	47,129	20,734	13,856	13,872	1.
18,818	54,688	53,501	34,570	49,084	1,211	261	10,561	2.
6,023	9,298	6,787	7,898	21,167	1,824	1,487	9,022	3.
-	-	-	-	-	-	-	-	4.
1,037	4,601	1,230	1,100	3,550	147	109	1,706	5.
7,839	33,275	32,376	10,005	37,620	1,096	766	5,695	6.
5,208	9,791	3,590	1,259	16,461	266	316	2,496	7.
250	381	285	374	903	113	79	426	8.
-	-	-	-	-	-	-	-	9.
3,288	8,846	1,412	1,543	13,059	61	16	375	10.
525	741	642	966	1,266	156	88	585	11.
962	1,528	1,295	773	2,834	178	116	1,163	12.
2,123	2,998	2,130	5,059	37,931	1,908	5,047	2,147	13.
1,066	765	641	1,388	2,212	280	340	1,260	14.
5,661	7,393	6,645	10,926	18,095	2,083	1,565	6,346	15.
1,624	5,682	702	877	4,311	78	65	1,215	16.
2,453	3,766	2,621	2,707	9,623	661	468	4,095	17.
1,268	1,524	894	1,053	5,672	214	294	5,177	18.
120	120	58	35	676	13	24	564	19.
11,396	21,338	14,961	19,500	38,143	4,339	3,833	13,716	20.
387	366	282	196	1,344	49	67	513	21.
11,584	20,003	16,957	9,590	36,056	2,034	1,098	11,119	22.
673	1,177	1,129	1,459	2,402	323	214	638	23.
340	491	406	423	1,746	246	182	1,094	24.
2,532	3,688	3,675	5,864	8,425	1,151	850	5,058	25.
3,314	4,443	4,510	6,966	9,835	1,712	1,492	4,281	26.
2,226	2,291	2,488	4,862	6,003	535	364	3,876	27.
14,178	32,473	34,585	27,900	43,084	2,609	1,444	11,310	N.C.
123,902	246,688	215,091	246,062	418,631	44,021	34,441	118,310	
192,663	383,712	323,478	387,123	656,172	72,207	55,688	192,902	

MALE EMPLOYMENT: 1871

Scotland

	49.Central & Fife	50. Tayside	51.Gram-pian	52.High-land	53. South East	54. East Anglia	55. South West	56. W Midla
1.	16,599	28,523	65,027	68,220	369,122	148,533	219,274	125
2.	11,205	1,437	1,941	761	11,584	1,458	45,182	60
3.	4,100	5,532	4,797	2,158	153,329	19,471	40,600	35
4.	-	-	-	-	-	-	-	
5.	461	376	539	106	17,220	1,438	3,284	4
6.	4,951	4,011	3,180	1,316	50,275	8,313	20,595	80
7.	1,180	2,115	865	239	27,088	2,243	6,697	21
8.	142	228	259	132	9,890	619	1,511	5
9.	-	-	-	-	-	-	-	
10.	465	850	1,010	414	12,007	1,115	4,701	
11.	220	286	352	199	18,348	3,386	5,162	7
12.	690	399	343	165	19,259	1,089	3,388	33
13.	11,405	20,682	2,886	1,066	39,341	5,332	17,599	16
14.	387	566	441	141	22,406	2,805	6,140	8
15.	3,122	4,900	5,542	3,456	106,021	16,489	34,967	30
16.	615	187	168	58	14,764	2,347	3,985	32
17.	1,391	2,155	2,160	1,259	69,315	5,046	14,746	14
18.	630	934	1,360	227	50,658	2,427	5,980	5
19.	287	227	860	12	10,580	230	730	3
20.	6,379	10,948	8,215	5,175	212,637	23,787	70,452	56
21.	163	303	229	52	7,341	545	1,139	1
22.	5,396	6,398	5,062	3,313	213,516	14,801	38,703	30
23.	431	673	608	332	25,462	3,480	4,812	3
24.	339	546	545	270	11,863	777	1,985	1
25.	1,695	2,710	2,562	1,779	73,862	7,121	19,414	13
26.	1,915	3,488	2,643	2,136	128,390	14,941	29,957	25
27.	1,298	1,551	1,785	1,312	134,399	4,575	31,407	7
N.C.	5,818	7,702	5,467	2,275	302,839	33,632	89,509	86
Total Employed	81,284	107,727	118,846	96,573	2,111,516	326,000	721,919	712
Total Population	132,218	171,976	182,334	139,646	3,441,561	500,010	1,125,668	1,103

57. East Midlands	58. North West	59. Yorks. & Humberside	60. North	61. Wales	62. Scotland	63. Great Britain	
159,770	92,035	85,571	86,954	110,058	273,960	1,670,854	1.
38,617	66,032	55,877	93,213	88,071	76,461	537,158	2.
28,331	49,574	34,027	22,560	14,685	50,087	448,254	3.
-	-	-	-	-	-	-	4.
2,769	12,467	7,146	6,329	2,330	6,994	64,275	5.
19,030	55,310	46,400	49,306	42,381	58,635	430,389	6.
8,820	35,110	20,386	17,012	4,849	23,938	167,357	7.
1,016	3,858	1,511	963	659	2,282	27,800	8.
-	-	-	-	-	-	-	9.
610	7,786	2,144	13,092	2,955	16,250	61,316	10.
5,328	7,597	4,681	1,948	1,608	3,152	58,512	11.
3,448	7,356	32,420	3,241	2,068	5,888	111,849	12.
46,085	219,063	139,497	10,978	7,189	83,072	584,304	13.
4,610	5,932	7,062	3,127	2,029	5,627	68,194	14.
40,698	45,818	29,796	21,343	17,571	45,109	388,397	15.
4,942	10,500	8,358	9,986	1,579	6,697	95,753	16.
7,578	20,383	12,205	9,561	5,328	21,812	180,703	17.
3,772	12,824	6,150	3,869	1,947	14,508	107,285	18.
2,261	2,198	1,395	347	93	2,663	24,260	19.
41,265	91,003	63,950	49,838	34,461	90,748	734,537	20.
1,037	3,625	2,271	990	478	2,720	21,796	21.
21,078	108,357	41,689	39,150	26,547	70,476	604,580	22.
4,121	8,937	5,221	2,814	2,588	5,621	67,015	23.
1,100	3,130	1,735	1,231	829	4,968	29,242	24.
10,621	20,894	12,869	10,154	9,539	24,230	202,378	25.
20,086	31,854	17,737	13,501	11,476	27,502	321,179	26.
5,328	16,737	8,295	6,325	7,350	16,724	238,171	27.
53,834	147,188	65,664	59,909	62,485	79,709	980,782	N.C.
536,155	1,085,568	714,057	537,741	461,153	1,019,833	8,226,340	
816,991	1,634,268	1,066,096	836,236	710,601	1,603,143	12,838,404	

FEMALE EMPLOYMENT: 1871

South East

	1. London	2. Middlesex	3. Kent	4. Surrey	5. Sussex	6. Hants.	7. Berks.	8. Oxon.
1.	883	810	1,370	772	630	1,128	2,126	1,543
2.	170	8	30	19	12	13	8	11
3.	8,652	537	1,310	696	1,019	1,133	448	358
4.	-	-	-	-	-	-	-	-
5.	2,151	104	62	28	15	10	5	9
6.	481	16	23	24	22	11	7	11
7.	98	2	-	1	-	2	3	1
8.	328	6	5	7	6	119	5	3
9.	-	-	-	-	-	-	-	-
10.	36	-	2	2	-	3	-	-
11.	148	13	10	6	2	5	5	2
12.	1,136	29	27	30	40	42	8	11
13.	16,118	617	916	616	586	862	320	1,584
14.	5,272	30	50	37	48	68	19	12
15.	118,501	4,177	9,689	5,227	7,564	10,601	4,609	5,177
16.	638	54	60	43	15	39	11	13
17.	8,190	160	188	178	240	254	125	58
18.	9,862	155	1,918	236	143	262	136	98
19.	1,348	70	62	32	38	48	24	13
20.	219	21	28	18	17	29	10	10
21.	1	1	-	-	-	3	-	-
22.	1,096	42	82	53	87	116	54	62
23.	7,287	353	703	482	531	549	239	175
24.	-	-	-	-	-	-	-	-
25.	30,263	2,880	4,825	3,474	4,228	4,155	1,905	1,478
26.	299,507	25,723	46,421	37,918	42,524	39,789	18,388	13,068
27.	1,591	90	230	208	151	185	86	71
N.C.	14,920	358	764	417	357	451	383	284
Total Employed	528,896	36,256	68,775	50,524	58,275	59,877	28,924	24,052
Total Population	1,731,109	138,713	316,195	188,952	219,660	263,936	114,348	90,769

East Anglia

9. Bucks.	10. Beds.	11. Herts.	12. Essex	13. Cambridge	14. Hunts.	15. Norfolk	16. Suffolk	
408	193	365	1,373	2,481	503	3,635	1,702	1.
-	4	7	9	6	3	13	4	2.
288	299	389	848	436	164	902	720	3.
-	-	-	-	-	-	-	-	4.
5	3	6	49	2	-	28	16	5.
9	1	18	33	10	3	21	13	6.
-	-	-	9	4	-	82	-	7.
-	2	-	9	-	-	7	1	8.
-	-	-	-	-	-	-	-	9.
-	-	-	-	-	-	5	-	10.
4	1	4	9	1	1	3	10	11.
13	6	8	20	6	1	47	21	12.
8,379	6,227	913	4,274	293	753	4,227	2,181	13.
60	10	37	82	28	3	631	666	14.
5,945	23,416	14,801	10,195	3,479	920	10,675	9,534	15.
13	10	12	27	105	4	27	22	16.
618	21	32	89	44	17	204	97	17.
321	15	355	106	209	213	237	100	18.
12	6	10	54	15	3	10	12	19.
10	1	10	22	6	2	17	14	20.
-	-	-	-	-	-	-	-	21.
26	11	32	65	44	16	82	55	22.
128	120	157	500	247	54	725	404	23.
-	-	-	-	-	-	-	-	24.
1,074	895	1,486	3,169	1,402	444	3,151	2,534	25.
9,210	7,007	12,094	26,063	12,542	3,650	27,667	21,342	26.
42	43	75	104	48	17	129	107	27.
109	68	151	621	252	100	1,251	584	N.C
26,674	38,359	30,962	47,730	21,660	6,871	53,776	40,139	
79,259	79,995	99,434	219,603	97,732	29,659	223,479	177,047	

FEMALE EMPLOYMENT: 1871

	South West						West Midlands	
	17.Cornwall	18. Devon	19.Somerset	20.Gloucs.	21.Wilts.	22.Dorset	23.Hereford	24.Shrops
1.	2,526	2,141	3,721	2,485	4,187	1,442	1,119	1,913
2.	3,994	292	63	53	11	–	6	518
3.	1,786	2,094	1,414	1,782	601	490	208	646
4.	–	–	–	–	–	–	–	–
5.	44	52	18	69	6	–	4	31
6.	627	37	24	24	15	8	8	264
7.	2	8	11	12	3	–	1	1
8.	1	5	9	18	4	1	1	1
9.	–	–	–	–	–	–	–	–
10.	–	3	11	5	–	–	–	–
11.	–	6	7	10	2	1	2	7
12.	21	66	70	129	11	8	16	9
13.	1,240	7,444	4,314	6,678	4,250	1,996	130	551
14.	20	93	321	143	30	30	11	129
15.	8,623	18,516	19,668	16,019	3,864	6,772	2,301	3,573
16.	21	101	69	178	23	15	20	346
17.	73	66	274	544	93	66	34	71
18.	62	568	559	462	66	47	18	52
19.	8	46	32	157	16	24	5	79
20.	4	34	25	39	10	6	6	10
21.	1	2	–	2	–	–	–	1
22.	116	190	175	196	100	52	54	130
23.	424	1,035	838	1,232	235	254	180	304
24.	–	–	–	–	–	–	–	–
25.	1,804	4,283	3,859	4,511	1,736	1,407	747	1,441
26.	23,361	49,176	39,328	41,858	15,018	12,214	9,313	19,910
27.	105	180	154	137	69	81	47	81
N.C.	703	1,446	1,872	1,518	675	401	146	393
Total Employed	45,566	87,884	76,836	78,261	31,025	25,315	14,377	30,461
Total Population	190,517	318,891	254,625	259,177	124,233	96,426	60,553	134,149

East Midlands

25.Staffs.	26.Warwick	27.Worcs.	28.Derby	29.Notts.	30.Leics.	31.Lincs.	32.North-ants.	
1,811	1,125	1,867	1,400	796	774	2,303	537	1.
907	87	154	43	33	17	14	12	2.
2,211	2,044	870	744	973	995	1,013	546	3.
-	-	-	-	-	-	-	-	4.
172	1,051	130	52	29	12	10	5	5.
1,111	3,287	218	23	22	11	16	11	6.
55	290	14	3	6	11	5	2	7.
27	281	4	5	9	1	7	3	8.
-	-	-	-	-	-	-	-	9.
-	-	-	-	-	-	1	1	10.
8	72	3	4	6	-	9	4	11.
7,428	7,812	6,131	66	24	23	21	7	12.
4,723	13,153	2,234	15,240	23,139	13,353	420	6,616	13.
1,053	1,008	290	40	121	29	77	14	14.
12,027	14,034	9,838	5,332	9,853	10,490	6,914	8,616	15.
15,117	333	852	198	61	113	25	12	16.
249	1,529	216	85	463	167	67	73	17.
216	1,439	189	436	242	69	37	78	18.
106	3,248	395	100	44	285	9	4	19.
24	66	16	19	11	11	28	13	20.
-	1	-	1	-	-	1	-	21.
785	2,958	226	186	443	695	73	72	22.
1,221	1,477	613	454	518	277	397	293	23.
-	-	-	-	-	-	-	-	24.
3,723	3,816	2,275	1,482	1,851	1,629	3,059	1,632	25.
41,737	36,828	24,381	16,862	18,764	15,290	30,623	14,146	26.
147	135	86	82	66	56	117	62	27.
1,325	1,547	746	439	555	721	390	1,070	N.C.
96,183	97,621	51,748	43,296	58,029	45,029	45,636	33,829	
436,024	323,062	174,291	162,860	182,118	141,037	215,575	124,870	

FEMALE EMPLOYMENT: 1871

| | East Midlands | North West | | Yorks. & Humberside | | North | | |
	33.Rut-land	34. Cheshire	35.Lancs.	36. West Riding	37. East Riding	38. North Riding	39.West-morland	40.Cum-berland
1.	105	2,258	4,444	3,773	961	1,702	582	2,237
2.	4	28	1,263	177	23	9	6	183
3.	52	1,691	11,488	5,263	890	588	284	1,001
4.	-	-	-	-	-	-	-	-
5.	-	55	435	305	141	14	3	20
6.	1	58	149	517	41	23	4	38
7.	-	8	152	197	4	2	1	4
8.	1	5	67	80	7	-	1	2
9.	-	-	-	-	-	-	-	-
10.	-	-	7	1	5	1	-	1
11.	-	2	41	14	3	-	-	-
12.	2	32	597	3,777	19	6	1	15
13.	88	29,354	261,132	133,767	946	405	454	3,525
14.	4	44	601	586	105	10	15	13
15.	324	9,176	50,129	27,075	6,242	3,702	1,085	3,739
16.	2	62	1,194	653	37	41	14	83
17.	1	226	2,459	945	185	29	18	42
18.	1	156	3,303	1,063	128	79	81	93
19.	-	53	511	307	35	10	9	9
20.	1	25	136	95	19	1	-	-
21.	-	-	1	2	-	1	-	-
22.	4	125	1,559	1,604	81	49	28	69
23.	19	791	8,088	3,016	566	208	75	430
24.	-	-	-	-	-	-	-	-
25.	177	2,742	11,259	7,064	2,164	1,172	320	837
26.	1,672	36,695	155,975	80,190	22,649	17,215	4,789	14,888
27.	10	97	597	205	77	62	20	59
N.C.	37	764	7,282	3,611	415	221	224	612
Total Employed	2,505	84,447	522,869	274,287	35,743	25,550	8,014	27,900
Total Population	11,718	278,181	1,476,595	939,510	155,146	117,087	32,078	111,174

		Wales		Scotland				
41.North-umberland	42.Durham	43.Glam-organ & Monmouth	44.North & West Wales	45.Strathclyde	46.Dumfries & Galloway	47.Borders	48.Lothian	
4,376	2,029	1,725	11,466	9,505	4,660	3,424	4,011	1.
23	74	1,383	523	171	6	6	71	2.
1,452	1,739	2,011	2,823	5,048	680	367	1,805	3.
-	-	-	-	-	-	-	-	4.
102	74	32	42	420	7	1	75	5.
60	59	2,353	693	99	3	1	24	6.
7	7	3	3	211	6	8	3	7.
11	3	3	7	9	-	1	5	8.
-	-	-	-	-	-	-	-	9.
8	3	3	-	6	-	-	-	10.
2	-	1	2	-	-	3	10	11.
34	63	48	48	93	4	1	64	12.
399	1,144	737	2,926	68,020	1,066	3,744	1,840	13.
45	27	21	45	343	3	2	73	14.
6,345	8,925	9,911	12,263	27,307	2,779	1,389	7,688	15.
259	637	490	191	1,204	18	20	322	16.
119	105	102	67	1,445	36	14	357	17.
223	440	115	167	2,421	15	95	2,597	18.
27	18	64	22	262	3	4	286	19.
-	-	19	22	19	-	1	23	20.
-	-	-	3	-	1	-	-	21.
89	101	106	212	2,556	52	48	453	22.
999	1,029	726	1,119	3,338	252	162	1,638	23.
-	-	-	-	1	-	-	-	24.
1,291	2,250	2,290	2,174	3,346	423	311	2,194	25.
23,679	29,249	34,109	59,132	49,605	8,403	5,890	28,360	26.
127	95	120	202	205	87	33	103	27.
659	761	815	684	3,575	468	45	1,630	N.C.
40,336	48,832	57,187	94,836	179,209	18,972	15,570	53,632	
193,983	358,493	302,028	409,041	684,789	83,324	60,804	214,370	

FEMALE EMPLOYMENT: 1871

<u>Scotland</u>

	49.Central & Fife	50. Tayside	51.Gram-pian	52.High-land	53. South East	54. East Anglia	55. South West	56. West Midland
1.	4,074	4,421	9,588	11,339	11,601	8,321	16,502	7,83⌇
2.	234	11	8	2	291	26	4,413	1,67⌇
3.	931	1,480	1,380	430	15,977	2,222	8,167	5,97⌇
4.	-	-	-	-	-	-	-	-
5.	14	17	75	3	2,447	46	189	1,38⌇
6.	9	14	3	4	656	47	735	4,88⌇
7.	7	23	2	-	116	86	36	36
8.	-	-	1	-	490	8	38	31⌇
9.	-	-	-	-	-	-	-	-
10.	-	1	-	-	43	5	19	-
11.	-	-	1	1	209	15	26	9⌇
12.	5	9	1	1	1,370	75	305	21,39⌇
13.	15,814	36,920	6,204	4,755	41,412	7,454	25,922	20,79⌇
14.	5	22	16	3	5,725	1,328	637	2,49⌇
15.	3,233	5,001	3,932	2,209	219,902	24,608	73,462	41,77⌇
16.	143	40	44	6	935	158	407	16,66⌇
17.	48	93	125	5	10,153	362	1,116	2,09⌇
18.	298	176	1,120	5	13,607	759	1,764	1,91⌇
19.	24	24	164	5	1,717	40	283	3,83⌇
20.	2	1	-	2	395	39	118	12⌇
21.	-	-	-	-	5	-	5	⌇
22.	125	138	105	22	1,726	197	829	4,15⌇
23.	494	592	742	212	11,224	1,430	4,018	3,79⌇
24.	-	-	-	-	-	-	-	-
25.	684	1,304	1,496	716	59,832	7,531	17,600	12,00⌇
26.	8,847	13,896	18,609	12,990	577,712	65,201	180,955	132,16⌇
27.	75	106	71	65	2,876	301	726	49⌇
N.C.	281	355	401	235	18,883	2,187	6,615	4,15⌇
Total Employed	35,347	64,644	44,088	33,010	999,304	122,446	344,887	290,39⌇
Total Population	144,286	204,541	202,493	162,268	3,730,925	527,917	1,243,869	1,128,07⌇

57. East Midlands	58. North West	59. Yorks. & Humberside	60. North	61. Wales	62. Scotland	63. Great Britain	
5,915	6,702	4,734	10,926	13,191	51,022	136,749	1.
123	1,291	200	295	1,906	509	10,726	2.
4,323	13,179	6,153	5,064	4,834	12,121	78,019	3.
-	-	-	-	-	-	-	4.
108	490	446	213	74	612	6,013	5.
84	207	558	184	3,046	157	10,562	6.
27	160	201	21	6	260	1,274	7.
26	72	87	17	10	16	1,078	8.
-	-	-	-	-	-	-	9.
2	7	6	13	3	7	105	10.
23	43	17	2	3	15	445	11.
143	629	3,796	119	96	178	28,107	12.
58,856	290,486	134,713	5,927	3,663	138,363	727,587	13.
285	645	691	110	66	467	12,445	14.
41,529	59,305	33,317	23,796	22,174	53,538	593,404	15.
411	1,256	690	1,034	681	1,797	24,037	16.
856	2,685	1,130	313	169	2,123	21,006	17.
863	3,459	1,191	916	282	6,727	31,482	18.
442	564	342	73	86	772	8,152	19.
83	161	114	1	41	48	1,122	20.
2	1	2	1	3	1	22	21.
1,473	1,684	1,685	336	318	3,499	15,900	22.
1,958	8,879	3,582	2,741	1,845	7,430	46,902	23.
-	-	-	-	-	1	1	24.
9,830	14,001	9,228	5,870	4,464	10,474	150,832	25.
97,357	192,670	102,839	89,820	93,241	146,600	1,678,564	26.
393	694	282	363	322	745	7,198	27.
3,212	8,046	4,026	2,477	1,499	6,990	58,092	N.C.
228,324	607,316	310,030	150,632	152,023	444,472	3,649,824	
838,178	1,754,776	1,094,656	812,815	711,069	1,756,875	13,599,159	

TOTAL EMPLOYMENT: 1871

South East

	1. London	2. Middlesex	3. Kent	4. Surrey	5. Sussex	6. Hants.	7. Berks.	8. Oxon.
1.	15,389	13,698	58,278	25,126	45,058	43,079	29,806	26,307
2.	6,074	380	1,345	586	642	712	322	357
3.	89,286	6,019	14,255	8,307	10,381	11,035	5,851	3,951
4.	-	-	-	-	-	-	-	-
5.	14,467	668	1,010	589	551	572	217	171
6.	26,920	1,314	4,364	2,053	2,625	3,685	1,797	1,387
7.	17,322	1,882	2,140	440	700	1,500	513	220
8.	7,726	255	435	329	334	441	170	102
9.	-	-	-	-	-	-	-	-
10.	6,171	109	2,171	102	418	2,211	90	47
11.	8,640	750	1,643	936	1,309	1,165	681	429
12.	16,236	544	667	520	602	684	280	236
13.	41,403	1,640	3,225	2,077	2,281	2,602	1,122	2,652
14.	21,163	407	1,101	872	780	812	506	349
15.	182,855	6,648	15,821	8,906	12,252	16,486	7,247	7,830
16.	6,303	1,107	2,558	810	1,099	1,040	536	327
17.	55,595	1,421	3,533	2,029	3,070	3,484	1,592	1,289
18.	50,087	1,049	4,515	1,356	1,147	1,346	659	865
19.	10,203	422	378	241	191	162	76	56
20.	107,034	9,137	18,047	13,246	14,175	14,710	7,134	4,928
21.	4,657	334	453	366	292	318	120	98
22.	142,248	5,630	15,701	6,761	9,201	13,376	3,337	2,242
23.	22,923	1,044	2,398	1,392	1,696	2,159	804	613
24.	7,961	517	635	766	417	453	196	119
25.	73,715	6,466	9,505	7,828	8,251	8,090	3,930	3,019
26.	362,508	31,200	56,561	46,128	51,299	49,588	23,477	16,769
27.	47,901	3,522	24,050	13,459	3,919	31,642	2,563	735
N.C.	176,282	15,654	25,493	18,444	14,303	18,828	8,845	5,764
Total Employed	1,521,069	111,817	270,282	163,669	186,993	230,180	101,871	80,862
Total Population	3,254,260	264,854	629,126	365,279	420,910	526,143	226,268	178,329

9. Bucks.	10. Beds.	11. Herts.	12. Essex	13. Cambridge	14. Hunts.	15. Norfolk	16. Suffolk	
21,868	20,567	24,574	56,973	33,011	11,096	60,269	52,478	1.
189	235	283	750	305	84	684	411	2.
3,016	3,118	4,487	9,600	3,914	1,332	9,218	7,229	3.
–	–	–	–	–	–	–	–	4.
200	137	174	911	175	55	721	533	5.
933	1,109	1,204	3,540	1,119	349	3,679	3,213	6.
314	209	276	1,688	231	86	986	1,026	7.
82	80	120	306	91	39	300	197	8.
–	–	–	–	–	–	–	–	9.
12	2	22	695	58	7	552	503	10.
603	375	585	1,441	546	204	1,365	1,286	11.
130	120	158	452	183	58	585	338	12.
8,855	6,764	1,857	6,275	836	909	6,809	4,232	13.
408	252	460	1,021	414	124	1,962	1,633	14.
8,290	27,655	17,561	14,372	6,038	1,708	18,999	14,352	15.
293	247	368	1,011	518	155	987	845	16.
3,876	614	961	2,004	843	198	2,638	1,729	17.
990	188	1,124	939	855	333	1,229	769	18.
33	36	56	443	50	17	143	60	19.
3,914	4,007	5,958	10,742	5,233	1,228	9,687	7,678	20.
72	54	117	465	94	47	242	162	21.
1,546	1,603	3,088	10,509	1,993	362	6,923	5,720	22.
517	632	688	1,820	705	199	2,507	1,499	23.
94	84	144	477	124	37	358	258	24.
2,088	1,793	2,891	6,118	2,769	863	6,196	4,824	25.
11,784	8,974	15,860	31,954	15,057	4,420	34,279	26,386	26.
617	556	899	7,412	689	238	2,184	1,765	27.
5,599	5,613	9,001	17,896	7,720	1,496	15,740	10,863	N.C.
76,323	85,024	92,916	189,814	83,571	25,644	189,242	149,989	
155,007	151,539	194,612	440,880	192,033	58,046	430,638	347,210	

TOTAL POPULATION: 1871

	South West						West Midlands	
	17.Corn-wall	18. Devon	19.Som-erset	20.Gloucs.	21.Wilts.	22.Dorset	23.Here-ford	24.Shrops
1.	34,571	57,319	49,380	33,770	36,609	24,127	18,772	31,991
2.	29,868	4,715	7,408	5,227	1,078	1,299	431	8,048
3.	5,709	11,737	10,388	11,577	4,817	4,539	1,759	4,402
4.	–	–	–	–	–	–	–	–
5.	364	869	657	1,247	211	125	125	358
6.	5,022	4,649	3,773	4,166	2,381	1,339	925	5,774
7.	830	1,177	1,042	1,759	1,704	221	162	787
8.	156	474	276	411	125	107	65	141
9.	–	–	–	–	–	–	–	–
10.	1,223	2,236	344	719	22	176	8	39
11.	466	1,423	1,065	1,309	604	321	429	1,080
12.	345	821	820	1,278	227	202	179	491
13.	2,404	10,607	8,087	11,467	7,551	3,405	437	1,600
14.	606	1,649	1,957	1,513	616	436	294	697
15.	12,539	27,892	27,382	24,672	6,641	9,303	3,928	7,442
16.	99	731	1,087	1,515	406	554	207	1,480
17.	1,363	3,574	3,481	4,990	1,399	1,055	820	1,555
18.	467	2,240	2,055	2,213	418	351	187	498
19.	32	155	190	517	77	42	19	127
20.	8,457	18,751	14,992	15,841	7,031	5,498	3,684	6,530
21.	73	254	251	388	112	66	42	118
22.	6,494	11,406	6,561	10,402	2,210	2,459	895	2,552
23.	919	2,103	1,784	2,473	774	777	396	770
24.	195	549	377	509	187	168	96	187
25.	3,923	9,398	7,994	9,402	3,542	2,755	1,719	3,402
26.	25,765	57,083	46,005	48,776	18,277	15,006	11,322	23,983
27.	2,685	19,159	2,672	3,051	1,222	3,344	517	1,043
N.C.	7,608	20,357	22,810	26,006	11,347	7,996	6,073	11,200
Total Employed	152,183	271,328	222,838	225,198	109,588	85,671	53,491	116,295
Total Population	358,356	606,102	482,652	488,760	244,667	189,000	120,723	267,003

5.Staffs.	26.War- wick	27.Worcs.	28. Derby	29.Notts.	30.Leics.	31.Lincs.	32.North- ants.	
31,398	28,235	23,016	18,617	23,679	21,756	68,736	29,186	1.
45,751	4,200	3,905	19,227	12,617	4,769	916	1,181	2.
15,873	13,695	5,840	5,319	7,444	5,687	9,114	4,643	3.
-	-	-	-	-	-	-	-	4.
1,607	2,501	1,095	776	593	352	921	218	5.
43,651	24,068	10,614	6,864	3,985	1,654	4,628	1,851	6.
6,613	11,624	2,389	2,803	2,509	1,056	1,687	784	7.
643	4,724	232	196	217	154	329	133	8.
-	-	-	-	-	-	-	-	9.
368	138	103	21	38	11	507	35	10.
2,482	2,446	957	1,001	946	742	1,725	852	11.
16,278	24,581	13,559	1,456	624	616	617	255	12.
8,986	19,943	5,973	26,475	42,660	26,068	2,216	7,388	13.
4,847	3,661	1,448	912	1,122	667	997	1,123	14.
23,480	23,247	14,261	9,172	15,293	19,856	12,538	24,737	15.
40,172	3,227	4,177	1,353	993	1,230	1,268	464	16.
4,990	7,374	2,089	1,566	2,327	1,459	1,778	1,217	17.
1,339	3,939	1,101	1,483	1,475	556	650	458	18.
348	6,099	1,003	616	238	1,695	58	96	19.
22,285	16,404	7,615	9,348	9,257	6,708	9,290	6,189	20.
634	650	208	246	283	173	210	123	21.
12,269	14,156	4,544	4,771	4,693	3,888	6,158	2,911	22.
2,563	2,905	1,120	1,155	1,481	1,035	1,400	943	23.
526	453	362	170	293	169	322	135	24.
7,746	7,844	4,965	3,374	3,961	3,394	6,119	3,223	25.
49,835	43,886	28,878	20,216	22,732	19,160	36,136	17,111	26.
2,155	2,549	1,263	990	1,021	865	1,487	1,296	27.
32,563	25,603	14,731	12,541	12,153	9,393	12,816	9,145	N.C.
379,402	298,152	155,448	150,668	172,634	133,113	182,623	115,697	
877,435	630,472	336,276	324,900	355,404	275,171	428,075	248,234	

TOTAL EMPLOYMENT: 1871

	East Midlands	North West	Yorks. & Humberside		North		
	33.Rutland	34. Cheshire	35.Lancs.	36. West Riding	37. East Riding	38. North Riding	39.Westmorland	40.Cumberland
1.	3,711	33,855	64,882	62,749	27,556	29,504	7,983	19,96(
2.	30	5,227	62,096	55,245	832	8,253	569	11,08.
3.	447	9,671	53,082	32,761	7,419	4,228	1,118	3,76(
4.	-	-	-	-	-	-	-	-
5.	17	3,429	9,528	5,202	2,390	338	76	31(
6.	132	7,278	48,239	42,500	4,458	3,553	462	4,24(
7.	8	6,078	29,192	17,961	2,626	423	484	1,11(
8.	13	293	3,637	1,276	322	137	40	15(
9.	-	-	-	-	-	-	-	-
10.	-	1,413	6,380	487	1,663	337	5	61(
11.	85	1,399	6,241	3,655	1,043	400	74	20(
12.	23	828	7,157	35,601	615	224	67	48(
13.	134	51,232	458,317	271,402	2,808	1,682	1,462	7,09(
14.	74	1,127	5,450	6,517	1,236	563	233	53(
15.	631	19,006	86,117	52,047	11,066	7,525	2,256	7,03(
16.	45	1,368	10,388	8,175	873	456	83	2,27(
17.	87	2,731	20,337	10,176	3,159	2,054	409	96(
18.	13	1,269	15,014	6,187	1,154	401	309	62(
19.	-	179	2,583	1,424	313	34	47	5(
20.	556	14,956	76,208	54,825	9,239	6,834	3,650	6,62(
21.	4	364	3,262	2,040	233	123	25	9(
22.	130	13,119	96,922	31,952	11,422	2,704	696	4,30(
23.	65	1,960	15,856	7,458	1,345	690	164	82.
24.	11	551	2,579	1,397	338	172	52	17(
25.	380	6,485	28,410	17,347	4,750	2,969	877	2,41(
26.	2,088	43,288	181,236	94,428	26,148	20,361	5,527	16,74(
27.	62	3,407	14,024	6,368	2,209	949	81	91(
N.C.	998	24,284	130,950	60,423	9,267	5,506	2,257	6,55(
Total Employed	9,744	254,797	1,438,087	889,603	134,484	100,420	29,006	99,18(
Total Population	23,385	539,785	2,849,259	1,854,172	306,580	234,817	65,130	220,25.

		Wales		Scotland				
41.North-umberland	42.Durham	43.Glam-organ & Monmouth	44.North & West Wales	45.Strathclyde	46.Dumfries & Galloway	47.Borders	48.Lothian	
23,383	17,050	23,014	100,235	56,634	25,394	17,280	17,883	1.
18,841	54,762	54,884	35,093	49,255	1,217	267	10,632	2.
7,475	11,037	8,798	10,721	26,215	2,504	1,854	10,827	3.
−	−	−	−	−	−	−	−	4.
1,139	4,675	1,262	1,142	3,970	154	110	1,781	5.
7,899	33,334	34,729	10,698	37,719	1,099	767	5,719	6.
5,215	9,798	3,593	1,262	16,672	272	324	2,499	7.
261	384	286	381	912	113	80	431	8.
−	−	−	−	−	−	−	−	9.
3,296	8,849	1,415	1,543	13,065	61	16	375	10.
527	741	643	968	1,266	156	91	595	11.
996	1,591	1,343	821	2,927	182	117	1,227	12.
2,522	4,142	2,867	7,985	105,951	2,974	8,791	3,987	13.
1,111	792	662	1,433	2,555	283	342	1,333	14.
12,006	16,318	16,556	23,189	45,402	4,862	2,954	14,034	15.
1,883	6,319	1,192	1,068	5,515	96	85	1,537	16.
2,572	3,871	2,723	2,774	11,068	697	482	4,452	17.
1,491	1,964	1,009	1,220	8,093	229	389	7,774	18.
147	138	122	57	938	16	28	850	19.
11,396	21,338	14,980	19,522	38,162	4,339	3,834	13,739	20.
387	366	282	199	1,344	50	67	513	21.
11,673	20,104	17,063	9,802	38,612	2,086	1,146	11,572	22.
1,672	2,206	1,855	2,578	5,740	575	376	2,276	23.
340	491	406	423	1,747	246	182	1,094	24.
3,823	5,938	5,965	8,038	11,771	1,574	1,161	7,252	25.
26,993	33,692	38,619	66,098	59,440	10,115	7,382	32,641	26.
2,353	2,386	2,608	5,064	6,208	622	397	3,979	27.
14,837	33,234	35,400	28,584	46,659	3,077	1,489	12,940	N.C.
164,238	295,520	272,278	340,898	597,840	62,993	50,011	171,942	
386,646	742,205	625,506	796,164	1,340,961	155,531	116,492	407,272	

TOTAL EMPLOYMENT: 1871

Scotland

	49.Central & Fife	50. Tayside	51.Grampian	52.Highland	53. South East	54. East Anglia	55. South West	56. Midl
1.	20,673	32,944	74,615	79,559	380,723	156,854	235,776	133
2.	11,439	1,448	1,949	763	11,875	1,484	49,595	62
3.	5,031	7,012	6,177	2,588	169,306	21,693	48,767	41
4.	–	–	–	–	–	–	–	
5.	475	393	614	109	19,667	1,484	3,473	5
6.	4,960	4,025	3,183	1,320	50,931	8,360	21,330	85
7.	1,187	2,138	867	239	27,204	2,329	6,733	21
8.	142	228	260	132	10,380	627	1,549	5
9.	–	–	–	–	–	–	–	
10.	465	851	1,010	414	12,050	1,120	4,720	
11.	220	286	353	200	18,557	3,401	5,188	7
12.	695	408	344	166	20,629	1,164	3,693	5
13.	27,219	57,602	9,090	5,821	80,753	12,786	43,521	36
14.	392	588	457	144	28,131	4,133	6,777	10
15.	6,355	9,901	9,474	5,665	325,923	41,097	108,429	72
16.	758	227	212	64	15,699	2,505	4,392	49
17.	1,439	2,248	2,285	1,264	79,468	5,408	15,862	16
18.	928	1,110	2,480	232	64,265	3,186	7,744	7
19.	311	251	1,024	17	12,297	270	1,013	7
20.	6,381	10,949	8,215	5,177	213,032	23,826	70,570	56
21.	163	303	229	52	7,346	545	1,144	
22.	5,521	6,536	5,167	3,335	215,242	14,998	39,532	3
23.	925	1,265	1,350	544	36,686	4,910	8,830	7
24.	339	546	545	270	11,863	777	1,985	
25.	2,379	4,014	4,058	2,495	133,694	14,652	37,014	25
26.	10,762	17,384	21,252	15,126	706,102	80,142	210,912	157
27.	1,373	1,657	1,856	1,377	137,275	4,876	32,133	7
N.C.	6,099	8,057	5,868	2,510	321,722	35,819	96,124	90
Total Employed	116,631	172,371	162,934	129,583	3,110,820	448,446	1,066,806	1,002
Total Population	276,504	376,517	384,827	301,914	7,172,486	1,027,927	2,369,537	2,23

57. East Midlands	58. North West	59. Yorks. & Humberside	60. North	61. Wales	62. Scotland	63. Great Britain	
165,685	98,737	90,305	97,880	123,249	324,982	1,807,603	1.
38,740	67,323	56,077	93,508	89,977	76,970	547,884	2.
32,654	62,753	40,180	27,624	19,519	62,208	526,273	3.
-	-	-	-	-	-	-	4.
2,877	12,957	7,592	6,542	2,404	7,606	70,288	5.
19,114	55,517	46,958	49,490	45,427	58,792	440,951	6.
8,847	35,270	20,587	17,033	4,855	24,198	168,631	7.
1,042	3,930	1,598	980	669	2,298	28,878	8.
-	-	-	-	-	-	-	9.
612	7,793	2,150	13,105	2,958	16,257	61,421	10.
5,351	7,640	4,698	1,950	1,611	3,167	58,957	11.
3,591	7,985	36,216	3,360	2,164	6,066	139,956	12.
104,941	509,549	274,210	16,905	10,852	221,435	1,311,891	13.
4,895	6,577	7,753	3,237	2,095	6,094	80,639	14.
82,227	105,123	63,113	45,139	39,745	98,647	981,801	15.
5,353	11,756	9,048	11,020	2,260	8,494	119,790	16.
8,434	23,068	13,335	9,874	5,497	23,935	201,709	17.
4,635	16,283	7,341	4,785	2,229	21,235	138,767	18.
2,703	2,762	1,737	420	179	3,435	32,412	19.
41,348	91,164	64,064	49,839	34,502	90,796	735,659	20.
1,039	3,626	2,273	991	481	2,721	21,818	21.
22,551	110,041	43,374	39,486	26,865	73,975	620,480	22.
6,079	17,816	8,803	5,555	4,433	13,051	113,917	23.
1,100	3,130	1,735	1,231	829	4,969	29,243	24.
20,451	34,895	22,097	16,024	14,003	34,704	353,210	25.
117,443	224,524	120,576	103,321	104,717	174,102	1,999,743	26.
5,721	17,431	8,577	6,688	7,672	17,469	245,369	27.
57,046	155,234	69,690	62,386	63,984	86,699	1,038,874	N.C.
764,479	1,692,884	1,024,087	688,373	613,176	1,464,305	11,876,164	
1,655,169	3,389,044	2,160,752	1,649,051	1,421,670	3,360,018	26,437,563	

MALE EMPLOYMENT: 1881

South East

	1. London	2. Middlesex	3. Kent	4. Surrey	5. Sussex	6. Hants.	7. Berks.	8. Oxon.
1.	11,636	9,763	52,478	21,566	40,647	36,466	24,965	21,215
2.	6,056	521	1,691	741	769	873	339	354
3.	83,914	7,099	13,761	9,006	10,589	10,376	6,389	3,462
4.	–	–	–	–	–	–	–	–
5.	12,229	802	1,207	724	603	658	205	128
6.	28,821	1,615	4,647	2,106	2,790	4,398	2,104	1,051
7.	19,440	1,404	3,029	554	1,028	2,695	722	243
8.	7,229	430	524	405	383	420	165	103
9.	1,321	46	56	44	10	29	5	1
10.	5,896	192	2,667	146	372	3,785	90	71
11.	9,320	846	1,819	1,030	1,444	1,146	668	380
12.	15,189	765	733	577	646	671	290	240
13.	22,790	1,424	2,120	1,482	1,546	1,568	665	903
14.	17,653	595	1,015	946	726	831	476	302
15.	63,824	2,672	5,412	3,748	4,135	5,295	2,326	2,174
16.	6,579	1,718	6,348	1,039	1,679	1,379	725	298
17.	49,865	1,739	3,463	1,879	3,083	3,200	1,383	1,046
18.	48,355	1,680	2,789	1,631	1,433	1,462	676	856
19.	10,384	836	394	300	175	133	66	64
20.	131,208	15,606	20,380	18,319	20,496	17,640	8,811	5,641
21.	5,695	467	645	448	421	385	170	124
22.	166,427	8,553	18,720	8,827	11,178	15,988	4,211	2,547
23.	17,883	877	1,888	1,192	1,329	1,811	500	432
24.	10,245	1,272	963	1,366	691	754	292	176
25.	50,544	5,081	5,749	5,687	4,897	4,778	2,324	1,737
26.	85,624	11,014	15,152	12,697	11,992	11,703	6,220	5,063
27.	42,077	3,962	17,070	11,844	3,734	21,129	2,997	793
N.C.	180,262	18,685	24,358	19,213	13,725	19,788	7,544	4,726
Total Employed	1,110,466	99,664	209,078	127,517	140,521	169,361	75,328	54,130
Total Population	1,797,486	180,622	350,615	219,076	234,248	281,310	123,301	88,908

East Anglia

9. Bucks.	10. Beds.	11. Herts.	12. Essex	13. Cambridge	14. Hunts.	15. Norfolk	16. Suffolk	
16,908	17,825	20,604	47,242	26,893	8,479	54,415	47,900	1.
256	278	611	1,175	599	69	749	481	2.
2,681	2,778	4,090	10,462	3,282	1,043	7,906	6,584	3.
-	-	-	-	-	-	-	-	4.
90	128	220	1,447	178	47	770	523	5.
784	1,259	1,148	4,074	1,011	317	3,579	3,140	6.
263	359	269	3,098	256	75	1,059	1,361	7.
76	75	127	385	110	33	295	218	8.
7	3	7	124	2	3	12	22	9.
15	10	28	861	50	6	555	636	10.
731	393	599	1,644	410	242	1,331	1,212	11.
128	148	190	637	160	56	567	340	12.
378	396	645	2,089	374	139	1,908	1,952	13.
338	229	393	1,134	382	104	1,289	909	14.
2,115	3,794	2,177	4,306	2,034	554	7,591	4,286	15.
423	504	427	1,797	391	182	1,043	1,058	16.
3,290	552	818	2,664	627	137	2,250	1,394	17.
676	253	784	1,485	741	118	1,182	921	18.
37	21	24	432	43	4	97	55	19.
3,979	3,984	5,875	15,769	4,371	1,140	11,557	8,322	20.
79	73	117	892	114	21	254	169	21.
1,774	1,782	3,366	17,744	3,651	553	7,995	6,109	22.
381	463	485	1,418	492	155	1,667	1,055	23.
144	164	238	842	173	56	535	322	24.
1,143	1,009	1,619	3,980	1,588	389	3,237	2,353	25.
3,902	2,599	5,766	8,689	3,906	983	7,425	5,662	26.
566	885	984	5,977	627	226	1,842	2,130	27.
4,966	3,882	6,370	23,446	4,398	1,227	11,162	6,680	N.C.
46,130	43,846	57,981	163,813	56,863	16,358	132,272	105,794	
76,796	72,576	98,963	276,176	93,903	26,067	211,806	172,728	

MALE EMPLOYMENT: 1881

South West   West Midlands

	17.Corn-wall	18. Devon	19.Som-erset	20.Gloucs.	21.Wilts.	22.Dorset	23.Here-ford	24.Shrops.
1.	32,431	49,943	41,077	27,784	29,395	20,518	16,426	27,338
2.	16,196	3,899	7,219	5,486	1,279	1,269	452	6,188
3.	3,636	9,080	8,271	9,655	4,113	3,558	1,478	3,631
4.	–	–	–	–	–	–	–	–
5.	310	754	609	1,181	157	110	111	272
6.	2,724	4,246	3,425	4,522	2,421	1,273	875	5,286
7.	741	2,077	1,193	2,079	2,204	330	163	790
8.	162	505	309	399	135	120	62	140
9.	5	17	12	15	10	5	2	2
10.	1,018	2,653	263	501	14	145	4	31
11.	478	1,433	1,073	1,464	1,044	354	410	1,080
12.	297	849	690	1,148	286	199	157	631
13.	842	2,590	3,277	3,729	2,359	1,201	235	945
14.	524	1,487	1,488	1,273	608	336	229	490
15.	3,146	8,121	7,555	9,039	2,155	1,902	1,315	2,932
16.	115	756	1,301	1,246	325	620	178	1,350
17.	1,032	3,230	2,964	4,305	1,164	783	592	1,161
18.	430	1,988	1,902	1,968	459	379	216	459
19.	34	151	187	388	83	19	11	35
20.	8,307	19,992	15,235	16,314	7,296	5,736	3,548	7,280
21.	81	297	242	565	102	73	30	148
22.	7,681	14,064	9,504	13,044	4,143	3,840	1,288	3,388
23.	510	1,161	1,012	1,404	524	486	157	434
24.	364	788	570	761	280	214	128	332
25.	2,377	5,422	4,386	5,040	1,846	1,359	1,068	2,069
26.	2,312	8,187	6,885	9,079	3,480	2,884	2,372	5,169
27.	2,773	14,398	2,488	3,376	1,228	3,297	593	1,323
N.C.	5,407	14,847	14,678	20,235	8,164	4,974	4,001	9,019
Total Employed	93,933	172,935	137,815	146,000	75,274	55,984	36,101	81,923
Total Population	153,015	287,461	231,394	245,627	122,766	90,835	58,525	132,992

East Midlands

5.Staffs.	26.Warwick	27.Worcs.	28.Derby	29.Notts.	30.Leics.	31.Lincs.	32.North-ants.	
25,578	24,844	20,573	15,651	19,873	18,111	63,419	24,154	1.
43,257	5,209	3,058	21,032	20,305	6,190	1,449	1,905	2.
15,732	12,591	5,529	5,012	7,621	5,214	8,500	4,410	3.
–	–	–	–	–	–	–	–	4.
1,522	1,106	829	705	562	313	853	176	5.
39,403	23,665	10,758	8,365	4,844	1,923	5,499	2,367	6.
6,690	9,016	2,687	3,865	3,553	1,250	2,364	764	7.
569	5,041	292	283	258	172	291	134	8.
22	80	29	60	28	15	–	3	9.
359	128	80	30	32	17	700	30	10.
2,981	3,188	1,132	1,552	1,133	763	1,513	1,024	11.
11,267	21,247	7,911	1,272	688	642	598	254	12.
3,986	4,916	4,595	10,397	19,943	11,819	1,595	603	13.
4,239	2,671	1,038	552	1,087	638	925	1,381	14.
10,384	8,970	4,056	3,452	5,106	14,023	4,633	17,608	15.
25,665	3,192	3,322	1,251	1,259	1,606	1,429	644	16.
4,262	4,986	1,752	1,539	2,061	1,274	1,595	1,093	17.
1,618	3,186	1,092	1,378	1,731	772	728	460	18.
307	3,103	780	417	235	1,004	55	74	19.
27,842	20,716	9,223	10,543	11,887	9,123	12,068	8,372	20.
804	867	201	320	455	272	228	143	21.
16,563	15,870	5,961	7,339	7,459	5,073	7,691	5,069	22.
1,518	1,763	634	844	1,234	839	1,121	618	23.
1,054	836	640	408	458	365	499	261	24.
5,644	4,395	3,212	2,533	2,748	2,119	3,300	1,833	25.
10,605	8,377	5,294	4,673	5,858	5,349	7,189	4,134	26.
3,142	2,769	1,414	1,310	1,235	1,135	1,574	1,257	27.
37,645	25,284	14,664	13,906	13,138	8,109	13,269	7,734	N.C.
302,658	218,016	110,756	118,689	134,791	98,130	143,085	86,505	
504,874	355,551	184,016	193,110	215,371	158,763	231,710	138,091	

MALE EMPLOYMENT: 1881

	East Midlands	North West	Yorks. & Humberside		North			
	33.Rut-land	34. Cheshire	35.Lancs.	36. West Riding	37. East Riding	38. North Riding	39.West-morland	40.Cum-berland
1.	3,444	28,331	53,292	56,043	24,915	27,264	6,919	17,060
2.	42	5,907	74,701	70,328	916	9,217	476	12,338
3.	380	9,290	52,054	32,451	6,744	4,641	776	3,138
4.	-	-	-	-	-	-	-	-
5.	11	4,543	10,626	4,240	2,369	339	116	356
6.	116	8,003	60,855	44,739	4,208	12,213	378	5,102
7.	13	7,118	34,988	23,741	2,881	1,734	137	1,166
8.	7	352	3,289	1,366	333	209	52	193
9.	-	36	249	111	7	5	4	3
10.	-	1,680	7,558	507	1,689	1,406	10	635
11.	55	1,558	7,843	4,709	990	370	64	231
12.	14	887	9,181	33,627	498	1,418	69	379
13.	41	18,856	202,169	129,477	1,747	1,232	823	2,284
14.	50	1,092	5,996	6,781	1,227	529	166	486
15.	260	9,739	35,621	24,756	4,236	3,981	914	3,227
16.	58	2,148	12,452	8,720	984	683	18	377
17.	52	2,616	20,118	10,514	2,971	1,052	616	954
18.	17	1,324	15,497	7,048	1,251	602	241	656
19.	2	180	2,733	1,394	343	33	24	148
20.	710	17,621	94,438	60,464	11,343	8,879	2,379	7,584
21.	9	509	4,667	2,836	299	218	47	180
22.	285	19,217	120,461	42,592	14,032	6,503	905	5,406
23.	28	1,288	9,215	5,229	956	702	130	448
24.	15	1,198	6,339	2,930	522	460	77	344
25.	184	4,655	21,927	13,436	2,907	2,429	544	1,865
26.	715	9,226	35,377	20,462	4,652	4,145	1,082	2,598
27.	83	3,035	15,309	7,653	3,480	1,174	225	1,004
N.C.	505	24,938	147,593	61,628	13,473	10,740	1,691	7,559
Total Employed	7,096	185,347	1,064,548	677,782	109,973	102,178	18,883	75,721
Total Population	11,519	301,768	1,684,905	1,075,334	179,394	169,197	31,585	124,746

		Wales		Scotland				
41.North-umberland	42.Durham	43.Glam-organ & Monmouth	44.North & West Wales	45.Strathclyde	46.Dumfries & Galloway	47.Borders	48.Lothian	
16,844	13,533	18,768	80,440	35,377	16,385	12,014	12,027	1.
22,940	70,892	64,129	37,047	53,980	1,379	229	10,030	2.
6,241	10,266	8,217	8,605	25,809	2,235	1,820	10,363	3.
-	-	-	-	-	-	-	-	4.
1,068	6,250	1,222	1,404	4,076	134	110	2,211	5.
6,802	26,858	31,845	10,588	45,507	1,096	729	5,995	6.
5,354	11,236	4,314	1,319	23,261	287	509	2,720	7.
276	453	321	441	1,138	130	88	519	8.
23	30	28	3	38	2	2	21	9.
4,506	10,939	1,680	1,972	14,844	47	22	621	10.
499	776	917	1,012	1,567	142	88	606	11.
808	1,480	1,185	879	4,222	215	122	1,373	12.
1,880	2,664	2,221	5,079	30,236	1,860	6,319	2,282	13.
897	670	601	1,285	2,845	269	280	1,337	14.
4,937	6,259	6,001	9,316	19,128	1,986	1,596	6,412	15.
1,474	4,992	893	1,240	4,456	94	52	1,211	16.
2,326	3,614	2,389	2,358	10,495	563	418	4,257	17.
1,457	1,906	1,203	1,310	6,765	249	381	6,019	18.
156	152	97	47	900	22	33	712	19.
11,855	21,479	19,082	21,075	44,751	5,164	4,375	17,299	20.
275	614	403	286	1,595	75	74	654	21.
14,077	23,884	25,220	13,096	43,752	2,369	1,313	13,394	22.
842	1,541	1,095	1,398	3,285	374	199	912	23.
666	916	836	913	2,684	249	174	1,372	24.
3,044	4,909	5,255	6,666	10,242	1,253	945	5,972	25.
5,178	6,275	6,601	9,135	15,793	2,317	2,062	7,364	26.
2,122	2,416	2,406	4,594	7,172	530	406	4,629	27.
15,728	34,023	34,987	24,945	62,341	3,617	2,733	16,235	N.C.
132,275	269,027	241,916	246,453	476,259	43,043	37,093	136,547	
215,882	447,816	386,093	402,981	769,739	73,990	61,000	225,560	

MALE EMPLOYMENT: 1881

Scotland

	49.Central & Fife	50.Tayside	51.Grampian	52.Highland	53. South East	54. East Anglia	55. South West	56. West Midlands
1.	13,657	22,565	47,472	49,005	321,315	137,687	201,148	114,759
2.	12,358	1,410	2,457	664	13,664	1,898	35,348	58,164
3.	5,067	6,501	5,775	2,618	164,607	18,815	38,313	38,961
4.	-	-	-	-	-	-	-	-
5.	558	383	562	113	18,441	1,518	3,121	3,840
6.	6,177	4,060	3,289	1,365	54,797	8,047	18,611	79,987
7.	1,598	3,130	1,183	224	33,104	2,751	8,624	19,346
8.	183	291	342	156	10,322	656	1,630	6,104
9.	-	8	5	2	1,653	39	64	135
10.	445	1,078	964	449	14,133	1,247	4,594	602
11.	222	390	397	229	20,020	3,195	5,846	8,791
12.	583	564	447	227	20,214	1,123	3,469	41,213
13.	8,859	18,521	2,921	1,047	36,006	4,373	13,998	14,677
14.	353	690	503	158	24,638	2,684	5,716	8,667
15.	2,962	5,134	5,492	3,133	101,978	14,465	31,918	27,657
16.	765	242	171	50	22,916	2,674	4,363	33,707
17.	1,464	2,225	2,772	1,227	72,982	4,408	13,478	12,753
18.	946	1,229	1,515	345	62,080	2,962	7,126	6,571
19.	768	146	746	19	12,866	199	862	4,236
20.	7,840	11,381	9,886	6,564	267,708	25,390	72,880	68,609
21.	227	372	243	42	9,516	558	1,360	2,050
22.	6,051	8,004	6,380	3,863	261,117	18,308	52,276	43,070
23.	450	782	798	766	28,659	3,369	5,097	4,506
24.	449	682	671	337	17,147	1,086	2,977	2,990
25.	1,948	2,908	2,790	1,901	88,548	7,567	20,430	16,388
26.	2,847	5,038	3,853	2,800	180,421	17,976	32,827	31,817
27.	1,230	1,600	1,400	2,004	112,018	4,825	27,560	9,241
N.C.	8,710	13,183	9,942	5,784	326,965	23,467	68,305	90,613
Total Employed	86,717	112,517	112,976	85,092	2,297,835	311,287	681,941	749,454
Total Population	146,053	186,539	195,790	140,804	3,800,077	504,504	1,131,098	1,235,958

57. East Midlands	58. North West	59. Yorks. & Humberside	60. North	61. Wales	62. Scotland	63. Great Britain	
144,652	81,623	80,958	81,620	99,208	208,502	1,471,472	1.
50,923	80,608	71,244	115,863	101,176	82,507	611,395	2.
31,137	61,344	39,195	25,062	16,822	60,188	494,444	3.
–	–	–	–	–	–	–	4.
2,620	15,169	6,609	8,129	2,626	8,147	70,220	5.
23,114	68,858	48,947	51,353	42,433	68,218	464,365	6.
11,809	42,106	26,622	19,627	5,633	32,912	202,534	7.
1,145	3,641	1,699	1,183	762	2,847	29,989	8.
106	285	118	65	31	78	2,574	9.
809	9,238	2,196	17,496	3,652	18,470	72,437	10.
6,040	9,401	5,699	1,940	1,929	3,641	66,502	11.
3,468	10,068	34,125	4,154	2,064	7,753	127,651	12.
44,398	221,025	131,224	8,883	7,300	72,045	553,929	13.
4,633	7,088	8,008	2,748	1,886	6,435	72,503	14.
45,082	45,360	28,992	19,318	15,317	45,843	375,930	15.
6,247	14,600	9,704	7,544	2,133	7,041	110,929	16.
7,614	22,734	13,485	8,562	4,747	23,421	184,184	17.
5,086	16,821	8,299	4,862	2,513	17,449	133,769	18.
1,787	2,913	1,737	513	144	3,346	28,603	19.
52,703	112,059	71,807	52,176	40,157	107,260	870,749	20.
1,427	5,176	3,135	1,334	689	3,282	28,527	21.
32,916	139,678	56,624	50,775	38,316	85,126	778,206	22.
4,684	10,503	6,185	3,663	2,493	7,566	76,725	23.
2,006	7,537	3,452	2,463	1,749	6,618	48,025	24.
12,717	26,582	16,343	12,791	11,921	27,959	241,246	25.
27,918	44,603	25,114	19,278	15,736	42,074	437,764	26.
6,594	18,344	11,133	6,941	7,000	18,971	222,627	27.
56,661	172,531	75,101	69,741	59,932	122,545	1,065,861	N.C.
588,296	1,249,895	787,755	598,084	488,369	1,090,244	8,843,160	
948,564	1,986,673	1,254,728	989,226	789,074	1,799,475	14,439,377	

FEMALE EMPLOYMENT: 1881

South East

	1. London	2. Middlesex	3. Kent	4. Surrey	5. Sussex	6. Hants.	7. Berks.	8. Oxon.
1.	891	752	1,521	576	539	748	1,286	837
2.	122	14	15	15	7	15	19	8
3.	11,524	701	1,399	812	1,159	1,389	683	424
4.	-	-	-	-	-	-	-	-
5.	1,999	136	76	61	35	20	5	5
6.	489	7	28	21	17	17	40	5
7.	111	5	2	4	3	5	2	-
8.	343	13	12	3	14	66	5	-
9.	16	-	-	1	-	-	-	-
10.	22	6	5	1	2	4	-	-
11.	102	8	16	4	4	7	2	2
12.	1,386	26	36	34	40	47	21	14
13.	16,843	1,078	1,250	944	932	1,114	431	1,009
14.	7,366	69	57	22	31	72	17	12
15.	133,016	5,308	11,038	6,790	8,420	12,340	4,674	4,776
16.	728	57	132	65	41	54	26	14
17.	7,051	191	221	209	229	252	116	69
18.	17,607	238	1,972	382	241	407	136	230
19.	1,769	178	75	38	42	39	21	8
20.	274	16	28	35	31	40	13	11
21.	145	3	-	-	1	-	-	-
22.	1,874	105	145	85	130	126	43	44
23.	8,321	356	863	632	679	706	250	248
24.	176	6	8	9	7	10	-	2
25.	37,236	4,507	6,331	5,101	5,249	4,980	2,398	1,687
26.	331,241	34,105	52,140	47,156	49,321	44,760	18,892	13,326
27.	1,386	74	209	210	134	204	112	78
N.C.	10,488	361	287	252	355	360	102	137
Total Employed	592,526	48,320	77,866	63,462	67,663	67,782	29,294	22,946
Total Population	2,018,997	200,192	357,912	241,978	259,946	294,099	124,591	92,662

East Anglia

9. Bucks.	10. Beds.	11. Herts.	12. Essex	13. Cambridge	14. Hunts.	15. Norfolk	16. Suffolk	
328	189	298	954	1,656	349	2,191	1,083	1.
4	13	8	15	12	1	13	9	2.
346	342	443	1,007	473	134	1,044	847	3.
-	-	-	-	-	-	-	-	4.
5	7	9	104	6	-	144	28	5.
28	5	8	32	9	1	14	18	6.
2	-	2	5	4	1	18	3	7.
-	2	5	13	2	-	14	3	8.
-	-	-	-	-	-	-	-	9.
-	-	-	5	-	-	2	1	10.
12	3	3	7	3	2	8	10	11.
7	10	9	20	11	3	28	19	12.
4,751	4,988	704	4,923	324	467	4,157	2,013	13.
191	8	84	143	48	-	835	784	14.
4,349	18,088	10,416	10,563	3,290	862	11,218	9,142	15.
17	5	9	46	3	2	50	37	16.
657	73	116	136	53	11	173	84	17.
390	32	483	233	191	250	407	279	18.
6	3	12	60	10	4	16	16	19.
9	3	13	15	9	-	26	17	20.
-	-	-	-	1	-	1	-	21.
29	30	40	128	36	16	100	59	22.
121	136	180	689	214	76	906	526	23.
-	-	2	4	-	-	2	1	24.
1,216	1,132	1,867	4,487	1,680	480	3,670	3,016	25.
9,215	7,535	13,022	30,170	12,102	3,231	26,906	21,510	26.
46	48	65	221	62	22	181	117	27.
69	24	86	258	81	10	169	86	N.C.
21,798	32,676	27,884	54,238	20,280	5,922	52,293	39,708	
79,073	81,683	103,412	276,092	97,211	27,156	225,905	180,817	

FEMALE EMPLOYMENT: 1881

South West West Midlands

	17.Cornwall	18. Devon	19.Somerset	20.Gloucs.	21.Wilts.	22.Dorset	23.Hereford	24.Shrops
1.	2,132	1,796	2,300	1,589	2,117	990	796	1,336
2.	2,152	131	36	56	18	–	2	386
3.	1,713	2,243	1,483	2,115	746	442	231	646
4.	–	–	–	–	–	–	–	–
5.	193	72	25	143	4	1	4	9
6.	18	11	12	79	9	7	14	23
7.	–	8	6	11	5	–	1	5
8.	5	17	13	15	2	2	–	1
9.	–	–	–	–	–	–	–	–
10.	2	3	1	1	2	–	–	–
11.	1	5	5	9	12	1	1	3
12.	35	90	34	184	14	10	17	29
13.	1,270	5,886	4,149	6,050	3,547	1,740	140	472
14.	24	115	294	149	34	20	3	37
15.	8,220	18,056	18,766	17,898	3,873	6,085	1,984	3,494
16.	15	123	60	139	18	18	17	217
17.	70	346	236	512	91	41	44	66
18.	62	722	926	859	63	64	40	64
19.	7	49	37	186	14	11	7	67
20.	20	23	18	67	20	12	2	16
21.	2	1	–	5	–	–	–	–
22.	79	178	102	162	53	44	28	46
23.	524	1,276	868	1,348	301	279	188	327
24.	2	5	2	1	1	1	1	1
25.	2,090	5,515	4,607	4,983	2,148	1,576	951	1,629
26.	19,482	47,888	37,754	41,643	15,005	11,716	8,724	18,184
27.	151	219	192	200	116	91	61	116
N.C.	85	219	238	320	116	86	52	69
Total Employed	38,354	84,997	72,164	78,724	28,329	23,237	13,308	27,243
Total Population	173,360	320,939	259,208	279,540	125,898	94,137	59,622	132,898

East Midlands

5.Staffs.	26.War-wick	27.Worcs.	28.Derby	29.Notts.	30.Leics.	31.Lincs.	32.North-ants.	
1,343	913	1,676	962	618	520	1,643	413	1.
433	76	46	38	67	15	12	6	2.
2,558	2,885	1,006	1,052	1,656	1,338	1,163	564	3.
-	-	-	-	-	-	-	-	4.
213	490	126	35	26	5	29	6	5.
1,183	3,686	347	12	15	6	9	8	6.
65	335	23	10	8	3	5	3	7.
30	445	11	31	22	5	8	4	8.
-	1	-	-	-	-	-	-	9.
2	-	-	1	-	2	1	-	10.
19	43	2	25	3	6	10	22	11.
7,312	11,289	5,667	80	34	39	20	15	12.
4,488	10,459	3,501	14,228	24,987	15,055	669	3,609	13.
1,241	1,259	296	48	116	32	64	18	14.
15,057	16,912	9,316	6,323	10,131	12,409	6,984	12,422	15.
16,813	379	1,148	269	35	157	25	14	16.
296	1,346	200	126	175	91	80	84.	17.
449	2,425	340	592	648	426	60	175	18.
108	3,794	591	112	55	505	15	50	19.
406	177	27	23	26	11	22	7	20.
1	-	7	1	-	-	-	-	21.
642	2,161	264	98	343	346	72	72	22.
1,459	1,848	720	422	683	462	440	321	23.
10	12	9	-	5	1	2	4	24.
5,252	4,736	3,054	2,043	2,488	2,280	3,335	2,080	25.
42,725	38,337	26,128	16,934	19,806	15,249	27,795	14,165	26.
190	177	106	112	92	93	106	99	27.
685	2,049	390	141	542	1,113	156	68	N.C.
102,980	106,234	55,001	43,718	62,581	50,169	42,725	34,229	
501,884	374,980	198,995	193,404	223,271	167,878	231,351	138,944	

FEMALE EMPLOYMENT: 1881

	East Midlands	North West		Yorks. & Humberside		North		
	33.Rutland	34. Cheshire	35.Lancs.	36. West Riding	37. East Riding	38. North Riding	39.Westmorland	40.Cumberland
1.	76	1,867	3,847	3,385	816	1,362	406	1,593
2.	1	30	1,497	226	19	18	–	200
3.	54	2,359	16,256	6,793	1,096	726	311	1,102
4.	–	–	–	–	–	–	–	–
5.	–	92	814	320	214	15	7	11
6.	–	48	169	378	23	32	2	31
7.	–	22	576	163	12	2	4	5
8.	1	4	90	90	7	–	–	–
9.	–	–	2	1	–	–	–	–
10.	–	2	12	–	3	2	–	–
11.	–	5	36	28	6	–	1	1
12.	–	41	795	5,211	25	33	8	19
13.	88	27,185	286,194	141,638	1,186	486	587	2,648
14.	2	62	873	802	100	16	6	9
15.	322	12,251	63,842	34,895	6,670	5,159	1,076	4,468
16.	–	76	1,245	613	31	94	9	39
17.	2	240	2,554	1,180	151	51	20	51
18.	6	360	5,890	2,042	255	107	74	164
19.	1	38	783	352	64	16	8	21
20.	4	31	177	369	20	16	5	8
21.	–	–	2	10	1	–	–	–
22.	5	213	1,342	881	109	55	18	60
23.	15	1,032	9,580	3,206	644	332	79	449
24.	–	6	52	24	9	4	1	1
25.	184	3,776	17,497	10,283	2,603	1,724	380	1,146
26.	1,716	39,202	154,178	80,626	22,988	19,599	4,428	14,716
27.	9	136	719	332	73	108	22	73
N.C.	14	362	2,653	1,897	141	82	58	367
Total Employed	2,500	89,440	571,675	295,745	37,266	30,039	7,510	27,182
Total Population	11,488	320,597	1,800,914	1,122,665	182,981	165,188	32,729	125,901

		Wales			Scotland			
41.North-umberland	42.Durham	43.Glam-organ & Monmouth	44.North & West Wales	45.Strathclyde	46.Dumfries & Galloway	47.Borders	48.Lothian	
3,742	1,591	1,503	9,316	10,660	3,779	3,853	5,063	1.
34	133	837	396	205	6	4	54	2.
1,792	2,029	2,210	3,306	7,658	646	401	2,263	3.
-	-	-	-	-	-	-	-	4.
157	106	109	50	682	10	7	137	5.
27	55	2,764	841	143	4	1	122	6.
7	4	6	4	161	-	13	13	7.
5	13	3	6	28	-	-	5	8.
1	4	-	-	-	-	-	-	9.
12	13	4	2	20	-	-	-	10.
1	1	4	4	3	-	-	1	11.
54	57	111	20	420	4	4	98	12.
535	1,393	1,057	2,857	58,939	1,398	5,519	2,137	13.
82	33	19	45	487	2	1	91	14.
6,929	11,417	11,691	13,547	31,016	2,674	1,671	8,993	15.
322	405	527	180	1,356	30	19	375	16.
152	158	109	66	1,783	25	6	424	17.
307	593	232	288	4,670	27	102	4,047	18.
37	32	49	32	341	-	15	346	19.
30	26	27	57	42	2	5	36	20.
3	1	6	3	2	-	-	1	21.
146	100	173	245	1,875	55	60	635	22.
1,112	1,275	900	1,229	5,320	279	217	1,929	23.
7	3	2	2	11	-	1	3	24.
2,007	3,481	3,557	2,847	5,396	613	468	3,104	25.
23,895	32,637	36,530	55,830	58,123	8,138	5,340	29,744	26.
117	111	128	252	372	97	52	188	27.
296	487	456	331	6,077	29	64	1,393	N.C.
41,809	56,158	63,014	91,756	195,790	17,818	17,823	61,202	
218,204	427,350	366,622	421,863	792,285	82,915	66,899	245,791	

FEMALE EMPLOYMENT: 1881

Scotland

	49.Central & Fife	50.Tayside	51.Grampian	52.Highland	53. South East	54. East Anglia	55. South West	56. W Mid
1.	3,848	5,319	8,378	13,423	8,919	5,279	10,924	6
2.	300	8	4	2	255	35	2,393	
3.	1,094	1,741	1,564	485	20,229	2,498	8,742	7
4.	–	–	–	–	–	–	–	
5.	24	16	34	6	2,462	178	438	
6.	17	21	9	22	697	42	136	5
7.	12	34	2	1	141	26	30	
8.	–	5	1	2	476	19	54	
9.	–	–	–	–	17	–	–	
10.	1	1	–	–	45	3	9	
11.	1	–	–	–	170	23	33	
12.	18	11	9	7	1,650	61	367	24
13.	15,200	39,381	4,410	5,803	38,967	6,961	22,642	19
14.	9	60	36	1	8,072	1,667	636	2
15.	3,757	5,639	4,672	2,659	229,778	24,512	72,898	46
16.	225	44	34	6	1,194	92	373	18
17.	66	108	154	13	9,320	321	1,296	1
18.	588	283	1,641	21	22,351	1,127	2,696	3
19.	24	31	159	1	2,251	46	304	4
20.	5	5	4	–	488	52	160	
21.	–	–	1	–	149	2	8	
22.	84	168	184	19	2,779	211	618	3
23.	643	1,006	801	319	13,181	1,722	4,596	4
24.	6	2	1	–	224	3	12	
25.	1,119	1,531	2,153	877	76,191	8,846	20,919	15
26.	10,503	13,921	20,963	12,198	650,883	63,749	173,488	134
27.	105	149	97	91	2,787	382	969	
N.C.	448	789	1,668	374	12,779	346	1,064	3
Total Employed	38,097	70,273	46,979	36,330	1,106,455	118,203	325,805	304
Total Population	156,986	219,726	213,613	157,883	4,130,637	531,089	1,253,082	1,268

57. East Midlands	58. North West	59. Yorks. & Humberside	60. North	61. Wales	62. Scotland	63. Great Britain	
4,232	5,714	4,201	8,694	10,819	54,323	119,169	1.
139	1,527	245	385	1,233	583	7,738	2.
5,827	18,615	7,889	5,960	5,516	15,852	98,454	3.
–	–	–	–	–	–	–	4.
101	906	534	296	159	916	6,832	5.
50	217	401	147	3,605	339	10,887	6.
29	598	175	22	10	236	1,696	7.
71	94	97	18	9	41	1,366	8.
–	2	1	5	–	–	26	9.
4	14	3	27	6	22	135	10.
66	41	34	4	8	5	452	11.
188	836	5,236	171	131	571	33,525	12.
58,636	313,379	142,824	5,649	3,914	132,787	744,819	13.
280	935	902	146	64	687	16,225	14.
48,591	76,093	41,565	29,049	25,238	61,081	655,568	15.
500	1,321	644	869	707	2,089	26,363	16.
558	2,794	1,331	432	175	2,579	20,758	17.
1,907	6,250	2,297	1,245	520	11,379	53,090	18.
738	821	416	114	81	917	10,255	19.
93	208	389	85	84	99	2,286	20.
1	2	11	4	9	4	198	21.
936	1,555	990	379	418	3,080	14,107	22.
2,343	10,612	3,850	3,247	2,129	10,514	56,736	23.
12	58	33	16	4	24	419	24.
12,410	21,273	12,886	8,738	6,404	15,261	198,550	25.
95,665	193,380	103,614	95,275	92,360	158,930	1,761,442	26.
511	855	405	431	380	1,151	8,521	27.
2,034	3,015	2,038	1,290	787	10,842	37,440	N.C.
235,922	661,115	333,011	162,698	154,770	484,312	3,887,057	
966,336	2,121,511	1,305,646	969,372	788,485	1,936,098	15,270,635	

TOTAL EMPLOYMENT: 1881

South East

	1. London	2. Middlesex	3. Kent	4. Surrey	5. Sussex	6. Hants.	7. Berks.	8. Oxon.
1.	12,527	10,515	53,999	22,142	41,186	37,214	26,251	22,052
2.	6,178	535	1,706	756	776	888	358	362
3.	95,438	7,800	15,160	9,818	11,748	11,765	7,072	3,886
4.	–	–	–	–	–	–	–	–
5.	14,228	938	1,283	785	638	678	210	133
6.	29,310	1,622	4,675	2,127	2,807	4,415	2,144	1,056
7.	19,551	1,409	3,031	558	1,031	2,700	724	243
8.	7,572	443	536	408	397	486	170	103
9.	1,337	46	56	45	10	29	5	1
10.	5,918	198	2,672	147	374	3,789	90	71
11.	9,422	854	1,835	1,034	1,448	1,153	670	382
12.	16,575	791	769	611	686	718	311	254
13.	39,633	2,502	3,370	2,426	2,478	2,682	1,096	1,912
14.	25,019	664	1,072	968	757	903	493	314
15.	196,840	7,980	16,450	10,538	12,555	17,635	7,000	6,950
16.	7,307	1,775	6,480	1,104	1,720	1,433	751	312
17.	56,916	1,930	3,684	2,088	3,312	3,452	1,499	1,115
18.	65,962	1,918	4,761	2,013	1,674	1,869	812	1,086
19.	12,153	1,014	469	338	217	172	87	72
20.	131,482	15,622	20,408	18,354	20,527	17,680	8,824	5,652
21.	5,840	470	645	448	422	385	170	124
22.	168,301	8,658	18,865	8,912	11,308	16,114	4,254	2,591
23.	26,204	1,233	2,751	1,824	2,008	2,517	750	680
24.	10,421	1,278	971	1,375	698	764	292	178
25.	87,780	9,588	12,080	10,788	10,146	9,758	4,722	3,424
26.	416,865	45,119	67,292	59,853	61,313	56,463	25,112	18,389
27.	43,463	4,036	17,279	12,054	3,868	21,333	3,109	871
N.C.	190,750	19,046	24,645	19,465	14,080	20,148	7,646	4,863
Total Employed	1,702,992	147,984	286,944	190,979	208,184	237,143	104,622	77,076
Total Population	3,816,483	380,814	708,527	461,054	494,194	575,409	247,892	181,570

East Anglia

9. Bucks.	10. Beds.	11. Herts.	12. Essex	13. Cambridge	14. Hunts.	15. Norfolk	16. Suffolk	
17,236	18,014	20,902	48,196	28,549	8,828	56,606	48,983	1.
260	291	619	1,190	611	70	762	490	2.
3,027	3,120	4,533	11,469	3,755	1,177	8,950	7,431	3.
-	-	-	-	-	-	-	-	4.
95	135	229	1,551	184	47	914	551	5.
812	1,264	1,156	4,106	1,020	318	3,593	3,158	6.
265	359	271	3,103	260	76	1,077	1,364	7.
76	77	132	398	112	33	309	221	8.
7	3	7	124	2	3	12	22	9.
15	10	28	866	50	6	557	637	10.
743	396	602	1,651	413	244	1,339	1,222	11.
135	158	199	657	171	59	595	359	12.
5,129	5,384	1,349	7,012	698	606	6,065	3,965	13.
529	237	477	1,277	430	104	2,124	1,693	14.
6,464	21,882	12,593	14,869	5,324	1,416	18,809	13,428	15.
440	509	436	1,843	394	184	1,093	1,095	16.
3,947	625	934	2,800	680	148	2,423	1,478	17.
1,066	285	1,267	1,718	932	368	1,589	1,200	18.
43	24	36	492	53	8	113	71	19.
3,988	3,987	5,888	15,784	4,380	1,140	11,583	8,339	20.
79	73	117	892	115	21	255	169	21.
1,803	1,812	3,406	17,872	3,687	569	8,095	6,168	22.
502	599	665	2,107	706	231	2,573	1,581	23.
144	164	240	846	173	56	537	323	24.
2,359	2,141	3,486	8,467	3,268	869	6,907	5,369	25.
13,117	10,134	18,788	38,859	16,008	4,214	34,331	27,172	26.
612	933	1,049	6,198	689	248	2,023	2,247	27.
5,035	3,906	6,456	23,704	4,479	1,237	11,331	6,766	N.C.
67,928	76,522	85,865	218,051	77,143	22,280	184,565	145,502	
155,869	154,259	202,375	552,268	191,114	53,223	437,711	353,545	

TOTAL EMPLOYMENT: 1881

South West   West Midlands

	17.Corn-wall	18. Devon	19.Som-erset	20.Gloucs.	21.Wilts.	22.Dorset	23.Here-ford	24.Shrops.
1.	34,563	51,739	43,377	29,373	31,512	21,508	17,222	28,674
2.	18,348	4,030	7,255	5,542	1,297	1,269	454	6,574
3.	5,349	11,323	9,754	11,770	4,859	4,000	1,709	4,277
4.	–	–	–	–	–	–	–	–
5.	503	826	634	1,324	161	111	115	281
6.	2,742	4,257	3,437	4,601	2,430	1,280	889	5,309
7.	741	2,085	1,199	2,090	2,209	330	164	795
8.	167	522	322	414	137	122	62	141
9.	5	17	12	15	10	5	2	2
10.	1,020	2,656	264	502	16	145	4	31
11.	479	1,438	1,078	1,473	1,056	355	411	1,083
12.	332	939	724	1,332	300	209	174	660
13.	2,112	8,476	7,426	9,779	5,906	2,941	375	1,417
14.	548	1,602	1,782	1,422	642	356	232	527
15.	11,366	26,177	26,321	26,937	6,028	7,987	3,299	6,426
16.	130	879	1,361	1,385	343	638	195	1,567
17.	1,102	3,576	3,200	4,817	1,255	824	636	1,227
18.	492	2,710	2,828	2,827	522	443	256	523
19.	41	200	224	574	97	30	18	102
20.	8,327	20,015	15,253	16,381	7,316	5,748	3,550	7,296
21.	83	298	242	570	102	73	30	148
22.	7,760	14,242	9,606	13,206	4,196	3,884	1,316	3,434
23.	1,034	2,437	1,880	2,752	825	765	345	761
24.	366	793	572	762	281	215	129	333
25.	4,467	10,937	8,993	10,023	3,994	2,935	2,019	3,698
26.	21,794	56,075	44,639	50,722	18,485	14,600	11,096	23,353
27.	2,924	14,617	2,680	3,576	1,344	3,388	654	1,439
N.C.	5,492	15,066	14,916	20,555	8,280	5,060	4,053	9,088
Total Employed	132,287	257,932	209,979	224,724	103,603	79,221	49,409	109,166
Total Population	326,375	608,400	490,602	525,167	248,664	184,972	118,147	265,890

East Midlands

25.Staffs.	26.Warwick	27.Worcs.	28.Derby	29.Notts.	30.Leics.	31.Lincs.	32.Northants.	
26,921	25,757	22,249	16,613	20,491	18,631	65,062	24,567	1.
43,690	5,285	3,104	21,070	20,372	6,205	1,461	1,911	2.
18,290	15,476	6,535	6,064	9,277	6,552	9,663	4,974	3.
-	-	-	-	-	-	-	-	4.
1,735	1,596	955	740	588	318	882	182	5.
40,586	27,351	11,105	8,377	4,859	1,929	5,508	2,375	6.
6,755	9,351	2,710	3,875	3,561	1,253	2,369	767	7.
599	5,486	303	314	280	177	299	138	8.
22	81	29	60	28	15	-	3	9.
361	128	80	31	32	19	701	30	10.
3,000	3,231	1,134	1,577	1,136	769	1,523	1,046	11.
18,579	32,536	13,578	1,352	722	681	618	269	12.
8,474	15,375	8,096	24,625	44,930	26,874	2,264	4,212	13.
5,480	3,930	1,334	600	1,203	670	989	1,399	14.
25,441	25,882	13,372	9,775	15,237	26,432	11,617	30,030	15.
42,478	3,571	4,470	1,520	1,294	1,763	1,454	658	16.
4,558	6,332	1,952	1,665	2,236	1,365	1,675	1,177	17.
2,067	5,611	1,432	1,970	2,379	1,198	788	635	18.
415	6,897	1,371	529	290	1,509	70	124	19.
28,248	20,893	9,250	10,566	11,913	9,134	12,090	8,379	20.
805	867	208	321	455	272	228	143	21.
17,205	18,031	6,225	7,437	7,802	5,419	7,763	5,141	22.
2,977	3,611	1,354	1,266	1,917	1,301	1,561	939	23.
1,064	848	649	408	463	366	501	265	24.
10,896	9,131	6,266	4,576	5,236	4,399	6,635	3,913	25.
53,330	46,714	31,422	21,607	25,664	20,598	34,984	18,299	26.
3,332	2,946	1,520	1,422	1,327	1,228	1,680	1,356	27.
38,330	27,333	15,054	14,047	13,680	9,222	13,425	7,802	N.C.
405,638	324,250	165,757	162,407	197,372	148,299	185,810	120,734	
1,006,758	730,531	383,011	386,514	438,642	326,641	463,061	277,035	

	East Midlands	North West		Yorks. & Humberside		North		
	33.Rut-land	34. Cheshire	35.Lancs.	36. West Riding	37. East Riding	38. North Riding	39.West-morland	40.Cum-berland
1.	3,520	30,198	57,139	59,428	25,731	28,626	7,325	18,653
2.	43	5,937	76,198	70,554	935	9,235	476	12,538
3.	434	11,649	68,310	39,244	7,840	5,367	1,087	4,240
4.	-	-	-	-	-	-	-	-
5.	11	4,635	11,440	4,560	2,583	354	123	367
6.	116	8,051	61,024	45,117	4,231	12,245	380	5,133
7.	13	7,140	35,564	23,904	2,893	1,736	141	1,171
8.	8	356	3,379	1,456	340	209	52	193
9.	-	36	251	112	7	5	4	3
10.	-	1,682	7,570	507	1,692	1,408	10	635
11.	55	1,563	7,879	4,737	996	370	65	232
12.	14	928	9,976	38,838	523	1,451	77	398
13.	129	46,041	488,363	271,115	2,933	1,718	1,410	4,932
14.	52	1,154	6,869	7,583	1,327	545	172	495
15.	582	21,990	99,463	59,651	10,906	9,140	1,990	7,695
16.	58	2,224	13,697	9,333	1,015	777	27	416
17.	54	2,856	22,672	11,694	3,122	1,103	636	1,005
18.	23	1,684	21,387	9,090	1,506	709	315	820
19.	3	218	3,516	1,746	407	49	32	169
20.	714	17,652	94,615	60,833	11,363	8,895	2,384	7,592
21.	9	509	4,669	2,846	300	218	47	180
22.	290	19,430	121,803	43,473	14,141	6,558	923	5,466
23.	43	2,320	18,795	8,435	1,600	1,034	209	897
24.	15	1,204	6,391	2,954	531	464	78	345
25.	368	8,431	39,424	23,719	5,510	4,153	924	3,011
26.	2,431	48,428	189,555	101,088	27,640	23,744	5,510	17,314
27.	92	3,171	16,028	7,985	3,553	1,282	247	1,077
N.C.	519	25,300	150,246	63,525	13,614	10,822	1,749	7,926
Total Employed	9,596	274,787	1,636,223	973,527	147,239	132,217	26,393	102,903
Total Population	23,007	622,356	3,485,819	2,197,999	362,375	334,385	64,314	250,647

		Wales		Scotland				
41.North-umberland	42.Durham	43.Glam-organ & Monmouth	44.North & West Wales	45.Strathclyde	46.Dumfries & Galloway	47.Borders	48.Lothian	
20,586	15,124	20,271	89,756	46,037	20,164	15,867	17,090	1.
22,974	71,025	64,966	37,443	54,185	1,385	233	10,084	2.
8,033	12,295	10,427	11,911	33,467	2,881	2,221	12,626	3.
-	-	-	-	-	-	-	-	4.
1,225	6,356	1,331	1,454	4,758	144	117	2,348	5.
6,829	26,913	34,609	11,429	45,650	1,100	730	6,117	6.
5,361	11,240	4,320	1,323	23,422	287	522	2,733	7.
281	466	324	447	1,166	130	88	524	8.
24	34	28	3	38	2	2	21	9.
4,518	10,952	1,684	1,974	14,864	47	22	621	10.
500	777	921	1,016	1,570	142	88	607	11.
862	1,537	1,296	899	4,642	219	126	1,471	12.
2,415	4,057	3,278	7,936	89,175	3,258	11,838	4,419	13.
979	703	620	1,330	3,332	271	281	1,428	14.
11,866	17,676	17,692	22,863	50,144	4,660	3,267	15,405	15.
1,796	5,397	1,420	1,420	5,812	124	71	1,586	16.
2,478	3,772	2,498	2,424	12,278	588	424	4,681	17.
1,764	2,499	1,435	1,598	11,435	276	483	10,066	18.
193	184	146	79	1,241	22	48	1,058	19.
11,885	21,505	19,109	21,132	44,793	5,166	4,380	17,335	20.
278	615	409	289	1,597	75	74	655	21.
14,223	23,984	25,393	13,341	45,627	2,424	1,373	14,029	22.
1,954	2,816	1,995	2,627	8,605	653	416	2,841	23.
673	919	838	915	2,695	249	175	1,375	24.
5,051	8,390	8,812	9,513	15,638	1,866	1,413	9,076	25.
29,073	38,912	43,131	64,965	73,916	10,455	7,402	37,108	26.
2,239	2,527	2,534	4,846	7,544	627	458	4,817	27.
16,024	34,510	35,443	25,276	68,418	3,646	2,797	17,628	N.C.
174,084	325,185	304,930	338,209	672,049	60,861	54,916	197,749	
434,086	875,166	752,715	824,844	1,562,024	156,905	127,899	471,351	

TOTAL EMPLOYMENT: 1881

Scotland

	49.Central & Fife	50.Tayside	51.Grampian	52.Highland	53. South East	54. East Anglia	55. South West	56. West Midlands
1.	17,505	27,884	55,850	62,428	330,234	142,966	212,072	120,823
2.	12,658	1,418	2,461	666	13,919	1,933	37,741	59,107
3.	6,161	8,242	7,339	3,103	184,836	21,313	47,055	46,287
4.	–	–	–	–	–	–	–	–
5.	582	399	596	119	20,903	1,696	3,559	4,682
6.	6,194	4,081	3,298	1,387	55,494	8,089	18,747	85,240
7.	1,610	3,164	1,185	225	33,245	2,777	8,654	19,775
8.	183	296	343	158	10,798	675	1,684	6,591
9.	–	8	5	2	1,670	39	64	136
10.	446	1,079	964	449	14,178	1,250	4,603	604
11.	223	390	397	229	20,190	3,218	5,879	8,859
12.	601	575	456	234	21,864	1,184	3,836	65,527
13.	24,059	57,902	7,331	6,850	74,973	11,334	36,640	33,737
14.	362	750	539	159	32,710	4,351	6,352	11,503
15.	6,719	10,773	10,164	5,792	331,756	38,977	104,816	74,420
16.	990	286	205	56	24,110	2,766	4,736	52,281
17.	1,530	2,333	2,926	1,240	82,302	4,729	14,774	14,705
18.	1,534	1,512	3,156	366	84,431	4,089	9,822	9,889
19.	792	177	905	20	15,117	245	1,166	8,803
20.	7,845	11,386	9,890	6,564	268,196	25,442	73,040	69,237
21.	227	372	244	42	9,665	560	1,368	2,058
22.	6,135	8,172	6,564	3,882	263,896	18,519	52,894	46,211
23.	1,093	1,788	1,599	1,085	41,840	5,091	9,693	9,048
24.	455	684	672	337	17,371	1,089	2,989	3,023
25.	3,067	4,439	4,943	2,778	164,739	16,413	41,349	32,010
26.	13,350	18,959	24,816	14,998	831,304	81,725	206,315	165,915
27.	1,335	1,749	1,497	2,095	114,805	5,207	28,529	9,891
N.C.	9,158	13,972	11,610	6,158	339,744	23,813	69,369	93,858
Total Employed	124,814	182,790	159,955	121,422	3,404,290	429,490	1,007,746	1,054,220
Total Population	303,039	406,265	409,403	298,687	7,930,714	1,035,593	2,384,180	2,504,337

57. East Midlands	58. North West	59.Yorks. & Humberside	60. North	61. Wales	62. Scotland	63.Great Britain	
148,884	87,337	85,159	90,314	110,027	262,825	1,590,641	1.
51,062	82,135	71,489	116,248	102,409	83,090	619,133	2.
36,964	79,959	47,084	31,022	22,338	76,040	592,898	3.
-	-	-	-	-		-	4.
2,721	16,075	7,143	8,425	2,785	9,063	77,052	5.
23,164	69,075	49,348	51,500	46,038	68,557	475,252	6.
11,838	42,704	26,797	19,649	5,643	33,148	204,230	7.
1,216	3,735	1,796	1,201	771	2,888	31,355	8.
106	287	119	70	31	78	2,600	9.
813	9,252	2,199	17,523	3,658	18,492	72,572	10.
6,106	9,442	5,733	1,944	1,937	3,646	66,954	11.
3,656	10,904	39,361	4,325	2,195	8,324	161,176	12.
103,034	534,404	274,048	14,532	11,214	204,832	1,298,748	13.
4,913	8,023	8,910	2,894	1,950	7,122	88,728	14.
93,673	121,453	70,557	48,367	40,555	106,924	1,031,498	15.
6,747	15,921	10,348	8,413	2,840	9,130	137,292	16.
8,172	25,528	14,816	8,994	4,922	26,000	204,942	17.
6,993	23,071	10,596	6,107	3,033	28,828	186,859	18.
2,525	3,734	2,153	627	225	4,263	38,858	19.
52,796	112,267	72,196	52,261	40,241	107,359	873,035	20.
1,428	5,178	3,146	1,338	698	3,286	28,725	21.
33,852	141,233	57,614	51,154	38,734	88,206	792,313	22.
7,027	21,115	10,035	6,910	4,622	18,080	133,461	23.
2,018	7,595	3,485	2,479	1,753	6,642	48,444	24.
25,127	47,855	29,229	21,529	18,325	43,220	439,796	25.
123,583	237,983	128,728	114,553	108,096	201,004	2,199,206	26.
7,105	19,199	11,538	7,372	7,380	20,122	231,148	27.
58,695	175,546	77,139	71,031	60,719	133,387	1,103,301	N.C.
824,218	1,911,010	1,120,766	760,782	643,139	1,574,556	12,730,217	
1,914,900	4,108,184	2,560,374	1,958,598	1,577,559	3,735,573	29,710,012	

MALE EMPLOYMENT: 1891

<u>South East</u>

	1. London	2. Middlesex	3. Kent	4. Surrey	5. Sussex	6. Hants.	7. Berks.	8. Oxon
1.	13,868	15,492	54,351	26,246	40,045	34,442	23,183	20,010
2.	7,519	944	1,913	921	988	1,029	340	412
3.	97,190	12,265	17,223	12,714	13,437	13,094	7,591	3,892
4.	-	-	-	-	-	-	-	-
5.	13,717	1,771	1,321	1,153	683	734	230	145
6.	32,465	2,787	4,939	2,492	2,710	4,415	2,196	1,286
7.	22,343	3,398	4,075	876	1,000	2,974	573	286
8.	7,135	753	584	566	476	492	173	110
9.	4,801	577	203	243	161	179	71	21
10.	4,576	194	3,439	206	302	4,791	108	80
11.	10,406	1,314	2,075	1,351	1,654	1,503	735	441
12.	16,616	1,641	989	941	768	906	342	257
13.	23,438	2,177	2,115	1,780	1,754	1,677	670	973
14.	18,438	990	1,112	1,390	820	921	456	288
15.	71,838	4,205	5,150	4,258	4,208	5,306	2,213	2,008
16.	6,430	1,589	6,772	888	1,168	1,258	692	270
17.	53,128	3,239	4,043	2,276	3,060	3,317	1,362	1,047
18.	60,929	4,067	3,943	2,822	1,965	2,112	816	1,108
19.	11,862	1,647	476	464	244	206	132	99
20.	126,715	19,649	21,453	19,877	17,902	20,227	9,409	5,848
21.	8,566	1,086	809	702	681	556	260	152
22.	215,897	18,702	26,040	17,469	19,984	25,545	8,850	5,107
23.	21,296	1,418	2,281	1,425	1,869	2,309	596	483
24.	13,886	2,739	1,648	2,404	1,204	1,268	433	270
25.	51,512	7,939	7,022	7,400	6,340	5,951	2,419	1,812
26.	82,328	6,861	9,986	8,025	9,603	9,003	3,932	3,019
27.	52,611	5,963	22,152	16,309	4,786	26,749	2,590	969
N.C.	204,817	28,461	31,513	23,737	14,910	23,246	10,487	5,438
Total Employed	1,254,327	151,868	237,627	158,935	152,722	194,210	80,859	55,831
Total Population	1,990,748	268,776	394,321	269,417	255,443	321,273	131,926	90,794

9. Bucks.	10. Beds.	11. Herts.	12. Essex	13. Cambridge	14. Hunts.	15. Norfolk	16. Suffolk	
17,464	17,248	22,030	46,547	28,483	8,612	55,653	45,637	1.
292	388	406	1,950	483	71	875	444	2.
3,063	3,470	4,906	16,011	3,996	1,100	9,499	7,398	3.
-	-	-	-	-	-	-	-	4.
113	142	280	2,469	207	39	671	617	5.
947	1,335	1,175	5,846	1,027	295	3,454	3,365	6.
267	455	371	5,642	289	101	1,220	1,361	7.
86	81	142	604	122	41	315	215	8.
31	25	48	638	44	4	64	50	9.
36	10	35	1,806	53	2	601	401	10.
947	564	683	2,369	428	347	1,319	1,236	11.
178	193	218	1,222	195	60	754	390	12.
322	440	631	2,635	439	117	1,489	2,048	13.
360	243	448	1,386	388	92	1,292	943	14.
2,509	4,443	2,009	5,886	1,798	472	8,250	3,953	15.
397	568	328	2,023	309	102	753	857	16.
4,426	676	909	4,279	685	158	2,297	1,284	17.
929	415	1,016	3,606	874	145	1,555	1,227	18.
55	34	80	852	64	10	138	165	19.
4,954	4,672	6,829	21,834	5,018	1,165	11,465	8,287	20.
119	130	177	2,979	137	24	318	248	21.
3,744	3,440	6,009	33,618	5,820	1,028	12,164	9,308	22.
365	506	558	2,058	480	138	1,933	1,052	23.
220	248	383	1,891	275	76	800	505	24.
1,179	1,283	1,803	5,726	1,714	371	3,385	2,415	25.
1,891	1,529	2,946	6,999	2,524	396	4,543	3,250	26.
756	1,053	1,128	10,100	910	260	2,902	2,224	27.
4,784	3,570	6,946	35,598	4,343	833	9,975	6,642	N.C.
50,434	47,161	62,494	226,574	61,105	16,059	137,684	105,522	
80,880	77,988	104,525	378,425	96,219	24,750	221,688	172,067	

MALE EMPLOYMENT: 1891

South West   West Midlands

	17.Corn- wall	18.Devon	19.Som- erset	20.Gloucs.	21.Wilts.	22.Dorset	23.Here- ford	24.Shrops
1.	28,944	48,057	37,675	25,767	26,220	18,636	14,943	26,332
2.	13,862	3,299	7,928	5,976	1,072	1,255	472	5,555
3.	4,288	10,932	9,671	11,007	4,800	3,690	1,606	4,112
4.	–	–	–	–	–	–	–	–
5.	283	730	665	1,245	166	112	80	219
6.	3,138	4,037	3,568	4,672	2,789	1,175	776	4,485
7.	875	2,027	1,339	2,148	3,165	261	126	816
8.	162	504	341	402	135	123	58	167
9.	30	99	125	111	21	21	4	37
10.	1,067	2,618	252	459	8	105	10	22
11.	528	1,572	1,202	1,610	1,591	397	393	947
12.	383	966	791	1,217	308	223	142	572
13.	832	2,663	3,128	3,390	2,231	1,023	213	832
14.	501	1,546	1,462	1,295	623	315	182	463
15.	2,737	7,589	9,462	11,028	1,883	1,620	1,088	2,399
16.	186	869	1,394	1,052	364	707	156	1,402
17.	917	3,292	3,201	4,506	1,274	819	497	1,022
18.	488	2,451	2,487	2,553	525	397	272	520
19.	51	180	264	471	111	31	17	56
20.	8,463	19,987	15,460	16,197	8,052	5,939	3,170	6,613
21.	103	463	429	795	157	115	45	153
22.	7,574	17,518	14,487	19,683	7,552	6,327	2,753	6,709
23.	591	1,546	1,004	1,483	515	548	192	453
24.	527	1,278	924	1,236	399	300	227	474
25.	2,446	5,909	4,583	4,979	1,935	1,632	1,065	2,092
26.	1,786	6,478	4,533	5,495	2,211	1,924	1,193	2,839
27.	3,323	19,012	2,886	3,385	1,395	3,726	621	1,373
N.C.	6,295	17,845	15,207	22,662	9,113	6,027	3,724	8,094
Total Employed	90,380	183,467	144,468	154,824	78,615	57,448	34,025	78,758
Total Population	147,460	299,676	238,638	255,341	125,696	92,118	54,943	126,008

East Midlands

25.Staffs.	26.War-wick	27.Worcs.	28.Derby	29.Notts.	30.Leics.	31.Lincs.	32.North-ants.	
25,494	22,976	20,725	15,765	20,282	17,564	61,161	22,649	1.
50,830	6,699	3,503	25,607	31,454	8,205	1,876	1,619	2.
18,946	13,624	6,686	6,355	9,630	6,497	9,767	5,168	3.
-	-	-	-	-	-	-	-	4.
1,796	1,301	999	820	760	428	965	171	5.
44,040	29,235	12,373	9,552	5,314	2,746	6,893	2,375	6.
7,445	10,201	2,810	4,060	3,503	1,601	3,424	957	7.
675	4,624	310	330	308	214	296	144	8.
314	280	91	155	102	76	64	43	9.
363	127	92	10	29	11	819	27	10.
3,897	9,425	1,638	2,177	1,384	1,146	1,558	1,404	11.
11,695	20,797	8,108	1,196	725	696	632	321	12.
4,381	3,853	4,948	11,362	19,558	11,080	1,633	583	13.
5,918	2,692	1,305	656	1,192	791	913	1,867	14.
10,154	8,509	3,888	3,449	4,739	23,950	3,955	26,923	15.
30,443	3,212	3,771	1,480	1,108	1,490	1,117	771	16.
4,719	6,310	2,118	1,865	2,620	1,608	1,885	1,147	17.
2,259	4,114	1,581	1,727	2,420	1,258	1,005	655	18.
338	2,803	969	282	316	952	94	99	19.
28,523	21,535	10,104	12,873	11,025	9,396	10,872	8,512	20.
1,386	1,340	345	463	652	465	345	269	21.
25,265	23,697	9,868	11,353	11,552	8,810	13,985	8,351	22.
2,019	1,985	737	910	1,522	955	1,103	703	23.
1,714	1,349	1,060	644	800	602	717	433	24.
6,235	4,569	3,743	2,900	3,121	2,361	3,382	2,013	25.
7,413	7,340	3,509	3,300	4,148	3,276	3,445	2,335	26.
3,693	3,505	1,881	1,509	1,457	1,346	1,981	1,567	27.
40,988	28,967	16,719	16,931	13,487	8,817	11,168	7,109	N.C.
340,943	245,069	123,881	137,731	153,208	116,341	145,055	98,215	
551,087	388,534	200,205	216,103	245,338	183,003	230,773	152,918	

MALE EMPLOYMENT: 1891

	East Midlands	North West	Yorks. & Humberside		North			
	33.Rut-land	34.Cheshire	35.Lancs.	36. West Riding	37. East Riding	38.North Riding	39.West-morland	40.Cum-berland
1.	2,962	31,443	55,204	54,580	23,464	25,727	6,825	16,977
2.	123	6,088	92,849	89,995	1,158	6,900	551	13,469
3.	379	11,942	65,084	39,784	8,322	5,537	867	3,666
4.	-	-	-	-	-	-	-	-
5.	10	5,821	14,690	5,255	2,699	533	142	386
6.	108	7,429	68,618	50,431	4,129	12,297	441	5,927
7.	13	8,095	44,361	32,768	3,853	2,482	192	1,385
8.	12	386	3,095	1,680	387	226	48	179
9.	3	190	1,354	757	78	64	6	37
10.	-	2,451	7,768	413	2,383	2,992	14	362
11.	53	1,820	8,364	5,926	1,038	337	57	266
12.	15	1,256	10,672	36,418	589	1,166	81	334
13.	47	19,248	226,837	140,054	1,827	1,163	809	1,839
14.	39	1,298	6,836	7,671	1,347	457	156	549
15.	275	10,819	37,129	28,592	3,824	3,445	964	2,822
16.	28	1,641	12,685	11,032	891	452	23	347
17.	51	3,045	23,296	13,441	3,259	1,135	597	878
18.	28	2,075	21,007	9,727	1,771	773	297	895
19.	3	312	4,257	1,929	460	96	32	165
20.	693	23,489	98,004	63,353	10,827	8,778	2,176	7,032
21.	12	795	6,523	4,460	588	362	803	187
22.	746	27,995	152,441	61,171	21,784	9,690	1,425	7,281
23.	34	1,513	11,339	6,885	1,113	861	107	521
24.	42	2,015	9,591	4,633	765	596	120	491
25.	215	5,555	24,359	15,496	3,224	2,768	610	2,107
26.	314	5,457	32,009	16,600	3,497	3,095	596	1,670
27.	101	3,067	18,271	9,024	3,548	1,654	280	1,132
N.C.	460	32,218	176,130	76,409	14,904	14,218	2,162	8,847
Total Employed	6,766	217,463	1,232,773	788,484	121,729	107,804	20,381	79,751
Total Population	10,984	342,935	1,905,115	1,200,332	196,249	177,172	32,385	132,080

		Wales		Scotland				
41.North- umberland	42.Durham	43.Glam- organ & Monmouth	44.North & West Wales	45.Strathclyde	46.Dumfries & Galloway	47.Borders	48.Lothian	
16,559	14,180	19,664	79,366	35,808	16,706	12,305	12,720	1.
29,322	85,930	107,815	36,526	61,466	1,330	253	14,897	2.
7,527	12,466	12,477	10,100	32,673	2,596	2,116	13,724	3.
-	-	-	-	-	-	-	-	4.
890	6,390	1,259	1,432	4,805	162	131	3,979	5.
7,751	27,670	31,858	12,490	49,232	889	703	6,055	6.
10,773	17,197	6,720	1,497	31,891	236	315	3,777	7.
327	542	475	448	1,380	115	83	639	8.
338	261	238	76	454	3	13	112	9.
7,103	19,575	2,551	2,020	18,430	30	16	920	10.
576	1,047	1,474	1,056	2,202	191	85	704	11.
921	1,580	1,637	930	6,004	229	128	1,574	12.
1,883	2,922	2,562	5,182	29,372	1,857	7,813	2,643	13.
877	673	697	1,259	3,026	195	257	1,372	14.
4,730	5,816	6,471	8,136	18,339	1,673	1,421	6,023	15.
1,434	4,798	1,211	1,592	5,449	85	30	1,334	16.
2,650	3,967	3,008	2,118	11,745	488	376	4,123	17.
1,648	2,517	1,821	1,539	8,971	275	373	7,132	18.
217	224	186	69	1,130	24	42	1,224	19.
12,969	24,705	25,389	18,953	45,354	4,092	3,319	15,485	20.
562	1,159	827	321	2,713	85	77	877	21.
17,791	32,849	36,402	16,759	59,424	3,250	2,223	19,114	22.
1,059	2,217	1,968	1,209	4,008	391	259	1,073	23.
986	1,372	1,647	1,189	3,585	278	241	1,852	24.
3,469	5,606	6,774	7,307	12,329	1,401	960	7,340	25.
4,221	5,885	5,853	5,414	12,203	1,161	982	4,989	26.
3,055	2,884	3,614	4,981	9,437	704	522	5,430	27.
19,203	36,189	48,087	21,308	74,651	3,153	2,196	17,530	N.C.
158,841	320,621	332,685	243,277	546,081	41,599	37,239	156,642	
252,283	521,776	505,584	388,925	865,590	70,776	60,105	251,880	

MALE EMPLOYMENT: 1891

Scotland

	49.Central & Fife	50.Tayside	51.Grampian	52.Highland	53. South East	54. East Anglia	55. South West	56. W Mid
1.	14,604	23,052	49,889	49,171	330,926	138,385	185,299	110
2.	17,612	1,684	2,977	574	17,102	1,873	33,392	67
3.	5,853	7,533	6,789	2,982	204,856	21,993	44,388	44
4.	-	-	-	-	-		-	
5.	938	533	745	125	22,758	1,534	3,201	4
6.	7,490	3,927	3,254	1,297	62,593	8,141	19,379	90
7.	1,699	3,487	1,643	270	42,260	2,971	9,815	21
8.	250	310	361	176	11,202	693	1,667	5
9.	18	43	18	21	6,998	162	407	
10.	779	1,947	1,029	282	15,583	1,057	4,509	
11.	294	429	532	196	24,042	3,330	6,900	16
12.	702	803	513	285	24,271	1,399	3,888	41
13.	7,857	20,981	2,939	987	38,612	4,093	13,267	14
14.	489	841	439	135	26,852	2,715	5,742	10
15.	2,812	4,719	4,993	2,801	114,033	14,473	34,319	26
16.	951	311	160	56	22,383	2,021	4,572	38
17.	1,932	2,296	2,970	1,248	81,762	4,424	14,009	14
18.	1,349	1,396	2,018	378	83,728	3,801	8,901	8
19.	1,317	229	800	28	16,151	377	1,108	4
20.	8,560	10,142	9,032	5,767	279,369	25,935	74,098	69
21.	234	419	310	71	16,217	727	2,062	3
22.	9,040	10,233	9,247	4,863	384,405	28,320	73,141	68
23.	521	912	1,318	959	35,164	3,603	5,687	5
24.	574	802	884	382	26,594	1,656	4,664	4
25.	2,319	3,319	3,122	2,133	100,386	7,885	21,484	17
26.	2,333	3,116	2,092	1,992	146,122	10,713	22,427	22
27.	1,498	2,094	2,138	2,422	145,166	6,296	33,727	11
N.C.	9,977	10,521	9,342	5,112	393,507	21,793	77,149	98
Total Employed	102,002	116,079	119,554	84,713	2,673,042	320,370	709,202	822
Total Population	165,839	186,400	202,624	139,503	4,364,516	514,724	1,158,929	1,320

57. East Midlands	58. North West	59. Yorks. & Humberside	60. North	61. Wales	62. Scotland	63. Great Britain	
140,383	86,647	78,044	80,268	99,030	214,255	1,463,707	1.
68,884	98,937	91,153	136,172	144,341	100,793	759,706	2.
37,796	77,026	48,106	30,063	22,577	74,266	606,045	3.
-	-	-	-	-	-	-	4.
3,154	20,511	7,954	8,341	2,691	11,418	85,957	5.
26,988	76,047	54,560	54,086	44,348	72,847	509,898	6.
13,558	52,456	36,621	32,029	8,217	43,318	262,643	7.
1,304	3,481	2,067	1,322	923	3,314	31,807	8.
443	1,544	835	706	314	682	12,817	9.
896	10,219	2,796	30,046	4,571	23,433	93,724	10.
7,722	10,184	6,964	2,283	2,530	4,633	84,888	11.
3,585	11,928	37,007	4,082	2,567	10,238	140,279	12.
44,263	246,085	141,881	8,616	7,744	74,449	593,237	13.
5,458	8,134	9,018	2,712	1,956	6,754	79,901	14.
63,291	47,948	32,416	17,777	14,607	42,781	407,683	15.
5,994	14,326	11,923	7,054	2,803	8,376	118,436	16.
9,176	26,341	16,700	9,227	5,126	25,178	206,609	17.
7,093	23,082	11,498	6,130	3,360	21,892	178,231	18.
1,746	4,569	2,389	734	255	4,794	36,306	19.
53,371	121,493	74,180	55,660	44,342	101,751	900,144	20.
2,206	7,318	5,048	3,073	1,148	4,786	45,854	21.
54,797	180,436	82,955	69,036	53,161	117,394	1,111,937	22.
5,227	12,852	7,998	4,765	3,177	9,441	93,300	23.
3,238	11,606	5,398	3,565	2,836	8,598	72,979	24.
13,992	29,914	18,720	14,560	14,081	32,923	271,649	25.
16,818	37,466	20,097	15,467	11,267	28,868	331,539	26.
7,961	21,338	12,572	9,005	8,595	24,245	279,978	27.
57,972	208,348	91,313	80,619	69,395	132,482	1,231,070	N.C.
657,316	1,450,236	910,213	687,398	575,962	1,203,909	10,010,324	
1,039,119	2,248,050	1,396,581	1,115,696	894,509	1,942,717	15,995,618	

FEMALE EMPLOYMENT: 1891

South East

	1. London	2. Middlesex	3. Kent	4. Surrey	5. Sussex	6. Hants.	7. Berks.	8. Oxon.
1.	1,299	996	1,496	507	552	823	895	466
2.	113	16	31	25	27	22	23	16
3.	19,546	1,717	2,257	1,710	1,885	2,163	923	620
4.	–	–	–	–	–	–	–	–
5.	3,096	473	165	112	47	14	10	3
6.	1,021	23	28	17	26	23	28	10
7.	190	38	14	4	9	19	3	–
8.	474	35	7	7	16	25	7	3
9.	129	148	2	3	1	1	–	–
10.	43	1	3	3	2	10	–	2
11.	124	11	9	10	9	4	5	8
12.	1,698	76	49	63	59	58	11	18
13.	19,775	1,604	1,868	1,379	1,354	1,622	575	883
14.	8,159	172	63	49	51	83	17	11
15.	145,005	8,809	11,890	8,443	9,583	14,132	4,992	4,427
16.	947	71	85	60	57	79	18	15
17.	7,064	266	260	199	256	303	104	66
18.	26,354	617	2,000	510	446	625	176	283
19.	2,815	249	83	50	63	38	13	14
20.	465	25	23	26	28	33	16	10
21.	134	1	2	4	1	–	–	–
22.	3,208	214	222	154	184	191	76	55
23.	8,326	515	1,114	653	727	818	310	232
24.	270	34	12	14	11	10	5	1
25.	43,568	7,120	8,121	7,264	7,261	6,387	2,853	1,934
26.	351,239	50,764	62,493	59,983	60,974	53,382	21,548	14,810
27.	2,727	534	439	490	305	391	186	154
N.C.	20,172	1,279	1,022	693	630	655	350	208
Total Employed	667,961	75,808	93,758	82,432	84,564	81,911	33,144	24,249
Total Population	2,220,995	306,223	411,976	302,675	299,099	344,977	136,431	97,426

East Anglia

9. Bucks.	10. Beds.	11. Herts.	12. Essex	13. Cambridge	14. Hunts.	15. Norfolk	16. Suffolk	
250	172	259	654	1,209	244	1,376	631	1.
3	3	5	17	7	2	14	11	2.
505	591	601	2,327	720	178	1,745	1,185	3.
-	-	-	-	-	-	-	-	4.
4	5	14	332	3	-	240	14	5.
15	5	6	67	3	1	21	32	6.
-	3	4	28	5	-	14	1	7.
5	2	8	40	5	-	12	8	8.
-	-	-	41	-	-	-	1	9.
-	-	-	4	2	-	3	3	10.
20	2	3	14	5	1	10	9	11.
12	16	17	49	18	4	49	18	12.
1,658	1,972	798	5,257	436	223	3,704	1,827	13.
241	16	148	267	41	2	888	701	14.
3,350	13,443	6,146	13,560	3,582	806	11,347	8,845	15.
13	9	20	78	11	1	34	33	16.
628	164	51	235	53	9	195	83	17.
523	80	582	672	275	86	643	391	18.
12	11	11	214	17	1	31	21	19.
9	4	17	37	9	6	25	13	20.
-	-	-	2	1	-	-	-	21.
41	48	53	221	49	22	109	74	22.
158	158	230	916	224	44	773	472	23.
-	2	7	29	6	-	2	-	24.
1,320	1,502	2,074	6,386	1,681	464	4,173	3,120	25.
10,579	10,546	15,508	41,059	14,381	3,505	29,689	23,931	26.
109	99	191	549	108	29	334	223	27.
106	98	179	1,447	136	17	679	341	N.C.
19,561	28,951	26,932	74,502	22,978	5,645	56,110	41,988	
83,562	88,011	110,654	382,766	100,050	25,539	238,674	181,691	

FEMALE EMPLOYMENT: 1891

South West   West Midlands

	17.Corn-wall	18. Devon	19.Som-erset	20.Gloucs.	21.Wilts.	22.Dorset	23.Here-ford	24.Shrops
1.	1,241	1,378	1,523	1,048	1,029	683	717	1,017
2.	1,298	60	37	25	11	6	2	193
3.	2,198	2,973	2,683	3,766	965	766	339	987
4.	-	-	-	-	-	-	-	-
5.	192	78	34	201	3	6	8	22
6.	142	22	23	41	18	7	12	24
7.	6	14	6	17	9	2	-	4
8.	-	15	8	19	1	4	-	5
9.	-	-	-	2	-	-	-	-
10.	1	11	2	2	-	-	-	-
11.	-	4	8	9	10	6	-	2
12.	38	87	55	279	11	16	12	33
13.	1,632	4,530	4,297	5,641	3,197	1,451	198	519
14.	42	209	318	166	33	32	2	45
15.	7,854	17,314	18,269	18,960	3,915	4,503	1,757	3,747
16.	32	152	83	173	23	43	45	289
17.	67	380	246	408	112	60	46	53
18.	131	872	1,127	1,487	110	97	49	100
19.	7	48	31	213	19	17	4	95
20.	13	28	25	32	14	5	9	7
21.	-	-	1	-	-	-	-	-
22.	98	174	144	196	57	47	47	117
23.	345	1,175	627	1,211	233	217	152	300
24.	5	10	5	9	2	1	-	-
25.	2,405	6,298	5,181	5,815	2,275	1,788	988	1,824
26.	21,073	52,994	40,058	43,638	15,822	13,587	9,297	19,847
27.	271	358	358	406	186	158	106	187
N.C.	161	749	705	1,019	224	157	92	80
Total Employed	39,252	89,933	75,854	84,783	28,279	23,659	13,882	29,497
Total Population	171,123	336,549	271,438	293,545	129,423	96,877	58,403	128,757

25.Staffs.	26.Warwick	27.Worcs.	28.Derby	29.Notts.	30.Leics.	31.Lincs.	32.Northants.	
1,128	686	1,107	844	530	481	1,426	381	1.
344	90	57	42	78	25	16	13	2.
4,368	4,185	2,266	1,773	3,331	2,438	2,127	943	3.
-	-	-	-	-	-	-	-	4.
333	1,076	110	35	35	40	35	11	5.
1,449	5,879	793	43	24	12	37	7	6.
142	457	53	29	44	18	10	5	7.
72	985	28	61	50	3	6	4	8.
18	5	-	15	-	4	1	-	9.
1	2	-	-	-	1	4	1	10.
43	575	55	31	24	11	14	9	11.
5,663	11,477	4,379	100	93	29	26	40	12.
5,298	7,697	4,308	14,568	26,167	18,471	960	1,295	13.
2,241	1,589	404	37	237	59	75	97	14.
18,131	17,130	9,662	6,743	8,990	16,656	7,209	15,944	15.
20,327	442	1,343	384	98	178	39	22	16.
322	2,047	303	202	184	167	176	32	17.
989	3,518	891	828	778	799	143	485	18.
149	3,189	853	94	90	803	19	119	19.
457	165	49	16	24	13	23	15	20.
5	1	6	-	-	1	-	-	21.
708	1,873	268	82	529	259	107	120	22.
1,717	2,091	689	518	650	437	456	355	23.
31	35	22	4	7	6	4	2	24.
6,717	5,656	3,868	2,806	3,439	2,653	3,639	2,539	25.
48,756	40,420	29,452	20,559	23,139	17,966	31,903	16,278	26.
388	458	200	209	167	191	258	180	27.
2,802	8,675	1,461	413	863	529	163	313	N.C.
122,599	120,403	62,627	50,436	69,571	62,250	48,876	39,210	
552,365	413,204	222,325	216,311	259,973	196,283	236,508	155,154	

FEMALE EMPLOYMENT: 1891

East Midlands	North West	Yorks. & Humberside		North		
33.Rut- land	34.Cheshire	35.Lancs.	36. West Riding	37. East Riding	38. North Riding	39.West- morland	40.Cum- berland

	33.Rutland	34.Cheshire	35.Lancs.	36. West Riding	37. East Riding	38. North Riding	39.West-morland	40.Cumberland
1.	73	1,916	3,383	2,652	519	965	318	1,251
2.	3	32	2,286	213	11	16	2	180
3.	89	4,018	26,120	12,251	2,012	1,365	372	1,691
4.	-	-	-	-	-	-	-	-
5.	-	197	1,216	867	343	21	23	12
6.	1	37	344	625	25	16	2	59
7.	-	47	827	474	14	5	15	11
8.	-	4	160	119	10	-	-	5
9.	-	13	72	9	-	-	-	-
10.	-	8	44	3	7	-	-	1
11.	-	11	56	68	9	1	2	1
12.	-	94	1,013	6,969	33	46	8	15
13.	56	26,842	315,643	157,122	1,543	709	714	2,283
14.	1	100	1,111	959	63	15	26	5
15.	380	15,373	76,403	50,523	7,196	5,503	1,227	4,751
16.	3	91	1,318	799	55	95	8	38
17.	1	324	2,776	1,877	202	52	29	50
18.	8	643	8,948	3,449	541	186	116	269
19.	1	57	1,941	431	83	12	6	27
20.	-	30	249	322	33	9	5	10
21.	-	-	10	3	-	-	-	-
22.	7	345	2,256	990	155	79	31	82
23.	17	884	9,089	3,091	605	359	62	357
24.	-	21	123	45	7	5	-	3
25.	186	5,359	23,972	13,874	3,171	2,220	422	1,641
26.	1,927	46,117	180,522	97,106	26,150	22,573	5,148	16,463
27.	26	253	1,257	734	134	170	58	143
N.C.	11	573	8,063	2,868	392	191	33	200
Total Employed	2,790	103,389	669,202	358,443	43,313	34,613	8,627	29,548
Total Population	11,139	365,043	2,052,791	1,264,083	203,836	177,210	33,830	134,469

	Wales				Scotland				
41.Northumberland	42.Durham	43.Glamorgan & Monmouth	44.North & West Wales	45.Strathclyde	46.Dumfries & Galloway	47.Borders	48.Lothian	
3,280	1,203	1,263	8,148	5,844	2,522	2,814	3,560	1.
45	80	585	162	172	4	7	56	2.
2,472	3,546	3,614	4,517	13,373	877	594	4,282	3.
-	-	-	-	-	-	-	-	4.
193	212	120	36	931	1	-	204	5.
38	41	3,116	1,265	163	2	2	151	6.
22	36	11	4	347	3	7	6	7.
7	4	3	6	33	2	2	14	8.
4	-	-	-	44	1	-	2	9.
18	34	7	3	78	-	-	3	10.
2	2	7	-	2	-	-	2	11.
61	155	157	61	751	10	7	108	12.
1,066	2,783	1,949	3,014	55,490	1,744	7,258	3,137	13.
141	63	28	43	792	5	-	143	14.
8,066	14,080	16,640	15,322	37,702	2,675	1,955	11,189	15.
305	473	490	188	2,080	15	26	434	16.
167	223	123	97	2,749	25	11	495	17.
501	1,059	469	356	6,515	40	96	4,403	18.
62	43	90	47	660	7	74	634	19.
31	49	40	26	142	2	7	64	20.
-	1	4	1	2	1	-	2	21.
194	210	254	180	3,463	39	94	822	22.
1,077	1,556	1,174	805	6,084	268	212	1,862	23.
10	7	7	3	10	-	-	1	24.
2,888	4,949	5,589	4,092	7,542	751	566	3,856	25.
28,974	39,965	51,455	64,651	69,796	10,003	6,259	33,078	26.
233	296	322	465	692	129	70	328	27.
539	667	653	246	6,860	144	174	2,040	N.C.
50,396	71,737	88,170	103,738	222,317	19,270	20,235	70,876	
253,747	502,593	462,730	419,166	888,010	79,516	68,147	272,581	

FEMALE EMPLOYMENT: 1891

Scotland

	49.Central & Fife	50.Tayside	51.Grampian	52.Highland	53. South East	54. East Anglia	55. South West	56. West Midlands
1.	2,820	1,888	2,482	8,152	8,369	3,460	6,902	4,655
2.	437	8	5	5	301	34	1,437	686
3.	1,707	2,433	2,463	832	34,845	3,828	13,351	12,145
4.	-	-	-	-	-	-	-	-
5.	38	35	17	-	4,275	257	514	1,549
6.	59	20	12	8	1,269	57	253	8,157
7.	-	57	2	-	312	20	54	656
8.	4	4	2	1	629	25	47	1,090
9.	29	-	-	-	325	1	2	23
10.	1	2	1	-	68	8	16	3
11.	-	-	2	-	219	25	37	675
12.	27	14	38	1	2,126	89	486	21,564
13.	15,704	40,156	4,981	6,991	38,745	6,190	20,748	18,020
14.	17	106	26	1	9,277	1,632	800	4,281
15.	5,046	7,026	5,724	3,017	243,780	24,580	70,815	50,427
16.	320	65	47	4	1,452	79	506	22,446
17.	156	212	163	12	9,596	340	1,273	2,771
18.	821	404	2,007	44	32,868	1,395	3,824	5,547
19.	38	50	289	2	3,573	70	335	4,290
20.	13	15	15	-	693	53	117	687
21.	-	-	-	-	144	1	1	12
22.	185	310	332	36	4,667	254	716	3,013
23.	701	1,015	985	392	14,157	1,513	3,808	4,949
24.	4	-	1	-	395	8	32	88
25.	1,601	2,039	2,595	1,154	95,790	9,438	23,762	19,053
26.	13,620	17,324	30,883	16,292	752,885	71,506	187,172	147,772
27.	149	197	135	128	6,174	694	1,737	1,339
N.C.	845	1,355	1,554	220	26,839	1,173	3,015	13,110
Total Employed	44,342	74,735	54,761	37,292	1,293,773	126,730	341,760	349,008
Total Population	175,687	220,193	222,059	156,737	4,784,795	545,954	1,298,955	1,375,054

57. East Midlands	58. North West	59. Yorks. & Humberside	60. North	61. Wales	62. Scotland	63. Great Britain	
3,735	5,299	3,171	7,017	9,411	30,082	82,101	1.
177	2,318	224	323	747	694	6,941	2.
10,701	30,138	14,263	9,446	8,131	26,561	163,409	3.
-	-	-	-	-	-	-	4.
156	1,413	1,210	461	156	1,226	11,217	5.
124	381	650	156	4,381	417	15,845	6.
106	874	488	89	15	422	3,036	7.
124	164	129	16	9	62	2,295	8.
20	85	9	4	-	76	545	9.
6	52	10	53	10	85	311	10.
89	67	77	8	7	6	1,210	11.
288	1,107	7,002	285	218	956	34,121	12.
61,517	342,485	158,665	7,555	4,963	135,461	794,349	13.
506	1,211	1,022	250	71	1,090	20,140	14.
55,922	91,776	57,719	33,627	31,962	74,334	734,942	15.
724	1,409	854	919	678	2,991	32,058	16.
762	3,100	2,079	521	220	3,823	24,485	17.
3,041	9,591	3,990	2,131	825	14,330	77,542	18.
1,126	1,998	514	150	137	1,754	13,947	19.
91	279	355	104	66	258	2,703	20.
1	10	3	1	5	5	183	21.
1,104	2,601	1,145	596	434	5,281	19,811	22.
2,433	9,973	3,696	3,411	1,979	11,519	57,438	23.
23	144	52	25	10	16	793	24.
15,262	29,331	17,045	12,120	9,681	20,104	251,586	25.
111,772	226,639	123,256	113,123	116,106	197,255	2,047,486	26.
1,031	1,510	868	900	787	1,828	16,868	27.
2,292	8,636	3,260	1,630	899	13,192	74,046	N.C.
273,133	772,591	401,756	194,921	191,908	543,828	4,489,408	
1,075,368	2,417,834	1,467,919	1,101,849	881,896	2,082,930	17,032,554	

TOTAL EMPLOYMENT: 1891

South East

	1. London	2. Middlesex	3. Kent	4. Surrey	5. Sussex	6. Hants.	7. Berks.	8. Oxon.
1.	15,167	16,488	55,847	26,753	40,597	35,265	24,078	20,476
2.	7,632	960	1,944	946	1,015	1,051	363	428
3.	116,736	13,982	19,480	14,424	15,322	15,257	8,514	4,512
4.	–	–	–	–	–	–	–	–
5.	16,813	2,244	1,486	1,265	730	748	240	148
6.	33,486	2,810	4,967	2,509	2,736	4,438	2,224	1,296
7.	22,533	3,436	4,089	880	1,009	2,993	576	286
8.	7,609	788	591	573	492	517	180	113
9.	4,930	725	205	246	162	180	71	21
10.	4,619	195	3,442	209	304	4,801	108	82
11.	10,530	1,325	2,084	1,361	1,663	1,507	740	449
12.	18,314	1,717	1,038	1,004	827	964	353	275
13.	43,213	3,781	3,983	3,159	3,108	3,299	1,245	1,856
14.	26,597	1,162	1,175	1,439	871	1,004	473	299
15.	216,843	13,014	17,040	12,701	13,791	19,438	7,205	6,435
16.	7,377	1,660	6,857	948	1,225	1,337	710	285
17.	60,192	3,505	4,303	2,475	3,316	3,620	1,466	1,113
18.	87,283	4,684	5,943	3,332	2,411	2,737	992	1,391
19.	14,677	1,896	559	514	307	244	145	113
20.	127,180	19,674	21,476	19,903	17,930	20,260	9,425	5,858
21.	8,700	1,087	811	706	682	556	260	152
22.	219,105	18,916	26,262	17,623	20,168	25,736	8,926	5,162
23.	29,622	1,933	3,395	2,078	2,596	3,127	906	715
24.	14,156	2,773	1,660	2,418	1,215	1,278	438	271
25.	95,080	15,059	15,143	14,664	13,601	12,338	5,272	3,746
26.	433,567	57,625	72,479	68,008	70,577	62,385	25,480	17,829
27.	55,338	6,497	22,591	16,799	5,091	27,140	2,776	1,123
N.C.	224,989	29,740	32,535	24,430	15,540	23,901	10,837	5,646
Total Employed	1,922,288	227,676	331,385	241,367	237,286	276,121	114,003	80,080
Total Population	4,211,743	574,999	806,297	572,092	554,542	666,250	268,357	188,220

East Anglia

9. Bucks.	10. Beds.	11. Herts.	12. Essex	13. Cambridge	14. Hunts.	15. Norfolk	16. Suffolk	
17,714	17,420	22,289	47,201	29,692	8,856	57,029	46,268	1.
295	391	411	1,967	490	73	889	455	2.
3,568	4,061	5,507	18,338	4,716	1,278	11,244	8,583	3.
-	-	-	-	-	-	-	-	4.
117	147	294	2,801	210	39	911	631	5.
962	1,340	1,181	5,913	1,030	296	3,475	3,397	6.
267	458	375	5,670	294	101	1,234	1,362	7.
91	83	150	644	127	41	327	223	8.
31	25	48	679	44	4	64	51	9.
36	10	35	1,810	55	2	604	404	10.
967	566	686	2,383	433	348	1,329	1,245	11.
190	209	235	1,271	213	64	803	408	12.
1,980	2,412	1,429	7,892	875	340	5,193	3,875	13.
601	259	596	1,653	429	94	2,180	1,644	14.
5,859	17,886	8,155	19,446	5,380	1,278	19,597	12,798	15.
410	577	348	2,101	320	103	787	890	16.
5,054	840	960	4,514	738	167	2,492	1,367	17.
1,452	495	1,598	4,278	1,149	231	2,198	1,618	18.
67	45	91	1,066	81	11	169	186	19.
4,963	4,676	6,846	21,871	5,027	1,171	11,490	8,300	20.
119	130	177	2,981	138	24	318	248	21.
3,785	3,488	6,062	33,839	5,869	1,050	12,273	9,382	22.
523	664	788	2,974	704	182	2,706	1,524	23.
220	250	390	1,920	281	76	802	505	24.
2,499	2,785	3,877	12,112	3,395	835	7,558	5,535	25.
12,470	12,075	18,454	48,058	16,905	3,901	34,232	27,181	26.
865	1,152	1,319	10,649	1,018	289	3,236	2,447	27.
4,890	3,668	7,125	37,045	4,479	850	10,654	6,983	N.C.
69,995	76,112	89,426	301,076	84,092	21,704	193,794	147,510	
164,442	165,999	215,179	761,191	196,269	50,289	460,362	353,758	

TOTAL EMPLOYMENT: 1891

South West   West Midlands

	17.Cornwall	18. Devon	19.Somerset	20.Gloucs.	21.Wilts.	22.Dorset	23.Hereford	24.Shrops
1.	30,185	49,435	39,198	26,815	27,249	19,319	15,660	27,349
2.	15,160	3,359	7,965	6,001	1,083	1,261	474	5,748
3.	6,486	13,905	12,354	14,773	5,765	4,456	1,945	5,099
4.	-	-	-	-	-	-	-	-
5.	475	808	699	1,446	169	118	88	241
6.	3,280	4,059	3,591	4,713	2,807	1,182	788	4,509
7.	881	2,041	1,345	2,165	3,174	263	126	820
8.	162	519	349	421	136	127	58	172
9.	30	99	125	113	21	21	4	37
10.	1,068	2,629	254	461	8	105	10	22
11.	528	1,576	1,210	1,619	1,601	403	393	949
12.	421	1,053	846	1,496	319	239	154	605
13.	2,464	7,193	7,425	9,031	5,428	2,474	411	1,351
14.	543	1,755	1,780	1,461	656	347	184	508
15.	10,591	24,903	27,731	29,988	5,798	6,123	2,845	6,146
16.	218	1,021	1,477	1,225	387	750	201	1,691
17.	984	3,672	3,447	4,914	1,386	879	543	1,075
18.	619	3,323	3,614	4,040	635	494	321	620
19.	58	228	295	684	130	48	21	151
20.	8,476	20,015	15,485	16,229	8,066	5,944	3,179	6,620
21.	103	463	430	795	157	115	45	153
22.	7,672	17,692	14,631	19,879	7,609	6,374	2,800	6,826
23.	936	2,721	1,631	2,694	748	765	344	753
24.	532	1,288	929	1,245	401	301	227	474
25.	4,851	12,207	9,764	10,794	4,210	3,420	2,053	3,916
26.	22,859	59,472	44,591	49,133	18,033	15,511	10,490	22,686
27.	3,594	19,370	3,244	3,791	1,581	3,884	727	1,560
N.C.	6,456	18,594	15,912	23,681	9,337	6,184	3,816	8,174
Total Employed	129,632	273,400	220,322	239,607	106,894	81,107	47,907	108,255
Total Population	318,583	636,225	510,076	548,886	255,119	188,995	113,346	254,765

East Midlands

25.Staffs.	26.War-wick	27.Worcs.	28.Derby	29.Notts.	30.Leics.	31.Lincs.	32.North-ants.	
26,622	23,662	21,832	16,609	20,812	18,045	62,587	23,030	1.
51,174	6,789	3,560	25,649	31,532	8,230	1,892	1,632	2.
23,314	17,809	8,952	8,128	12,961	8,935	11,894	6,111	3.
-	-	-	-	-	-	-	-	4.
2,129	2,377	1,109	855	795	468	1,000	182	5.
45,489	35,114	13,166	9,595	5,338	2,758	6,930	2,382	6.
7,587	10,658	2,863	4,089	3,547	1,619	3,434	962	7.
747	5,609	338	391	358	217	302	148	8.
332	285	91	170	102	80	65	43	9.
364	129	92	10	29	12	823	28	10.
3,940	10,000	1,693	2,208	1,408	1,157	1,572	1,413	11.
17,358	32,274	12,487	1,296	818	725	658	361	12.
9,679	11,550	9,256	25,930	45,725	29,551	2,593	1,878	13.
8,159	4,281	1,709	693	1,429	850	988	1,964	14.
28,285	25,639	13,550	10,192	13,729	40,606	11,164	42,867	15.
50,770	3,654	5,114	1,864	1,206	1,668	1,156	793	16.
5,041	8,357	2,421	2,067	2,804	1,775	2,061	1,179	17.
3,248	7,632	2,472	2,555	3,198	2,057	1,148	1,140	18.
487	5,992	1,822	376	406	1,755	113	218	19.
28,980	21,700	10,153	12,889	11,049	9,409	10,895	8,527	20.
1,391	1,341	351	463	652	466	345	269	21.
25,973	25,570	10,136	11,435	12,081	9,069	14,092	8,471	22.
3,736	4,076	1,426	1,428	2,172	1,392	1,559	1,058	23.
1,745	1,384	1,082	648	807	608	721	435	24.
12,952	10,225	7,611	5,706	6,560	5,014	7,021	4,552	25.
56,169	47,760	32,961	23,859	27,287	21,242	35,348	18,613	26.
4,081	3,963	2,081	1,718	1,624	1,537	2,239	1,747	27.
43,790	37,642	18,180	17,344	14,350	9,346	11,331	7,422	N.C.
463,542	365,472	186,508	188,167	222,779	178,591	193,931	137,425	
,103,452	801,738	422,530	432,414	505,311	379,286	467,281	308,072	

TOTAL EMPLOYMENT: 1891

	East Midlands	North West		Yorks. & Humberside		North		
	33.Rut-land	34.Cheshire	35.Lancs.	36. West Riding	37. East Riding	38. North Riding	39.West-morland	40.Cum-berland
1.	3,035	33,359	58,587	57,232	23,983	26,692	7,143	18,228
2.	126	6,120	95,135	90,208	1,169	6,916	553	13,649
3.	468	15,960	91,204	52,035	10,334	6,902	1,239	5,357
4.	−	−	−	−	−	−	−	−
5.	10	6,018	15,906	6,122	3,042	554	165	398
6.	109	7,466	68,962	51,056	4,154	12,313	443	5,986
7.	13	8,142	45,188	33,242	3,867	2,487	207	1,396
8.	12	390	3,255	1,799	397	226	48	184
9.	3	203	1,426	766	78	64	6	37
10.	−	2,459	7,812	416	2,390	2,992	14	363
11.	53	1,831	8,420	5,994	1,047	338	59	267
12.	15	1,350	11,685	43,387	622	1,212	89	349
13.	103	46,090	542,480	297,176	3,370	1,872	1,523	4,122
14.	40	1,398	7,947	8,630	1,410	472	182	554
15.	655	26,192	113,532	79,115	11,020	8,948	2,191	7,573
16.	31	1,732	14,003	11,831	946	547	31	385
17.	52	3,369	26,072	15,318	3,461	1,187	626	928
18.	36	2,718	29,955	13,176	2,312	959	413	1,164
19.	4	369	6,198	2,360	543	108	38	192
20.	693	23,519	98,253	63,675	10,860	8,787	2,181	7,042
21.	12	795	6,533	4,463	588	362	803	187
22.	753	28,340	154,697	62,161	21,939	9,769	1,456	7,363
23.	51	2,397	20,428	9,976	1,718	1,220	169	878
24.	42	2,036	9,714	4,678	772	601	120	494
25.	401	10,914	48,331	29,370	6,395	4,988	1,032	3,748
26.	2,241	51,574	212,531	113,706	29,647	25,668	5,744	18,133
27.	127	3,320	19,528	9,758	3,682	1,824	338	1,275
N.C.	471	32,791	184,193	79,277	15,296	14,409	2,195	9,047
Total Employed	9,556	320,852	1,901,975	1,146,927	165,042	142,417	29,008	109,299
Total Population	22,123	707,978	3,957,906	2,464,415	400,085	354,382	66,215	266,549

		Wales		Scotland				
41.North- umberland	42.Durham	43.Glam- organ & Monmouth	44.North & West Wales	45.Strathclyde	46.Dumfries & Galloway	47.Borders	48.Lothian	
19,839	15,383	20,927	87,514	41,652	19,228	15,119	16,280	1.
29,367	86,010	108,400	36,688	61,638	1,334	260	14,953	2.
9,999	16,012	16,091	14,617	46,046	3,473	2,710	18,006	3.
-	-	-	-	-	-	-	-	4.
1,083	6,602	1,379	1,468	5,736	163	131	4,183	5.
7,789	27,711	34,974	13,755	49,395	891	705	6,206	6.
10,795	17,233	6,731	1,501	32,238	239	322	3,783	7.
334	546	478	454	1,413	117	85	653	8.
342	261	238	76	498	4	13	114	9.
7,121	19,609	2,558	2,023	18,508	30	16	923	10.
578	1,049	1,481	1,056	2,204	191	85	706	11.
982	1,735	1,794	991	6,755	239	135	1,682	12.
2,949	5,705	4,511	8,196	84,862	3,601	15,071	5,780	13.
1,018	736	725	1,302	3,818	200	257	1,515	14.
12,796	19,896	23,111	23,458	56,041	4,348	3,376	17,212	15.
1,739	5,271	1,701	1,780	7,529	100	56	1,768	16.
2,817	4,190	3,131	2,215	14,494	513	387	4,618	17.
2,149	3,576	2,290	1,895	15,486	315	469	11,535	18.
279	267	276	116	1,790	31	116	1,858	19.
13,000	24,754	25,429	18,979	45,496	4,094	3,326	15,549	20.
562	1,160	831	322	2,715	86	77	879	21.
17,985	33,059	36,656	16,939	62,887	3,289	2,317	19,936	22.
2,136	3,773	3,142	2,014	10,092	659	471	2,935	23.
996	1,379	1,654	1,192	3,595	278	241	1,853	24.
6,357	10,555	12,363	11,399	19,871	2,152	1,526	11,196	25.
33,195	45,850	57,308	70,065	81,999	11,164	7,241	38,067	26.
3,288	3,180	3,936	5,446	10,129	833	592	5,758	27.
19,742	36,856	48,740	21,554	81,511	3,297	2,370	19,570	N.C.
209,237	392,358	420,855	347,015	768,398	60,869	57,474	227,518	
506,030	1,024,369	968,314	808,091	1,753,600	150,292	128,252	524,461	

TOTAL EMPLOYMENT: 1891

Scotland

	49.Central & Fife	50.Tayside	51.Grampian	52.Highland	53. South East	54. East Anglia	55. South West	56. We Midl
1.	17,424	24,940	52,371	57,323	339,295	141,845	192,201	115,
2.	18,049	1,692	2,982	579	17,403	1,907	34,829	67,
3.	7,560	9,966	9,252	3,814	239,701	25,821	57,739	57,
4.	-	-	-	-	-	-		
5.	976	568	762	125	27,033	1,791	3,715	5,
6.	7,549	3,947	3,266	1,305	63,862	8,198	19,632	99,
7.	1,699	3,544	1,645	270	42,572	2,991	9,869	22,
8.	254	314	363	177	11,831	718	1,714	6,
9.	47	43	18	21	7,323	163	409	
10.	780	1,949	1,030	282	15,651	1,065	4,525	
11.	294	429	534	196	24,261	3,355	6,937	16,
12.	729	817	551	286	26,397	1,488	4,374	62,
13.	23,561	61,137	7,920	7,978	77,357	10,283	34,015	32,
14.	506	947	465	136	36,129	4,347	6,542	14,
15.	7,858	11,745	10,717	5,818	357,813	39,053	105,134	76,
16.	1,271	376	207	60	23,835	2,100	5,078	61,
17.	2,088	2,508	3,133	1,260	91,358	4,764	15,282	17,
18.	2,170	1,800	4,025	422	116,596	5,196	12,725	14,
19.	1,355	279	1,089	30	19,724	447	1,443	8,
20.	8,573	10,157	9,047	5,767	280,062	25,988	74,215	70,
21.	234	419	310	71	16,361	728	2,063	3,
22.	9,225	10,543	9,579	4,899	389,072	28,574	73,857	71,
23.	1,222	1,927	2,303	1,351	49,321	5,116	9,495	10,
24.	578	802	885	382	26,989	1,664	4,696	4,
25.	3,920	5,358	5,717	3,287	196,176	17,323	45,246	36,
26.	15,953	20,440	32,975	18,284	899,007	82,219	209,599	170,
27.	1,647	2,291	2,273	2,550	151,340	6,990	35,464	12,
N.C.	10,822	11,876	10,896	5,332	420,346	22,966	80,164	111,
Total Employed	146,344	190,814	174,315	122,005	3,966,815	447,100	1,050,962	1,171,
Total Population	341,526	406,593	424,683	296,240	9,149,311	1,060,678	2,457,884	2,695,

57. East Midlands	58. North West	59. Yorks. & Humberside	60. North	61. Wales	62. Scotland	63. Great Britain	
144,118	91,946	81,215	87,285	108,441	244,337	1,545,808	1.
69,061	101,255	91,377	136,495	145,088	101,487	766,647	2.
48,497	107,164	62,369	39,509	30,708	100,827	769,454	3.
-	-	-	-	-	-	-	4.
3,310	21,924	9,164	8,802	2,847	12,644	97,174	5.
27,112	76,428	55,210	54,242	48,729	73,264	525,743	6.
13,664	53,330	37,109	32,118	8,232	43,740	265,679	7.
1,428	3,645	2,196	1,338	932	3,376	34,102	8.
463	1,629	844	710	314	758	13,362	9.
902	10,271	2,806	30,099	4,581	23,518	94,035	10.
7,811	10,251	7,041	2,291	2,537	4,639	86,098	11.
3,873	13,035	44,009	4,367	2,785	11,194	174,400	12.
105,780	588,570	300,546	16,171	12,707	209,910	1,387,586	13.
5,964	9,345	10,040	2,962	2,027	7,844	100,041	14.
119,213	139,724	90,135	51,404	46,569	117,115	1,142,625	15.
6,718	15,735	12,777	7,973	3,481	11,367	150,494	16.
9,938	29,441	18,779	9,748	5,346	29,001	231,094	17.
10,134	32,673	15,488	8,261	4,185	36,222	255,773	18.
2,872	6,567	2,903	884	392	6,548	50,253	19.
53,462	121,772	74,535	55,764	44,408	102,009	902,847	20.
2,207	7,328	5,051	3,074	1,153	4,791	46,037	21.
55,901	183,037	84,100	69,632	53,595	122,675	1,131,748	22.
7,660	22,825	11,694	8,176	5,156	20,960	150,738	23.
3,261	11,750	5,450	3,590	2,846	8,614	73,772	24.
29,254	59,245	35,765	26,680	23,762	53,027	523,235	25.
128,590	264,105	143,353	128,590	127,373	226,123	2,379,025	26.
8,992	22,848	13,440	9,905	9,382	26,073	296,846	27.
60,264	216,984	94,573	82,249	70,294	145,674	1,305,116	N.C.
930,449	2,222,827	1,311,969	882,319	767,870	1,747,737	14,499,732	
2,114,487	4,665,884	2,864,500	2,217,545	1,776,405	4,025,647	33,028,172	

MALE EMPLOYMENT: 1901

South East

	1. London	2. Middlesex	3. Kent	4. Surrey	5. Sussex	6. Hants.	7. Berks.	8. Oxon.
1.	9,356	12,205	46,804	19,539	34,376	30,777	15,020	15,845
2.	8,575	1,459	3,826	1,425	1,292	1,809	335	553
3.	104,968	17,554	20,898	14,948	15,295	16,404	9,188	4,037
4.	–	–	–	–	–	–	–	–
5.	17,309	2,494	2,127	1,459	854	968	235	158
6.	28,734	3,400	5,634	2,309	2,432	4,387	2,073	1,122
7.	36,255	6,167	9,700	1,824	1,778	5,842	1,065	679
8.	7,072	1,085	678	670	521	499	171	102
9.	12,788	2,044	1,512	1,146	918	898	292	115
10.	3,731	512	4,629	171	277	5,631	96	101
11.	12,048	2,147	2,920	2,015	2,102	2,695	971	548
12.	24,428	3,286	1,904	1,644	1,361	1,665	584	346
13.	24,161	3,310	2,445	2,074	1,646	1,802	626	867
14.	19,238	1,550	1,448	1,560	778	986	389	317
15.	74,125	6,156	5,712	4,402	4,230	6,139	2,003	1,749
16.	7,735	2,013	10,742	1,556	1,880	1,766	1,029	275
17.	60,974	5,710	4,916	3,245	3,730	4,263	1,526	1,183
18.	63,566	6,983	5,637	3,766	2,286	2,652	1,033	1,268
19.	11,895	2,545	692	720	314	326	56	84
20.	154,037	38,075	36,951	32,835	26,401	30,580	10,746	6,940
21.	11,784	2,010	1,671	1,497	1,135	1,104	308	226
22.	234,746	29,391	30,412	18,195	18,734	28,786	6,730	4,587
23.	20,438	1,727	2,311	1,553	1,821	2,135	529	414
24.	19,077	4,942	2,727	3,724	1,708	1,916	551	401
25.	55,843	11,139	8,934	9,502	7,270	7,192	2,403	2,087
26.	108,114	13,498	21,314	21,111	18,867	19,066	8,789	5,723
27.	65,381	8,629	34,751	9,646	6,200	46,441	3,928	1,426
N.C.	203,651	36,073	29,381	24,485	12,827	23,227	6,499	4,123
Total Employed	1,399,969	226,104	300,676	187,021	171,033	249,956	77,175	55,276
Total Population	2,142,085	371,061	471,436	303,263	273,724	389,118	122,807	88,316

East Anglia

9. Bucks.	10. Beds.	11. Herts.	12. Essex	13. Cambridge	14. Hunts.	15. Norfolk	16. Suffolk	
16,131	13,692	16,445	41,826	24,100	7,691	50,566	40,372	1.
350	632	686	2,992	363	99	964	558	2.
3,795	3,648	6,064	23,883	4,020	1,139	10,788	8,427	3.
–	–	–	–	–	–	–	–	4.
176	170	734	5,510	227	49	956	765	5.
1,246	1,690	1,193	6,939	824	299	3,398	3,277	6.
700	1,473	1,083	11,158	504	148	1,900	2,967	7.
82	80	188	856	139	34	296	193	8.
167	209	251	3,039	139	15	460	208	9.
41	10	42	2,644	39	8	481	524	10.
2,741	564	878	3,796	477	347	1,428	1,262	11.
327	353	542	2,899	345	70	990	655	12.
303	410	666	4,079	393	86	1,262	2,032	13.
429	291	609	2,145	331	92	1,304	1,077	14.
2,450	5,048	2,290	8,481	1,495	393	8,443	3,600	15.
882	1,002	470	3,650	897	1,210	754	880	16.
5,088	865	1,334	7,559	705	166	2,760	1,672	17.
1,295	614	2,001	7,604	920	160	1,809	1,361	18.
82	34	139	2,150	61	10	217	240	19.
7,351	6,157	12,133	43,476	6,216	1,771	15,770	12,381	20.
228	221	353	4,840	147	65	440	437	21.
4,523	3,626	7,380	48,740	5,044	1,220	12,086	10,683	22.
373	458	503	2,639	443	117	1,652	965	23.
353	352	823	3,771	346	81	1,186	718	24.
1,476	1,387	2,717	9,344	1,689	410	3,660	2,814	25.
5,218	2,876	8,257	15,794	3,519	944	9,032	7,212	26.
969	1,095	1,981	13,928	997	295	3,262	3,039	27.
4,226	3,040	6,775	45,469	3,455	709	8,845	6,082	N.C
61,002	49,997	76,537	329,211	57,835	17,628	144,709	114,401	
96,486	80,448	123,719	535,602	89,658	26,735	228,429	181,846	

MALE EMPLOYMENT: 1901

<u>South West</u>   <u>West Midlands</u>

	17.Corn-wall	18. Devon	19.Som-erset	20.Gloucs.	21.Wilts.	22.Dorset	23.Here-ford	24.Shrops
1.	27,532	42,625	31,729	24,740	24,189	17,158	14,896	21,750
2.	13,625	3,521	7,029	11,178	1,604	1,566	281	5,902
3.	4,801	11,653	8,769	16,564	5,246	4,154	1,778	4,314
4.	–	–	–	–	–	–	–	–
5.	549	965	498	2,281	218	146	84	220
6.	2,624	3,993	2,506	5,987	3,240	1,191	647	4,335
7.	1,302	3,744	1,368	4,844	5,048	860	163	1,517
8.	152	437	258	501	146	120	41	134
9.	74	419	310	678	148	99	44	144
10.	874	3,502	84	457	9	126	7	19
11.	568	1,667	1,335	2,836	2,197	481	423	1,327
12.	500	1,303	863	2,487	499	331	187	890
13.	729	2,453	2,915	3,383	1,476	936	218	774
14.	444	1,444	1,202	1,951	770	284	191	378
15.	2,342	6,485	5,876	13,402	1,773	1,471	889	1,869
16.	230	1,090	1,419	1,708	369	874	207	1,700
17.	943	3,586	2,984	6,720	1,485	942	513	1,126
18.	559	2,771	2,228	4,223	581	468	227	475
19.	48	234	194	673	231	35	40	59
20.	10,350	25,766	15,909	26,151	12,165	7,873	4,053	8,395
21.	167	756	529	1,888	318	348	85	284
22.	7,749	18,559	10,612	25,959	7,329	5,216	2,186	5,650
23.	589	1,532	786	1,547	410	468	167	276
24.	736	1,826	1,169	2,145	543	433	256	594
25.	2,613	6,391	4,273	6,208	2,129	1,784	1,098	1,990
26.	3,168	11,182	8,012	11,553	5,218	4,614	2,830	4,787
27.	5,227	21,470	2,947	4,939	2,543	7,497	741	1,600
N.C.	5,555	18,220	9,127	21,805	6,364	5,113	2,683	5,753
Total Employed	94,050	197,594	124,931	206,808	86,248	64,588	34,935	76,262
Total Population	149,937	312,536	200,493	331,558	134,540	99,637	55,196	118,675

East Midlands

25.Staffs.	26.Warwick	27.Worcs.	28.Derby	29.Notts.	30.Leics.	31.Lincs.	32.Northants.	
22,508	18,603	20,320	17,166	16,543	14,656	59,022	18,374	1.
55,146	11,848	4,702	50,067	27,408	10,649	2,570	2,193	2.
22,656	26,206	8,337	9,297	11,002	7,958	11,473	6,010	3.
-	-	-	-	-	-	-	-	4.
2,253	2,181	1,815	1,148	1,015	569	1,054	223	5.
46,417	30,764	10,915	12,073	5,020	3,347	7,544	2,522	6.
14,909	14,990	4,099	7,716	5,702	3,267	7,580	1,375	7.
795	3,328	275	401	299	244	318	131	8.
1,679	1,519	403	683	649	592	207	162	9.
357	149	156	12	67	13	700	28	10.
5,652	15,385	3,290	3,065	2,483	1,665	1,908	1,334	11.
22,172	29,110	10,188	2,865	1,106	1,023	888	468	12.
4,445	3,415	4,425	11,610	15,992	10,242	1,606	570	13.
6,897	3,175	1,260	871	1,220	920	1,009	2,216	14.
9,892	8,432	3,937	4,022	4,377	27,117	3,681	31,043	15.
33,211	4,152	3,009	4,097	1,590	2,129	1,436	1,039	16.
6,626	8,661	2,464	2,538	4,277	2,303	2,688	1,497	17.
2,905	5,268	1,618	2,325	3,095	1,986	1,269	804	18.
460	2,900	1,216	348	441	1,171	128	162	19.
39,112	31,272	15,577	19,556	16,153	14,412	14,613	11,467	20.
2,239	2,532	747	1,038	1,137	1,051	528	481	21.
30,724	28,747	10,900	17,346	15,460	11,215	16,227	9,292	22.
2,048	2,058	758	1,027	1,486	968	1,071	692	23.
2,926	2,406	1,321	1,340	1,307	996	1,079	666	24.
7,249	5,957	3,726	3,706	3,349	2,745	3,558	2,261	25.
13,100	13,962	6,997	6,912	6,572	6,503	6,717	4,962	26.
4,891	5,001	2,339	2,296	1,992	1,975	2,405	1,955	27.
32,006	25,502	12,729	14,702	12,005	8,546	9,194	5,716	N.C.
393,275	297,523	137,523	198,227	161,747	138,262	160,473	107,643	
614,740	453,179	216,680	306,545	248,098	210,226	245,773	165,235	

MALE EMPLOYMENT: 1901

	East Midlands	North West		Yorks. & Humberside		North		
	33.Rut-land	34.Cheshire	35.Lancs.	36. West Riding	37. East Riding	38. North Riding	39.West-morland	40.Cum-berland
1.	2,351	28,610	48,880	46,235	24,607	25,280	6,124	15,749
2.	200	5,729	104,347	113,628	1,477	8,002	758	13,698
3.	358	15,619	79,398	45,482	11,799	6,153	956	4,262
4.	-	-	-	-	-	-	-	-
5.	10	7,705	17,908	6,835	3,896	661	207	407
6.	104	8,832	65,872	57,156	3,790	16,396	404	6,230
7.	38	14,189	75,382	49,713	4,635	3,593	237	1,935
8.	11	462	3,529	1,846	507	221	36	182
9.	7	1,545	7,928	3,386	443	430	64	168
10.	-	2,480	8,564	878	2,568	3,105	34	279
11.	60	2,268	12,638	8,373	1,795	391	133	362
12.	22	2,253	17,907	35,299	1,317	2,131	114	431
13.	40	22,856	216,763	124,184	1,265	1,011	531	1,747
14.	26	1,704	7,841	7,476	1,707	353	138	585
15.	216	10,827	40,088	30,636	3,723	2,866	956	2,497
16.	16	1,506	16,023	15,110	1,239	860	24	447
17.	48	4,028	32,548	17,359	4,785	1,314	523	997
18.	32	3,107	25,725	12,038	2,099	854	345	1,022
19.	4	491	7,410	2,131	292	138	57	83
20.	700	30,103	135,562	82,000	15,867	13,094	2,429	8,045
21.	18	1,713	10,632	7,759	984	628	71	325
22.	420	31,843	183,815	81,162	30,747	12,572	1,550	8,290
23.	25	1,674	12,436	7,872	1,170	872	103	485
24.	41	3,330	15,138	7,398	1,197	829	169	677
25.	187	6,709	27,367	17,346	3,479	2,839	606	2,217
26.	882	13,095	50,024	29,728	5,995	5,624	1,290	2,889
27.	97	5,213	23,524	12,560	3,916	2,440	359	1,477
N.C.	217	28,877	148,584	70,211	15,045	9,369	1,352	6,089
Total Employed	6,130	256,768	1,395,833	893,801	150,344	122,026	19,570	81,575
Total Population	9,849	395,017	2,107,605	1,337,332	226,862	186,702	30,550	130,613

		Wales		Scotland				
41.North-umberland	42.Durham	43.Glam-organ & Monmouth	44.North & West Wales	45.Strathclyde	46.Dumfries & Galloway	47.Borders	48.Lothian	
15,029	12,021	16,729	76,783	32,567	15,450	11,303	11,636	1.
39,253	105,117	144,716	46,327	77,309	2,326	281	18,643	2.
9,019	14,895	17,098	11,881	38,150	2,478	2,121	14,672	3.
-	-	-	-	-	-	-	-	4.
1,378	6,703	2,376	1,198	5,851	138	133	2,587	5.
8,848	28,590	30,508	11,233	59,331	1,026	660	6,816	6.
16,036	25,770	10,213	2,778	46,854	467	650	4,831	7.
347	597	513	438	1,603	119	88	661	8.
1,195	1,354	967	418	3,103	44	17	843	9.
10,579	28,077	2,416	2,047	29,789	78	21	1,022	10.
901	1,708	2,462	1,437	3,969	213	120	895	11.
1,547	3,018	2,731	1,465	8,383	246	115	1,918	12.
2,048	3,123	2,697	4,559	25,916	1,430	5,821	2,392	13.
913	657	716	1,179	3,335	204	290	1,241	14.
4,437	5,712	6,954	7,287	19,303	1,537	1,307	5,773	15.
1,847	5,852	1,530	2,910	5,772	113	26	1,557	16.
3,201	5,066	3,792	2,121	16,818	460	424	5,218	17.
1,869	3,016	2,455	1,738	9,510	291	450	7,998	18.
278	293	256	107	1,619	32	53	1,740	19.
19,771	35,500	32,032	26,895	69,627	4,449	3,610	22,484	20.
1,079	2,555	1,484	554	4,851	120	109	1,504	21.
20,601	37,350	41,542	17,999	74,320	3,301	2,062	23,677	22.
1,290	2,690	2,389	1,023	3,508	280	176	926	23.
1,504	2,237	3,198	1,859	5,064	352	269	2,227	24.
4,212	6,426	8,828	8,393	15,101	1,400	1,041	8,463	25.
7,302	9,866	10,050	10,492	21,073	2,300	2,349	8,307	26.
3,720	3,704	5,551	5,578	10,075	758	646	6,230	27.
17,717	28,743	34,638	18,209	75,551	2,717	2,079	18,342	N.C.
195,921	380,640	388,841	266,908	668,352	42,329	36,221	182,603	
302,433	602,411	597,146	414,312	1,031,023	68,388	54,876	284,517	

MALE EMPLOYMENT: 1901

Scotland

	49.Central & Fife	50.Tayside	51.Grampian	52.Highland	53. South East	54. East Anglia	55. South West	56. West Midland
1.	12,473	20,946	46,556	47,193	272,016	122,729	167,973	98,077
2.	26,732	2,058	4,319	765	23,874	1,984	38,523	77,879
3.	7,248	7,699	8,474	3,524	240,682	24,374	51,187	53,291
4.	-	-	-	-	-	-	-	-
5.	876	487	873	187	32,194	1,997	4,657	6,553
6.	9,780	4,283	3,566	1,322	61,159	7,798	19,541	93,078
7.	3,098	4,137	2,173	482	77,724	5,519	17,166	35,678
8.	247	327	394	152	12,004	662	1,614	4,573
9.	106	215	239	97	23,379	822	1,728	3,789
10.	604	1,514	1,237	262	17,885	1,052	5,052	688
11.	432	533	775	279	33,425	3,514	9,084	26,077
12.	776	711	641	398	39,339	2,060	5,983	62,547
13.	6,252	19,377	2,769	962	42,389	3,773	11,892	13,277
14.	374	652	471	131	29,740	2,804	6,095	11,901
15.	2,573	4,406	4,601	2,433	122,785	13,931	31,349	25,019
16.	1,262	278	222	41	33,000	3,741	5,690	42,279
17.	2,397	2,757	4,044	1,464	100,393	5,303	16,660	19,390
18.	1,667	1,626	2,225	342	98,705	4,250	10,830	10,493
19.	2,263	189	794	41	19,037	528	1,415	4,675
20.	12,068	13,433	13,132	7,090	405,682	36,138	98,214	98,409
21.	474	701	589	102	25,377	1,089	4,006	5,887
22.	10,148	12,035	12,128	6,228	435,850	29,033	75,424	78,207
23.	581	655	911	681	34,901	3,177	5,332	5,307
24.	793	1,003	1,175	486	40,345	2,331	6,852	7,503
25.	2,875	3,667	3,594	2,264	119,294	8,573	23,398	20,020
26.	3,949	5,788	3,957	3,211	248,627	20,707	43,747	41,676
27.	1,780	2,674	2,459	2,629	194,375	7,593	44,623	14,572
N.C.	10,036	9,175	8,738	4,671	399,776	19,091	66,184	78,673
Total Employed	121,864	121,326	131,056	87,437	3,183,957	334,573	774,219	939,518
Total Population	193,092	189,097	215,375	137,387	4,998,065	526,668	1,228,701	1,458,470

57. East Midlands	58. North West	59.Yorks. & Humberside	60. North	61. Wales	62. Scotland	63. Great Britain	
128,112	77,490	70,842	74,203	93,512	198,124	1,303,078	1.
93,087	110,076	115,105	166,828	191,043	132,433	950,832	2.
46,098	95,017	57,281	35,285	28,979	84,366	716,560	3.
-	-	-	-	-	-	-	4.
4,019	25,613	10,731	9,356	3,574	11,132	109,826	5.
30,610	74,704	60,946	60,468	41,741	86,784	536,829	6.
25,678	89,571	54,348	47,571	12,991	62,692	428,938	7.
1,404	3,991	2,353	1,383	951	3,591	32,526	8.
2,300	9,473	3,829	3,211	1,385	4,664	54,580	9.
820	11,044	3,446	42,074	4,463	34,527	121,051	10.
10,515	14,906	10,168	3,495	3,899	7,216	122,299	11.
6,372	20,160	36,616	7,241	4,196	13,188	197,702	12.
40,060	239,619	125,449	8,460	7,256	64,919	557,094	13.
6,262	9,545	9,183	2,646	1,895	6,698	86,769	14.
70,456	50,915	34,359	16,468	14,241	41,933	421,456	15.
10,307	17,529	16,349	9,030	4,440	9,271	151,636	16.
13,351	36,576	22,144	11,101	5,913	33,582	264,413	17.
9,511	28,832	14,137	7,106	4,193	24,109	212,166	18.
2,254	7,901	2,423	849	363	6,731	46,176	19.
76,901	165,665	97,867	78,839	58,927	145,893	1,262,535	20.
4,253	12,345	8,743	4,658	2,038	8,450	76,846	21.
69,960	215,658	111,909	80,363	59,541	143,899	1,299,844	22.
5,269	14,110	9,042	5,440	3,412	7,718	93,708	23.
5,429	18,468	8,595	5,416	5,057	11,369	111,365	24.
15,806	34,076	20,825	16,300	17,221	38,405	313,918	25.
32,548	63,119	35,723	26,971	20,542	50,934	584,594	26.
10,720	28,737	16,476	11,700	11,129	27,251	367,176	27.
50,380	177,461	85,256	63,270	52,847	131,309	1,124,247	N.C.
772,482	1,652,601	1,044,145	799,732	655,749	1,391,188	11,548,164	
1,185,726	2,502,622	1,564,194	1,252,709	1,011,458	2,173,755	17,902,368	

FEMALE EMPLOYMENT: 1901

South East

	1. London	2. Middlesex	3. Kent	4. Surrey	5. Sussex	6. Hants.	7. Berks.	8. Oxon
1.	1,458	691	1,397	376	505	615	352	224
2.	194	11	23	14	26	13	10	14
3.	26,085	2,741	2,762	1,808	2,005	2,429	1,302	548
4.	-	-	-	-	-	-	-	-
5.	4,817	781	561	190	58	67	18	9
6.	1,733	44	16	13	16	18	82	3
7.	84	14	7	2	1	5	1	-
8.	883	63	11	10	4	11	-	-
9.	566	476	1	14	-	2	-	-
10.	13	2	-	4	1	-	2	-
11.	121	8	11	5	7	6	2	1
12.	2,878	230	72	92	89	111	42	28
13.	22,917	2,706	2,864	1,992	1,778	2,323	685	1,047
14.	9,468	271	78	136	71	81	14	42
15.	155,108	13,656	13,396	9,318	9,952	16,112	4,430	4,121
16.	977	114	96	115	66	90	35	11
17.	7,800	326	277	258	231	350	113	63
18.	33,369	1,456	2,615	669	612	906	362	386
19.	2,777	303	94	75	80	115	15	9
20.	603	19	16	21	11	17	6	5
21.	119	1	7	1	-	-	-	-
22.	3,860	483	356	264	290	352	92	88
23.	8,350	855	1,421	805	919	1,111	322	264
24.	528	112	33	34	7	9	2	-
25.	47,626	9,975	10,506	8,451	8,569	8,571	2,939	2,241
26.	357,841	61,814	69,892	65,781	63,156	58,868	19,762	14,662
27.	5,796	1,056	847	911	532	705	261	207
N.C.	23,344	3,172	1,429	1,424	1,255	1,204	359	168
Total Employed	719,315	101,380	108,788	92,783	90,241	94,091	31,208	24,141
Total Population	2,394,456	421,253	489,703	350,286	328,531	410,464	129,764	98,144

East Anglia

	9. Bucks.	10. Beds.	11. Herts.	12. Essex	13. Cambridge	14. Hunts.	15. Norfolk	16. Suffolk	
	218	165	213	695	605	177	808	490	1.
	6	4	19	88	4	2	11	14	2.
	612	582	876	4,235	633	152	1,998	1,223	3.
	–	–	–	–	–	–	–	–	4.
	3	8	116	907	2	–	439	31	5.
	13	9	5	117	5	2	17	12	6.
	–	–	–	6	–	1	2	2	7.
	–	–	72	57	2	–	3	–	8.
	–	60	2	228	–	–	7	2	9.
	–	–	–	6	–	–	2	1	10.
	1	–	3	9	4	1	3	5	11.
	15	21	29	161	14	5	47	37	12.
	1,451	1,584	772	6,014	509	152	3,869	2,262	13.
	367	17	211	540	61	10	790	993	14.
	3,078	11,344	5,747	20,841	2,965	703	11,845	8,007	15.
	17	31	29	126	11	1	34	33	16.
	596	97	59	411	53	4	176	95	17.
	975	420	1,130	1,956	289	92	888	560	18.
	7	13	64	982	15	7	79	27	19.
	7	5	6	21	5	4	13	14	20.
	–	–	–	1	–	–	–	–	21.
	72	56	98	568	65	15	150	111	22.
	226	185	210	1,212	214	42	734	526	23.
	2	1	8	51	1	2	2	7	24.
	1,824	1,633	2,841	10,406	1,763	484	4,617	3,462	25.
	11,472	10,108	18,854	50,184	12,094	2,860	27,633	22,865	26.
	217	131	330	999	158	56	491	309	27.
	166	151	411	2,598	173	29	480	346	N.C.
	21,345	26,625	32,105	103,419	19,645	4,801	55,138	41,434	
	100,560	91,259	134,704	548,396	95,101	27,390	248,124	191,507	

FEMALE EMPLOYMENT: 1901

<u>South West</u>   <u>West Midlands</u>

	17.Corn-wall	18. Devon	19.Som-erset	20.Gloucs.	21.Wilts.	22.Dorset	23.Here-ford	24.Shrops
1.	946	917	1,093	708	541	473	595	876
2.	394	21	29	58	12	3	7	100
3.	1,847	2,928	1,559	8,030	1,003	651	351	928
4.	-	-	-	-	-	-	-	-
5.	413	115	21	454	5	3	3	12
6.	15	10	9	71	22	2	7	17
7.	1	1	8	1	-	-	-	1
8.	-	9	6	15	11	-	1	2
9.	-	1	-	15	-	-	-	-
10.	-	-	-	1	-	-	-	-
11.	3	5	2	7	1	-	2	1
12.	44	128	56	485	35	14	18	37
13.	1,672	4,917	3,944	5,940	1,947	1,444	228	647
14.	31	182	223	284	61	12	1	42
15.	6,669	15,961	14,182	23,253	4,453	4,015	1,456	3,077
16.	35	165	73	236	31	47	42	287
17.	58	317	257	422	160	55	37	45
18.	157	1,044	921	3,314	138	168	72	117
19.	8	67	20	408	43	10	8	89
20.	12	14	14	9	6	7	3	5
21.	-	-	-	-	-	-	-	-
22.	90	248	160	281	62	69	67	112
23.	343	1,125	489	1,264	226	209	125	226
24.	4	13	4	11	6	2	1	6
25.	2,629	6,675	5,047	7,668	2,530	1,990	1,036	1,910
26.	17,157	48,457	33,946	44,679	14,919	13,230	8,492	16,030
27.	380	517	413	623	301	236	167	243
N.C.	177	691	464	1,201	229	148	76	91
Total Employed	33,085	84,528	62,940	99,438	26,742	22,788	12,795	24,901
Total Population	172,397	349,660	234,457	376,881	136,854	102,426	58,929	121,108

East Midlands

25.Staffs.	26.Warwick	27.Worcs.	28.Derby	29.Notts.	30.Leics.	31.Lincs.	32.North-ants.	
848	423	783	820	362	439	1,464	237	1.
190	99	57	52	36	23	18	12	2.
5,341	5,601	3,406	2,123	4,471	3,449	2,392	1,082	3.
-	-	-	-	-	-	-	-	4.
855	1,931	224	101	198	82	83	22	5.
1,334	6,016	542	45	305	30	37	5	6.
234	499	30	14	38	5	1	1	7.
169	1,164	47	131	72	11	2	5	8.
203	146	6	74	9	21	-	-	9.
2	3	-	-	-	-	-	-	10.
145	2,391	259	5	45	7	18	9	11.
8,366	19,678	4,603	231	76	88	61	47	12.
6,456	7,024	5,031	16,231	26,717	21,944	1,550	1,140	13.
4,300	2,520	365	115	313	84	86	161	14.
19,152	17,621	9,077	8,266	10,873	20,356	6,901	18,671	15.
23,149	573	1,095	991	91	84	57	24	16.
555	2,576	291	317	475	223	186	77	17.
1,710	4,736	1,300	1,232	1,268	1,408	354	692	18.
339	3,421	1,382	102	90	936	37	128	19.
652	327	11	10	39	8	21	9	20.
7	1	-	1	-	-	-	-	21.
713	1,115	239	168	777	407	133	130	22.
1,670	2,107	680	511	597	433	480	366	23.
67	144	41	15	9	2	11	5	24.
8,986	7,330	4,312	4,454	3,899	3,274	4,122	2,754	25.
45,133	44,975	25,646	22,941	20,988	16,451	27,781	15,047	26.
686	649	368	323	248	303	400	269	27.
3,080	6,378	1,116	648	1,137	718	324	366	N.C.
134,342	139,448	60,911	59,921	73,133	70,786	46,519	41,259	
622,179	486,725	237,054	303,977	266,361	227,264	254,249	170,393	

FEMALE EMPLOYMENT: 1901

	East Midlands	North West		Yorks. & Humberside		North		
	33.Rutland	34.Cheshire	35.Lancs.	36. West Riding	37. East Riding	38.North Riding	39.West-morland	40.Cum-berland
1.	45	1,553	2,212	1,740	553	923	262	861
2.	1	44	2,281	137	43	13	3	238
3.	56	5,573	35,780	14,452	4,509	1,626	401	2,023
4.	-	-	-	-	-	-	-	-
5.	-	940	2,943	1,027	1,358	32	28	29
6.	-	115	701	320	436	2	1	351
7.	-	79	748	387	2	-	12	7
8.	-	27	546	119	21	3	-	1
9.	-	32	372	22	-	1	-	-
10.	-	4	37	-	3	1	-	-
11.	1	8	142	133	7	4	-	-
12.	1	204	2,085	9,626	108	78	8	25
13.	48	33,149	306,883	146,747	1,793	897	568	2,153
14.	2	157	1,548	1,154	105	16	58	13
15.	269	16,662	87,233	56,374	6,700	4,602	1,158	4,658
16.	3	92	1,559	1,040	64	64	7	39
17.	4	348	3,274	2,284	343	95	36	50
18.	8	1,443	13,057	5,699	1,035	258	130	466
19.	-	186	3,206	454	34	21	9	15
20.	-	25	95	101	1	2	5	4
21.	-	-	-	1	-	-	-	-
22.	6	493	3,012	1,712	311	80	25	133
23.	9	968	8,186	3,089	401	367	57	358
24.	-	41	372	77	23	9	-	10
25.	193	6,851	31,487	18,427	3,999	2,886	544	2,028
26.	1,639	46,236	174,278	93,458	24,230	20,769	4,651	13,367
27.	40	509	2,339	1,323	265	237	63	233
N.C.	7	1,047	7,265	3,856	607	280	46	304
Total Employed	2,330	116,786	691,641	363,759	46,951	33,266	8,072	27,366
Total Population	9,860	432,174	2,279,438	1,413,161	236,059	190,636	33,859	136,320

| | Wales | | | Scotland | | | | |
41.North-umberland	42.Durham	43.Glam-organ & Monmouth	44.North & West Wales	45.Strathclyde	46.Dumfries & Galloway	47.Borders	48.Lothian	
2,552	888	890	6,372	6,690	2,361	2,621	3,207	1.
23	44	236	88	535	11	8	112	2.
3,126	5,202	4,227	4,102	20,623	885	708	5,824	3.
–	–	–	–	–	–	–	–	4.
230	325	146	36	1,499	5	7	400	5.
44	35	1,503	657	109	2	3	137	6.
12	36	–	1	837	5	3	50	7.
7	8	5	4	59	1	2	42	8.
89	90	3	48	22	–	–	12	9.
16	15	–	–	122	–	–	1	10.
4	6	3	–	42	1	–	7	11.
168	342	199	84	2,129	22	7	245	12.
1,575	4,115	2,924	2,615	51,823	1,533	6,699	3,757	13.
129	84	30	44	1,164	1	–	197	14.
7,929	13,995	17,455	14,656	44,555	2,725	1,791	11,138	15.
448	568	327	171	2,390	22	36	563	16.
209	282	165	78	3,878	19	13	709	17.
743	1,414	904	427	8,918	74	158	6,185	18.
98	67	114	51	1,085	4	45	1,487	19.
14	23	25	11	123	7	3	81	20.
–	1	–	1	1	–	–	5	21.
359	351	414	238	5,277	110	89	1,059	22.
1,170	1,651	1,256	732	4,814	149	150	1,767	23.
16	30	29	9	29	–	–	4	24.
3,802	7,078	8,310	5,599	12,746	975	654	5,568	25.
27,431	37,515	43,329	54,138	70,175	8,679	6,565	35,391	26.
383	498	643	835	704	155	115	279	27.
1,196	1,325	784	288	9,634	377	189	4,651	N.C.
51,773	75,988	83,921	91,285	249,983	18,123	19,866	82,878	
300,686	585,063	560,861	440,557	1,038,046	76,251	63,174	308,652	

Scotland

	49.Central & Fife	50.Tayside	51.Grampian	52.Highland	53. South East	54. East Anglia	55. South West	56. W Mid
1.	2,584	1,699	2,570	6,638	6,909	2,080	4,678	3
2.	656	14	2	3	422	31	517	
3.	2,191	3,404	4,856	2,346	45,985	4,006	16,018	15
4.	-	-	-	-	-	-	-	
5.	161	49	57	4	7,535	472	1,011	3
6.	79	36	31	27	2,069	36	129	7
7.	-	9	1	1	120	5	11	
8.	1	12	10	4	1,111	5	41	1
9.	-	-	-	-	1,349	9	16	
10.	-	1	5	-	28	3	1	
11.	10	2	1	-	174	13	18	2
12.	135	50	62	2	3,768	103	762	32
13.	14,313	40,392	5,644	7,316	46,133	6,792	19,864	19
14.	21	146	31	-	11,296	1,854	793	7
15.	5,600	6,640	6,213	2,851	267,103	23,520	68,533	50
16.	552	70	52	6	1,707	79	587	25
17.	242	188	225	28	10,581	328	1,269	3
18.	1,061	675	2,467	94	44,856	1,829	5,742	7
19.	154	19	357	2	4,534	128	556	5
20.	20	19	17	-	737	36	62	
21.	4	1	-	-	129	-	-	
22.	398	479	523	142	6,579	341	910	2
23.	751	770	774	276	15,880	1,516	3,656	4
24.	8	7	4	1	787	12	40	
25.	2,346	2,690	3,488	1,722	115,582	10,326	26,539	23
26.	14,458	16,731	21,554	13,077	802,394	65,452	172,388	140
27.	207	280	202	261	11,992	1,014	2,470	2
N.C.	886	1,416	1,498	290	35,681	1,028	2,910	10
Total Employed	46,838	75,799	50,644	35,091	1,445,441	121,018	329,521	372
Total Population	200,068	225,249	236,275	150,633	5,497,520	562,122	1,372,675	1,525

57. East Midlands	58. North West	59. Yorks. & Humberside	60. North	61. Wales	62. Scotland	63. Great Britain	
3,367	3,765	2,293	5,486	7,262	28,370	67,735	1.
142	2,325	180	321	324	1,341	6,056	2.
13,573	41,353	18,961	12,378	8,329	40,837	217,067	3.
-	-	-	-	-	-	-	4.
486	3,883	2,385	644	182	2,182	21,805	5.
422	816	756	433	2,160	424	15,161	6.
59	827	389	67	1	906	3,149	7.
221	573	140	19	9	131	3,633	8.
104	404	22	180	51	34	2,524	9.
-	41	3	32	-	129	242	10.
85	150	140	14	3	63	3,458	11.
504	2,289	9,734	621	283	2,652	53,418	12.
67,628	340,032	148,540	9,308	5,539	131,477	794,699	13.
761	1,705	1,259	300	74	1,560	26,830	14.
65,336	103,895	63,074	32,342	32,111	81,513	787,810	15.
1,250	1,651	1,104	1,126	498	3,691	36,839	16.
1,282	3,622	2,627	672	243	5,302	29,430	17.
4,962	14,500	6,734	3,011	1,331	19,632	110,532	18.
1,293	3,392	488	210	165	3,153	19,158	19.
87	120	102	48	36	270	2,496	20.
1	-	1	1	1	11	152	21.
1,621	3,505	2,023	948	652	8,077	26,902	22.
2,396	9,154	3,490	3,603	1,988	9,451	55,942	23.
42	413	100	65	38	53	1,809	24.
18,696	38,338	22,426	16,338	13,909	30,189	315,917	25.
104,847	220,514	117,688	103,733	97,467	186,630	2,011,389	26.
1,583	2,848	1,588	1,414	1,478	2,203	28,703	27.
3,200	8,312	4,463	3,151	1,072	18,941	89,499	N.C.
293,948	808,427	410,710	196,465	175,206	579,222	4,732,355	
1,232,104	2,711,612	1,649,220	1,246,564	1,001,418	2,298,348	19,097,578	

TOTAL EMPLOYMENT: 1901

South East

	1. London	2. Middlesex	3. Kent	4. Surrey	5. Sussex	6. Hants.	7. Berks.	8. Oxon.
1.	10,814	12,896	48,201	19,915	34,881	31,392	15,372	16,069
2.	8,709	1,470	3,849	1,439	1,318	1,822	345	567
3.	131,053	20,295	23,660	16,756	17,300	18,833	10,490	4,585
4.	—	—	—	—	—	—	—	—
5.	22,126	3,275	2,688	1,649	912	1,035	253	167
6.	30,467	3,444	5,650	2,322	2,448	4,405	2,155	1,125
7.	36,339	6,181	9,707	1,826	1,779	5,847	1,066	679
8.	7,955	1,148	689	680	525	510	171	102
9.	13,354	2,520	1,513	1,160	918	900	292	115
10.	3,744	514	4,629	175	278	5,631	98	101
11.	12,169	2,155	2,931	2,020	2,109	2,701	973	549
12.	27,306	3,516	1,976	1,736	1,450	1,776	626	374
13.	47,078	6,016	5,309	4,066	3,424	4,125	1,311	1,914
14.	28,706	1,821	1,526	1,696	849	1,067	403	359
15.	229,233	19,812	19,108	13,720	14,182	22,251	6,433	5,870
16.	8,712	2,127	10,838	1,671	1,946	1,856	1,064	286
17.	68,774	6,036	5,193	3,503	3,961	4,613	1,639	1,246
18.	96,935	8,439	8,252	4,435	2,898	3,558	1,395	1,654
19.	14,672	2,848	786	795	394	441	71	93
20.	154,640	38,094	36,967	32,856	26,412	30,597	10,752	6,945
21.	11,903	2,011	1,678	1,498	1,135	1,104	308	226
22.	238,606	29,874	30,768	18,459	19,024	29,138	6,822	4,675
23.	28,788	2,582	3,732	2,358	2,740	3,246	851	678
24.	19,605	5,054	2,760	3,758	1,715	1,925	553	401
25.	103,469	21,114	19,440	17,953	15,839	15,763	5,342	4,328
26.	465,955	75,312	91,206	86,892	82,023	77,934	28,551	20,385
27.	71,177	9,685	35,598	10,557	6,732	47,146	4,189	1,633
N.C.	226,995	39,245	30,810	25,909	14,082	24,431	6,858	4,291
Total Employed	2,119,284	327,484	409,464	279,804	261,274	344,047	108,383	79,417
Total Population	4,536,541	792,314	961,139	653,549	602,255	799,582	252,571	186,460

East Anglia

9. Bucks.	10. Beds.	11. Herts.	12. Essex	13. Cambridge	14. Hunts.	15. Norfolk	16. Suffolk	
16,349	13,857	16,658	42,521	24,705	7,868	51,374	40,862	1.
356	636	705	3,080	367	101	975	572	2.
4,407	4,230	6,940	28,118	4,653	1,291	12,786	9,650	3.
–	–	–	–	–	–	–	–	4.
179	178	850	6,417	229	49	1,395	796	5.
1,259	1,699	1,198	7,056	829	301	3,415	3,289	6.
700	1,473	1,083	11,164	504	149	1,902	2,969	7.
82	80	260	913	141	34	299	193	8.
167	269	253	3,267	139	15	467	210	9.
41	10	42	2,650	39	8	483	525	10.
2,742	564	881	3,805	481	348	1,431	1,267	11.
342	374	571	3,060	359	75	1,037	692	12.
1,754	1,994	1,438	10,093	902	238	5,131	4,294	13.
796	308	820	2,685	392	102	2,094	2,070	14.
5,528	16,392	8,037	29,322	4,460	1,096	20,288	11,607	15.
899	1,033	499	3,776	908	1,211	788	913	16.
5,684	962	1,393	7,970	758	170	2,936	1,767	17.
2,270	1,034	3,131	9,560	1,209	252	2,697	1,921	18.
89	47	203	3,132	76	17	296	267	19.
7,358	6,162	12,139	43,497	6,221	1,775	15,783	12,395	20.
228	221	353	4,841	147	65	440	437	21.
4,595	3,682	7,478	49,308	5,109	1,235	12,236	10,794	22.
599	643	713	3,851	657	159	2,386	1,491	23.
355	353	831	3,822	347	83	1,188	725	24.
3,300	3,020	5,558	19,750	3,452	894	8,277	6,276	25.
16,690	12,984	27,111	65,978	15,613	3,804	36,665	30,077	26.
1,186	1,226	2,311	14,927	1,155	351	3,753	3,348	27.
4,392	3,191	7,186	48,067	3,628	738	9,325	6,428	N.C
82,347	76,622	108,642	432,630	77,480	22,429	199,847	155,835	
197,046	171,707	258,423	1,083,998	184,759	54,125	476,553	373,353	

TOTAL EMPLOYMENT: 1901

<u>South West</u>

<u>West Midlands</u>

	17.Corn-wall	18. Devon	19.Som-erset	20.Gloucs.	21.Wilts.	22.Dorset	23.Here-ford	24.Shrops.
1.	28,478	43,542	32,822	25,448	24,730	17,631	15,491	22,626
2.	14,019	3,542	7,058	11,236	1,616	1,569	288	6,002
3.	6,648	14,581	10,328	24,594	6,249	4,805	2,129	5,242
4.	-	-	-	-	-	-	-	-
5.	962	1,080	519	2,735	223	149	87	232
6.	2,639	4,003	2,515	6,058	3,262	1,193	654	4,352
7.	1,303	3,745	1,376	4,845	5,048	860	163	1,518
8.	152	446	264	516	157	120	42	136
9.	74	420	310	693	148	99	44	144
10.	874	3,502	84	458	9	126	7	19
11.	571	1,672	1,337	2,843	2,198	481	425	1,328
12.	544	1,431	919	2,972	534	345	205	927
13.	2,401	7,370	6,859	9,323	3,423	2,380	446	1,421
14.	475	1,626	1,425	2,235	831	296	192	420
15.	9,011	22,446	20,058	36,655	6,226	5,486	2,345	4,946
16.	265	1,255	1,492	1,944	400	921	249	1,987
17.	1,001	3,903	3,241	7,142	1,645	997	550	1,171
18.	716	3,815	3,149	7,537	719	636	299	592
19.	56	301	214	1,081	274	45	48	148
20.	10,362	25,780	15,923	26,160	12,171	7,880	4,056	8,400
21.	167	756	529	1,888	318	348	85	284
22.	7,839	18,807	10,772	26,240	7,391	5,285	2,253	5,762
23.	932	2,657	1,275	2,811	636	677	292	502
24.	740	1,839	1,173	2,156	549	435	257	600
25.	5,242	13,066	9,320	13,876	4,659	3,774	2,134	3,900
26.	20,325	59,639	41,958	56,232	20,137	17,844	11,322	20,817
27.	5,607	21,987	3,360	5,562	2,844	7,733	908	1,843
N.C.	5,732	18,911	9,591	23,006	6,593	5,261	2,759	5,844
Total Employed	127,135	282,122	187,871	306,246	112,990	87,376	47,730	101,163
Total Population	322,334	662,196	434,950	708,439	271,394	202,063	114,125	239,783

East Midlands

25.Staffs.	26.War- wick	27.Worcs.	28.Derby	29.Notts.	30.Leics.	31.Lincs.	32.North- ants.	
23,356	19,026	21,103	17,986	16,905	15,095	60,486	18,611	1.
55,336	11,947	4,759	50,119	27,444	10,672	2,588	2,205	2.
27,997	21,807	11,743	11,420	15,473	11,407	13,865	7,092	3.
-	-	-	-	-	-	-	-	4.
3,108	4,112	2,039	1,249	1,213	651	1,137	245	5.
47,751	36,780	11,457	12,118	5,325	3,377	7,581	2,527	6.
15,143	15,489	4,129	7,730	5,740	3,272	7,581	1,376	7.
964	4,492	322	532	371	255	320	136	8.
1,882	1,665	409	757	658	613	207	162	9.
359	152	156	12	67	13	700	28	10.
5,797	17,776	3,549	3,070	2,528	1,672	1,926	1,343	11.
30,538	48,788	14,791	3,096	1,182	1,111	949	515	12.
10,901	10,439	9,456	27,841	42,709	32,186	3,156	1,710	13.
11,197	5,695	1,625	986	1,533	1,004	1,095	2,377	14.
29,044	26,053	13,014	12,288	15,250	47,473	10,582	49,714	15.
56,360	4,725	4,104	5,088	1,681	2,213	1,493	1,063	16.
7,181	11,237	2,755	2,855	4,752	2,526	2,874	1,574	17.
4,615	10,004	2,918	3,557	4,363	3,394	1,623	1,496	18.
799	6,321	2,598	450	531	2,107	165	290	19.
39,764	31,599	15,588	19,566	16,192	14,420	14,634	11,476	20.
2,246	2,533	747	1,039	1,137	1,051	528	481	21.
31,437	29,862	11,139	17,514	16,237	11,622	16,360	9,422	22.
3,718	4,165	1,438	1,538	2,083	1,401	1,551	1,058	23.
2,993	2,550	1,362	1,355	1,316	998	1,090	671	24.
16,235	13,287	8,038	8,160	7,248	6,019	7,680	5,015	25.
58,233	58,937	32,643	29,853	27,560	22,954	34,498	20,009	26.
5,577	5,650	2,707	2,619	2,240	2,278	2,805	2,224	27.
35,086	31,880	13,845	15,350	13,142	9,264	9,518	6,082	N.C.
527,617	436,971	198,434	258,148	234,880	209,048	206,992	148,902	
1,236,919	939,904	453,734	610,522	514,459	437,490	500,022	335,628	

TOTAL EMPLOYMENT: 1901

	East Midlands	North West		Yorks. & Humberside		North		
	33.Rut-land	34. Cheshire	35.Lancs.	36. West Riding	37. East Riding	38. North Riding	39.West-morland	40.Cum-berland
1.	2,396	30,163	51,092	47,975	25,160	26,203	6,386	16,610
2.	201	5,773	106,628	113,765	1,520	8,015	761	13,936
3.	414	21,192	115,178	59,934	16,308	7,779	1,357	6,285
4.	-	-	-	-	-	-	-	-
5.	10	8,645	20,851	7,862	5,254	693	235	436
6.	104	8,947	66,573	57,476	4,226	16,398	405	6,581
7.	38	14,268	76,130	50,100	4,637	3,593	249	1,942
8.	11	489	4,075	1,965	528	224	36	183
9.	7	1,577	8,300	3,408	443	431	64	168
10.	-	2,484	8,601	878	2,571	3,106	34	279
11.	61	2,276	12,780	8,506	1,802	395	133	362
12.	23	2,457	19,992	44,925	1,425	2,209	122	456
13.	86	56,005	523,646	270,931	3,058	1,908	1,099	3,900
14.	28	1,861	9,389	8,630	1,812	369	196	598
15.	485	27,489	127,321	87,010	10,423	7,468	2,114	7,155
16.	19	1,598	17,582	16,150	1,303	924	31	486
17.	52	4,376	35,822	19,643	5,128	1,409	559	1,047
18.	40	4,550	38,782	17,737	3,134	1,112	475	1,488
19.	4	677	10,616	2,585	326	159	66	98
20.	700	30,128	135,657	82,101	15,868	13,096	2,434	8,049
21.	18	1,713	10,632	7,760	984	628	71	325
22.	426	32,336	186,827	82,874	31,058	12,652	1,575	8,423
23.	34	2,642	20,622	10,961	1,571	1,239	160	843
24.	41	3,371	15,510	7,475	1,220	838	169	687
25.	380	13,560	58,854	35,773	7,478	5,725	1,150	4,245
26.	2,521	59,331	224,302	123,186	30,225	26,393	5,941	16,256
27.	137	5,722	25,863	13,883	4,181	2,677	422	1,710
N.C.	224	29,924	155,849	74,067	15,652	9,649	1,398	6,393
Total Employed	8,460	373,554	2,087,474	1,257,560	197,295	155,292	27,642	108,941
Total Population	19,709	827,191	4,387,043	2,750,493	462,921	377,338	64,409	266,933

	Wales			Scotland				
41.North-umberland	42.Durham	43.Glam-organ & Monmouth	44.North & West Wales	45.Strathclyde	46.Dumfries & Galloway	47.Borders	48.Lothian	
17,581	12,909	17,619	83,155	39,257	17,811	13,924	14,843	1.
39,276	105,161	144,952	46,415	77,844	2,337	289	18,755	2.
12,145	20,097	21,325	15,983	58,773	3,363	2,829	20,496	3.
-	-	-	-	-	-	-	-	4.
1,608	7,028	2,522	1,234	7,350	143	140	2,987	5.
8,892	28,625	32,011	11,890	59,440	1,028	663	6,953	6.
16,048	25,806	10,213	2,779	47,691	472	653	4,881	7.
354	605	518	442	1,662	120	90	703	8.
1,284	1,444	970	466	3,125	44	17	855	9.
10,595	28,092	2,416	2,047	29,911	78	21	1,023	10.
905	1,714	2,465	1,437	4,011	214	120	902	11.
1,715	3,360	2,930	1,549	10,512	268	122	2,163	12.
3,623	7,238	5,621	7,174	77,739	2,963	12,520	6,149	13.
1,042	741	746	1,223	4,499	205	290	1,438	14.
12,366	19,707	24,409	21,943	63,858	4,262	3,098	16,911	15.
2,295	6,420	1,857	3,081	8,162	135	62	2,120	16.
3,410	5,348	3,957	2,199	20,696	479	437	5,927	17.
2,612	4,430	3,359	2,165	18,428	365	608	14,183	18.
376	360	370	158	2,704	36	98	3,227	19.
19,785	35,523	32,057	26,906	69,750	4,456	3,613	22,565	20.
1,079	2,556	1,484	555	4,852	120	109	1,509	21.
20,960	37,701	41,956	18,237	79,597	3,411	2,151	24,736	22.
2,460	4,341	3,645	1,755	8,322	429	326	2,693	23.
1,520	2,267	3,227	1,868	5,093	352	269	2,231	24.
8,014	13,504	17,138	13,992	27,847	2,375	1,695	14,031	25.
34,733	47,381	53,379	64,630	91,248	10,979	8,914	43,698	26.
4,103	4,202	6,194	6,413	10,779	913	761	6,509	27.
18,913	30,068	35,422	18,497	85,185	3,094	2,268	22,993	N.C.
247,694	456,628	472,762	358,193	918,335	60,452	56,087	265,481	
603,119	1,187,474	1,158,007	854,869	2,069,069	144,639	118,050	593,169	

TOTAL EMPLOYMENT: 1901

Scotland

	49.Central & Fife	50.Tayside	51.Gram- pian	52.High- land	53. South East	54. East Anglia	55. South West	56. West Midland
1.	15,057	22,645	49,126	53,831	278,925	124,809	172,651	101,602
2.	27,388	2,072	4,321	768	24,296	2,015	39,040	78,332
3.	9,439	11,103	13,330	5,870	286,667	28,380	67,205	68,918
4.	-	-	-	-	-	-	-	-
5.	1,037	536	930	191	39,729	2,469	5,668	9,578
6.	9,859	4,319	3,597	1,349	63,228	7,834	19,670	100,994
7.	3,098	4,146	2,174	483	77,844	5,524	17,177	36,442
8.	248	339	404	156	13,115	667	1,655	5,956
9.	106	215	239	97	24,728	831	1,744	4,144
10.	604	1,515	1,242	262	17,913	1,055	5,053	693
11.	442	535	776	279	33,599	3,527	9,102	28,875
12.	911	761	703	400	43,107	2,163	6,745	95,249
13.	20,565	59,769	8,413	8,278	88,522	10,565	31,756	32,663
14.	395	798	502	131	41,036	4,658	6,888	19,129
15.	8,173	11,046	10,814	5,284	389,888	37,451	99,882	75,402
16.	1,814	348	274	47	34,707	3,820	6,277	67,425
17.	2,639	2,945	4,269	1,492	110,974	5,631	17,929	22,894
18.	2,728	2,301	4,692	436	143,561	6,079	16,572	18,428
19.	2,417	208	1,151	43	23,571	656	1,971	9,914
20.	12,088	13,452	13,149	7,090	406,419	36,174	98,276	99,407
21.	478	702	589	102	25,506	1,089	4,006	5,895
22.	10,546	12,514	12,651	6,370	442,429	29,374	76,334	80,453
23.	1,332	1,425	1,685	957	50,781	4,693	8,988	10,115
24.	801	1,010	1,179	487	41,132	2,343	6,892	7,762
25.	5,221	6,357	7,082	3,986	234,876	18,899	49,937	43,594
26.	18,407	22,519	25,511	16,288	1,051,021	86,159	216,135	181,952
27.	1,987	2,954	2,661	2,890	206,367	8,607	47,093	16,685
N.C.	10,922	10,591	10,236	4,961	435,457	20,119	69,094	89,414
Total Employed	168,702	197,125	181,700	122,528	4,629,398	455,591	1,103,740	1,311,915
Total Population	393,160	414,346	451,650	288,020	10,495,585	1,088,790	2,601,376	2,984,465

57. East Midlands	58. North West	59. Yorks. & Humberside	60. North	61. Wales	62. Scotland	63. Great Britain	
131,479	81,255	73,135	79,689	100,774	226,494	1,370,813	1.
93,229	112,401	115,285	167,149	191,367	133,774	956,888	2.
59,671	136,370	76,242	47,663	37,308	125,203	933,627	3.
–	–	–	–	–	–	–	4.
4,505	29,496	13,116	10,000	3,756	13,314	131,631	5.
31,032	75,520	61,702	60,901	43,901	87,208	551,990	6.
25,737	90,398	54,737	47,638	12,992	63,598	432,087	7.
1,625	4,564	2,493	1,402	960	3,722	36,159	8.
2,404	9,877	3,851	3,391	1,436	4,698	57,104	9.
820	11,085	3,449	42,106	4,463	34,656	121,293	10.
10,600	15,056	10,308	3,509	3,902	7,279	125,757	11.
6,876	22,449	46,350	7,862	4,479	15,840	251,120	12.
107,688	579,651	273,989	17,768	12,795	196,396	1,351,793	13.
7,023	11,250	10,442	2,946	1,969	8,258	113,599	14.
135,792	154,810	97,433	48,810	46,352	123,446	1,209,266	15.
11,557	19,180	17,453	10,156	4,938	12,962	188,475	16.
14,633	40,198	24,771	11,773	6,156	38,884	293,843	17.
14,473	43,332	20,871	10,117	5,524	43,741	322,698	18.
3,547	11,293	2,911	1,059	528	9,884	65,334	19.
76,988	165,785	97,969	78,887	58,963	146,163	1,265,031	20.
4,254	12,345	8,744	4,659	2,039	8,461	76,998	21.
71,581	219,163	113,932	81,311	60,193	151,976	1,326,746	22.
7,665	23,264	12,532	9,043	5,400	17,169	149,650	23.
5,471	18,881	8,695	5,481	5,095	11,422	113,174	24.
34,502	72,414	43,251	32,638	31,130	68,594	629,835	25.
137,395	283,633	153,411	130,704	118,009	237,564	2,595,983	26.
12,303	31,585	18,064	13,114	12,607	29,454	395,879	27.
53,580	185,773	89,719	66,421	53,919	150,250	1,213,746	N.C.
,066,430	2,461,028	1,454,855	996,197	830,955	1,970,410	16,280,519	
,417,830	5,214,234	3,213,414	2,499,273	2,012,876	4,472,103	36,999,946	

MALE EMPLOYMENT: 1911

South East

	1. London	2. Middlesex	3. Kent	4. Surrey	5. Sussex	6. Hants.	7. Berks.	8. Oxor
1.	9,079	14,513	50,994	21,801	37,676	34,367	16,073	17,150
2.	8,660	2,264	4,194	1,848	1,546	2,194	499	652
3.	110,600	27,022	24,621	21,164	18,016	20,539	9,722	4,640
4.	-	-	-	-	-	-	-	-
5.	18,990	4,132	2,847	2,138	1,066	1,178	298	182
6.	22,984	3,714	5,319	2,354	2,278	4,661	2,138	1,081
7.	32,530	8,215	11,419	3,080	2,116	9,475	1,196	697
8.	7,829	2,025	791	984	527	573	144	124
9.	20,275	5,730	2,977	2,641	1,499	2,359	489	299
10.	3,220	342	4,687	192	231	9,876	83	101
11.	19,020	6,526	3,882	3,467	2,642	3,903	1,268	690
12.	26,108	6,255	2,308	2,833	1,689	2,152	700	404
13.	22,893	5,273	2,442	2,903	1,734	1,829	547	1,026
14.	19,558	2,367	1,566	1,836	704	982	361	362
15.	73,484	10,155	6,268	6,034	4,748	6,986	1,985	1,820
16.	7,436	1,653	8,739	1,240	1,516	1,647	960	265
17.	58,753	9,946	5,331	4,284	4,003	4,731	1,717	1,541
18.	65,395	12,196	7,872	6,545	2,618	3,163	1,582	1,676
19.	13,547	4,373	829	1,081	414	528	101	97
20.	131,822	42,504	31,984	33,630	24,403	29,792	10,702	7,243
21.	13,963	3,778	2,355	2,450	1,521	1,779	433	351
22.	234,561	43,640	32,937	24,119	20,410	35,937	7,852	5,230
23.	29,004	4,372	3,811	3,014	2,988	3,494	918	591
24.	26,053	10,126	4,363	7,018	2,638	3,199	908	575
25.	55,017	16,102	10,501	13,415	8,160	8,086	2,636	2,291
26.	132,676	21,757	26,910	29,480	25,313	26,473	11,552	7,461
27.	76,718	17,164	37,255	16,020	7,251	69,890	3,792	1,635
N.C.	164,087	44,346	27,198	28,846	12,793	22,493	6,489	3,897
Total Employed	1,404,262	330,490	324,400	244,417	190,500	312,286	85,145	62,081
Total Population	2,126,341	525,431	506,870	390,395	299,188	470,102	131,809	94,937

East Anglia

9. Bucks.	10. Beds.	11. Herts.	12. Essex	13. Cambridge	14. Hunts.	15. Norfolk	16. Suffolk	
17,243	14,560	18,090	46,838	27,578	8,678	54,596	43,218	1.
419	684	797	3,569	473	122	1,247	634	2.
4,629	4,508	7,730	32,996	4,660	1,248	12,080	9,707	3.
-	-	-	-	-	-	-	-	4.
279	212	937	8,253	237	38	1,229	1,049	5.
1,049	2,573	1,282	7,340	796	269	3,164	3,618	6.
822	2,532	1,283	13,777	652	172	2,028	4,370	7.
98	100	465	1,437	203	24	260	174	8.
400	552	545	5,680	179	21	861	422	9.
44	19	35	3,197	46	7	605	718	10.
3,485	1,618	1,226	5,682	572	390	1,603	1,580	11.
489	437	760	5,297	399	80	1,374	818	12.
324	508	785	5,250	371	78	1,259	1,621	13.
485	307	869	2,892	316	75	1,180	1,039	14.
2,492	6,209	2,749	11,079	1,472	336	8,802	3,259	15.
548	906	352	3,085	917	843	428	571	16.
5,351	1,182	1,781	10,681	836	148	3,239	1,991	17.
1,723	1,086	3,515	12,707	1,128	228	2,043	1,665	18.
185	89	412	4,054	93	11	339	361	19.
7,403	6,302	12,517	41,948	5,979	1,540	14,086	10,813	20.
303	399	659	5,767	269	56	623	556	21.
5,461	4,242	9,191	62,554	5,272	1,198	12,651	11,269	22.
605	638	972	5,335	572	120	2,367	1,400	23.
641	555	1,664	8,106	480	123	1,715	1,049	24.
1,983	1,532	3,971	12,480	1,863	426	3,885	2,913	25.
7,204	3,779	10,783	23,240	4,871	1,201	11,691	9,585	26.
1,402	1,354	2,866	22,648	1,208	338	4,138	5,403	27.
4,702	3,954	8,117	50,117	3,254	648	8,951	6,533	N.C.
69,769	60,837	94,353	416,009	64,696	18,418	156,444	126,336	
107,326	93,006	148,632	660,662	96,899	27,533	241,159	193,376	

MALE EMPLOYMENT: 1911

South West   West Midlands

	17.Corn-wall	18. Devon	19.Som-erset	20.Gloucs.	21.Wilts.	22.Dorset	23.Here-ford	24.Shrops
1.	28,207	44,572	33,679	26,580	25,830	18,446	15,418	23,494
2.	14,479	4,097	8,362	11,965	1,306	2,244	313	6,574
3.	5,343	13,231	10,049	18,970	5,867	5,029	2,010	4,713
4.	–	–	–	–	–	–	–	–
5.	408	1,262	605	3,295	212	180	101	257
6.	2,356	3,535	2,490	6,067	2,949	1,064	637	4,168
7.	1,537	4,557	2,085	5,454	6,990	1,106	179	1,576
8.	125	442	269	472	101	108	42	136
9.	340	1,113	536	1,030	239	243	86	249
10.	878	5,170	62	481	7	115	4	15
11.	735	1,986	1,632	4,188	3,441	645	498	1,299
12.	654	1,507	1,076	3,917	685	416	202	1,260
13.	676	2,438	3,124	3,136	1,354	939	156	773
14.	354	1,365	1,207	1,904	788	265	213	374
15.	2,293	6,460	6,579	13,059	2,091	1,475	795	1,726
16.	158	1,121	1,412	1,567	225	1,086	242	1,728
17.	982	3,932	3,188	7,247	1,487	1,195	512	998
18.	577	3,166	2,594	5,736	691	577	274	537
19.	77	326	337	971	855	63	33	50
20.	9,248	22,454	15,613	21,271	8,656	7,797	3,773	7,102
21.	250	1,160	747	1,705	456	432	103	331
22.	8,414	20,038	11,891	28,737	8,027	6,028	2,357	6,043
23.	966	2,545	1,180	2,569	672	704	200	494
24.	1,011	2,703	1,732	3,251	783	652	344	869
25.	2,760	6,554	4,478	6,474	2,251	1,947	1,095	2,016
26.	4,612	15,349	10,641	14,359	7,256	6,335	3,412	6,204
27.	4,404	32,517	3,439	5,757	5,676	10,656	856	1,900
N.C.	5,939	15,703	9,052	20,353	5,261	4,732	2,168	4,746
Total Employed	97,783	219,303	138,059	220,515	94,156	74,479	36,023	79,632
Total Population	151,614	332,813	212,732	343,605	143,137	110,805	55,168	121,835

East Midlands

25.Staffs.	26.Warwick	27.Worcs.	28.Derby	29.Notts.	30.Leics.	31.Lincs.	32.Northants.	
23,823	19,250	21,987	18,164	17,284	15,537	62,894	19,689	1.
64,124	18,484	4,662	63,409	40,797	13,761	3,532	3,302	2.
24,354	17,639	10,830	10,643	12,767	8,953	13,768	6,881	3.
–	–	–	–	–	–	–	–	4.
3,131	2,296	1,967	1,438	1,416	820	1,310	263	5.
47,113	26,196	12,281	13,370	5,742	3,840	9,692	3,398	6.
17,217	17,493	5,322	9,331	8,210	5,966	12,750	2,588	7.
888	2,269	368	384	373	285	262	158	8.
4,043	5,323	1,017	1,309	1,687	772	513	463	9.
293	140	104	10	74	8	836	23	10.
10,598	27,860	6,525	5,145	2,789	2,125	2,463	1,937	11.
32,319	34,684	14,161	2,500	1,517	1,392	1,303	582	12.
4,450	3,726	4,712	15,268	16,459	12,062	1,473	535	13.
7,050	2,665	1,314	848	1,357	1,083	981	2,422	14.
9,734	8,114	4,376	3,889	4,335	26,178	3,739	30,341	15.
34,597	3,950	2,761	4,053	1,540	1,546	1,149	566	16.
7,040	8,371	3,022	2,444	4,617	2,723	3,280	1,881	17.
3,718	5,909	2,218	2,672	3,833	2,735	1,574	1,172	18.
661	4,465	1,600	358	661	2,169	179	292	19.
35,475	29,051	14,232	17,309	15,329	11,627	16,522	9,618	20.
2,635	2,912	953	1,257	1,421	1,370	834	635	21.
33,912	30,619	13,039	18,921	17,810	11,449	19,952	9,438	22.
3,184	3,344	1,326	1,617	2,304	1,368	1,582	1,015	23.
4,431	3,379	2,329	2,271	2,209	1,567	1,490	952	24.
7,757	6,549	4,597	3,864	3,869	3,031	3,902	2,460	25.
15,486	17,374	9,288	8,922	9,390	8,209	8,653	6,918	26.
7,350	6,600	3,648	2,941	2,873	2,556	4,071	2,380	27.
27,971	24,265	12,961	12,624	12,520	9,497	10,167	5,954	N.C.
433,354	332,927	161,600	224,961	193,183	152,629	188,871	115,863	
668,694	505,737	250,446	342,964	291,720	228,353	281,279	170,841	

MALE EMPLOYMENT: 1911

	East Midlands	North West		Yorks. & Humberside		North		
	33.Rut-land	34. Cheshire	35.Lancs.	36. West Riding	37. East Riding	38. North Riding	39.West-morland	40.Cum-berland
1.	2,427	29,778	49,379	47,631	25,383	26,110	6,194	15,979
2.	250	5,508	118,073	151,137	1,909	10,632	593	16,235
3.	388	18,912	88,420	51,309	13,297	6,929	1,046	4,384
4.	-	-	-	-	-	-	-	-
5.	12	10,800	22,571	9,560	5,447	923	234	614
6.	111	9,306	64,109	68,257	4,483	19,680	326	5,194
7.	39	18,117	93,093	56,614	5,265	4,096	300	1,965
8.	9	601	3,122	1,849	509	221	35	153
9.	34	2,888	16,232	5,924	773	756	63	246
10.	-	5,947	9,896	1,148	3,367	4,074	36	174
11.	68	3,286	16,062	11,042	2,374	515	156	424
12.	25	4,818	23,436	42,414	1,575	2,547	123	555
13.	43	28,308	260,263	144,443	1,470	1,235	509	1,972
14.	26	1,903	8,390	7,775	1,779	369	89	579
15.	220	11,505	42,165	31,692	3,803	2,990	885	2,270
16.	17	1,340	16,235	14,101	1,160	803	18	369
17.	52	4,857	34,245	18,070	4,974	1,361	632	1,072
18.	40	4,253	29,548	13,967	2,426	992	444	1,047
19.	9	841	13,120	2,593	355	170	59	99
20.	663	28,296	118,501	77,042	14,910	12,356	2,393	7,244
21.	23	2,531	13,712	9,255	1,177	741	165	368
22.	503	39,172	205,011	86,961	32,989	13,388	1,491	7,973
23.	52	2,696	16,873	11,550	1,715	1,289	146	677
24.	44	5,427	21,556	10,857	1,753	1,222	208	914
25.	211	8,090	30,398	19,425	3,886	3,178	602	2,148
26.	970	17,189	63,359	37,915	7,624	7,163	1,610	3,542
27.	116	6,484	29,892	16,505	5,136	3,204	417	1,669
N.C.	285	28,978	131,276	66,100	14,209	8,788	1,273	4,986
Total Employed	6,637	301,831	1,538,937	1,015,136	163,748	135,732	20,047	82,852
Total Population	10,314	454,718	2,285,464	1,480,180	251,799	208,943	30,105	129,783

		Wales		Scotland				
41.North-amberland	42.Durham	43.Glam-organ & Monmouth	44.North & West Wales	45.Strathclyde	46.Dumfries & Galloway	47.Borders	48.Lothian	
15,504	13,016	17,717	80,077	31,962	15,776	11,074	12,001	1.
56,053	151,824	206,060	52,269	86,904	2,144	244	27,299	2.
10,460	16,478	23,550	13,557	40,419	2,542	2,109	15,073	3.
–	–	–	–	–	–	–	–	4.
1,850	7,961	3,547	1,485	7,440	203	139	4,269	5.
8,734	28,396	41,572	14,650	67,217	822	588	5,953	6.
15,808	25,593	11,557	3,286	58,774	527	367	5,162	7.
366	541	638	411	1,529	75	67	602	8.
2,360	2,871	2,618	943	4,981	86	77	1,214	9.
13,634	29,198	3,625	1,786	45,314	21	17	1,323	10.
1,300	2,437	3,565	1,697	6,685	296	148	986	11.
1,641	3,864	4,681	2,316	10,295	315	158	2,025	12.
2,042	2,695	2,700	4,156	27,065	1,555	6,841	2,533	13.
823	655	806	1,189	3,365	185	270	1,077	14.
4,230	5,567	8,233	6,857	17,655	1,346	1,142	5,137	15.
1,714	5,054	2,406	2,690	6,021	109	24	1,527	16.
3,245	5,405	5,086	2,561	15,822	457	417	4,879	17.
2,094	3,266	3,304	1,945	10,442	308	400	9,013	18.
432	428	437	158	2,043	30	60	1,901	19.
16,719	30,155	41,069	26,469	52,682	4,147	3,313	16,507	20.
1,346	2,687	2,178	739	5,954	167	166	1,443	21.
22,526	38,633	54,458	19,462	83,584	3,309	2,114	24,724	22.
2,275	4,080	4,154	1,978	4,768	322	207	1,325	23.
2,580	3,610	5,752	2,902	7,311	448	330	3,133	24.
4,928	7,061	10,871	8,854	17,388	1,422	1,096	8,884	25.
9,647	11,970	15,091	13,104	25,427	3,000	2,888	9,774	26.
5,081	4,920	7,333	6,978	16,080	853	783	8,992	27.
16,735	23,878	35,989	17,078	59,112	2,489	1,781	15,136	N.C.
224,127	432,243	518,997	289,597	716,239	42,954	36,820	191,892	
346,713	690,441	789,609	442,130	1,116,379	68,171	54,173	299,617	

MALE EMPLOYMENT: 1911

Scotland

	49.Central & Fife	50.Tayside	51.Grampian	52.High-land	53. South East	54. East Anglia	55. South West	56. W Midl
1.	12,490	21,404	46,779	43,688	298,384	134,070	177,314	103
2.	41,726	1,812	3,856	528	27,326	2,476	42,453	94
3.	7,692	7,868	8,664	3,453	286,187	27,695	58,489	59
4.	-	-	-	-	-	-	-	
5.	1,240	708	1,213	254	40,512	2,553	5,962	7
6.	10,677	3,752	3,016	1,320	56,773	7,847	18,461	90
7.	3,531	4,664	2,766	420	87,142	7,222	21,729	41
8.	196	253	328	123	15,097	661	1,517	3
9.	619	459	339	134	43,446	1,483	3,501	10
10.	651	1,502	1,771	257	22,027	1,376	6,713	
11.	573	607	801	367	53,409	4,145	12,627	46
12.	1,070	836	813	326	49,432	2,671	8,255	82
13.	6,268	20,398	3,332	1,052	45,514	3,329	11,667	13
14.	391	471	400	98	32,289	2,610	5,883	11
15.	2,489	3,467	4,163	2,036	134,009	13,869	31,957	24
16.	1,535	507	192	49	28,347	2,759	5,569	43
17.	2,577	2,591	4,746	1,867	109,301	6,214	18,031	19
18.	2,052	1,805	2,309	323	120,078	5,064	13,341	12
19.	2,851	352	650	43	25,710	804	2,629	6
20.	12,128	10,419	9,475	6,035	380,250	32,418	85,039	89
21.	851	839	722	122	33,758	1,504	4,750	6
22.	12,173	12,359	13,995	6,240	486,134	30,390	83,135	85
23.	738	817	1,269	919	55,742	4,459	8,636	8
24.	1,189	1,462	1,562	599	65,846	3,367	10,132	11
25.	3,288	3,855	3,736	2,280	136,174	9,087	24,464	22
26.	5,334	6,778	4,995	3,927	326,628	27,348	58,552	51
27.	2,473	3,278	2,987	7,030	257,995	11,087	62,449	20
N.C.	8,579	7,297	7,721	3,821	377,039	19,386	61,040	72
Total Employed	145,381	120,560	132,600	87,311	3,594,549	365,894	844,295	1,043
Total Population	229,125	188,619	217,365	135,390	5,554,699	558,967	1,294,906	1,601

57. East Midlands	58. North West	59.Yorks. & Humberside	60.North	61.Wales	62.Scotland	63.Great Britain	
135,995	79,157	73,014	76,803	97,794	195,174	1,371,677	1.
125,051	123,581	153,046	235,337	258,329	164,513	1,226,269	2.
53,400	107,332	64,606	39,297	37,107	87,820	821,479	3.
-	-	-	-	-	-	-	4.
5,259	33,371	15,007	11,582	5,032	15,466	142,496	5.
36,153	73,415	72,740	62,330	56,222	93,345	567,681	6.
38,884	111,210	61,879	47,762	14,843	76,211	508,669	7.
1,471	3,723	2,358	1,316	1,049	3,173	34,068	8.
4,778	19,120	6,697	6,296	3,561	7,909	107,509	9.
951	15,843	4,515	47,116	5,411	50,856	155,364	10.
14,527	19,348	13,416	4,832	5,262	10,463	184,809	11.
7,319	28,254	43,989	8,730	6,997	15,838	254,111	12.
45,840	288,571	145,913	8,453	6,856	69,044	639,004	13.
6,717	10,293	9,554	2,515	1,995	6,257	89,729	14.
68,702	53,670	35,495	15,942	15,090	37,435	430,914	15.
8,871	17,575	15,261	7,958	5,096	9,964	144,678	16.
14,997	39,102	23,044	11,715	7,647	33,356	283,350	17.
12,026	33,801	16,393	7,843	5,249	26,652	253,103	18.
3,668	13,961	2,948	1,188	595	7,930	66,242	19.
71,068	146,797	91,952	68,867	67,538	114,706	1,148,268	20.
5,540	16,243	10,432	5,307	2,917	10,264	97,649	21.
78,073	244,183	119,950	84,011	73,920	158,498	1,444,264	22.
7,938	19,569	13,265	8,467	6,132	10,365	143,121	23.
8,533	26,983	12,610	8,534	8,654	16,034	172,045	24.
17,337	38,488	23,311	17,917	19,725	41,949	350,466	25.
43,062	80,548	45,539	33,932	28,195	62,123	757,691	26.
14,937	36,376	21,641	15,291	14,311	42,476	496,917	27.
51,047	160,254	80,309	55,660	53,067	105,936	1,035,849	N.C.
882,144	1,840,768	1,178,884	895,001	808,594	1,473,757	12,927,422	
1,325,471	2,740,182	1,731,979	1,405,985	1,231,739	2,308,839	19,754,447	

FEMALE EMPLOYMENT: 1911

South East

	1. London	2. Middlesex	3. Kent	4. Surrey	5. Sussex	6. Hants.	7. Berks.	8. Oxon.
1.	372	758	1,926	468	573	597	273	220
2.	235	32	36	30	43	46	10	13
3.	39,808	6,355	5,060	3,969	3,506	4,507	2,224	914
4.	-	-	-	-	-	-	-	-
5.	5,881	1,884	862	338	190	156	61	11
6.	3,629	80	15	14	12	10	87	10
7.	197	43	11	70	5	5	-	-
8.	1,396	147	27	28	7	21	3	3
9.	2,139	1,684	7	157	4	2	1	-
10.	15	1	17	-	-	13	1	4
11.	203	23	13	19	7	11	8	1
12.	3,766	738	217	224	174	248	54	37
13.	22,910	4,808	3,480	2,949	2,426	2,978	817	1,280
14.	12,127	712	87	99	81	86	32	28
15.	157,675	21,420	13,658	11,913	10,578	16,939	4,203	3,963
16.	1,052	200	135	124	99	121	39	19
17.	8,306	942	376	379	266	501	132	65
18.	37,979	3,421	2,931	1,416	860	1,320	587	501
19.	3,992	494	115	94	94	154	36	28
20.	1,085	28	79	69	11	8	4	5
21.	68	7	-	-	-	-	-	-
22.	5,105	862	368	326	255	439	120	63
23.	10,660	1,581	2,294	1,325	1,282	1,927	477	339
24.	1,646	547	109	197	33	43	9	7
25.	53,359	14,464	13,073	12,567	11,417	10,597	3,350	2,621
26.	348,209	79,568	76,083	80,239	70,037	67,781	21,270	16,171
27.	11,619	2,677	1,450	1,809	970	1,348	476	344
N.C.	36,098	9,015	2,718	3,683	2,047	2,295	704	395
Total Employed	769,531	152,491	125,147	122,506	104,977	112,153	34,978	27,042
Total Population	2,395,344	601,034	538,721	455,183	364,190	480,477	139,200	104,332

East Anglia

9. Bucks.	10. Beds.	11. Herts.	12. Essex	13. Cambridge	14. Hunts.	15. Norfolk	16. Suffolk	
270	184	248	764	689	170	837	504	1.
16	1	16	130	7	3	27	23	2.
1,008	1,126	1,832	9,392	1,238	292	3,141	2,016	3.
–	–	–	–	–	–	–	–	4.
30	48	387	1,578	11	13	486	25	5.
14	19	11	380	11	1	14	18	6.
–	5	–	99	1	–	5	17	7.
2	8	297	139	4	–	9	9	8.
1	84	21	899	–	–	24	–	9.
–	–	–	8	1	–	–	1	10.
11	5	12	28	–	3	6	8	11.
27	42	59	448	20	9	92	57	12.
921	1,359	1,098	6,840	556	135	3,630	2,785	13.
286	22	389	1,224	48	2	587	923	14.
2,945	12,094	5,579	28,666	2,976	754	11,457	6,830	15.
23	27	36	191	21	2	47	39	16.
521	76	114	924	108	15	231	113	17.
1,244	940	1,870	4,240	284	118	1,114	590	18.
48	14	73	2,413	22	3	111	68	19.
4	5	12	117	2	1	12	11	20.
–	–	–	3	–	–	–	–	21.
80	61	138	1,003	54	14	132	101	22.
330	314	384	2,270	254	79	1,291	770	23.
8	11	27	420	4	3	20	16	24.
2,247	1,815	4,178	13,192	1,936	563	5,112	3,999	25.
14,559	10,862	22,940	62,763	13,152	3,167	29,424	24,216	26.
405	191	561	2,426	267	86	815	535	27.
368	382	1,161	7,213	284	48	882	623	N.C
25,368	29,695	41,443	147,770	21,950	5,481	59,506	44,297	
112,225	101,582	162,652	690,219	101,175	28,044	257,957	200,684	

FEMALE EMPLOYMENT: 1911

South West   West Midlands

	17.Corn-wall	18. Devon	19.Som-erset	20.Gloucs.	21.Wilts.	22.Dorset	23.Here-ford	24.Shrops.
1.	907	1,129	1,032	692	404	444	588	905
2.	172	44	43	74	22	4	7	44
3.	2,491	4,179	2,403	11,358	1,543	1,067	506	1,312
4.	–	–	–	–	–	–	–	–
5.	642	203	66	713	13	25	10	10
6.	6	22	4	50	25	5	1	9
7.	–	10	82	12	17	–	1	2
8.	–	14	11	22	9	1	4	6
9.	1	1	–	28	–	–	–	–
10.	2	14	–	–	–	–	–	–
11.	1	9	4	26	4	1	3	2
12.	112	255	85	751	69	26	23	97
13.	1,717	5,216	4,127	5,699	1,859	1,435	271	700
14.	28	233	247	297	139	18	10	29
15.	6,094	15,632	14,868	22,386	5,132	3,755	1,311	2,648
16.	43	204	83	317	31	71	48	293
17.	52	399	306	577	168	70	36	61
18.	220	1,291	1,224	5,562	217	195	88	210
19.	11	98	51	619	146	15	2	75
20.	4	9	8	8	7	2	–	9
21.	–	1	–	–	–	–	–	–
22.	83	219	172	274	64	76	43	68
23.	752	1,717	727	1,781	402	412	159	315
24.	4	35	16	107	5	5	1	7
25.	2,730	7,892	5,836	8,449	2,859	2,605	1,281	2,228
26.	17,876	50,774	34,516	45,026	15,525	15,567	8,615	16,204
27.	521	907	647	1,036	455	344	267	409
N.C.	319	1,334	821	2,279	347	337	137	238
Total Employed	34,788	91,841	67,379	108,143	29,462	26,480	13,412	25,881
Total Population	176,484	366,890	245,293	392,492	143,685	112,461	59,101	124,472

East Midlands

25.Staffs.	26.Warwick	27.Worcs.	28.Derby	29.Notts.	30.Leics.	31.Lincs.	32.Northants.	
850	399	774	708	371	381	1,381	281	1.
240	123	78	51	54	22	35	26	2.
7,808	7,335	5,437	3,184	4,765	3,578	4,256	1,661	3.
-	-	-	-	-	-	-	-	4.
770	1,384	237	160	337	171	110	84	5.
1,641	7,278	807	113	671	19	55	7	6.
363	687	39	96	178	13	31	2	7.
250	917	89	194	122	15	4	6	8.
334	1,231	116	94	199	52	3	2	9.
2	1	-	-	-	-	1	-	10.
700	4,864	975	21	237	12	78	35	11.
12,954	20,869	5,649	261	212	373	105	62	12.
7,897	8,422	5,740	20,273	30,535	27,128	1,887	989	13.
4,301	2,673	627	107	231	100	64	263	14.
19,664	17,993	9,804	7,787	13,140	20,817	6,437	21,470	15.
27,783	521	1,014	1,288	78	79	55	35	16.
818	2,437	400	397	520	290	284	116	17.
2,796	5,913	1,535	1,623	2,048	1,828	573	1,052	18.
858	4,878	1,900	212	163	1,496	55	219	19.
1,219	905	47	19	29	13	20	9	20.
1	-	2	-	-	-	-	-	21.
811	1,037	352	224	1,136	508	169	156	22.
2,888	3,113	1,187	893	924	646	859	607	23.
159	337	142	26	51	24	37	11	24.
9,980	8,381	5,635	5,102	4,375	3,780	4,785	3,092	25.
46,828	45,308	27,761	24,228	23,409	17,257	28,448	15,158	26.
1,177	1,159	726	578	584	553	570	407	27.
5,103	8,071	2,450	1,157	2,239	1,673	805	955	N.C.
158,195	156,236	73,523	68,796	86,608	80,828	51,107	46,705	
679,565	534,672	275,641	340,459	312,378	248,200	282,681	177,674	

FEMALE EMPLOYMENT: 1911

	East Midlands	North West		Yorks. & Humberside		North		
	33.Rutland	34.Cheshire	35.Lancs.	36. West Riding	37. East Riding	38. North Riding	39.Westmorland	40.Cumberland
1.	42	1,469	2,102	1,647	525	873	241	799
2.	-	69	2,792	183	57	18	3	317
3.	79	8,607	48,502	21,126	6,585	2,371	535	2,743
4.	-	-	-	-	-	-	-	-
5.	1	1,671	4,598	1,549	2,049	47	45	22
6.	1	98	1,187	735	1,001	6	1	371
7.	-	295	2,154	754	2	1	36	14
8.	1	83	231	181	32	5	1	8
9.	-	161	1,403	91	-	1	1	1
10.	-	14	48	-	7	1	-	-
11.	-	21	247	164	9	5	-	1
12.	3	340	3,375	10,778	115	93	13	42
13.	27	35,727	346,902	158,859	1,862	987	560	2,401
14.	2	320	1,594	1,351	122	19	36	17
15.	243	18,728	95,459	60,474	7,201	4,903	1,107	4,092
16.	2	127	1,973	1,063	66	66	7	27
17.	4	457	4,273	2,668	399	112	35	73
18.	10	2,789	17,493	8,235	1,496	378	209	580
19.	2	224	4,911	799	60	38	17	21
20.	2	130	121	849	12	13	4	2
21.	-	-	11	1	1	-	-	-
22.	1	649	4,487	2,467	449	114	24	110
23.	26	1,555	10,468	6,625	861	781	76	441
24.	-	176	820	262	79	28	1	11
25.	221	8,727	36,671	21,906	4,738	3,431	668	2,266
26.	1,610	52,135	177,118	103,775	26,991	23,038	4,692	12,981
27.	49	1,101	4,916	2,649	531	474	95	342
N.C.	13	2,696	13,413	7,604	1,200	555	89	460
Total Employed	2,339	138,369	787,269	416,795	56,450	38,358	8,496	28,142
Total Population	10,032	500,061	2,482,368	1,565,197	263,242	210,603	33,470	135,963

	Wales			Scotland				
41.North-umberland	42.Durham	43.Glam-organ & Monmouth	44.North & West Wales	45.Strathclyde	46.Dumfries & Galloway	47.Borders	48.Lothian	
2,354	1,162	880	6,393	5,575	1,909	1,945	2,824	1.
37	81	162	90	1,125	14	-	277	2.
4,513	7,741	8,161	5,801	22,885	733	535	6,210	3.
-	-	-	-	-	-	-	-	4.
343	675	264	103	2,161	17	9	618	5.
104	61	2,214	926	307	3	3	97	6.
225	70	5	1	1,916	3	11	106	7.
6	10	18	4	83	-	3	57	8.
154	388	2	5	55	-	1	22	9.
42	47	2	-	268	-	-	3	10.
10	4	7	16	82	1	3	15	11.
309	552	288	204	2,629	23	17	287	12.
1,845	4,433	4,097	3,261	50,853	1,542	7,143	4,453	13.
364	153	40	90	923	2	1	214	14.
7,868	12,952	19,379	13,961	39,518	2,804	1,473	10,834	15.
596	595	304	180	1,868	17	28	489	16.
264	393	351	104	3,536	19	16	723	17.
882	1,772	1,363	579	10,562	122	141	6,888	18.
129	125	120	41	1,278	3	40	1,607	19.
12	20	15	12	67	10	5	25	20.
2	2	1	-	25	-	-	13	21.
461	461	458	219	5,426	60	59	1,003	22.
1,831	3,098	2,452	1,354	4,888	181	123	1,559	23.
81	74	107	14	128	6	1	55	24.
4,887	8,232	10,737	7,081	16,497	1,087	757	6,585	25.
31,148	43,089	52,092	53,595	68,228	7,662	5,355	32,928	26.
770	986	1,521	1,222	2,132	219	149	694	27.
2,399	2,452	1,831	550	17,429	418	310	6,475	N.C.
61,636	89,628	106,871	95,806	260,444	16,855	18,128	85,061	
350,180	679,419	727,020	462,162	1,142,463	75,019	62,521	331,458	

FEMALE EMPLOYMENT: 1911

Scotland

	49.Central & Fife	50.Tayside	51.Grampian	52.Highland	53. South East	54. East Anglia	55. South West	56. West Midland
1.	1,954	1,465	2,190	4,876	6,653	2,200	4,608	3,516
2.	1,110	13	4	2	608	60	359	492
3.	2,335	3,647	5,179	3,460	79,701	6,687	23,041	22,398
4.	-	-	-	-	-	-	-	-
5.	363	125	115	18	11,426	535	1,662	2,411
6.	131	55	64	10	4,281	44	112	9,736
7.	38	24	9	2	435	23	121	1,092
8.	7	6	9	1	2,078	22	57	1,266
9.	16	-	-	-	4,999	24	30	1,681
10.	2	4	2	-	59	2	16	3
11.	5	5	4	-	341	17	45	6,544
12.	207	106	113	20	6,034	178	1,298	39,592
13.	13,896	37,220	5,567	5,229	51,866	7,106	20,053	23,030
14.	34	118	31	-	15,173	1,560	962	7,640
15.	4,875	5,650	5,856	2,086	289,633	22,017	67,867	51,420
16.	510	84	41	17	2,066	109	749	29,659
17.	254	169	210	37	12,602	467	1,572	3,752
18.	1,308	906	2,605	96	57,309	2,106	8,709	10,542
19.	303	17	308	4	7,555	204	940	7,713
20.	13	17	9	3	1,427	26	38	2,180
21.	2	1	1	-	78	-	1	3
22.	284	407	489	78	8,820	301	888	2,311
23.	861	796	848	412	23,183	2,394	5,791	7,662
24.	15	63	16	3	3,057	43	172	646
25.	3,048	3,379	3,909	1,947	142,880	11,610	30,371	27,505
26.	12,745	15,501	21,641	11,407	870,482	69,959	179,284	144,716
27.	396	447	440	455	24,276	1,703	3,910	3,738
N.C.	1,906	2,418	2,450	514	66,079	1,837	5,437	15,999
Total Employed	46,618	72,643	52,110	30,677	1,693,101	131,234	358,093	427,247
Total Population	230,726	224,667	240,649	144,562	6,145,159	587,860	1,437,305	1,673,451

57. East Midlands	58. North West	59. Yorks. & Humberside	60. North	61. Wales	62. Scotland	63. Great Britain	
3,164	3,571	2,172	5,429	7,273	22,738	61,324	1.
188	2,861	240	456	252	2,545	8,061	2.
17,523	57,109	27,711	17,903	13,962	44,984	311,019	3.
–	–	–	–	–	–	–	4.
863	6,269	3,598	1,132	367	3,426	31,689	5.
866	1,285	1,736	543	3,140	670	22,413	6.
320	2,449	756	346	6	2,109	7,657	7.
342	314	213	30	22	166	4,510	8.
350	1,564	91	545	7	94	9,385	9.
1	62	7	90	2	279	521	10.
383	268	173	20	23	115	7,929	11.
1,016	3,715	10,893	1,009	492	3,402	67,629	12.
80,839	382,629	160,721	10,226	7,358	125,903	869,731	13.
767	1,914	1,473	589	130	1,323	31,531	14.
69,894	114,187	67,675	30,922	33,340	73,096	820,051	15.
1,537	2,100	1,129	1,291	484	3,054	42,178	16.
1,611	4,730	3,067	877	455	4,964	34,097	17.
7,134	20,282	9,731	3,821	1,942	22,628	144,204	18.
2,147	5,135	859	330	161	3,560	28,604	19.
92	251	861	51	27	149	5,102	20.
–	11	2	4	1	42	142	21.
2,194	5,136	2,916	1,170	677	7,806	32,219	22.
3,955	12,023	7,486	6,227	3,806	9,668	82,195	23.
149	996	341	195	121	287	6,007	24.
21,355	45,398	26,644	19,484	17,818	37,209	380,274	25.
110,110	229,253	130,766	114,948	105,687	175,467	2,130,672	26.
2,741	6,017	3,180	2,667	2,743	4,932	55,907	27.
6,842	16,109	8,804	5,955	2,381	31,920	161,363	N.C.
336,383	925,638	473,245	226,260	202,677	582,536	5,356,414	
1,371,424	2,982,429	1,828,439	1,409,635	1,189,182	2,452,065	21,076,949	

TOTAL EMPLOYMENT: 1911

South East

	1. London	2. Middlesex	3. Kent	4. Surrey	5. Sussex	6. Hants.	7. Berks.	8. Oxon
1.	9,451	15,271	52,920	22,269	38,249	34,964	16,346	17,370
2.	8,895	2,296	4,230	1,878	1,589	2,240	509	665
3.	150,408	33,377	29,681	25,133	21,522	25,046	11,946	5,554
4.	-	-	-	-	-	-	-	-
5.	24,871	6,016	3,709	2,476	1,256	1,334	359	193
6.	26,613	3,794	5,334	2,368	2,290	4,671	2,225	1,091
7.	32,727	8,258	11,430	3,150	2,121	9,480	1,196	697
8.	9,225	2,172	818	1,012	534	594	147	127
9.	22,414	7,414	2,984	2,798	1,503	2,361	490	299
10.	3,235	343	4,704	192	231	9,889	84	105
11.	19,223	6,549	3,895	3,486	2,649	3,914	1,276	691
12.	29,874	6,993	2,525	3,057	1,863	2,400	754	441
13.	45,803	10,081	5,922	5,852	4,160	4,807	1,364	2,306
14.	31,685	3,079	1,653	1,935	785	1,068	393	390
15.	231,159	31,575	19,926	17,947	15,326	23,925	6,188	5,783
16.	8,488	1,853	8,874	1,364	1,615	1,768	999	284
17.	67,059	10,888	5,707	4,663	4,269	5,232	1,849	1,606
18.	103,374	15,617	10,803	7,961	3,478	4,483	2,169	2,177
19.	17,539	4,867	944	1,175	508	682	137	125
20.	132,907	42,532	32,063	33,699	24,414	29,800	10,706	7,248
21.	14,031	3,785	2,355	2,450	1,521	1,779	433	351
22.	239,666	44,502	33,305	24,445	20,665	36,376	7,972	5,293
23.	39,664	5,953	6,105	4,339	4,270	5,421	1,395	930
24.	27,699	10,673	4,472	7,215	2,671	3,242	917	582
25.	108,376	30,566	23,574	25,982	19,577	18,683	5,986	4,912
26.	480,885	101,325	102,993	109,719	95,350	94,254	32,822	23,632
27.	88,337	19,841	38,705	17,829	8,221	71,238	4,268	1,979
N.C.	200,185	53,361	29,916	32,529	14,840	24,788	7,193	4,292
Total Employed	2,173,793	482,981	449,547	366,923	295,477	424,439	120,123	89,123
Total Population	4,521,685	1,126,465	1,045,591	845,578	663,378	950,579	271,009	199,269

East Anglia

9. Bucks.	10.Beds.	11. Herts.	12. Essex	13. Cambridge	14. Hunts.	15. Norfolk	16. Suffolk	
17,513	14,744	18,338	47,602	28,267	8,848	55,433	43,722	1.
435	685	813	3,699	480	125	1,274	657	2.
5,637	5,634	9,562	42,388	5,898	1,540	15,221	11,723	3.
-	-	-	-	-	-	-	-	4.
309	260	1,324	9,831	248	51	1,715	1,074	5.
1,063	2,592	1,293	7,720	807	270	3,178	3,636	6.
822	2,537	1,283	13,876	653	172	2,033	4,387	7.
100	108	762	1,576	207	24	269	183	8.
401	636	566	6,579	179	21	885	422	9.
44	19	35	3,205	47	7	605	719	10.
3,496	1,623	1,238	5,710	572	393	1,609	1,588	11.
516	479	819	5,745	419	89	1,466	875	12.
1,245	1,867	1,883	12,090	927	213	4,889	4,406	13.
771	329	1,258	4,116	364	77	1,767	1,962	14.
5,437	18,303	8,328	39,745	4,448	1,090	20,259	10,089	15.
571	933	388	3,276	938	845	475	610	16.
5,872	1,258	1,895	11,605	944	163	3,470	2,104	17.
2,967	2,026	5,385	16,947	1,412	346	3,157	2,255	18.
233	103	485	6,467	115	14	450	429	19.
7,407	6,307	12,529	42,065	5,981	1,541	14,098	10,824	20.
303	399	659	5,770	269	56	623	556	21.
5,541	4,303	9,329	63,557	5,326	1,212	12,783	11,370	22.
935	952	1,356	7,605	826	199	3,658	2,170	23.
649	566	1,691	8,526	484	126	1,735	1,065	24.
4,230	3,347	8,149	25,672	3,799	989	8,997	6,912	25.
21,763	14,641	33,723	86,003	18,023	4,368	41,115	33,801	26.
1,807	1,545	3,427	25,074	1,475	424	4,953	5,938	27.
5,070	4,336	9,278	57,330	3,538	696	9,833	7,156	N.C
95,137	90,532	135,796	563,779	86,646	23,899	215,950	170,633	
219,551	194,588	311,284	1,350,881	198,074	55,577	499,116	394,060	

TOTAL EMPLOYMENT: 1911

South West   West Midlands

	17.Corn-wall	18. Devon	19.Som-erset	20.Gloucs.	21.Wilts.	22.Dorset	23.Here-ford	24.Shrop
1.	29,114	45,701	34,711	27,272	26,234	18,890	16,006	24,399
2.	14,651	4,141	8,405	12,039	1,328	2,248	320	6,618
3.	7,834	17,410	12,452	30,328	7,410	6,096	2,516	6,025
4.	–	–	–	–	–	–	–	–
5.	1,050	1,465	671	4,008	225	205	111	267
6.	2,362	3,557	2,494	6,117	2,974	1,069	638	4,177
7.	1,537	4,567	2,167	5,466	7,007	1,106	180	1,578
8.	125	456	280	494	110	109	46	142
9.	341	1,114	536	1,058	239	243	86	249
10.	880	5,184	62	481	7	115	4	15
11.	736	1,995	1,636	4,214	3,445	646	501	1,301
12.	766	1,762	1,161	4,668	754	442	225	1,357
13.	2,393	7,654	7,251	8,835	3,213	2,374	427	1,473
14.	382	1,598	1,454	2,201	927	283	223	403
15.	8,387	22,092	21,447	35,445	7,223	5,230	2,106	4,374
16.	201	1,325	1,495	1,884	256	1,157	290	2,021
17.	1,034	4,331	3,494	7,824	1,655	1,265	548	1,059
18.	797	4,457	3,818	11,298	908	772	362	747
19.	88	424	388	1,590	1,001	78	35	125
20.	9,252	22,463	15,621	21,279	8,663	7,799	3,773	7,111
21.	250	1,161	747	1,705	456	432	103	331
22.	8,497	20,257	12,063	29,011	8,091	6,104	2,400	6,111
23.	1,718	4,262	1,907	4,350	1,074	1,116	359	809
24.	1,015	2,738	1,748	3,358	788	657	345	876
25.	5,490	14,446	10,314	14,923	5,110	4,552	2,376	4,244
26.	22,488	66,123	45,157	59,385	22,781	21,902	12,027	22,408
27.	4,925	33,424	4,086	6,793	6,131	11,000	1,123	2,309
N.C.	6,258	17,037	9,873	22,632	5,608	5,069	2,305	4,984
Total Employed	132,571	311,144	205,438	328,658	123,618	100,959	49,435	105,513
Total Population	328,098	699,703	458,025	736,097	286,822	223,266	114,269	246,307

East Midlands

5.Staffs.	26.War-wick	27.Worcs.	28.Derby	29.Notts.	30.Leics.	31.Lincs.	32.North-ants.	
24,673	19,649	22,761	18,872	17,655	15,918	64,275	19,970	1.
64,364	18,607	4,740	63,460	40,851	13,783	3,567	3,328	2.
32,162	24,974	16,267	13,827	17,532	12,531	18,024	8,542	3.
-	-	-	-	-	-	-	-	4.
3,901	3,680	2,204	1,598	1,753	991	1,420	347	5.
48,754	33,474	13,088	13,483	6,413	3,859	9,747	3,405	6.
17,580	18,180	5,361	9,427	8,388	5,979	12,781	2,590	7.
1,138	3,186	457	578	495	300	266	164	8.
4,377	6,554	1,133	1,403	1,886	824	516	465	9.
295	141	104	10	74	8	837	23	10.
11,298	32,724	7,500	5,166	3,026	2,137	2,541	1,972	11.
45,273	55,553	19,810	2,761	1,729	1,765	1,408	644	12.
12,347	12,148	10,452	35,541	46,994	39,190	3,360	1,524	13.
11,351	5,338	1,941	955	1,588	1,183	1,045	2,685	14.
29,398	26,107	14,180	11,676	17,475	46,995	10,176	51,811	15.
62,380	4,471	3,775	5,341	1,618	1,625	1,204	601	16.
7,858	10,808	3,422	2,841	5,137	3,013	3,564	1,997	17.
6,514	11,822	3,753	4,295	5,881	4,563	2,147	2,224	18.
1,519	9,343	3,500	570	824	3,665	234	511	19.
36,694	29,956	14,279	17,328	15,358	11,640	16,542	9,627	20.
2,636	2,912	955	1,257	1,421	1,370	834	635	21.
34,723	31,656	13,391	19,145	18,946	11,957	20,121	9,594	22.
6,072	6,457	2,513	2,510	3,228	2,014	2,441	1,622	23.
4,590	3,716	2,471	2,297	2,260	1,591	1,527	963	24.
17,737	14,930	10,232	8,966	8,244	6,811	8,687	5,552	25.
62,314	62,682	37,049	33,150	32,799	25,466	37,101	22,076	26.
8,527	7,759	4,374	3,519	3,457	3,109	4,641	2,787	27.
33,074	32,336	15,411	13,781	14,759	11,170	10,972	6,909	N.C.
591,549	489,163	235,123	293,757	279,791	233,457	239,978	162,568	
,348,259	1,040,409	526,087	683,423	604,098	476,553	563,960	348,515	

TOTAL EMPLOYMENT: 1911

	East Midlands	North West	Yorks. & Humberside		North			
	33.Rut-land	34.Cheshire	35.Lancs.	36. West Riding	37. East Riding	38. North Riding	39.West-morland	40.Cum-berland
1.	2,469	31,247	51,481	49,278	25,908	26,983	6,435	16,778
2.	250	5,577	120,865	151,320	1,966	10,650	596	16,552
3.	467	27,519	136,922	72,435	19,882	9,300	1,581	7,127
4.	-	-	-	-	-	-	-	-
5.	13	12,471	27,169	11,109	7,496	970	279	636
6.	112	9,404	65,296	68,992	5,484	19,686	327	5,565
7.	39	18,412	95,247	57,368	5,267	4,097	336	1,979
8.	10	684	3,353	2,030	541	226	36	161
9.	34	3,049	17,635	6,015	773	757	64	247
10.	-	5,961	9,944	1,148	3,374	4,075	36	174
11.	68	3,307	16,309	11,206	2,383	520	156	425
12.	28	5,158	26,811	53,192	1,690	2,640	136	597
13.	70	64,035	607,165	303,302	3,332	2,222	1,069	4,373
14.	28	2,223	9,984	9,126	1,901	388	125	596
15.	463	30,233	137,624	92,166	11,004	7,893	1,992	6,362
16.	19	1,467	18,208	15,164	1,226	869	25	396
17.	56	5,314	38,518	20,738	5,373	1,473	667	1,145
18.	50	7,042	47,041	22,202	3,922	1,370	653	1,627
19.	11	1,065	18,031	3,392	415	208	76	120
20.	665	28,426	118,622	77,891	14,922	12,369	2,397	7,246
21.	23	2,531	13,723	9,256	1,178	741	165	368
22.	504	39,821	209,498	89,428	33,438	13,502	1,515	8,083
23.	78	4,251	27,341	18,175	2,576	2,070	222	1,118
24.	44	5,603	22,376	11,119	1,832	1,250	209	925
25.	432	16,817	67,069	41,331	8,624	6,609	1,270	4,414
26.	2,580	69,324	240,477	141,690	34,615	30,201	6,302	16,523
27.	165	7,585	34,808	19,154	5,667	3,678	512	2,011
N.C.	298	31,674	144,689	73,704	15,409	9,343	1,362	5,446
Total Employed	8,976	440,200	2,326,206	1,431,931	220,198	174,090	28,543	110,994
Total Population	20,346	954,779	4,767,832	3,045,377	515,041	419,546	63,575	265,746

| | Wales | | | Scotland | | | |
41.North-umberland	42.Durham	43.Glam-organ & Monmouth	44.North & West Wales	45.Strathclyde	46.Dumfries & Galloway	47.Borders	48.Lothian	
17,858	14,178	18,597	86,470	37,537	17,685	13,019	14,825	1.
56,090	151,905	206,222	52,359	88,029	2,158	244	27,576	2.
14,973	24,219	31,711	19,358	63,304	3,275	2,644	21,283	3.
-	-	-	-	-	-	-	-	4.
2,193	8,636	3,811	1,588	9,601	220	148	4,887	5.
8,838	28,457	43,786	15,576	67,524	825	591	6,050	6.
16,033	25,663	11,562	3,287	60,690	530	378	5,268	7.
372	551	656	415	1,612	75	70	659	8.
2,514	3,259	2,620	948	5,036	86	78	1,236	9.
13,676	29,245	3,627	1,786	45,582	21	17	1,326	10.
1,310	2,441	3,572	1,713	6,767	297	151	1,001	11.
1,950	4,416	4,969	2,520	12,924	338	175	2,312	12.
3,887	7,128	6,797	7,417	77,918	3,097	13,984	6,986	13.
1,187	808	846	1,279	4,288	187	271	1,291	14.
12,098	18,519	27,612	20,818	57,173	4,150	2,615	15,971	15.
2,310	5,649	2,710	2,870	7,889	126	52	2,016	16.
3,509	5,798	5,437	2,665	19,358	476	433	5,602	17.
2,976	5,038	4,667	2,524	21,004	430	541	15,901	18.
561	553	557	199	3,321	33	100	3,508	19.
16,731	30,175	41,084	26,481	52,749	4,157	3,318	16,532	20.
1,348	2,689	2,179	739	5,979	167	166	1,456	21.
22,987	39,094	54,916	19,681	89,010	3,369	2,173	25,727	22.
4,106	7,178	6,606	3,332	9,656	503	330	2,884	23.
2,661	3,684	5,859	2,916	7,439	454	331	3,188	24.
9,815	15,293	21,608	15,935	33,885	2,509	1,853	15,469	25.
40,795	55,059	67,183	66,699	93,655	10,662	8,243	42,702	26.
5,851	5,906	8,854	8,200	18,212	1,072	932	9,686	27.
19,134	26,330	37,820	17,628	76,541	2,907	2,091	21,611	N.C.
285,763	521,871	625,868	385,403	976,683	59,809	54,948	276,953	
696,893	1,369,860	1,516,629	904,292	2,258,842	143,190	116,694	631,075	

TOTAL EMPLOYMENT: 1911

Scotland

	49.Central & Fife	50.Tayside	51.Grampian	52.High-land	53. South East	54. East Anglia	55. South West	56. Mi
1.	14,444	22,869	48,969	48,564	305,037	136,270	181,922	10
2.	42,836	1,825	3,860	530	27,934	2,536	42,812	9
3.	10,027	11,515	13,843	6,913	365,888	34,382	81,530	8
4.	-	-	-	-	-	-	-	
5.	1,603	833	1,328	272	51,938	3,088	7,624	1
6.	10,808	3,807	3,080	1,330	61,054	7,891	18,573	100
7.	3,569	4,688	2,775	422	87,577	7,245	21,850	4
8.	203	259	337	124	17,175	683	1,574	
9.	635	459	339	134	48,445	1,507	3,531	1
10.	653	1,506	1,773	257	22,086	1,378	6,729	
11.	578	612	805	367	53,750	4,162	12,672	5
12.	1,277	942	926	346	55,466	2,849	9,553	12
13.	20,164	57,618	8,899	6,281	97,380	10,435	31,720	3
14.	425	589	431	98	47,462	4,170	6,845	1
15.	7,364	9,117	10,019	4,122	423,642	35,886	99,824	7
16.	2,045	591	233	66	30,413	2,868	6,318	7
17.	2,831	2,760	4,956	1,904	121,903	6,681	19,603	2
18.	3,360	2,711	4,914	419	177,387	7,170	22,050	2
19.	3,154	369	958	47	33,265	1,008	3,569	1
20.	12,141	10,436	9,484	6,038	381,677	32,444	85,077	9
21.	853	840	723	122	33,836	1,504	4,751	
22.	12,457	12,766	14,484	6,318	494,954	30,691	84,023	88
23.	1,599	1,613	2,117	1,331	78,925	6,853	14,427	1
24.	1,204	1,525	1,578	602	68,903	3,410	10,304	1
25.	6,336	7,234	7,645	4,227	279,054	20,697	54,835	4
26.	18,079	22,279	26,636	15,334	1,197,110	97,307	237,836	19
27.	2,869	3,725	3,427	7,485	282,271	12,790	66,359	2
N.C.	10,485	9,715	10,171	4,335	443,118	21,223	66,477	88
Total Employed	191,999	193,203	184,710	117,988	5,287,650	497,128	1,202,388	1,47
Total Population	459,851	413,286	458,014	279,952	11,699,858	1,146,827	2,732,011	3,27

57. East Midlands	58. North West	59. Yorks. & Humberside	60. North	61. Wales	62. Scotland	63. Great Britain	
139,159	82,728	75,186	82,232	105,067	217,912	1,433,001	1.
125,239	126,442	153,286	235,793	258,581	167,058	1,234,330	2.
70,923	164,441	92,317	57,200	51,069	132,804	1,132,498	3.
-	-	-	-	-	-	-	4.
6,122	39,640	18,605	12,714	5,399	18,892	174,185	5.
37,019	74,700	74,476	62,873	59,362	94,015	590,094	6.
39,204	113,659	62,635	48,108	14,849	78,320	516,326	7.
1,813	4,037	2,571	1,346	1,071	3,339	38,578	8.
5,128	20,684	6,788	6,841	3,568	8,003	116,894	9.
952	15,905	4,522	47,206	5,413	51,135	155,885	10.
14,910	19,616	13,589	4,852	5,285	10,578	192,738	11.
8,335	31,969	54,882	9,739	7,489	19,240	321,740	12.
126,679	671,200	306,634	18,679	14,214	194,947	1,508,735	13.
7,484	12,207	11,027	3,104	2,125	7,580	121,260	14.
138,596	167,857	103,170	46,864	48,430	110,531	1,250,965	15.
10,408	19,675	16,390	9,249	5,580	13,018	186,856	16.
16,608	43,832	26,111	12,592	8,102	38,320	317,447	17.
19,160	54,083	26,124	11,664	7,191	49,280	397,307	18.
5,815	19,096	3,807	1,518	756	11,490	94,846	19.
71,160	147,048	92,813	68,918	67,565	114,855	1,153,370	20.
5,540	16,254	10,434	5,311	2,918	10,306	97,791	21.
80,267	249,319	122,866	85,181	74,597	166,304	1,476,483	22.
11,893	31,592	20,751	14,694	9,938	20,033	225,316	23.
8,682	27,979	12,951	8,729	8,775	16,321	178,052	24.
38,692	83,886	49,955	37,401	37,543	79,158	730,740	25.
153,172	309,801	176,305	148,880	133,882	237,590	2,888,363	26.
17,678	42,393	24,821	17,958	17,054	47,408	552,824	27.
57,889	176,363	89,113	61,615	55,448	137,856	1,197,212	N.C.
1,218,527	2,766,406	1,652,129	1,121,261	1,011,271	2,056,293	18,283,836	
2,696,895	5,722,611	3,560,418	2,815,620	2,420,921	4,760,904	40,831,396	

PART III

STATISTICAL TABLES

Series B, county and regional employment 1901–1971

MALE EMPLOYMENT: 1901

South East

	1. London	2. Middlesex	3. Kent	4. Surrey	5. Sussex	6. Hants.	7. Berks.	8. Oxon.
1.	8,454	12,092	46,664	19,428	34,261	30,612	14,966	15,790
2.	1,349	164	1,986	402	426	208	48	226
3.	30,918	3,913	5,619	3,472	4,158	5,043	5,498	1,431
4.	-	-	-	-	-	-	-	-
5.	8,074	1,045	1,157	619	199	259	25	13
6.	6,281	440	1,306	323	289	570	247	252
7.	36,255	6,167	9,700	1,824	1,778	5,842	1,065	679
8.	7,072	1,085	678	670	521	499	171	102
9.	11,665	1,961	1,463	1,083	820	851	273	109
10.	3,731	512	4,629	171	277	5,631	96	101
11.	12,048	2,147	2,920	2,015	2,102	2,695	971	548
12.	41,411	5,144	5,125	2,719	2,753	4,485	2,082	982
13.	5,297	461	477	267	262	315	88	505
14.	14,757	1,085	1,273	1,357	640	804	337	297
15.	64,227	4,563	4,374	3,375	3,389	4,922	1,659	1,530
16.	6,339	1,787	10,843	1,629	1,856	1,749	1,004	251
17.	54,943	4,652	4,082	2,555	3,016	3,371	1,335	1,007
18.	55,308	5,913	5,064	3,117	1,819	2,213	910	1,190
19.	13,981	2,658	666	727	325	396	77	72
20.	153,804	38,053	36,948	32,829	26,395	30,579	10,745	6,939
21.	9,372	1,614	1,443	1,131	986	959	286	191
22.	234,746	29,391	30,412	18,195	18,734	28,786	6,730	4,587
23.	164,512	26,517	26,484	20,227	18,914	21,157	6,351	4,674
24.	30,923	7,501	4,135	5,897	2,416	2,660	744	487
25.	55,843	11,139	8,934	9,502	7,270	7,192	2,403	2,087
26.	108,114	13,498	21,314	21,111	18,867	19,066	8,789	5,723
27.	68,916	9,108	35,028	10,075	6,447	46,633	3,969	1,467
N.C.	191,629	33,494	27,952	22,301	12,113	22,459	6,306	4,036
Total Employed	1,399,969	226,104	300,676	187,021	171,033	249,956	77,175	55,276
Total Population	2,142,085	371,061	471,436	303,263	273,724	389,118	122,807	88,316

East Anglia

9. Bucks.	10. Beds.	11. Herts.	12. Essex	13. Cambridge	14. Hunts.	15. Norfolk	16. Suffolk	
16,042	13,613	16,380	41,510	23,990	7,635	50,274	40,205	1.
63	198	313	361	52	16	188	78	2.
1,254	1,029	2,334	7,538	1,349	440	4,123	3,383	3.
-	-	-	-	-	-	-	-	4.
65	39	499	3,937	72	21	596	506	5.
186	788	176	2,094	72	20	556	1,119	6.
700	1,473	1,083	11,158	504	148	1,900	2,967	7.
82	80	188	856	139	34	296	193	8.
158	201	237	2,911	124	14	431	199	9.
41	10	42	2,644	39	8	481	524	10.
2,741	564	878	3,796	477	347	1,428	1,262	11.
1,210	1,057	1,241	6,665	899	292	3,346	2,431	12.
43	67	136	1,279	88	17	538	1,418	13.
253	254	494	1,634	314	86	675	768	14.
2,275	4,686	2,012	6,623	1,292	358	7,921	3,165	15.
879	1,175	455	3,583	913	1,208	779	902	16.
4,941	720	1,136	6,654	602	150	2,446	1,442	17.
1,227	554	1,871	6,525	844	149	1,609	1,224	18.
238	43	213	2,389	50	9	743	492	19.
7,351	6,157	12,133	43,460	6,216	1,771	15,770	12,379	20.
181	183	322	4,417	135	28	367	309	21.
4,523	3,626	7,380	48,740	5,044	1,220	12,086	10,683	22.
4,251	4,685	6,418	31,631	4,587	1,180	12,094	8,756	23.
483	470	1,207	5,360	450	98	1,490	917	24.
1,476	1,387	2,717	9,344	1,689	410	3,660	2,814	25.
5,218	2,876	8,257	15,794	3,519	944	9,032	7,212	26.
1,025	1,141	2,026	14,479	1,024	333	3,364	3,176	27.
4,096	2,921	6,389	43,829	3,351	692	8,516	5,877	N.C.
61,002	49,997	76,537	329,211	57,835	17,628	144,709	114,401	
96,486	80,448	123,719	535,602	89,658	26,735	228,429	181,846	

MALE EMPLOYMENT: 1901

South West   West Midlands

	17.Corn-wall	18. Devon	19.Som-erset	20.Gloucs.	21.Wilts.	22.Dorset	23.Here-ford	24.Shrops.
1.	27.418	42,486	31,537	24,561	24,088	17,099	14,862	21,638
2.	13,098	2,368	6,359	10,178	1,230	1,239	156	5,510
3.	1,295	3,761	3,148	6,944	2,095	1,490	657	1,519
4.	-	-	-	-	-	-	-	-
5.	375	401	157	1,524	65	8	21	60
6.	536	635	466	2,196	1,037	142	35	2,683
7.	1,302	3,744	1,368	4,844	5,048	860	163	1,517
8.	152	437	258	501	146	120	41	134
9.	69	408	291	627	142	85	43	133
10.	874	3,502	84	457	9	126	7	19
11.	568	1,667	1,335	2,836	2,197	481	423	1,327
12.	2,237	3,751	2,400	5,410	2,427	1,136	654	2,191
13.	209	1,171	2,140	1,966	1,103	649	31	308
14.	395	1,219	973	1,439	616	222	183	354
15.	1,985	5,674	5,419	12,316	1,480	1,256	743	1,640
16.	201	1,015	1,455	1,650	366	863	201	1,730
17.	865	3,164	2,710	6,019	1,325	844	426	1,002
18.	498	2,443	2,015	3,674	502	397	199	415
19.	68	359	365	973	349	79	35	54
20.	10,350	25,763	15,908	26,149	12,165	7,873	4,053	8,395
21.	137	630	449	1,286	276	293	73	262
22.	7,749	18,559	10,612	25,959	7,329	5,216	2,186	5,650
23.	6,349	15,226	9,859	18,014	5,408	4,604	2,122	4,964
24.	1,000	2,311	1,464	2,907	644	532	310	736
25.	2,613	6,391	4,273	6,208	2,129	1,784	1,098	1,990
26.	3,168	11,182	8,012	11,553	5,218	4,614	2,830	4,787
27.	5,262	21,607	3,046	5,592	2,591	7,566	754	1,633
N.C.	5,277	17,720	8,828	21,025	6,263	5,010	2,629	5,611
Total Employed	94,050	197,594	124,931	206,808	86,248	64,588	34,935	76,262
Total Population	149,937	312,536	200,493	331,558	134,540	99,637	55,196	118,675

East Midlands

25.Staffs.	26.Warwick	27.Worcs.	28.Derby	29.Notts.	30.Leics.	31.Lincs.	32.Northants.	
22,392	18,480	20,230	17,054	16,425	14,551	58,756	18,281	1.
53,054	10,010	3,965	49,039	26,655	9,908	1,358	1,778	2.
9,548	5,028	3,039	2,039	3,848	2,330	3,709	1,975	3.
-	-	-	-	-	-	-	-	4.
1,473	1,274	1,399	722	466	140	532	23	5.
34,805	13,367	6,345	8,347	2,690	1,604	4,096	1,261	6.
14,909	14,990	4,099	7,716	5,702	3,267	7,580	1,375	7.
795	3,328	275	401	299	244	318	131	8.
1,631	1,476	380	663	626	572	200	145	9.
357	149	156	12	67	13	700	28	10.
5,652	15,385	3,290	3,065	2,483	1,665	1,908	1,334	11.
37,790	45,967	14,272	6,220	2,996	2,372	3,859	1,419	12.
2,781	1,726	3,572	10,622	14,782	9,216	542	55	13.
6,467	2,660	1,066	766	1,093	701	874	1,996	14.
8,693	7,266	3,403	3,460	3,621	26,431	3,088	30,658	15.
33,122	4,241	2,974	4,470	1,611	2,270	1,445	1,047	16.
5,979	7,894	2,160	2,244	3,845	2,026	2,394	1,260	17.
2,494	4,621	1,412	2,064	2,734	1,770	1,061	688	18.
721	3,223	1,323	401	484	1,226	153	211	19.
33,701	30,421	15,461	19,555	16,152	14,404	14,611	11,463	20.
1,869	2,132	579	815	909	910	431	431	21.
30,724	28,747	10,900	17,346	15,460	11,215	16,227	9,292	22.
23,732	21,875	9,923	12,012	13,328	10,502	13,589	7,165	23.
3,982	3,519	1,847	1,724	1,843	1,433	1,431	956	24.
7,249	5,957	3,726	3,706	3,349	2,745	3,558	2,261	25.
13,100	13,962	6,997	6,912	6,572	6,503	6,717	4,962	26.
5,309	5,444	2,530	2,539	2,243	2,136	2,509	2,022	27.
30,946	24,381	12,200	14,313	11,464	8,108	8,827	5,426	N.C.
393,275	297,523	137,523	198,227	161,747	138,262	160,473	107,643	
614,740	453,179	216,680	306,545	248,098	210,226	245,773	165,235	

MALE EMPLOYMENT: 1901

	East Midlands	North West	Yorks. & Humberside			North		
	33.Rutland	34.Cheshire	35.Lancs.	36. West Riding	37. East Riding	38. North Riding	39.Westmorland	40.Cumberland
1.	2,333	28,323	48,240	45,759	24,405	25,167	6,099	15,675
2.	153	4,283	96,995	109,906	117	7,398	669	13,372
3.	117	4,172	21,276	9,840	4,495	1,112	253	1,199
4.	–	–	–	–	–	–	–	–
5.	–	6,744	13,178	4,367	3,044	374	150	174
6.	4	4,157	41,677	33,265	859	11,134	91	4,597
7.	38	14,189	75,382	49,713	4,636	3,592	237	1,935
8.	11	462	3,529	1,846	507	221	36	182
9.	7	1,495	7,545	3,238	425	384	58	149
10.	–	2,480	8,564	878	2,568	3,105	34	279
11.	60	2,268	12,638	8,373	1,795	391	133	362
12.	105	6,049	38,280	58,728	4,325	4,528	351	1,746
13.	5	19,971	199,689	114,691	346	346	361	927
14.	24	1,403	5,981	6,003	1,503	320	113	557
15.	211	9,890	34,982	27,771	3,064	2,464	898	2,258
16.	26	1,382	15,524	14,452	1,212	947	22	488
17.	39	3,479	29,047	15,765	4,328	1,125	498	897
18.	28	2,507	21,860	9,986	1,735	668	327	911
19.	3	609	8,168	2,817	350	132	73	73
20.	700	30,099	135,416	86,290	16,720	13,914	2,429	8,045
21.	14	1,404	8,120	6,002	771	573	67	284
22.	420	31,843	183,815	77,629	28,800	12,089	1,550	8,290
23.	404	22,012	118,560	68,461	13,027	8,356	1,335	5,771
24.	46	5,361	22,685	10,099	1,809	1,106	195	872
25.	187	6,709	27,367	17,346	3,478	2,840	606	2,217
26.	882	13,095	50,024	29,729	5,995	5,623	1,290	2,889
27.	101	5,572	26,419	14,321	4,315	2,517	369	1,537
N.C.	212	26,810	140,872	69,630	14,827	9,384	1,326	5,889
Total Employed	6,130	256,768	1,395,833	896,905	149,456	119,810	19,570	81,575
Total Population	9,849	395,017	2,107,605	1,337,332	226,862	186,702	30,550	130,613

		Wales			Scotland			
41.North-umberland	42.Durham	43.Glam-organ & Monmouth	44.North & West Wales	45.Strathclyde	46.Dumfries & Galloway	47.Borders	48.Lothian	
14,915	11,939	16,604	76,370	32,213	15,313	11,266	11,468	1.
38,091	103,166	140,550	45,059	74,424	2,178	161	17,711	2.
1,676	2,286	3,911	2,795	13,480	810	689	6,085	3.
–	–	–	–	–	–	–	–	4.
815	5,975	1,659	578	3,912	14	12	1,540	5.
3,484	17,687	23,778	6,316	39,601	164	74	2,448	6.
16,036	25,770	10,213	2,778	46,854	467	650	4,831	7.
347	597	513	438	1,603	119	88	661	8.
1,139	1,299	918	380	2,751	39	13	762	9.
10,579	28,077	2,416	2,047	29,789	78	21	1,022	10.
901	1,708	2,462	1,437	3,969	213	120	895	11.
6,288	13,156	8,294	5,424	25,576	923	601	5,506	12.
289	707	359	2,114	18,896	949	5,396	941	13.
747	536	627	1,121	2,781	198	285	1,056	14.
3,857	4,614	5,311	6,660	17,341	1,463	1,229	5,123	15.
1,807	5,850	1,502	2,944	5,626	103	5	1,455	16.
2,885	4,541	3,182	1,875	15,841	435	375	4,913	17.
1,446	2,411	2,095	1,550	8,089	237	396	7,222	18.
315	318	225	95	1,868	28	52	1,827	19.
19,771	35,499	32,029	26,894	69,566	4,449	3,610	22,461	20.
946	2,232	1,295	503	4,085	86	85	1,171	21.
20,601	37,350	41,542	17,999	74,320	3,301	2,062	23,677	22.
14,440	23,633	27,016	16,926	47,835	3,198	2,621	15,851	23.
2,325	3,097	4,422	2,343	7,873	437	360	2,932	24.
4,212	6,426	8,828	8,393	15,101	1,400	1,041	8,463	25.
7,302	9,866	10,050	10,492	21,073	2,300	2,349	8,307	26.
3,909	4,082	5,789	5,667	11,193	797	674	6,644	27.
16,798	27,818	33,251	17,710	72,692	2,630	1,986	17,631	N.C.
195,921	380,640	388,841	266,908	668,352	42,329	36,221	182,603	
302,433	602,411	597,146	414,312	1,031,023	68,388	54,876	284,517	

MALE EMPLOYMENT: 1901

Scotland

	49.Central & Fife	50.Tayside	51.Gram-pian	52.High-land	53. South East	54. East Anglia	55. South West	56. West Midland
1.	12,386	20,813	46,295	47,048	269,812	122,104	167,189	97,602
2.	26,159	1,477	3,885	665	5,744	334	34,472	72,695
3.	2,929	2,732	4,088	1,532	72,207	9,295	18,733	19,791
4.	-	-	-	-	-	-	-	-
5.	568	119	353	52	15,931	1,195	2,530	4,227
6.	7,676	1,640	571	60	12,952	1,767	5,012	57,235
7.	3,098	4,137	2,173	482	77,724	5,519	17,166	35,678
8.	247	327	394	152	12,004	662	1,614	4,573
9.	97	192	227	79	21,732	768	1,622	3,663
10.	604	1,514	1,237	262	17,885	1,052	5,052	688
11.	432	533	775	279	33,425	3,514	9,084	26,077
12.	2,443	2,873	3,225	1,460	74,874	6,968	17,361	100,874
13.	5,224	18,210	1,593	336	9,197	2,061	7,238	8,418
14.	327	569	399	120	23,185	1,843	4,864	10,730
15.	2,396	4,082	4,287	2,353	103,635	12,736	28,130	21,745
16.	1,254	234	196	38	31,550	3,802	5,550	42,268
17.	2,260	2,598	3,891	1,421	88,412	4,640	14,927	17,461
18.	1,523	1,389	2,090	297	85,711	3,826	9,529	9,141
19.	2,292	239	825	42	21,785	1,294	2,193	5,356
20.	12,061	13,431	13,128	7,089	405,393	36,136	98,208	92,031
21.	371	515	384	72	21,085	839	3,071	4,915
22.	10,148	12,035	12,128	6,228	435,850	29,033	75,424	78,207
23.	7,844	9,164	8,779	4,066	335,821	26,617	59,460	62,616
24.	1,022	1,430	1,516	751	62,283	2,955	8,858	10,394
25.	2,875	3,667	3,594	2,264	119,294	8,573	23,398	20,020
26.	3,949	5,788	3,957	3,211	248,627	20,707	43,747	41,676
27.	1,892	2,883	2,676	2,677	200,314	7,897	45,664	15,670
N.C.	9,787	8,735	8,390	4,401	377,525	18,436	64,123	75,767
Total Employed	121,864	121,326	131,056	87,437	3,183,957	334,573	774,219	939,518
Total Population	193,092	189,097	215,375	137,387	4,998,065	526,668	1,228,701	1,458,470

57. East Midlands	58. North West	59. Yorks. & Humberside	60. North	61. Wales	62. Scotland	63. Great Britain	
127,400	76,563	70,164	73,795	92,974	196,802	1,294,405	1.
88,891	101,278	110,023	162,696	185,609	126,660	888,402	2.
14,018	25,448	14,335	6,526	6,706	32,345	219,404	3.
-	-	-	-	-	-	-	4.
1,883	19,922	7,411	7,488	2,237	6,570	69,394	5.
18,002	45,834	34,124	36,993	30,094	52,234	294,247	6.
25,678	89,571	54,349	47,570	12,991	62,692	428,938	7.
1,404	3,991	2,353	1,383	951	3,591	32,526	8.
2,213	9,040	3,663	3,029	1,298	4,160	51,188	9.
820	11,044	3,446	42,074	4,463	34,527	121,051	10.
10,515	14,906	10,168	3,495	3,899	7,216	122,299	11.
16,971	44,329	63,053	26,069	13,718	42,607	406,824	12.
35,222	219,660	115,037	2,630	2,473	51,545	453,481	13.
5,454	7,384	7,506	2,273	1,748	5,735	70,722	14.
67,469	44,872	30,835	14,091	11,971	38,274	373,758	15.
10,869	16,906	15,664	9,114	4,446	8,911	149,080	16.
11,808	32,526	20,093	9,946	5,057	31,734	236,604	17.
8,345	24,367	11,721	5,763	3,645	21,243	183,291	18.
2,478	8,777	3,167	911	320	7,173	53,454	19.
76,885	165,515	103,010	79,658	58,923	145,795	1,261,554	20.
3,510	9,524	6,773	4,102	1,798	6,769	62,386	21.
69,960	215,658	106,429	79,880	59,541	143,899	1,293,881	22.
57,000	140,572	81,488	53,535	43,942	99,358	960,409	23.
7,433	28,046	11,908	7,595	6,765	16,321	162,558	24.
15,806	34,076	20,824	16,301	17,221	38,405	313,918	25.
32,548	63,119	35,724	26,970	20,542	50,934	584,594	26.
11,550	31,991	18,636	12,414	11,456	29,436	385,028	27.
48,350	167,682	84,457	61,215	50,961	126,252	1,074,768	N.C.
772,482	1,652,601	1,046,361	797,516	655,749	1,391,188	11,548,164	
1,185,726	2,502,622	1,564,194	1,252,709	1,011,458	2,173,755	17,902,368	

South East

	1. London	2. Middlesex	3. Kent	4. Surrey	5. Sussex	6. Hants.	7. Berks.	8. Oxon.
1.	1,342	706	1,523	412	601	727	386	277
2.	2	-	-	4	-	-	-	-
3.	12,613	821	453	115	108	191	650	81
4.	-	-	-	-	-	-	-	-
5.	3,647	685	505	160	12	14	-	-
6.	-	-	-	-	-	1	2	-
7.	84	14	7	2	1	5	1	-
8.	883	63	11	10	4	11	-	-
9.	566	476	1	14	-	2	-	-
10.	13	2	-	4	1	-	2	-
11.	121	8	11	5	7	6	2	1
12.	4,757	194	32	44	41	49	90	6
13.	10,365	574	389	215	195	230	65	556
14.	4,692	149	39	107	42	25	6	39
15.	152,057	13,169	13,011	8,990	9,615	15,753	4,301	4,033
16.	655	33	20	27	5	5	1	1
17.	7,474	287	226	226	191	286	101	56
18.	30,395	1,035	2,242	392	290	544	248	321
19.	7,100	343	37	41	43	108	6	4
20.	80	14	16	12	11	17	6	5
21.	28	-	-	1	-	-	-	-
22.	3,860	483	356	264	290	352	92	88
23.	43,392	6,213	7,323	5,177	5,366	6,525	1,961	1,450
24.	725	136	63	42	23	44	8	6
25.	47,626	9,975	10,506	8,451	8,569	8,571	2,939	2,241
26.	357,841	61,814	69,892	65,781	63,156	58,868	19,762	14,662
27.	5,887	1,057	854	911	532	705	261	207
N.C.	23,126	3,147	1,397	1,416	1,239	1,167	353	162
Total Employed	719,331	101,398	108,914	92,823	90,342	94,206	31,243	24,196
Total Population	2,394,456	421,253	489,703	350,286	328,531	410,464	129,764	98,144

East Anglia

9. Bucks.	10. Beds.	11. Herts.	12. Essex	13. Cambridge	14. Hunts.	15. Norfolk	16. Suffolk	
252	202	251	761	656	194	912	628	1.
1	-	-	-	-	-	-	-	2.
88	31	208	1,581	161	4	746	158	3.
-	-	-	-	-	-	-	-	4.
-	1	101	768	2	-	421	13	5.
3	-	-	5	-	-	3	1	6.
-	-	-	6	-	1	2	2	7.
-	-	72	57	2	-	3	-	8.
-	60	2	228	-	-	7	2	9.
-	-	-	6	-	-	2	1	10.
1	-	3	9	4	1	3	5	11.
13	9	8	214	11	2	24	13	12.
1,123	1,198	234	3,445	106	59	2,343	1,330	13.
18	7	60	198	34	10	83	257	14.
3,019	11,257	5,657	20,371	2,899	688	11,620	7,873	15.
3	19	9	96	-	-	5	4	16.
588	78	48	375	44	2	154	73	17.
929	364	1,025	1,542	247	86	761	425	18.
349	13	202	1,229	26	4	753	743	19.
7	5	6	20	5	4	13	14	20.
-	-	-	-	-	-	-	-	21.
72	56	98	568	65	15	150	111	22.
1,232	1,339	1,716	7,783	1,246	317	4,017	2,931	23.
6	3	11	79	2	2	14	14	24.
1,824	1,633	2,841	10,406	1,763	484	4,617	3,462	25.
11,472	10,108	18,854	50,184	12,094	2,860	27,633	22,865	26.
217	131	330	1,000	158	56	491	309	27.
162	149	408	2,567	172	29	468	339	N.C.
21,379	26,663	32,144	103,498	19,697	4,818	55,245	41,573	
100,560	91,259	134,704	548,396	95,101	27,390	248,124	191,507	

FEMALE EMPLOYMENT: 1901

South West   West Midlands

	17.Corn-wall	18. Devon	19.Som-erset	20.Gloucs.	21.Wilts.	22.Dorset	23.Here-ford	24.Shrops
1.	1,376	2,127	1,599	899	664	611	816	1,317
2.	387	–	1	–	–	–	–	91
3.	64	514	74	5,307	198	66	25	165
4.	–	–	–	–	–	–	–	–
5.	403	75	5	370	–	–	–	2
6.	5	–	–	10	–	1	–	4
7.	1	1	8	1	–	–	–	1
8.	–	9	6	15	11	–	1	2
9.	–	1	–	15	–	–	–	–
10.	–	–	–	1	–	–	–	–
11.	3	5	2	7	1	–	2	1
12.	11	32	27	438	35	3	9	33
13.	310	2,524	2,575	3,751	1,384	906	16	355
14.	11	33	66	75	24	2	–	15
15.	6,534	15,626	13,992	22,849	4,363	3,957	1,421	2,939
16.	3	71	25	167	5	16	30	257
17.	46	274	228	352	141	39	30	34
18.	55	709	753	2,861	80	86	25	47
19.	21	172	152	551	64	9	1	107
20.	12	14	14	9	6	7	3	5
21.	–	–	–	–	–	–	–	–
22.	90	248	160	281	62	69	67	112
23.	3,836	6,957	3,885	7,490	1,844	1,548	798	1,575
24.	10	48	20	32	18	6	4	11
25.	2,629	6,675	5,047	7,668	2,530	1,990	1,036	1,910
26.	17,157	48,457	33,946	44,679	14,919	13,230	8,492	16,030
27.	380	517	413	623	301	236	167	243
N.C.	171	654	448	1,180	217	144	73	86
Total Employed	33,515	85,743	63,446	99,631	26,867	22,926	13,016	25,342
Total Population	172,397	349,660	234,457	376,881	136,854	102,426	58,929	121,108

East Midlands

25.Staffs.	26.Warwick	27.Worcs.	28.Derby	29.Notts.	30.Leics.	31.Lincs.	32.Northants.	
1,467	535	926	1,314	484	570	1,845	287	1.
63	3	6	3	2	-	-	-	2.
417	1,426	1,634	225	2,569	1,741	717	75	3.
-	-	-	-		-	-	-	4.
762	1,759	190	53	98	35	38	2	5.
265	450	96	32	2	22	10	2	6.
234	499	30	14	38	5	1	1	7.
169	1,164	47	131	72	11	2	5	8.
203	146	6	74	9	21	-	-	9.
2	3	-	-	-	-	-	-	10.
145	2,391	259	5	45	7	18	9	11.
9,846	25,166	4,978	208	365	52	41	10	12.
4,736	5,311	4,229	15,435	26,014	21,098	682	523	13.
3,853	2,008	158	33	294	47	44	138	14.
18,379	16,705	8,714	8,025	10,494	20,041	6,660	18,521	15.
23,069	478	1,024	981	53	65	11	2	16.
458	2,425	259	287	438	202	152	65	17.
1,341	4,202	1,129	1,080	1,099	1,267	239	603	18.
731	3,830	1,571	152	83	953	44	125	19.
23	21	4	7	10	8	21	9	20.
-	-	-	1	-	-	-	-	21.
713	1,115	239	168	777	407	133	130	22.
10,128	10,452	4,077	3,808	4,028	3,618	3,605	2,361	23.
114	209	64	30	26	14	31	11	24.
8,986	7,330	4,312	4,454	3,899	3,274	4,122	2,754	25.
45,133	44,975	25,646	22,941	20,988	16,451	27,781	15,047	26.
693	650	368	323	248	303	400	269	27.
3,033	6,313	1,092	633	1,120	706	303	360	N.C.
134,963	139,566	61,058	60,417	73,255	70,918	46,900	41,309	
622,179	486,725	237,054	303,977	266,361	227,264	254,249	170,393	

FEMALE EMPLOYMENT: 1901

| | East Midlands | North West | Yorks. & Humberside | | North | | |
	33.Rut-land	34.Cheshire	35.Lancs.	36. West Riding	37. East Riding	38. North Riding	39.West-morland	40.Cum-berland
1.	56	2,544	4,628	2,482	850	1,786	542	1,861
2.	–	–	2,035	18	–	–	–	225
3.	1	1,407	10,953	3,073	2,533	137	85	778
4.	–	–	–	–	–	–	–	–
5.	–	863	2,133	520	1,386	11	26	8
6.	–	38	39	136	–	1	–	3
7.	–	79	748	387	2	–	12	7
8.	–	27	546	119	21	3	–	1
9.	–	32	372	23	–	–	–	–
10.	–	4	37	–	3	1	–	–
11.	1	8	142	133	7	4	–	–
12.	–	149	1,927	9,094	813	10	1	352
13.	25	31,636	298,132	142,902	720	287	497	1,867
14.	2	96	741	716	33	6	52	10
15.	265	16,036	83,727	55,037	6,305	4,334	1,127	4,520
16.	–	18	1,130	780	53	15	1	12
17.	3	263	2,732	2,103	273	58	32	36
18.	4	1,117	11,175	4,795	844	145	107	396
19.	–	192	3,696	751	61	6	15	6
20.	–	25	87	79	12	13	5	4
21.	–	–	–	–	–	–	–	–
22.	6	493	3,012	1,584	328	191	25	133
23.	99	8,069	50,364	22,241	3,832	2,737	521	2,205
24.	1	65	597	206	52	30	–	16
25.	193	6,851	31,487	18,427	3,999	2,886	544	2,028
26.	1,639	46,236	174,278	93,459	24,230	20,768	4,651	13,367
27.	40	509	2,339	1,455	223	148	63	233
N.C.	6	1,023	7,034	4,241	666	297	46	298
Total Employed	2,341	117,780	694,091	364,761	47,246	33,874	8,352	28,366
Total Population	9,860	432,174	2,279,438	1,413,161	236,059	190,636	33,859	136,320

		Wales		Scotland				
41.North- umberland	42.Durham	43.Glam- organ & Monmouth	44.North & West Wales	45.Strathclyde	46.Dumfries & Galloway	47.Borders	48.Lothian	
2,806	1,039	1,270	11,199	9,590	3,328	2,829	3,510	1.
10	15	199	34	450	1	-	85	2.
617	1,097	470	142	8,040	122	175	1,790	3.
-	-	-	-	-	-	-	-	4.
126	188	95	10	1,019	-	2	236	5.
12	-	1,382	559	7	-	-	64	6.
12	36	-	1	837	5	3	50	7.
7	8	5	4	59	1	2	42	8.
89	90	3	48	18	-	-	12	9.
16	15	-	-	122	-	-	1	10.
4	6	3	-	42	1	-	7	11.
90	235	262	118	1,265	5	3	239	12.
543	2,070	430	1,347	47,145	1,368	6,592	2,277	13.
92	41	9	34	444	1	-	117	14.
7,586	13,291	17,087	14,404	42,324	2,686	1,746	10,527	15.
380	498	256	85	1,771	-	3	407	16.
161	199	109	52	3,636	14	9	632	17.
557	1,127	557	253	7,368	34	125	5,510	18.
105	65	71	4	1,667	4	42	1,533	19.
13	21	25	10	123	6	3	77	20.
-	-	-	1	5	-	-	4	21.
359	351	414	238	5,277	110	89	1,059	22.
5,620	9,312	8,565	6,710	28,441	1,221	930	9,120	23.
55	110	64	23	81	2	3	35	24.
3,802	7,078	8,310	5,599	12,746	975	654	5,568	25.
27,431	37,515	43,329	54,138	70,175	8,679	6,565	35,391	26.
383	499	643	835	704	155	115	280	27.
1,152	1,240	747	271	9,552	375	184	4,614	N.C.
52,028	76,146	84,305	96,119	252,908	19,093	20,074	83,187	
300,686	585,063	560,861	440,557	1,038,046	76,251	63,174	308,652	

FEMALE EMPLOYMENT: 1901

Scotland

	49.Central & Fife	50.Tayside	51.Grampian	52.Highland	53. South East	54. East Anglia	55. South West	56. West Midland
1.	3,040	2,372	4,340	11,721	7,440	2,390	7,276	5,061
2.	649	3	–	–	7	–	388	163
3.	190	767	2,711	1,495	16,940	1,069	6,223	3,667
4.	–	–	–	–	–	–	–	–
5.	139	20	27	–	5,893	436	853	2,713
6.	69	1	1	–	11	4	16	815
7.	–	9	1	1	120	5	11	764
8.	1	12	10	4	1,111	5	41	1,383
9.	–	–	–	–	1,349	9	16	355
10.	–	1	5	–	28	3	1	5
11.	10	2	1	–	174	13	18	2,798
12.	96	36	67	27	5,457	50	546	40,032
13.	13,820	39,632	4,998	7,170	18,589	3,838	11,450	14,647
14.	7	71	16	–	5,382	384	211	6,034
15.	5,346	6,392	6,017	2,816	261,233	23,080	67,321	48,158
16.	485	13	3	–	874	9	287	24,858
17.	215	145	179	21	9,936	273	1,080	3,206
18.	919	497	2,322	62	39,327	1,519	4,544	6,744
19.	162	84	368	–	9,475	1,526	969	6,240
20.	20	19	17	–	199	36	62	56
21.	–	–	–	–	29	–	–	–
22.	398	479	523	142	6,579	341	910	2,246
23.	3,824	4,798	4,066	1,364	89,477	8,511	25,560	27,030
24.	9	20	9	12	1,146	32	134	402
25.	2,346	2,690	3,488	1,722	115,582	10,326	26,539	23,574
26.	14,458	16,731	21,554	13,077	802,394	65,452	172,388	140,276
27.	211	281	202	261	12,092	1,014	2,470	2,121
N.C.	884	1,399	1,491	279	35,293	1,008	2,814	10,597
Total Employed	47,298	76,474	52,416	40,174	1,446,137	121,333	332,128	373,945
Total Population	200,068	225,249	236,275	150,633	5,497,520	562,122	1,372,675	1,525,995

57. East Midlands	58. North West	59. Yorks. & Humberside	60. North	61. Wales	62. Scotland	63. Great Britain	
4,556	7,172	3,332	8,034	12,469	40,730	98,460	1.
5	2,035	18	250	233	1,188	4,287	2.
5,328	12,360	5,606	2,714	612	15,290	69,809	3.
–	–	–	–	–	–	–	4.
226	2,996	1,906	359	105	1,443	16,930	5.
68	77	136	16	1,941	142	3,226	6.
59	827	389	67	1	906	3,149	7.
221	573	140	19	9	131	3,633	8.
104	404	23	179	51	30	2,520	9.
–	41	3	32	–	129	242	10.
85	150	140	14	3	63	3,458	11.
676	2,076	9,907	688	380	1,738	61,550	12.
63,777	329,768	143,622	5,264	1,777	123,002	715,734	13.
558	837	749	201	43	656	15,055	14.
64,006	99,763	61,342	30,858	31,491	77,854	765,106	15.
1,112	1,148	833	906	341	2,682	33,050	16.
1,147	2,995	2,376	486	161	4,851	26,511	17.
4,292	12,292	5,639	2,332	810	16,837	94,336	18.
1,357	3,888	812	197	75	3,860	28,399	19.
55	112	91	56	35	265	967	20.
1	–	–	–	1	9	40	21.
1,621	3,505	1,912	1,059	652	8,077	26,902	22.
17,519	58,433	26,073	20,395	15,275	53,764	342,037	23.
113	662	258	211	87	171	3,216	24.
18,696	38,338	22,426	16,338	13,909	30,189	315,917	25.
104,847	220,514	117,689	103,732	97,467	186,630	2,011,389	26.
1,583	2,848	1,678	1,326	1,478	2,209	28,819	27.
3,128	8,057	4,907	3,033	1,018	18,778	88,633	N.C.
295,140	811,871	412,007	198,766	180,424	591,624	4,763,375	
,232,104	2,711,612	1,649,220	1,246,564	1,001,418	2,298,348	19,097,578	

TOTAL EMPLOYMENT: 1901

South East

	1. London	2. Middlesex	3. Kent	4. Surrey	5. Sussex	6. Hants.	7. Berks.	8. Oxon
1.	9,796	12,798	48,187	19,840	34,862	31,339	15,352	16,067
2.	1,351	164	1,986	406	426	208	48	226
3.	43,531	4,734	6,072	3,587	4,266	5,234	6,148	1,512
4.	-	-	-	-	-	-	-	-
5.	11,721	1,730	1,662	779	211	273	25	13
6.	6,281	440	1,306	323	289	571	249	252
7.	36,339	6,181	9,707	1,826	1,779	5,847	1,066	679
8.	7,955	1,148	689	680	525	510	171	102
9.	12,231	2,437	1,464	1,097	820	853	273	109
10.	3,744	514	4,629	175	278	5,631	98	101
11.	12,169	2,155	2,931	2,020	2,109	2,701	973	549
12.	46,168	5,338	5,157	2,763	2,794	4,534	2,172	988
13.	15,662	1,035	866	482	457	545	153	1,061
14.	19,449	1,234	1,312	1,464	682	829	343	336
15.	216,284	17,732	17,385	12,365	13,004	20,675	5,960	5,563
16.	6,994	1,820	10,863	1,656	1,861	1,754	1,005	252
17.	62,417	4,939	4,308	2,781	3,207	3,657	1,436	1,063
18.	85,703	6,948	7,306	3,509	2,109	2,757	1,158	1,511
19.	21,081	3,001	703	768	368	504	83	76
20.	153,884	38,067	36,964	32,841	26,406	30,596	10,751	6,944
21.	9,400	1,614	1,443	1,132	986	959	286	191
22.	238,606	29,874	30,768	18,459	19,024	29,138	6,822	4,675
23.	207,904	32,730	33,807	25,404	24,280	27,682	8,312	6,124
24.	31,648	7,637	4,198	5,939	2,439	2,704	752	493
25.	103,469	21,114	19,440	17,953	15,839	15,763	5,342	4,328
26.	465,955	75,312	91,206	86,892	82,023	77,934	28,551	20,385
27.	74,803	10,165	35,882	10,986	6,979	47,338	4,230	1,674
N.C.	214,755	36,641	29,349	23,717	13,352	23,626	6,659	4,198
Total Employed	2,119,300	327,502	409,590	279,844	261,375	344,162	108,418	79,472
Total Population	4,536,541	792,314	961,139	653,549	602,255	799,582	252,571	186,460

East Anglia

9. Bucks.	10. Beds.	11. Herts.	12. Essex	13. Cambridge	14. Hunts.	15. Norfolk	16. Suffolk	
16,294	13,815	16,631	42,271	24,646	7,829	51,186	40,833	1.
64	198	313	361	52	16	188	78	2.
1,342	1,060	2,542	9,119	1,510	444	4,869	3,541	3.
-	-	-	-	-	-	-	-	4.
65	40	600	4,705	74	21	1,017	519	5.
189	788	176	2,099	72	20	559	1,120	6.
700	1,473	1,083	11,164	504	149	1,902	2,969	7.
82	80	260	913	141	34	299	193	8.
158	261	239	3,139	124	14	438	201	9.
41	10	42	2,650	39	8	483	525	10.
2,742	564	881	3,805	481	348	1,431	1,267	11.
1,223	1,066	1,249	6,879	910	294	3,370	2,444	12.
1,166	1,265	370	4,724	194	76	2,881	2,748	13.
271	261	554	1,832	348	96	758	1,025	14.
5,294	15,943	7,669	26,994	4,191	1,046	19,541	11,038	15.
882	1,194	464	3,679	913	1,208	784	906	16.
5,529	798	1,184	7,029	646	152	2,600	1,515	17.
2,156	918	2,896	8,067	1,091	235	2,370	1,649	18.
587	56	415	3,618	76	13	1,496	1,235	19.
7,358	6,162	12,139	43,480	6,221	1,775	15,783	12,393	20.
181	183	322	4,417	135	28	367	309	21.
4,595	3,682	7,478	49,308	5,109	1,235	12,236	10,794	22.
5,483	6,024	8,134	39,414	5,833	1,497	16,111	11,687	23.
489	473	1,218	5,439	452	100	1,504	931	24.
3,300	3,020	5,558	19,750	3,452	894	8,277	6,276	25.
16,690	12,984	27,111	65,978	15,613	3,804	36,665	30,077	26.
1,242	1,272	2,356	15,479	1,182	389	3,855	3,485	27.
4,258	3,070	6,797	46,396	3,523	721	8,984	6,216	N.C.
82,381	76,660	108,681	432,709	77,532	22,446	199,954	155,974	
197,046	171,707	258,423	1,083,998	184,759	54,125	476,553	373,353	

TOTAL EMPLOYMENT: 1901

South West   West Midlands

	17.Corn-wall	18. Devon	19.Som-erset	20.Gloucs.	21.Wilts.	22.Dorset	23.Here-ford	24.Shrops
1.	28,794	44,613	33,136	25,460	24,752	17,710	15,678	22,955
2.	13,485	2,368	6,360	10,178	1,230	1,239	156	5,601
3.	1,359	4,275	3,222	12,251	2,293	1,556	682	1,684
4.	–	–	–	–	–	–	–	–
5.	778	476	162	1,894	65	8	21	62
6.	541	635	466	2,206	1,037	143	35	2,687
7.	1,303	3,745	1,376	4,845	5,048	860	163	1,518
8.	152	446	264	516	157	120	42	136
9.	69	409	291	642	142	85	43	133
10.	874	3,502	84	458	9	126	7	19
11.	571	1,672	1,337	2,843	2,198	481	425	1,328
12.	2,248	3,783	2,427	5,848	2,462	1,139	663	2,224
13.	519	3,695	4,715	5,717	2,487	1,555	47	663
14.	406	1,252	1,039	1,514	640	224	183	369
15.	8,519	21,300	19,411	35,165	5,843	5,213	2,164	4,579
16.	204	1,086	1,480	1,817	371	879	231	1,987
17.	911	3,438	2,938	6,371	1,466	883	456	1,036
18.	553	3,152	2,768	6,535	582	483	224	462
19.	89	531	517	1,524	413	88	36	161
20.	10,362	25,777	15,922	26,158	12,171	7,880	4,056	8,400
21.	137	630	449	1,286	276	293	73	262
22.	7,839	18,807	10,772	26,240	7,391	5,285	2,253	5,762
23.	10,185	22,183	13,744	25,504	7,252	6,152	2,920	6,539
24.	1,010	2,359	1,484	2,939	662	538	314	747
25.	5,242	13,066	9,320	13,876	4,659	3,774	2,134	3,900
26.	20,325	59,639	41,958	56,232	20,137	17,844	11,322	20,817
27.	5,642	22,124	3,459	6,215	2,892	7,802	921	1,876
N.C.	5,448	18,374	9,276	22,205	6,480	5,154	2,702	5,697
Total Employed	127,565	283,337	188,377	306,439	113,115	87,514	47,951	101,604
Total Population	322,334	662,196	434,950	708,439	271,394	202,063	114,125	239,783

East Midlands

25.Staffs.	26.War-wick	27.Worcs.	28.Derby	29.Notts.	30.Leics.	31.Lincs.	32.North-ants.	
23,859	19,015	21,156	18,368	16,909	15,121	60,601	18,568	1.
53,117	10,013	3,971	49,042	26,657	9,908	1,358	1,778	2.
9,965	6,454	4,673	2,264	6,417	4,071	4,426	2,050	3.
–	–	–	–	–	–	–	–	4.
2,235	3,033	1,589	775	564	175	570	25	5.
35,070	13,817	6,441	8,379	2,692	1,626	4,106	1,263	6.
15,143	15,489	4,129	7,730	5,740	3,272	7,581	1,376	7.
964	4,492	322	532	371	255	320	136	8.
1,834	1,622	386	737	635	593	200	145	9.
359	152	156	12	67	13	700	28	10.
5,797	17,776	3,549	3,070	2,528	1,672	1,926	1,343	11.
47,636	71,133	19,250	6,428	3,361	2,424	3,900	1,429	12.
7,517	7,037	7,801	26,057	40,796	30,314	1,224	578	13.
10,320	4,668	1,224	799	1,387	748	918	2,134	14.
27,072	23,971	12,117	11,485	14,115	46,472	9,748	49,179	15.
56,191	4,719	3,998	5,451	1,664	2,335	1,456	1,049	16.
6,437	10,319	2,419	2,531	4,283	2,228	2,546	1,325	17.
3,835	8,823	2,541	3,144	3,833	3,037	1,300	1,291	18.
1,452	7,053	2,894	553	567	2,179	197	336	19.
33,724	30,442	15,465	19,562	16,162	14,412	14,632	11,472	20.
1,869	2,132	579	816	909	910	431	431	21.
31,437	29,862	11,139	17,514	16,237	11,622	16,360	9,422	22.
33,860	32,327	14,000	15,820	17,356	14,120	17,194	9,526	23.
4,096	3,728	1,911	1,754	1,869	1,447	1,462	967	24.
16,235	13,287	8,038	8,160	7,248	6,019	7,680	5,015	25.
58,233	58,937	32,643	29,853	27,560	22,954	34,498	20,009	26.
6,002	6,094	2,898	2,862	2,491	2,439	2,909	2,291	27.
33,979	30,694	13,292	14,946	12,584	8,814	9,130	5,786	N.C.
528,238	437,089	198,581	258,644	235,002	209,180	207,373	148,952	
1,236,919	939,904	453,734	610,522	514,459	437,490	500,022	335,628	

TOTAL EMPLOYMENT: 1901

	East Midlands	North West	Yorks. & Humberside			North		
	33.Rutland	34.Cheshire	35.Lancs.	36. West Riding	37. East Riding	38. North Riding	39.Westmorland	40.Cumberland
1.	2,389	30,867	52,868	48,241	25,255	26,953	6,641	17,536
2.	153	4,283	99,030	109,924	117	7,398	669	13,597
3.	118	5,579	32,229	12,913	7,028	1,249	338	1,977
4.	-	-	-	-	-	-	-	-
5.	-	7,607	15,311	4,887	4,430	385	176	182
6.	4	4,195	41,716	33,401	859	11,135	91	4,600
7.	38	14,268	76,130	50,100	4,638	3,592	249	1,942
8.	11	489	4,075	1,965	528	224	36	183
9.	7	1,527	7,917	3,261	425	384	58	149
10.	-	2,484	8,601	878	2,571	3,106	34	279
11.	61	2,276	12,780	8,506	1,802	395	133	362
12.	105	6,198	40,207	67,822	5,138	4,538	352	2,098
13.	30	51,607	497,821	257,593	1,066	633	858	2,794
14.	26	1,499	6,722	6,719	1,536	326	165	567
15.	476	25,926	118,709	82,808	9,369	6,798	2,025	6,778
16.	26	1,400	16,654	15,232	1,265	962	23	500
17.	42	3,742	31,779	17,868	4,601	1,183	530	933
18.	32	3,624	33,035	14,781	2,579	813	434	1,307
19.	3	801	11,864	3,568	411	138	88	79
20.	700	30,124	135,503	86,369	16,732	13,927	2,434	8,049
21.	14	1,404	8,120	6,002	771	573	67	284
22.	426	32,336	186,827	79,213	29,128	12,280	1,575	8,423
23.	503	30,081	168,924	90,702	16,859	11,093	1,856	7,976
24.	47	5,426	23,282	10,305	1,861	1,136	195	888
25.	380	13,560	58,854	35,773	7,477	5,726	1,150	4,245
26.	2,521	59,331	224,302	123,188	30,225	26,391	5,941	16,256
27.	141	6,081	28,758	15,776	4,538	2,665	432	1,770
N.C.	218	27,833	147,906	73,871	15,493	9,681	1,372	6,187
Total Employed	8,471	374,548	2,089,924	1,261,666	196,702	153,684	27,922	109,941
Total Population	19,709	827,191	4,387,043	2,750,493	462,921	377,338	64,409	266,933

	Wales				Scotland				
41.North-umberland	42.Durham	43.Glam-organ & Monmouth	44.North & West Wales	45.Strathclyde	46.Dumfries & Galloway	47.Borders	48.Lothian		
17,721	12,978	17,874	87,569	41,803	18,641	14,095	14,978	1.
38,101	103,181	140,749	45,093	74,874	2,179	161	17,796	2.
2,293	3,383	4,381	2,937	21,520	932	864	7,875	3.
-	-	-	-	-	-	-	-	4.
941	6,163	1,754	588	4,931	14	14	1,776	5.
3,496	17,687	25,160	6,875	39,608	164	74	2,512	6.
16,048	25,806	10,213	2,779	47,691	472	653	4,881	7.
354	605	518	442	1,662	120	90	703	8.
1,228	1,389	921	428	2,769	39	13	774	9.
10,595	28,092	2,416	2,047	29,911	78	21	1,023	10.
905	1,714	2,465	1,437	4,011	214	120	902	11.
6,378	13,391	8,556	5,542	26,841	928	604	5,745	12.
832	2,777	789	3,461	66,041	2,317	11,988	3,218	13.
839	577	636	1,155	3,225	199	285	1,173	14.
11,443	17,905	22,398	21,064	59,665	4,149	2,975	15,650	15.
2,187	6,348	1,758	3,029	7,397	103	8	1,862	16.
3,046	4,740	3,291	1,927	19,477	449	384	5,545	17.
2,003	3,538	2,652	1,803	15,457	271	521	12,732	18.
420	383	296	99	3,535	32	94	3,360	19.
19,784	35,520	32,054	26,904	69,689	4,455	3,613	22,538	20.
946	2,232	1,295	504	4,090	86	85	1,175	21.
20,960	37,701	41,956	18,237	79,597	3,411	2,151	24,736	22.
20,060	32,945	35,581	23,636	76,276	4,419	3,551	24,971	23.
2,380	3,207	4,486	2,366	7,954	439	363	2,967	24.
8,014	13,504	17,138	13,992	27,847	2,375	1,695	14,031	25.
34,733	47,381	53,379	64,630	91,248	10,979	8,914	43,698	26.
4,292	4,581	6,432	6,502	11,897	952	789	6,924	27.
17,950	29,058	33,998	17,981	82,244	3,005	2,170	22,245	N.C.
247,949	456,786	473,146	363,027	921,260	61,422	56,295	265,790	
603,119	1,187,474	1,158,007	854,869	2,069,069	144,639	118,050	593,169	

TOTAL EMPLOYMENT: 1901

Scotland

	49.Central & Fife	50.Tayside	51.Grampian	52.Highland	53. South East	54. East Anglia	55. South West	56. West Midland
1.	15,426	23,185	50,635	58,769	277,252	124,494	174,465	102,663
2.	26,808	1,480	3,885	665	5,751	334	34,860	72,858
3.	3,119	3,499	6,799	3,027	89,147	10,364	24,956	23,458
4.	-	-	-	-	-	-	-	-
5.	707	139	380	52	21,824	1,631	3,383	6,940
6.	7,745	1,641	572	60	12,963	1,771	5,028	58,050
7.	3,098	4,146	2,174	483	77,844	5,524	17,177	36,442
8.	248	339	404	156	13,115	667	1,655	5,956
9.	97	192	227	79	23,081	777	1,638	4,018
10.	604	1,515	1,242	262	17,913	1,055	5,053	693
11.	442	535	776	279	33,599	3,527	9,102	28,875
12.	2,539	2,909	3,292	1,487	80,331	7,018	17,907	140,906
13.	19,044	57,842	6,591	7,506	27,786	5,899	18,688	23,065
14.	334	640	415	120	28,567	2,227	5,075	16,764
15.	7,742	10,474	10,304	5,169	364,868	35,816	95,451	69,903
16.	1,739	247	199	38	32,424	3,811	5,837	67,126
17.	2,475	2,743	4,070	1,442	98,348	4,913	16,007	20,667
18.	2,442	1,886	4,412	359	125,038	5,345	14,073	15,885
19.	2,454	323	1,193	42	31,260	2,820	3,162	11,596
20.	12,081	13,450	13,145	7,089	405,592	36,172	98,270	92,087
21.	371	515	384	72	21,114	839	3,071	4,915
22.	10,546	12,514	12,651	6,370	442,429	29,374	76,334	80,453
23.	11,668	13,962	12,845	5,430	425,298	35,128	85,020	89,646
24.	1,031	1,450	1,525	763	63,429	2,987	8,992	10,796
25.	5,221	6,357	7,082	3,986	234,876	18,899	49,937	43,594
26.	18,407	22,519	25,511	16,288	1,051,021	86,159	216,135	181,952
27.	2,103	3,164	2,878	2,938	212,406	8,911	48,134	17,791
N.C.	10,671	10,134	9,881	4,680	412,818	19,444	66,937	86,364
Total Employed	169,162	197,800	183,472	127,611	4,630,094	455,906	1,106,347	1,313,463
Total Population	393,160	414,346	451,650	288,020	10,495,585	1,088,790	2,601,376	2,984,465

7. East Midlands	58. North West	59. Yorks. & Humberside	60. North	61. Wales	62. Scotland	63. Great Britain	
131,956	83,735	73,496	81,829	105,443	237,532	1,392,865	1.
88,896	103,313	110,041	162,946	185,842	127,848	892,689	2.
19,346	37,808	19,941	9,240	7,318	47,635	289,213	3.
-	-	-	-	-	-	-	4.
2,109	22,918	9,317	7,847	2,342	8,013	86,324	5.
18,070	45,911	34,260	37,009	32,035	52,376	297,473	6.
25,737	90,398	54,738	47,637	12,992	63,598	432,087	7.
1,625	4,564	2,493	1,402	960	3,722	36,159	8.
2,317	9,444	3,686	3,208	1,349	4,190	53,708	9.
820	11,085	3,449	42,106	4,463	34,656	121,293	10.
10,600	15,056	10,308	3,509	3,902	7,279	125,757	11.
17,647	46,405	72,960	26,757	14,098	44,345	468,374	12.
98,999	549,428	258,659	7,894	4,250	174,547	1,169,215	13.
6,012	8,221	8,255	2,474	1,791	6,391	85,777	14.
131,475	144,635	92,177	44,949	43,462	116,128	1,138,864	15.
11,981	18,054	16,497	10,020	4,787	11,593	182,130	16.
12,955	35,521	22,469	10,432	5,218	36,585	263,115	17.
12,637	36,659	17,360	8,095	4,455	38,080	277,627	18.
3,835	12,665	3,979	1,108	395	11,033	81,853	19.
76,940	165,627	103,101	79,714	58,958	146,060	1,262,521	20.
3,511	9,524	6,773	4,102	1,799	6,778	62,426	21.
71,581	219,163	108,341	80,939	60,193	151,976	1,320,783	22.
74,519	199,005	107,561	73,930	59,217	153,122	1,302,446	23.
7,546	28,708	12,166	7,806	6,852	16,492	165,774	24.
34,502	72,414	43,250	32,639	31,130	68,594	629,835	25.
137,395	283,633	153,413	130,702	118,009	237,564	2,595,983	26.
13,133	34,839	20,314	13,740	12,934	31,645	413,847	27.
51,478	175,739	89,364	64,248	51,979	145,030	1,163,401	N.C.
,067,622	2,464,472	1,458,368	996,282	836,173	1,982,812	16,311,539	
,417,830	5,214,234	3,213,414	2,499,273	2,012,876	4,472,103	36,999,946	

MALE EMPLOYMENT: 1911

South East

	1. London	2. Middlesex	3. Kent	4. Surrey	5. Sussex	6. Hants.	7. Berks.	8. Oxon
1.	8,137	14,325	50,867	21,642	37,507	34,183	16,007	17,08
2.	372	167	1,919	446	460	251	86	24
3.	33,100	5,694	5,950	4,334	4,277	5,577	5,255	1,50
4.	-	-	-	-	-	-	-	-
5.	10,279	2,072	1,794	939	283	306	54	1
6.	6,311	651	1,483	387	293	839	264	22
7.	32,530	8,215	11,419	3,080	2,116	9,475	1,196	69
8.	7,829	2,025	791	984	527	573	144	12
9.	17,466	4,900	2,500	2,183	1,149	1,952	390	23
10.	3,220	342	4,687	192	231	9,876	83	10
11.	19,020	6,526	3,882	3,467	2,642	3,903	1,268	69
12.	33,881	6,734	4,586	3,080	2,424	4,469	2,116	93
13.	4,831	770	605	413	348	322	94	67
14.	14,418	1,482	1,362	1,513	573	759	304	32
15.	61,943	7,019	4,460	4,237	3,495	5,147	1,497	1,48
16.	6,697	1,546	8,915	1,330	1,518	1,672	943	27
17.	51,700	8,133	4,258	3,207	3,121	3,631	1,420	1,35
18.	56,881	10,445	6,958	5,457	1,904	2,396	1,355	1,53
19.	15,041	4,458	747	1,015	361	512	107	7
20.	131,157	42,411	31,966	33,583	24,393	29,782	10,701	7,24
21.	11,891	3,595	2,295	2,333	1,467	1,783	440	32
22.	254,804	49,484	35,998	27,649	22,692	38,799	8,811	5,86
23.	182,122	44,490	33,099	30,918	24,317	28,290	8,056	5,72
24.	38,768	13,969	6,079	10,096	3,579	4,092	1,191	74
25.	55,017	16,102	10,501	13,415	8,160	8,086	2,636	2,29
26.	132,676	21,757	26,910	29,480	25,313	26,473	11,552	7,46
27.	61,356	12,333	34,731	13,065	5,373	67,431	2,925	1,09
N.C.	152,815	40,845	25,638	25,972	11,977	21,707	6,250	3,74
Total Employed	1,404,262	330,490	324,400	244,417	190,500	312,286	85,145	62,08
Total Population	2,126,341	525,431	506,870	390,395	299,188	470,102	131,809	94,93

East Anglia

9. Bucks.	10. Beds.	11. Herts.	12. Essex	13. Cambridge	14. Hunts.	15. Norfolk	16. Suffolk	
17,150	14,485	17,999	46,496	27,452	8,634	54,166	43,010	1.
78	258	279	398	124	43	370	51	2.
1,340	1,205	2,540	9,880	1,559	430	4,568	3,603	3.
–	–	–	–	–	–	–	–	4.
126	79	663	6,183	75	7	842	778	5.
191	1,610	224	2,468	78	22	546	1,401	6.
822	2,532	1,283	13,777	652	172	2,028	4,370	7.
98	100	465	1,437	203	24	260	174	8.
348	496	452	4,909	136	20	693	280	9.
44	19	35	3,197	46	7	605	718	10.
3,485	1,618	1,226	5,682	572	390	1,603	1,580	11.
1,081	1,104	1,323	8,142	833	258	3,296	2,484	12.
61	130	200	1,381	65	15	560	1,144	13.
289	274	567	2,006	299	70	574	723	14.
2,228	5,695	2,224	7,966	1,193	284	8,092	2,673	15.
558	1,048	348	3,143	916	843	445	605	16.
5,156	995	1,501	9,109	700	127	2,877	1,642	17.
1,614	987	3,281	10,968	1,016	213	1,737	1,456	18.
343	92	639	4,352	76	10	823	603	19.
7,397	6,301	12,513	41,852	5,977	1,540	14,079	10,813	20.
280	375	602	5,570	255	35	627	530	21.
6,020	4,632	10,210	68,104	5,831	1,357	13,961	12,355	22.
5,597	5,918	9,190	46,780	5,446	1,314	14,401	10,756	23.
893	738	2,337	10,546	654	161	2,158	1,317	24.
1,983	1,532	3,971	12,480	1,863	426	3,885	2,913	25.
7,204	3,779	10,783	23,240	4,871	1,201	11,691	9,585	26.
918	1,044	1,997	18,066	706	201	2,992	4,485	27.
4,465	3,791	7,501	47,877	3,098	614	8,565	6,287	N.C.
69,769	60,837	94,353	416,009	64,696	18,418	156,444	126,336	
107,326	93,006	148,632	660,662	96,899	27,533	241,159	193,376	

MALE EMPLOYMENT: 1911

South West   West Midlands

	17.Cornwall	18. Devon	19.Somerset	20.Gloucs.	21.Wilts.	22.Dorset	23.Hereford	24.Shrops
1.	28,061	44,399	33,451	26,416	25,722	18,396	15,382	23,372
2.	13,008	2,437	7,301	10,236	614	1,199	168	6,060
3.	1,334	3,944	3,460	8,153	2,371	1,710	671	1,577
4.	-	-	-	-	-	-	-	-
5.	199	601	234	2,454	44	32	20	81
6.	528	556	611	2,783	895	143	40	2,753
7.	1,537	4,557	2,085	5,454	6,990	1,106	179	1,576
8.	125	442	269	472	101	108	42	136
9.	230	890	409	800	188	167	71	215
10.	878	5,170	62	481	7	115	4	15
11.	735	1,986	1,632	4,188	3,441	645	498	1,299
12.	1,982	3,295	2,204	5,990	2,314	991	625	2,265
13.	270	1,173	2,333	1,984	943	674	15	336
14.	303	1,066	940	1,356	644	209	194	346
15.	1,748	5,200	5,900	11,607	1,653	1,132	615	1,359
16.	975	1,260	1,782	2,026	522	1,629	244	1,835
17.	860	3,358	2,818	6,449	1,281	1,035	417	853
18.	473	2,691	2,300	4,958	550	437	227	427
19.	75	481	495	1,014	952	88	30	47
20.	9,248	22,438	15,611	21,260	8,654	7,797	3,773	7,102
21.	312	1,112	711	1,394	424	457	105	325
22.	9,322	22,431	13,314	31,036	8,856	6,733	2,775	6,922
23.	7,690	19,027	11,982	21,439	6,476	5,983	2,444	5,808
24.	1,301	3,248	2,130	4,132	935	807	428	1,048
25.	2,760	6,554	4,478	6,474	2,251	1,947	1,095	2,016
26.	4,612	15,349	10,641	14,359	7,256	6,335	3,412	6,204
27.	3,544	30,395	2,179	3,999	4,930	10,002	451	1,061
N.C.	5,673	15,243	8,727	19,601	5,142	4,602	2,098	4,594
Total Employed	97,783	219,303	138,059	220,515	94,156	74,479	36,023	79,632
Total Population	151,614	332,813	212,732	343,605	143,137	110,805	55,168	121,835

25.Staffs.	26.War-wick	27.Worcs.	28.Derby	29.Notts.	30.Leics.	31.Lincs.	32.North-ants.	
23,690	19,132	21,878	18,061	17,168	15,421	62,604	19,559	1.
61,463	16,579	3,671	61,966	39,949	12,729	1,952	2,768	2.
9,610	4,923	3,929	2,184	3,951	2,306	4,420	1,992	3.
-	-	-	-	-	-	-	-	4.
2,280	1,331	1,462	994	861	371	818	71	5.
36,605	7,704	7,141	9,744	3,459	2,193	6,034	2,151	6.
17,217	17,493	5,322	9,331	8,210	5,966	12,750	2,588	7.
888	2,269	368	384	373	285	262	158	8.
3,517	4,967	883	1,129	1,526	672	391	364	9.
293	140	104	10	74	8	836	23	10.
10,598	27,860	6,525	5,145	2,789	2,125	2,463	1,937	11.
47,140	53,284	18,643	5,516	3,095	2,465	4,211	1,446	12.
2,869	2,215	3,737	14,370	15,013	12,061	474	73	13.
6,607	2,095	1,124	718	1,183	725	857	2,143	14.
8,059	6,657	3,493	3,072	3,342	24,939	2,835	29,784	15.
34,688	3,947	2,774	4,849	1,587	1,914	1,299	628	16.
6,233	7,445	2,580	2,079	4,056	2,389	2,900	1,599	17.
3,074	4,948	1,858	2,282	3,253	2,432	1,251	925	18.
865	4,682	1,672	293	590	1,267	191	326	19.
29,311	26,982	13,884	17,302	15,321	11,625	16,520	9,613	20.
2,487	2,628	867	1,116	1,195	1,162	718	606	21.
35,969	33,028	14,461	19,913	18,893	12,365	21,165	10,136	22.
28,128	25,989	13,499	14,484	17,037	12,894	16,640	8,842	23.
5,590	4,598	3,029	2,726	2,810	2,075	1,935	1,244	24.
7,757	6,549	4,597	3,864	3,869	3,031	3,902	2,460	25.
15,486	17,374	9,288	8,922	9,390	8,209	8,653	6,918	26.
5,967	4,831	2,446	2,270	2,177	1,948	3,096	1,810	27.
26,963	23,277	12,365	12,237	12,012	9,052	9,764	5,699	N.C.
433,354	332,927	161,600	224,961	193,183	152,629	188,871	115,863	
668,694	505,737	250,446	342,964	291,720	228,353	281,279	170,841	

MALE EMPLOYMENT: 1911

	East Midlands	North West		Yorks. & Humberside		North		
	33.Rut-land	34. Cheshire	35.Lancs.	36.West Riding	37.East Riding	38.North Riding	39.West-morland	40.Cu berl
1.	2,417	29,508	48,673	47,206	25,192	25,975	6,173	15,
2.	197	3,463	108,787	145,626	175	9,814	474	15,
3.	112	4,742	23,346	10,522	4,805	1,190	233	1,
4.	-	-	-	-	-	-	-	
5.	-	9,682	17,584	6,850	4,775	582	171	
6.	23	6,463	42,683	52,492	1,355	17,534	76	3,
7.	39	18,117	93,093	56,614	5,265	4,096	300	1,
8.	9	601	3,122	1,849	509	221	35	
9.	29	2,541	14,358	4,828	636	573	40	
10.	-	5,947	9,896	1,148	3,367	4,074	36	
11.	68	3,286	16,062	11,042	2,374	515	156	
12.	94	6,278	38,777	54,858	4,022	4,198	283	1,
13.	4	24,508	238,874	131,088	355	361	349	1,
14.	25	1,608	6,518	6,158	1,543	329	67	
15.	201	10,007	34,603	27,165	3,006	2,398	777	1,
16.	30	1,380	16,356	15,729	1,327	1,037	57	
17.	40	4,074	29,973	16,024	4,407	1,132	589	
18.	30	3,477	24,666	11,147	1,935	748	416	
19.	9	902	13,519	3,312	418	156	73	
20.	663	28,261	118,275	76,830	14,900	12,352	2,391	7,
21.	24	2,243	10,650	7,492	958	717	174	
22.	560	41,452	213,690	91,860	34,108	14,247	1,707	8,
23.	485	28,693	142,021	86,131	16,415	10,557	1,555	6,
24.	60	8,000	29,336	14,081	2,524	1,536	257	1,
25.	211	8,090	30,398	19,425	3,886	3,178	602	2,
26.	970	17,189	63,359	37,915	7,624	7,163	1,610	3,
27.	63	4,839	26,149	14,465	4,373	2,552	215	1,
N.C.	274	26,480	124,169	63,279	13,494	8,497	1,231	4,
Total Employed	6,637	301,831	1,538,937	1,015,136	163,748	135,732	20,047	82,
Total Population	10,314	454,718	2,285,464	1,480,180	251,799	208,943	30,105	129,

		Wales		Scotland				
41.North-umberland	42.Durham	43.Glamorgan & Monmouth	44.North & West Wales	45.Strathclyde	46.Dumfries & Galloway	47.Borders	48.Lothian	
15,383	12,927	17,598	79,715	31,672	15,675	11,038	11,868	1.
54,501	149,032	200,680	48,863	82,406	1,784	120	25,885	2.
1,814	2,358	5,366	2,865	13,678	859	711	6,154	3.
-	-	-	-	-	-	-	-	4.
1,238	7,138	2,556	758	5,495	81	27	3,373	5.
3,846	18,511	35,742	10,655	48,748	73	109	2,398	6.
15,808	25,593	11,557	3,286	58,774	527	367	5,162	7.
366	541	638	411	1,529	75	67	602	8.
1,866	2,344	2,059	754	4,560	82	55	1,071	9.
13,634	29,198	3,625	1,786	45,314	21	17	1,323	10.
1,300	2,437	3,565	1,697	6,685	296	148	986	11.
5,692	12,682	8,712	4,965	25,784	798	498	4,680	12.
313	614	323	1,878	20,052	1,095	6,463	1,137	13.
702	519	689	1,135	2,825	172	262	911	14.
3,409	4,126	5,457	5,593	15,597	1,264	1,069	4,439	15.
1,791	5,398	2,720	4,715	6,539	310	9	1,604	16.
2,822	4,701	4,172	2,232	14,702	436	372	4,473	17.
1,526	2,487	2,574	1,606	8,699	240	349	8,179	18.
426	390	316	128	2,300	29	53	1,958	19.
16,702	30,152	41,066	26,463	52,682	4,147	3,313	16,507	20.
1,533	2,688	2,279	809	4,885	113	122	1,136	21.
23,990	40,122	56,875	21,963	88,441	3,809	2,507	26,874	22.
17,654	27,769	37,400	20,715	52,611	3,293	2,586	16,876	23.
3,533	4,564	7,035	3,466	10,936	549	414	3,849	24.
4,928	7,061	10,871	8,854	17,388	1,422	1,096	8,884	25.
9,647	11,970	15,091	13,104	25,427	3,000	2,888	9,774	26.
3,924	3,957	5,374	4,596	12,713	411	456	7,292	27.
15,779	22,964	34,657	16,585	55,797	2,393	1,704	14,497	N.C.
224,127	432,243	518,997	289,597	716,239	42,954	36,820	191,892	
346,713	690,441	789,609	442,130	1,116,379	68,171	54,173	299,617	

MALE EMPLOYMENT: 1911

Scotland

	49.Central & Fife	50. Tayside	51.Grampian	52. High-land	53. South East	54. East Anglia	55. South West	56. West Midland
1.	12,431	21,269	46,581	43,583	295,887	133,262	176,445	103,454
2.	40,828	1,047	891	314	4,961	588	34,795	87,941
3.	2,887	2,767	4,098	1,457	80,655	10,160	20,972	20,710
4.	-	-	-	-	-	-	-	-
5.	880	379	685	119	22,792	1,702	3,564	5,174
6.	8,566	1,677	531	227	14,949	2,047	5,516	54,243
7.	3,531	4,664	2,766	420	87,142	7,222	21,729	41,787
8.	196	253	328	123	15,097	661	1,517	3,703
9.	546	411	304	104	36,983	1,129	2,684	9,653
10.	651	1,502	1,771	257	22,027	1,376	6,713	556
11.	573	607	801	367	53,409	4,145	12,627	46,780
12.	2,662	2,350	2,794	1,159	69,878	6,871	16,776	121,957
13.	5,304	19,402	2,266	537	9,832	1,784	7,377	9,172
14.	338	390	347	84	23,875	1,666	4,518	10,366
15.	2,242	3,109	3,825	1,934	107,397	12,242	27,240	20,183
16.	1,673	524	2,444	107	27,990	2,809	8,194	43,488
17.	2,416	2,403	4,549	1,821	93,581	5,346	15,801	17,528
18.	1,848	1,517	2,110	272	103,784	4,422	11,409	10,534
19.	2,884	400	662	48	27,738	1,512	3,105	7,296
20.	12,128	10,419	9,475	6,035	379,297	32,409	85,008	81,052
21.	767	621	498	103	30,953	1,447	4,410	6,412
22.	12,945	13,532	15,408	7,413	533,068	33,504	91,692	93,155
23.	8,812	9,500	9,588	4,291	424,501	31,917	72,597	75,868
24.	1,531	1,919	2,078	881	93,036	4,290	12,553	14,693
25.	3,288	3,855	3,736	2,280	136,174	9,087	24,464	22,014
26.	5,334	6,778	4,995	3,927	326,628	27,348	58,552	51,764
27.	1,858	2,371	1,833	5,906	220,329	8,384	55,049	14,756
N.C.	8,262	6,894	7,236	3,542	352,586	18,564	58,988	69,297
Total Employed	145,381	120,560	132,600	87,311	3,594,549	365,894	844,295	1,043,536
Total Population	229,125	188,619	217,365	135,390	5,554,699	558,967	1,294,706	1,601,880

7. East Midlands	58. North West	59. Yorks. & Humberside	60. North	61. Wales	62. Scotland	63. Great Britain	
135,230	78,181	72,398	76,366	97,313	194,117	1,362,653	1.
119,561	112,250	145,801	229,682	249,543	153,275	1,138,397	2.
14,965	28,088	15,327	6,795	8,231	32,611	238,514	3.
–	–	–	–	–	–	–	4.
3,115	27,266	11,625	9,504	3,314	11,039	99,095	5.
23,604	49,146	53,847	43,703	46,397	62,329	355,781	6.
38,884	111,210	61,879	47,762	14,843	76,211	508,669	7.
1,471	3,723	2,358	1,316	1,049	3,173	34,068	8.
4,111	16,899	5,464	5,010	2,813	7,133	91,879	9.
951	15,843	4,515	47,116	5,411	50,856	155,364	10.
14,527	19,348	13,416	4,832	5,262	10,463	184,809	11.
16,827	45,055	58,880	24,467	13,677	40,725	415,113	12.
41,995	263,382	131,443	2,904	2,201	56,256	526,346	13.
5,651	8,126	7,701	2,164	1,824	5,329	71,220	14.
64,173	44,610	30,171	12,633	11,050	33,479	363,178	15.
10,237	17,736	17,056	8,688	7,435	13,210	156,843	16.
13,063	34,047	20,431	10,188	6,404	31,172	247,561	17.
10,173	28,143	13,082	6,051	4,180	23,214	214,992	18.
2,676	14,421	3,730	1,131	444	8,334	70,387	19.
71,044	146,536	91,730	68,841	67,529	114,706	1,138,152	20.
4,821	12,893	8,450	5,471	3,088	8,245	86,190	21.
83,032	255,142	125,968	88,679	78,838	170,929	1,554,007	22.
70,382	170,714	102,546	63,819	58,115	107,557	1,178,016	23.
10,850	37,336	16,605	11,040	10,501	22,157	233,061	24.
17,337	38,488	23,311	17,917	19,725	41,949	350,466	25.
43,062	80,548	45,539	33,932	28,195	62,123	757,691	26.
11,364	30,988	18,838	11,745	9,970	32,840	414,263	27.
49,038	150,649	76,773	53,245	51,242	100,325	980,707	N.C.
882,144	1,840,768	1,178,884	895,001	808,594	1,473,757	12,927,422	
1,325,471	2,740,182	1,731,979	1,405,985	1,231,739	2,308,839	19,754,447	

South East

	1. London	2. Middlesex	3. Kent	4. Surrey	5. Sussex	6. Hants.	7. Berks.	8. Oxon.
1.	168	829	2,466	641	1,127	1,147	432	435
2.	1	-	-	-	-	-	-	-
3.	19,057	1,746	635	372	209	263	1,190	113
4.	-	-	-	-	-	-	-	-
5.	4,234	1,698	766	214	101	14	13	-
6.	89	3	-	2	-	-	1	-
7.	197	43	11	70	5	5	-	-
8.	1,396	147	27	28	7	21	3	3
9.	2,125	1,684	7	157	4	2	1	-
10.	15	1	17	-	-	13	1	4
11.	203	23	13	19	7	11	8	1
12.	7,335	559	110	128	27	27	89	11
13.	9,420	1,366	603	361	379	327	81	708
14.	7,065	348	37	37	35	25	14	21
15.	151,644	20,093	13,018	11,116	9,939	16,231	3,995	3,817
16.	547	53	24	18	9	12	-	-
17.	7,629	832	259	297	192	339	98	53
18.	34,121	2,682	2,250	912	319	746	448	424
19.	8,202	703	57	66	38	100	16	5
20.	40	17	17	13	10	7	4	5
21.	31	5	-	-	-	-	-	-
22.	9,879	2,471	1,182	1,346	862	1,291	393	305
23.	59,858	12,604	11,579	9,420	8,382	10,925	2,820	2,060
24.	2,214	655	164	274	99	128	38	18
25.	53,359	14,464	13,073	12,567	11,417	10,597	3,350	2,621
26.	348,209	79,568	76,083	80,239	70,037	67,781	21,270	16,171
27.	6,896	1,070	636	789	363	496	203	102
N.C.	35,618	8,917	2,666	3,607	1,986	2,211	675	384
Total Employed	769,552	152,581	125,700	122,693	105,554	112,719	35,143	27,261
Total Population	2,395,344	601,034	538,721	455,183	364,190	480,477	139,200	104,332

9. Bucks.	10. Beds.	11. Herts.	12. Essex	13. Cambridge	14. Hunts.	15. Norfolk	16. Suffolk	
523	333	367	1,129	1,052	296	1,655	1,067	1.
1	–	–	–	–	–	–	–	2.
105	236	518	3,613	456	52	922	384	3.
–	–	–	–	–	–	–	–	4.
19	37	364	1,256	–	13	458	7	5.
2	16	–	19	–	–	–	–	6.
–	5	–	99	1	–	5	17	7.
2	8	297	139	4	–	9	9	8.
1	84	21	899	–	–	24	–	9.
–	–	–	8	1	–	–	1	10.
11	5	12	28	–	3	6	8	11.
16	16	26	672	15	1	26	21	12.
485	830	417	3,251	120	32	2,081	1,738	13.
18	10	72	535	33	2	62	260	14.
2,838	11,929	5,350	27,488	2,848	737	11,152	6,598	15.
4	16	2	123	–	–	1	5	16.
503	53	75	798	94	7	185	86	17.
1,151	857	1,698	3,543	237	108	919	415	18.
307	14	368	2,954	14	1	601	698	19.
4	5	10	7	2	1	12	11	20.
–	–	–	1	–	–	–	–	21.
344	186	482	2,400	248	84	676	456	22.
1,965	2,072	2,963	14,568	1,742	474	5,830	4,053	23.
23	25	46	505	15	7	59	44	24.
2,247	1,815	4,178	13,192	1,936	563	5,112	3,999	25.
14,559	10,862	22,940	62,763	13,152	3,167	29,424	24,216	26.
141	66	217	1,031	73	16	271	180	27.
352	368	1,143	7,150	273	44	845	598	N.C.
25,621	29,848	41,566	148,171	22,316	5,608	60,335	44,871	
112,225	101,582	162,652	690,219	101,175	28,044	257,957	200,684	

FEMALE EMPLOYMENT: 1911

<u>South West</u>   <u>West Midlands</u>

	17.Corn- wall	18. Devon	19.Som- erset	20.Gloucs.	21.Wilts.	22.Dorset	23.Here- ford	24.Shrops.
1.	3,520	5,056	3,007	1,463	871	1,060	1,361	2,253
2.	159	2		2	–	–	–	33
3.	96	471	187	7,488	324	104	69	199
4.	–	–	–	–	–	–	–	–
5.	624	129	18	594	–	11	–	–
6.	2	6	–	3	–	–	–	2
7.	–	10	82	12	17	–	1	2
8.	–	14	11	22	9	1	4	6
9.	1	1	–	28	–	–	–	–
10.	2	14	–	–	–	–	–	–
11.	1	9	4	26	4	1	3	2
12.	10	26	17	613	44	7	1	56
13.	252	2,413	2,613	3,535	1,200	786	14	284
14.	8	47	89	78	47	10	10	16
15.	5,842	15,068	14,570	21,641	4,985	3,627	1,248	2,480
16.	–	76	33	230	–	31	35	264
17.	35	290	251	449	142	50	27	34
18.	73	842	964	5,077	89	72	34	86
19.	12	204	164	539	210	8	–	69
20.	4	9	8	8	7	2	–	9
21.	–	1	–	–	–	–	–	–
22.	518	870	617	973	383	330	248	368
23.	5,234	9,940	5,335	9,946	2,723	2,397	1,034	2,287
24.	17	86	45	168	26	16	11	29
25.	2,730	7,892	5,836	8,449	2,859	2,605	1,281	2,228
26.	17,876	50,774	34,516	45,026	15,525	15,567	8,615	16,204
27.	86	256	202	337	136	90	62	109
N.C.	300	1,274	793	2,218	330	326	128	215
Total Employed	37,402	95,780	69,363	108,925	29,931	27,101	14,186	27,235
Total Population	176,484	366,890	245,293	392,492	143,685	112,461	59,101	124,472

25.Staffs.	26.Warwick	27.Worcs.	28.Derby	29.Notts.	30.Leics.	31.Lincs.	32.Northants.	
2,369	907	1,307	2,132	950	933	3,130	599	1.
41	-	18	2	1	-	-	2	2.
542	1,624	2,689	249	1,777	1,124	1,451	123	3.
-	-	-	-	-	-	-	-	4.
591	1,125	143	92	235	101	37	48	5.
236	240	131	98	1	11	33	-	6.
363	687	39	96	178	13	31	2	7.
250	917	89	194	122	15	4	6	8.
334	1,231	116	94	199	52	3	2	9.
2	1	-	-	-	-	1	-	10.
700	4,864	975	21	237	12	78	35	11.
15,182	28,226	6,201	173	755	272	26	16	12.
5,439	6,542	4,555	19,377	29,582	27,450	807	471	13.
3,870	1,979	369	60	191	54	27	237	14.
18,428	16,619	9,189	7,361	12,587	20,052	6,026	21,251	15.
27,620	372	940	1,246	31	57	12	1	16.
642	2,187	311	332	432	222	226	70	17.
2,211	5,233	1,267	1,366	1,787	1,647	337	923	18.
1,184	5,220	2,099	65	96	125	37	37	19.
13	11	5	6	12	13	20	7	20.
-						-		21.
1,462	1,665	790	634	1,446	844	580	435	22.
15,640	14,473	6,556	5,946	6,218	5,436	5,757	3,413	23.
254	440	168	60	96	49	77	35	24.
9,980	8,381	5,635	5,102	4,375	3,780	4,785	3,092	25.
46,828	45,308	27,761	24,228	23,409	17,257	28,448	15,158	26.
527	531	290	168	274	217	159	128	27.
5,009	7,970	2,425	1,122	2,200	1,648	767	933	N.C.
159,717	156,753	74,068	70,224	87,191	81,384	52,859	47,024	
679,565	534,672	275,641	340,459	312,378	248,200	282,681	177,674	

FEMALE EMPLOYMENT: 1911

| | East Midlands | North West | | Yorks & Humberside | | | North | |
	33. Rutland	34. Cheshire	35.Lancs.	36.West Riding	37.East Riding	38.North Riding	39.Westmorland	40.Cumberland
1.	105	3,918	6,605	4,530	1,547	3,260	1,300	2,968
2.	–	1	2,384	11	–	–	1	308
3.	2	1,858	13,117	4,398	3,626	197	114	934
4.	–	–	–	–	–	–	–	–
5.	–	1,508	3,404	732	1,951	16	30	1
6.	–	23	150	213	–	2	–	1
7.	–	295	2,154	754	2	1	36	14
8.	1	83	231	181	32	5	1	8
9.	–	161	1,403	91	–	1	1	1
10.	–	14	48	–	7	1	–	–
11.	–	21	247	164	9	5	–	1
12.	2	252	2,767	11,370	1,012	16	3	372
13.	8	33,540	334,465	153,058	823	293	458	1,986
14.	2	243	641	707	33	6	30	12
15.	236	17,744	89,430	57,572	6,563	4,518	1,060	3,873
16.	–	13	1,516	774	52	15	–	4
17.	3	317	3,314	2,283	296	64	24	44
18.	3	2,230	14,539	6,799	1,197	208	178	453
19.	–	225	5,295	1,105	89	10	17	8
20.	2	19	92	80	12	13	2	2
21.	–	–	–	1	–	–	–	–
22.	43	1,287	6,607	3,710	767	446	98	371
23.	143	12,883	72,600	36,214	6,237	4,475	730	3,149
24.	2	259	1,314	495	125	72	4	27
25.	221	8,727	36,671	21,906	4,738	3,431	668	2,266
26.	1,610	52,135	177,118	103,775	26,991	23,038	4,692	12,981
27.	7	463	2,807	1,406	214	142	21	81
N.C.	12	2,612	12,917	7,371	1,154	513	87	446
Total Employed	2,402	140,831	791,836	419,700	57,477	40,748	9,555	30,311
Total Population	10,032	500,061	2,482,368	1,565,197	263,242	210,603	33,470	135,963

41.North-umberland	42.Durham	43.Glamorgan & Monmouth	44.North & West Wales	45.Strathclyde	46.Dumfries & Galloway	47.Borders	48.Lothian	
3,444	2,312	2,547	17,702	7,625	2,396	2,094	2,944	1.
9	37	57	9	1,048	5	–	257	2.
944	1,503	1,198	230	8,775	113	109	2,037	3.
–	–	–	–	–	–	–	–	4.
172	374	135	39	1,471	1	1	389	5.
5	6	2,007	784	150	1	–	36	6.
225	70	5	1	1,916	3	11	106	7.
6	10	18	4	83	–	3	57	8.
152	388	2	5	55	–	–	22	9.
42	47	2	–	268	–	–	3	10.
10	4	7	16	82	1	3	15	11.
190	299	295	165	1,462	5	7	195	12.
476	1,909	417	1,384	45,082	1,363	6,997	2,673	13.
319	92	13	74	427	2	1	150	14.
7,268	11,797	18,472	13,417	36,894	2,724	1,394	10,138	15.
520	492	213	58	1,497	2	–	376	16.
169	224	167	48	3,292	12	8	635	17.
595	1,231	798	315	8,711	83	98	6,238	18.
119	90	57	7	1,690	1	40	1,638	19.
12	20	15	12	67	10	5	25	20.
2	2	1	–	7	–	1	11	21.
984	1,034	1,469	1,215	7,033	261	193	1,512	22.
8,306	14,581	15,370	10,189	32,086	1,176	877	9,521	23.
161	198	166	44	269	11	7	120	24.
4,887	8,232	10,737	7,081	16,497	1,087	757	6,585	25.
31,148	43,089	52,092	53,595	68,228	7,662	5,355	32,928	26.
249	413	510	226	543	18	15	187	27.
2,316	2,327	1,773	518	17,247	409	302	6,390	N.C.
62,730	90,781	108,543	107,138	262,505	17,346	18,278	85,188	
350,180	679,419	727,020	462,162	1,142,463	75,019	62,521	331,458	

FEMALE EMPLOYMENT: 1911

Scotland

	49.Central & Fife	50. Tayside	51.Grampian	52.Highland	53.South East	54.East Anglia	55.South West	56.West Midland
1.	2,316	2,034	3,553	10,419	9,597	4,070	14,977	8,19
2.	1,104	1	–	1	2	–	164	9
3.	366	1,256	3,295	2,881	28,057	1,814	8,670	5,12
4.	–	–	–	–	–		–	–
5.	274	36	56	1	8,716	478	1,376	1,85
6.	128	–	8	–	132	–	11	60
7.	38	24	9	2	435	23	121	1,09
8.	7	6	9	1	2,078	22	57	1,26
9.	14	–	–	–	4,985	24	30	1,68
10.	2	4	2	–	59	2	16	
11.	5	5	4	–	341	17	45	6,54
12.	110	73	87	16	9,016	63	717	49,66
13.	13,191	36,198	4,810	5,055	18,228	3,971	10,799	16,83
14.	12	81	18	–	8,217	357	279	6,24
15.	4,547	5,344	5,584	2,039	277,458	21,335	65,733	47,96
16.	453	24	4	2	808	6	370	29,23
17.	210	118	175	27	11,128	372	1,217	3,20
18.	1,085	672	2,343	51	49,151	1,679	7,117	8,83
19.	309	43	315	1	12,830	1,314	1,137	8,57
20.	13	17	9	3	139	26	38	3
21.	3	1	–	–	37	–	1	–
22.	642	782	835	489	21,141	1,464	3,691	4,53
23.	4,412	5,071	4,252	1,323	139,216	12,099	35,575	39,99
24.	33	107	60	30	4,189	125	358	90
25.	3,048	3,379	3,909	1,947	142,880	11,610	30,371	27,50
26.	12,745	15,501	21,641	11,407	870,482	69,959	179,284	144,71
27.	39	72	95	44	12,010	540	1,107	1,51
N.C.	1,877	2,367	2,401	481	65,077	1,760	5,241	15,74
Total Employed	46,983	73,216	53,474	36,220	1,696,409	133,130	368,502	431,95
Total Population	230,726	224,667	240,649	144,562	6,145,159	587,860	1,437,305	1,673,45

7.East Midlands	58.North West	59.Yorks. & Humberside	60. North	61.Wales	62.Scotland	63.Great Britain	
7,849	10,523	6,077	13,284	20,249	33,381	128,204	1.
5	2,385	11	355	66	2,416	5,496	2.
4,726	14,975	8,024	3,692	1,428	18,832	95,341	3.
-	-	-	-	-	-	-	4.
513	4,912	2,683	593	174	2,229	23,533	5.
143	173	213	14	2,791	323	4,409	6.
320	2,449	756	346	6	2,109	7,657	7.
342	314	213	30	22	166	4,510	8.
350	1,564	91	543	7	91	9,366	9.
1	62	7	90	2	279	521	10.
383	268	173	20	23	115	7,929	11.
1,244	3,019	12,382	880	460	1,955	79,402	12.
77,695	368,005	153,881	5,122	1,801	115,369	771,705	13.
571	884	740	459	87	691	18,529	14.
67,513	107,174	64,135	28,516	31,889	68,664	780,381	15.
1,347	1,529	826	1,031	271	2,358	37,777	16.
1,285	3,631	2,579	525	215	4,477	28,630	17.
6,063	16,769	7,996	2,665	1,113	19,281	120,665	18.
360	5,520	1,194	244	64	4,037	35,272	19.
60	111	92	49	27	149	729	20.
-	-	1	4	1	23	67	21.
3,982	7,894	4,477	2,933	2,684	11,747	64,546	22.
26,913	85,483	42,451	31,241	25,559	58,718	497,245	23.
319	1,573	620	462	210	637	9,395	24.
21,355	45,398	26,644	19,484	17,818	37,209	380,274	25.
110,110	229,253	130,766	114,948	105,687	175,467	2,130,672	26.
953	3,270	1,620	906	736	1,013	23,674	27.
6,682	15,529	8,525	5,689	2,291	31,474	158,015	N.C.
341,084	932,667	477,177	234,125	215,681	593,210	5,423,944	
,371,424	2,982,429	1,828,439	1,409,635	1,189,182	2,452,065	21,076,949	

TOTAL EMPLOYMENT: 1911

South East

	1. London	2. Middlesex	3. Kent	4. Surrey	5. Sussex	6. Hants.	7. Berks.	8. Oxon.
1.	8,305	15,154	53,333	22,283	38,634	35,330	16,439	17,524
2.	373	167	1,919	446	460	251	86	247
3.	52,157	7,440	6,585	4,706	4,486	5,840	6,445	1,616
4.	−	−	−	−	−	−	−	−
5.	14,513	3,770	2,560	1,153	384	320	67	14
6.	6,400	654	1,483	389	293	839	265	228
7.	32,727	8,258	11,430	3,150	2,121	9,480	1,196	697
8.	9,225	2,172	818	1,012	534	594	147	127
9.	19,591	6,584	2,507	2,340	1,153	1,954	391	238
10.	3,235	343	4,704	192	231	9,889	84	105
11.	19,223	6,549	3,895	3,486	2,649	3,914	1,276	691
12.	41,216	7,293	4,696	3,208	2,451	4,496	2,205	949
13.	14,251	2,136	1,208	774	727	649	175	1,385
14.	21,483	1,830	1,399	1,550	608	784	318	349
15.	213,587	27,112	17,478	15,353	13,434	21,378	5,492	5,303
16.	7,244	1,599	8,939	1,348	1,527	1,684	943	272
17.	59,329	8,965	4,517	3,504	3,313	3,970	1,518	1,403
18.	91,002	13,127	9,208	6,369	2,223	3,142	1,803	1,962
19.	23,243	5,161	804	1,081	399	612	123	76
20.	131,197	42,428	31,983	33,596	24,403	29,789	10,705	7,246
21.	11,922	3,600	2,295	2,333	1,467	1,783	440	322
22.	264,683	51,955	37,180	28,995	23,554	40,090	9,204	6,170
23.	241,980	57,094	44,678	40,338	32,699	39,215	10,876	7,784
24.	40,982	14,624	6,243	10,370	3,678	4,220	1,229	766
25.	108,376	30,566	23,574	25,982	19,577	18,683	5,986	4,912
26.	480,885	101,325	102,993	109,719	95,350	94,254	32,822	23,632
27.	68,252	13,403	35,367	13,854	5,736	67,927	3,128	1,192
N.C.	188,433	49,762	28,304	29,579	13,963	23,918	6,925	4,132
Total Employed	2,173,814	483,071	450,100	367,110	296,054	425,005	120,288	89,342
Total Population	4,521,685	1,126,465	1,045,591	845,578	663,378	950,579	271,009	199,269

East Anglia

9. Bucks.	10. Beds.	11. Herts.	12. Essex	13. Cambridge	14. Hunts.	15. Norfolk	16. Suffolk	
17,673	14,818	18,366	47,625	28,504	8,930	55,821	44,077	1.
79	258	279	398	124	43	370	51	2.
1,445	1,441	3,058	13,493	2,015	482	5,490	3,987	3.
–	–	–	–	–	–	–	–	4.
145	116	1,027	7,439	75	20	1,300	785	5.
193	1,626	224	2,487	78	22	546	1,401	6.
822	2,537	1,283	13,876	653	172	2,033	4,387	7.
100	108	762	1,576	207	24	269	183	8.
349	580	473	5,808	136	20	717	280	9.
44	19	35	3,205	47	7	605	719	10.
3,496	1,623	1,238	5,710	572	393	1,609	1,588	11.
1,097	1,120	1,349	8,814	848	259	3,322	2,505	12.
546	960	617	4,632	185	47	2,641	2,882	13.
307	284	639	2,541	332	72	636	983	14.
5,066	17,624	7,574	35,454	4,041	1,021	19,244	9,271	15.
562	1,064	350	3,266	916	843	446	610	16.
5,659	1,048	1,576	9,907	794	134	3,062	1,728	17.
2,765	1,844	4,979	14,511	1,253	321	2,656	1,871	18.
650	106	1,007	7,306	90	11	1,424	1,301	19.
7,401	6,306	12,523	41,859	5,979	1,541	14,091	10,824	20.
280	375	602	5,571	255	35	627	530	21.
6,364	4,818	10,692	70,504	6,079	1,441	14,637	12,811	22.
7,562	7,990	12,153	61,348	7,188	1,788	20,231	14,809	23.
916	763	2,383	11,051	669	168	2,217	1,361	24.
4,230	3,347	8,149	25,672	3,799	989	8,997	6,912	25.
21,763	14,641	33,723	86,003	18,023	4,368	41,115	33,801	26.
1,059	1,110	2,214	19,097	779	217	3,263	4,665	27.
4,817	4,159	8,644	55,027	3,371	658	9,410	6,885	N.C.
95,390	90,685	135,919	564,180	87,012	24,026	216,779	171,207	
219,551	194,588	311,284	1,350,881	198,074	55,577	499,116	394,060	

South West   West Midlands

	17.Corn- wall	18. Devon	19.Som- erset	20.Gloucs.	21.Wilts.	22.Dorset	23.Here- ford	24.Shrops.
1.	31,581	49,455	36,458	27,879	26,593	19,456	16,743	25,625
2.	13,167	2,439	7,302	10,238	614	1,199	168	6,093
3.	1,430	4,415	3,647	15,641	2,695	1,814	740	1,776
4.	–	–	–	–	–	–	–	–
5.	823	730	252	3,048	44	43	20	81
6.	530	562	611	2,786	895	143	40	2,755
7.	1,537	4,567	2,167	5,466	7,007	1,106	180	1,578
8.	125	456	280	494	110	109	46	142
9.	231	891	409	828	188	167	71	215
10.	880	5,184	62	481	7	115	4	15
11.	736	1,995	1,636	4,214	3,445	646	501	1,301
12.	1,992	3,321	2,221	6,603	2,358	998	626	2,321
13.	522	3,586	4,946	5,519	2,143	1,460	29	620
14.	311	1,113	1,029	1,434	691	219	204	362
15.	7,590	20,268	20,470	33,248	6,638	4,759	1,863	3,839
16.	975	1,336	1,815	2,256	522	1,660	279	2,099
17.	895	3,648	3,069	6,898	1,423	1,085	444	887
18.	546	3,533	3,264	10,035	639	509	261	513
19.	87	685	659	1,553	1,162	96	30	116
20.	9,252	22,447	15,619.	21,268	8,661	7,799	3,773	7,111
21.	312	1,113	711	1,394	424	457	105	325
22.	9,840	23,301	13,931	32,009	9,239	7,063	3,023	7,290
23.	12,924	28,967	17,317	31,385	9,199	8,380	3,478	8,095
24.	1,318	3,334	2,175	4,300	961	823	439	1,077
25.	5,490	14,446	10,314	14,923	5,110	4,552	2,376	4,244
26.	22,488	66,123	45,157	59,385	22,781	21,902	12,027	22,408
27.	3,630	30,651	2,381	4,336	5,066	10,092	513	1,170
N.C.	5,973	16,517	9,520	21,819	5,472	4,928	2,226	4,809
Total Employed	135,185	315,083	207,422	329,440	124,087	101,580	50,209	106,867
Total Population	328,098	699,703	458,025	736,097	286,822	223,266	114,269	246,307

East Midlands

25.Staffs.	26.War-wick	27.Worcs.	28.Derby	29.Notts.	30.Leics.	31.Lincs.	32.North-ants.	
26,059	20,039	23,185	20,193	18,118	16,354	65,734	20,158	1.
61,504	16,579	3,689	61,968	39,950	12,729	1,952	2,770	2.
10,152	6,547	6,618	2,433	5,728	3,430	5,871	2,115	3.
-	-	-	-	-	-	-	-	4.
2,871	2,456	1,605	1,086	1,096	472	855	119	5.
36,841	7,944	7,272	9,842	3,460	2,204	6,067	2,151	6.
17,580	18,180	5,361	9,427	8,388	5,979	12,781	2,590	7.
1,138	3,186	457	578	495	300	266	164	8.
3,851	6,198	999	1,223	1,725	724	394	366	9.
295	141	104	10	74	8	837	23	10.
11,298	32,724	7,500	5,166	3,026	2,137	2,541	1,972	11.
62,322	81,510	24,844	5,689	3,850	2,737	4,237	1,462	12.
8,308	8,757	8,292	33,747	44,595	39,511	1,281	544	13.
10,477	4,074	1,493	778	1,374	779	884	2,380	14.
26,487	23,276	12,682	10,433	15,929	44,991	8,861	51,035	15.
62,308	4,319	3,714	6,095	1,618	1,971	1,241	629	16.
6,875	9,632	2,891	2,411	4,488	2,611	3,126	1,669	17.
5,285	10,181	3,125	3,648	5,040	4,079	1,588	1,848	18.
2,049	9,902	3,771	358	686	1,392	228	363	19.
29,324	26,993	13,889	17,308	15,333	11,638	16,540	9,620	20.
2,487	2,628	867	1,116	1,195	1,162	718	606	21.
37,431	34,693	15,251	20,547	20,339	13,209	21,745	1.,571	22.
43,768	40,462	20,055	20,430	23,255	18,330	22,397	12,255	23.
5,844	5,038	3,197	2,786	2,906	2,124	2,012	1,279	24.
17,737	14,930	10,232	8,966	8,244	6,811	8,687	5,552	25.
62,314	62,682	37,049	33,150	32,799	25,466	37,101	22,076	26.
6,494	5,362	2,736	2,438	2,451	2,165	3,255	1,938	27.
31,972	31,247	14,790	13,359	14,212	10,700	10,531	6,632	N.C.
593,071	489,680	235,668	295,185	280,374	234,013	241,730	162,887	
1,348,259	1,040,409	526,087	683,423	604,098	476,553	563,960	348,575	

TOTAL EMPLOYMENT: 1911

| | East Midlands | North West | | Yorks. & Humberside | | | North | |
	33.Rut-land	34. Cheshire	35.Lancs.	36.West Riding	37.East Riding	38.North Riding	39.West-morland	40.Cumberla
1.	2,522	33,426	55,278	51,736	26,739	29,235	7,473	18,8
2.	197	3,464	111,171	145,637	175	9,814	475	16,1
3.	114	6,600	36,463	14,920	8,431	1,387	347	2,1
4.	-	-	-	-	-	-	-	-
5.	-	11,190	20,988	7,582	6,726	598	201	3
6.	23	6,486	42,833	52,705	1,355	17,536	76	3,7
7.	39	18,412	95,247	57,368	5,267	4,097	336	1,9
8.	10	684	3,353	2,030	541	226	36	1
9.	29	2,702	15,761	4,919	636	574	41	1
10.	-	5,961	9,944	1,148	3,374	4,075	36	1
11.	68	3,307	16,309	11,206	2,383	520	156	4
12.	96	6,530	41,544	66,228	5,034	4,214	286	1,9
13.	12	58,048	573,339	284,146	1,178	654	807	3,2
14.	27	1,851	7,159	6,865	1,576	335	97	5
15.	437	27,751	124,033	84,737	9,569	6,916	1,837	5,7
16.	30	1,393	17,872	16,503	1,379	1,052	57	4
17.	43	4,391	33,287	18,307	4,703	1,196	613	9
18.	33	5,707	39,205	17,946	3,132	956	594	1,3
19.	9	1,127	18,814	4,417	507	166	90	
20.	665	28,280	118,367	76,910	14,912	12,365	2,393	7,2
21.	24	2,243	10,650	7,493	958	717	174	3
22.	603	42,739	220,297	95,570	34,875	14,693	1,805	8,9
23.	628	41,576	214,621	122,345	22,652	15,032	2,285	9,4
24.	62	8,259	30,650	14,576	2,649	1,608	261	1,1
25.	432	16,817	67,069	41,331	8,624	6,609	1,270	4,4
26.	2,580	69,324	240,477	141,690	34,615	30,201	6,302	16,5
27.	70	5,302	28,956	15,871	4,587	2,694	236	1,1
N.C.	286	29,092	137,086	70,650	14,648	9,010	1,318	5,2
Total Employed	9,039	442,662	2,330,773	1,434,836	221,225	176,480	29,602	113,1
Total Population	20,346	954,779	4,767,832	3,045,377	515,041	419,546	63,575	265,7

		Wales		Scotland				
41.North-umberland	42.Durham	43.Glamorgan & Monmouth	44.North & West Wales	45.Strathclyde	46.Dumfries & Galloway	47.Borders	48.Lothian	
18,827	15,239	20,145	97,417	39,297	18,071	13,132	14,812	1.
54,510	149,069	200,737	48,872	83,454	1,789	120	26,142	2.
2,758	3,861	6,564	3,095	22,453	972	820	8,191	3.
-	-	-	-	-	-	-	-	4.
1,410	7,512	2,691	797	6,966	82	28	3,762	5.
3,851	18,517	37,749	11,439	48,898	74	109	2,434	6.
16,033	25,663	11,562	3,287	60,690	530	378	5,268	7.
372	551	656	415	1,612	75	70	659	8.
2,018	2,732	2,061	759	4,615	82	55	1,093	9.
13,676	29,245	3,627	1,786	45,582	21	17	1,326	10.
1,310	2,441	3,572	1,713	6,767	297	151	1,001	11.
5,882	12,981	9,007	5,130	27,246	803	505	4,875	12.
789	2,523	740	3,262	65,134	2,458	13,460	3,810	13.
1,021	611	702	1,209	3,252	174	263	1,061	14.
10,677	15,923	23,929	19,010	52,491	3,988	2,463	14,577	15.
2,311	5,890	2,933	4,773	8,036	312	9	1,980	16.
2,991	4,925	4,339	2,280	17,994	448	380	5,108	17.
2,121	3,718	3,372	1,921	17,410	323	447	14,417	18.
545	480	373	135	3,990	30	93	3,596	19.
16,714	30,172	41,081	26,475	52,749	4,157	3,318	16,532	20.
1,535	2,690	2,280	809	4,892	113	123	1,147	21.
24,974	41,156	58,344	23,178	95,474	4,070	2,700	28,386	22.
25,960	42,350	52,770	30,904	84,697	4,469	3,463	26,397	23.
3,694	4,762	7,201	3,510	11,205	560	421	3,969	24.
9,815	15,293	21,608	15,935	33,885	2,509	1,853	15,469	25.
40,795	55,059	67,183	66,699	93,655	10,662	8,243	42,702	26.
4,173	4,370	5,884	4,822	13,256	429	471	7,479	27.
18,095	25,291	36,430	17,103	73,044	2,802	2,006	20,887	N.C.
286,857	523,024	627,540	396,735	978,744	60,300	55,098	277,080	
696,893	1,369,860	1,516,629	904,292	2,258,842	143,190	116,694	631,075	

TOTAL EMPLOYMENT: 1911

Scotland

	49.Central & Fife	50. Tayside	51.Grampian	52.Highland	53.South East	54.East Anglia	55.South West	56.West Midlands
1.	14,747	23,303	50,134	54,002	305,484	137,332	191,422	111,65
2.	41,932	1,048	891	315	4,963	588	34,959	88,03
3.	3,253	4,023	7,393	4,338	108,712	11,974	29,642	25,83
4.	–	–	–	–	–	–	–	–
5.	1,154	415	741	120	31,508	2,180	4,940	7,03
6.	8,694	1,677	539	227	15,081	2,047	5,527	54,85
7.	3,569	4,688	2,775	422	87,577	7,245	21,850	42,87
8.	203	259	337	124	17,175	683	1,574	4,96
9.	560	411	304	104	41,968	1,153	2,714	11,33
10.	653	1,506	1,773	257	22,086	1,378	6,729	55
11.	578	612	805	367	53,750	4,162	12,672	53,32
12.	2,772	2,423	2,881	1,175	78,894	6,934	17,493	171,62
13.	18,495	55,600	7,076	5,592	28,060	5,755	18,176	26,00
14.	350	471	365	84	32,092	2,023	4,797	16,61
15.	6,789	8,453	9,409	3,973	384,855	33,577	92,973	68,14
16.	2,126	548	2,448	109	28,798	2,815	8,564	72,71
17.	2,626	2,521	4,724	1,848	104,709	5,718	17,018	20,72
18.	2,933	2,189	4,453	323	152,935	6,101	18,526	19,36
19.	3,193	443	977	49	40,568	2,826	4,242	15,86
20.	12,141	10,436	9,484	6,038	379,436	32,435	85,046	81,09
21.	770	622	498	103	30,990	1,447	4,411	6,41
22.	13,587	14,314	16,243	7,902	554,209	34,968	95,383	97,68
23.	13,224	14,571	13,840	5,614	563,717	44,016	108,172	115,85
24.	1,564	2,026	2,138	911	97,225	4,415	12,911	15,59
25.	6,336	7,234	7,645	4,227	279,054	20,697	54,835	49,51
26.	18,079	22,279	26,636	15,334	1,197,110	97,307	237,836	196,48
27.	1,897	2,443	1,928	5,950	232,339	8,924	56,156	16,27
N.C.	10,139	9,261	9,637	4,023	417,663	20,324	64,229	85,04
Total Employed	192,364	193,776	186,074	123,531	5,290,958	499,024	1,212,797	1,475,49
Total Population	459,851	413,286	458,014	279,952	11,699,858	1,146,827	2,732,011	3,275,33

7.East Midlands	58.North West	59.Yorks. & Humberside	60.North	61.Wales	62.Scotland	63.Great Britain	
143,079	88,704	78,475	89,650	117,562	227,498	1,490,857	1.
119,566	114,635	145,812	230,037	249,609	155,691	1,143,893	2.
19,691	43,063	23,351	10,487	9,659	51,443	333,855	3.
-	-	-	-	-	-	-	4.
3,628	32,178	14,308	10,097	3,488	13,268	122,628	5.
23,747	49,319	54,060	43,717	49,188	62,652	360,190	6.
39,204	113,659	62,635	48,108	14,849	78,320	516,326	7.
1,813	4,037	2,571	1,346	1,071	3,339	38,578	8.
4,461	18,463	5,555	5,553	2,820	7,224	101,245	9.
952	15,905	4,522	47,206	5,413	51,135	155,885	10.
14,910	19,616	13,589	4,852	5,285	10,578	192,738	11.
18,071	48,074	71,262	25,347	14,137	42,680	494,515	12.
119,690	631,387	285,324	8,026	4,002	171,625	1,298,051	13.
6,222	9,010	8,441	2,623	1,911	6,020	89,749	14.
131,686	151,784	94,306	41,149	42,939	102,143	1,143,559	15.
11,584	19,265	17,882	9,719	7,706	15,568	194,620	16.
14,348	37,678	23,010	10,713	6,619	35,649	276,191	17.
16,236	44,912	21,078	8,716	5,293	42,495	335,657	18.
3,036	19,941	4,924	1,375	508	12,371	105,659	19.
71,104	146,647	91,822	68,890	67,556	114,855	1,138,881	20.
4,821	12,893	8,451	5,475	3,089	8,268	86,257	21.
87,014	263,036	130,445	91,612	81,522	182,676	1,618,553	22.
97,295	256,197	144,997	95,060	83,674	166,275	1,675,261	23.
11,169	38,909	17,225	11,502	10,711	22,794	242,456	24.
38,692	83,886	49,955	37,401	37,543	79,158	730,740	25.
153,172	309,801	176,305	148,880	133,882	237,590	2,888,363	26.
12,317	34,258	20,458	12,651	10,706	33,853	437,937	27.
55,720	166,178	85,298	58,934	53,533	131,799	1,138,722	N.C.
1,223,228	2,773,435	1,656,061	1,129,126	1,024,275	2,066,967	18,351,366	
2,696,895	5,722,611	3,560,418	2,815,620	2,420,921	4,760,904	40,831,396	

MALE EMPLOYMENT: 1921

South East

	1. London	2. Middlesex	3. Kent	4. Surrey	5. Sussex	6. Hants.	7. Berks.	8. Oxon.
1.	2,129	9,606	43,201	15,239	31,074	28,505	13,206	13,749
2.	770	235	2,786	398	436	232	123	474
3.	56,998	7,844	8,043	6,130	5,215	7,508	6,097	1,586
4.	–	–	–	–	–	–	–	–
5.	23,702	3,398	3,454	1,253	435	906	63	93
6.	8,715	1,309	609	418	106	188	135	16
7.	60,958	9,369	13,893	3,295	2,851	3,808	2,216	1,086
8.	10,032	1,607	145	543	161	149	32	16
9.	25,059	8,080	3,858	1,567	1,570	1,249	160	135
10.	8,332	470	15,267	323	265	31,977	376	153
11.	28,448	15,210	6,331	9,281	3,654	7,870	2,141	1,344
12.	30,897	3,941	1,901	1,908	2,122	1,750	1,004	520
13.	8,392	932	632	281	301	279	89	660
14.	15,656	619	1,124	1,211	465	610	486	180
15.	67,064	4,387	3,460	3,323	2,951	4,370	1,279	1,249
16.	9,165	1,850	12,448	1,380	1,827	1,367	1,049	282
17.	49,635	5,262	3,923	3,452	3,329	4,214	2,101	1,435
18.	80,281	4,289	9,804	2,938	1,452	2,414	1,416	1,430
19.	27,089	7,589	1,002	869	318	536	96	94
20.	85,148	20,916	18,750	20,390	15,448	16,202	5,873	4,150
21.	29,403	7,114	3,991	4,472	2,824	3,609	926	481
22.	200,888	23,771	19,214	13,700	12,851	21,580	5,626	3,350
23.	273,032	28,473	30,732	25,588	24,066	30,274	9,160	5,858
24.	87,897	2,866	3,421	2,532	2,968	3,548	997	598
25.	68,900	5,234	6,027	5,766	6,482	6,154	2,555	3,681
26.	105,864	14,764	21,699	24,426	22,165	21,479	10,483	5,188
27.	176,677	22,996	26,369	20,588	11,372	29,234	8,568	3,047
N.C.	1,877	97	89	118	74	159	45	20
Total Employed	1,543,008	212,228	262,173	171,389	156,782	230,171	76,302	50,875
Total Population	2,071,579	578,385	542,088	425,023	320,111	480,316	140,640	90,281

East Anglia

9. Bucks.	10. Beds.	11. Herts.	12. Essex	13. Cambridge	14. Hunts.	15. Norfolk	16. Suffolk	
14,032	12,723	15,317	37,448	24,573	7,417	48,079	35,053	1.
82	362	242	349	116	18	477	78	2.
1,972	1,980	3,929	14,763	2,572	636	7,509	5,423	3.
-	-	-	-	-	-	-	-	4.
167	362	577	10,938	123	60	582	1,014	5.
71	1,285	550	1,030	19	3	136	1,337	6.
1,467	6,831	2,086	15,250	589	254	2,452	5,680	7.
20	78	477	1,025	293	-	45	28	8.
162	526	522	6,780	84	7	1,061	234	9.
53	23	105	6,427	47	8	1,117	1,625	10.
8,713	3,760	2,082	7,099	802	548	2,496	1,605	11.
643	680	758	3,637	529	196	1,988	1,012	12.
80	75	184	1,335	97	27	505	1,243	13.
232	269	423	702	247	51	463	702	14.
1,684	4,726	2,082	5,137	1,000	205	8,417	2,114	15.
675	1,509	265	3,980	1,497	1,370	243	575	16.
7,017	1,314	1,884	5,251	982	265	3,714	2,304	17.
2,169	1,149	4,220	3,500	937	241	1,417	1,258	18.
433	104	1,315	3,933	118	9	884	700	19.
5,785	3,986	9,347	25,383	3,461	1,095	6,972	6,838	20.
539	654	1,368	10,145	429	43	1,391	1,051	21.
4,057	2,368	5,693	41,979	4,879	726	9,251	6,976	22.
5,347	5,933	8,809	35,884	5,782	1,236	14,127	11,743	23.
542	524	1,093	3,522	581	123	1,939	1,245	24.
1,387	1,093	2,296	4,616	3,499	289	2,784	2,038	25.
6,506	3,110	8,958	16,018	2,997	889	9,616	8,666	26.
3,357	3,280	5,405	22,784	2,917	617	7,978	6,212	27.
16	20	31	598	23	11	67	61	N.C.
67,208	58,724	80,018	289,513	59,193	16,344	135,710	108,815	
113,979	98,232	155,724	703,042	98,456	26,736	239,697	194,328	

MALE EMPLOYMENT: 1921

South West   West Midlands

	17.Corn-wall	18. Devon	19.Som-erset	20.Gloucs.	21.Wilts.	22.Dorset	23.Here-ford	24.Shrops.
1.	23,209	36,249	29,511	22,062	22,341	15,551	13,632	20,408
2.	10,175	2,650	9,119	11,573	605	1,390	736	6,736
3.	1,828	5,072	4,296	14,207	3,665	2,293	1,011	1,793
4.	–	–	–	–	–	–	–	–
5.	300	869	341	3,922	66	940	122	212
6.	316	298	106	3,013	180	41	12	3,170
7.	1,514	1,883	4,019	7,772	10,137	1,394	219	3,425
8.	9	79	55	116	21	11	7	9
9.	84	423	429	983	102	69	37	87
10.	1,985	16,793	101	3,261	5	224	12	14
11.	1,059	2,568	2,758	8,744	4,442	979	593	1,869
12.	934	1,547	1,329	2,891	597	507	341	939
13.	371	1,259	2,618	1,908	786	649	29	322
14.	254	935	825	1,189	491	162	159	281
15.	1,263	3,594	5,102	9,685	1,215	820	374	857
16.	260	1,202	1,600	1,707	312	1,258	202	1,574
17.	1,551	4,611	3,488	7,160	1,480	1,320	641	1,042
18.	388	2,744	2,403	6,887	461	306	218	358
19.	51	437	326	1,463	1,849	66	9	52
20.	4,736	11,870	8,795	14,416	5,597	3,708	1,394	3,578
21.	537	2,059	1,345	2,448	688	959	266	546
22.	4,641	13,159	7,883	23,285	7,100	3,153	1,844	5,401
23.	7,917	20,982	12,635	25,057	7,363	5,838	2,514	5,957
24.	833	2,536	1,614	3,458	804	654	318	867
25.	1,608	4,907	3,332	5,586	1,701	1,333	732	1,578
26.	4,064	13,267	8,823	11,382	6,593	5,262	2,905	5,128
27.	5,447	15,772	6,818	13,546	6,632	4,595	2,018	3,870
N.C.	16	62	56	124	13	126	12	27
Total Employed	75,350	167,827	119,727	207,845	85,246	53,608	30,357	70,100
Total Population	147,463	331,984	214,092	353,466	144,917	108,709	54,199	119,542

East Midlands

25.Staffs.	26.War-wick	27.Worcs.	28.Derby	29.Notts.	30.Leics.	31.Lincs.	32.North-ants.	
19,390	16,193	17,916	15,695	14,251	13,730	57,559	16,579	1.
66,338	19,109	4,016	69,172	50,455	15,129	1,593	2,790	2.
16,095	12,737	2,692	3,186	6,557	2,800	5,340	2,711	3.
-	-	-	-	-	-	-	-	4.
3,101	2,369	1,986	1,893	1,460	662	1,200	164	5.
51,509	23,473	9,716	13,242	2,158	2,646	8,163	2,043	6.
25,680	24,611	3,918	11,215	9,171	10,023	17,271	5,520	7.
81	966	19	118	96	221	40	21	8.
3,946	15,942	563	1,016	1,504	964	257	342	9.
277	171	95	35	176	20	2,625	30	10.
15,778	62,261	6,767	12,729	5,879	4,278	4,028	2,532	11.
38,834	54,321	11,536	2,185	1,569	1,463	1,718	778	12.
4,027	3,983	3,849	13,855	13,974	15,848	321	98	13.
2,915	1,502	707	473	979	707	687	2,810	14.
6,234	6,378	2,508	2,437	3,230	24,522	2,086	28,952	15.
34,287	5,019	1,828	5,220	1,826	2,486	1,171	579	16.
5,035	7,691	1,704	2,202	4,258	2,862	3,911	2,078	17.
2,989	6,992	849	2,628	2,965	2,445	1,370	1,094	18.
702	11,950	771	312	709	1,358	288	191	19.
17,810	20,508	5,827	7,560	8,403	7,363	8,682	5,067	20.
4,954	6,512	1,111	2,116	1,708	1,862	1,178	1,310	21.
23,778	27,808	6,701	16,794	15,034	8,945	15,800	9,933	22.
26,102	36,913	8,753	14,383	19,565	13,877	17,931	9,153	23.
3,288	5,923	1,066	1,877	2,520	1,599	1,781	950	24.
4,223	8,315	2,004	2,535	2,991	2,643	3,140	1,851	25.
11,034	14,368	5,585	7,017	7,140	5,900	6,914	5,530	26.
14,705	23,197	5,224	6,996	10,684	7,010	8,574	4,917	27.
49	73	28	43	56	22	71	36	N.C.
403,161	419,555	107,739	216,934	189,318	151,385	173,699	108,059	
662,821	663,854	192,938	352,975	307,551	234,517	296,524	168,517	

	East Midlands	North West		Yorks. & Humberside		North		
	33.Rut-land	34. Cheshire	35.Lancs.	36.West Riding	37.East Riding	38.North Riding	39.West-morland	40.Cum-berland
1.	2,155	24,135	40,168	38,316	21,369	22,223	5,665	13,762
2.	217	6,342	111,017	159,347	303	8,956	493	17,245
3.	166	8,501	42,210	16,364	8,893	1,716	284	1,886
4.	-	-	-	-	-	-	-	-
5.	1	17,793	34,182	12,998	10,005	659	351	1,102
6.	16	4,956	28,407	83,725	939	30,405	36	5,818
7.	19	25,109	124,804	71,509	3,634	3,288	565	1,985
8.	-	192	1,297	845	434	27	3	10
9.	2	2,298	28,397	5,831	456	280	41	87
10.	5	12,576	33,294	2,317	7,747	7,359	68	99
11.	88	6,426	33,903	17,563	4,366	816	236	621
12.	78	2,953	25,174	44,474	2,050	1,688	165	677
13.	16	24,170	236,225	138,240	477	244	290	1,545
14.	18	1,740	6,742	4,366	1,249	237	37	394
15.	124	6,338	35,054	23,522	2,360	1,635	688	1,112
16.	43	1,537	19,304	15,774	1,454	569	44	313
17.	106	2,760	26,679	15,300	5,305	1,856	612	1,472
18.	16	2,642	29,093	11,924	1,793	716	592	723
19.	7	1,207	17,448	3,468	417	218	75	106
20.	207	15,006	71,060	45,348	6,110	4,869	927	3,041
21.	27	3,632	19,608	14,246	1,890	1,303	127	628
22.	403	27,563	148,913	65,382	24,090	9,123	1,542	8,477
23.	416	24,029	184,046	91,235	18,766	9,832	1,522	6,162
24.	46	2,863	27,343	10,867	2,103	1,498	256	952
25.	198	4,319	27,989	15,188	3,029	2,036	448	1,271
26.	601	12,883	49,787	28,958	6,560	6,172	1,502	2,655
27.	230	13,786	83,687	46,337	10,173	6,131	856	3,722
N.C.	4	88	471	162	211	63	-	22
Total Employed	5,209	255,844	1,486,302	983,606	146,183	123,919	17,425	75,887
Total Population	9,080	485,098	2,332,931	1,487,398	263,915	222,873	30,239	132,677

| | Wales | | | Scotland | | | | |
41.North-umberland	42.Durham	43.Glam-organ & Monmouth	44.North & West Wales	45.Strathclyde	46.Dumfries & Galloway	47.Borders	48.Lothian	
12,961	10,395	14,463	70,192	31,604	16,478	11,211	12,330	1.
55,912	162,693	226,416	56,110	90,217	2,241	231	33,534	2.
3,258	3,986	9,061	3,961	21,951	1,208	869	8,605	3.
-	-	-	-	-			-	4.
2,056	8,029	7,683	1,066	8,040	670	61	3,137	5.
5,019	23,475	48,418	15,232	68,127	187	167	3,855	6.
14,077	20,981	4,761	2,539	79,384	876	525	6,109	7.
168	103	191	20	1,866	7	5	321	8.
1,834	1,882	1,193	312	5,027	78	77	1,860	9.
36,134	59,638	9,988	4,598	95,976	134	150	7,000	10.
2,574	4,467	5,138	2,260	10,000	1,394	322	1,727	11.
1,819	3,883	3,118	2,744	10,278	634	380	2,571	12.
267	671	376	1,961	19,779	968	6,100	1,576	13.
695	230	451	887	2,476	113	271	727	14.
2,361	2,640	4,825	3,983	13,274	897	736	3,242	15.
1,805	4,407	3,105	3,213	6,311	255	16	1,637	16.
2,992	5,445	4,260	4,152	17,825	1,045	905	4,785	17.
2,074	2,800	2,861	1,403	9,728	226	395	7,983	18.
674	585	496	132	3,322	88	50	3,199	19.
9,305	13,301	15,497	10,305	31,783	2,148	1,785	9,718	20.
3,156	4,475	4,230	1,922	10,037	159	193	2,028	21.
18,465	25,794	47,244	17,658	81,294	3,677	2,268	22,698	22.
21,071	26,028	37,588	20,246	71,386	4,507	3,698	24,502	23.
3,247	3,206	5,990	2,988	10,298	550	438	3,936	24.
4,390	4,076	7,490	6,141	14,407	994	767	9,649	25.
7,764	8,694	12,431	12,083	23,540	2,420	2,613	7,747	26.
10,611	16,084	23,447	13,471	43,495	2,621	2,157	19,129	27.
152	214	236	263	377	13	3	179	N.C.
224,841	418,182	500,957	259,842	781,802	44,588	36,393	203,784	
367,810	740,005	870,029	459,965	1,174,252	67,338	50,621	301,823	

MALE EMPLOYMENT: 1921

Scotland

	49.Central & Fife	50.Tayside	51.Grampian	52.Highland	53.South East	54.East Anglia	55.South West	56.West Midland
1.	12,494	21,983	47,735	40,133	236,229	115,122	148,923	87,5:
2.	47,826	1,371	716	246	6,489	689	35,512	96,9:
3.	4,014	3,940	6,748	2,431	122,065	16,140	31,361	34,3:
4.	-	-	-	-	-	-	-	-
5.	1,208	480	1,121	139	45,348	1,779	6,438	7,7:
6.	11,711	1,100	492	573	14,432	495	3,954	87,8:
7.	3,003	7,104	3,414	737	123,110	11,975	26,719	57,8:
8.	29	43	65	12	14,285	366	291	1,0:
9.	622	458	332	69	49,668	1,386	2,090	20,5:
10.	8,678	5,405	4,384	647	63,771	2,797	22,369	5:
11.	873	1,046	1,236	528	95,933	5,451	20,550	87,2:
12.	1,282	1,406	1,823	974	49,761	3,725	7,805	105,9:
13.	4,709	17,378	1,904	419	13,240	1,872	7,591	12,2:
14.	290	335	294	77	21,977	1,463	3,856	5,5:
15.	1,817	2,483	3,115	1,404	101,712	11,736	21,679	16,3:
16.	1,769	558	1,709	69	35,797	3,685	6,339	42,9:
17.	3,481	3,879	5,074	2,252	88,817	7,265	19,610	16,1:
18.	2,456	1,843	2,932	243	115,062	3,853	13,189	11,4:
19.	3,156	444	595	50	43,378	1,711	4,192	13,4:
20.	5,812	6,286	5,313	2,788	231,378	18,366	49,122	49,1:
21.	1,114	1,485	858	140	65,526	2,914	8,036	13,3:
22.	12,952	11,777	10,833	7,358	355,077	21,832	59,221	65,5:
23.	11,336	13,669	15,784	6,722	483,156	32,888	79,792	80,2:
24.	1,629	1,948	2,025	1,531	110,508	3,888	9,899	11,4:
25.	2,535	2,996	3,660	1,754	114,191	8,610	18,467	16,8:
26.	4,845	7,544	4,991	3,792	260,660	22,168	49,391	39,2:
27.	10,718	8,691	8,378	6,162	333,677	17,724	52,810	49,0:
N.C.	32	37	75	2	3,144	162	397	18
Total Employed	160,391	125,689	135,606	81,252	3,198,391	320,062	709,603	1,030,9:
Total Population	240,043	183,870	207,386	122,309	5,719,400	559,217	1,300,631	1,693,35

.East dlands	58.North West	59.Yorks. & Humberside	60.North	61.Wales	England & Wales: place of work not specified	62.Scotland	63.Great Britain	
119,969	64,303	59,685	65,006	84,655	95,675	193,968	1,271,074	1.
139,356	117,359	159,650	245,299	282,526	139,118	176,382	1,399,315	2.
20,760	50,711	25,257	11,130	13,022	16,198	49,766	390,738	3.
-	-	-	-	-	-	-	-	4.
5,380	51,975	23,003	12,197	8,749	8,072	14,856	185,587	5.
28,268	33,363	84,664	64,753	63,650	6,130	86,212	473,801	6.
53,219	149,913	75,143	40,896	7,300	14,715	101,152	661,995	7.
496	1,489	1,279	311	211	848	2,348	23,006	8.
4,085	30,695	6,287	4,124	1,505	6,761	8,523	135,699	9.
2,891	45,870	10,064	103,298	14,586	12,133	122,374	400,722	10.
29,534	40,329	21,929	8,714	7,398	8,688	17,126	342,920	11.
7,791	28,127	46,524	8,232	5,862	7,794	19,348	290,940	12.
44,112	260,395	138,717	3,017	2,337	7,947	52,833	544,271	13.
5,674	8,482	5,615	1,593	1,338	2,543	4,583	62,688	14.
61,351	41,392	25,882	8,436	8,808	13,383	26,968	337,698	15.
11,325	20,841	17,228	7,138	6,318	4,760	12,324	168,665	16.
15,417	29,439	20,605	12,377	8,412	19,514	39,246	276,815	17.
10,518	31,735	13,717	6,905	4,264	7,513	25,806	243,968	18.
2,865	18,655	3,885	1,658	628	5,989	10,904	107,349	19.
37,282	86,066	51,458	31,443	25,802	135,323	65,633	780,990	20.
8,201	23,240	16,136	9,689	6,152	4,889	16,014	174,186	21.
66,909	176,476	89,472	63,401	64,902	201,637	152,857	1,317,316	22.
75,325	208,075	110,001	64,615	57,834	116,498	151,604	1,460,027	23.
8,773	30,206	12,970	9,159	8,978	19,138	22,355	247,336	24.
13,358	32,308	18,217	12,221	13,631	24,412	36,762	309,029	25.
33,102	62,670	35,518	26,787	24,514	60,137	57,492	671,729	26.
38,411	97,473	56,510	37,404	36,918	261,203	101,351	1,082,495	27.
232	559	373	451	499	2,517	718	9,241	N.C.
844,604	1,742,146	1,129,789	860,254	760,799	1,203,535	1,569,505	13,369,600	
369,164	2,818,029	1,751,313	1,493,604	1,329,994		2,347,642	20,382,348	

FEMALE EMPLOYMENT: 1921

South East

	1. London	2. Middlesex	3. Kent	4. Surrey	5. Sussex	6. Hants.	7. Berks.	8. Oxon
1.	238	1,844	4,749	1,348	1,663	1,907	733	486
2.	91	4	14	6	3	4	-	2
3.	43,078	5,867	3,214	3,208	1,757	2,483	1,982	299
4.	-	-	-	-	-	-	-	-
5.	11,807	2,639	1,196	626	301	109	32	9
6.	1,153	112	39	30	4	10	5	-
7.	5,941	748	919	436	65	104	88	62
8.	4,084	847	20	196	31	44	12	7
9.	10,360	4,238	593	296	256	453	7	7
10.	448	14	325	8	5	457	4	5
11.	2,706	1,408	289	512	106	534	104	79
12.	9,924	1,543	86	313	132	109	317	34
13.	10,163	1,389	563	536	273	294	94	671
14.	9,111	314	109	188	100	90	129	30
15.	115,793	8,474	5,627	5,167	4,574	8,886	2,487	1,705
16.	1,768	177	262	32	24	18	11	1
17.	6,955	672	220	362	159	306	134	101
18.	40,338	3,108	2,695	1,468	444	1,027	533	433
19.	21,147	3,402	686	836	66	187	43	5
20.	2,007	280	203	290	160	164	62	31
21.	1,187	221	97	130	87	159	23	18
22.	11,537	473	494	287	346	732	107	87
23.	135,069	14,273	16,296	13,318	12,991	18,011	4,578	2,916
24.	39,781	749	824	721	650	909	249	178
25.	48,728	7,568	7,454	7,047	9,779	6,312	2,825	1,787
26.	233,440	49,962	54,103	59,461	56,201	52,081	16,274	11,207
27.	78,204	11,797	10,629	9,646	5,261	8,229	2,720	1,836
N.C.	528	9	11	7	8	15	2	-
Total Employed	845,586	122,132	111,717	106,475	95,446	103,634	33,555	21,996
Total Population	2,412,944	674,617	599,578	505,063	407,886	524,602	154,181	99,334

East Anglia

9. Bucks.	10. Beds.	11. Herts.	12. Essex	13. Cambridge	14. Hunts.	15. Norfolk	16. Suffolk	
647	427	1,132	2,132	1,665	433	3,204	1,633	1.
2	1	2	8	1	–	4	2	2.
586	884	1,416	5,728	1,542	201	2,926	1,418	3.
–	–	–	–	–	–	–	–	4.
43	54	491	3,291	14	30	155	61	5.
3	101	36	68	1	–	2	16	6.
109	700	191	1,113	18	8	138	288	7.
–	9	336	666	66	–	11	4	8.
7	346	139	3,039	8	1	92	11	9.
–	1	5	107	1	–	7	23	10.
374	301	254	350	36	8	137	78	11.
54	29	89	687	35	8	85	62	12.
148	176	506	2,164	262	48	1,207	1,563	13.
99	45	152	353	12	2	86	342	14.
1,449	8,668	3,747	12,426	1,461	278	7,959	3,683	15.
7	12	11	184	20	77	5	13	16.
734	109	85	413	73	9	188	160	17.
1,309	1,145	2,628	2,161	288	153	1,002	480	18.
437	68	1,144	3,652	69	1	521	84	19.
52	40	88	190	58	6	47	60	20.
12	22	52	189	7	2	31	29	21.
78	34	90	816	88	6	254	150	22.
2,468	2,770	4,025	16,903	2,610	554	7,543	5,879	23.
117	132	194	775	169	33	480	321	24.
1,548	1,085	2,850	5,274	1,962	163	2,325	1,903	25.
11,118	7,003	15,999	38,639	8,061	2,146	20,618	16,829	26.
1,823	1,474	3,051	10,709	1,710	524	4,136	3,340	27.
3	–	3	42	–	–	1	3	N.C.
23,227	25,636	38,716	112,079	20,237	4,691	53,164	38,435	
122,192	108,230	177,471	767,215	104,963	28,005	264,596	205,730	

FEMALE EMPLOYMENT: 1921

South West   West Midlands

	17.Corn-wall	18. Devon	19.Som-erset	20.Gloucs.	21.Wilts.	22.Dorset	23.Here-ford	24.Shrops.
1.	1,906	2,703	2,317	1,511	913	936	1,215	1,824
2.	114	27	9	33	4	5	-	45
3.	394	1,808	1,018	13,630	1,747	463	459	547
4.	-	-	-	-	-	-	-	-
5.	376	222	91	1,241	4	165	8	9
6.	17	22	3	140	1	1	-	69
7.	38	51	176	285	295	46	6	122
8.	1	23	15	48	16	-	6	2
9.	2	33	21	217	5	4	3	4
10.	18	222	1	51	1	2	-	-
11.	22	86	134	404	120	33	25	59
12.	8	33	70	840	19	11	4	21
13.	985	1,803	2,171	2,859	1,282	679	20	292
14.	4	113	256	152	48	17	2	32
15.	2,105	7,645	10,044	13,567	2,322	1,444	450	1,074
16.	3	146	46	246	3	121	50	345
17.	53	187	244	494	85	84	19	56
18.	63	1,028	1,168	6,147	101	58	99	95
19.	14	270	172	846	567	21	1	87
20.	44	121	91	141	57	30	18	34
21.	20	62	38	60	5	13	7	14
22.	128	325	163	638	288	80	42	141
23.	5,056	13,199	7,176	13,448	3,603	3,003	1,399	3,257
24.	124	592	325	1,025	182	137	67	180
25.	1,382	4,520	3,468	5,741	1,518	1,457	564	1,373
26.	13,302	38,071	24,289	28,631	11,107	11,537	6,017	11,106
27.	2,273	5,556	3,803	6,317	2,608	1,927	1,147	2,007
N.C.	3	11	12	11	1	1	4	1
Total Employed	28,455	78,879	57,321	98,723	26,902	22,275	11,632	22,796
Total Population	173,242	377,630	251,618	404,185	147,291	119,451	58,990	123,520

East Midlands

25.Staffs.	26.Warwick	27.Worcs.	28.Derby	29.Notts.	30.Leics.	31.Lincs.	32.Northants.	
1,751	1,040	2,076	1,333	914	710	4,139	630	1.
108	43	60	121	55	30	9	12	2.
3,042	8,661	959	1,378	4,531	1,456	2,353	493	3.
-	-	-	-	-	-	-	-	4.
902	1,527	237	432	761	419	239	133	5.
3,898	3,887	558	565	96	90	215	21	6.
2,524	3,948	225	308	931	726	694	308	7.
49	628	7	22	67	81	7	3	8.
991	5,923	113	491	378	150	26	48	9.
12	16	-	4	15	3	40	-	10.
1,379	14,319	597	776	633	181	272	170	11.
18,201	40,780	6,173	408	1,249	420	78	25	12.
8,181	7,706	4,780	19,500	26,980	34,913	439	364	13.
2,542	1,621	353	100	356	145	129	619	14.
10,731	13,324	4,955	4,362	9,418	17,775	2,456	21,418	15.
34,180	874	879	2,039	133	206	27	17	16.
733	1,822	175	293	505	247	284	81	17.
2,434	5,714	535	1,868	1,594	1,552	489	1,114	18.
680	10,695	1,639	130	365	717	62	117	19.
226	366	65	103	120	81	87	51	20.
180	226	48	67	18	24	40	46	21.
629	978	201	664	224	148	499	198	22.
16,352	24,032	5,525	7,891	10,655	6,321	8,414	4,420	23.
1,125	3,146	329	435	594	493	402	218	24.
3,512	6,876	2,266	2,345	2,042	1,743	1,842	1,370	25.
26,949	39,179	13,173	16,565	16,197	11,396	21,330	10,212	26.
9,541	12,036	3,274	4,721	4,749	3,492	4,447	2,662	27.
5	15	3	5	6	1	7	3	N.C.
150,857	209,382	49,205	66,926	83,586	83,520	49,026	44,753	
686,056	726,123	212,904	361,687	333,598	259,952	305,678	180,846	

FEMALE EMPLOYMENT: 1921

	East Midlands	North West		Yorks. & Humberside		North		
	33.Rutland	34. Cheshire	35.Lancs.	36.West Riding	37.East Riding	38.North Riding	39.West-morland	40.C ber?
1.	104	2,731	4,508	2,763	941	1,487	599	1,
2.	1	576	2,420	166	5	34	5	
3.	12	5,405	36,745	12,238	7,008	1,116	282	2,
4.	–	–	–	–	–	–	–	
5.	–	4,536	10,660	2,361	3,526	75	96	
6.	–	228	1,294	3,544	31	481	1	
7.	–	1,135	7,137	4,293	186	72	74	
8.	1	120	513	394	42	8	1	
9.	2	889	7,396	830	31	29	2	
10.	–	177	697	32	122	90	1	
11.	4	370	1,761	1,295	144	32	4	
12.	4	358	6,177	17,263	462	66	6	
13.	39	35,705	326,675	153,062	819	237	555	1,
14.	1	425	1,975	989	101	16	3	
15.	95	11,339	69,154	47,798	3,325	2,618	711	1,
16.	1	144	3,413	1,659	147	72	3	
17.	1	257	3,183	2,152	392	126	29	
18.	4	1,811	15,650	6,976	1,132	358	165	
19.	–	1,082	11,726	1,768	147	32	44	
20.	1	186	1,322	675	105	81	7	
21.	–	71	410	296	53	65	1	
22.	3	670	7,321	1,968	1,292	457	29	
23.	199	13,984	95,339	45,656	9,327	6,627	700	3,
24.	5	741	9,630	3,310	584	364	68	
25.	182	4,157	19,526	10,940	2,659	1,695	563	1,
26.	952	36,170	116,115	72,049	18,323	17,323	4,222	9,
27.	161	7,185	40,199	24,508	4,506	3,497	565	2,
N.C.	–	7	77	25	13	4	–	
Total Employed	1,772	130,459	801,023	419,010	55,423	37,062	8,736	26,
Total Population	9,296	540,626	2,594,553	1,609,737	281,004	233,563	35,507	140,

	Wales			Scotland				
41.North-umberland	42.Durham	43.Glam-organ & Monmouth	44.North & West Wales	45.Strathclyde	46.Dumfries & Galloway	47.Borders	48.Lothian	
2,953	2,409	1,642	9,786	6,813	2,115	1,723	3,197	1.
56	747	250	63	2,201	57	7	747	2.
3,111	4,253	3,430	1,160	18,614	345	286	4,075	3.
-	-	-	-	-	-	-	-	4.
569	957	157	75	2,424	52	5	827	5.
173	358	2,832	1,092	1,831	4	5	114	6.
993	528	177	80	7,068	54	26	432	7.
43	25	47	4	462	1	-	118	8.
251	327	175	17	702	3	3	181	9.
1,116	769	179	33	2,242	7	5	101	10.
152	177	190	73	711	152	22	162	11.
496	577	726	371	2,460	19	5	446	12.
639	1,705	285	1,405	42,008	2,271	6,716	3,279	13.
280	37	111	97	1,058	6	21	228	14.
4,757	5,441	9,423	5,934	26,129	957	736	4,493	15.
606	1,029	264	180	1,924	7	2	479	16.
361	442	273	109	3,214	20	14	478	17.
1,120	1,402	1,102	248	8,229	103	98	5,936	18.
295	356	136	41	2,147	7	36	2,799	19.
194	291	167	71	1,374	32	28	401	20.
177	127	147	41	598	6	12	55	21.
1,185	1,166	1,300	342	4,755	123	47	977	22.
16,233	21,793	24,713	11,388	62,162	2,244	1,761	18,649	23.
1,399	1,203	1,748	482	4,350	72	62	1,512	24.
3,160	3,549	5,091	3,735	13,074	781	539	8,322	25.
24,922	29,321	37,818	40,075	62,254	7,114	5,140	24,711	26.
5,909	10,098	13,614	7,602	21,700	1,455	895	7,476	27.
13	6	22	80	26	-	-	7	N.C.
71,163	89,093	106,019	84,584	300,530	18,007	18,194	90,202	
378,286	739,028	833,246	493,234	1,224,801	75,970	60,553	336,003	

FEMALE EMPLOYMENT: 1921

Scotland

	49.Central & Fife	50.Tayside	51.Grampian	52.Highland	53.South East	54.East Anglia	55.South West	56.West Midlands
1.	2,125	1,794	2,102	5,022	17,306	6,935	10,286	7,90
2.	1,715	26	13	3	137	7	192	25
3.	1,055	1,955	4,154	3,102	70,502	6,087	19,060	13,66
4.	–	–	–	–	–	–	–	–
5.	525	83	144	12	20,598	260	2,099	2,68
6.	892	28	25	31	1,561	19	184	8,41
7.	132	349	166	19	10,476	452	891	6,82
8.	16	14	33	3	6,252	81	103	69
9.	106	30	43	1	19,741	112	282	7,03
10.	102	115	74	6	1,379	31	295	2
11.	64	74	68	25	7,017	259	799	16,37
12.	148	122	155	11	13,317	190	981	65,17
13.	9,585	31,652	4,108	2,018	16,977	3,080	9,779	20,97
14.	69	184	40	2	10,720	442	590	4,55
15.	2,812	2,866	2,954	1,100	179,003	13,381	37,127	30,53
16.	643	79	34	3	2,507	115	565	36,32
17.	337	230	425	36	10,250	430	1,147	2,80
18.	1,217	928	2,203	38	57,289	1,923	8,565	8,87
19.	1,310	88	462	11	31,673	675	1,890	13,10
20.	174	200	211	41	3,567	171	484	70
21.	79	39	12	6	2,197	69	198	47
22.	495	398	392	174	15,081	498	1,622	1,99
23.	9,094	9,221	8,797	2,436	243,618	16,586	45,485	50,56
24.	409	569	535	133	45,279	1,003	2,385	4,84
25.	2,320	2,800	3,304	1,151	102,257	6,353	18,086	14,59
26.	13,016	16,786	20,495	11,495	605,488	47,654	126,937	96,42
27.	4,109	3,833	4,288	2,505	145,379	9,710	22,484	28,00
N.C.	1	2	6	–	628	4	39	28
Total Employed	52,550	74,465	55,243	29,384	1,640,199	116,527	312,555	443,87
Total Population	247,143	220,648	234,265	135,472	6,553,313	603,294	1,473,417	1,807,59

7.East Midlands	58.North West	59.Yorks. & Humberside	60.North	61.Wales	England & Wales: place of work not specified	62.Scotland	63.Great Britain	
7,830	7,239	3,704	8,975	11,428	5,493	24,891	111,993	1.
228	2,996	171	1,100	313	3,399	4,769	13,568	2.
10,223	42,150	19,246	11,259	4,590	2,964	33,586	233,335	3.
-	-	-	-	-	-	-	-	4.
1,984	15,196	5,887	1,723	232	685	4,072	55,419	5.
987	1,522	3,575	1,046	3,924	271	2,930	24,431	6.
2,967	8,272	4,479	1,767	257	430	8,246	45,062	7.
181	633	436	78	51	163	647	9,317	8.
1,095	8,285	861	612	192	438	1,069	39,721	9.
62	874	154	1,977	212	83	2,652	7,747	10.
2,036	2,131	1,439	383	263	476	1,278	32,460	11.
2,184	6,535	17,725	1,388	1,097	1,732	3,366	113,694	12.
82,235	362,380	153,881	5,007	1,690	6,376	101,637	764,021	13.
1,350	2,400	1,090	375	208	642	1,608	23,975	14.
55,524	80,493	51,123	15,338	15,357	17,068	42,047	536,995	15.
2,433	3,557	1,806	1,725	444	468	3,171	53,119	16.
1,411	3,440	2,544	1,014	382	864	4,754	29,041	17.
6,621	17,461	8,108	3,479	1,350	1,947	18,752	134,372	18.
1,391	12,808	1,915	793	177	1,437	6,860	72,721	19.
443	1,508	780	620	238	384	2,461	11,365	20.
195	481	349	382	188	61	807	5,402	21.
1,736	7,991	3,260	2,994	1,642	2,292	7,361	46,468	22.
37,900	109,323	54,983	49,319	36,101	19,852	114,364	778,096	23.
2,147	10,371	3,894	3,269	2,230	2,587	7,642	85,654	24.
9,524	23,683	13,599	10,002	8,826	35,588	32,291	274,800	25.
76,652	152,285	90,372	84,896	77,893	212,527	161,011	1,732,139	26.
20,232	47,384	29,014	22,694	21,216	8,617	46,261	400,996	27.
22	84	38	24	102	76	42	1,087	N.C
329,593	931,482	474,433	232,239	190,603	326,920	638,575	5,636,998	
,451,057	3,135,179	1,890,741	1,526,880	1,326,480		2,534,855	22,302,809	

TOTAL EMPLOYMENT: 1921

South East

	1. London	2. Middlesex	3. Kent	4. Surrey	5. Sussex	6. Hants.	7. Berks.	8. Oxon.
1.	2,367	11,450	47,950	16,587	32,737	30,412	13,939	14,235
2.	861	239	2,800	404	439	236	123	476
3.	100,076	13,711	11,257	9,338	6,972	9,991	8,079	1,885
4.	–	–	–	–	–	–	–	–
5.	35,509	6,037	4,650	1,879	736	1,015	95	102
6.	9,868	1,421	648	448	110	198	140	16
7.	66,899	10,117	14,812	3,731	2,916	3,912	2,304	1,148
8.	14,116	2,454	165	739	192	193	44	23
9.	35,419	12,318	4,451	1,863	1,826	1,702	167	142
10.	8,780	484	15,592	331	270	32,434	380	158
11.	31,154	16,618	6,620	9,793	3,760	8,404	2,245	1,423
12.	40,821	5,484	1,987	2,221	2,254	1,859	1,321	554
13.	18,555	2,321	1,195	817	574	573	183	1,331
14.	24,767	933	1,233	1,399	565	700	615	210
15.	182,857	12,861	9,087	8,490	7,525	13,256	3,766	2,954
16.	10,933	2,027	12,710	1,412	1,851	1,385	1,060	283
17.	56,590	5,934	4,143	3,814	3,488	4,520	2,235	1,536
18.	120,619	7,397	12,499	4,406	1,896	3,441	1,949	1,863
19.	48,236	10,991	1,688	1,705	384	723	139	99
20.	87,155	21,196	18,953	20,680	15,608	16,366	5,935	4,181
21.	30,590	7,335	4,088	4,602	2,911	3,768	949	499
22.	212,425	24,244	19,708	13,987	13,197	22,312	5,733	3,437
23.	408,101	42,746	47,028	38,906	37,057	48,285	13,738	8,774
24.	127,678	3,615	4,245	3,253	3,618	4,457	1,246	776
25.	117,628	12,802	13,481	12,813	16,261	12,466	5,380	5,468
26.	339,304	64,726	75,802	83,887	78,366	73,560	26,757	16,395
27.	254,881	34,793	36,998	30,234	16,633	37,463	11,288	4,883
N.C.	2,405	106	100	125	82	174	47	20
Total Employed	2,388,594	334,360	373,890	277,864	252,228	333,805	109,857	72,871
Total Population	4,484,523	1,253,002	1,141,666	930,086	727,997	1,004,918	294,821	189,615

East Anglia

9. Bucks.	10. Beds.	11. Herts.	12. Essex	13. Cambridge	14. Hunts.	15. Norfolk	16. Suffolk	
14,679	13,150	16,449	39,580	26,238	7,850	51,283	36,686	1.
84	363	244	357	117	18	481	80	2.
2,558	2,864	5,345	20,491	4,114	837	10,435	6,841	3.
-	-	-	-	-	-	-	-	4.
210	416	1,068	14,229	137	90	737	1,075	5.
74	1,386	586	1,098	20	3	138	353	6.
1,576	7,531	2,277	16,363	607	262	2,590	8,968	7.
20	87	813	1,691	359	-	56	32	8.
169	872	661	9,819	92	8	1,153	245	9.
53	24	110	6,534	48	8	1,124	1,648	10.
9,087	4,061	2,336	7,449	838	556	2,633	1,683	11.
697	709	847	4,324	564	204	2,073	1,074	12.
228	251	690	3,499	359	75	1,712	2,806	13.
331	314	575	1,055	259	53	549	1,044	14.
3,133	13,394	5,829	17,563	2,461	483	16,376	5,797	15.
682	1,521	276	4,164	1,517	1,447	248	588	16.
7,751	1,423	1,969	5,664	1,055	274	3,902	2,464	17.
3,478	2,294	6,848	5,661	1,225	394	2,419	1,738	18.
870	172	2,459	7,585	187	10	1,405	784	19.
5,837	4,026	9,435	25,573	3,519	1,101	7,019	6,898	20.
551	676	1,420	10,334	436	45	1,422	1,080	21.
4,135	2,402	5,783	42,795	4,967	732	9,505	7,126	22.
7,815	8,703	12,834	52,787	8,392	1,790	21,670	17,622	23.
659	656	1,287	4,297	750	156	2,419	1,566	24.
2,935	2,178	5,146	9,890	5,461	452	5,109	3,941	25.
17,624	10,113	24,957	54,657	11,058	3,035	30,234	25,495	26.
5,180	4,754	8,456	33,493	4,627	1,141	12,114	9,552	27.
19	20	34	640	23	11	68	64	N.C.
90,435	84,360	118,734	401,592	79,430	21,035	188,874	147,250	
236,171	206,462	333,195	1,470,257	203,419	54,741	504,293	400,058	

TOTAL EMPLOYMENT: 1921

South West   West Midlands

	17.Corn-wall	18. Devon	19.Som-erset	20.Gloucs.	21.Wilts.	22.Dorset	23.Here-ford	24.Shrops.
1.	25,115	38,952	31,828	23,573	23,254	16,487	14,847	22,232
2.	10,289	2,677	9,128	11,606	609	1,395	736	6,781
3.	2,222	6,880	5,314	27,837	5,412	2,756	1,470	2,340
4.	–	–	–	–	–	–	–	–
5.	676	1,091	432	5,163	70	1,105	130	221
6.	333	320	109	3,153	181	42	12	3,239
7.	1,552	1,934	4,195	8,057	10,432	1,440	225	3,547
8.	10	102	70	164	37	11	13	11
9.	86	456	450	1,200	107	73	40	91
10.	2,003	17,015	102	3,312	6	226	12	14
11.	1,081	2,654	2,892	9,148	4,562	1,012	618	1,928
12.	942	1,580	1,399	3,731	616	518	345	960
13.	1,356	3,062	4,789	4,767	2,068	1,328	49	614
14.	258	1,048	1,081	1,341	539	179	161	313
15.	3,368	11,239	15,146	23,252	3,537	2,264	824	1,931
16.	263	1,348	1,646	1,953	315	1,379	252	1,919
17.	1,604	4,798	3,732	7,654	1,565	1,404	660	1,098
18.	451	3,772	3,571	13,034	562	364	317	453
19.	65	707	498	2,309	2,416	87	10	139
20.	4,780	11,991	8,886	14,557	5,654	3,738	1,412	3,612
21.	557	2,121	1,383	2,508	693	972	273	560
22.	4,769	13,484	8,046	23,923	7,388	3,233	1,886	5,542
23.	12,973	34,181	19,811	38,505	10,966	8,841	3,913	9,214
24.	957	3,128	1,939	4,483	986	791	385	1,047
25.	2,990	9,427	6,800	11,327	3,219	2,790	1,296	2,951
26.	17,366	51,338	33,112	40,013	17,700	16,799	8,922	16,234
27.	7,720	21,328	10,621	19,863	9,240	6,522	3,165	5,877
N.C.	19	73	68	135	14	127	16	28
Total Employed	103,805	246,706	177,048	306,568	112,148	75,883	41,989	92,896
Total Population	320,705	709,614	465,710	757,651	292,208	228,160	113,189	243,062

25.Staffs.	26.Warwick	27.Worcs.	28.Derby	29.Notts.	30.Leics.	31.Lincs.	32.Northants.	
21,141	17,233	19,992	17,028	15,165	14,440	61,698	17,209	1.
66,446	19,152	4,076	69,293	50,510	15,159	1,602	2,802	2.
19,137	21,398	3,651	4,564	11,088	4,256	7,693	3,204	3.
-	-	-	-	-	-	-	-	4.
4,003	3,896	2,223	2,325	2,221	1,081	1,439	297	5.
55,407	27,360	10,274	13,807	2,254	2,736	8,378	2,064	6.
28,204	28,559	4,143	11,523	10,102	10,749	17,965	5,828	7.
130	1,594	26	140	163	302	47	24	8.
4,937	21,865	676	1,507	1,882	1,114	283	390	9.
289	187	95	39	191	23	2,665	30	10.
17,157	76,580	7,364	13,505	6,512	4,459	4,300	2,702	11.
57,035	95,101	17,709	2,593	2,818	1,883	1,796	803	12.
12,208	11,689	8,629	33,355	40,954	50,761	760	462	13.
5,457	3,123	1,060	573	1,335	852	816	3,429	14.
16,965	19,702	7,463	6,799	12,648	42,297	4,542	50,370	15.
68,467	5,893	2,707	7,259	1,959	2,692	1,198	596	16.
5,768	9,513	1,879	2,495	4,763	3,109	4,195	2,159	17.
5,423	12,706	1,384	4,496	4,559	3,997	1,859	2,208	18.
1,382	22,645	2,410	442	1,074	2,075	350	308	19.
18,036	20,874	5,892	7,663	8,523	7,444	8,769	5,118	20.
5,134	6,738	1,159	2,183	1,726	1,886	1,218	1,356	21.
24,407	28,786	6,902	17,458	15,258	9,093	16,299	10,131	22.
42,454	60,945	14,278	22,274	30,220	20,198	26,345	13,573	23.
4,413	9,069	1,395	2,312	3,114	2,092	2,183	1,168	24.
7,735	15,191	4,270	4,880	5,033	4,386	4,982	3,221	25.
37,983	53,817	18,758	23,582	23,337	17,296	28,244	15,742	26.
24,246	35,233	8,498	11,717	15,433	10,502	13,021	7,579	27.
54	88	31	48	62	23	78	39	N.C.
554,018	628,937	156,944	283,860	272,904	234,905	222,725	152,812	
1,348,877	1,389,977	405,842	714,662	641,149	494,469	602,202	349,363	

TOTAL EMPLOYMENT: 1921

	East Midlands	North West	Yorks. & Humberside			North		
	33.Rutland	34. Cheshire	35.Lancs.	36.West Riding	37.East Riding	38.North Riding	39.Westmorland	40.Cumberland
1.	2,259	26,866	44,676	41,079	22,310	23,710	6,264	15,289
2.	218	6,918	113,437	159,513	308	8,990	498	17,503
3.	178	13,906	78,955	28,602	15,901	2,832	566	4,383
4.	–	–	–	–	–	–	–	–
5.	1	22,329	44,842	15,359	13,531	734	447	1,128
6.	16	5,184	29,701	87,269	970	30,886	37	5,851
7.	19	26,244	131,941	75,802	3,820	3,360	639	2,085
8.	1	312	1,810	1,239	476	35	4	11
9.	4	3,187	35,793	6,661	487	309	43	90
10.	5	12,753	33,991	2,349	7,869	7,449	69	100
11.	92	6,796	35,664	18,858	4,510	848	240	639
12.	82	3,311	31,351	61,737	2,512	1,754	171	920
13.	55	59,875	562,900	291,302	1,296	481	845	3,416
14.	19	2,165	8,717	5,355	1,350	253	40	433
15.	219	17,677	104,208	71,320	5,685	4,253	1,399	2,923
16.	44	1,681	22,717	17,433	1,601	641	47	328
17.	107	3,017	29,862	17,452	5,697	1,982	641	1,528
18.	20	4,453	44,743	18,900	2,925	1,074	757	1,157
19.	7	2,289	29,174	5,236	564	250	119	172
20.	208	15,192	72,382	46,023	6,215	4,950	934	3,088
21.	27	3,703	20,018	14,542	1,943	1,368	128	640
22.	406	28,233	156,234	67,350	25,382	9,580	1,571	8,634
23.	615	38,013	279,385	136,891	28,093	16,459	2,222	10,128
24.	51	3,604	36,973	14,177	2,687	1,862	324	1,187
25.	380	8,476	47,515	26,128	5,688	3,731	1,011	2,306
26.	1,553	49,053	165,902	101,007	24,883	23,495	5,724	11,763
27.	391	20,971	123,886	70,845	14,679	9,628	1,421	6,347
N.C.	4	95	548	187	224	67	–	23
Total Employed	6,981	386,303	2,287,325	1,402,616	201,606	160,981	26,161	102,072
Total Population	18,376	1,025,724	4,927,484	3,097,135	544,919	456,436	65,746	273,173

	Wales			Scotland				
41.North-umberland	42.Durham	43.Glam-organ & Monmouth	44.North & West Wales	45.Strathclyde	46.Dumfries & Galloway	47.Borders	48.Lothian	
15,914	12,804	16,105	79,978	38,417	18,593	12,934	15,527	1.
55,968	163,440	226,666	56,173	92,418	2,298	238	34,281	2.
6,369	8,239	12,491	5,121	40,565	1,553	1,155	12,680	3.
-	-	-	-	-	-	-	-	4.
2,625	8,986	7,840	1,141	10,464	722	66	3,964	5.
5,192	23,833	51,250	16,324	69,958	191	172	3,969	6.
15,070	21,509	4,938	2,619	86,452	930	551	6,541	7.
211	128	238	24	2,328	8	5	439	8.
2,085	2,209	1,368	329	5,729	81	80	2,041	9.
37,250	60,407	10,167	4,631	98,218	141	155	7,101	10.
2,726	4,644	5,328	2,333	10,711	1,546	344	1,889	11.
2,315	4,460	3,844	3,115	12,738	653	385	3,017	12.
906	2,376	661	3,366	61,787	3,239	12,816	4,855	13.
975	267	562	984	3,534	119	292	955	14.
7,118	8,081	14,248	9,917	39,403	1,854	1,472	7,735	15.
2,411	5,436	3,369	3,393	8,235	262	18	2,116	16.
3,353	5,887	4,533	4,261	21,039	1,065	919	5,263	17.
3,194	4,202	3,963	1,651	17,957	329	493	13,919	18.
969	941	632	173	5,469	95	86	5,998	19.
9,499	13,592	15,664	10,376	33,157	2,180	1,813	10,119	20.
3,333	4,602	4,377	1,963	10,635	165	205	2,083	21.
19,650	26,960	48,544	18,000	86,049	3,800	2,315	23,675	22.
37,304	47,821	62,301	31,634	133,548	6,751	5,459	43,151	23.
4,646	4,409	7,738	3,470	14,648	622	500	5,448	24.
7,550	7,625	12,581	9,876	27,481	1,775	1,306	17,971	25.
32,686	38,015	50,249	52,158	85,794	9,534	7,753	32,458	26.
16,520	26,182	37,061	21,073	65,195	4,076	3,052	26,605	27.
165	220	258	343	403	13	3	186	N.C.
296,004	507,275	606,976	344,426	1,082,332	62,595	54,587	293,986	
746,096	1,479,033	1,703,275	953,199	2,399,053	143,308	111,174	637,826	

TOTAL EMPLOYMENT: 1921

Scotland

	49.Central & Fife	50.Tayside	51.Grampian	52.Highland	53.South East	54.East Anglia	55.South West	56.West Midlands
1.	14,619	23,777	49,837	45,155	253,535	122,057	159,209	95,445
2.	49,541	1,397	729	249	6,626	696	35,704	97,191
3.	5,069	5,895	10,902	5,533	192,567	22,227	50,421	47,996
4.	-	-	-	-	-	-	-	-
5.	1,733	563	1,265	151	65,946	2,039	8,537	10,473
6.	12,603	1,128	517	604	15,993	514	4,138	96,292
7.	3,135	7,453	3,580	756	133,586	12,427	27,610	64,678
8.	45	57	98	15	20,537	447	394	1,774
9.	728	488	375	70	69,409	1,498	2,372	27,609
10.	8,780	5,520	4,458	653	65,150	2,828	22,664	597
11.	937	1,120	1,304	553	102,950	5,710	21,349	103,647
12.	1,430	1,528	1,978	985	63,078	3,915	8,786	171,150
13.	14,294	49,030	6,012	2,437	30,217	4,952	17,370	33,189
14.	359	519	334	79	32,697	1,905	4,446	10,114
15.	4,629	5,349	6,069	2,504	280,715	25,117	58,806	46,885
16.	2,412	637	1,743	72	38,304	3,800	6,904	79,238
17.	3,818	4,109	5,499	2,288	99,067	7,695	20,757	18,918
18.	3,673	2,771	5,135	281	172,351	5,776	21,754	20,283
19.	4,466	532	1,057	61	75,051	2,386	6,082	26,586
20.	5,986	6,486	5,524	2,829	234,945	18,537	49,606	49,826
21.	1,193	1,524	870	146	67,723	2,983	8,234	13,864
22.	13,447	12,175	11,225	7,532	370,158	22,330	60,843	67,523
23.	20,430	22,890	24,581	9,158	726,774	49,474	125,277	130,804
24.	2,038	2,517	2,560	1,664	155,787	4,891	12,284	16,309
25.	4,855	5,796	6,964	2,905	216,448	14,963	36,553	31,443
26.	17,861	24,330	25,486	15,287	866,148	69,822	176,328	135,714
27.	14,827	12,524	12,666	8,667	479,056	27,434	75,294	77,019
N.C.	33	39	81	2	3,772	166	436	217
Total Employed	212,941	200,154	190,849	110,636	4,838,590	436,589	1,022,158	1,474,784
Total Population	487,186	404,518	441,651	257,781	12,272,713	1,162,511	2,774,048	3,500,947

7.East idlands	58.North West	59.Yorks. & Humberside	60.North	61.Wales	England & Wales: place of work not specified	62.Scotland	63.Great Britain	
127,799	71,542	63,389	73,981	96,083	101,168	218,859	1,383,067	1.
139,584	120,355	159,821	246,399	282,839	142,517	181,151	1,412,883	2.
30,983	92,861	44,503	22,389	17,612	19,162	83,352	624,073	3.
–	–	–	–	–	–	–	–	4.
7,364	67,171	28,890	13,920	8,981	8,757	18,928	241,006	5.
29,255	34,885	88,239	65,799	67,574	6,401	89,142	498,232	6.
56,186	158,185	79,622	42,663	7,557	15,145	109,398	707,057	7.
677	2,122	1,715	389	262	1,011	2,995	32,323	8.
5,180	38,980	7,148	4,736	1,697	7,199	9,592	175,420	9.
2,953	46,744	10,218	105,275	14,798	12,216	125,026	408,469	10.
31,570	42,460	23,368	9,097	7,661	9,164	18,404	375,380	11.
9,975	34,662	64,249	9,620	6,959	9,526	22,714	404,634	12.
126,347	622,775	292,598	8,024	4,027	14,323	154,470	1,308,292	13.
7,024	10,882	6,705	1,968	1,546	3,185	6,191	86,663	14.
116,875	121,885	77,005	23,774	24,165	30,451	69,015	874,693	15.
13,758	24,398	19,034	8,863	6,762	5,228	15,495	221,784	16.
16,828	32,879	23,149	13,391	8,794	20,378	44,000	305,856	17.
17,139	49,196	21,825	10,384	5,614	9,460	44,558	378,340	18.
4,256	31,463	5,800	2,451	805	7,426	17,764	180,070	19.
37,725	87,574	52,238	32,063	26,040	135,707	68,094	792,355	20.
8,396	23,721	16,485	10,071	6,340	4,950	16,821	179,588	21.
68,645	184,467	92,732	66,395	66,544	203,929	160,218	1,363,784	22.
113,225	317,398	164,984	113,934	93,935	136,350	265,968	2,238,123	23.
10,920	40,577	16,864	12,428	11,208	21,725	29,927	332,990	24.
22,882	55,991	31,816	22,223	22,457	60,000	69,053	583,829	25.
109,754	214,955	125,890	111,683	102,407	272,664	218,503	2,403,868	26.
58,643	144,857	85,524	60,098	58,134	269,820	147,612	1,483,491	27.
254	643	411	475	601	2,593	760	10,328	N.C.
,174,197	2,673,628	1,604,222	1,092,493	951,402	1,530,455	2,208,080	19,006,598	
,820,221	5,953,208	3,642,054	3,020,484	2,656,474		4,882,497	42,685,157	

MALE EMPLOYMENT: 1931

South East

	1. London	2. Middlesex	3. Kent	4. Surrey	5. Sussex	6. Hants.	7. Berks.	8. Oxon
1.	3,575	9,769	38,644	14,492	28,636	26,355	11,185	10,470
2.	645	898	7,651	749	612	429	165	346
3.	46,240	14,088	9,428	9,510	5,962	8,664	5,824	1,729
4.	1,244	493	396	186	26	642	8	5
5.	17,130	5,082	3,332	3,197	686	846	372	96
6.	7,407	2,982	720	1,228	233	328	182	326
7.	42,801	14,429	9,359	7,358	1,860	2,709	1,700	842
8.	8,921	4,023	812	1,802	607	580	189	93
9.	26,889	15,996	6,158	6,576	3,132	3,051	663	371
10.	2,782	505	12,022	250	304	19,890	440	152
11.	21,254	19,734	9,617	10,375	5,505	9,661	2,905	6,168
12.	20,156	7,244	1,623	2,625	1,225	1,183	747	687
13.	6,121	2,592	896	1,473	392	446	100	688
14.	11,604	2,099	1,124	1,386	384	439	259	116
15.	55,185	11,079	3,698	5,442	2,682	4,012	1,219	1,005
16.	9,196	3,657	10,874	2,961	2,522	2,271	1,619	517
17.	42,704	13,244	3,918	4,392	3,060	3,918	1,800	1,489
18.	57,436	17,778	16,505	11,234	2,406	3,112	2,216	1,743
19.	19,348	13,352	1,809	3,553	603	1,009	312	114
20.	100,448	58,749	32,684	43,897	26,829	31,387	9,640	6,341
21.	28,780	13,619	6,861	9,204	4,666	5,416	1,533	809
22.	185,152	68,210	35,553	35,734	21,293	34,881	9,332	5,233
23.	249,796	89,169	52,891	61,404	37,168	46,712	13,781	7,920
24.	48,422	26,136	10,353	20,532	6,047	6,011	1,937	957
25.	50,753	22,286	12,611	18,365	10,290	9,537	3,919	4,119
26.	129,044	32,701	28,901	38,929	30,848	31,003	13,150	6,681
27.	91,557	36,911	44,650	36,377	14,815	74,849	8,453	4,247
N.C.	5,269	1,138	936	1,325	813	1,066	293	213
Total Employed	1,289,859	507,963	364,026	354,556	213,606	330,407	93,943	63,477
Total Population	2,044,108	768,657	584,335	544,054	340,363	490,501	148,310	102,419

East Anglia

9. Bucks.	10. Beds.	11. Herts.	12. Essex	13. Cambridge	14. Hunts.	15. Norfolk	16. Suffolk	
10,977	10,435	14,012	33,960	22,820	6,540	43,743	32,051	1.
221	417	674	1,126	180	40	474	212	2.
2,389	2,081	4,209	20,116	2,814	664	7,583	5,226	3.
15	11	33	2,133	6	–	32	21	4.
454	533	1,131	9,822	154	30	580	764	5.
197	1,724	762	3,088	41	8	177	289	6.
1,020	5,830	2,714	13,749	465	289	1,716	5,808	7.
147	152	705	2,353	434	23	227	175	8.
1,225	865	1,808	10,391	663	44	1,462	484	9.
32	17	43	4,177	48	4	579	789	10.
5,475	3,883	2,765	10,204	827	363	2,735	2,078	11.
672	183	869	7,541	328	90	1,539	670	12.
292	272	559	3,068	82	123	669	794	13.
181	327	549	2,083	219	44	383	510	14.
1,404	5,415	2,342	10,254	862	169	7,859	1,808	15.
1,296	3,071	630	5,886	1,418	1,621	335	592	16.
9,139	1,072	2,211	12,228	749	170	2,841	2,127	17.
2,713	1,633	7,401	17,789	1,402	238	1,795	1,525	18.
898	211	1,683	8,245	187	50	894	535	19.
9,011	5,506	14,856	51,079	5,164	993	9,269	8,337	20.
1,061	1,052	2,661	14,760	675	149	1,785	1,522	21.
7,247	4,262	13,142	80,892	6,663	1,329	12,491	8,824	22.
9,672	9,070	17,180	92,544	8,203	1,859	20,326	16,093	23.
1,902	984	4,224	20,274	832	216	2,616	1,731	24.
3,011	1,732	5,143	16,046	3,918	402	3,969	3,109	25.
9,063	4,186	12,613	29,582	4,064	1,142	11,215	10,753	26.
7,680	5,012	7,340	37,135	3,696	558	10,787	8,592	27.
280	244	364	1,397	231	58	478	345	N.C.
87,674	70,180	122,623	521,922	67,145	17,216	148,559	115,764	
132,490	106,449	189,663	844,625	108,488	27,786	243,536	195,477	

MALE EMPLOYMENT: 1931

South West   West Midlands

	17. Corn-wall	18. Devon	19.Som-erset	20.Gloucs.	21.Wilts.	22.Dorset	23.Hereford	24.Shrops
1.	25,076	36,720	27,006	19,252	18,874	14,035	12,287	19,895
2.	7,104	2,508	6,585	8,094	431	1,692	238	5,386
3.	1,908	5,843	5,501	14,417	4,089	2,581	1,142	1,772
4.	7	25	17	71	3	5	4	10
5.	182	924	465	3,613	93	1,114	170	131
6.	256	483	268	3,282	93	50	31	2,551
7.	1,440	2,124	3,221	6,181	1,555	1,236	295	1,774
8.	103	391	432	408	100	98	36	112
9.	234	1,091	862	1,787	281	255	158	311
10.	1,995	11,117	53	628	7	190	4	13
11.	937	2,764	2,818	7,765	15,237	921	451	2,030
12.	667	1,080	976	2,520	374	356	256	1,166
13.	223	1,205	1,827	1,764	802	515	27	399
14.	163	605	833	1,018	466	77	74	213
15.	1,039	3,197	4,810	6,937	1,261	782	305	734
16.	349	1,674	2,151	2,495	423	2,281	342	1,740
17.	1,319	3,538	3,016	6,635	1,157	1,098	340	754
18.	456	3,237	3,476	7,262	647	529	249	487
19.	104	519	453	1,695	1,711	115	31	140
20.	6,656	19,957	12,424	18,267	7,580	7,198	1,994	4,092
21.	869	3,307	2,115	3,652	1,039	1,590	370	870
22.	9,006	21,159	12,721	28,776	8,013	6,149	2,637	7,174
23.	11,391	28,949	18,263	34,723	10,039	9,373	3,671	8,424
24.	1,257	4,062	2,413	4,514	1,122	1,142	480	1,141
25.	2,705	7,120	4,938	7,167	2,329	2,296	1,007	2,187
26.	6,068	18,826	12,163	15,487	8,301	7,535	3,560	6,047
27.	6,681	31,760	6,831	13,656	12,852	9,948	1,706	4,037
N.C.	418	889	578	648	247	237	165	259
Total Employed	88,613	215,074	137,216	222,714	99,126	73,398	32,030	73,849
Total Population	148,849	345,887	219,970	370,054	151,377	115,395	53,681	120,585

25.Staffs.	26.Warwick	27.Worcs.	28.Derby	29.Notts.	30.Leics.	31.Lincs.	32.Northants.	
19,052	14,579	16,046	14,826	12,730	11,983	60,701	13,168	1.
57,525	17,816	2,598	63,785	53,439	14,179	1,495	1,704	2.
14,659	14,146	3,647	3,503	7,775	3,251	6,626	3,120	3.
328	108	14	1,336	76	29	161	15	4.
2,650	2,857	1,173	1,025	1,483	756	1,287	225	5.
37,690	23,582	9,159	11,037	2,465	2,508	7,398	1,863	6.
16,482	24,437	4,348	5,399	7,311	9,410	11,107	3,879	7.
424	1,952	155	269	355	382	201	116	8.
6,638	19,399	2,000	1,932	2,176	1,963	605	661	9.
127	90	81	11	62	6	1,213	20	10.
17,877	59,402	7,754	12,608	5,243	2,165	2,951	2,185	11.
31,190	38,237	10,118	2,149	1,478	1,161	1,461	567	12.
5,605	5,440	4,821	16,222	14,618	17,828	371	163	13.
2,108	1,093	562	423	767	593	515	2,346	14.
6,082	6,119	2,386	2,452	3,206	22,530	1,700	27,056	15.
36,339	5,839	3,270	6,822	2,412	4,646	1,397	1,399	16.
4,175	8,867	1,306	2,150	3,923	2,341	3,532	1,699	17.
4,411	7,658	1,190	3,055	3,908	3,673	1,796	1,512	18.
3,013	8,634	771	616	916	1,579	290	409	19.
23,850	32,030	8,356	10,730	12,772	11,487	9,789	6,988	20.
6,095	8,144	2,403	2,715	2,720	2,639	1,494	1,907	21.
29,082	36,699	9,544	20,807	18,439	11,853	19,546	11,434	22.
39,865	55,801	13,724	21,503	27,354	20,339	25,213	13,264	23.
5,012	8,188	1,749	2,932	3,333	2,195	2,289	1,457	24.
8,094	11,286	3,216	4,687	4,688	4,053	4,199	2,851	25.
14,686	21,183	7,261	8,619	9,613	8,326	9,087	7,084	26.
16,979	20,073	5,973	8,998	9,454	6,108	12,318	6,431	27.
580	920	294	278	279	241	575	241	N.C.
410,618	454,579	123,919	230,889	212,995	168,224	189,317	113,764	
702,401	735,517	201,115	375,073	344,596	258,267	309,637	175,240	

	East Midlands	North West	Yorks. & Humberside			North		
	33. Rut-land	34. Cheshire	35.Lancs.	36. West Riding	37. East Riding	38. North Riding	39.West-morland	40.Cum-berla~
1.	1,678	24,122	45,203	37,969	24,185	22,340	5,441	13,458
2.	230	4,816	80,710	177,980	320	4,115	599	13,060
3.	124	9,712	45,649	20,020	8,586	2,466	291	1,743
4.	–	719	1,196	3,900	110	571	–	566
5.	2	14,710	25,682	8,880	7,243	2,178	250	239
6.	22	5,441	22,678	53,932	706	19,968	18	3,491
7.	108	10,707	61,313	42,677	3,535	2,552	504	1,05~
8.	1	556	2,751	1,981	660	154	22	89
9.	12	5,046	31,681	6,979	1,081	513	71	256
10.	–	3,969	16,882	755	2,850	1,988	56	182
11.	91	12,181	34,911	17,250	4,076	924	191	667
12.	33	3,318	19,526	35,025	1,696	1,110	118	566
13.	5	19,426	179,457	112,739	437	188	256	1,542
14.	11	2,376	7,602	3,958	1,155	173	27	232
15.	79	8,216	35,700	24,568	2,054	1,481	752	1,006
16.	173	2,172	20,953	14,752	1,508	1,075	135	476
17.	56	3,052	22,076	15,037	3,937	1,723	500	1,034
18.	19	5,659	31,647	14,395	2,256	983	526	842
19.	7	2,289	17,167	3,607	463	366	65	133
20.	284	22,018	77,164	46,733	10,432	7,542	1,661	3,693
21.	36	5,044	24,383	15,553	2,495	1,570	599	756
22.	478	42,030	165,694	80,327	30,413	13,063	1,945	8,191
23.	582	48,951	214,689	122,424	27,401	14,534	2,096	8,302
24.	57	8,839	28,733	15,003	2,638	1,864	358	1,315
25.	212	9,937	35,630	23,179	4,276	3,326	603	1,956
26.	835	17,913	64,523	38,896	8,401	8,129	1,835	3,628
27.	205	16,649	75,496	47,212	10,783	15,214	915	3,827
N.C.	7	515	2,689	1,260	582	427	41	167
Total Employed	5,347	310,383	1,391,785	986,991	164,279	130,537	19,875	72,472
Total Population	8,446	513,447	2,383,723	1,614,623	275,353	232,896	30,393	127,676

	Wales			Scotland				
.North-berland	42.Durham	43.Glamorgan & Monmouth	44.North & West Wales	45.Strathclyde	46.Dumfries & Galloway	47.Borders	48.Lothian	
3,956	11,293	15,307	70,469	32,174	15,835	10,449	12,350	1.
9,244	131,641	158,435	46,457	71,622	2,382	160	27,070	2.
4,129	5,272	9,800	4,317	24,120	1,214	812	10,130	3.
167	2,652	3,107	66	844	52	1	2,977	4.
1,590	8,502	1,073	887	7,866	111	40	1,972	5.
1,438	11,184	37,119	12,245	50,214	50	111	2,956	6.
6,513	8,461	3,227	1,419	51,753	675	333	4,679	7.
343	342	459	290	2,226	35	40	446	8.
2,296	3,472	1,560	702	5,130	107	82	1,848	9.
2,729	14,265	3,180	760	65,884	50	35	2,229	10.
2,461	8,287	5,145	1,802	19,461	790	325	2,246	11.
1,397	3,363	2,593	2,172	9,337	439	270	2,262	12.
363	608	389	2,723	19,206	738	6,709	1,517	13.
438	204	283	532	2,672	86	262	630	14.
2,096	2,454	3,879	3,218	10,657	508	352	2,247	15.
1,538	4,034	3,003	3,374	9,608	83	19	1,665	16.
2,319	4,102	3,176	3,006	19,287	1,025	785	5,451	17.
2,615	3,533	3,264	1,754	12,486	227	380	8,349	18.
639	628	629	211	5,328	45	60	3,368	19.
0,270	14,814	15,223	14,603	48,174	2,675	2,061	15,254	20.
3,192	6,025	4,588	2,169	9,703	254	249	2,620	21.
1,621	32,968	57,865	24,101	85,012	3,793	2,348	24,397	22.
7,104	38,663	51,149	28,313	100,695	5,520	4,001	31,643	23.
3,971	4,598	7,431	4,191	12,577	553	465	4,713	24.
5,574	8,261	12,376	9,336	20,993	1,371	884	10,760	25.
9,483	11,545	15,879	14,621	31,066	2,370	2,426	11,092	26.
0,361	16,976	19,466	14,509	35,551	1,971	1,564	12,655	27.
412	501	1,013	905	8,968	652	386	4,344	N.C.
8,259	358,648	440,618	269,152	772,614	43,611	35,609	211,870	
0,446	742,923	839,287	454,518	1,160,780	66,970	50,741	308,385	

MALE EMPLOYMENT: 1931

Scotland

	49.Central & Fife	50. Tayside	51.Grampian	52.Highland	53. South East	54. East Anglia	55. South West	56. West Midland
1.	11,974	21,043	43,827	34,478	212,510	105,154	140,963	81,85?
2.	39,337	843	625	152	13,933	906	26,414	83,56?
3.	4,190	3,866	6,640	2,207	130,240	16,287	34,339	35,366
4.	365	23	56	5	5,192	59	128	46?
5.	1,769	566	875	146	42,681	1,528	6,391	6,98?
6.	11,793	796	327	785	19,177	515	4,432	73,01?
7.	2,503	4,490	1,994	280	104,371	8,278	15,757	47,33?
8.	121	158	220	53	20,384	859	1,532	2,67?
9.	790	702	328	133	77,125	2,653	4,510	28,50?
10.	1,976	3,043	2,923	247	40,614	1,420	13,990	31?
11.	1,343	1,215	1,438	510	107,546	6,003	30,442	87,51?
12.	847	961	1,177	610	44,755	2,627	5,973	80,96?
13.	3,799	17,457	1,810	475	16,899	1,668	6,336	16,29?
14.	203	195	204	47	20,551	1,156	3,162	4,05?
15.	911	1,556	1,838	811	103,737	10,698	18,026	15,62?
16.	2,270	384	635	49	44,500	3,966	9,373	47,53?
17.	3,573	3,526	4,403	1,780	99,175	5,887	16,763	15,44?
18.	3,316	1,985	2,967	252	141,966	4,960	15,607	13,99?
19.	4,617	536	442	44	51,137	1,666	4,597	12,58?
20.	8,162	8,420	7,607	5,261	390,427	23,763	72,082	70,32?
21.	1,309	1,492	972	208	90,422	4,131	12,572	17,88?
22.	14,038	11,929	12,073	7,988	500,931	29,307	85,824	85,13?
23.	15,896	17,110	20,708	7,346	687,307	46,481	112,738	121,48?
24.	1,920	2,231	2,207	765	147,779	5,395	14,510	16,57?
25.	3,597	3,784	4,272	2,115	157,812	11,398	26,555	25,79?
26.	5,728	7,719	5,351	2,949	366,701	27,174	68,380	52,73?
27.	7,885	5,738	6,592	4,686	369,026	23,633	81,728	48,76?
N.C.	1,732	1,494	1,957	2,246	13,338	1,112	3,017	2,21?
Total Employed	155,964	123,262	134,468	76,628	4,020,236	348,684	836,141	1,094,995
Total Population	233,531	182,782	206,898	115,436	6,295,974	575,287	1,351,532	1,813,299

57. East Midlands	58. North West	59. Yorks. & Humberside	60. North	61. Wales	62. Scotland	63. Great Britain	
511,086	69,325	62,154	66,488	85,776	182,130	1,121,445	1.
134,832	85,526	178,300	198,659	204,892	142,191	1,069,216	2.
24,399	55,361	28,606	13,901	14,117	53,179	405,795	3.
1,617	1,915	4,010	3,956	3,173	4,323	24,837	4.
4,778	40,392	16,123	12,759	1,960	13,345	146,938	5.
25,293	28,119	54,638	36,099	49,364	67,032	357,682	6.
37,214	72,020	46,212	19,085	4,646	66,707	421,626	7.
1,324	3,307	2,641	950	749	3,299	37,724	8.
7,349	36,727	8,060	6,608	2,262	9,120	182,920	9.
1,312	20,851	3,605	29,220	3,940	76,387	191,654	10.
25,243	47,092	21,326	12,530	6,947	27,328	371,971	11.
6,849	22,844	36,721	6,554	4,765	15,903	227,958	12.
49,207	198,883	113,176	2,957	3,112	51,711	460,241	13.
4,655	9,978	5,113	1,074	815	4,299	54,853	14.
57,023	43,916	26,622	7,789	7,097	18,880	309,414	15.
16,849	23,125	16,260	7,258	6,377	14,713	189,951	16.
13,701	25,128	18,974	9,678	6,182	39,830	250,760	17.
13,963	37,306	16,651	8,499	5,018	29,962	287,927	18.
3,817	19,456	4,070	1,831	840	14,440	114,443	19.
52,050	99,182	57,165	37,980	29,826	97,614	930,411	20.
11,511	29,427	18,048	12,142	6,757	16,807	219,699	21.
82,557	207,724	110,740	77,788	81,966	161,578	1,423,551	22.
108,255	263,640	149,825	90,699	79,462	202,919	1,862,811	23.
12,263	37,572	17,641	12,106	11,622	25,431	300,889	24.
20,690	45,567	27,455	19,720	21,712	47,776	404,475	25.
43,564	82,436	47,297	34,620	30,500	68,701	822,110	26.
43,514	92,145	57,995	47,293	33,975	76,642	874,719	27.
1,621	3,204	1,842	1,548	1,918	21,779	51,597	N.C.
920,536	1,702,168	1,151,270	779,791	709,770	1,554,026	13,117,617	
,471,259	2,897,170	1,889,976	1,504,334	1,293,805	2,325,523	21,418,159	

FEMALE EMPLOYMENT: 1931

South East

	1. London	2. Middlesex	3. Kent	4. Surrey	5. Sussex	6. Hants.	7. Berks.	8. Oxon.
1.	235	1,536	2,440	1,107	1,360	1,394	498	282
2.	140	54	29	29	7	5	1	3
3.	39,568	9,813	2,770	3,536	1,851	3,074	2,964	381
4.	315	107	30	35	–	9	2	–
5.	9,904	3,366	1,291	1,221	423	103	155	6
6.	908	384	75	122	11	9	11	6
7.	4,981	2,277	851	1,261	130	187	129	51
8.	3,360	1,295	117	597	64	62	34	16
9.	12,265	9,124	1,290	1,790	478	735	181	18
10.	136	30	187	9	4	408	17	4
11.	2,279	2,323	567	934	163	568	176	484
12.	8,583	2,506	195	610	129	119	380	72
13.	9,463	3,235	672	1,287	265	457	71	683
14.	9,035	1,074	162	350	74	104	50	24
15.	115,163	18,449	4,952	6,863	3,500	6,866	2,168	1,438
16.	1,918	470	291	196	40	55	36	4
17.	6,503	1,850	406	516	192	365	290	80
18.	34,055	6,604	3,781	3,173	587	1,138	787	548
19.	14,399	6,450	685	1,616	176	301	62	17
20.	1,711	786	331	599	290	222	67	37
21.	1,434	487	213	350	129	160	35	23
22.	16,707	7,935	2,798	4,426	1,657	2,330	680	443
23.	118,956	38,008	22,143	24,828	15,971	21,484	5,334	3,300
24.	24,650	8,671	2,611	5,116	1,183	1,191	418	212
25.	61,228	20,422	15,686	17,020	14,211	12,510	4,855	3,466
26.	266,855	82,479	67,848	84,880	67,459	63,659	19,144	13,138
27.	27,434	8,450	5,374	7,761	2,390	3,935	908	530
N.C.	2,005	307	219	467	267	254	35	55
Total Employed	794,190	238,492	138,014	170,699	113,011	121,704	39,488	25,321
Total Population	2,352,895	870,071	634,938	636,824	429,496	523,815	163,143	107,202

9. Bucks.	10. Beds.	11. Herts.	12. Essex	13. Cambridge	14. Hunts.	15. Norfolk	16. Suffolk	
482	254	835	1,803	1,284	201	1,646	1,150	1.
5	6	13	44	3	-	2	1	2.
1,004	859	1,398	10,354	1,600	214	2,528	1,349	3.
-	4	2	158	1	-	2	1	4.
259	94	848	3,914	13	10	76	89	5.
18	128	31	251	2	-	2	12	6.
92	944	289	2,085	19	9	113	337	7.
40	56	246	1,092	95	1	18	17	8.
330	351	752	4,402	411	13	171	27	9.
-	1	4	114	-	-	3	17	10.
425	302	298	319	65	7	173	175	11.
151	21	134	2,236	16	3	65	16	12.
258	261	858	3,676	211	213	1,537	1,111	13.
127	63	185	1,348	9	5	77	222	14.
1,327	10,557	3,897	24,438	1,070	359	8,223	3,144	15.
35	11	34	595	14	7	9	6	16.
1,325	164	136	1,383	175	4	220	150	17.
1,573	1,253	3,879	7,235	437	152	1,202	496	18.
685	98	1,253	6,565	87	7	431	71	19.
69	52	140	406	48	12	72	60	20.
30	41	117	348	14	13	71	43	21.
700	251	1,314	5,879	351	110	918	587	22.
3,386	3,259	6,128	34,871	3,005	582	7,653	6,106	23.
291	165	904	6,571	196	32	504	325	24.
3,359	2,029	5,752	17,654	3,143	569	5,422	4,643	25.
14,487	8,211	21,671	60,989	9,903	2,192	22,085	19,236	26.
665	556	1,744	6,885	374	114	1,227	1,006	27.
52	42	62	280	21	10	78	34	N.C.
31,175	30,033	52,924	205,895	22,567	4,839	54,528	40,431	
139,096	114,076	211,543	910,834	109,214	28,420	261,404	205,637	

FEMALE EMPLOYMENT: 1931

South West   West Midlands

	17.Corn-wall	18. Devon	19.Som-erset	20.Gloucs.	21.Wilts.	22.Dorset	23.Here-ford	24.Shrop
1.	1,209	1,810	1,341	866	472	669	688	1,302
2.	71	26	22	32	3	5	1	27
3.	367	1,729	1,487	11,999	1,572	490	362	393
4.	–	2	2	14	–	–	–	–
5.	248	227	69	1,298	9	58	6	6
6.	9	47	10	185	1	3	1	74
7.	52	91	223	358	362	35	11	34
8.	5	55	73	76	10	6	3	13
9.	16	56	85	230	28	12	19	13
10.	18	156	1	15	–	1	–	1
11.	22	115	182	418	555	43	24	114
12.	5	30	64	513	12	17	7	66
13.	635	1,259	1,660	2,118	1,043	577	12	310
14.	4	151	363	166	78	11	10	18
15.	1,257	4,671	8,579	9,761	2,022	1,085	280	666
16.	22	146	71	406	4	159	171	186
17.	39	198	299	522	63	71	8	37
18.	89	1,039	1,569	5,063	125	90	52	89
19.	16	159	164	804	568	13	2	360
20.	43	149	102	186	75	59	15	31
21.	39	81	74	109	33	22	16	22
22.	655	1,462	903	1,752	629	451	251	501
23.	5,456	14,285	7,779	14,811	3,950	4,041	1,465	3,414
24.	183	680	416	1,164	184	145	76	160
25.	3,095	9,043	6,842	9,777	3,127	3,122	1,331	2,782
26.	15,735	42,510	27,729	35,856	13,120	14,280	6,830	12,381
27.	512	1,569	955	2,256	833	530	244	574
N.C.	45	127	59	163	26	37	21	23
Total Employed	29,847	81,873	61,123	100,918	28,904	26,032	11,906	23,597
Total Population	169,119	387,081	255,172	415,946	151,996	123,957	58,086	123,571

East Midlands

25.Staffs.	26.Warwick	27.Worcs.	28.Derby	29.Notts.	30.Leics.	31.Lincs.	32.North-ants.	
1,226	691	1,107	875	534	488	4,031	391	1.
219	78	75	272	133	75	13	1	2.
3,665	8,914	1,412	1,446	4,934	1,216	2,537	611	3.
24	18	5	8	2	1	14	2	4.
1,014	1,732	191	759	924	423	277	83	5.
4,082	5,680	793	507	78	69	182	18	6.
1,881	4,164	314	379	989	873	719	305	7.
206	1,197	38	32	73	116	20	11	8.
3,381	9,510	982	605	462	263	32	198	9.
4	12	4	1	3	–	17	–	10.
3,527	15,593	1,788	650	701	78	339	139	11.
19,080	26,412	6,326	401	1,513	386	47	30	12.
9,751	11,521	5,307	22,281	27,962	37,397	765	237	13.
2,948	1,325	263	151	324	126	138	460	14.
11,602	13,290	4,853	3,652	9,542	17,423	1,547	21,998	15.
36,027	1,046	1,244	1,531	101	308	21	9	16.
906	2,435	193	761	892	190	270	92	17.
3,479	5,940	778	2,012	1,971	2,132	644	1,315	18.
1,788	7,193	1,386	245	280	899	71	114	19.
314	453	81	124	146	158	71	76	20.
211	320	131	76	18	54	45	62	21.
2,021	3,077	712	1,592	946	677	1,017	616	22.
21,942	29,137	7,047	9,162	11,738	7,515	9,178	4,924	23.
1,040	2,933	374	520	659	462	382	240	24.
10,635	14,494	4,566	6,124	5,776	4,537	4,962	3,426	25.
34,328	48,847	15,696	20,517	20,780	14,359	25,276	11,758	26.
3,884	5,282	1,046	1,741	1,739	1,146	1,309	661	27.
182	338	63	64	75	75	65	40	N.C.
179,367	221,632	56,775	76,488	93,295	91,446	53,989	47,817	
728,958	799,490	218,941	382,301	368,135	283,594	314,952	186,073	

FEMALE EMPLOYMENT: 1931

	East Midlands	North West		Yorks. & Humberside		North		
	33.Rut-land	34. Cheshire	35.Lancs.	36.West Riding	37.East Riding	38. North Riding	39.West-morland	40.Cum-berland
1.	50	2,178	3,680	2,067	559	1,004	434	1,162
2.	1	612	2,136	383	12	27	2	273
3.	13	5,981	37,392	12,704	6,517	1,399	256	2,610
4.	–	47	143	82	8	2	–	1
5.	1	3,321	9,094	2,939	2,128	136	32	19
6.	1	234	1,379	3,245	36	420	2	48
7.	4	972	5,214	3,188	286	85	45	71
8.	–	225	659	725	58	11	–	3
9.	2	1,530	8,764	1,396	44	32	2	10
10.	–	101	489	14	57	26	1	1
11.	4	353	1,545	1,012	204	35	5	32
12.	–	825	5,863	15,464	1,781	66	5	339
13.	6	24,666	243,255	132,535	1,092	93	456	1,815
14.	–	377	2,311	1,100	173	13	5	23
15.	60	13,133	74,373	55,574	2,406	1,905	679	1,230
16.	3	238	3,256	1,438	175	42	4	8
17.	–	322	3,158	2,196	298	72	39	31
18.	–	2,876	17,996	7,619	1,420	389	196	380
19.	–	759	8,312	1,736	128	46	21	71
20.	–	283	1,243	678	105	102	9	56
21.	–	123	519	466	87	55	8	17
22.	34	2,883	9,206	4,638	1,423	908	136	407
23.	161	21,404	106,988	53,155	10,872	7,569	778	3,820
24.	3	2,178	8,009	3,327	583	298	91	204
25.	285	11,380	43,146	27,185	5,373	4,421	912	2,654
26.	1,140	47,747	145,057	94,446	24,165	21,433	4,637	10,223
27.	9	3,351	18,025	10,211	1,999	1,254	132	500
N.C.	–	104	661	390	65	58	3	35
Total Employed	1,777	148,203	761,873	439,913	62,054	41,901	8,890	26,043
Total Population	8,955	574,208	2,655,732	1,737,932	292,396	236,479	35,015	135,475

41.North-umberland	42.Durham	43.Glamorgan & Monmouth	44.North & West Wales	45.Strathclyde	46.Dumfries & Galloway	47.Borders	48.Lothian	
2,077	1,418	1,070	7,604	4,402	1,290	1,136	2,312	1.
210	953	369	89	983	16	8	293	2.
3,509	4,879	3,632	1,067	20,948	438	281	6,384	3.
17	13	34	–	147	–	–	62	4.
696	1,234	129	109	2,309	5	–	718	5.
95	352	2,140	896	1,396	1	7	84	6.
781	456	212	43	6,201	43	15	323	7.
60	56	70	12	549	6	3	115	8.
272	621	190	47	751	11	7	273	9.
505	412	51	5	1,230	–	1	34	10.
148	193	127	60	882	47	30	243	11.
700	585	806	388	2,134	13	6	539	12.
477	1,422	333	2,232	42,366	1,896	6,623	3,878	13.
156	98	79	34	1,068	3	10	247	14.
2,935	3,822	5,334	3,382	20,040	382	364	2,416	15.
481	810	132	106	1,902	4	1	342	16.
349	389	176	108	3,504	30	20	482	17.
1,163	1,756	990	317	9,163	98	102	5,878	18.
388	337	206	26	2,646	2	39	2,895	19.
191	293	158	71	1,831	45	50	579	20.
329	178	151	61	374	9	16	103	21.
1,651	1,869	2,726	1,639	8,332	329	239	1,957	22.
16,118	25,447	24,045	11,435	70,677	2,265	1,681	20,760	23.
1,094	1,046	1,355	440	3,851	56	53	1,614	24.
6,901	11,195	15,205	10,408	28,505	1,873	1,201	12,717	25.
29,252	37,606	43,189	41,572	73,559	7,206	5,336	29,908	26.
1,986	3,289	3,736	1,460	9,278	319	264	3,166	27.
103	112	174	90	5,066	181	92	2,535	N.C.
72,644	100,841	106,819	83,701	324,094	16,568	17,585	100,857	
386,336	743,252	821,388	478,139	1,228,687	73,749	59,318	346,680	

FEMALE EMPLOYMENT: 1931

Scotland

	49.Central & Fife	50. Tayside	51.Gram-pian	52.High-land	53. South East	54. East Anglia	55. South West	56. West Midlands
1.	1,582	1,144	1,966	2,617	12,226	4,281	6,367	5,014
2.	778	8	9	2	336	6	159	400
3.	1,419	2,850	4,210	2,842	77,572	5,691	17,644	14,746
4.	2	6	7	–	662	4	18	47
5.	571	90	121	3	21,584	188	1,909	2,949
6.	919	34	67	27	1,954	16	255	10,630
7.	173	264	107	13	13,277	478	1,121	6,404
8.	15	23	30	7	6,979	131	225	1,457
9.	113	61	37	6	31,716	622	427	13,905
10.	36	54	62	2	914	20	191	21
11.	83	92	91	27	8,838	420	1,335	21,046
12.	111	71	60	5	15,136	100	641	51,891
13.	9,085	30,987	4,187	1,641	21,186	3,072	7,292	26,901
14.	45	87	53	4	12,596	313	773	4,564
15.	1,257	1,484	1,408	437	199,618	12,796	27,375	30,691
16.	396	58	9	4	3,685	36	808	38,674
17.	260	184	463	45	13,210	549	1,192	3,579
18.	1,682	1,057	2,100	32	64,613	2,287	7,975	10,338
19.	1,585	61	210	6	32,307	596	1,724	10,729
20.	264	243	274	56	4,710	192	614	894
21.	103	46	29	9	3,367	141	358	700
22.	1,834	923	1,039	615	45,120	1,966	5,852	6,562
23.	9,684	9,984	9,919	2,722	297,668	17,346	50,322	63,005
24.	335	676	475	88	51,983	1,057	2,772	4,583
25.	5,393	5,555	6,459	3,194	178,192	13,777	35,006	33,808
26.	14,777	16,687	18,364	10,024	770,820	53,416	149,230	118,082
27.	1,162	1,214	1,085	480	66,632	2,721	6,655	11,030
N.C.	900	586	1,037	366	4,045	143	457	627
Total Employed	54,564	74,529	53,878	25,274	1,960,946	122,365	328,697	493,277
Total Population	241,232	215,655	229,116	123,020	7,093,933	604,675	1,503,271	1,929,046

57. East Midlands	58. North West	59. Yorks. & Humberside	60. North	61. Wales	62. Scotland	63. Great Britain	
6,369	5,858	2,626	6,095	8,674	16,449	73,959	1.
495	2,748	395	1,465	458	2,097	8,559	2.
10,757	43,373	19,221	12,653	4,699	39,372	245,728	3.
27	190	90	33	34	224	1,329	4.
2,467	12,415	5,067	2,117	238	3,817	52,751	5.
855	1,613	3,281	917	3,036	2,535	25,092	6.
3,269	6,186	3,474	1,438	255	7,139	43,041	7.
252	884	783	130	82	748	11,671	8.
1,562	10,294	1,440	937	237	1,259	62,399	9.
21	590	71	945	56	1,419	4,248	10.
1,911	1,898	1,216	413	187	1,495	38,759	11.
2,377	6,688	17,245	1,695	1,194	2,939	99,906	12.
88,648	267,921	133,627	4,263	2,565	100,663	656,138	13.
1,199	2,688	1,273	295	113	1,517	25,331	14.
54,222	87,506	57,980	10,571	8,716	27,788	517,263	15.
1,973	3,494	1,613	1,345	238	2,716	54,582	16.
2,205	3,480	2,494	880	284	4,988	32,861	17.
8,074	20,872	9,039	3,884	1,307	20,112	148,501	18.
1,609	9,071	1,864	863	232	7,444	66,439	19.
575	1,526	783	651	229	3,342	13,516	20.
255	642	553	587	212	689	7,504	21.
4,882	12,089	6,061	4,971	4,365	15,268	107,136	22.
42,678	128,392	64,027	53,732	35,480	127,692	880,342	23.
2,266	10,187	3,910	2,733	1,795	7,148	88,434	24.
25,110	54,526	32,558	26,083	25,613	64,897	489,570	25.
93,830	192,804	118,611	103,151	84,761	175,861	1,860,566	26.
6,605	21,376	12,210	7,161	5,196	16,968	156,554	27.
319	765	455	311	264	10,763	18,149	N.C.
364,812	910,076	501,967	250,319	190,520	667,349	5,790,328	
,544,010	3,229,940	2,030,328	1,536,557	1,299,527	2,517,457	23,288,744	

TOTAL EMPLOYMENT: 1931

South East

	1. London	2. Middlesex	3. Kent	4. Surrey	5. Sussex	6. Hants.	7. Berks.	8. Oxon
1.	3,810	11,305	41,084	15,599	29,996	27,749	11,683	10,752
2.	785	952	7,680	778	619	434	166	349
3.	85,808	23,901	12,198	13,046	7,813	11,738	8,788	2,110
4.	1,559	600	426	221	26	651	10	5
5.	27,034	8,448	4,623	4,418	1,109	949	527	102
6.	8,315	3,366	795	1,350	244	337	193	332
7.	47,782	16,706	10,210	8,619	1,990	2,896	1,829	893
8.	12,281	5,318	929	2,399	671	642	223	109
9.	39,154	25,120	7,448	8,366	3,610	3,786	844	389
10.	2,918	535	12,209	259	308	20,298	457	156
11.	23,533	22,057	10,184	11,309	5,668	10,229	3,081	6,652
12.	28,739	9,750	1,818	3,235	1,354	1,302	1,127	759
13.	15,584	5,827	1,568	2,760	657	903	171	1,371
14.	20,639	3,173	1,286	1,736	458	543	309	140
15.	170,348	29,528	8,650	12,305	6,182	10,878	3,387	2,443
16.	11,114	4,127	11,165	3,157	2,562	2,326	1,655	521
17.	49,207	15,094	4,324	4,908	3,252	4,283	2,090	1,569
18.	91,491	24,382	20,286	14,407	2,993	4,250	3,003	2,291
19.	33,747	19,802	2,494	5,169	779	1,310	374	131
20.	102,159	59,535	33,015	44,496	27,119	31,609	9,707	6,378
21.	30,214	14,106	7,074	9,554	4,795	5,576	1,568	832
22.	201,859	76,145	38,351	40,160	22,950	37,211	10,012	5,676
23.	368,752	127,177	75,034	86,232	53,139	68,196	19,115	11,220
24.	73,072	34,807	12,964	25,648	7,230	7,202	2,355	1,169
25.	111,981	42,708	28,297	35,385	24,501	22,047	8,774	7,585
26.	395,899	115,180	96,749	123,809	98,307	94,662	32,294	19,819
27.	118,991	45,361	50,024	44,138	17,205	78,784	9,361	4,777
N.C.	7,274	1,445	1,155	1,792	1,080	1,320	328	268
Total Employed	2,084,049	746,455	502,040	525,255	326,617	452,111	133,431	88,798
Total Population	4,397,003	1,638,728	1,219,273	1,180,878	769,859	1,014,316	311,453	209,621

East Anglia

9. Bucks.	10. Beds.	11. Herts.	12. Essex	13. Cambridge	14. Hunts.	15. Norfolk	16. Suffolk	
11,459	10,689	14,847	35,763	24,104	6,741	45,389	33,201	1.
226	423	687	1,170	183	40	476	213	2.
3,393	2,940	5,607	30,470	4,414	878	10,111	6,575	3.
15	15	35	2,291	7	–	34	22	4.
713	627	1,979	13,736	167	40	656	853	5.
215	1,852	193	3,339	43	8	179	301	6.
1,112	6,774	3,003	15,834	484	298	1,829	6,145	7.
187	208	951	3,445	529	24	245	192	8.
1,555	1,216	2,560	14,793	1,074	57	1,633	511	9.
32	18	47	4,291	48	4	582	806	10.
5,900	4,185	3,063	10,523	892	370	2,908	2,253	11.
823	204	1,003	9,777	344	93	1,604	686	12.
550	533	1,417	6,744	293	336	2,206	1,905	13.
308	390	734	3,431	228	49	460	732	14.
2,731	15,972	6,239	34,692	1,932	528	16,082	4,952	15.
1,331	3,082	664	6,481	1,432	1,628	344	598	16.
10,464	1,236	2,347	13,611	924	174	3,061	2,277	17.
4,286	2,886	11,280	25,024	1,839	390	2,997	2,021	18.
1,583	309	2,936	14,810	274	57	1,325	606	19.
9,080	5,558	14,996	51,485	5,212	1,005	9,341	8,397	20.
1,091	1,093	2,778	15,108	689	162	1,856	1,565	21.
7,947	4,513	14,456	86,771	7,014	1,439	13,409	9,411	22.
13,058	12,329	23,308	127,415	11,208	2,441	27,979	22,199	23.
2,193	1,149	5,128	26,845	1,028	248	3,120	2,056	24.
6,370	3,761	10,895	33,700	7,061	971	9,391	7,752	25.
23,550	12,397	34,284	90,571	13,967	3,334	33,300	29,989	26.
8,345	5,568	9,084	44,020	4,070	672	12,014	9,598	27.
332	286	426	1,677	252	68	556	379	N.C.
118,849	100,213	175,547	727,817	89,712	22,055	203,087	156,195	
271,586	220,525	401,206	1,755,459	217,702	56,206	504,940	401,114	

TOTAL EMPLOYMENT: 1931

<u>South West</u>   <u>West Midlands</u>

	17.Corn-wall	18. Devon	19.Som-erset	20.Gloucs.	21.Wilts.	22.Dorset	23.Here-ford	24.Shrops
1.	26,285	38,530	28,347	20,118	19,346	14,704	12,975	21,197
2.	7,175	2,534	6,607	8,126	434	1,697	239	5,413
3.	2,275	7,572	6,988	26,416	5,661	3,071	1,504	2,165
4.	7	27	19	85	3	5	4	10
5.	430	1,151	534	4,911	102	1,172	176	137
6.	265	530	278	3,467	94	53	32	2,625
7.	1,492	2,215	3,444	6,539	1,917	1,271	306	1,808
8.	108	446	505	484	110	104	39	125
9.	250	1,147	947	2,017	309	267	177	324
10.	2,013	11,273	54	643	7	191	4	14
11.	959	2,879	3,000	8,183	15,792	964	475	2,144
12.	672	1,110	1,040	3,033	386	373	263	1,232
13.	858	2,464	3,487	3,882	1,845	1,092	39	709
14.	167	756	1,196	1,184	544	88	84	231
15.	2,296	7,868	13,389	16,698	3,283	1,867	585	1,400
16.	371	1,820	2,222	2,901	427	2,440	513	1,926
17.	1,358	3,736	3,315	7,157	1,220	1,169	348	791
18.	545	4,276	5,045	12,325	772	619	301	576
19.	120	678	617	2,499	2,279	128	33	500
20.	6,699	20,106	12,526	18,453	7,655	7,257	2,009	4,123
21.	908	3,388	2,189	3,761	1,072	1,612	386	892
22.	9,661	22,621	13,624	30,528	8,642	6,600	2,888	7,675
23.	16,847	43,234	26,042	49,534	13,989	13,414	5,136	11,838
24.	1,440	4,742	2,829	5,678	1,306	1,287	556	1,301
25.	5,800	16,163	11,780	16,944	5,456	5,418	2,338	4,969
26.	21,803	61,336	39,892	51,343	21,421	21,815	10,390	18,428
27.	7,193	33,329	7,786	15,912	13,685	10,478	1,950	4,611
N.C.	463	1,016	637	811	273	274	186	282
Total Employed	118,460	296,947	198,339	323,632	128,030	99,430	43,936	97,446
Total Population	317,968	732,968	475,142	786,000	303,373	239,352	111,767	244,156

East Midlands

25.Staffs.	26.War-Wick	27.Worcs.	28.Derby	29.Notts.	30.Leics.	31.Lincs.	32. North-ants.	
20,278	15,270	17,153	15,701	13,264	12,471	64,732	13,559	1.
57,744	17,894	2,673	64,057	53,572	14,254	1,508	1,705	2.
18,324	23,060	5,059	4,949	12,709	4,467	9,163	3,731	3.
352	126	19	1,344	78	30	175	17	4.
3,664	4,589	1,364	1,784	2,407	1,179	1,564	308	5.
41,772	29,262	9,952	11,544	2,543	2,577	7,580	1,881	6.
18,363	28,601	4,662	5,778	8,300	10,283	11,826	4,184	7.
630	3,149	193	301	428	498	221	127	8.
10,019	28,909	2,982	2,537	2,638	2,226	637	859	9.
131	102	85	12	65	6	1,230	20	10.
21,404	74,995	9,542	13,258	5,944	2,243	3,290	2,324	11.
50,270	64,649	16,444	2,550	2,991	1,547	1,508	597	12.
15,356	16,961	10,128	38,503	42,580	55,225	1,136	400	13.
5,056	2,418	825	574	1,091	719	653	2,806	14.
17,684	19,409	7,239	6,104	12,748	39,953	3,247	49,054	15.
72,366	6,885	4,514	8,353	2,513	4,954	1,418	1,408	16.
5,081	11,302	1,499	2,911	4,815	2,531	3,802	1,791	17.
7,890	13,598	1,968	5,067	5,879	5,805	2,440	2,827	18.
4,801	15,827	2,157	861	1,196	2,478	361	523	19.
24,164	32,483	8,437	10,854	12,918	11,645	9,860	7,064	20.
6,306	8,464	2,534	2,791	2,738	2,693	1,539	1,969	21.
31,103	39,776	10,256	22,399	19,385	12,530	20,563	12,050	22.
61,807	84,938	20,771	30,665	39,092	27,854	34,391	18,188	23.
6,052	11,121	2,123	3,452	3,992	2,657	2,671	1,697	24.
18,729	25,780	7,782	10,811	10,464	8,590	9,161	6,277	25.
49,014	70,030	22,957	29,136	30,393	22,685	34,363	18,842	26.
20,863	25,355	7,019	10,739	11,193	7,254	13,627	7,092	27.
762	1,258	357	342	354	316	640	281	N.C.
589,985	676,211	180,694	307,377	306,290	259,670	243,306	161,581	
1,431,359	1,535,007	420,056	757,374	712,731	541,861	624,589	361,313	

| | East Midlands | North West | | Yorks. & Humberside | | North | | |
	33.Rut-land	34.Cheshire	35.Lancs.	36. West Riding	37. East Riding	38. North Riding	39.West-morland	40.Cum...la
1.	1,728	26,300	48,883	40,036	24,744	23,344	5,875	14,62*
2.	231	5,428	82,846	178,363	332	4,142	601	13,33*
3.	137	15,693	83,041	32,724	15,103	3,865	547	4,35*
4.	-	766	1,339	3,982	118	573	-	56*
5.	3	18,031	34,776	11,819	9,371	2,314	282	25*
6.	23	5,675	24,057	57,177	742	20,388	20	3,53*
7.	112	11,679	66,527	45,865	3,821	2,637	549	1,12*
8.	1	781	3,410	2,706	718	165	22	9*
9.	14	6,576	40,445	8,375	1,125	545	73	26*
10.	-	4,070	17,371	769	2,907	2,014	57	18*
11.	95	12,534	36,456	18,262	4,280	959	196	69*
12.	33	4,143	25,389	50,489	3,477	1,176	123	90*
13.	11	44,092	422,712	245,274	1,529	281	712	3,35*
14.	11	2,753	9,913	5,058	1,328	186	32	25*
15.	139	21,349	110,073	80,142	4,460	3,386	1,431	2,23*
16.	176	2,410	24,209	16,190	1,683	1,117	139	48*
17.	56	3,374	25,234	17,233	4,235	1,795	539	1,06*
18.	19	8,535	49,643	22,014	3,676	1,372	722	1,22*
19.	7	3,048	25,479	5,343	591	412	86	20*
20.	284	22,301	78,407	47,411	10,537	7,644	1,670	3,74*
21.	36	5,167	24,902	16,019	2,582	1,625	607	77*
22.	512	44,913	174,900	84,965	31,836	13,971	2,081	8,59*
23.	743	70,355	321,677	175,579	38,273	22,103	2,874	12,12*
24.	60	11,017	36,742	18,330	3,221	2,162	449	1,51*
25.	497	21,317	78,776	50,364	9,649	7,747	1,515	4,61*
26.	1,975	65,660	209,580	133,342	32,566	29,562	6,472	13,85*
27.	214	20,000	93,521	57,423	12,782	16,468	1,047	4,32*
N.C.	7	619	3,350	1,650	647	485	44	20*
Total Employed	7,124	458,586	2,153,658	1,426,904	226,333	172,438	28,765	98,51*
Total Population	17,401	1,087,655	5,039,455	3,352,555	567,749	469,375	65,408	263,15*

	Wales			Scotland			
41.North-umberland	42.Durham	43.Glamorgan & Monmouth	44.North & West Wales	45.Strathclyde	46.Dumfries & Galloway	47.Borders	48.Lothian	
16,033	12,711	16,377	78,073	36,576	17,125	11,585	14,662	1.
49,454	132,594	158,804	46,546	72,605	2,398	168	27,363	2.
7,638	10,151	13,432	5,384	45,068	1,652	1,093	16,514	3.
184	2,665	3,141	66	991	52	1	3,039	4.
2,286	9,736	1,202	996	10,175	116	40	2,690	5.
1,533	11,536	39,259	13,141	51,610	51	118	3,040	6.
7,294	8,917	3,439	1,462	57,954	718	348	5,002	7.
403	398	529	302	2,775	41	43	561	8.
2,568	4,093	1,750	749	5,881	118	89	2,121	9.
13,234	14,677	3,231	765	67,114	50	36	2,263	10.
2,609	8,480	5,272	1,862	20,343	837	355	2,489	11.
2,097	3,948	3,399	2,560	11,471	452	276	2,801	12.
840	2,030	722	4,955	61,572	2,634	13,332	5,395	13.
594	302	362	566	3,740	89	272	877	14.
5,031	6,276	9,213	6,600	30,697	890	716	4,663	15.
2,019	4,844	3,135	3,480	11,510	87	20	2,007	16.
2,668	4,491	3,352	3,114	22,791	1,055	805	5,933	17.
3,778	5,289	4,254	2,071	21,649	325	482	14,227	18.
1,027	965	835	237	7,974	47	99	6,263	19.
10,461	15,107	15,381	14,674	50,005	2,720	2,111	15,833	20.
3,521	6,203	4,739	2,230	10,077	263	265	2,723	21.
23,272	34,837	60,591	25,740	93,344	4,122	2,587	26,354	22.
43,222	64,110	75,194	39,748	171,372	7,785	5,682	52,403	23.
5,065	5,644	8,786	4,631	16,428	609	518	6,327	24.
12,475	19,456	27,581	19,744	49,498	3,244	2,085	23,477	25.
38,735	49,151	59,068	56,193	104,625	9,576	7,762	41,000	26.
12,347	20,265	23,202	15,969	44,829	2,290	1,828	15,821	27.
515	613	1,187	995	14,034	833	478	6,879	N.C.
270,903	459,489	547,437	352,853	1,096,708	60,179	53,194	312,727	
756,782	1,486,175	1,660,675	932,657	2,389,467	140,719	110,059	655,065	

TOTAL EMPLOYMENT: 1931

Scotland

	49.Central & Fife	50. Tayside	51.Grampian	52.Highland	53. South East	54. East Anglia	55. South West	56. West Midlands
1.	13,556	22,187	45,793	37,095	224,736	109,435	147,330	86,873
2.	40,115	851	634	154	14,269	912	26,573	83,963
3.	5,609	6,716	10,850	5,049	207,812	21,978	51,983	50,112
4.	367	29	63	5	5,854	63	146	511
5.	2,340	656	996	149	64,265	1,716	8,300	9,930
6.	12,712	830	394	812	21,131	531	4,687	83,643
7.	2,676	4,754	2,101	293	117,648	8,756	16,878	53,740
8.	136	181	250	60	27,363	990	1,757	4,136
9.	903	763	365	139	108,841	3,275	4,937	42,411
10.	2,012	3,097	2,985	249	41,528	1,440	14,181	336
11.	1,426	1,307	1,529	537	116,384	6,423	31,777	108,560
12.	958	1,032	1,237	615	59,891	2,727	6,614	132,858
13.	12,884	48,444	5,997	2,116	38,085	4,740	13,628	43,193
14.	248	282	257	51	33,147	1,469	3,935	8,614
15.	2,168	3,040	3,246	1,248	303,355	23,494	45,401	46,317
16.	2,666	442	644	53	48,185	4,002	10,181	86,204
17.	3,833	3,710	4,866	1,825	112,385	6,436	17,955	19,021
18.	4,998	3,042	5,067	284	206,579	7,247	23,582	24,333
19.	6,202	597	652	50	83,444	2,262	6,321	23,318
20.	8,426	8,663	7,881	5,317	395,137	23,955	72,696	71,216
21.	1,412	1,538	1,001	217	93,789	4,272	12,930	18,582
22.	15,872	12,852	13,112	8,603	546,051	31,273	91,676	91,698
23.	25,580	27,094	30,627	10,068	984,975	63,827	163,060	184,490
24.	2,255	2,907	2,682	853	199,762	6,452	17,282	21,153
25.	8,990	9,339	10,731	5,309	336,004	25,175	61,561	59,598
26.	20,505	24,406	23,715	12,973	1,137,521	80,590	217,610	170,819
27.	9,047	6,952	7,677	5,166	435,658	26,354	88,383	59,798
N.C.	2,632	2,080	2,994	2,612	17,383	1,255	3,474	2,845
Total Employed	210,528	197,791	188,346	101,902	5,981,182	471,049	1,164,838	1,588,272
Total Population	474,763	398,437	436,014	238,456	13,389,907	1,179,962	2,854,803	3,742,345

57. East Midlands	58. North West	59. Yorks. & Humberside	60. North	61. Wales	62. Scotland	63. Great Britain	
121,455	75,183	64,780	72,583	94,450	198,579	1,195,404	1.
135,327	88,274	178,695	200,124	205,350	144,288	1,077,775	2.
35,156	98,734	47,827	26,554	18,816	92,551	651,523	3.
1,644	2,105	4,100	3,989	3,207	4,547	26,166	4.
7,245	52,807	21,190	14,876	2,198	17,162	199,689	5.
26,148	29,732	57,919	37,016	52,400	69,567	382,774	6.
40,483	78,206	49,686	20,523	4,901	73,846	464,667	7.
1,576	4,191	3,424	1,080	831	4,047	49,395	8.
8,911	47,021	9,500	7,545	2,499	10,379	245,319	9.
1,333	21,441	3,676	30,165	3,996	77,806	195,902	10.
27,154	48,990	22,542	12,943	7,134	28,823	410,730	11.
9,226	29,532	53,966	8,249	5,959	18,842	327,864	12.
137,855	466,804	246,803	7,220	5,677	152,374	1,116,379	13.
5,854	12,666	6,386	1,369	928	5,816	80,184	14.
111,245	131,422	84,602	18,360	15,813	46,668	826,677	15.
18,822	26,619	17,873	8,603	6,615	17,429	244,533	16.
15,906	28,608	21,468	10,558	6,466	44,818	283,621	17.
22,037	58,178	25,690	12,383	6,325	50,074	436,428	18.
5,426	28,527	5,934	2,694	1,072	21,884	180,882	19.
52,625	100,708	57,948	38,631	30,055	100,956	943,927	20.
11,766	30,069	18,601	12,729	6,969	17,496	227,203	21.
87,439	219,813	116,801	82,759	86,331	176,846	1,530,687	22.
150,933	392,032	213,852	144,431	114,942	330,611	2,743,153	23.
14,529	47,759	21,551	14,839	13,417	32,579	389,323	24.
45,800	100,093	60,013	45,803	47,325	112,673	894,045	25.
137,394	275,240	165,908	137,771	115,261	244,562	2,682,676	26.
50,119	113,521	70,205	54,454	39,171	93,610	1,031,273	27.
1,940	3,969	2,297	1,859	2,182	32,542	69,746	N.C.
1,285,348	2,612,244	1,653,237	1,030,110	900,290	2,221,375	18,907,945	
3,015,269	6,127,110	3,920,304	3,040,891	2,593,332	4,842,980	44,706,903	

MALE EMPLOYMENT: 1951

South East

	1. London	2. Middlesex	3. Kent	4. Surrey	5. Sussex	6. Hants.	7. Berks.	8. Oxon.
1.	1,232	4,428	35,620	12,454	28,192	24,893	10,284	9,425
2.	1,254	465	7,794	560	723	303	225	345
3.	51,732	20,481	8,564	8,077	5,570	8,593	5,116	1,850
4.	2,901	585	317	79	4	1,338	131	7
5.	24,432	10,162	5,727	4,492	1,102	2,491	2,860	112
6.	7,906	7,063	1,526	2,453	321	607	235	2,721
7.	67,742	36,502	18,215	19,773	5,951	8,823	3,945	2,190
8.	17,316	11,887	1,075	5,685	1,061	1,344	423	239
9.	38,203	43,974	7,905	12,728	3,194	4,109	822	858
10.	7,068	809	13,780	506	758	28,454	566	376
11.	15,383	36,888	6,932	18,111	4,021	24,010	4,609	14,785
12.	30,310	18,816	2,703	6,156	1,915	1,628	1,696	262
13.	6,847	2,319	1,177	1,334	500	545	147	792
14.	9,174	1,054	705	1,304	334	300	291	22
15.	47,766	4,565	933	1,593	947	1,426	528	461
16.	12,252	7,352	10,087	3,738	3,017	1,667	959	539
17.	41,214	20,301	4,433	6,112	3,716	4,888	2,152	1,157
18.	88,675	14,270	19,604	7,201	2,643	4,611	2,849	1,860
19.	16,309	16,094	2,866	5,757	992	1,388	882	182
20.	146,445	55,463	42,644	43,987	31,444	38,490	13,882	9,420
21.	39,724	15,648	10,125	10,886	6,873	9,119	2,899	1,474
22.	234,288	62,997	35,233	29,626	21,408	37,995	10,418	6,512
23.	235,586	56,290	42,078	41,922	31,102	38,436	12,298	8,360
24.	97,804	8,163	5,529	7,454	5,388	5,962	1,767	1,088
25.	110,197	21,595	18,442	22,744	14,464	14,918	6,146	6,807
26.	140,998	41,743	31,191	35,416	30,041	33,965	11,373	8,698
27.	149,498	47,275	57,464	38,660	22,148	110,584	24,268	15,746
N.C.	1,646	537	427	385	312	312	127	60
Total Employed	1,643,902	567,726	393,096	349,193	228,141	411,199	121,898	96,348
Total Population	1,565,888	1,067,582	743,668	742,568	413,941	629,836	195,528	137,717

9. Bucks.	10. Beds.	11. Herts.	12. Essex	13. Cambridge	14. Hunts.	15. Norfolk	16. Suffolk	
10,600	9,788	12,484	32,077	21,558	6,292	42,299	30,215	1.
192	337	425	653	174	86	373	172	2.
3,827	2,647	4,467	17,921	3,335	1,016	8,180	6,367	3.
18	3	19	2,870	8	-	15	13	4.
2,664	1,506	4,862	13,822	474	45	854	2,790	5.
2,948	2,554	2,803	5,234	14	2	327	2,030	6.
6,096	8,296	9,234	20,908	1,381	664	3,456	9,439	7.
1,563	1,740	2,432	3,272	789	12	215	141	8.
3,838	3,543	8,660	17,856	1,562	828	3,148	717	9.
164	19	89	6,657	79	16	813	1,050	10.
7,536	17,051	13,002	28,564	967	70	1,625	1,767	11.
1,866	676	2,304	8,514	197	74	1,132	468	12.
936	284	1,814	2,950	59	59	793	883	13.
252	535	378	1,075	278	15	288	299	14.
684	2,650	1,174	5,871	241	30	5,379	752	15.
2,732	5,865	1,705	7,729	1,590	2,356	439	609	16.
10,602	873	2,703	12,474	927	196	3,441	2,441	17.
4,281	2,179	11,929	8,524	1,763	156	1,987	1,917	18.
1,710	1,149	2,935	8,634	276	137	835	359	19.
10,698	8,457	19,812	57,073	7,804	2,002	18,631	14,607	20.
1,979	2,151	4,470	18,033	1,466	390	3,050	3,095	21.
7,441	5,220	11,173	61,665	7,869	1,136	13,690	9,777	22.
8,763	8,558	14,772	55,285	7,901	1,568	17,118	14,068	23.
1,236	1,210	2,228	6,066	909	181	2,915	1,763	24.
4,794	3,579	9,579	20,054	5,941	588	5,704	4,893	25.
10,432	5,446	13,218	29,603	6,610	2,360	14,820	13,243	26.
15,035	12,163	9,954	42,013	8,848	3,641	25,016	16,472	27.
118	76	140	393	143	22	228	107	N.C.
123,005	108,555	168,765	495,790	83,163	23,942	176,771	140,454	
188,457	155,436	289,892	980,313	125,650	35,965	272,060	217,911	

MALE EMPLOYMENT: 1951

South West   West Midlands

	17. Corn-wall	18. Devon	19. Som-erset	20.Gloucs.	21.Wilts.	22.Dorset	23. Here-ford	24.Shrops.
1.	23,905	34,893	25,475	17,812	17,551	13,473	12,240	20,175
2.	5,355	2,628	4,874	5,118	211	823	117	4,215
3.	2,205	6,317	7,360	14,080	5,211	2,819	1,709	2,216
4.	1	93	23	47	–	2	3	8
5.	302	1,840	1,303	4,837	162	1,062	51	165
6.	114	641	121	4,548	101	103	28	2,834
7.	3,013	4,138	5,717	17,946	1,825	2,990	919	5,083
8.	89	485	380	2,080	299	225	36	75
9.	199	1,086	1,614	3,093	2,612	429	265	413
10.	3,072	15,024	56	1,616	29	1,454	7	15
11.	306	1,485	3,192	30,805	16,427	729	504	4,633
12.	330	882	1,222	3,910	233	853	171	1,249
13.	361	1,531	1,602	1,853	798	568	50	270
14.	68	522	1,240	657	485	46	76	113
15.	235	1,136	4,308	2,903	581	261	35	137
16.	1,782	2,397	2,146	2,456	463	2,572	710	919
17.	1,106	3,311	3,643	6,513	1,154	989	386	569
18.	437	2,699	5,023	11,364	661	618	221	478
19.	131	489	738	2,003	2,703	261	41	293
20.	8,898	26,988	16,046	26,305	11,778	9,656	3,262	6,915
21.	2,265	5,592	4,058	6,510	2,074	2,717	634	1,936
22.	9,412	21,504	12,320	32,725	10,103	5,646	3,221	7,775
23.	10,004	24,631	15,291	31,152	9,116	7,715	3,368	7,224
24.	1,256	3,968	2,075	4,493	1,250	1,168	460	1,376
25.	3,670	10,598	7,640	12,984	4,172	3,568	1,406	3,092
26.	8,288	21,373	12,826	18,546	8,670	7,729	2,893	5,722
27.	14,473	42,289	19,883	27,281	48,684	18,818	6,227	26,555
N.C.	159	220	189	309	112	71	80	102
Total Employed	101,436	238,760	160,365	293,946	147,465	87,365	39,120	104,557
Total Population	164,777	378,276	259,257	451,713	203,237	141,266	62,747	149,519

East Midlands

25.Staffs.	26. Warwick	27. Worcs.	28. Derby	29. Notts.	30. Leics.	31. Lincs.	32. Northants.	
17,991	13,498	15,137	13,664	12,062	12,168	55,247	12,433	1.
42,997	16,656	1,161	49,365	53,575	14,326	1,779	1,625	2.
16,689	16,480	3,063	4,108	10,632	3,793	8,010	3,711	3.
442	62	8	1,856	202	9	441	151	4.
5,662	5,512	3,259	2,136	4,835	1,224	2,498	698	5.
57,083	31,749	16,889	19,813	2,451	3,340	15,330	8,527	6.
35,899	43,872	10,016	9,449	15,811	21,336	15,242	10,701	7.
432	2,747	365	375	711	938	158	231	8.
15,691	45,666	4,082	1,983	4,614	5,447	352	517	9.
393	116	100	12	118	21	2,835	23	10.
24,207	130,507	6,214	22,528	10,136	3,969	5,968	5,675	11.
46,349	49,883	13,920	3,033	3,794	2,552	1,453	696	12.
6,234	6,343	5,943	24,149	13,656	18,682	518	383	13.
1,908	860	563	291	582	569	395	3,485	14.
3,038	2,435	1,083	1,126	2,719	15,843	343	21,272	15.
40,387	6,507	2,461	6,731	3,997	3,765	2,106	822	16.
6,041	8,819	1,750	2,273	4,624	2,798	3,255	1,599	17.
4,935	8,877	1,155	2,818	4,062	3,892	1,803	1,857	18.
9,451	13,404	1,213	636	991	3,681	446	1,208	19.
37,621	42,480	11,313	19,109	20,463	15,903	19,681	11,834	20.
10,444	11,452	3,623	4,523	4,337	3,539	3,319	3,066	21.
31,463	38,541	9,376	20,434	21,512	12,541	21,746	11,778	22.
37,207	53,630	13,060	18,192	25,033	19,996	22,540	12,176	23.
4,360	8,796	1,489	2,404	3,484	2,240	2,189	1,666	24.
13,988	21,217	5,308	7,084	8,961	7,198	6,582	4,527	25.
19,743	28,864	8,802	10,458	13,545	10,495	11,687	7,613	26.
30,482	31,408	11,615	12,664	26,491	12,053	28,183	7,628	27.
298	361	122	99	96	166	213	60	N.C.
521,435	640,742	153,090	261,313	273,494	202,484	234,319	135,962	
795,373	904,369	253,661	405,938	411,257	303,403	353,374	205,472	

MALE EMPLOYMENT: 1951

		North West		Yorks. & Humberside		North		
	33. Rut-land	34. Cheshire	35.Lancs.	36. West Riding	37. East Riding	38. North Riding	39. West-morland	40. Cum-berland
1.	1,892	20,560	36,047	33,164	22,557	21,928	5,128	12,264
2.	237	3,014	55,846	144,015	341	2,751	731	8,451
3.	96	11,617	54,548	25,738	12,518	3,008	569	2,446
4.	1	6,004	2,122	4,394	44	558	2	200
5.	19	23,340	50,839	15,455	8,161	3,134	72	2,961
6.	34	5,162	32,469	80,997	2,613	28,167	10	4,456
7.	206	24,896	100,152	83,419	3,976	5,802	727	3,437
8.	–	643	4,119	3,078	395	781	16	132
9.	4	4,859	62,343	12,814	489	514	32	355
10.	–	13,682	21,733	1,860	5,091	3,112	61	52
11.	86	17,774	50,944	28,937	6,721	1,002	40	4,116
12.	18	5,875	30,280	43,987	2,153	1,560	62	715
13.	37	16,287	150,007	105,370	861	343	233	1,833
14.	6	1,948	7,791	4,606	1,282	285	10	630
15.	44	4,122	26,106	18,341	496	619	851	759
16.	239	2,497	31,191	19,275	2,361	1,028	293	793
17.	46	2,995	27,711	16,451	4,657	1,578	517	1,290
18.	10	5,895	38,978	16,012	2,390	875	629	1,055
19.	20	3,765	30,065	4,775	862	239	81	638
20.	583	36,660	122,179	74,957	15,885	13,097	1,593	9,641
21.	40	8,620	32,902	23,234	3,652	2,283	513	1,824
22.	435	37,385	188,989	82,528	32,514	12,653	1,840	9,099
23.	349	29,839	178,830	103,501	21,353	11,485	1,802	6,992
24.	77	4,161	27,521	14,772	2,667	1,989	467	1,143
25.	248	11,048	60,061	36,669	7,186	4,812	814	2,710
26.	440	19,717	90,694	53,046	11,294	9,455	1,910	4,800
27.	2,022	30,894	102,923	57,412	16,767	33,621	1,205	9,514
N.C.	6	266	1,290	472	106	163	11	51
Total Employed	7,195	353,525	1,618,680	1,109,279	189,392	166,842	20,219	92,357
Total Population	10,720	599,741	2,422,666	1,670,352	296,155	263,914	31,706	140,389

41. North- umberland	42.Durham	Wales 43.Glam- organ & Monmouth	44. North & West Wales	Scotland 45.Strathclyde	46.Dumfries & Galloway	47. Borders	48.Lothian	
13,548	11,039	13,204	62,845	26,320	14,786	9,839	10,354	1.
47,856	116,739	106,553	23,925	36,872	2,091	142	24,991	2.
6,448	7,385	10,944	5,703	26,386	1,660	767	12,361	3.
61	4,169	4,114	42	932	4	-	1,722	4.
3,620	21,844	9,105	4,779	15,434	962	56	3,107	5.
2,041	19,135	57,680	15,845	41,611	15	38	2,784	6.
13,649	23,783	12,804	3,369	69,052	898	584	4,438	7.
672	315	966	1,237	4,109	17	17	485	8.
5,722	10,365	7,664	562	6,716	43	39	2,644	9.
23,274	31,568	5,020	1,291	55,450	19	21	3,294	10.
2,346	9,734	10,907	6,274	27,302	225	74	2,336	11.
2,339	4,769	9,191	2,717	15,030	304	153	3,294	12.
803	2,393	4,651	6,143	18,878	478	5,665	1,207	13.
589	325	637	526	2,630	54	328	450	14.
936	2,216	2,545	620	6,716	110	130	1,074	15.
2,828	7,833	6,179	3,901	10,544	190	28	2,667	16.
3,922	5,527	5,535	2,641	14,684	1,229	985	4,538	17.
2,731	3,288	4,106	1,455	12,603	204	349	8,083	18.
1,791	1,470	3,778	570	5,132	479	22	3,473	19.
20,221	31,621	40,509	27,264	68,439	4,419	3,177	21,060	20.
4,937	6,813	10,165	5,136	12,637	645	447	4,046	21.
26,570	35,446	57,957	25,119	78,392	3,919	2,194	23,238	22.
25,766	30,420	40,616	23,924	70,107	3,836	2,682	21,025	23.
4,309	3,915	6,102	4,262	10,356	458	362	4,534	24.
9,792	12,381	17,587	12,588	29,378	1,648	1,122	11,453	25.
12,508	14,802	20,124	17,513	38,377	2,695	2,449	14,490	26.
19,925	23,232	34,221	31,023	44,056	4,598	1,530	18,440	27.
131	199	325	454	507	39	14	219	N.C.
259,335	442,726	503,189	291,728	748,650	46,025	33,214	211,807	
385,780	718,056	798,714	471,389	1,199,555	72,135	50,571	332,856	

MALE EMPLOYMENT: 1951

Scotland

	49. Central & Fife	50. Tayside	51.Grampian	52. Highland	53. South East	54. East Anglia	55. South West	56. West Midland
1.	10,263	18,832	34,164	22,678	191,477	100,364	133,109	79,04
2.	32,190	483	648	453	13,276	805	19,009	65,14
3.	5,409	4,077	6,870	1,821	138,845	18,898	37,992	40,15
4.	1,165	9	10	5	8,272	36	166	52
5.	3,619	932	1,150	186	74,232	4,163	9,506	14,64
6.	12,145	143	188	852	36,371	2,373	5,628	108,58
7.	3,573	7,858	3,614	413	207,675	14,940	35,629	95,78
8.	96	468	159	36	48,037	1,157	3,558	3,65
9.	834	631	158	40	145,690	6,255	9,033	66,11
10.	8,282	2,493	3,505	256	59,246	1,958	21,251	63
11.	2,389	678	923	186	190,892	4,429	52,944	166,06
12.	1,626	992	890	260	76,846	1,871	7,430	111,57
13.	2,854	11,736	1,477	1,698	19,645	1,794	6,713	18,84
14.	130	168	74	21	15,424	880	3,018	3,52
15.	282	546	437	157	68,598	6,402	9,424	6,72
16.	3,419	483	1,750	84	57,642	4,994	11,816	50,98
17.	3,710	2,906	3,884	1,814	110,625	7,005	16,716	17,56
18.	4,330	2,206	3,198	243	168,626	5,823	20,802	15,66
19.	4,629	757	287	33	58,898	1,607	6,325	24,40
20.	14,123	11,806	12,804	8,817	477,815	43,044	99,671	101,59
21.	2,057	2,108	1,619	611	123,381	8,001	23,216	28,08
22.	12,444	11,836	12,921	7,230	523,976	32,472	91,710	90,37
23.	11,206	12,841	14,682	5,696	553,450	40,655	97,909	144,48
24.	1,443	1,980	1,806	706	143,895	5,768	14,210	16,48
25.	4,677	5,518	5,410	2,725	253,319	17,126	42,632	45,01
26.	8,456	8,786	7,591	4,053	392,124	37,033	77,432	66,02
27.	12,976	8,406	10,952	6,472	544,808	53,977	171,428	106,28
N.C.	60	54	114	107	4,533	500	1,060	96.
Total Employment	168,387	119,733	131,285	67,653	4,707,618	424,330	1,029,337	1,458,94
Total Population	260,180	190,716	215,755	112,590	7,110,826	651,586	1,598,526	2,165,66

57. East Midlands	58. North West	59. Yorks. & Humber- side	60. North	61. Wales	62. Scotland	63. Great Britain	
107,466	56,607	55,721	63,907	76,049	147,236	1,010,977	1.
120,907	58,860	144,356	176,528	130,478	97,870	827,235	2.
30,350	66,165	38,256	19,856	16,647	59,351	466,517	3.
2,660	8,126	4,438	4,990	4,156	3,847	37,214	4.
11,410	74,179	23,616	31,631	13,884	25,446	282,716	5.
49,495	37,631	83,610	53,809	73,525	57,776	508,801	6.
72,745	125,048	87,395	47,398	16,173	90,430	793,222	7.
2,413	4,762	3,473	1,916	2,203	5,387	76,561	8.
12,917	67,202	13,303	16,988	8,226	11,105	356,836	9.
3,009	35,415	6,951	58,067	6,311	73,320	266,159	10.
48,362	68,718	35,658	17,238	17,181	34,113	635,600	11.
11,546	36,155	46,140	9,445	11,908	22,549	335,462	12.
57,425	166,294	106,231	5,605	10,794	43,993	437,334	13.
5,328	9,739	5,888	1,839	1,163	3,855	50,654	14.
41,347	30,228	18,837	5,381	3,165	9,452	199,562	15.
17,660	33,688	21,636	12,775	10,080	19,165	240,440	16.
14,595	30,706	21,108	12,834	8,176	33,750	273,080	17.
14,442	44,873	18,402	8,578	5,561	31,216	333,989	18.
6,982	33,830	5,637	4,219	4,348	14,812	161,060	19.
87,573	158,839	90,842	76,173	67,773	144,645	1,347,966	20.
18,824	41,522	26,886	16,370	15,301	24,170	325,760	21.
88,446	226,374	115,042	85,608	83,076	152,174	1,489,254	22.
98,286	208,669	124,854	76,465	64,540	142,075	1,521,392	23.
12,060	31,682	17,439	11,823	10,364	21,645	285,367	24.
34,600	71,109	43,855	30,509	30,175	61,931	630,267	25.
54,238	110,411	64,340	43,475	37,637	86,897	969,611	26.
89,041	133,817	74,179	87,497	65,244	107,430	1,433,708	27.
640	1,556	578	555	779	1,114	12,278	N.C.
1,114,767	1,972,205	1,298,671	981,479	794,917	1,526,754	15,309,022	
1,690,164	3,022,407	1,966,507	1,539,845	1,270,103	2,434,358	23,449,991	

FEMALE EMPLOYMENT: 1951

South East

	1. London	2. Middlesex	3. Kent	4. Surrey	5. Sussex	6. Hants.	7. Berks.	8. Oxon
1.	305	1,168	6,713	2,113	3,562	2,993	1,256	920
2.	626	46	96	30	7	17	11	
3.	31,400	14,007	3,292	4,894	2,152	3,917	2,910	606
4.	1,186	126	41	15	–	72	40	
5.	16,645	10,738	2,664	2,370	973	963	797	4
6.	2,236	1,553	246	410	30	67	67	442
7.	13,015	8,953	2,496	4,723	883	967	946	247
8.	6,303	5,845	267	3,597	768	458	151	74
9.	21,704	27,925	5,992	7,966	1,467	1,685	485	130
10.	440	81	612	54	31	908	52	80
11.	3,393	6,515	1,263	2,542	271	3,648	738	1,555
12.	11,921	9,117	733	2,396	733	537	573	48
13.	7,037	3,747	1,118	1,489	540	597	76	66
14.	6,885	932	192	564	199	173	84	6
15.	93,900	12,270	3,604	3,647	2,684	4,462	1,415	1,417
16.	3,196	1,235	1,024	468	198	148	100	15
17.	7,436	3,732	824	1,467	432	942	366	162
18.	40,518	9,943	6,255	4,202	905	2,258	1,051	874
19.	12,617	10,111	2,329	5,546	790	984	465	44
20.	6,819	2,052	1,053	1,479	781	882	270	190
21.	4,402	1,649	950	1,176	707	896	376	114
22.	43,851	9,743	4,170	4,685	2,759	4,915	1,519	1,088
23.	148,118	40,967	31,799	32,310	22,097	30,905	8,833	6,003
24.	62,778	3,680	2,396	4,307	2,343	2,688	934	470
25.	124,691	35,673	29,291	35,370	22,509	21,891	9,216	8,340
26.	191,247	61,741	44,279	53,377	43,221	43,907	13,424	9,794
27.	53,298	12,967	7,637	8,934	4,206	9,181	4,649	2,109
N.C.	1,052	340	210	310	219	204	50	26
Total Employed	917,019	296,856	161,546	190,441	115,467	141,265	50,854	35,468
Total Population	1,782,094	1,201,733	820,656	859,915	523,398	662,959	207,613	138,091

East Anglia

9. Bucks.	10. Beds.	11. Herts.	12. Essex	13. Cambridge	14. Hunts.	15. Norfolk	16. Suffolk	
1,168	684	1,816	3,647	2,582	553	3,536	2,139	1.
9	9	20	33	9	5	13	8	2.
2,223	1,710	2,197	7,661	1,790	729	3,543	2,310	3.
5	1	4	193	-	-	2	2	4.
1,749	269	3,465	6,925	74	2	117	594	5.
529	551	511	942	2	-	28	313	6.
1,108	2,780	1,879	3,975	185	75	395	1,085	7.
631	514	1,008	1,499	211	-	70	30	8.
2,133	1,533	3,839	12,923	1,419	645	1,511	496	9.
9	1	13	249	15	1	34	40	10.
1,142	2,436	2,034	2,045	29	2	111	107	11.
796	244	985	2,669	14	19	242	85	12.
872	397	1,911	3,164	121	112	1,071	1,116	13.
173	165	233	1,019	77	2	135	208	14.
2,138	6,554	3,509	18,363	614	139	7,247	3,065	15.
189	227	304	2,013	110	57	56	35	16.
1,872	104	455	2,484	373	29	377	189	17.
2,166	1,428	5,073	5,702	820	97	1,201	868	18.
1,495	682	2,205	8,365	109	79	491	421	19.
261	164	527	1,317	153	35	335	222	20.
138	224	512	1,163	138	36	293	349	21.
1,244	991	1,830	5,219	1,009	164	1,786	1,173	22.
6,203	5,960	11,256	36,069	5,076	983	10,514	8,736	23.
540	490	1,172	2,134	409	38	1,362	625	24.
7,028	4,661	13,657	29,714	5,757	805	7,734	6,700	25.
11,853	7,255	17,397	43,887	6,772	1,578	13,983	12,357	26.
1,990	1,475	2,734	6,695	1,732	338	2,227	1,580	27.
57	23	94	263	69	8	62	24	N.C.
49,721	41,532	80,640	210,332	29,669	6,531	58,476	44,877	
197,834	156,501	319,883	1,064,651	130,286	33,337	276,002	224,650	

FEMALE EMPLOYMENT: 1951

<u>South West</u>   West Midlands

	17. Corn-wall	18. Devon	19.Som-erset	20. Gloucs.	21.Wilts.	22.Dorset	23. Here-ford	24.Shro
1.	2,630	3,918	2,703	1,727	1,346	1,479	1,424	2,319
2.	154	47	108	127	7	8	4	59
3.	627	2,238	2,989	9,319	2,575	785	812	717
4.	-	3	8	10	-	-	-	-
5.	143	311	233	2,033	116	221	3	69
6.	3	149	9	438	6	6	2	400
7.	251	1,014	591	2,947	226	331	158	683
8.	12	115	91	1,032	203	41	4	13
9.	15	850	847	1,226	2,270	229	155	311
10.	57	233	1	50	-	83	-	-
11.	6	147	348	3,969	1,579	91	70	519
12.	13	128	258	1,490	18	690	51	484
13.	879	1,170	1,228	1,991	959	506	76	334
14.	13	179	265	217	100	2	9	30
15.	526	3,723	7,462	5,452	1,577	553	125	393
16.	63	413	164	423	43	363	373	178
17.	152	471	467	1,389	167	63	25	53
18.	120	1,059	2,230	7,010	224	164	82	167
19.	55	137	376	1,102	803	127	7	633
20.	148	521	323	636	279	150	58	120
21.	298	564	347	778	201	127	52	163
22.	1,010	2,667	1,602	4,157	1,540	698	447	1,174
23.	7,146	18,505	11,459	20,847	6,642	5,451	2,376	5,639
24.	340	1,546	769	2,320	405	335	132	405
25.	4,566	14,275	11,078	18,533	5,974	4,804	2,102	5,130
26.	10,205	27,079	16,807	25,098	9,656	9,554	4,235	8,390
27.	1,699	3,629	3,827	5,843	2,878	1,084	717	2,866
N.C.	51	105	56	177	50	28	22	16
Total Employed	31,182	85,196	66,646	120,341	39,844	27,973	13,521	31,251
Total Population	180,665	419,462	292,196	487,720	183,455	150,057	64,412	140,283

East Midlands

25.Staffs.	26.Warwick	27. Worcs.	28. Derby	29. Netts.	30. Leics.	31. Lincs.	32. North-ants.	
2,280	1,539	2,036	1,387	1,122	1,150	6,705	1,040	1.
647	208	122	512	719	236	44	19	2.
6,212	10,673	1,860	2,597	6,180	1,875	4,779	1,201	3.
32	33	2	58	8	–	5	–	4.
1,736	1,995	651	1,222	4,558	863	371	143	5.
8,999	7,629	3,147	1,698	180	161	1,181	510	6.
6,885	10,469	1,404	1,218	2,597	3,097	2,155	1,628	7.
192	1,788	152	115	387	254	13	25	8.
10,812	23,136	1,750	973	1,580	1,940	38	407	9.
43	32	6	–	4	–	70	1	10.
6,471	29,742	2,168	2,331	1,892	545	1,017	664	11.
28,181	34,769	7,650	1,125	3,990	1,110	71	227	12.
7,725	8,066	5,294	20,589	25,604	33,630	1,138	562	13.
2,768	1,063	410	46	202	152	168	804	14.
9,342	7,673	3,631	4,266	12,160	17,474	1,622	21,233	15.
38,145	1,387	1,221	2,180	334	273	90	222	16.
1,486	2,420	584	685	865	424	488	179	17.
4,528	5,827	792	2,023	2,312	2,236	860	1,750	18.
4,231	7,564	1,746	447	490	1,963	343	893	19.
1,198	1,521	303	532	559	486	328	223	20.
941	1,202	637	417	303	286	314	247	21.
4,611	9,455	1,513	3,462	2,799	1,739	2,825	1,734	22.
32,884	45,549	11,220	14,704	17,480	12,473	14,980	8,610	23.
1,902	5,699	604	786	1,510	1,020	803	619	24.
21,104	32,358	8,359	10,758	12,068	8,787	8,706	6,238	25.
31,124	48,651	13,756	15,860	17,938	13,297	16,825	8,874	26.
5,966	8,314	2,526	2,731	5,570	2,253	2,944	1,210	27.
164	201	52	65	61	94	64	21	N.C.
240,609	308,963	73,596	92,787	123,472	107,818	68,947	59,284	
825,661	957,301	269,185	420,499	429,954	327,674	352,448	218,009	

FEMALE EMPLOYMENT: 1951

| | East Midlands | North West | | Yorks & Humberside | | North | | |
	33. Rutland	34. Cheshire	35.Lancs.	36. West Riding	37. East Riding	38. North Riding	39. Westmorland	40. Cuerlan
1.	185	3,128	4,445	3,479	1,244	1,735	724	1,6
2.	3	781	1,773	1,395	16	26	19	2
3.	13	6,230	41,953	16,723	9,287	1,735	290	2,6
4.	-	527	268	129	1	4	-	
5.	2	5,625	17,588	5,678	2,698	346	30	2
6.	2	629	4,513	9,165	257	1,605	-	2
7.	18	3,766	17,568	14,181	425	453	81	2
8.	-	242	2,061	1,485	143	103	4	
9.	-	2,813	27,968	7,779	210	576	2	1
10.	-	263	1,039	91	126	149	1	
11.	5	1,790	6,055	3,251	1,333	137	2	3
12.	13	2,024	12,053	22,760	2,149	323	3	80
13.	162	20,618	195,084	109,135	1,937	1,282	273	2,4
14.	1	488	3,901	1,792	251	21	7	2
15.	75	14,309	76,593	51,592	1,199	3,584	800	2,8
16.	6	361	7,670	3,116	327	90	24	
17.	1	794	7,066	3,750	838	151	51	1
18.	1	3,581	21,903	10,352	1,799	515	176	5
19.	74	1,725	16,736	2,989	642	140	46	4
20.	10	865	3,357	2,103	415	254	22	2
21.	3	731	3,009	1,780	293	255	58	1
22.	54	3,706	19,737	12,688	3,405	2,250	203	90
23.	224	25,645	137,924	78,423	14,978	11,151	1,263	5,58
24.	7	1,534	15,086	7,325	1,081	583	253	3
25.	355	18,160	85,062	53,143	10,141	7,655	1,328	3,9
26.	559	33,410	142,410	80,879	15,405	14,388	2,910	7,2
27.	89	5,519	24,256	13,023	2,556	2,377	187	1,3
N.C.	1	107	553	306	56	27	5	
Total Employed	1,863	159,371	897,631	518,512	73,212	51,915	8,762	33,38
Total Population	9,817	658,766	2,695,187	1,810,551	320,120	261,567	35,686	144,9

41. North-umberland	42. Durham	43. Glamorgan & Monmouth	44. North & West Wales	45. Strathclyde	46. Dumfries & Galloway	47. Borders	48. Lothian	
1,764	1,312	1,481	8,924	4,195	1,519	836	1,755	1.
805	1,346	1,530	258	641	17	4	388	2.
5,541	6,200	5,590	1,759	20,667	541	104	7,128	3.
8	30	197	-	117	-	-	80	4.
2,094	3,846	1,643	767	5,669	54	12	1,133	5.
290	1,195	5,471	998	2,591	-	-	150	6.
2,336	2,651	2,000	348	12,650	86	46	555	7.
132	32	470	1,011	2,465	5	-	216	8.
1,557	8,041	4,947	431	4,705	3	1	1,898	9.
990	1,074	137	27	2,708	-	1	148	10.
159	349	1,851	1,792	2,063	15	1	123	11.
1,307	1,349	5,810	1,378	4,270	19	7	1,106	12.
1,137	4,011	1,912	2,901	36,806	1,767	5,860	3,011	13.
334	574	484	210	1,511	7	33	189	14.
4,252	15,380	10,844	1,814	24,195	161	274	2,462	15.
849	1,624	861	273	1,632	15	-	422	16.
917	1,458	709	302	3,671	43	39	633	17.
1,859	2,662	1,852	519	9,164	88	97	5,575	18.
732	1,652	3,878	346	2,082	553	6	1,533	19.
667	753	732	345	3,378	121	104	1,172	20.
829	539	919	557	1,114	92	62	416	21.
3,872	4,009	5,421	2,726	16,112	627	337	3,684	22.
24,134	30,677	33,718	16,456	69,555	2,818	1,865	18,996	23.
2,196	1,437	2,442	878	5,301	173	98	2,797	24.
13,791	20,099	24,556	14,766	48,166	2,564	1,629	18,818	25.
21,571	26,931	30,302	25,191	49,413	4,330	3,170	18,944	26.
7,083	4,331	7,163	3,815	9,561	730	338	6,279	27.
97	99	196	112	245	5	6	135	N.C.
101,303	143,661	157,116	88,904	344,647	16,353	14,930	99,746	
412,644	745,812	828,982	499,590	1,307,618	75,870	57,015	373,714	

FEMALE EMPLOYMENT: 1951

Scotland

	49. Central & Fife	50. Tayside	51. Grampian	52. Highland	53. South East	54. East Anglia	55. South West	56. West Midlands
1.	1,369	1,612	2,020	1,828	26,345	8,810	13,803	9,598
2.	540	12	17	8	908	35	451	1,036
3.	2,009	2,853	3,110	388	76,969	8,372	18,533	20,270
4.	57	2	−	1	1,683	4	21	67
5.	1,311	156	254	15	47,605	787	3,057	4,454
6.	2,047	9	14	85	7,584	343	611	20,177
7.	300	1,459	380	14	41,972	1,740	5,360	19,599
8.	10	575	36	−	21,115	311	1,494	2,148
9.	163	764	19	3	87,782	4,071	5,437	36,164
10.	453	76	149	10	2,530	90	424	81
11.	233	41	35	5	27,582	249	6,140	38,966
12.	944	237	232	7	30,752	360	2,597	71,135
13.	7,209	14,954	3,272	692	21,611	2,420	6,733	21,495
14.	26	186	25	1	10,625	422	776	4,280
15.	1,110	1,657	798	152	153,963	11,065	19,293	21,164
16.	508	69	75	10	9,117	258	1,469	41,304
17.	383	252	462	76	20,276	968	2,709	4,568
18.	2,475	1,575	1,795	48	80,375	2,986	10,807	11,396
19.	1,632	115	137	3	45,633	1,100	2,600	14,180
20.	529	515	501	175	15,795	745	2,057	3,200
21.	294	187	127	59	12,307	816	2,315	2,995
22.	2,831	1,714	1,899	1,184	82,014	4,132	11,674	17,200
23.	11,284	10,878	11,329	3,589	380,520	25,309	70,050	97,668
24.	502	1,103	777	221	83,932	2,434	5,715	8,742
25.	8,450	9,571	9,369	3,894	342,041	20,996	59,230	69,053
26.	10,045	11,433	11,401	6,092	541,382	34,690	98,399	106,156
27.	2,405	1,715	1,691	813	115,875	5,877	18,960	20,389
N.C.	38	14	25	22	2,848	163	467	455
Total Employed	59,157	63,734	49,949	19,395	2,291,141	139,553	371,182	667,940
Total Population	271,657	219,607	238,022	118,554	7,935,328	664,275	1,713,555	2,256,842

57. East Midlands	58. North West	59. Yorks. & Humberside	60. North	61. Wales	62. Scotland	63. Great Britain	
11,589	7,573	4,723	7,162	10,405	15,134	115,142	1.
1,533	2,554	1,411	2,436	1,788	1,627	13,779	2.
16,645	48,183	26,010	16,444	7,349	36,800	275,575	3.
71	795	130	44	197	257	3,269	4.
7,159	23,213	8,376	6,600	2,410	8,604	112,265	5.
3,732	5,142	9,422	3,388	6,469	4,896	61,764	6.
10,713	21,334	14,606	5,814	2,348	15,490	138,976	7.
794	2,303	1,628	341	1,481	3,307	34,922	8.
4,938	30,781	7,989	10,328	5,378	7,556	200,424	9.
75	1,302	217	2,216	164	3,545	10,644	10.
6,454	7,845	4,584	1,037	3,643	2,516	99,016	11.
6,536	14,077	24,909	3,789	7,188	6,822	168,165	12.
81,685	215,702	111,072	9,126	4,813	73,571	548,228	13.
1,373	4,389	2,043	1,202	694	1,978	27,782	14.
56,830	90,902	52,791	26,861	12,658	30,809	476,336	15.
3,105	8,031	3,443	2,628	1,134	2,731	73,220	16.
2,642	7,860	4,588	2,703	1,011	5,559	52,884	17.
9,182	25,484	12,151	5,716	2,371	20,817	181,285	18.
4,210	18,461	3,631	3,047	4,224	6,061	103,147	19.
2,138	4,222	2,518	1,915	1,077	6,495	40,162	20.
1,570	3,740	2,073	1,811	1,476	2,351	31,454	21.
12,613	23,443	16,093	11,237	8,147	28,388	214,941	22.
68,471	163,569	93,401	72,812	50,174	130,314	1,152,288	23.
4,745	16,620	8,406	4,868	3,320	10,972	149,754	24.
46,912	103,222	63,284	46,818	39,322	102,461	893,339	25.
73,353	175,820	96,284	73,060	55,493	114,828	1,369,465	26.
14,797	29,775	15,579	15,361	10,978	23,532	271,123	27.
306	660	362	259	308	490	6,318	N.C
454,171	1,057,002	591,724	339,023	246,020	667,911	6,825,667	
1,758,401	3,353,953	2,130,671	1,600,658	1,328,572	2,662,057	25,404,312	

TOTAL EMPLOYMENT: 1951

South East

	1. London	2. Middlesex	3. Kent	4. Surrey	5. Sussex	6. Hants.	7. Berks.	8. Oxon.
1.	1,537	5,596	42,333	14,567	31,754	27,886	11,540	10,345
2.	1,880	511	7,890	590	730	320	236	349
3.	83,132	34,488	11,856	12,971	7,722	12,510	8,026	2,456
4.	4,087	711	358	94	4	1,410	171	7
5.	41,077	20,900	8,391	6,862	2,075	3,454	3,657	159
6.	10,142	8,616	1,772	2,863	351	674	302	3,163
7.	80,757	45,455	20,711	24,496	6,834	9,790	4,891	2,437
8.	23,619	17,732	1,342	9,282	1,829	1,802	574	313
9.	59,907	71,899	13,897	20,694	4,661	5,794	1,307	988
10.	7,508	890	14,392	560	789	29,362	618	456
11.	18,776	43,403	8,195	20,653	4,292	27,658	5,347	16,340
12.	42,231	27,933	3,436	8,552	2,648	2,165	2,269	310
13.	13,884	6,066	2,295	2,823	1,040	1,142	223	1,455
14.	16,059	1,986	897	1,868	533	473	375	28
15.	141,666	16,835	4,537	5,240	3,631	5,888	1,943	1,878
16.	15,448	8,587	11,111	4,206	3,215	1,815	1,059	554
17.	48,650	24,033	5,257	7,579	4,148	5,830	2,518	1,319
18.	129,193	24,213	25,859	11,403	3,548	6,869	3,900	2,734
19.	28,926	26,205	5,195	11,303	1,782	2,372	1,347	226
20.	153,264	57,515	43,697	45,466	32,225	39,372	14,152	9,610
21.	44,126	17,297	11,075	12,062	7,580	10,015	3,275	1,588
22.	278,139	72,740	39,403	34,311	24,167	42,910	11,937	7,600
23.	383,704	97,257	73,877	74,232	53,199	69,341	21,131	14,363
24.	160,582	11,843	7,925	11,761	7,731	8,650	2,701	1,558
25.	234,888	57,268	47,733	58,114	36,973	36,809	15,362	15,147
26.	332,245	103,484	75,470	88,793	73,262	77,872	24,797	18,492
27.	202,796	60,242	65,101	47,594	26,354	119,765	28,917	17,855
N.C.	2,698	877	637	695	531	516	177	86
Total Employed	2,560,921	864,582	554,642	539,634	343,608	552,464	172,752	131,816
Total Population	3,347,982	2,269,315	1,564,324	1,602,483	937,339	1,292,795	403,141	275,808

9. Bucks.	10. Beds.	11. Herts.	12. Essex	13. Cambridge	14. Hunts.	15. Norfolk	16. Suffolk	
11,768	10,472	14,300	35,724	24,140	6,845	45,835	32,354	1.
201	346	445	686	183	91	386	180	2.
6,050	4,357	6,664	25,582	5,125	1,745	11,723	8,677	3.
23	4	23	3,063	8	–	17	15	4.
4,413	1,775	8,327	20,747	548	47	971	3,384	5.
3,477	3,105	3,314	6,176	16	2	355	2,343	6.
7,204	11,076	11,113	24,883	1,566	739	3,851	10,524	7.
2,194	2,254	3,440	4,771	1,000	12	285	171	8.
5,971	5,076	12,499	30,779	2,981	1,473	4,659	1,213	9.
173	20	102	6,906	94	17	847	1,090	10.
8,678	19,487	15,036	30,609	996	72	1,736	1,874	11.
2,662	920	3,289	11,183	211	93	1,374	553	12.
1,808	681	3,725	6,114	180	171	1,864	1,999	13.
425	700	611	2,094	355	17	423	507	14.
2,822	9,204	4,683	24,234	855	169	12,626	3,817	15.
2,921	6,092	2,009	9,742	1,700	2,413	495	644	16.
12,474	977	3,158	14,958	1,300	225	3,818	2,630	17.
6,447	3,607	17,002	14,226	2,583	253	3,188	2,785	18.
3,205	1,831	5,140	16,999	385	216	1,326	780	19.
10,959	8,621	20,339	58,390	7,957	2,037	18,966	14,829	20.
2,117	2,375	4,982	19,196	1,604	426	3,343	3,444	21.
8,685	6,211	13,003	66,884	8,878	1,300	15,476	10,950	22.
14,966	14,518	26,028	91,354	12,977	2,551	27,632	22,804	23.
1,776	1,700	3,400	8,200	1,318	219	4,277	2,388	24.
11,822	8,240	23,236	49,768	11,698	1,393	13,438	11,593	25.
22,285	12,701	30,615	73,490	13,382	3,938	28,803	25,600	26.
17,025	13,638	12,688	48,708	10,580	3,979	27,243	18,052	27.
175	99	234	656	212	30	290	131	N.C.
172,726	150,087	249,405	706,122	112,832	30,473	235,247	185,331	
386,291	311,937	609,775	2,044,964	255,936	69,302	548,062	442,561	

TOTAL EMPLOYMENT: 1951

South West   West Midlands

	17. Corn-wall	18. Devon	19.Som-erset	20.Gloucs	21.Wilts.	22.Dorset	23. Here-ford	24.Shrop*
1.	26,535	38,811	28,178	19,539	18,897	14,952	13,664	22,494
2.	5,509	2,675	4,982	5,245	218	831	121	4,270
3.	2,832	8,555	10,349	23,399	7,786	3,604	2,521	2,929
4.	1	96	31	57	-	2	3	8
5.	445	2,151	1,536	6,870	278	1,283	54	234
6.	117	790	130	4,986	107	109	30	3,234
7.	3,264	5,152	6,308	20,893	2,051	3,321	1,077	5,766
8.	101	600	471	3,112	502	266	40	87
9.	214	1,936	2,461	4,319	4,882	658	420	724
10.	3,129	15,257	57	1,666	29	1,537	7	15
11.	312	1,632	3,540	34,774	18,006	820	574	5,148
12.	343	1,010	1,480	5,400	251	1,543	222	1,733
13.	1,240	2,701	2,830	3,844	1,757	1,074	126	604
14.	81	701	1,505	874	585	48	85	143
15.	761	4,859	11,770	8,355	2,158	814	160	530
16.	1,845	2,810	2,310	2,879	506	2,935	1,083	1,097
17.	1,258	3,782	4,110	7,902	1,321	1,052	411	622
18.	557	3,758	7,253	18,374	885	782	303	645
19.	186	626	1,114	3,105	3,506	388	48	925
20.	9,046	27,509	16,369	26,941	12,057	9,806	3,320	7,035
21.	2,563	6,156	4,405	7,288	2,275	2,844	686	2,099
22.	10,422	24,171	13,922	36,882	11,643	6,344	3,668	8,949
23.	17,150	43,136	26,750	51,999	15,758	13,166	5,744	12,863
24.	1,596	5,514	2,844	6,813	1,655	1,503	592	1,781
25.	8,236	24,873	18,718	31,517	10,146	8,372	3,508	8,222
26.	18,493	48,452	29,633	43,644	18,326	17,283	7,128	14,112
27.	16,172	45,918	23,710	33,124	51,562	19,902	6,944	29,421
N.C.	210	325	245	486	162	99	102	118
Total Employed	132,618	323,956	227,011	414,287	187,309	115,338	52,641	135,808
Total Population	345,442	797,738	551,453	939,433	386,692	291,323	127,159	289,802

East Midlands

25.Staffs.	26.Warwick	27.Worcs.	28. Derby	29. Notts.	30. Leics.	31. Lincs.	32. North-ants.	
20,271	15,137	17,173	15,051	13,184	13,318	61,952	13,473	1.
43,644	16,864	1,283	49,877	54,294	14,562	1,823	1,644	2.
22,901	27,153	4,923	6,705	16,812	5,668	12,789	4,912	3.
474	95	10	1,914	210	9	446	151	4.
7,398	7,507	3,910	3,358	9,393	2,087	2,869	841	5.
66,082	39,378	20,036	21,511	2,631	3,501	16,511	9,037	6.
42,784	54,341	11,420	10,667	18,408	24,433	17,397	12,329	7.
624	4,535	517	490	1,098	1,192	171	256	8.
26,503	68,802	5,832	2,956	6,194	7,387	390	924	9.
436	148	106	12	122	21	2,905	24	10.
30,678	160,249	8,382	24,859	12,028	4,514	6,985	6,339	11.
74,530	84,652	21,570	4,158	7,784	3,662	1,524	923	12.
13,959	14,409	11,237	44,738	39,260	52,312	1,656	945	13.
4,676	1,923	973	337	784	721	563	4,289	14.
12,380	10,108	4,714	5,392	14,879	33,317	1,965	42,505	15.
78,532	7,894	3,682	8,911	4,331	4,038	2,196	1,044	16.
7,527	11,239	2,334	2,958	5,489	3,222	3,743	1,778	17.
9,463	14,704	1,947	4,841	6,374	6,128	2,663	3,607	18.
13,682	20,968	2,959	1,083	1,481	5,644	789	2,101	19.
38,819	44,001	11,616	19,641	21,022	16,389	20,009	12,057	20.
11,385	12,654	4,260	4,940	4,640	3,825	3,633	3,313	21.
36,074	47,996	10,889	23,896	24,311	14,280	24,571	13,512	22.
70,091	99,179	24,280	32,896	42,513	32,469	37,520	20,786	23.
6,262	14,495	2,093	3,190	4,994	3,260	2,992	2,285	24.
35,092	53,575	13,667	17,842	21,029	15,985	15,288	10,765	25.
50,867	77,515	22,558	26,318	31,483	23,792	28,512	16,487	26.
36,448	39,722	14,141	15,395	32,061	14,306	31,127	8,838	27.
462	562	174	164	157	260	277	81	N.C.
762,044	949,705	226,686	354,100	396,966	310,302	303,266	195,246	
1,621,034	1,861,670	522,846	826,437	841,211	631,077	705,822	423,481	

TOTAL EMPLOYMENT: 1951

	East Midlands	North West		Yorks. & Humberside		North		
	33. Rutland	34. Cheshire	35. Lancs.	36. West Riding	37. East Riding	38. North Riding	39. Westmorland	40. Cumberland
1.	2,077	23,688	40,492	36,643	23,801	23,663	5,852	13,891
2.	240	3,795	57,619	145,410	357	2,777	750	8,691
3.	109	17,847	96,501	42,461	21,805	4,743	859	5,124
4.	1	6,531	2,390	4,523	45	562	2	202
5.	21	28,965	68,427	21,133	10,859	3,480	102	3,245
6.	36	5,791	36,982	90,162	2,870	29,772	10	4,754
7.	224	28,662	117,720	97,600	4,401	6,255	808	3,730
8.	–	885	6,180	4,563	538	884	20	202
9.	4	7,672	90,311	20,593	699	1,090	34	507
10.	–	13,945	22,772	1,951	5,217	3,261	62	54
11.	91	19,564	56,999	32,188	8,054	1,139	42	4,506
12.	31	7,899	42,333	66,747	4,302	1,883	65	1,522
13.	199	36,905	345,091	214,505	2,798	1,625	506	4,256
14.	7	2,436	11,692	6,398	1,533	306	17	896
15.	119	18,431	102,699	69,933	1,695	4,203	1,651	3,604
16.	245	2,858	38,861	22,391	2,688	1,118	317	834
17.	47	3,789	34,777	20,201	5,495	1,729	568	1,416
18.	11	9,476	60,881	26,364	4,189	1,390	805	1,559
19.	94	5,490	46,801	7,764	1,504	379	127	1,115
20.	593	37,525	125,536	77,060	16,300	13,351	1,615	9,860
21.	43	9,351	35,911	25,014	3,945	2,538	571	1,954
22.	489	41,091	208,726	95,216	35,919	14,903	2,043	10,002
23.	573	55,484	316,754	181,924	36,331	22,636	3,065	12,579
24.	84	5,695	42,607	22,097	3,748	2,572	720	1,542
25.	603	29,208	145,123	89,812	17,327	12,467	2,142	6,655
26.	999	53,127	233,104	133,925	26,699	23,843	4,820	12,060
27.	2,111	36,413	127,179	70,435	19,323	35,998	1,392	10,897
N.C.	7	373	1,843	778	162	190	16	82
Total Employed	9,058	512,896	2,516,311	1,627,791	262,604	218,757	28,981	125,739
Total Population	20,537	1,258,507	5,117,853	3,480,903	616,275	525,481	67,392	285,338

		Wales		Scotland				
41.North-umberland	42.Durham	43.Glamorgan & Monmouth	44.North & West Wales	45.Strathclyde	46.Dumfries & Galloway	47.Borders	48.Lothian	
15,312	12,351	14,685	71,769	30,515	16,305	10,675	12,109	1.
48,661	118,085	108,083	24,183	37,513	2,108	146	25,379	2.
11,989	13,585	16,534	7,462	47,053	2,201	871	19,489	3.
69	4,199	4,311	42	1,049	4	–	1,802	4.
5,714	25,690	10,748	5,546	21,103	1,016	68	4,240	5.
2,331	20,330	63,151	16,843	44,202	15	38	2,934	6.
15,985	26,434	14,804	3,717	81,702	984	630	4,993	7.
804	347	1,436	2,248	6,574	22	17	701	8.
7,279	18,406	12,611	993	11,421	46	40	4,542	9.
24,264	32,642	5,157	1,318	58,158	19	22	3,442	10.
2,505	10,083	12,758	8,066	29,365	240	75	2,459	11.
3,646	6,118	15,001	4,095	19,300	323	160	4,400	12.
1,940	6,404	6,563	9,044	55,684	2,245	11,525	4,218	13.
923	899	1,121	736	4,141	61	361	639	14.
5,188	17,596	13,389	2,434	30,911	271	404	3,536	15.
3,677	9,457	7,040	4,174	12,176	205	28	3,089	16.
4,839	6,985	6,244	2,943	18,355	1,272	1,024	5,171	17.
4,590	5,950	5,958	1,974	21,767	292	446	13,658	18.
2,523	3,122	7,656	916	7,214	1,032	28	5,006	19.
20,888	32,374	41,241	27,609	71,817	4,540	3,281	22,232	20.
5,766	7,352	11,084	5,693	13,751	737	509	4,462	21.
30,442	39,455	63,378	27,845	94,504	4,546	2,531	26,922	22.
49,900	61,097	74,334	40,380	139,662	6,654	4,547	40,021	23.
6,505	5,352	8,544	5,140	15,657	631	460	7,331	24.
23,583	32,480	42,143	27,354	77,544	4,212	2,751	30,271	25.
34,079	41,733	50,426	42,704	87,790	7,025	5,619	33,434	26.
27,008	27,563	41,384	34,838	53,617	5,328	1,868	24,719	27.
228	298	521	566	752	44	20	354	N.C.
360,638	586,387	660,305	380,632	1,093,297	62,378	48,144	311,553	
798,424	1,463,868	1,627,696	970,979	2,507,173	148,005	107,586	706,570	

TOTAL EMPLOYMENT: 1951

Scotland

	49.Central & Fife	50. Tayside	51.Gram-pian	52. High-land	53. South East	54. East Anglia	55. South West	56. West Midlands
1.	11,632	20,444	36,184	24,506	217,822	109,174	146,912	88,639
2.	32,730	495	665	461	14,184	840	19,460	66,182
3.	7,418	6,930	9,980	2,209	215,814	27,270	56,525	60,427
4.	1,222	11	10	6	9,955	40	187	590
5.	4,930	1,088	1,404	201	121,837	4,950	12,563	19,103
6.	14,192	152	202	937	43,955	2,716	6,239	128,760
7.	3,873	9,317	3,994	427	249,647	16,680	40,989	115,388
8.	106	1,043	195	36	69,152	1,468	5,052	5,803
9.	997	1,395	177	43	233,472	10,326	14,470	102,281
10.	8,735	2,569	3,654	266	61,776	2,048	21,675	712
11.	2,622	719	958	191	218,474	4,678	59,084	205,031
12.	2,570	1,229	1,122	267	107,598	2,231	10,027	182,707
13.	10,063	26,690	4,749	2,390	41,256	4,214	13,446	40,335
14.	156	354	99	22	26,049	1,302	3,794	7,800
15.	1,392	2,203	1,235	309	222,561	17,467	28,717	27,892
16.	3,927	552	1,825	94	66,759	5,252	13,285	92,288
17.	4,093	3,158	4,346	1,890	130,901	7,973	19,425	22,133
18.	6,805	3,781	4,993	291	249,001	8,809	31,609	27,062
19.	6,261	872	424	36	104,531	2,707	8,925	38,582
20.	14,652	12,321	13,305	8,992	493,610	43,789	101,728	104,791
21.	2,351	2,295	1,746	670	135,688	8,817	25,531	31,084
22.	15,275	13,550	14,820	8,414	605,990	36,604	103,384	107,576
23.	22,490	23,719	26,011	9,285	933,970	65,964	167,959	212,157
24.	1,945	3,083	2,583	927	227,827	8,202	19,925	25,223
25.	13,127	15,089	14,779	6,619	595,360	38,122	101,862	114,064
26.	18,501	20,219	18,992	10,145	933,506	71,723	175,831	172,180
27.	15,381	10,121	12,643	7,285	660,683	59,854	190,388	126,676
N.C.	98	68	139	129	7,381	663	1,527	1,418
Total Employed	227,544	183,467	181,234	87,048	6,998,759	563,883	1,400,519	2,126,884
Total Population	531,837	410,323	453,777	231,144	15,046,154	1,315,861	3,312,081	4,422,511

57. East Midlands	58. North West	59. Yorks.& Humberside	60. North	61. Wales	62. Scotland	63. Great Britain	
119,055	64,180	60,444	71,069	86,454	162,370	1,126,119	1.
122,440	61,414	145,767	178,964	132,266	99,497	841,014	2.
46,995	114,348	64,266	36,300	23,996	96,151	742,092	3.
2,731	8,921	4,568	5,034	4,353	4,104	40,483	4.
18,569	97,392	31,992	38,231	16,294	34,050	394,981	5.
53,227	42,773	93,032	57,197	79,994	62,672	570,565	6.
83,458	146,382	102,001	53,212	18,521	105,920	932,198	7.
3,207	7,065	5,101	2,257	3,684	8,694	111,483	8.
17,855	97,983	21,292	27,316	13,604	18,661	557,260	9.
3,084	36,717	7,168	60,283	6,475	76,865	276,803	10.
54,816	76,563	40,242	18,275	20,824	36,629	734,616	11.
18,082	50,232	71,049	13,234	19,096	29,371	503,627	12.
139,110	381,996	217,303	14,731	15,607	117,564	985,562	13.
6,701	14,128	7,931	3,041	1,857	5,833	78,436	14.
98,177	121,130	71,628	32,242	15,823	40,261	675,898	15.
20,765	41,719	25,079	15,403	11,214	21,896	313,660	16.
17,237	38,566	25,696	15,537	9,187	39,309	325,964	17.
23,624	70,357	30,553	14,294	7,932	52,033	515,274	18.
11,192	52,291	9,268	7,266	8,572	20,873	264,207	19.
89,711	163,061	93,360	78,088	68,850	151,140	1,388,128	20.
20,394	45,262	28,959	18,181	16,777	26,521	357,214	21.
101,059	249,817	131,135	96,845	91,223	180,562	1,704,195	22.
166,757	372,238	218,255	149,277	114,714	272,389	2,673,680	23.
16,805	48,302	25,845	16,691	13,684	32,617	435,121	24.
81,512	174,331	107,139	77,327	69,497	164,392	1,523,606	25.
127,591	286,231	160,624	116,535	93,130	201,725	2,339,076	26.
103,838	163,592	89,758	102,858	76,222	130,962	1,704,831	27.
946	2,216	940	814	1,087	1,604	18,596	N.C.
1,568,938	3,029,207	1,890,395	1,320,502	1,040,937	2,194,665	22,134,689	
3,448,565	6,376,360	4,097,178	3,140,503	2,598,675	5,096,415	48,854,303	

MALE EMPLOYMENT: 1961

South East

	1. London	2. Middlesex	3. Kent	4. Surrey	5. Sussex	6. Hants.	7. Berks.	8. Oxon.
1.	780	2,340	24,980	9,550	19,830	18,150	7,810	6,460
2.	1,770	440	7,050	870	800	270	270	400
3.	40,350	21,420	7,630	6,260	4,950	8,110	3,760	1,600
4.	6,010	860	3,210	190	40	3,380	30	10
5.	18,590	11,210	7,060	7,280	1,710	4,260	1,020	150
6.	8,140	6,760	1,830	2,530	1,390	660	720	2,450
7.	59,420	51,230	22,930	25,750	12,450	13,790	9,460	1,530
8.	16,000	17,000	3,930	7,680	1,780	1,470	560	170
9.	35,120	57,680	13,690	23,530	6,910	10,930	2,950	1,300
10.	4,600	660	9,000	390	620	24,130	310	110
11.	11,730	31,650	7,750	20,650	3,880	24,910	4,760	22,980
12.	29,020	18,090	3,710	7,960	3,080	2,530	2,700	300
13.	6,620	1,810	1,390	2,210	450	750	150	900
14.	6,810	480	440	890	220	120	170	-
15.	34,980	2,930	350	1,000	720	650	290	280
16.	13,570	8,460	11,990	3,420	3,600	1,620	1,000	910
17.	33,800	17,340	4,970	5,870	4,720	5,290	2,500	990
18.	100,710	16,350	27,460	9,660	3,610	7,180	4,270	2,330
19.	14,620	13,690	3,860	6,110	2,370	2,560	1,070	100
20.	138,460	57,010	47,710	47,450	37,480	47,750	18,350	11,280
21.	35,470	14,580	10,250	9,940	6,910	9,660	3,290	1,140
22.	232,930	70,250	36,890	29,300	21,060	36,190	10,130	6,290
23.	232,850	63,040	46,260	48,000	37,020	46,670	15,160	8,980
24.	116,410	9,770	6,440	10,590	6,720	7,860	2,850	1,300
25.	116,090	29,910	24,300	29,150	18,140	29,460	21,950	9,610
26.	186,160	47,080	31,330	37,070	31,050	34,430	12,820	9,840
27.	132,040	36,820	38,580	31,610	19,120	77,380	20,030	8,390
N.C.	8,050	2,740	1,250	1,400	900	1,130	510	360
Total Employed	1,641,100	611,600	406,240	386,310	251,530	421,290	148,870	100,160
Total Population	1,524,359	1,068,817	813,134	813,035	482,765	687,728	247,591	155,554

East Anglia

9. Bucks.	10. Beds.	11. Herts.	12. Essex	13. Cambridge	14. Hunts.	15. Norfolk	16. Suffolk	
7,580	7,700	8,740	21,530	15,830	4,390	32,890	23,360	1.
330	480	520	1,020	210	280	560	150	2.
4,490	2,530	4,820	16,700	2,280	700	9,160	6,940	3.
20	10	40	3,440	20	10	30	20	4.
4,600	1,330	6,380	14,060	910	60	1,000	4,890	5.
3,550	1,500	3,830	5,640	20	–	610	2,650	6.
13,310	11,840	15,950	26,980	1,290	740	4,700	9,170	7.
1,920	1,950	4,680	7,270	1,200	–	190	110	8.
4,970	4,230	14,670	29,920	2,790	2,040	3,400	2,430	9.
110	2,250	100	7,230	180	50	1,050	1,560	10.
7,830	29,100	25,740	45,780	2,000	60	970	2,350	11.
2,870	940	3,930	10,660	580	70	1,100	440	12.
850	340	1,200	3,050	40	30	720	610	13.
240	360	260	800	140	10	140	240	14.
310	1,810	980	5,090	90	40	4,790	590	15.
3,290	6,090	3,720	8,620	1,800	2,450	690	820	16.
9,080	750	4,510	17,130	1,070	210	3,910	2,590	17.
5,340	2,660	15,020	12,660	2,030	290	2,840	2,790	18.
2,880	1,080	5,100	7,940	310	410	680	510	19.
14,040	11,290	22,330	63,400	9,560	2,070	18,900	15,680	20.
1,760	2,140	4,670	17,570	1,360	390	3,280	3,150	21.
8,180	5,490	12,820	64,500	7,640	1,080	12,220	9,190	22.
11,800	9,730	19,300	64,090	9,740	2,010	20,610	16,250	23.
1,640	1,480	3,140	7,730	1,370	180	3,330	2,150	24.
8,360	6,560	15,870	28,860	8,870	810	7,630	6,840	25.
12,200	6,890	15,930	36,030	5,320	4,180	16,370	16,970	26.
11,030	7,940	9,560	35,760	7,870	4,690	17,570	14,520	27.
700	720	620	2,530	320	40	240	220	N.C.
143,280	129,190	224,430	565,990	84,840	27,290	169,580	147,190	
240,810	190,549	405,015	1,108,402	139,688	41,129	274,356	232,143	

MALE EMPLOYMENT: 1961

South West   West Midlands

	17. Corn-wall	18. Devon	19.Som-erset	20.Gloucs.	21.Wilts.	22.Dorset	23.Here-ford	24.Shrop
1.	17,840	28,600	19,530	13,370	13,390	10,420	9,860	16,270
2.	5,170	2,580	3,080	3,250	240	1,020	120	3,900
3.	1,270	5,430	8,320	14,430	4,880	3,190	1,620	2,160
4.	–	80	40	150	20	30	10	50
5.	390	980	2,060	4,320	250	650	120	210
6.	180	450	350	3,890	140	60	1,740	3,400
7.	3,190	4,840	6,450	22,770	5,700	3,850	1,270	5,020
8.	–	430	410	3,700	90	170	20	10
9.	240	3,050	2,070	4,750	2,180	680	720	740
10.	3,140	9,740	220	1,530	30	1,040	–	–
11.	350	1,510	7,390	34,870	18,130	2,250	250	7,110
12.	190	770	1,240	2,840	230	640	260	700
13.	180	1,850	1,200	3,060	760	520	10	180
14.	90	550	1,190	340	420	10	80	20
15.	120	730	5,540	1,760	700	100	10	190
16.	1,120	2,460	1,870	2,260	370	2,590	460	750
17.	690	3,050	3,270	5,750	1,250	950	370	670
18.	410	3,320	5,350	13,480	910	830	440	590
19.	130	350	3,260	3,120	3,230	160	130	390
20.	9,480	26,050	18,590	33,710	15,670	10,880	4,190	7,030
21.	2,280	6,430	5,220	6,510	1,880	2,460	870	2,530
22.	9,670	21,750	11,630	33,040	10,700	5,360	2,770	7,380
23.	12,450	29,830	17,990	35,690	11,260	8,970	3,650	8,520
24.	1,600	4,950	2,540	5,840	1,420	1,410	690	1,490
25.	5,360	14,250	10,060	17,430	7,510	7,020	2,040	4,610
26.	8,760	20,920	12,220	20,580	9,170	7,560	2,900	6,130
27.	11,160	39,540	18,930	22,400	31,050	13,780	4,430	15,770
N.C.	580	760	470	670	240	340	130	220
Total Employed	96,040	235,250	170,490	315,510	141,820	86,940	39,160	96,040
Total Population	162,428	390,095	284,921	486,824	212,570	150,526	64,605	149,189

East Midlands

25.Staffs.	26. Warwick	27. Worcs.	28. Derby	29. Notts.	30. Leics.	31. Lincs.	32.Northants.	
12,940	9,500	10,780	9,710	9,260	8,410	40,620	8,770	1.
33,810	12,600	650	46,040	55,580	12,630	2,310	1,230	2.
16,600	15,790	3,320	3,520	10,170	4,660	8,800	3,100	3.
490	130	240	2,580	340	10	610	190	4.
5,530	7,820	4,380	2,870	4,360	1,420	4,520	990	5.
64,280	28,370	17,970	23,070	2,870	3,230	20,100	12,830	6.
43,230	56,560	14,350	12,340	18,900	26,810	17,820	13,720	7.
440	2,880	540	370	840	1,030	40	150	8.
23,450	48,480	2,600	2,470	7,690	8,630	980	2,210	9.
60	160	60	20	140	40	2,250	40	10.
21,660	147,540	3,140	28,360	10,130	5,240	2,960	9,620	11.
48,760	55,720	15,120	3,820	4,030	2,750	1,760	610	12.
5,440	6,620	6,790	17,290	14,560	19,310	1,330	110	13.
1,520	500	390	140	340	500	280	2,700	14.
1,890	1,290	670	920	2,570	11,620	120	18,540	15.
35,490	6,030	2,820	7,160	4,620	3,510	2,290	1,160	16.
6,380	7,660	1,890	2,460	4,770	3,990	2,320	1,560	17.
6,480	10,230	1,510	3,480	4,490	4,540	2,710	2,680	18.
11,710	12,250	1,510	880	1,150	5,200	920	1,520	19.
51,250	55,370	15,250	22,500	24,760	18,790	21,940	14,150	20.
11,340	11,960	4,170	5,540	5,590	3,910	3,560	2,760	21.
20,930	37,690	8,690	19,970	21,180	11,940	19,610	11,860	22.
43,680	60,190	15,140	20,570	29,460	22,110	26,050	15,050	23.
5,070	9,950	1,610	2,500	4,050	2,900	2,760	1,890	24.
18,910	27,240	9,100	9,460	12,920	10,320	8,960	5,640	25.
22,850	34,020	9,710	11,040	15,760	13,070	13,340	9,830	26.
21,690	27,550	9,630	10,070	18,940	8,470	24,500	8,070	27.
1,120	3,050	460	270	550	360	440	240	N.C.
547,000	697,150	162,490	269,420	290,020	215,400	233,900	151,220	
858,183	1,001,070	278,046	432,779	443,601	333,380	369,386	232,367	

MALE EMPLOYMENT: 1961

East Midlands	North West		Yorks. & Humberside				
33.Rutland	34. Cheshire	35.Lancs.	36. West Riding	37. East Riding	38. North Riding	39. West-morland	40. Cu...berl
1.	1,290	15,710	25,370	24,390	18,540	16,970	4,170	9,7
2.	290	2,370	42,620	123,460	410	1,440	530	6,7
3.	60	12,150	53,660	22,300	13,160	2,660	310	2,3
4.	-	7,490	3,270	4,610	170	690	20	1
5.	10	29,780	55,080	15,430	8,320	9,610	40	5,7
6.	80	4,690	32,270	88,050	3,570	29,620	-	6,1
7.	260	29,320	97,480	94,060	5,160	6,970	480	2,9
8.	-	1,120	4,010	2,410	250	650	20	4
9.	10	5,700	84,090	11,310	590	810	20	1
10.	-	11,470	18,810	1,710	4,440	2,380	70	
11.	80	19,530	68,770	28,570	9,710	1,620	40	8
12.	20	6,820	33,730	42,990	2,320	1,120	20	5
13.	-	11,110	99,370	93,890	410	2,260	350	1,8
14.	10	1,070	5,040	2,950	1,090	210	30	4
15.	80	3,320	19,400	13,710	200	260	1,180	8
16.	270	3,780	32,650	22,090	2,680	990	450	7
17.	40	2,940	24,330	16,730	4,850	1,020	420	1,1
18.	-	8,620	46,120	19,120	3,330	1,060	780	7
19.	60	3,850	35,660	5,400	800	210	50	1,1
20.	590	38,490	139,400	89,560	17,510	15,770	1,570	7,8
21.	40	8,730	32,330	26,150	3,790	2,600	640	1,6
22.	440	35,690	173,930	75,940	30,500	12,010	1,470	8,6
23.	270	34,180	185,240	113,690	24,670	12,670	2,160	6,8
24.	60	4,450	29,070	16,040	3,040	2,310	590	1,2
25.	340	14,850	74,020	46,950	9,210	6,740	1,070	4,3
26.	430	19,110	92,310	57,060	11,660	9,710	2,090	5,5
27.	2,890	17,150	76,980	49,640	12,960	20,530	1,300	9,1
N.C.	-	890	3,400	2,050	180	390	50	
Total Employed	7,620	354,380	1,588,410	1,110,260	193,520	163,280	19,920	88,2
Total Population	12,290	654,508	2,456,420	1,716,361	304,549	274,159	31,825	144,4

| | Wales | | | Scotland | | | |
41.North-umberland	42. Durham	43.Glamorgan & Monmouth	44. North & West Wales	45.Strathclyde	46.Dumfries & Galloway	47.Borders	48.Lothian	
11,080	8,010	9,370	47,250	19,710	12,290	8,080	7,150	1.
40,080	97,990	83,160	18,330	30,310	1,660	130	23,340	2.
6,970	6,650	9,130	3,680	22,510	1,180	200	11,230	3.
150	2,930	5,220	690	1,170	10	–	900	4.
3,880	26,050	10,880	3,820	12,640	1,660	50	2,340	5.
1,380	20,130	65,560	20,740	40,570	20	70	3,480	6.
14,170	29,090	15,070	3,770	77,660	930	520	4,340	7.
540	260	640	1,020	4,690	–	10	520	8.
8,020	14,250	10,910	2,380	12,260	40	20	5,420	9.
23,720	27,110	3,120	1,680	44,810	–	10	2,480	10.
1,240	9,690	9,650	6,230	25,540	160	–	870	11.
2,070	4,620	12,430	1,350	10,760	110	80	3,060	12.
800	2,940	6,040	4,780	15,680	680	5,840	1,030	13.
330	150	400	680	1,840	30	310	320	14.
530	2,120	1,920	200	4,720	–	40	340	15.
3,430	8,020	5,240	4,040	9,570	140	80	1,980	16.
3,430	5,010	4,040	2,250	10,970	990	590	3,050	17.
2,750	3,930	5,450	1,570	14,420	260	430	9,040	18.
3,310	2,460	5,690	1,020	5,550	670	30	2,100	19.
24,580	36,330	53,590	27,890	80,430	5,000	3,010	24,880	20.
5,270	7,900	11,200	6,510	13,580	900	380	3,730	21.
23,000	30,400	52,980	22,960	78,200	3,440	1,630	22,220	22.
26,710	32,450	44,180	27,140	75,850	4,210	3,140	24,360	23.
4,690	3,890	6,700	4,490	11,890	500	470	5,880	24.
11,740	15,530	22,560	17,940	34,330	2,090	1,470	13,900	25.
14,200	15,390	23,460	17,270	40,630	2,570	2,230	14,750	26.
17,880	20,190	29,890	28,850	37,460	2,050	1,120	15,350	27.
640	810	1,570	2,070	1,780	90	90	630	N.C.
256,590	434,300	510,050	280,600	739,530	41,680	30,030	208,690	
397,936	744,546	822,510	469,254	1,233,134	71,190	47,577	343,129	

MALE EMPLOYMENT: 1961

Scotland

	49.Central & Fife	50. Tayside	51.Gram-pian	52.High-land	53. South East	54. East Anglia	55. South West	56. West Midlands
1.	7,980	16,030	29,540	16,280	135,450	76,470	103,150	59,350
2.	27,910	390	410	190	14,220	1,200	15,340	51,080
3.	4,030	3,300	5,900	940	122,620	19,080	37,520	39,490
4.	1,110	160	30	20	17,240	80	320	920
5.	5,290	700	900	560	77,650	6,860	8,650	18,060
6.	11,160	690	190	840	39,000	3,280	5,070	115,760
7.	2,540	8,550	3,860	450	264,640	15,900	46,800	120,430
8.	50	580	40	–	64,410	1,500	4,800	3,890
9.	750	1,320	420	50	205,900	10,660	12,970	75,990
10.	8,000	1,460	3,100	370	49,510	2,840	15,700	280
11.	890	610	430	110	236,760	5,380	64,500	179,700
12.	1,440	740	460	190	85,790	2,190	5,910	120,560
13.	2,310	10,580	1,730	1,900	19,720	1,400	7,570	19,040
14.	80	120	70	20	10,790	530	2,600	2,510
15.	110	260	80	10	49,390	5,510	8,950	4,050
16.	3,670	390	1,560	220	66,290	5,760	10,670	45,550
17.	2,640	1,920	2,700	870	106,950	7,780	14,960	16,970
18.	4,950	2,610	3,880	250	207,250	7,950	24,300	19,250
19.	4,370	750	280	30	61,380	1,910	10,250	25,990
20.	17,960	11,800	11,660	9,890	516,550	46,210	114,380	133,090
21.	3,010	2,040	1,790	940	117,380	8,180	24,780	30,870
22.	12,360	10,630	11,350	7,110	534,030	30,130	92,150	87,460
23.	12,860	14,230	16,720	7,400	602,900	48,610	116,190	131,180
24.	1,680	2,460	2,130	830	175,930	7,030	17,760	18,810
25.	6,520	7,350	7,490	5,340	338,240	24,150	61,630	61,900
26.	7,270	8,830	7,920	4,240	460,830	42,840	79,210	75,610
27.	13,100	7,660	9,700	5,490	428,260	44,650	136,860	79,070
N.C.	240	280	300	460	20,910	820	3,060	4,980
Total Employed	164,280	116,440	124,640	65,000	5,029,990	428,900	1,046,050	1,541,840
Total Population	271,644	194,361	210,591	111,108	7,737,759	687,316	1,687,364	2,351,093

57. East Midlands	58. North West	59. Yorks. & Humberside	60. North	61. Wales	62. Scotland	63. Great Britain	
78,060	41,080	42,930	49,940	56,620	117,060	760,110	1.
118,080	44,990	123,870	146,810	101,490	84,340	701,420	2.
30,310	65,810	35,460	18,930	12,810	49,290	431,320	3.
3,730	10,760	4,780	3,960	5,910	3,400	51,100	4.
14,170	84,860	23,750	45,340	14,700	24,140	318,180	5.
62,180	36,960	91,620	57,320	86,300	57,020	554,510	6.
89,850	126,800	99,220	53,680	18,840	98,850	935,010	7.
2,430	5,130	2,660	1,940	1,660	5,890	94,310	8.
21,990	89,790	11,900	28,280	13,290	20,280	486,050	9.
2,490	30,280	6,150	53,320	4,800	60,230	225,600	10.
56,390	88,300	38,280	13,470	15,880	28,610	727,270	11.
12,990	40,550	45,310	8,390	13,780	16,840	352,310	12.
52,600	110,480	94,300	8,150	10,820	39,750	363,830	13.
3,970	6,110	4,040	1,170	1,080	2,790	35,590	14.
33,850	22,720	13,910	4,920	2,120	5,560	150,980	15.
19,010	36,430	24,770	13,600	9,280	17,610	248,970	16.
15,140	27,270	21,580	10,990	6,290	23,730	251,660	17.
17,900	54,740	22,450	9,310	7,020	35,840	406,010	18.
9,730	39,510	6,200	7,190	6,710	13,780	182,650	19.
102,730	177,890	107,070	86,130	81,480	164,630	1,530,160	20.
21,400	41,060	29,940	18,010	17,710	26,370	335,700	21.
85,000	209,620	106,440	75,520	75,940	146,940	1,443,230	22.
113,510	219,420	138,360	80,840	71,320	158,770	1,681,100	23.
14,160	33,520	19,080	12,730	11,190	25,840	336,050	24.
47,640	88,870	56,160	39,470	40,500	78,490	837,050	25.
63,470	111,420	68,720	46,930	40,730	88,440	1,078,200	26.
72,940	94,130	62,600	69,050	58,740	91,930	1,138,230	27.
1,860	4,290	2,230	1,980	3,640	3,870	47,640	N.C.
1,167,580	1,942,790	1,303,780	962,370	790,650	1,490,290	15,704,240	
1,823,803	3,110,928	2,020,910	1,592,896	1,291,764	2,482,734	24,786,567	

FEMALE EMPLOYMENT: 1961

South East

	1. London	2. Middlesex	3. Kent	4. Surrey	5. Sussex	6. Hants.	7. Berks.	8. Oxon.
1.	190	700	6,540	2,260	3,400	2,920	1,290	820
2.	1,130	30	210	60	40	20	30	20
3.	25,340	15,220	4,220	3,780	2,090	3,650	1,940	610
4.	3,010	230	330	40	–	70	10	–
5.	13,190	10,270	3,220	3,970	1,320	2,630	640	10
6.	2,510	1,530	250	540	190	10	280	370
7.	14,940	14,530	3,920	6,770	2,750	2,400	2,330	420
8.	6,930	8,390	860	4,560	1,880	380	240	120
9.	21,210	32,730	8,970	13,880	3,640	6,400	1,490	170
10.	380	100	300	100	–	960	–	10
11.	2,590	5,840	950	3,140	260	3,110	790	2,980
12.	10,870	7,880	1,070	3,370	1,400	920	1,210	50
13.	6,120	2,710	1,020	1,610	500	700	160	880
14.	5,830	720	190	340	190	50	120	–
15.	67,670	7,900	3,240	2,550	2,840	4,390	910	1,000
16.	4,200	1,710	1,450	750	350	230	180	40
17.	6,810	3,500	1,220	1,590	870	920	710	270
18.	42,150	10,710	8,070	4,710	1,370	3,240	1,630	1,180
19.	11,870	8,430	4,040	5,780	2,020	1,460	530	60
20.	10,200	4,040	1,770	2,680	1,370	1,520	560	280
21.	4,720	1,850	1,120	1,880	770	1,240	480	130
22.	47,060	13,240	5,980	5,900	3,290	5,150	2,100	1,460
23.	167,650	56,090	40,300	44,240	29,540	43,270	13,260	8,610
24.	85,060	7,080	4,460	8,560	4,540	5,440	2,170	740
25.	138,070	49,830	42,130	46,960	31,380	33,990	16,350	11,640
26.	194,740	51,490	37,520	45,910	37,900	38,820	12,950	9,650
27	50,230	11,320	7,610	10,950	4,320	10,140	4,800	2,340
N.C.	6,410	1,340	660	920	680	560	310	160
Total Employed	951,080	329,410	191,620	227,800	138,900	174,590	67,470	44,020
Total Population	1,676,125	1,165,726	888,717	918,007	594,752	744,818	256,563	153,898

9. Bucks.	10. Beds.	11. Herts.	12. Essex	13. Cambridge	14. Hunts.	15. Norfolk	16. Suffolk	
900	730	1,630	3,130	2,260	430	3,310	1,930	1.
20	20	90	50	50	40	10	20	2.
2,710	1,670	2,910	8,670	1,310	460	5,070	2,980	3.
-	-	-	380	-	-	-	60	4.
2,900	260	3,820	6,360	230	10	290	1,120	5.
750	230	1,000	1,420	20	-	40	430	6.
3,190	4,260	4,310	5,510	130	60	700	1,230	7.
910	660	2,510	4,100	340	-	300	30	8.
2,400	1,970	6,250	17,040	1,950	870	1,980	1,820	9.
20	440	20	320	20	-	60	100	10.
780	2,980	4,690	2,850	170	-	70	170	11.
1,310	340	1,130	3,400	240	20	330	110	12.
900	690	1,520	2,450	100	30	780	910	13.
260	50	260	750	60	-	290	220	14.
1,380	5,990	3,520	18,850	420	340	6,020	2,340	15.
270	380	610	2,110	90	110	130	40	16.
1,860	120	890	3,480	280	30	490	310	17.
2,940	1,410	5,570	7,960	1,120	130	1,140	1,080	18.
2,450	800	3,900	8,220	170	150	370	660	19.
510	560	1,110	2,090	210	70	410	390	20.
180	280	680	1,500	250	20	300	400	21.
1,610	1,230	2,310	6,920	880	150	1,260	1,060	22.
9,840	8,770	18,530	51,090	6,860	1,310	13,800	11,150	23.
1,150	1,060	2,310	5,240	840	40	2,210	1,100	24.
12,160	8,060	23,920	47,400	8,640	1,190	12,190	9,990	25.
11,730	6,970	16,830	40,320	5,980	1,450	12,240	11,190	26.
2,550	1,780	3,130	8,450	1,460	760	1,970	1,500	27.
250	370	330	1,050	190	20	160	130	N.C.
65,930	52,080	113,780	261,110	34,270	7,690	65,920	52,470	
247,423	190,288	427,886	1,179,656	139,876	38,795	286,715	239,831	

South West   West Midlands

	17. Corn-wall	18. Devon	19.Som-erset	20.Gloucs.	21.Wilts.	22.Dorset	23.Here-ford	24.Shrops
1.	1,660	2,480	2,270	1,690	1,230	1,040	1,090	2,060
2.	230	150	160	170	30	30	–	140
3.	320	2,220	4,080	8,660	2,460	860	910	660
4.	–	40	–	40	–	–	–	10
5.	150	230	170	1,170	230	310	20	10
6.	10	120	50	470	10	20	290	580
7.	330	1,670	830	4,010	2,340	580	230	890
8.	–	210	130	1,590	80	50	–	10
9.	30	2,510	1,160	1,770	2,110	930	360	720
10.	40	80	30	130	–	90	–	10
11.	20	230	1,470	4,960	1,760	350	60	910
12.	10	140	170	1,180	10	450	80	380
13.	490	950	780	2,030	800	530	30	300
14.	30	260	370	90	150	20	–	10
15.	490	3,120	8,030	4,090	1,320	520	160	1,460
16.	70	480	180	380	20	400	160	270
17.	50	410	600	1,290	160	70	20	80
18.	100	1,080	2,470	6,540	230	230	210	230
19.	30	180	910	1,950	1,010	130	60	500
20.	150	700	550	1,290	530	280	150	120
21.	130	630	970	990	230	240	90	190
22.	820	2,130	1,450	4,420	1,410	800	330	1,150
23.	8,400	24,500	14,120	30,390	10,690	7,150	3,010	7,570
24.	750	3,130	1,610	3,920	890	710	290	690
25.	6,380	20,690	16,980	26,280	9,580	7,680	3,130	7,950
26.	8,690	23,360	14,190	23,530	8,760	8,260	3,420	6,340
27.	1,590	3,990	3,530	7,060	4,320	1,510	690	3,520
N.C.	290	380	170	320	140	130	30	70
Total Employed	31,260	96,070	77,430	140,410	50,500	33,370	14,820	36,830
Total Population	179,873	433,656	314,125	514,882	210,415	162,934	66,323	148,277

East Midlands

25.Staffs.	26.Warwick	27.Worcs.	28.Derby	29. Notts.	30.Leics.	31.Lincs.	32. North-ants.	
1,750	1,200	1,920	1,140	1,120	1,000	6,060	1,300	1.
1,190	370	280	940	1,610	560	100	60	2.
7,740	10,750	2,550	3,050	6,600	2,640	6,940	1,530	3.
80	–	40	170	10	10	–	–	4.
1,950	4,000	1,270	990	2,870	830	550	460	5.
12,100	6,450	3,640	2,230	190	230	1,600	1,160	6.
8,640	15,600	2,770	1,960	2,750	4,580	2,570	2,370	7.
190	1,970	500	80	450	380	20	20	8.
15,520	26,280	2,150	1,330	2,970	2,990	680	1,880	9.
40	20	–	–	–	–	90	–	10.
4,970	28,320	1,370	3,560	2,060	750	390	1,120	11.
31,670	36,070	8,730	1,440	3,240	1,240	110	50	12.
6,140	7,300	4,680	16,870	23,790	31,760	1,380	270	13.
2,910	840	400	40	140	220	110	830	14.
7,440	5,740	2,680	5,250	11,460	14,700	1,600	19,530	15.
31,860	1,250	1,550	2,330	810	430	170	320	16.
1,600	1,770	590	760	1,410	620	420	380	17.
4,830	6,430	1,010	2,290	2,330	2,320	1,020	1,740	18.
4,590	6,080	1,770	730	590	2,110	430	1,270	19.
2,250	3,260	680	750	990	920	760	450	20.
1,440	2,040	820	510	490	500	420	260	21.
4,800	9,450	1,460	3,230	2,730	1,560	2,760	2,010	22.
43,510	61,710	15,710	19,550	25,090	17,350	20,180	11,860	23.
3,620	9,500	1,190	1,360	2,810	1,840	1,580	1,710	24.
33,720	49,960	14,180	16,880	19,670	14,380	15,100	9,420	25.
28,100	44,940	11,780	13,160	18,390	11,330	15,120	8,910	26.
6,600	8,330	3,360	3,480	5,390	2,180	3,600	1,790	27.
530	1,750	290	170	450	180	240	120	N.C.
269,780	351,380	87,370	104,250	140,410	117,610	84,000	70,820	
875,336	1,024,406	291,911	444,841	459,387	349,188	374,210	240,396	

FEMALE EMPLOYMENT: 1961

	East Midlands	North West		Yorks. & Humberside		North		
	33. Rut-land	34. Cheshire	35.Lancs.	36. West Riding	37. East Riding	38.North Riding	39. West-morland	40.Cumber-land
1.	130	2,060	3,770	2,940	1,170	1,450	430	1,230
2.	–	510	1,590	2,380	70	30	–	240
3.	–	7,110	40,710	17,060	10,080	1,700	170	1,950
4.	–	910	420	300	80	–	–	–
5.	10	7,500	20,260	5,690	3,740	990	10	640
6.	10	580	4,860	10,950	420	1,270	–	420
7.	30	4,820	20,270	18,440	1,210	680	100	300
8.	–	450	1,930	1,400	200	160	10	230
9.	–	3,620	38,350	7,890	180	1,070	–	180
10.	–	410	1,010	50	150	220	10	–
11.	–	2,200	10,970	3,440	1,770	820	–	80
12.	–	2,670	12,700	20,890	2,240	180	–	840
13.	20	11,740	124,420	96,280	940	1,220	480	2,080
14.	–	490	3,580	1,830	270	10	10	170
15.	340	13,860	62,480	43,130	940	2,610	620	2,680
16.	30	690	7,260	4,310	440	160	40	80
17.	–	760	6,200	3,390	1,300	140	20	160
18.	–	4,220	23,480	11,760	1,770	500	200	480
19.	180	2,280	18,940	3,320	640	130	30	710
20.	30	1,620	5,950	3,750	850	600	40	340
21.	–	930	3,860	3,020	290	320	150	130
22.	50	3,580	21,080	12,390	3,090	2,460	120	980
23.	400	34,880	183,750	105,180	20,220	14,830	1,830	7,240
24.	30	2,770	21,960	11,100	2,050	1,170	490	630
25.	460	29,990	123,170	81,340	15,800	11,750	1,760	6,790
26.	520	26,740	118,540	68,520	13,890	11,820	2,630	6,070
27.	120	4,810	24,160	13,340	2,760	2,440	190	1,840
N.C.	20	410	2,130	1,220	180	190	20	20
Total Employed	2,380	172,610	907,800	555,310	86,740	58,920	9,360	36,510
Total Population	11,214	714,471	2,672,996	1,823,829	327,135	279,943	35,355	149,873

	Wales			Scotland				
41.North-umberland	42. Durham	43.Glamorgan & Monmouth	44.North & West Wales	45.Strathclyde	46.Dumfries & Galloway	47.Borders	48.Lothian	
1,260	1,060	970	5,790	2,890	1,190	640	1,260	1.
1,030	2,220	2,300	510	680	10	10	530	2.
4,260	4,250	5,630	1,140	17,320	460	40	7,300	3.
20	90	270	80	200	–	–	70	4.
2,840	4,640	2,380	650	4,610	100	–	1,070	5.
260	1,530	5,440	980	3,290	10	–	410	6.
2,830	4,190	2,750	700	14,380	100	60	490	7.
80	80	350	1,510	4,070	–	–	140	8.
2,650	10,520	7,780	1,240	7,220	–	10	2,920	9.
1,270	1,170	220	100	2,400	–	–	160	10.
90	470	1,570	1,880	3,210	–	–	130	11.
1,000	1,060	6,330	800	3,200	–	10	860	12.
1,060	4,610	2,660	2,920	26,590	1,610	6,880	3,000	13.
220	390	610	180	1,080	–	40	50	14.
3,190	14,870	8,600	1,920	19,750	50	170	1,080	15.
650	1,350	820	420	1,280	30	–	390	16.
850	1,140	620	420	2,560	60	20	390	17.
1,660	3,290	2,570	550	9,310	100	70	5,540	18.
1,390	1,560	4,250	470	2,260	510	20	830	19.
1,290	1,020	1,600	870	4,710	80	100	1,490	20.
1,090	800	1,230	590	1,670	120	20	660	21.
3,730	3,990	5,420	2,370	15,370	660	120	3,960	22.
30,200	39,900	44,320	20,440	82,720	3,340	2,360	24,420	23.
2,990	2,320	4,290	1,510	7,430	230	140	4,680	24.
20,850	29,910	36,130	23,060	62,110	3,170	1,920	24,470	25.
19,450	23,050	27,970	19,020	49,070	4,110	2,790	20,510	26.
6,660	4,800	7,760	4,000	9,570	750	430	6,030	27.
410	480	1,090	720	650	50	20	170	N.C.
113,280	164,760	185,930	94,840	359,600	16,740	15,870	113,010	
423,307	771,097	851,897	500,362	1,334,103	75,244	53,251	382,645	

FEMALE EMPLOYMENT: 1961

Scotland

	49.Central & Fife	50. Tayside	51.Grampian	52. Highland	53. South East	54. East Anglia	55. South West	56. West Midlands
1.	1,250	1,480	1,390	1,070	24,510	7,930	10,370	8,020
2.	460	10	–	–	1,720	120	770	1,980
3.	2,030	3,170	2,900	240	72,810	9,820	18,600	22,610
4.	80	–	–	–	4,070	60	80	130
5.	1,020	210	230	50	48,590	1,650	2,260	7,250
6.	1,940	230	30	80	9,080	490	680	23,060
7.	390	1,490	440	50	65,330	2,120	9,760	28,130
8.	120	990	20	–	31,540	670	2,060	2,670
9.	160	950	160	10	116,150	6,620	8,510	45,030
10.	230	50	170	20	2,650	180	370	70
11.	60	50	30	–	30,960	410	8,790	35,630
12.	780	290	170	10	32,950	700	1,960	76,930
13.	6,050	10,930	2,730	620	19,260	1,820	5,580	18,450
14.	–	100	30	–	8,760	570	920	4,160
15.	510	860	140	–	120,240	9,120	17,570	17,480
16.	890	100	130	10	12,280	370	1,530	35,090
17.	500	190	400	20	22,240	1,110	2,580	4,060
18.	2,550	1,320	2,020	90	90,940	3,470	10,650	12,710
19.	1,480	150	70	20	49,560	1,350	4,210	13,000
20.	750	590	520	220	26,690	1,080	3,500	6,460
21.	320	320	210	130	14,830	970	3,190	4,580
22.	2,630	1,610	1,680	840	96,250	3,350	11,030	17,190
23.	14,260	13,060	12,580	5,050	491,190	33,120	95,250	131,510
24.	920	1,400	1,150	330	127,810	4,190	11,010	15,290
25.	12,400	11,510	12,250	5,870	461,890	32,010	87,590	108,940
26.	10,150	11,560	11,020	6,250	504,830	30,860	86,790	94,580
27.	3,120	1,830	1,960	1,010	117,620	5,690	22,000	22,500
N.C.	70	130	20	110	13,040	500	1,430	2,670
Total Employed	65,120	64,580	52,450	22,100	2,617,790	160,350	429,040	760,180
Total Population	285,318	217,796	232,380	115,873	8,443,859	705,217	1,815,885	2,406,253

57. East Midlands	58. North West	59. Yorks. & Humberside	60. North	61. Wales	62. Scotland	63. Great Britain	
10,750	5,830	4,110	5,430	6,760	11,170	94,880	1.
3,270	2,100	2,450	3,520	2,810	1,700	20,440	2.
20,760	47,820	27,140	12,330	6,770	33,460	272,120	3.
190	1,330	380	110	350	350	7,050	4.
5,710	27,760	9,430	9,120	3,030	7,290	122,090	5.
5,420	5,440	11,370	3,480	6,420	5,990	71,430	6.
14,260	25,090	19,650	8,100	3,450	17,400	193,290	7.
950	2,380	1,600	560	1,860	5,340	49,630	8.
9,850	41,970	8,070	14,420	9,020	11,430	271,070	9.
90	1,420	200	2,670	320	3,030	11,000	10.
7,880	13,170	5,210	1,460	3,450	3,480	110,440	11.
6,080	15,370	23,130	3,080	7,130	5,320	172,650	12.
74,090	136,160	97,220	9,450	5,580	58,410	426,020	13.
1,340	4,070	2,100	800	790	1,300	24,810	14.
52,880	76,340	44,070	23,970	10,520	22,560	394,750	15.
4,090	7,950	4,750	2,280	1,240	2,830	72,410	16.
3,590	6,960	4,690	2,310	1,040	4,140	52,720	17.
9,700	27,700	13,530	6,130	3,120	21,000	198,950	18.
5,310	21,220	3,960	3,820	4,720	5,340	112,490	19.
3,900	7,570	4,600	3,290	2,470	8,460	68,020	20.
2,180	4,790	3,310	2,490	1,820	3,450	41,610	21.
12,340	24,660	15,480	11,280	7,790	26,870	226,240	22.
94,430	218,630	125,400	94,000	64,760	157,790	1,506,080	23.
9,330	24,730	13,150	7,600	5,800	16,280	235,190	24.
75,910	153,160	97,140	71,060	59,190	133,700	1,280,590	25.
67,430	145,280	82,410	63,020	46,990	115,460	1,237,650	26.
16,560	28,970	16,100	15,930	11,760	24,700	281,830	27.
1,180	2,540	1,400	1,120	1,810	1,220	26,910	N.C.
519,470	1,080,410	642,050	382,830	280,770	709,470	7,582,360	
1,879,236	3,387,467	2,150,964	1,659,575	1,352,259	2,696,610	26,497,325	

TOTAL EMPLOYMENT: 1961

South East

	1. London	2. Middlesex	3. Kent	4. Surrey	5. Sussex	6. Hants.	7. Berks.	8. Oxon.
1.	970	3,040	31,520	11,810	23,230	21,070	9,100	7,280
2.	2,900	470	7,260	930	840	290	300	420
3.	65,690	36,640	11,850	10,040	7,040	11,760	5,700	2,210
4.	9,020	1,090	3,540	230	40	3,450	40	10
5.	31,780	21,480	10,280	11,250	3,030	6,890	1,660	160
6.	10,650	8,290	2,080	3,070	1,580	670	1,000	2,820
7.	74,360	65,760	26,850	32,520	15,200	16,190	11,790	1,950
8.	22,930	25,390	4,790	12,240	3,660	1,850	800	290
9.	56,330	90,410	22,660	37,410	10,550	17,330	4,440	1,470
10.	4,980	760	9,300	490	620	25,090	310	120
11.	14,320	37,490	8,700	23,790	4,140	28,020	5,550	25,960
12.	39,890	25,970	4,780	11,330	4,480	3,450	3,910	350
13.	12,740	4,250	2,410	3,820	950	1,450	310	1,780
14.	12,640	1,200	630	1,230	410	170	290	–
15.	102,650	10,830	3,590	3,550	3,560	5,040	1,200	1,280
16.	17,770	10,170	13,440	4,170	3,950	1,850	1,180	950
17.	40,610	20,840	6,190	7,460	5,590	6,210	3,210	1,260
18.	142,860	27,060	35,530	14,370	4,980	10,420	5,900	3,510
19.	26,490	22,120	7,900	11,890	4,390	4,020	1,600	160
20.	148,660	61,050	49,480	50,130	38,850	49,270	18,910	11,560
21.	40,190	16,430	11,370	11,820	7,680	10,900	3,770	1,270
22.	279,990	83,490	42,870	35,200	24,350	41,340	12,230	7,750
23.	400,500	119,130	86,560	92,240	66,560	89,940	28,420	17,590
24.	201,470	16,850	10,900	19,150	11,260	13,300	5,020	2,040
25.	254,160	79,740	66,430	76,110	49,520	63,450	38,280	21,250
26.	380,900	98,570	68,850	82,980	68,950	73,250	25,770	19,490
27.	182,270	48,140	46,190	42,560	23,440	87,520	24,830	10,730
N.C.	14,460	4,080	1,910	2,320	1,580	1,690	820	520
Total Employed	2,592,180	941,010	597,860	614,110	390,430	595,880	216,340	144,180
Total Population	3,200,484	2,234,543	1,701,851	1,731,042	1,077,517	1,432,546	504,154	309,452

East Anglia

9. Bucks.	10. Beds.	11. Herts.	12. Essex	13. Cambridge	14. Hunts.	15. Norfolk	16. Suffolk	
8,480	8,430	10,370	24,660	18,090	4,820	36,200	25,290	1.
350	500	610	1,070	260	320	570	170	2.
7,200	4,200	7,730	25,370	3,590	1,160	14,230	9,920	3.
20	10	40	3,820	20	10	30	80	4.
7,500	1,590	10,200	20,420	1,140	70	1,290	6,010	5.
4,300	1,730	4,830	7,060	40	–	650	3,080	6.
16,500	16,100	20,260	32,490	1,420	800	5,400	10,400	7.
2,830	2,610	7,190	11,370	1,540	–	490	140	8.
7,370	6,200	20,920	46,960	4,740	2,910	5,380	4,250	9.
130	2,690	120	7,550	200	50	1,110	1,660	10.
8,610	32,080	30,430	48,630	2,170	60	1,040	2,520	11.
4,180	1,280	5,060	14,060	820	90	1,430	550	12.
1,750	1,030	2,720	5,500	140	60	1,500	1,520	13.
500	410	520	1,550	200	10	430	460	14.
1,690	7,800	4,500	23,940	510	380	10,810	2,930	15.
3,560	6,470	4,330	10,730	1,890	2,560	820	860	16.
10,940	870	5,400	20,610	1,350	240	4,400	2,900	17.
8,280	4,070	20,590	20,620	3,150	420	3,980	3,870	18.
5,330	1,880	9,000	16,160	480	560	1,050	1,170	19.
14,550	11,850	23,440	65,490	9,770	2,140	19,310	16,070	20.
1,940	2,420	5,350	19,070	1,610	410	3,580	3,550	21.
9,790	6,720	15,130	71,420	8,520	1,230	13,480	10,250	22.
21,640	18,500	37,830	115,180	16,600	3,320	34,410	27,400	23.
2,790	2,540	5,450	12,970	2,210	220	5,540	3,250	24.
20,520	14,620	39,790	76,260	17,510	2,000	19,820	16,830	25.
23,930	13,860	32,760	76,350	11,300	5,630	28,610	28,160	26.
13,580	9,720	12,690	44,210	9,330	5,450	19,540	16,020	27.
950	1,090	950	3,580	510	60	400	350	N.C.
209,210	181,270	338,210	827,100	119,110	34,980	235,500	199,660	
488,233	380,837	832,901	2,288,058	279,564	79,924	561,071	471,974	

TOTAL EMPLOYMENT: 1961

South West   West Midlands

	17. Corn-wall	18. Devon	19.Som-erset	20.Gloucs.	21.Wilts.	22.Dorset	23.Here-ford	24.Shrops.
1.	19,500	31,080	21,800	15,060	14,620	11,460	10,950	18,330
2.	5,400	2,730	3,240	3,420	270	1,050	120	4,040
3.	1,590	7,650	12,400	23,090	7,340	4,050	2,530	2,820
4.	-	120	40	190	20	30	10	60
5.	540	1,210	2,230	5,490	480	960	140	220
6.	190	570	400	4,360	150	80	2,030	3,980
7.	3,520	6,510	7,280	26,780	8,040	4,430	1,500	5,910
8.	-	640	540	5,290	170	220	20	20
9.	270	5,560	3,230	6,520	4,290	1,610	1,080	1,460
10.	3,180	9,820	250	1,660	30	1,130	-	10
11.	370	1,740	8,860	39,830	19,890	2,600	310	8,020
12.	200	910	1,410	4,020	240	1,090	340	1,080
13.	670	2,800	1,980	5,090	1,560	1,050	40	480
14.	120	810	1,560	430	570	30	80	30
15.	610	3,850	13,570	5,850	2,020	620	170	1,650
16.	1,190	2,940	2,050	2,640	390	2,990	620	1,020
17.	740	3,460	3,870	7,040	1,410	1,020	390	750
18.	510	4,400	7,820	20,020	1,140	1,060	650	820
19.	160	530	4,170	5,070	4,240	290	190	890
20.	9,630	26,750	19,140	35,000	16,200	11,160	4,340	7,150
21.	2,410	7,060	6,190	7,500	2,110	2,700	960	2,720
22.	10,490	23,880	13,080	37,460	12,110	6,160	3,100	8,530
23.	20,850	54,330	32,110	66,080	21,950	16,120	6,660	16,090
24.	2,350	8,080	4,150	9,760	2,310	2,120	980	2,180
25.	11,740	34,940	27,040	43,710	17,090	14,700	5,170	12,560
26.	17,450	44,280	26,410	44,110	17,930	15,820	6,320	12,470
27.	12,750	43,530	22,460	29,460	35,370	15,290	5,120	19,290
N.C.	870	1,140	640	990	380	470	160	290
Total Employed	127,300	331,320	247,920	455,920	192,320	120,310	53,980	132,870
Total Population	342,301	823,751	599,046	1,001,706	422,985	313,460	130,928	297,466

East Midlands

25.Staffs.	26.Warwick	27.Worcs.	28.Derby	29.Notts.	30.Leics.	31.Lincs.	32.Northants.	
14,690	10,700	12,700	10,850	10,380	9,410	46,680	10,070	1.
35,000	12,970	930	46,980	57,190	13,190	2,410	1,290	2.
24,340	26,540	5,870	6,570	16,770	7,300	15,740	4,630	3.
570	130	280	2,750	350	20	610	190	4.
7,480	11,820	5,650	3,860	7,230	2,250	5,070	1,450	5.
76,380	34,820	21,610	25,300	3,060	3,460	21,700	13,990	6.
51,870	72,160	17,120	14,300	21,650	31,390	20,390	16,090	7.
630	4,850	1,040	450	1,290	1,410	60	170	8.
38,970	74,760	4,750	3,800	10,660	11,620	1,660	4,090	9.
100	180	60	20	140	40	2,340	40	10.
26,630	175,860	4,510	31,920	12,190	5,990	3,350	10,740	11.
80,430	91,790	23,850	5,260	7,270	3,990	1,870	660	12.
11,580	13,920	11,470	34,160	38,350	51,070	2,710	380	13.
4,430	1,340	790	180	480	720	390	3,530	14.
9,330	7,030	3,350	6,170	14,030	26,320	1,720	38,070	15.
67,350	7,280	4,370	9,490	5,430	3,940	2,460	1,480	16.
7,980	9,430	2,480	3,220	6,180	4,610	2,740	1,940	17.
11,310	16,660	2,520	5,770	6,820	6,860	3,730	4,420	18.
16,300	18,330	3,280	1,610	1,740	7,310	1,350	2,790	19.
53,500	58,630	15,930	23,250	25,750	19,710	22,700	14,600	20.
12,780	14,000	4,990	6,050	6,080	4,410	3,980	3,020	21.
35,730	47,140	10,150	23,200	23,910	13,500	22,370	13,870	22.
87,190	121,900	30,850	40,120	54,550	39,460	46,230	26,910	23.
8,690	19,450	2,800	3,860	6,860	4,740	4,340	3,600	24.
52,630	77,200	23,280	26,340	32,590	24,700	24,060	15,060	25.
50,950	78,960	21,490	24,200	34,150	24,400	28,460	18,740	26.
28,290	35,880	12,990	13,550	24,330	10,650	28,100	9,860	27.
1,650	4,800	750	440	1,000	540	680	360	N.C.
816,780	1,048,530	249,860	373,670	430,430	333,010	317,900	222,040	
1,733,519	2,025,476	569,957	877,620	902,988	682,568	743,596	472,763	

TOTAL EMPLOYMENT: 1961

	East Midlands	North West	Yorks. & Humberside			North		
	33.Rutland	34. Cheshire	35.Lancs.	36. West Riding	37. East Riding	38.North Riding	39.Westmorland	40.Cumberland
1.	1,420	17,770	29,140	27,330	19,710	18,420	4,600	10,940
2.	290	2,880	44,210	125,840	480	1,470	530	7,010
3.	60	19,260	94,370	39,360	23,240	4,360	480	4,290
4.	–	8,400	3,690	4,910	250	690	20	170
5.	20	37,280	75,340	21,120	12,060	10,600	50	6,400
6.	90	5,270	37,130	99,000	3,990	30,890	–	6,610
7.	290	34,140	117,750	112,500	6,370	7,650	580	3,270
8.	–	1,570	5,940	3,810	450	810	30	700
9.	10	9,320	122,440	19,200	770	1,880	20	360
10.	–	11,880	19,820	1,760	4,590	2,600	80	40
11.	80	21,730	79,740	32,010	11,480	2,440	40	960
12.	20	9,490	46,430	63,880	4,560	1,300	20	1,400
13.	20	22,850	223,790	190,170	1,350	3,480	830	3,880
14.	10	1,560	8,620	4,780	1,360	220	40	620
15.	420	17,180	81,880	56,840	1,140	2,870	1,800	3,510
16.	300	4,470	39,910	26,400	3,120	1,150	490	790
17.	40	3,700	30,530	20,120	6,150	1,160	440	1,270
18.	–	12,840	69,600	30,880	5,100	1,560	980	1,270
19.	240	6,130	54,600	8,720	1,440	340	80	1,870
20.	620	40,110	145,350	93,310	18,360	16,370	1,610	8,220
21.	40	9,660	36,190	29,170	4,080	2,920	790	1,730
22.	490	39,270	195,010	88,330	33,590	14,470	1,590	9,620
23.	670	69,060	368,990	218,870	44,890	27,500	3,990	14,090
24.	90	7,220	51,030	27,140	5,090	3,480	1,080	1,880
25.	800	44,840	197,190	128,290	25,010	18,490	2,830	11,180
26.	950	45,850	210,850	125,580	25,550	21,530	4,720	11,610
27.	3,010	21,960	101,140	62,980	15,720	22,970	1,490	10,990
N.C.	20	1,300	5,530	3,270	360	580	70	110
Total Employed	10,000	526,990	2,496,210	1,665,570	280,260	222,200	29,280	124,790
Total Population	23,504	1,368,979	5,129,416	3,540,190	631,684	554,102	67,180	294,303

		Wales		Scotland				
41.North-umberland	42. Durham	43.Glamorgan & Monmouth	44.North & West Wales	45.Strathclyde	46.Dumfries & Galloway	47.Borders	48.Lothian	
12,340	9,070	10,340	53,040	22,600	13,480	8,720	8,410	1.
41,110	100,210	85,460	18,840	30,990	1,670	140	23,870	2.
11,230	10,900	14,760	4,820	39,830	1,640	240	18,530	3.
170	3,020	5,490	770	1,370	10	–	970	4.
6,720	30,690	13,260	4,470	17,250	1,760	50	3,410	5.
1,640	21,660	71,000	21,720	43,860	30	70	3,890	6.
17,000	33,280	17,820	4,470	92,040	1,030	580	4,830	7.
620	340	990	2,530	8,760	–	10	660	8.
10,670	24,770	18,690	3,620	19,480	40	30	8,340	9.
24,990	28,280	3,340	1,780	47,210	–	10	2,640	10.
1,330	10,160	11,220	8,110	28,750	160	–	1,000	11.
3,070	5,680	18,760	2,150	13,960	110	90	3,920	12.
1,860	7,550	8,700	7,700	42,270	2,290	12,720	4,030	13.
550	540	1,010	860	2,920	30	350	370	14.
3,720	16,990	10,520	2,120	24,470	50	210	1,420	15.
4,080	9,370	6,060	4,460	10,850	170	80	2,370	16.
4,280	6,150	4,660	2,670	13,530	1,050	610	3,440	17.
4,410	7,220	8,020	2,120	23,730	360	500	14,580	18.
4,700	4,020	9,940	1,490	7,810	1,180	50	2,930	19.
25,870	37,350	55,190	28,760	85,140	5,080	3,110	26,370	20.
6,360	8,700	12,430	7,100	15,250	1,020	400	4,390	21.
26,730	34,390	58,400	25,330	93,570	4,100	1,750	26,180	22.
56,910	72,350	88,500	47,580	158,570	7,550	5,500	48,780	23.
7,680	6,210	10,990	6,000	19,320	730	610	10,560	24.
32,590	45,440	58,690	41,000	96,440	5,260	3,390	38,370	25.
33,650	38,440	51,430	36,290	89,700	6,680	5,020	35,260	26.
24,540	24,990	37,650	32,850	47,030	2,800	1,550	21,380	27.
1,050	1,290	2,660	2,790	2,430	140	110	800	N.C.
369,870	599,060	695,980	375,440	1,099,130	58,420	45,900	321,700	
821,243	1,515,643	1,674,407	969,616	2,567,237	146,434	100,828	725,774	

TOTAL EMPLOYMENT: 1961

Scotland

	49.Central & Fife	50. Tayside	51.Grampian	52.Highland	53.South East	54.East Anglia	55. South West	56. West Midlan
1.	9,230	17,510	30,930	17,350	159,960	84,400	113,520	67,3
2.	28,370	400	410	190	15,940	1,320	16,110	53,0
3.	6,060	6,470	8,800	1,180	195,430	28,900	56,120	62,1
4.	1,190	160	30	20	21,310	140	400	1,0
5.	6,310	910	1,130	610	126,240	8,510	10,910	25,3
6.	13,100	920	220	920	48,080	3,770	5,750	138,8
7.	2,930	10,040	4,300	500	329,970	18,020	56,560	148,5
8.	170	1,570	60	–	95,950	2,170	6,860	6,5
9.	910	2,270	580	60	322,050	17,280	21,480	121,0
10.	8,230	1,510	3,270	390	52,160	3,020	16,070	3
11.	950	660	460	110	267,720	5,790	73,290	215,3
12.	2,220	1,030	630	200	118,740	2,890	7,870	197,4
13.	8,360	21,510	4,460	2,520	38,980	3,220	13,150	37,4
14.	80	220	100	20	19,550	1,100	3,520	6,6
15.	620	1,120	220	10	169,630	14,630	26,520	21,5
16.	4,560	490	1,690	230	78,570	6,130	12,200	80,6
17.	3,140	2,110	3,100	890	129,190	8,890	17,540	21,0
18.	7,500	3,930	5,900	340	298,190	11,420	34,950	31,9
19.	5,850	900	350	50	110,940	3,260	14,460	38,9
20.	18,710	12,390	12,180	10,110	543,240	47,290	117,880	139,5
21.	3,330	2,360	2,000	1,070	132,210	9,150	27,970	35,4
22.	14,990	12,240	13,030	7,950	630,280	33,480	103,180	104,6
23.	27,120	27,290	29,300	12,450	1,094,090	81,730	211,440	262,6
24.	2,600	3,860	3,280	1,160	303,740	11,220	28,770	34,1
25.	18,920	18,860	19,740	11,210	800,130	56,160	149,220	170,8
26.	17,420	20,390	18,940	10,490	965,660	73,700	166,000	170,1
27.	16,220	9,490	11,660	6,500	545,880	50,340	158,860	101,5
N.C.	310	410	320	570	33,950	1,320	4,490	7,6
Total Employed	229,400	181,020	177,090	87,100	7,647,780	589,250	1,475,090	2,302,0
Total Population	556,962	412,157	442,971	226,981	16,181,618	1,392,533	3,503,249	4,757,3

7. East Midlands	58. North West	59. Yorks. & Humberside	60. North	61. Wales	62. Scotland	63. Great Britain	
88,810	46,910	47,040	55,370	63,380	128,230	854,990	1.
121,350	47,090	126,320	150,330	104,300	86,040	721,860	2.
51,070	113,630	62,600	31,260	19,580	82,750	703,440	3.
3,920	12,090	5,160	4,070	6,260	3,750	58,150	4.
19,880	112,620	33,180	54,460	17,730	31,430	440,270	5.
67,600	42,400	102,990	60,800	92,720	63,010	625,940	6.
104,110	151,890	118,870	61,780	22,290	116,250	1,128,300	7.
3,380	7,510	4,260	2,500	3,520	11,230	143,940	8.
31,840	131,760	19,970	37,700	22,310	31,710	757,120	9.
2,580	31,700	6,350	55,990	5,120	63,260	236,600	10.
64,270	101,470	43,490	14,930	19,330	32,090	837,710	11.
19,070	55,920	68,440	11,470	20,910	22,160	524,960	12.
126,690	246,640	191,520	17,600	16,400	98,160	789,850	13.
5,310	10,180	6,140	1,970	1,870	4,090	60,400	14.
86,730	99,060	57,980	28,890	12,640	28,120	545,730	15.
23,100	44,380	29,520	15,880	10,520	20,440	321,380	16.
18,730	34,230	26,270	13,300	7,330	27,870	304,380	17.
27,600	82,440	35,980	15,440	10,140	56,840	604,960	18.
15,040	60,730	10,160	11,010	11,430	19,120	295,140	19.
106,630	185,460	111,670	89,420	83,950	173,090	1,598,180	20.
23,580	45,850	33,250	20,500	19,530	29,820	377,310	21.
97,340	234,280	121,920	86,800	83,730	173,810	1,669,470	22.
207,940	438,050	263,760	174,840	136,080	316,560	3,187,180	23.
23,490	58,250	32,230	20,330	16,990	42,120	571,240	24.
123,550	242,030	153,300	110,530	99,690	212,190	2,117,640	25.
130,900	256,700	151,130	109,950	87,720	203,900	2,315,850	26.
89,500	123,100	78,700	84,980	70,500	116,630	1,420,060	27.
3,040	6,830	3,630	3,100	5,450	5,090	74,550	N.C.
,687,050	3,023,200	1,945,830	1,345,200	1,071,420	2,199,760	23,286,600	
,703,039	6,498,395	4,171,874	3,252,471	2,644,023	5,179,344	51,283,892	

MALE EMPLOYMENT: 1971

South East

	1. London	2. Middlesex	3. Kent	4. Surrey	5. Sussex	6. Hants.	7. Berks.	8. Oxon.
1.	4,210		14,940	5,710	15,600	13,250	5,340	5,080
2.	3,240		4,730	650	310	540	460	250
3.	67,270		6,250	2,510	5,550	7,510	3,440	2,310
4.	6,380		2,540	1,390	30	2,140	200	10
5.	45,170		5,290	3,590	3,000	6,060	1,170	230
6.	17,040		1,770	500	2,520	1,260	1,020	1,280
7.	100,120		17,040	17,090	15,460	25,470	11,550	2,180
8.	25,130		1,720	4,220	3,310	2,260	840	350
9.	106,010		9,910	9,730	12,840	22,050	8,380	1,370
10.	5,160		7,610	450	820	18,510	320	310
11.	57,240		6,290	11,030	1,290	20,380	4,380	21,950
12.	51,270		5,180	6,010	5,010	5,660	4,590	420
13.	9,890	Included	840	530	540	810	210	630
14.	7,480	Under	390	230	210	60	330	10
15.	32,950	'London'	520	260	650	730	280	150
16.	18,070		8,760	2,940	3,650	1,980	1,740	1,200
17.	44,660		5,780	3,360	6,380	6,740	2,790	1,660
18.	110,030		23,680	4,150	5,020	8,620	6,180	3,430
19.	30,700		5,360	4,930	3,240	4,470	1,170	370
20.	230,700		39,030	26,160	38,160	52,650	19,690	12,990
21.	49,740		8,250	4,550	6,720	9,830	3,430	1,420
22.	341,880		33,140	20,090	21,030	39,070	10,780	6,320
23.	293,600		32,350	22,200	34,970	45,060	15,620	9,380
24.	198,390		8,170	8,660	11,370	10,400	4,570	2,200
25.	202,370		25,360	23,420	24,990	33,610	23,310	13,230
26.	227,390		26,450	21,150	30,010	36,980	13,750	11,000
27.	210,790		28,570	19,470	21,320	78,950	14,730	12,990
N.C.	29,440		1,620	1,500	1,820	2,330	1,080	510
Total Employed	2,526,320		331,540	226,480	275,820	457,380	161,350	113,230
Total Population	3,578,240		673,460	483,295	566,455	809,405	315,530	191,835

9. Bucks.	10. Beds.	11. Herts.	12. Essex	East Anglia 13. Cambridge	14. Hunts.	15. Norfolk	16. Suffolk	
5,700	4,690	5,370	14,300	9,910	4,230	22,030	15,350	1.
210	140	800	760	80	260	760	300	2.
7,310	2,320	4,160	8,040	2,900	1,200	9,930	7,610	3.
90	10	50	3,520	20	10	30	50	4.
5,560	1,210	9,490	7,230	1,580	240	1,960	4,200	5.
3,000	1,340	3,220	2,260	60	220	800	2,860	6.
14,820	11,050	17,460	20,590	2,240	6,410	6,340	9,840	7.
2,710	2,380	4,620	2,540	2,290	80	780	820	8.
5,730	5,670	17,280	21,180	2,630	2,710	4,240	3,210	9.
290	1,520	270	2,000	230	40	1,680	1,560	10.
7,840	29,380	22,740	11,530	1,810	7,560	3,160	3,680	11.
5,030	2,670	6,790	7,820	880	320	1,730	1,520	12.
1,060	310	690	1,570	110	50	810	960	13.
100	350	170	210	200	10	110	210	14.
410	1,350	620	2,370	80	60	3,400	550	15.
3,180	5,520	3,480	5,660	2,200	2,650	1,640	1,000	16.
7,330	1,090	4,960	8,170	860	840	4,960	3,300	17.
7,080	3,700	14,910	11,360	3,250	1,650	3,580	3,390	18.
4,180	1,990	5,720	4,080	420	1,720	1,900	1,170	19.
16,210	11,660	23,410	38,980	10,420	6,430	22,940	19,520	20.
2,320	1,870	4,690	7,570	1,030	1,310	2,770	3,710	21.
8,430	7,660	13,200	27,910	6,290	4,770	11,210	10,750	22.
14,490	10,150	23,610	31,980	8,270	5,170	19,700	15,230	23.
3,430	2,440	5,660	7,340	1,840	950	4,350	2,950	24.
11,970	9,250	20,720	24,240	11,650	3,390	10,470	8,690	25.
12,840	9,240	17,060	21,880	5,730	6,050	13,800	19,330	26.
12,430	8,210	10,910	22,570	6,500	7,610	12,500	11,620	27.
1,060	630	1,170	2,020	290	250	460	860	N.C
164,810	137,800	243,230	319,680	83,770	66,190	168,040	154,240	
291,130	232,415	453,870	661,065	150,830	101,601	300,595	269,435	

MALE EMPLOYMENT: 1971

South West							West Midlands	
	17. Corn-wall	18. Devon	19. Som-erset	20. Gloucs.	21. Wilts.	22. Dorset	23. Here-ford	24. Shrops
1.	12,660	19,830	13,350	9,830	9,230	7,290	7,000	11,610
2.	6,290	2,270	2,000	960	100	490	170	1,230
3.	2,010	6,520	7,500	13,690	6,600	3,210	2,580	2,390
4.	10	140	100	140	10	–	10	130
5.	220	700	3,730	5,130	670	990	190	340
6.	180	940	870	4,240	200	150	2,600	3,700
7.	4,310	7,350	8,670	25,800	9,580	5,700	1,670	7,810
8.	610	1,020	930	6,340	320	310	20	30
9.	570	4,180	1,850	6,190	7,510	3,170	450	1,010
10.	2,450	11,920	60	760	40	1,510	–	10
11.	200	2,060	8,610	30,640	10,850	2,590	320	6,520
12.	560	1,380	2,010	5,250	1,750	1,270	610	2,040
13.	840	2,260	1,190	3,810	460	810	30	350
14.	260	270	1,280	310	250	10	–	–
15.	230	1,300	5,090	1,500	720	100	40	250
16.	1,010	2,340	1,990	1,960	750	1,710	480	790
17.	800	3,830	4,000	5,680	2,290	1,030	500	1,080
18.	790	3,660	6,340	14,560	1,260	1,000	200	530
19.	280	720	2,240	4,520	4,800	220	510	560
20.	12,780	29,450	19,580	31,660	16,190	11,320	3,790	9,870
21.	2,200	5,340	5,380	6,110	1,870	2,170	470	2,020
22.	7,240	17,520	10,250	27,050	8,040	4,580	2,350	6,100
23.	10,970	26,650	17,000	33,180	11,880	9,040	3,000	7,640
24.	1,790	5,740	3,530	8,400	2,190	2,150	740	1,830
25.	5,500	16,970	13,260	22,470	9,190	8,400	2,060	5,380
26.	9,470	22,160	13,970	20,650	9,030	7,460	2,950	6,150
27.	9,850	33,030	18,190	22,660	23,930	12,040	3,720	11,500
N.C.	600	1,150	740	1,500	590	520	190	400
Total Employed	94,680	230,700	173,710	314,990	140,300	89,240	36,650	91,270
Total Population	181,735	426,785	327,630	524,375	240,160	173,295	68,160	167,045

25.Staffs.	26. War- wick	27. Worcs.	28. Derby	29. Notts.	30. Leics.	31. Lincs.	32. North- ants.	
9,740	6,480	7,340	7,180	6,480	5,700	29,290	4,960	1.
18,680	6,870	250	21,160	44,250	9,330	1,150	280	2.
14,870	14,420	4,980	3,490	10,440	5,460	9,520	4,170	3.
630	190	20	1,690	420	30	1,190	10	4.
5,650	6,350	3,200	4,430	4,850	2,490	6,380	2,150	5.
54,060	27,780	22,200	19,200	2,230	3,830	19,220	13,380	6.
49,820	42,540	18,740	15,400	18,640	31,370	16,180	11,300	7.
1,020	2,140	630	720	1,160	1,980	210	180	8.
22,960	40,370	3,450	2,610	7,920	8,450	2,200	2,780	9.
310	1,860	150	50	150	80	1,970	120	10.
19,970	139,350	4,940	22,810	8,570	6,550	3,050	2,900	11.
45,620	53,900	27,300	4,930	6,180	4,780	2,280	2,490	12.
4,340	4,550	7,760	15,140	14,610	18,680	2,960	360	13.
1,240	330	430	140	370	300	250	2,600	14.
2,290	1,300	600	1,020	2,440	7,230	210	11,280	15.
31,870	5,610	4,010	7,410	5,180	3,750	2,540	950	16.
7,860	5,530	2,960	4,030	4,230	3,910	3,100	1,790	17.
7,230	10,570	2,030	4,130	4,710	4,910	3,650	2,370	18.
19,040	12,460	1,650	1,730	1,880	5,860	2,150	1,660	19.
48,550	52,990	17,420	23,440	24,550	20,330	24,100	14,020	20.
9,070	10,540	3,130	5,440	7,100	4,690	3,390	2,030	21.
28,260	36,320	9,990	17,930	16,600	12,520	18,080	8,100	22.
41,770	51,350	16,400	16,900	26,260	21,130	23,500	11,980	23.
7,090	15,140	3,170	3,640	5,450	4,280	3,580	2,680	24.
24,810	38,150	10,020	12,210	16,000	14,290	10,680	6,620	25.
26,340	33,870	11,120	12,850	17,520	14,260	13,980	8,890	26.
21,020	28,150	9,800	7,820	16,250	8,980	23,110	6,040	27.
2,360	4,270	1,000	890	940	770	890	420	N.C.
526,470	653,380	194,690	238,390	275,380	225,940	228,810	126,510	
921,275	1,030,690	340,645	436,360	481,100	380,500	399,750	230,254	

MALE EMPLOYMENT: 1971

	East Midlands	North West		Yorks. & Humberside		North		
	33. Rutland	34. Cheshire	35. Lancs.	36. West Riding	37. East Riding	38. North-Riding	39. Westmorland	40. Cumberland
1.	870	10,700	16,780	16,940	11,890	13,100	3,380	7,070
2.	50	1,270	14,910	81,910	280	810	480	2,970
3.	110	12,610	55,230	30,290	6,410	3,260	770	2,780
4.	–	6,720	3,130	3,930	70	1,280	–	60
5.	40	31,450	50,840	15,190	6,000	27,980	50	5,300
6.	30	4,610	22,440	71,740	1,690	23,330	–	5,320
7.	380	30,440	90,730	81,250	6,970	10,010	870	2,560
8.	–	1,250	4,200	3,000	210	610	–	550
9.	110	8,920	71,530	16,930	670	1,580	160	240
10.	–	10,080	15,630	1,290	3,450	4,890	40	60
11.	30	30,370	70,710	27,660	8,130	2,490	60	820
12.	40	7,720	39,160	51,760	1,430	2,560	20	1,170
13.	–	8,370	74,290	75,700	490	2,860	260	2,360
14.	90	720	4,230	2,380	1,030	150	–	600
15.	120	3,050	15,180	12,560	300	690	1,270	1,240
16.	430	4,300	31,450	22,540	2,630	1,620	740	820
17.	30	3,930	24,170	17,740	3,880	2,290	380	720
18.	50	10,570	48,050	20,200	2,180	1,310	860	1,550
19.	20	3,660	29,310	8,160	1,260	490	50	1,570
20.	770	44,420	134,270	97,170	14,150	22,080	2,630	8,420
21.	20	8,530	27,130	24,020	2,790	3,340	460	1,360
22.	290	32,910	139,290	74,170	17,810	12,630	1,160	7,350
23.	370	34,150	144,660	98,250	16,000	15,170	1,650	6,160
24.	30	7,800	38,050	21,940	2,700	3,060	570	1,300
25.	430	22,260	90,230	61,750	9,800	9,450	1,140	5,110
26.	500	23,320	85,730	63,640	9,340	12,570	2,350	5,340
27.	2,630	19,050	78,410	51,550	9,530	19,900	1,030	6,810
N.C.	20	1,690	6,380	3,630	420	880	30	190
Total Employed	7,460	384,870	1,426,120	1,057,290	141,510	200,390	20,410	79,800
Total Population	14,155	745,895	2,472,610	1,792,130	312,765	357,475	34,800	142,660

		Wales			Scotland				
41.North- umberland	42. Durham	43. Mon- mouth & Glamorgan	44.North & West Wales	45.Strathclyde	46.Dumfries & Galloway	47.Borders	48.Lothian	
7,930	5,310	6,240	33,920	12,770	8,370	5,240	4,890	1.
17,110	40,570	40,740	9,050	11,330	290	200	11,360	2.
8,160	7,000	8,020	4,350	26,650	1,720	370	10,650	3.
60	1,750	10,100	890	710	-	-	90	4.
5,660	6,310	9,630	2,960	11,120	2,180	100	1,950	5.
2,450	17,740	55,130	20,020	33,540	90	40	2,730	6.
13,050	31,210	23,280	5,850	60,990	1,380	510	5,240	7.
520	820	1,110	1,610	5,180	-	20	870	8.
9,320	20,640	12,740	3,980	17,750	50	540	7,400	9.
15,330	15,430	1,060	1,340	27,170	-	40	2,000	10.
610	6,210	14,240	8,680	26,060	230	50	5,110	11.
2,780	5,340	13,230	2,700	14,510	390	300	3,380	12.
1,280	6,820	6,550	6,240	13,000	820	4,880	1,160	13.
240	120	360	420	1,500	-	230	200	14.
920	2,490	2,090	620	3,660	170	80	340	15.
3,660	7,730	4,580	3,410	9,030	220	100	2,990	16.
3,270	4,810	5,700	2,730	11,390	760	570	2,970	17.
3,220	5,570	7,140	2,000	13,020	210	220	6,710	18.
2,720	5,250	7,450	2,370	5,170	780	120	1,900	19.
26,980	38,120	54,610	33,180	78,210	4,390	2,850	25,020	20.
5,750	5,380	10,120	7,120	10,970	920	420	4,710	21.
18,540	26,420	39,450	17,060	62,800	2,870	1,250	19,140	22.
19,520	26,630	38,840	21,070	56,970	3,570	2,620	18,950	23.
5,330	5,010	8,670	4,630	14,860	770	560	7,240	24.
17,180	19,200	27,700	17,390	42,800	2,140	1,460	19,370	25.
14,040	15,840	25,120	17,970	38,010	2,600	2,210	14,510	26.
18,120	18,480	30,320	21,960	43,450	2,140	1,320	18,490	27.
570	1,080	2,130	1,140	2,060	130	30	400	N.C.
224,320	347,280	466,350	254,660	654,680	37,190	26,330	199,770	
384,125	689,945	840,055	487,455	1,230,120	69,440	46,100	361,845	

MALE EMPLOYMENT: 1971

Scotland

	49.Central & Fife	50. Tayside	51.Grampian	52.Highland	53. South East	54. East Anglia	55. South West	56. West Midlands
1.	5,650	10,060	19,610	10,210	94,190	51,520	72,190	42,170
2.	10,490	1,400	340	210	12,090	1,400	12,110	27,200
3.	4,620	3,920	8,910	2,360	116,670	21,640	39,530	39,240
4.	1,340	90	90	-	16,360	110	400	980
5.	5,740	840	620	100	88,000	7,980	11,440	15,730
6.	6,250	620	110	950	35,210	3,940	6,580	110,340
7.	6,240	9,390	3,930	1,070	252,830	24,830	61,410	120,580
8.	480	2,220	70	70	50,080	3,970	9,530	3,840
9.	2,460	1,560	340	160	220,150	12,790	23,470	68,240
10.	5,270	1,100	2,780	180	37,260	3,510	16,740	2,330
11.	1,310	210	560	60	194,050	16,210	54,950	171,100
12.	1,850	1,370	1,030	170	100,450	4,450	12,220	129,470
13.	2,150	8,280	1,970	1,740	17,080	1,930	9,370	17,030
14.	20	40	20	40	9,540	530	2,380	2,000
15.	400	260	80	10	40,290	4,090	8,940	4,480
16.	4,840	530	1,240	310	56,180	7,490	9,760	42,760
17.	2,970	1,990	2,920	820	92,920	9,960	17,630	17,930
18.	5,150	3,030	4,180	1,130	198,160	11,870	27,610	20,560
19.	2,860	190	500	90	66,210	5,210	12,780	34,220
20.	18,580	13,240	13,630	10,320	509,640	59,310	120,980	132,620
21.	3,360	1,870	1,650	820	100,390	8,820	23,070	25,230
22.	9,900	7,300	8,620	5,800	529,510	33,020	74,680	83,020
23.	10,570	10,670	12,440	5,250	533,410	48,370	108,720	120,160
24.	2,090	2,770	2,140	1,100	262,630	10,090	23,800	27,970
25.	9,250	8,250	8,690	5,650	412,470	34,200	75,790	80,420
26.	7,810	8,400	8,540	5,310	427,750	44,910	82,740	80,430
27.	14,880	7,600	10,510	7,710	440,940	38,230	119,700	74,190
N.C.	290	250	400	300	43,180	1,860	5,100	8,220
Total Employed	146,820	107,450	115,920	61,940	4,957,640	472,240	1,043,620	1,502,460
Total Population	282,710	196,975	211,160	116,270	8,256,700	822,461	1,873,980	2,527,815

57. East Midlands	58. North West	59. Yorks. & Humberside	60. North	61. Wales	62. Scotland	63. Great Britain	
54,480	27,480	28,830	36,790	40,160	76,800	524,610	1.
76,220	16,180	82,190	61,940	49,790	35,620	374,740	2.
33,190	67,840	36,700	21,970	12,370	59,200	448,350	3.
3,340	9,850	4,000	3,150	10,990	2,320	51,500	4.
20,340	82,290	21,190	45,300	12,590	22,650	327,510	5.
57,890	27,050	73,430	48,840	75,150	44,330	482,760	6.
93,270	121,170	88,220	57,700	29,130	88,750	937,890	7.
4,250	5,450	3,210	2,500	2,720	8,910	94,460	8.
24,070	80,450	17,600	31,940	16,720	30,260	525,690	9.
2,370	25,710	4,740	35,750	2,400	38,540	169,350	10.
43,910	101,080	35,790	10,190	22,920	33,590	683,790	11.
20,700	46,880	53,190	11,870	15,930	23,000	418,160	12.
51,750	82,660	76,190	13,580	12,790	34,000	316,380	13.
3,750	4,950	3,410	1,110	780	2,050	30,500	14.
22,300	18,230	12,860	6,610	2,710	5,000	125,510	15.
20,260	35,750	25,170	14,570	7,990	19,260	239,190	16.
17,090	28,100	21,620	11,470	8,430	24,390	249,540	17.
19,820	58,620	22,380	12,510	9,140	33,650	414,320	18.
13,300	32,970	9,420	10,080	9,820	11,610	205,620	19.
107,210	178,690	111,320	98,230	87,790	166,240	1,572,030	20.
22,670	35,660	26,810	16,290	17,240	24,720	300,900	21.
73,520	172,200	91,980	66,100	56,510	117,680	1,298,220	22.
100,140	178,810	114,250	69,130	59,910	121,040	1,453,940	23.
19,660	45,850	24,640	15,270	13,300	31,530	474,740	24.
60,230	112,490	71,550	52,080	45,090	97,610	1,041,930	25.
68,000	109,050	72,980	'50,140	43,090	87,390	1,066,480	26.
64,830	97,460	61,080	64,340	52,280	106,100	1,119,150	27.
3,930	8,070	4,050	2,750	3,270	3,860	84,290	N.C
1,102,490	1,810,990	1,198,800	872,200	721,010	1,350,100	15,031,550	
1,942,119	3,218,505	2,104,895	1,609,005	1,327,510	2,514,620	26,197,610	

FEMALE EMPLOYMENT: 1971

South East

	1. London	2. Middlesex	3. Kent	4. Surrey	5. Sussex	6. Hants.	7. Berks.	8. Oxon.
1.	1,030		5,830	1,620	4,990	3,320	1,310	1,020
2.	1,460		230	60	30	70	30	10
3.	38,420		4,240	1,270	2,600	3,950	1,470	1,130
4.	2,840		250	370	–	110	50	–
5.	27,250		3,240	2,540	2,370	3,750	890	100
6.	4,380		280	100	470	250	330	270
7.	27,510		3,440	4,760	3,430	4,670	3,000	340
8.	12,770		1,370	1,960	1,490	640	430	180
9.	59,650		4,380	5,280	7,020	13,760	3,750	630
10.	540		630	120	110	920	–	90
11.	8,740		1,200	2,000	460	2,390	750	3,020
12.	20,670		1,780	1,910	1,980	2,040	1,760	270
13.	7,900	Included	400	430	560	690	80	560
14.	5,610	Under	140	220	300	110	120	–
15.	57,020	'London'	3,240	900	3,050	4,450	630	790
16.	5,280		1,280	1,030	540	360	420	90
17.	9,160		1,220	660	1,220	1,260	780	690
18.	49,190		7,660	2,160	2,380	4,670	2,500	1,660
19.	21,800		4,650	3,180	2,550	3,500	750	160
20.	18,850		2,270	2,180	2,030	2,580	1,260	550
21.	12,520		1,190	980	1,290	2,400	770	280
22.	80,330		5,480	5,270	4,770	8,580	2,720	1,560
23.	253,940		35,700	24,640	35,360	50,220	16,910	9,880
24.	180,950		8,850	10,470	11,910	11,210	6,110	3,060
25.	304,350		45,690	38,470	43,650	54,720	26,230	19,080
26.	218,010		32,280	25,340	36,890	44,570	16,180	11,030
27.	105,190		9,300	8,840	10,670	19,320	5,900	4,270
N.C.	23,850		2,190	1,590	2,520	2,760	1,200	910
Total Employed	1,559,210		188,410	148,350	184,640	247,270	96,330	61,630
Total Population	3,874,110		726,005	519,595	674,015	865,585	321,330	189,755

9. Bucks.	10. Beds.	11. Herts.	12. Essex	13. Cambridge	14. Hunts.	15. Norfolk	16. Suffolk	
1,390	1,080	1,700	3,010	2,300	710	4,000	2,880	1.
50	10	110	30	-	30	70	10	2.
2,940	910	2,270	4,830	2,000	720	6,920	5,350	3.
40	10	10	530	-	-	10	-	4.
3,510	680	5,090	3,570	410	130	1,180	1,740	5.
730	260	880	310	20	60	110	470	6.
4,050	2,780	4,140	3,770	220	1,200	810	1,300	7.
1,250	870	2,690	1,070	820	20	580	460	8.
3,630	3,670	8,110	13,590	1,780	1,460	3,950	2,700	9.
40	220	100	280	-	10	180	170	10.
1,130	4,200	4,250	1,590	210	610	200	520	11.
1,910	690	1,980	1,850	210	20	430	290	12.
830	450	710	790	210	150	640	990	13.
200	220	210	160	90	30	320	190	14.
1,330	4,650	2,210	7,260	390	620	5,560	2,340	15.
280	580	850	1,120	200	110	180	190	16.
1,610	180	760	2,070	260	270	760	520	17.
3,790	2,180	6,680	6,040	1,410	780	1,670	1,620	18.
2,950	1,040	4,400	3,470	320	1,470	1,360	1,050	19.
980	1,040	1,930	2,350	520	440	950	680	20.
580	410	1,060	1,130	60	120	250	780	21.
1,920	2,880	3,270	5,360	1,230	1,060	1,680	1,670	22.
14,190	11,090	25,560	30,850	7,920	5,690	16,440	13,380	23.
4,760	2,780	7,540	8,800	1,600	1,130	4,410	2,860	24.
21,780	14,390	35,080	41,600	14,370	6,160	18,120	15,610	25.
12,780	9,010	17,860	26,850	7,220	4,360	15,250	14,120	26.
4,180	3,810	8,540	10,230	2,260	2,130	3,220	3,080	27.
1,330	910	1,350	1,950	470	190	930	750	N.C.
94,160	71,000	149,340	184,460	46,500	29,680	90,180	75,720	
296,425	231,865	470,760	696,965	152,215	101,019	317,020	276,760	

FEMALE EMPLOYMENT: 1971

| | South West | | | | | | West Midlands | |
	17. Corn-wall	18. Devon	19.Som-erset	20.Gloucs.	21.Wilts.	22.Dorset	23.Here-ford	24.Shrops.
1.	2,590	4,410	2,790	2,030	1,640	1,450	1,440	1,980
2.	510	150	80	90	20	30	–	90
3.	670	2,850	4,310	9,650	4,680	1,330	1,650	1,120
4.	–	20	20	10	–	–	20	10
5.	40	290	640	1,180	480	450	30	60
6.	–	180	230	340	40	40	270	860
7.	630	2,050	1,710	4,710	2,330	870	250	1,510
8.	340	1,070	340	1,770	210	200	10	20
9.	810	2,780	1,320	1,920	5,810	1,800	320	1,230
10.	120	320	–	20	10	190	–	10
11.	40	270	1,070	3,700	330	360	120	870
12.	100	350	440	1,440	400	740	150	910
13.	560	1,130	670	1,580	410	450	20	230
14.	100	310	460	120	90	–	–	–
15.	1,300	4,300	7,290	2,760	1,580	410	260	1,970
16.	370	680	230	290	40	440	160	200
17.	80	470	810	1,190	510	150	110	150
18.	410	1,230	2,640	6,450	700	320	140	260
19.	290	520	1,070	2,100	1,580	190	350	370
20.	410	1,490	930	2,090	830	540	250	340
21.	240	770	970	1,320	270	210	90	290
22.	920	2,540	1,840	5,670	1,370	730	290	1,050
23.	9,790	26,270	17,720	33,010	12,760	8,270	3,610	8,360
24.	1,580	5,180	3,380	9,480	2,510	1,770	610	1,750
25.	8,980	26,830	23,570	40,200	16,200	11,410	4,460	11,390
26.	10,790	26,940	17,200	27,200	12,310	9,130	3,960	8,290
27.	1,960	5,800	5,760	9,520	6,420	3,190	1,370	4,180
N.C.	600	1,460	960	1,940	530	950	260	660
Total Employed	44,230	120,660	98,450	171,780	74,060	45,620	20,200	48,160
Total Population	199,935	471,620	355,035	552,335	246,585	188,625	70,480	170,060

East Midlands

25.Staffs.	26.Warwick	27.Worcs.	28.Derby	29.Notts.	30.Leics.	31.Lincs.	32.Northants.	
2,200	1,470	2,220	1,620	1,300	1,010	6,500	920	1.
1,190	400	50	590	1,600	420	70	20	2.
6,350	9,000	3,340	2,950	6,830	3,590	7,910	2,410	3.
140	40	10	210	40	-	90	-	4.
2,030	3,000	990	2,980	3,460	1,410	1,100	1,490	5.
9,430	7,180	3,880	2,470	160	220	1,830	1,240	6.
10,500	11,540	3,900	2,260	3,280	4,760	2,270	2,120	7.
670	1,530	780	470	520	510	10	10	8.
14,290	21,700	5,270	1,550	3,460	4,000	1,010	2,380	9.
50	390	90	-	30	10	110	50	10.
5,130	22,300	2,160	3,010	1,730	850	330	530	11.
25,140	27,020	12,050	1,510	2,970	1,580	190	530	12.
4,200	4,080	4,970	13,430	22,670	28,690	2,470	220	13.
2,790	490	210	30	110	160	90	870	14.
9,590	3,320	1,440	6,130	11,150	12,980	2,180	16,640	15.
25,380	970	1,800	2,590	1,230	460	260	110	16.
1,980	1,440	740	1,160	860	830	600	550	17.
5,190	6,200	1,160	2,160	2,450	2,410	1,650	1,650	18.
7,010	5,860	1,820	920	1,110	2,850	1,020	1,140	19.
3,310	4,130	1,170	1,450	1,360	1,250	1,310	610	20.
1,610	3,720	870	760	970	1,580	750	380	21.
5,050	10,430	2,050	4,900	3,020	2,580	2,790	1,560	22.
48,560	59,920	18,580	19,860	26,700	19,840	21,920	11,690	23.
8,690	18,200	3,290	3,120	5,050	4,240	3,750	3,820	24.
52,450	75,780	20,280	25,600	28,480	22,280	22,650	12,700	25.
34,720	44,000	14,850	17,990	20,500	15,000	19,960	9,380	26.
10,840	16,990	4,700	4,220	7,190	3,590	5,540	2,480	27.
2,800	4,160	1,010	910	1,360	1,040	1,510	620	N.C.
301,290	365,260	113,680	124,850	159,590	138,140	109,870	76,120	
937,080	1,051,540	352,610	448,770	495,310	391,600	409,395	238,371	

FEMALE EMPLOYMENT: 1971

| | East Midlands | North West | | Yorks. & Humberside | | North | | |
	33.Rut-land	34.Cheshire	35.Lancs.	36. West Riding	37. East Riding	38.North Riding	39.West-morland	40.Cum-berland
1.	60	2,250	4,240	3,890	1,400	2,070	630	1,580
2.	–	380	960	2,780	10	20	60	60
3.	–	8,110	42,130	23,600	4,100	3,380	360	2,570
4.	–	820	430	270	30	50	–	–
5.	–	8,800	18,330	5,470	3,660	2,610	30	620
6.	–	760	4,170	10,490	190	1,590	10	410
7.	50	5,660	17,290	13,460	2,410	1,220	90	230
8.	–	380	1,850	1,410	130	150	–	420
9.	40	4,670	38,820	11,740	290	1,590	–	270
10.	–	400	1,540	100	100	250	–	–
11.	–	2,680	11,080	3,690	2,150	390	–	90
12.	20	2,070	12,530	22,420	1,540	350	10	800
13.	20	7,040	57,980	53,960	710	810	330	1,760
14.	60	440	2,780	1,930	210	60	10	350
15.	330	12,020	48,750	36,340	1,140	3,420	740	3,550
16.	20	710	6,610	4,090	510	270	70	60
17.	–	920	5,910	4,080	940	500	70	120
18.	10	4,760	20,110	11,070	1,650	670	240	610
19.	20	3,250	12,390	5,520	790	380	50	760
20.	60	2,790	7,940	5,970	670	1,270	110	370
21.	–	2,260	5,500	3,770	140	580	200	150
22.	80	4,990	23,280	13,410	2,290	2,570	340	820
23.	410	42,130	173,060	109,310	16,560	20,830	1,780	7,900
24.	60	8,110	41,750	22,760	2,630	2,860	500	1,160
25.	890	46,250	176,470	129,030	18,300	21,710	2,360	10,080
26.	750	33,930	112,040	85,960	13,030	18,680	2,970	7,470
27.	240	9,370	37,560	22,620	2,880	5,960	350	2,700
N.C.	20	2,340	8,060	4,670	670	1,160	100	300
Total Employed	3,140	218,290	893,560	613,810	79,130	95,400	11,410	45,210
Total Population	13,315	800,490	2,645,815	1,888,105	335,330	368,185	38,040	149,525

	Wales			Scotland				
41.North-umberland	42.Durham	43.Mon-mouth & Glamorgan	44.North & West Wales	45.Strathclyde	46.Dumfries & Galloway	47.Borders	48.Lothian	
1,300	1,010	1,280	7,070	2,690	1,160	630	880	1.
440	1,410	1,670	280	150	20	-	530	2.
4,560	5,810	5,490	1,680	20,210	830	100	6,730	3.
10	70	550	50	120	-	-	10	4.
3,020	2,010	2,120	670	5,270	290	30	1,140	5.
430	1,140	5,150	1,430	2,930	60	-	240	6.
2,380	4,190	4,960	1,260	9,280	210	40	540	7.
130	450	310	1,530	4,130	-	-	600	8.
3,840	18,130	10,440	3,070	12,780	20	170	3,650	9.
890	720	70	100	1,820	-	-	70	10.
150	920	3,220	2,840	3,020	-	10	500	11.
1,190	1,190	5,060	680	3,990	20	140	1,090	12.
960	3,580	2,530	2,610	18,130	1,740	4,980	1,900	13.
80	390	570	220	1,110	20	90	110	14.
4,360	15,140	9,410	3,950	20,450	860	150	2,040	15.
740	1,890	980	390	1,190	20	10	220	16.
720	770	1,180	750	2,030	20	30	450	17.
1,650	3,910	3,150	1,110	8,960	90	80	4,230	18.
1,310	2,310	6,010	1,170	2,250	370	130	530	19.
1,520	1,830	2,490	1,270	5,400	220	150	2,130	20.
1,530	680	1,870	970	2,310	90	110	1,410	21.
3,800	3,710	6,860	2,410	14,540	400	190	4,620	22.
28,100	40,230	44,630	21,880	77,960	3,890	2,490	24,910	23.
5,120	6,080	9,270	3,220	16,180	410	370	7,870	24.
32,070	39,700	56,010	30,510	89,940	4,370	2,480	36,170	25.
21,840	29,040	35,200	22,720	50,920	4,290	3,130	21,420	26.
10,960	8,200	13,530	5,980	15,300	930	650	8,950	27.
1,020	1,410	2,530	1,860	2,250	210	130	710	N.C.
134,120	195,920	236,540	121,680	395,310	20,540	16,290	133,650	
411,630	719,690	880,845	522,850	1,328,175	73,750	51,190	398,335	

FEMALE EMPLOYMENT: 1971

Scotland

	49.Central & Fife	50.Tayside	51.Grampian	52.Highland	53. South East	54. East Anglia	55. South West	56. West Midlands
1.	1,270	1,790	1,890	1,290	26,300	9,890	14,910	9,310
2.	350	50	40	–	2,090	110	880	1,730
3.	2,430	2,950	6,910	480	64,030	14,990	23,490	21,460
4.	190	10	10	–	4,210	10	50	220
5.	610	200	170	40	52,990	3,460	3,080	6,110
6.	1,350	260	30	100	8,260	660	830	21,620
7.	1,130	2,000	370	80	61,890	3,530	12,300	27,700
8.	490	3,740	–	20	24,720	1,880	3,930	3,010
9.	4,240	940	460	60	123,470	9,890	14,440	42,810
10.	70	30	100	–	3,050	360	660	540
11.	140	50	30	10	29,730	1,540	5,770	30,580
12.	810	310	280	10	36,840	950	3,470	65,270
13.	4,920	7,030	2,450	490	13,400	1,990	4,800	13,500
14.	–	40	20	110	7,290	630	1,080	3,490
15.	2,910	740	400	100	85,530	8,910	17,640	16,580
16.	770	90	140	70	11,830	680	2,050	28,510
17.	480	160	430	50	19,610	1,810	3,210	4,420
18.	2,680	1,550	1,910	210	88,910	5,480	11,750	12,950
19.	930	60	170	80	48,450	4,200	5,750	15,410
20.	900	790	770	370	36,020	2,590	6,290	9,200
21.	460	400	260	90	22,610	1,210	3,780	6,580
22.	2,470	1,460	1,690	1,200	122,140	5,640	13,070	18,870
23.	16,260	12,890	12,760	5,440	508,340	43,430	107,820	139,030
24.	1,830	2,210	1,510	670	256,440	10,000	23,900	32,540
25.	18,550	17,320	17,220	7,240	645,040	54,260	127,190	164,360
26.	12,810	10,940	11,630	7,630	450,800	40,950	103,570	105,820
27.	4,870	2,720	2,610	1,450	190,250	10,690	32,650	38,080
N.C.	490	480	620	430	40,560	2,340	6,440	8,890
Total Employed	84,410	71,210	64,880	27,720	2,984,800	242,080	554,800	848,590
Total Population	298,930	216,060	229,930	117,970	8,866,410	847,014	2,014,135	2,581,770

57. East Midlands	58. North West	59. Yorks. & Humberside	60. North	61. Wales	62. Scotland	63. Great Britain	
11,410	6,490	5,290	6,590	8,350	11,600	110,140	1.
2,700	1,340	2,790	1,990	1,950	1,140	16,720	2.
23,690	50,240	27,700	16,680	7,170	40,640	290,090	3.
340	1,250	300	130	600	340	7,450	4.
10,440	27,130	9,130	8,290	2,790	7,750	131,170	5.
5,920	4,930	10,680	3,580	6,580	4,970	68,030	6.
14,740	22,950	15,870	8,110	6,220	13,650	186,960	7.
1,520	2,230	1,540	1,150	1,840	8,980	50,800	8.
12,440	43,490	12,030	23,830	13,510	22,320	318,230	9.
200	1,940	200	1,860	170	2,090	11,070	10.
6,450	13,760	5,840	1,550	6,060	3,760	105,040	11.
6,800	14,600	23,960	3,540	5,740	6,650	167,820	12.
67,500	65,020	54,670	7,440	5,140	41,640	275,100	13.
1,320	3,220	2,140	890	790	1,500	22,350	14.
49,410	60,770	37,480	27,210	13,360	27,650	344,540	15.
4,670	7,320	4,600	3,030	1,370	2,510	66,570	16.
4,000	6,830	5,020	2,180	1,930	3,650	52,660	17.
10,330	24,870	12,720	7,080	4,260	19,710	198,060	18.
7,060	15,640	6,310	4,810	7,180	4,520	119,330	19.
6,040	10,730	6,640	5,100	3,760	10,730	97,100	20.
4,440	7,760	3,910	3,140	2,840	5,130	61,400	21.
14,930	28,270	15,700	11,240	9,270	26,570	265,700	22.
100,420	215,190	125,870	98,840	66,510	156,600	1,562,050	23.
20,040	49,860	25,390	15,720	12,490	31,050	477,430	24.
112,600	222,720	147,330	105,920	86,520	193,290	1,859,230	25.
83,580	145,970	98,990	80,000	57,920	122,770	1,290,370	26.
23,260	46,930	25,500	28,170	19,510	37,480	452,520	27.
5,460	10,400	5,340	3,990	4,390	5,320	93,130	N.C.
611,710	1,111,850	692,940	482,060	358,220	814,010	8,701,060	
1,996,761	3,446,305	2,223,435	1,687,070	1,403,695	2,714,340	27,780,935	

TOTAL EMPLOYMENT: 1971

South East

	1. London	2. Middlesex	3. Kent	4. Surrey	5. Sussex	6. Hants.	7. Berks.	8. Oxo
1.	5,240		20,770	7,330	20,590	16,570	6,650	6,10
2.	4,700		4,960	710	340	610	490	26
3.	105,690		10,490	3,780	8,150	11,460	4,910	3,44
4.	9,220		2,790	1,760	30	2,250	250	1
5.	72,420		8,530	6,130	5,370	9,810	2,060	33
6.	21,420		2,050	600	2,990	1,510	1,350	1,55
7.	127,630		20,480	21,850	18,890	30,140	14,550	2,52
8.	37,900		3,090	6,180	4,800	2,900	1,270	53
9.	165,660		14,290	15,010	19,860	35,810	12,130	2,00
10.	5,700		8,240	570	930	19,430	320	40
11.	65,980		7,490	13,030	1,750	22,770	5,130	24,97
12.	71,940	Included	6,960	7,920	6,990	7,700	6,350	69
13.	17,790	Under	1,240	960	1,100	1,500	290	1,19
14.	13,090	'London'	530	450	510	170	450	1
15.	89,970		3,760	1,160	3,700	5,180	910	94
16.	23,350		10,040	3,970	4,190	2,340	2,160	1,29
17.	53,820		7,000	4,020	7,600	8,000	3,570	2,35
18.	159,220		31,340	6,310	7,400	13,290	8,680	5,09
19.	52,500		10,010	8,110	5,790	7,970	1,920	53
20.	249,550		41,300	28,340	40,190	55,230	20,950	13,54
21.	62,260		9,440	5,530	8,010	12,230	4,200	1,70
22.	422,210		38,620	25,360	25,800	47,650	13,500	7,88
23.	547,540		68,050	46,840	70,330	95,280	32,530	19,26
24.	379,340		17,020	19,130	23,280	21,610	10,680	5,26
25.	506,720		71,050	61,890	68,640	88,330	49,540	32,31
26.	445,400		58,730	46,490	66,900	81,550	29,930	22,03
27.	315,980		37,870	28,310	31,990	98,270	20,630	17,26
N.C.	53,290		3,810	3,090	4,340	5,090	2,280	1,42
Total Employed	4,085,530		519,950	374,830	460,460	704,650	257,680	174,86
Total Population	7,452,350		1,399,465	1,002,890	1,240,470	1,674,990	636,860	381,59

9. Bucks.	10. Beds.	11. Herts.	12. Essex	13. Cambridge	14. Hunts.	15. Norfolk	16. Suffolk	
7,090	5,770	7,070	17,310	12,210	4,940	26,030	18,230	1.
260	150	910	790	80	290	830	310	2.
10,250	3,230	6,430	12,870	4,900	1,920	16,850	12,960	3.
130	20	60	4,050	20	10	40	50	4.
9,070	1,890	14,580	10,800	1,990	370	3,140	5,940	5.
3,730	1,600	4,100	2,570	80	280	910	3,330	6.
18,870	13,830	21,600	24,360	2,460	7,610	7,150	11,140	7.
3,960	3,250	7,310	3,610	3,110	100	1,360	1,280	8.
9,360	9,340	25,390	34,770	4,410	4,170	8,190	5,910	9.
330	1,740	370	2,280	230	50	1,860	1,730	10.
8,970	33,580	26,990	13,120	2,020	8,170	3,360	4,200	11.
6,940	3,360	8,770	9,670	1,090	340	2,160	1,810	12.
1,890	760	1,400	2,360	320	200	1,450	1,950	13.
300	570	380	370	290	40	430	400	14.
1,740	6,000	2,830	9,630	470	680	8,960	2,890	15.
3,460	6,100	4,330	6,780	2,400	2,760	1,820	1,190	16.
8,940	1,270	5,720	10,240	1,120	1,110	5,720	3,820	17.
10,870	5,880	21,590	17,400	4,660	2,430	5,250	5,010	18.
7,130	3,030	10,120	7,550	740	3,190	3,260	2,220	19.
17,190	12,700	25,340	41,330	10,940	6,870	23,890	20,200	20.
2,900	2,280	5,750	8,700	1,090	1,430	3,020	4,490	21.
10,350	10,540	16,470	33,270	7,520	5,830	12,890	12,420	22.
28,680	21,240	49,170	62,830	16,190	10,860	36,140	28,610	23.
8,190	5,220	13,200	16,140	3,440	2,080	8,760	5,810	24.
33,750	23,640	55,800	65,840	26,020	9,550	28,590	24,300	25.
25,620	18,250	34,920	48,730	12,950	10,410	29,050	33,450	26.
16,610	12,020	19,450	32,800	8,760	9,740	15,720	14,700	27.
2,390	1,540	2,520	3,970	760	440	1,390	1,610	N.C.
258,970	208,800	392,570	504,140	130,270	95,870	258,220	229,960	
587,555	464,280	924,630	1,358,030	303,045	202,620	617,615	546,195	

TOTAL EMPLOYMENT: 1971

	South West						West Midlands	
	17.Corn- wall	18. Devon	19.Som- erset	20.Gloucs.	21.Wilts.	22.Dorset	23.Here- ford	24.Shrops
1.	15,250	24,240	16,140	11,860	10,870	8,740	8,440	13,590
2.	6,800	2,420	2,080	1,050	120	520	170	1,320
3.	2,680	9,370	11,810	23,340	11,280	4,540	4,230	3,510
4.	10	160	120	150	10	–	30	140
5.	260	990	4,370	6,310	1,150	1,440	220	400
6.	180	1,120	1,100	4,580	240	190	2,870	4,560
7.	4,940	9,400	10,380	30,510	11,910	6,570	1,920	9,320
8.	950	2,090	1,270	8,110	530	510	30	50
9.	1,380	6,960	3,170	8,110	13,320	4,970	770	2,240
10.	2,570	12,240	60	780	50	1,700	–	20
11.	240	2,330	9,680	34,360	11,180	2,950	440	7,390
12.	660	1,730	2,450	6,690	2,150	2,010	760	2,950
13.	1,400	3,390	1,860	5,390	870	1,260	50	580
14.	360	580	1,740	430	340	10	–	–
15.	1,530	5,600	12,380	4,260	2,300	510	300	2,220
16.	1,380	3,020	2,220	2,250	790	2,150	640	990
17.	880	4,300	4,810	6,870	2,800	1,180	610	1,230
18.	1,200	4,890	8,980	21,010	1,960	1,320	340	790
19.	570	1,240	3,310	6,620	6,380	410	860	930
20.	13,190	30,940	20,510	33,750	17,020	11,860	4,040	10,210
21.	2,440	6,110	6,350	7,430	2,140	2,380	560	2,310
22.	8,160	20,060	12,090	32,720	9,410	5,310	2,640	7,150
23.	20,760	52,920	34,720	66,190	24,640	17,310	6,610	16,000
24.	3,370	10,920	6,910	17,880	4,700	3,920	1,350	3,580
25.	14,480	43,800	36,830	62,670	25,390	19,810	6,520	16,770
26.	20,260	49,100	31,170	47,850	21,340	16,590	6,910	14,440
27.	11,810	38,830	23,950	32,180	30,350	15,230	5,090	15,680
N.C.	1,200	2,610	1,700	3,440	1,120	1,470	450	1,060
Total Employed	138,910	351,360	272,160	486,770	214,360	134,860	56,850	139,430
Total Population	381,670	898,405	682,665	1,076,710	486,745	361,920	138,640	337,105

East Midlands

25.Staffs.	26.Warwick	27.Worcs.	28.Derby	29.Notts.	30.Leics.	31.Lincs.	32.Northants.	
11,940	7,950	9,560	8,800	7,780	6,710	35,790	5,880	1.
19,870	7,270	300	21,750	45,850	9,750	1,220	300	2.
21,220	23,420	8,320	6,440	17,270	9,050	17,430	6,580	3.
770	230	30	1,900	460	30	1,280	10	4.
7,680	9,350	4,190	7,410	8,310	3,900	7,480	3,640	5.
63,490	34,960	26,080	21,670	2,390	4,050	21,050	14,620	6.
60,320	54,080	22,640	17,660	21,920	36,130	18,450	13,420	7.
1,690	3,670	1,410	1,190	1,680	2,490	220	190	8.
37,250	62,070	8,720	4,160	11,380	12,450	3,210	5,160	9.
360	2,250	240	50	180	90	2,080	170	10.
25,100	161,650	7,100	25,820	10,300	7,400	3,380	3,430	11.
70,760	80,920	39,350	6,440	9,150	6,360	2,470	3,020	12.
8,540	8,630	12,730	28,570	37,280	47,370	5,430	580	13.
4,030	820	640	170	480	460	340	3,470	14.
11,880	4,620	2,040	7,150	13,590	20,210	2,390	27,920	15.
57,250	6,580	5,810	10,000	6,410	4,210	2,800	1,060	16.
9,840	6,970	3,700	5,190	5,090	4,740	3,700	2,340	17.
12,420	16,770	3,190	6,290	7,160	7,320	5,300	4,020	18.
26,050	18,320	3,470	2,650	2,990	8,710	3,170	2,800	19.
51,860	57,120	18,590	24,890	25,910	21,580	25,410	14,630	20.
10,680	14,260	4,000	6,200	8,070	6,270	4,140	2,410	21.
33,310	46,750	12,040	22,830	19,620	15,100	20,870	9,660	22.
90,330	111,270	34,980	36,760	52,960	40,970	45,420	23,670	23.
15,780	33,340	6,460	6,760	10,500	8,520	7,330	6,500	24.
77,260	113,930	30,300	37,810	44,480	36,570	33,330	19,320	25.
61,060	77,870	25,970	30,840	38,020	29,260	33,940	18,270	26.
31,860	45,140	14,500	12,040	23,440	12,570	28,650	8,520	27.
5,160	8,430	2,010	1,800	2,300	1,810	2,400	1,040	N.C.
827,760	1,018,640	308,370	363,240	434,970	364,080	338,680	202,630	
1,858,355	2,082,230	693,255	885,130	976,410	772,100	809,145	468,625	

TOTAL EMPLOYMENT: 1971

	East Midlands	North West		Yorks. & Humberside		North		
	33.Rutland	34.Cheshire	35.Lancs.	36. West Riding	37. East Riding	38.North Riding	39.Westmorland	40.Cumberland
1.	930	12,950	21,020	20,830	13,290	15,170	4,010	8,650
2.	50	1,650	15,870	84,690	290	830	540	3,030
3.	110	20,720	97,360	53,890	10,510	6,640	1,130	5,350
4.	–	7,540	3,560	4,200	100	1,330	–	60
5.	40	40,250	69,170	20,660	9,660	30,590	80	5,920
6.	30	5,370	26,610	82,230	1,880	24,920	10	5,730
7.	430	36,100	108,020	94,710	9,380	11,230	960	2,790
8.	–	1,630	6,050	4,410	340	760	–	970
9.	150	13,590	110,350	28,670	960	3,170	160	510
10.	–	10,480	17,170	1,390	3,550	5,140	40	60
11.	30	33,050	81,790	31,350	10,280	2,880	60	910
12.	60	9,790	51,690	74,180	2,970	2,910	30	1,970
13.	20	15,410	132,270	129,660	1,200	3,670	590	4,120
14.	150	1,160	7,010	4,310	1,240	210	10	950
15.	450	15,070	63,930	48,900	1,440	4,110	2,010	4,790
16.	450	5,010	38,060	26,630	3,140	1,890	810	880
17.	30	4,850	30,080	21,820	4,820	2,790	450	840
18.	60	15,330	68,160	31,270	3,830	1,980	1,100	2,160
19.	40	6,910	41,700	13,680	2,050	870	100	2,330
20.	830	47,210	142,210	103,140	14,820	23,350	2,740	8,790
21.	20	10,790	32,630	27,790	2,930	3,920	660	1,510
22.	370	37,900	162,570	87,580	20,100	15,200	1,500	8,170
23.	780	76,280	317,720	207,560	32,560	36,000	3,430	14,060
24.	90	15,910	79,800	44,700	5,330	5,920	1,070	2,460
25.	1,320	68,510	266,700	190,780	28,100	31,160	3,500	15,190
26.	1,250	57,250	197,770	149,600	22,370	31,250	5,320	12,810
27.	2,870	28,420	115,970	74,170	12,410	25,860	1,380	9,510
N.C.	40	4,030	14,440	8,300	1,090	2,040	130	490
Total Employed	10,600	603,160	2,319,680	1,671,100	220,640	295,790	31,820	125,010
Total Population	27,470	1,546,385	5,118,425	3,680,235	648,095	725,660	72,840	292,185

| | | Wales | | Scotland | | | | |
41.North-umberland	42.Durham	43.Mon-mouth & Glamorgan	44.North & West Wales	45.Strathclyde	46.Dumfries & Galloway	47.Borders	48.Lothian	
9,230	6,320	7,520	40,990	15,460	9,530	5,870	5,770	1.
17,550	41,980	42,410	9,330	11,480	310	200	11,890	2.
12,720	12,810	13,510	6,030	46,860	2,550	470	17,380	3.
70	1,820	10,650	940	830	–	–	100	4.
8,680	8,320	11,750	3,630	16,390	2,470	130	3,090	5.
2,880	18,880	60,280	21,450	36,470	150	40	2,970	6.
15,430	35,400	28,240	7,110	70,270	1,590	550	5,780	7.
650	1,270	1,420	3,140	9,310	–	20	1,470	8.
13,160	38,770	23,180	7,050	30,530	70	710	11,050	9.
16,220	16,150	1,130	1,440	28,990	–	40	2,070	10.
760	7,130	17,460	11,520	29,080	230	60	5,610	11.
3,970	6,530	18,290	3,380	18,500	410	440	4,470	12.
2,240	10,400	9,080	8,850	31,130	2,560	9,860	3,060	13.
320	510	930	640	2,610	20	320	310	14.
5,280	17,630	11,500	4,570	24,110	1,030	230	2,380	15.
4,400	9,620	5,560	3,800	10,220	240	110	3,210	16.
3,990	5,580	6,880	3,480	13,420	780	600	3,420	17.
4,870	9,480	10,290	3,110	21,980	300	300	10,940	18.
4,030	7,560	13,460	3,540	7,420	1,150	250	2,430	19.
28,500	39,950	57,100	34,450	83,610	4,610	3,000	27,150	20.
7,280	6,060	11,990	8,090	13,280	1,010	530	6,120	21.
22,340	30,130	46,310	19,470	77,340	3,270	1,440	23,760	22.
47,620	66,860	83,470	42,950	134,930	7,460	5,110	43,860	23.
10,450	11,090	17,940	7,850	31,040	1,180	930	15,110	24.
49,250	58,900	83,710	47,900	132,740	6,510	3,940	55,540	25.
35,880	44,880	60,320	40,690	88,930	6,890	5,340	35,930	26.
29,080	26,680	43,850	27,940	58,750	3,070	1,970	27,440	27.
1,590	2,490	4,660	3,000	4,310	340	160	1,110	N.C.
358,440	543,200	702,890	376,340	1,049,990	57,730	42,620	333,420	
795,755	1,409,635	1,720,900	1,010,305	2,558,295	143,190	97,290	760,180	

TOTAL EMPLOYMENT: 1971

Scotland

	49.Central & Fife	50.Tayside	51.Grampian	52.Highland	53. South East	54. East Anglia	55. South West	56. West Midlands
1.	6,920	11,850	21,500	11,500	120,490	61,410	87,100	51,480
2.	10,840	1,450	380	210	14,180	1,510	12,990	28,930
3.	7,050	6,870	15,820	2,840	180,700	36,630	63,020	60,700
4.	1,530	100	100	–	20,570	120	450	1,200
5.	6,350	1,040	790	140	140,990	11,440	14,520	21,840
6.	7,600	880	140	1,050	43,470	4,600	7,410	131,960
7.	7,370	11,390	4,300	1,150	314,720	28,360	73,710	148,280
8.	970	5,960	70	90	74,800	5,850	13,460	6,850
9.	6,700	2,500	800	220	343,620	22,680	37,910	111,050
10.	5,340	1,130	2,880	180	40,310	3,870	17,400	2,870
11.	1,450	260	590	70	223,780	17,750	60,720	201,680
12.	2,660	1,680	1,310	180	137,290	5,400	15,690	194,740
13.	7,070	15,310	4,420	2,230	30,480	3,920	14,170	30,530
14.	20	80	40	150	16,830	1,160	3,460	5,490
15.	3,310	1,000	480	110	125,820	13,000	26,580	21,060
16.	5,610	620	1,380	380	68,010	8,170	11,810	71,270
17.	3,450	2,150	3,350	870	112,530	11,770	20,840	22,350
18.	7,830	4,580	6,090	1,340	287,070	17,350	39,360	33,510
19.	3,790	250	670	170	114,660	9,410	18,530	49,630
20.	19,480	14,030	14,400	10,690	545,660	61,900	127,270	141,820
21.	3,820	2,270	1,910	910	123,000	10,030	26,850	31,810
22.	12,370	8,760	10,310	7,000	651,650	38,660	87,750	101,890
23.	26,830	23,560	25,200	10,690	1,041,750	91,800	216,540	259,190
24.	3,920	4,980	3,650	1,770	519,070	20,090	47,700	60,510
25.	27.800	25,570	25,910	12,890	1,057,510	88,460	202,980	244,780
26.	20,620	19,340	20,170	12,940	878,550	85,860	186,310	186,250
27.	19,750	10,320	13,120	9,160	631,190	48,920	152,350	112,270
N.C.	780	730	1,020	730	83,740	4,200	11,540	17,110
Total Employed	231,230	178,660	180,800	89,660	7,942,440	714,320	1,598,420	2,351,050
Total Population	581,640	413,035	441,090	234,240	17,123,110	1,669,475	3,888,115	5,109,585

57. East Midlands	58. North West	59. Yorks. & Humberside	60. North	61. Wales	62. Scotland	63. Great Britain	
65,890	33,970	34,120	43,380	48,510	88,400	634,750	1.
78,920	17,520	84,980	63,930	51,740	36,760	391,460	2.
56,880	118,080	64,400	38,650	19,540	99,840	738,440	3.
3,680	11,100	4,300	3,280	11,590	2,660	58,950	4.
30,780	109,420	30,320	53,590	15,380	30,400	458,680	5.
63,810	31,980	84,110	52,420	81,730	49,300	550,790	6.
108,010	144,120	104,090	65,810	35,350	102,400	1,124,850	7.
5,770	7,680	4,750	3,650	4,560	17,890	145,260	8.
36,510	123,940	29,630	55,770	30,230	52,580	843,920	9.
2,570	27,650	4,940	37,610	2,570	40,630	180,420	10.
50,360	114,840	41,630	11,740	28,980	37,350	788,830	11.
27,500	61,480	77,150	15,410	21,670	29,650	585,980	12.
119,250	147,680	130,860	21,020	17,930	75,640	591,480	13.
5,070	8,170	5,550	2,000	1,570	3,550	52,850	14.
71,710	79,000	50,340	33,820	16,070	32,650	470,050	15.
24,930	43,070	29,770	17,600	9,360	21,770	305,760	16.
21,090	34,930	26,640	13,650	10,360	28,040	302,200	17.
30,150	83,490	35,100	19,590	13,400	53,360	612,380	18.
20,360	48,610	15,730	14,890	17,000	16,130	324,950	19.
113,250	189,420	117,960	103,330	91,550	176,970	1,669,130	20.
27,110	43,420	30,720	19,430	20,080	29,850	362,300	21.
88,450	200,470	107,680	77,340	65,780	144,250	1,563,920	22.
200,560	394,000	240,120	167,970	126,420	277,640	3,015,990	23.
39,700	95,710	50,030	30,990	25,790	62,580	952,170	24.
172,830	335,210	218,880	158,000	131,610	290,900	2,901,160	25.
151,580	255,020	171,970	130,140	101,010	210,160	2,356,850	26.
88,090	144,390	86,580	92,510	71,790	143,580	1,571,670	27.
9,390	18,470	9,390	6,740	7,660	9,180	177,420	N.C.
1,714,200	2,922,840	1,891,740	1,354,260	1,079,230	2,164,110	23,732,610	
3,938,880	6,664,810	4,328,330	3,296,075	2,731,205	5,228,960	53,978,545